Lecture Notes in Computer Science 4472

Commenced Publication in 1973
Founding and Former Series Editors:
Gerhard Goos, Juris Hartmanis, and Jan van Leeuwen

T0223157

Michal Haindl   Josef Kittler
Fabio Roli (Eds.)

Multiple
Classifier Systems

7th International Workshop, MCS 2007
Prague, Czech Republic, May 23-25, 2007
Proceedings

 Springer

Volume Editors

Michal Haindl
Academy of Sciences CR
Institute of Information Theory and Automation
Prague, CZ182 08, Czech Republic
E-mail: haindl@utia.cas.cz

Josef Kittler
University of Surrey
Centre for Vision, Speech and Signal Processing
Guildford, Surrey GU27XH , UK
E-mail: j.kittler@eim.surrey.ac.uk

Fabio Roli
University of Cagliari
Department of Electrical and Electronic Engineering
Piazza d'Armi, 09123 Cagliari, Italy
E-mail: roli@diee.unica.it

Library of Congress Control Number: 2007926908

CR Subject Classification (1998): I.5, I.4, I.2.10, I.2, F.1

LNCS Sublibrary: SL 6 – Image Processing, Computer Vision, Pattern Recognition, and Graphics

ISSN   0302-9743
ISBN-10   3-540-72481-8 Springer Berlin Heidelberg New York
ISBN-13   978-3-540-72481-0 Springer Berlin Heidelberg New York

Springer is a part of Springer Science+Business Media

springer.com

© Springer-Verlag Berlin Heidelberg 2007

Typesetting: Camera-ready by author, data conversion by Scientific Publishing Services, Chennai, India
Printed on acid-free paper   SPIN: 12062539   06/3180   5 4 3 2 1 0

Preface

These proceedings are a record of the Multiple Classifier Systems Workshop, MCS 2007, held at the Institute of Information Theory and Automation, Czech Academy of Sciences, Prague in May 2007. Being the seventh in a well-established series of meetings providing an international forum for the discussion of issues in multiple classifier system design, the workshop achieved its objective of bringing together researchers from diverse communities (neural networks, pattern recognition, machine learning and statistics) concerned with this research topic.

From more than 80 submissions, the Programme Committee selected 49 papers to create an interesting scientific programme. The special focus of MCS 2007 was on the application of multiple classifier systems in biometrics. This particular application area exercises all aspects of multiple classifier fusion, from intramodal classifier combination, through confidence-based fusion, to multimodal biometric systems. The sponsorship of MCS 2007 by the European Union Network of Excellence in Biometrics BioSecure and in Multimedia Understanding through Semantics, Computation and Learning MUSCLE and their assistance in selecting the contributions to the MCS 2007 programme consistent with this theme is gratefully acknowledged.

The 'icing' on the technical programme, created from the regular submissions, was provided by the contributions made by invited speakers Samy Bengio from Google, Pramod Varshney from Syracuse University, USA, and Jon Benediktsson from the University of Iceland. Written versions of two of these talks are included in these workshop proceedings. Dr Bengio's and Professor Varshney's expertise in multiple biometric system fusion made the discussions on this topic at MCS 2007 particularly fruitful.

As usual, the workshop would not have been possible without the help of many individuals and organizations. First of all, our thanks go to the members of the MCS 2007 Programme Committee, whose expertise and dedication helped us to create an interesting event that marks the progress made in this field over the last two years and aspires to chart its future research. The help of James Field from the University of Surrey, who administered the submitted papers review, and of Ilias Kolonias, also from the University of Surrey, who compiled the camera-ready manuscripts into a well-structured volume deserve a particular mention. The co-sponsorship of the event by the International Association for Pattern Recognition and its Technical Committee TC1: Statistical Pattern Recognition, the Czech Society for Cybernetics and Informatics (CSKI), the Institute of Information Theory and Automation of the Czech Academy of Sciences, the University of Cagliari and the University of Surrey is also greatly appreciated.

May 2007

Michal Haindl
Josef Kittler
Fabio Roli

Organization

MCS 2007 was organized by the Institute of Information Theory and Automation of the Czech Republic Academy of Sciences (UTIA) in assosiation with the Centre for Vision, Speech and Signal Prosessing (CVSSP) of the University of Surrey, UK and the Department of Electrical and Electronic Engineering (Diee) of the University of Cagliari, Italy.

Programme Committee

Conference Chairs   Josef Kittler (University of Surrey, UK)
Fabio Roli (University of Cagliari, Italy)
Michal Haindl (Academy of Sciences of the Czech Republic)

Scientific Committee

J. A. Benediktsson (Iceland)
S. Bengio (USA)
H. Bunke (Switzerland)
G. Chollet (France)
L. P. Cordella (Italy)
B. V. Dasarathy (USA)
R. P.W. Duin (The Netherlands)
C. Furlanello (Italy)
J. Ghosh (USA)
V. Govindaraju (USA)
T. K. Ho (USA)
N. Intrator (Israel)
A.K. Jain (USA)

M. Kamel (Canada)
L.I. Kuncheva (UK)
N.C. Oza (USA)
P. Paclik (The Netherlands)
D. Partridge (UK)
R. Polikar (USA)
S. Raudys (Lithuania)
A. Ross (USA)
A.J.C. Sharkey (UK)
C.Y. Suen (Canada)
T. Windeatt (UK)
Z-H. Zhou (China)

Sponsoring Institutions

International Association for Pattern Recognition (IAPR)
EU IST FP6 BioSecure Network of Excellence (IST-2002-507634)
EU IST FP6 MUSCLE Network of Excellence (IST-2002-507752)
Centre for Vision, Speech and Signal Processing, University of Surrey, UK
Department of Electrical and Electronic Engineering, University of Cagliari, Italy
Institute of Information Theory and Automation, Academy of Sciences of the Czech Republic

Table of Contents

Kernel-Based Fusion

Combining Pattern Recognition Modalities at the Sensor Level Via
Kernel Fusion 1
  *Vadim Mottl, Alexander Tatarchuk, Valentina Sulimova,
  Olga Krasotkina, and Oleg Seredin*

The Neutral Point Method for Kernel-Based Combination of Disjoint
Training Data in Multi-modal Pattern Recognition 13
  *David Windridge, Vadim Mottl, Alexander Tatarchuk, and
  Andrey Eliseyev*

Kernel Combination Versus Classifier Combination 22
  Wan-Jui Lee, Sergey Verzakov, and Robert P.W. Duin

Deriving the Kernel from Training Data 32
  Stefano Merler, Giuseppe Jurman, and Cesare Furlanello

Applications

On the Application of SVM-Ensembles Based on Adapted Random
Subspace Sampling for Automatic Classification of NMR Data 42
  Kai Lienemann, Thomas Plötz, and Gernot A. Fink

A New HMM-Based Ensemble Generation Method for Numeral
Recognition 52
  Albert Hung-Ren Ko, Robert Sabourin, and Alceu de Souza Britto Jr.

Classifiers Fusion in Recognition of Wheat Varieties 62
  *Sarunas Raudys, Ömer Kaan Baykan, Ahmet Babalik,
  Vitalij Denisov, and Antanas Andrius Bielskis*

Multiple Classifier Methods for Offline Handwritten Text Line
Recognition 72
  Roman Bertolami and Horst Bunke

Applying Data Fusion Methods to Passage Retrieval in QAS 82
  Hans Ulrich Christensen and Daniel Ortiz-Arroyo

A Co-training Approach for Time Series Prediction with Missing
Data 93
  Tawfik A. Mohamed, Neamat El Gayar, and Amir F. Atiya

An Improved Random Subspace Method and Its Application to EEG
Signal Classification 103
  Shiliang Sun

Ensemble Learning Methods for Classifying EEG Signals   113
    Shiliang Sun

Confidence Based Gating of Colour Features for Face Authentication . . .   121
    Mohammad T. Sadeghi, Samaneh Khoshrou, and Josef Kittler

View-Based Eigenspaces with Mixture of Experts for View-Independent
Face Recognition   131
    Reza Ebrahimpour, Ehsanollah Kabir, and Mohammad Reza Yousefi

Fusion of Support Vector Classifiers for Parallel Gabor Methods
Applied to Face Verification   141
    Ángel Serrano, Isaac Martín de Diego, Cristina Conde,
    Enrique Cabello, Li Bai, and Linlin Shen

Serial Fusion of Fingerprint and Face Matchers   151
    Gian Luca Marcialis and Fabio Roli

Boosting

Boosting Lite – Handling Larger Datasets and Slower Base
Classifiers   161
    Lawrence O. Hall, Robert E. Banfield, Kevin W. Bowyer, and
    W. Philip Kegelmeyer

Information Theoretic Combination of Classifiers with Application to
AdaBoost   171
    Julien Meynet and Jean-Philippe Thiran

Interactive Boosting for Image Classification   180
    Yijuan Lu, Qi Tian, and Thomas S. Huang

Cluster and Graph Ensembles

Group-Induced Vector Spaces   190
    Manuele Bicego, Elżbieta Pękalska, and Robert P.W. Duin

Selecting Diversifying Heuristics for Cluster Ensembles   200
    Stefan T. Hadjitodorov and Ludmila I. Kuncheva

Unsupervised Texture Segmentation Using Multiple Segmenters
Strategy   210
    Michal Haindl and Stanislav Mikeš

Classifier Ensembles for Vector Space Embedding of Graphs   220
    Kaspar Riesen and Horst Bunke

Cascading for Nominal Data   231
    Jesús Maudes, Juan J. Rodríguez, and César García-Osorio

Feature Subspace Ensembles

A Combination of Sample Subsets and Feature Subsets in
One-Against-Other Classifiers 241
 Mineichi Kudo, Satoshi Shirai, and Hiroshi Tenmoto

Random Feature Subset Selection for Ensemble Based Classification of
Data with Missing Features 251
 Joseph DePasquale and Robi Polikar

Feature Subspace Ensembles: A Parallel Classifier Combination Scheme
Using Feature Selection 261
 Hugo Silva and Ana Fred

Stopping Criteria for Ensemble-Based Feature Selection............... 271
 Terry Windeatt and Matthew Prior

Multiple Classifier System Theory

On Rejecting Unreliably Classified Patterns 282
 *Pasquale Foggia, Gennaro Percannella, Carlo Sansone, and
 Mario Vento*

Bayesian Analysis of Linear Combiners 292
 Battista Biggio, Giorgio Fumera, and Fabio Roli

Applying Pairwise Fusion Matrix on Fusion Functions for Classifier
Combination 302
 Albert Hung-Ren Ko, Robert Sabourin, and Alceu de Souza Britto Jr.

Modelling Multiple-Classifier Relationships Using Bayesian Belief
Networks 312
 Samuel Chindaro, Konstantinos Sirlantzis, and Michael Fairhurst

Classifier Combining Rules Under Independence Assumptions 322
 Shoushan Li and Chengqing Zong

Embedding Reject Option in ECOC Through LDPC Codes 333
 Claudio Marrocco, Paolo Simeone, and Francesco Tortorella

Intramodal and Multimodal Fusion of Biometric Experts

On Combination of Face Authentication Experts by a Mixture of
Quality Dependent Fusion Classifiers 344
 Norman Poh, Guillaume Heusch, and Josef Kittler

Index Driven Combination of Multiple Biometric Experts for AUC
Maximisation... 357
 Roberto Tronci, Giorgio Giacinto, and Fabio Roli

$Q - stack$: Uni- and Multimodal Classifier Stacking with Quality
Measures 367
   Krzysztof Kryszczuk and Andrzej Drygajlo

Reliability-Based Voting Schemes Using Modality-Independent Features
in Multi-classifier Biometric Authentication 377
   Jonas Richiardi and Andrzej Drygajlo

Optimal Classifier Combination Rules for Verification and Identification
Systems 387
   Sergey Tulyakov, Venu Govindaraju, and Chaohong Wu

Majority Voting

Exploiting Diversity in Ensembles: Improving the Performance on
Unbalanced Datasets 397
   Nitesh V. Chawla and Jared Sylvester

On the Diversity-Performance Relationship for Majority Voting in
Classifier Ensembles 407
   Yun-Sheng Chung, D. Frank Hsu, and Chuan Yi Tang

Hierarchical Behavior Knowledge Space 421
   Hubert Cecotti and Abdel Belaïd

Ensemble Learning

A New Dynamic Ensemble Selection Method for Numeral
Recognition 431
   Albert Hung-Ren Ko, Robert Sabourin, and Alceu de Souza Britto Jr.

Ensemble Learning in Linearly Combined Classifiers Via Negative
Correlation 440
   Manuela Zanda, Gavin Brown, Giorgio Fumera, and Fabio Roli

Naïve Bayes Ensembles with a Random Oracle 450
   Juan J. Rodríguez and Ludmila I. Kuncheva

An Experimental Study on Rotation Forest Ensembles 459
   Ludmila I. Kuncheva and Juan J. Rodríguez

Cooperative Coevolutionary Ensemble Learning 469
   Daniel Kanevskiy and Konstantin Vorontsov

Robust Inference in Bayesian Networks with Application to Gene
Expression Temporal Data 479
   Omer Berkman and Nathan Intrator

An Ensemble Approach for Incremental Learning in Nonstationary
Environments 490
   Michael D. Muhlbaier and Robi Polikar

Invited Papers

Multiple Classifier Systems in Remote Sensing: From Basics to Recent
Developments 501
    Jon Atli Benediktsson, Jocelyn Chanussot, and Mathieu Fauvel

Biometric Person Authentication Is a Multiple Classifier Problem 513
    Samy Bengio and Johnny Mariéthoz

Author Index 523

Combining Pattern Recognition Modalities at the Sensor Level Via Kernel Fusion

Vadim Mottl, Alexander Tatarchuk[1],
Valentina Sulimova, Olga Krasotkina, and Oleg Seredin [2]

[1] Computing Center of the Russian Academy of Sciences
Vavilov St., 40, 117968 Moscow, Russia
`vmottl@yandex.ru`, `aitech@yandex.ru`
[2] Tula State University, Lenin Ave. 92, 300600 Tula, Russia
`vsulimova@yandex.ru`, `krasotkina@uic.tula.ru`, `oseredin@yandex.ru`

Abstract. The problem of multi-modal pattern recognition is considered under the assumption that the kernel-based approach is applicable within each particular modality. The Cartesian product of the linear spaces into which the respective kernels embed the output scales of single sensor is employed as an appropriate joint scale corresponding to the idea of combining modalities, actually, at the sensor level. From this point of view, the known kernel fusion techniques, including Relevance and Support Kernel Machines, offer a toolkit of combining pattern recognition modalities. We propose an SVM-based quasi-statistical approach to multi-modal pattern recognition which covers both of these modes of kernel fusion.

Keywords: Kernel-based pattern recognition; support vector machines, combining modalities, kernel fusion.

1 Introduction

It is clear that no physical object can be immediately perceived by a computer. As an intermediary between real-world objects $\omega \in \Omega$ and the computer, always serves a formal variable $x(\omega): \Omega \to \mathbb{X}$ which plays the role of some computer-perceptible generalized feature of objects of a certain kind.

The space (scale) $\mathbb{X}$ of the generalized feature may have quite a complicated structure. For instance, the set of biometric traits used for establishing the identity of a person [1] includes face image, fingerprints, off-line and on-line signature, iris and retina images, ear form etc. In medical diagnosis, the typical kinds of information on a patient [2] are, in particular, numerical or nominal results of laboratory tests, X-ray, ultrasonic and MR images or tomograms, electro- and magneto-encephalograms. In public surveys, target properties of population representatives are measured in the form of answers to special-purpose questions each of which produces a specific set of possible response alternatives $\mathbb{X}$.

Any specific type of physical, biological, social or other phenomenon which is considered as characteristic for some real-world objects and expressed by a formal

M. Haindl, J. Kittler, and F. Roli (Eds.): MCS 2007, LNCS 4472, pp. 1–12, 2007.

variable is called the specific modality of object representation in data analysis. In terms of the given modality, the original set of objects is substituted for their representations in the value space of an appropriate generalized feature $x(\omega) \in \mathbb{X}$, for instance, in the form of signals, images, questionnaire answers, or, in relatively rare simple situations, real-valued vectors.

The essence of the pattern recognition problem is extension of the information contained in the training set $(X,Y) = \{x(\omega_j), y(\omega_j), j=1,...,N\}$, $y(\omega_j) \in \mathbb{Y} = \{y^{(1)},..., y^{(m)}\}$, onto the entire scale of the respective feature $\hat{y}(x(\omega)): \mathbb{X} \to \mathbb{Y}$. In many practical cases, no single modality is able to provide the acceptable reliability of recognition. The intent to increase the generalization performance of the resulting recognition rule has led to the concept of multimodal systems $\hat{y}(x_1(\omega),...,x_n(\omega))$. In the comprehensive survey of multimodal biometrics [1], three levels of fusing several modalities are considered.

(a) Sensor or data level implies fusion of signals acquired immediately from sensors forming different initial object representations, and final decision making $\hat{y}(x(\omega))$ on the basis of some resulting unified feature $x(\omega) = \varphi(x_i(\omega), i=1,...,n)$.

(b) Classifier score level presupposes fusion of scores of multiple classifiers produced by different modalities to be combined. The score of a single classifier usually has the meaning of posterior probability vector associated with class-membership hypotheses $\left[p^{(1)}(x_i(\omega)),..., p^{(m)}(x_i(\omega)); i=1,...,n \right]$. The final decision is to be made from the vector of classifier scores $\hat{y}(p_i^{(1)},..., p_i^{(m)}, i=1,...,n)$.

(c) Decision level implies fusing final decisions $\hat{y}(\hat{y}_i, i=1,...,n)$ made separately by single classifiers on the basis of each modality $\left[\hat{y}_i(x_i(\omega)), i=1,...,n \right]$.

Fusing modalities at the decision level (c) is considered in [1] to be rigid. As to the sensor (a) and classifier score level (b), the latter one is rated in [1] as the most preferable level of fusing several modalities, because the signals of initial sensors are of different physical nature and hardly lend themselves to combination. Therefore, over a long time, the researchers paid the main attention to classifier score fusion [3]. At the same time, it is noted in [1] that the sensor level of fusing modalities might yield better results, if only there were a chance to algorithmize it. The aim of this paper is studying the ways of such algorithmization under the assumption that the kernel-based methodology is applied as a means of inferring a recognition rule for each particular modality.

The essence of the kernel-based methodology [4,5] is expressed by the notion of a kernel function $K(x',x'')$ defined in the output scale of a particular sensor $\mathbb{X} \times \mathbb{X} \to \mathbb{R}$ and meant to be the only means of perceiving real-world objects $\omega \in \Omega$ by pair-wise comparing their generalized features $x' = x(\omega')$, $x'' = x(\omega'')$. A two-argument function $K(x',x'')$ is said to be kernel if it forms a positive semidefinite matrix $\left[K(x(\omega_j), x(\omega_l)), j,l=1,...,N \right]$ for any finite collection of objects. In this case, it embeds the scale of the respective sensor $\mathbb{X}$ into a hypothetical linear space with inner product $\tilde{\mathbb{X}} \supseteq \mathbb{X}$ [6] in which the null element $\phi \in \tilde{\mathbb{X}}$ and linear operations $x' + x'': \tilde{\mathbb{X}} \times \tilde{\mathbb{X}} \to \tilde{\mathbb{X}}$

and $\alpha x: \mathbb{R} \times \tilde{\mathbb{X}} \to \tilde{\mathbb{X}}$ are defined in a special way. The role of the inner product is played by the kernel function $K(x', x'')$, which will be linear with respect to its arguments $K(\alpha'x' + \alpha''x'', x) = \alpha'K(x', x) + \alpha''K(x'', x)$ and produce the Euclidean metric along with Euclidean norm

$$\rho(x', x'') = \sqrt{K(x', x') + K(x'', x'') - 2K(x', x'')}, \quad \| x \| = \rho(x, \phi) = \sqrt{K(x, x)}. \qquad (1)$$

If, at least, one kernel is defined in the output scale of each of several sensors $K_i(x_i', x_i'')$, $x_i', x_i'' \in \mathbb{X}_i$, $i = 1, ..., n$, it appears natural to consider the Cartesian product of the respective linear spaces $\tilde{\mathbb{X}} = \tilde{\mathbb{X}}_1 \times ... \times \tilde{\mathbb{X}}_n$ and define an appropriate combined kernel (inner product) in it $K(x', x'')$, $x = (x_1, ..., x_n) \in \tilde{\mathbb{X}}$. The recent progress in the methodology of kernel fusion [7,8,9,10 has cleared the way for combining any modalities, actually, at the sensor level.

In terms of the kernel-based pattern recognition, the training set has the structure of n matrices of kernel values and N class-indices of objects:

$$(X, Y) = \left\{ x(\omega_j), y(\omega_j), j = 1, ..., N \right\} \Rightarrow \left\{ \mathbf{K}_i, i = 1, ..., n, \ y(\omega_j), j = 1, ..., N \right\}. \qquad (2)$$

In addition, it is required to hold the ability of computing the kernel values $K_i\left(x_i(\omega), x_i(\omega_j) \right)$, $i = 1, ..., n$, for any new real-world object $\omega \in \Omega$ and all the objects ω_j represented in the training set. Thus, the burden of dealing with the initial representation of objects in terms of the given modalities completely falls on the kernel computing procedures which are not considered here.

In this paper, like all the above-cited papers, we restrict our consideration only to the two-class patter recognition problem $\mathbb{Y} = \{-1, 1\}$. The common idea of all the known kernel fusion methods is the search for a combined kernel as linear combination of the particular ones $K(x', x'') = K(x'', x') = \sum_{i=1}^{n} \alpha_i K_i(x_i', x_i'')$, $\alpha_i \geq 0$. The particular kernel fusion methods differ from each other by the choice of the training criterion which essentially affects the coefficients forming the combined kernel.

The framework proposed in [7] is referred to as Support Kernel Machines (SKM) due to the fact that it produces coefficients $(\alpha_1, ..., \alpha_n)$ the most part of which equals zero, so that only the remaining positive coefficients $\alpha_i > 0$ indicate the active (support) kernels. However, this framework leads to the dual quadratically-constrained quadratic optimization problem (QCQP), which is essentially more challenging than the standard quadratic programming, or, in more detailed characterization, linearly constrained quadratic optimization problem (LCQP), which underlies the original SVM learning technique.

Another approach [8] leads to coefficients $(\alpha_1, ..., \alpha_n)$ which tend to zeros at redundant kernels without complete nulling. We propose here to call kernel fusion techniques of such a kind Relevance Kernel Machines (RKM) due to their analogy with the idea of Relevance Vector Machines (RVM) proposed by Bishop and Tipping in [11] for another purpose, namely, for constructing single-kernel discriminant hyperplanes on a different basis than SVM. The technique proposed in [8] results in the so-called semi-infinite linear programming procedure (SILP), i.e. an algorithm of minimizing a linear function of a finite number of variables under a continuum set of inequality constraints.

The quasi-statistical approach to the problem of kernel fusion we develop in this paper covers both RKM and SKM modes. Like our earlier publication [9,10], the combined kernel is assumed to be simply the sum of the initial kernels $K(x', x'') = \sum_{i=1}^{n} K_i(x_i', x_i'')$. The discriminant hyperplane is sought immediately in the linear space of the combined generalized feature $\tilde{\mathbb{X}} = \tilde{\mathbb{X}}_1 \times ... \times \tilde{\mathbb{X}}_n$ in the form

$$f(x(\omega)) = f(x_1(\omega),...,x_n(\omega)) = K(\vartheta, x(\omega)) + b = \sum_{i=1}^{n} K_i(\vartheta_i, x_i(\omega)) + b \gtrless 0. \qquad (3)$$

It is well seen that if the norm $\sqrt{K_i(\vartheta_i, \vartheta_i)}$ of a component of the direction vector $\vartheta = (\vartheta_1,...,\vartheta_n) \in \tilde{\mathbb{X}}$ is small in its linear space $\vartheta_i \in \tilde{\mathbb{X}}_i$, the respective kernel $K_i(x_i', x_i'')$ will little affect the recognition rule.

We call the approach quasi-statistical, because the improper densities we use may have no finite integral over the respective space. Our approach leans upon a quasi-probabilistic assumption on the a priori distribution of independent random elements of the direction vector $\vartheta = (\vartheta_1,...,\vartheta_n) \in \tilde{\mathbb{X}}$ in (3). Let $\psi(\vartheta)$ be a basic "spherical" density in some linear space, namely, the density with null mathematical expectation $E(\vartheta) = \phi$ and mean-square distance from the null element $E(\rho^2(\vartheta, \phi)) = 1$. Then, if we assume m_i to be the dimensionality of a modality-specific linear space $\tilde{\mathbb{X}}_i$, the density

$$\psi_i(\vartheta_i \mid r_i) = \sqrt{1/r_i^{m_i}} \, \psi(\vartheta_i / \sqrt{r_i}) \qquad (4)$$

will determine, in accordance with (1), the mean-square distance from the respective null element $E(\rho_i^2(\vartheta_i, \phi_i)) = E(K_i(\vartheta_i, \vartheta_i)) = r_i$.

We consider two kinds of basic a priori densities $\psi(\vartheta)$, namely, the quasi-normal and quasi-Laplace density. The kernel fusion problem is formulated as that of estimating the spatial variances $(r_1,...,r_n)$ along with the elementary direction vectors $(\vartheta_1,...,\vartheta_n)$ from the given training set (2). The normality assumption on the a priori distribution of the hidden direction elements ϑ_i leads to the RKM mode of kernel fusion, and the assumed Laplace distribution results in the SKM fusion mode.

We illustrate the proposed kernel fusion framework by its application to the problem of multi-kernel on-line signature verification.

2   The Quasi-statistical Approach to Kernel Fusion

Let $\{x_i(\omega) \in \mathbb{X}_i, i=1,...,n\}$ be the given set of generalized features $x(\omega) = (x_1(\omega),...,x_n(\omega)) \in \mathbb{X} = \mathbb{X}_1 \times ... \times \mathbb{X}_n$ defined in a universe of real-world objects $\omega \in \Omega$. We shall consider the universe $\omega \in \Omega$ with its genuine partition into two subsets $y(\omega) \in \mathbb{Y} = \{-1, 1\}$ as probability space producing a probability distribution in the set of pairs $(x(\omega), y(\omega)) \in \mathbb{X} \times \mathbb{Y}$, and treat the training set

$(X,Y) = \{ \boldsymbol{x}(\omega_j), y(\omega_j), j=1,...,N \}$ as result of repeated independent sampling from this distribution.

It is assumed that some kernel $K_i(x_i', x_i'')$ is defined in each scale $\mathbb{X}_i$, and, so, all the scales as well as its Cartesian product are embedded into respective linear spaces $\tilde{\mathbb{X}}_i \supseteq \mathbb{X}_i$, $\tilde{\mathbb{X}} = \tilde{\mathbb{X}}_1 \times ... \times \tilde{\mathbb{X}}_n \supseteq \mathbb{X} = \mathbb{X}_1 \times ... \times \mathbb{X}_n$. So, any choice of a point $\vartheta = (\vartheta_1,...,\vartheta_n) \in \tilde{\mathbb{X}}$ and a real number $b \in \mathbb{R}$ defines a discriminant hyperplane in $\tilde{\mathbb{X}}$ (3).

Let $\vartheta \in \tilde{\mathbb{X}}$ be a fixed point in the Cartesian product of the linear spaces produced by the elementary kernels. If we assume this point as the direction vector of the discriminant hyperplane (3), it will remain to choose the threshold $b \in \mathbb{R}$. Let the accepted training strategy be expressed by the criterion

$$b(\vartheta) = \arg\min_{b \in \mathbb{R}} Q(b \mid \vartheta, X, Y). \tag{5}$$

The main heuristic idea of our approach is treating the function

$$\Phi(\vartheta, b \mid X, Y) = \frac{\exp(-u Q(b \mid \vartheta, X, Y))}{\int_{\tilde{\mathbb{X}} \times \mathbb{R}} \exp[-u Q(b' \mid \vartheta', X, Y)] d\vartheta' db'} = \frac{1}{D(X,Y)} \exp(-u Q(b \mid \vartheta, X, Y)),$$

where $u > 0$ is free parameter, as a posteriori joint distribution density of the direction vector and threshold value under the assumption that no a priori information is available on the direction vector.

In addition, we assume that a priori information is available only on the direction vector $\vartheta \in \tilde{\mathbb{X}}$, so, the respective density will be expressed in the improper form $\Psi(\vartheta, b) = \Psi(\vartheta)$ which is constant with respect to b. Thus, the a posteriori joint probability density of ϑ and b will be the product $P(\vartheta, b \mid X, Y) = \Psi(\vartheta) \Phi(\vartheta, b \mid X, Y) = (1/D(X,Y)) \Psi(\vartheta) \exp(-u Q(b \mid \vartheta, X, Y))$. Under these assumptions, we obtain the training criterion $(\hat{\vartheta}, \hat{b}) = \arg\max_{\vartheta \in \tilde{\mathbb{X}}, b \in \mathbb{R}} P(\vartheta, b \mid X, Y)$, or, in the equivalent form,

$$(\hat{\vartheta}, \hat{b}) = \arg\min_{\vartheta \in \tilde{\mathbb{X}}, b \in \mathbb{R}} J(\vartheta, b \mid X, Y), \quad J(\vartheta, b \mid X, Y) = -\ln \Psi(\vartheta) + u Q(b \mid \vartheta, X, Y). \tag{6}$$

3 The General SVM-Based Kernel Fusion Framework

Let the initial threshold-oriented training criterion (5) that occurs in the resulting criterion (6) be taken in the form

$$Q(b \mid \vartheta, X, Y) = \sum_{\substack{j: y(\omega_j)=1, \\ K(\vartheta, \boldsymbol{x}(\omega))+b < 1}} \{ 1 - [K(\vartheta, \boldsymbol{x}(\omega)) + b] \} - \sum_{\substack{j: y(\omega_j)=-1, \\ K(\vartheta, \boldsymbol{x}(\omega))+b > -1}} \{ 1 + [K(\vartheta, \boldsymbol{x}(\omega)) + b] \} \to \min_b,$$

or, what is equivalent,

$$\sum_j \delta_j \to \min(b \in \mathbb{R}, \delta_j \in \mathbb{R}), \quad y_j [K(\vartheta, \boldsymbol{x}(\omega_j)) + b] \geq 1 - \delta_j, \quad \delta_j \geq 0.$$

In this case, in accordance with (6), we come to the following general training criterion:

$$\begin{cases} -\ln \Psi(\vartheta) + u \sum_j \delta_j \to \min \left(\vartheta \in \tilde{\mathbb{X}}, b \in \mathbb{R}, \delta_j \in \mathbb{R} \right), \\ y_j \left[K \left(\vartheta, x(\omega_j) \right) + b \right] \ge 1 - \delta_j, \ \delta_j \ge 0. \end{cases} \quad (7)$$

This training criterion differs from the usual kernel-based SVM [5] only in two aspects. First, the direction vector of the sought discriminant hyperplane ϑ is interpreted as element of a hypothetical linear space $\tilde{\mathbb{X}}$ "spanned", by the accepted kernel $K(x', x'')$, over the Cartesian product of the particular scales $\mathbb{X}_i$ of single object representation modalities. Second, the deflection of this vector from the null is penalized by the a priori probability density $-\ln\Psi(\vartheta)$ assumed to have the maximum value if $\vartheta = (\vartheta_1, ..., \vartheta_n) = (\phi_1, ..., \phi_n)$ instead of the usual squared norm $K(\vartheta, \vartheta)$ (1).

Kernel $K(x', x'')$ is the inner product in the combined linear space $\tilde{\mathbb{X}} = \tilde{\mathbb{X}}_1 \times ... \times \tilde{\mathbb{X}}_n$ of the object-representation modalities $x(\omega) = \left(x_1(\omega), ..., x_n(\omega) \right)$. For instance, any linear combination of the inner products in the particular modalities, i.e. particular kernels, with nonnegative coefficients will produce a combined kernel $K(x', x'') = \sum_{i=1}^n \alpha_i K_i(x_i', x_i'')$. However, in our case there is no need to consider more sophisticated combined kernels than the simple sum $K(x', x'') = \sum_{i=1}^n K_i(x_i', x_i'')$.

We restrict our consideration only to independent a priori distributions of the components in the combined direction vector $\vartheta = (\vartheta_1, ..., \vartheta_n)$, assuming that each of them $\psi_i(\vartheta_i \mid r_i)$ (4) depends on the specific unknown value of the spatial variance r_i. Then,

$$\Psi(\vartheta \mid r_1, ..., r_n) = \prod_{i=1}^n \psi_i(\vartheta_i \mid r_i) = \sqrt{1 / \left(\prod_{i=1}^n r_i^{m_i} \right)} \prod_{i=1}^n \psi\left(\vartheta_i / \sqrt{r_i} \right),$$

where the product in the denominator has the meaning of the concentration volume of this distribution in $\tilde{\mathbb{X}}$. Estimation of the concentration volume makes no sense in this problem, and we shall assume it to be preset, for instance, $\prod_{i=1}^n r_i^{m_i} = 1$. So,

$$\Psi(\vartheta \mid r_1, ..., r_n) = \prod_{i=1}^n \psi\left(\vartheta_i / \sqrt{r_i} \right), \quad (8)$$

and we shall have in (7) $-\ln \Psi(\vartheta) = -\sum_{i=1}^n \left[-\ln \psi\left(\vartheta_i / \sqrt{r_i} \right) \right]$ under the additional assumption $\sum_{i=1}^n m_i \ln r_i = 0$.

The unknown variances r_i of kernel-specific a priori distributions will be of crucial importance for the result of kernel fusion, therefore, we optimize (7) by $(r_1, ..., r_n)$ along with other variables. Thus, we shall use the general kernel fusion criterion having the following structure:

$$\begin{cases} \sum_{i=1}^n \left[-\ln \psi\left(\vartheta_i / \sqrt{r_i} \right) \right] + u \sum_j \delta(\omega_j) \to \min \left(\vartheta_i \in \tilde{\mathbb{X}}_i, r_i \in \mathbb{R}^+, b \in \mathbb{R}, \delta(\omega_j) \in \mathbb{R}^+ \right), \\ \sum_{i=1}^n m_i \ln r_i = 0, \quad y(\omega_j) \left[\sum_{i=1}^n K_i \left(\vartheta_i, x_i(\omega_j) \right) + b \right] \ge 1 - \delta(\omega_j). \end{cases} \quad (9)$$

Any particular kernel fusion technique will be specified only by the choice of the basic a priori density $\psi(\vartheta)$.

Generally speaking, it is problematic to evaluate the dimensionalities m_i of the kernel-specific linear spaces $\tilde{\mathbb{X}}_i$, which may be infinite. But for the given training set (2), the observed dimensionality cannot exceed the number of objects N , and the lower bound of m_i can be estimated from the respective positive semidefinite kernel matrix $\mathbf{K}_i = \left\{ K_i\big(x_i(\omega_j), x_i(\omega_k)\big), j, k = 1, ..., N \right\}$ as the number of its essentially positive eigenvalues.

4   Quasi-normal a Priori Distributions of Modality-Specific Direction Vectors: The Relevance Kernel Machine

For the standard normal density $\psi(\vartheta) = \left(1/\sqrt{2\pi}\right)\exp\left(-(1/2)\|\vartheta\|^2\right)$, we have $\ln\psi\left(\vartheta_i/\sqrt{r_i}\right) = -\ln\sqrt{2\pi} - (1/2r_i)K_i(\vartheta_i, \vartheta_i)$, and the training criterion (9) gets the form with $C = 2u$:

$$\begin{cases} \sum_{i=1}^{n}(1/r_i)K_i(\vartheta_i, \vartheta_i) + C\sum_j \delta_j \to \min\left(\vartheta_i \in \tilde{\mathbb{X}}_i, r_i \in \mathbb{R}, b \in \mathbb{R}, \delta_j \in \mathbb{R}\right), \\ \sum_{i=1}^{n} m_i \ln r_i = 0, \quad y_j\left[\sum_{i=1}^{n} K_i\big(\vartheta_i, x_i(\omega_j)\big) + b\right] \geq 1 - \delta_j, \ \delta_j \geq 0. \end{cases} \quad (10)$$

Theorem 1. *For fixed variances* $(r_i, i = 1, ..., n)$, *the combined recognition rule following from the optimization problem (10) has the structure*

$$\hat{f}(x(\omega)) = \hat{y}\big(x_1(\omega), ..., x_n(\omega)\big) = \sum_{j: \hat{\lambda}_j > 0} y_j \hat{\lambda}_j \sum_{i=1}^{n} r_i K_i\big(x_i(\omega_j), x_i(\omega)\big) + \hat{b} \gtrless 0,$$

$$\hat{b} = -\frac{\sum_{j: 0 < \hat{\lambda}_j < C/2} \hat{\lambda}_j \sum_{l: \lambda_l > 0} y_l \hat{\lambda}_l \sum_{i=1}^{n} r_i K_i\big(x_i(\omega_j), x_i(\omega_l)\big) + (C/2)\sum_{j: \hat{\lambda}_j = C/2} y_j}{\sum_{j: 0 < \hat{\lambda}_j < C/2} \hat{\lambda}_j}. \quad (11)$$

Here Lagrange multipliers $\hat{\lambda}_j$ *at the inequality constraints in (10) are solutions of the dual quadratic programming problem*

$$\begin{cases} \sum_{j=1}^{N} \lambda_j - (1/2)\sum_{j=1}^{N}\sum_{l=1}^{N}\Big(y_j y_l \sum_{i=1}^{n} r_i K_i\big(x_i(\omega_j), x_i(\omega_l)\big)\Big)\lambda_j \lambda_l \to \max, \\ \sum_{j=1}^{N} y_j \lambda_j = 0, \ 0 \leq \lambda_j \leq C/2, \ j = 1, ..., N. \end{cases} \quad (12)$$

The training criterion (10) with fixed variances r_i is a generalization of the well-known SVM criterion [5]. The training-set objects ω_j whose Lagrange multipliers are positive $\lambda_j > 0$ correspond to active constraints and are called support objects. It is easy to show that the hypothetical constituents $\hat{\vartheta}_i \in \tilde{\mathbb{X}}_i$ of the direction vectors of the optimal discriminant hyperplane in the combined linear space $\tilde{\mathbb{X}} = \tilde{\mathbb{X}}_1 \times ... \times \tilde{\mathbb{X}}_n$ are linear combinations of the support objects in the sense of specific linear operations produced by the respective kernels:

$$\hat{\vartheta}_i = r_i \sum_{j:\hat{\lambda}_j>0} y_j \hat{\lambda}_j x_i(\omega_j) \in \tilde{\mathbb{X}}_i . \qquad (13)$$

However, there is no need to deal with these products of mathematical imagination, because they do not occur in the final formulas (11).

For finding the optimal values variances $(r_i, i=1,...,n)$, we apply to (10) the Gauss-Seidel iteration with respect to both groups of variables $(\vartheta_i, i=1,...,n,b)$ and $(r_i, i=1,...,n)$:

$$(r_i^{(k)}, i=1,...,n) \to \left(\lambda_j^{(k+1)}, j=1,...,N\right) \text{ from (12)},$$

$$\left(\lambda_j^{(k+1)}, j=1,...,N\right) \to \vartheta_i^{(k+1)} = r_i^{(k)} \sum_{j:\lambda_j^{(k+1)}>0} y_j \lambda_j^{(k+1)} x_i(\omega_j) \text{ from (13)},$$

$$\left(\vartheta_i^{(k+1)}, i=1,...,n\right) \to \begin{cases} (r_i^{(k+1)}, i=1,...,n) = \arg\min \sum_{i=1}^{n}(1/r_i)K_i(\vartheta_i,\vartheta_i), \\ \sum_{i=1}^{n} m_i \ln r_i = 0, \end{cases} \text{ from (10).} \quad (14)$$

It is easy to show that the solution of the problem (14) is expressed by the formulas

$$r_i^{(k+1)} = \frac{K_i(\vartheta_i^{(k+1)},\vartheta_i^{(k+1)})}{m_i \exp\left\{\left(\sum_{l=1}^{n} m_l \ln\left[(1/m_l)K_l(\vartheta_l^{(k+1)},\vartheta_l^{(k+1)})\right]\right)\Big/\sum_{l=1}^{n} m_l\right\}} , \qquad (15)$$

where, according to (13),

$$K_i(\vartheta_i^{(k+1)},\vartheta_i^{(k+1)}) = (r_i^{(k)})^2 \sum_j \sum_l y_j y_l \lambda_j^{(k+1)} \lambda_l^{(k+1)} K_i\left(x_i(\omega_j), x_i(\omega_l)\right)$$

with summation only over the support objects $j:\lambda_j^{(k+1)} > 0$.

It is well seen from (11) that variances r_i occur in the recognition rule as weights at the respective kernels – the greater r_i, the greater the contribution of kernel $K_i(x_i', x_i'')$ to the recognition rule. The iterative process of estimating the variances usually converges in 10-15 steps and displays a tendency to suppressing the weights at "redundant" kernels $r_i \to 0$ along with emphasizing $r_i \gg 0$ the kernels which are "adequate" to the trainer's data. We name this training mode the Relevance Kernel Machine, because it results in soft extraction of a relatively small number of most adequate kernels without full suppression of the others.

5 Quasi-laplace a Priori Distributions of Direction Vectors: The Support Kernel Machine

Let us consider now the standard Laplace density $\psi(\vartheta)=(1/2)\exp\left(-(1/2)\|\vartheta\|\right)$. In this case, $\ln\psi\left(\vartheta/\sqrt{r_i}\right) = -\ln 2 - (1/2)\left(1/\sqrt{r_i}\right)\sqrt{K_i(\vartheta_i,\vartheta_i)}$, and we come to the criterion (9) in the following form with $C = 2u$:

$$\begin{cases} \sum_{i=1}^{n} \sqrt{(1/r_i)K_i(\vartheta_i,\vartheta_i)} + C\sum_j \delta_j \to \min\left(\vartheta_i \in \tilde{\mathbb{X}}_i, r_i \in \mathbb{R}, b \in \mathbb{R}, \delta_j \in \mathbb{R}\right), \\ \sum_{i=1}^{n} m_i \ln r_i = 0, \quad y_j\left[\sum_{i=1}^{n} K(\vartheta_i, x_i(\omega_j)) + b\right] \geq 1-\delta_j, \delta_j \geq 0. \end{cases} \qquad (16)$$

We have come to the formulation of the training problem which differs from the formulation proposed in [7] by the norm of the combined kernel, which is not squared in the criterion (16) in contrast to $\left(\sum_{i=1}^{n} d_i \sqrt{K_i(\vartheta_i, \vartheta_i)} \right)^2$ in the cited paper. We shall see that this distinction results in a considerable simplification of the optimization problem.

Theorem 2. *For fixed variances* $(r_1, ..., r_n)$*, the combined recognition rule following from the optimization problem (16) has the structure*

$$\hat{f}(x(\omega)) = \hat{y}(x_1(\omega), ..., x_n(\omega)) = \sum_{j:\lambda_j>0} \hat{\lambda}_j y_j \sum_{i \in \hat{I}} \hat{\mu}_i K_i (x_i(\omega_j), x_i(\omega)) + \hat{b}. \qquad (17)$$

Here $\hat{\lambda}_j$ *are the solutions of the first dual optimization problem*

$$\begin{cases} \sum_{j=1}^{N} \lambda_j \to \max, & \sum_{j=1}^{N} \lambda_j y_j = 0, \ 0 \le \lambda_j \le C, \ j = 1, ..., N, \\ \sum_{j=1}^{N} \sum_{l=1}^{N} y_j y_l K_i (x_i(\omega_j), x_i(\omega_l)) \lambda_j \lambda_l \le 1/r_i^2, \ i = 1, ..., n, \end{cases} \qquad (18)$$

set $\hat{I} \subseteq \{1, ..., n\}$ *is the set of active inequality constraints in (18) at the maximum point,* $\hat{\mu}_i$ *are the solutions of the system of linear equations*

$$\sum_{i \in \hat{I}} \left[\sum_{q:\hat{\lambda}_q>0} \sum_{l:0<\hat{\lambda}_l<C} g_l g_q \left(K_i(\omega_q, \omega_j) - K_i(\omega_q, \omega_l) \right) \hat{\lambda}_l \hat{\lambda}_q \right] \mu_i = $$

$$g_j \sum_{q:0<\hat{\lambda}_q<C} g_q \hat{\lambda}_q - \sum_{q:0<\hat{\lambda}_q<C} \hat{\lambda}_q, \ j : 0 < \hat{\lambda}_j < C, \qquad (19)$$

and $\hat{b}$ *is determined by the formula*

$$\hat{b} = \frac{\sum_{j:0<\hat{\lambda}_j<C} \hat{\lambda}_j - \sum_{i \in \hat{I}} \left(\sum_{j:\lambda_j>0} \sum_{l:0<\lambda_l<C} g_j g_l K_i(\omega_j, \omega_l) \hat{\lambda}_j \hat{\lambda}_l \right) \hat{\mu}_i}{\sum_{j:0<\hat{\lambda}_j<C} g_j \hat{\lambda}_j} \qquad (20)$$

In accordance with the terminology introduced in [7], the kernels $\{K_i(x_i', x_i''), i \in \hat{I}\}$ indicated by the subset of active constraints in (18) are the support kernels for the given training set, because only these kernels participate in the recognition rule (17). This is an alternative version of Support Kernel Machine first considered in [7].

The dual optimization problem (18) is that of maximizing a linear function under linear and quadratic constraints. The problems of this class, let us name it Quadratically Constraint Linear Programming (QCLP) is much simpler than those of Quadratically Constraint Quadratic Programming (QCQP) resulting from the framework studied in [7]. The QCLP problems lend themselves to an easy numerical solution by publicly available instruments.

The abstract constituents $\hat{\vartheta}_i \in \tilde{\mathbb{X}}_i$ of the direction vectors of the optimal discriminant hyperplane are linear combinations of the support objects:

$$\hat{\vartheta}_i = \hat{\mu}_i \sum_{j:\hat{\lambda}_j > 0} \hat{\lambda}_j y_j x_i(\omega_j) \in \tilde{\mathbb{X}}_i . \tag{21}$$

This fact is exploited in the Gauss-Seidel iterative procedure which is applied to the training criterion (16) for jointly optimizing it by $(r_i, i = 1,...,n)$ and $(\vartheta_i, i = 1,...,n, b)$:

$(r_i^{(k)}, i = 1,...,n) \to \left(\lambda_j^{(k+1)}, j = 1,...,N\right)$ and $\hat{I}^{(k+1)} \subseteq \{1,...,n\}$ from (18),

$\left(\lambda_j^{(k+1)}, j = 1,...,N\right)$ and $\hat{I}^{(k+1)} \subseteq \{1,...,n\} \to \left(\hat{\mu}_i^{(k+1)}, i \in I^{(k+1)}\right)$ from (19),

$\left(\lambda_j^{(k+1)}, j = 1,...,N\right)$ and $\left(\hat{\mu}_i^{(k+1)}, i \in I^{(k+1)}\right) \to \left(\vartheta_i^{(k+1)}, i = 1,...,n\right)$ from (21),

$$\left(\vartheta_i^{(k+1)}, i=1,...,n\right) \to \begin{cases} (r_i^{(k+1)}, i=1,...,n) = \arg\min \sum_{i=1}^{n} \sqrt{(1/r_i) K_i(\vartheta_i^{(k+1)}, \vartheta_i^{(k+1)})}, \\ \sum_{i=1}^{n} m_i \ln r_i = 0, \end{cases}$$ from (16).

The following formulas give the solution of the last optimization problem:

$$\sqrt{r_i^{(k+1)}} = \frac{\sqrt{K_i(\vartheta_i^{(k+1)}, \vartheta_i^{(k+1)})}}{m_i \exp\left\{\left(\sum_{k=1}^{n} m_k \ln\left[(1/m_k)\sqrt{K_k(\vartheta_k^{(k+1)}, \vartheta_k^{(k+1)})}\right]\right) \Big/ \sum_{k=1}^{n} m_k\right\}},$$

where $K_i(\vartheta_i^{(k+1)}, \vartheta_i^{(k+1)}) = (\hat{\mu}_i^{(k+1)})^2 \sum_j \sum_l y_j y_l \lambda_j^{(k+1)} \lambda_l^{(k+1)} K_i\left(x_i(\omega_j), x_i(\omega_l)\right)$ with summation over the support objects.

6 Experiments: Multi-kernel On-Line Signature Verification

The problem of signature verification consists in testing the null hypothesis that the given signature belongs to the person who has claimed his/her identity against the alternative hypothesis that this is forgery. The approach to on-line signature verification presented in [12] is completely based on evaluating one or several kernels on the set of "all feasible" signals that may be produced by the pen's trajectory. Twelve different kernels were simultaneously computed for each pair of signature signals.

In the experiment, we used the database that contains signatures of 40 persons. For each person, the training set consists of 800 signatures, namely, 10 signatures of the respective person, 10 skilled forgeries (attempts to emulate the signature dynamics of this person), and 780 random forgeries formed by 390 original signatures of other 39 persons and 390 skilled forgeries for them. The test set for each person consists of 59 signatures, namely, 10 original signatures, 10 skilled forgeries, and 39 random forgeries. Thus, the total number of the test signatures for 40 persons amounts to 2360.

We tested 13 ways of training, namely, based on each of the initial kernels separately and RKM principle of fusing all the kernels. The errors rates of single kernels in the total test set of 2360 signatures range from 0.51% to 23.81%. The RKM kernel fusion technique essentially outperforms each of the single kernels with 0.38% error rate.

For each of 40 persons whose signatures made the data set, the RKM procedure has selected only one relevance kernel which turned out to be most adequate to his/her handwriting. In each case, the relevance kernel obtained nonzero weight $r_i \geq 1.0$, whereas the weights at other kernels were assigned negligibly small values $r_i \leq 10^{-5}$.

7 Conclusions

The kernel-based view of the multi-modal pattern recognition problem stems from the assumption that, at least, one kernel is defined in the output scale of each of several sensors, and, so, each of the scales is embedded into a hypothetical kernel-specific linear space with inner product. The Cartesian product of these linear spaces appears to be just the expedient joint scale corresponding to the idea of combining modalities at the sensor level.

In these terms, the choice of a particular method of multi-modal pattern recognition boils down to the choice of an appropriate kernel in the resulting combined linear space. From this point of view, the known kernel fusion techniques, including Relevance and Support Kernel Machines, offer an appropriate toolkit of combining patter recognition modalities, actually, at the sensor level.

However, it remains open to question whether the sensor level of fusing modalities is really more preferable than the classifier combination level. In the companion paper [13], we set out to show that our approach to combining kernels leads, under some additional assumptions, to a new method of combining kernel-based classifiers, and offers a mathematical basis for comparison of two competing or, maybe, cooperating principles of kernel and classifier fusion.

Acknowledgments. This work is supported by the Russian Foundation for Basic Research, Grants 05-01-00679, 06-01-08042, 06-07-89249, and INTAS Grant 04-77-7347.

References

1. Ross A., Jain A.K. Multimodal biometrics: An overview. Proceedings of the 12th European Signal Processing Conference (EUSIPCO), 2004. Vienna, Austria, pp. 1221-1224.
2. Jannin P, Fleig O.J, Seigneuret E, Grova C, Morandi X, Scarabin J.M. A data fusion environment for multimodal and multi-informational neuronavigation. Comput Aided Surg., 2000, Vol. 5, No. 1, pp. 1-10.
3. Multiple Classifier Systems. Proceedings of the 1st - 6th International Workshops: Lecture Notes in Computer Science, Springer, 2001, 2002, 2003, 2004, 2005.
4. Aizerman M.A., Braverman E.M., Rozonoer L.I. Theoretical foundations of the potential function method in pattern recognition learning. Automation and Remote Control, 1964, Vol. 25, pp. 821-837.
5. Vapnik V. Statistical Learning Theory. John-Wiley & Sons, Inc. 1998.
6. Mottl V. Metric spaces admitting linear operations and inner product. Doklady Mathematics 67(1), 2003, 140–143.
7. Bach F.R., Lankriet G.R.G., Jordan M.I. Multiple kernel learning, conic duality, and the SMO algorithm. Proceedings of the 21th International Conference on Machine Learning, Banff, Canada, 2004.
8. Sonnenburg S., Rätsch G., Schäfer C. A general and efficient multiple kernel learning algorithm. Proceedings of the 19th Annual Conference on Neural Information Processing Systems, Vancouver, Canada, December 5-8, 2005.

9. Mottl V., Krasotkina O., Seredin O., Muchnik I. Principles of multi-kernel data mining. Proceedings of the 4th International Conference on Machine Learning and Data Mining in Pattern Recognition, Leipzig, Germany, 2005. Lecture Notes in Computer Science, 3587 Springer, 2005, pp. 52-61.
10. Mottl V., Krasotkina O., Seredin O., Muchnik I. Kernel fusion and feature selection in machine learning. Proceedings of the 8th IASTED International Conference on Intelligent Systems and Control. Cambridge, USA, October 31 - November 2, 2005.
11. Bishop C.M., Tipping M.E. Variational relevance vector machines. In: *C. Boutilier and M. Goldszmidt (Eds.)*, Proceedings of the 16th Conference on Uncertainty in Artificial Intelligence. Morgan Kaufmann, 2000, pp. 46–53.
12. Sulimova V., Mottl V., Tatarchuk A. Multi-kernel approach to on-line signature verification. Proceedings of the 8th IASTED International Conference on Signal and Image Processing. Honolulu, Hawaii, USA, August 14-16, 2006.
13. Windridge D., Mottl V., Tatarchuk A., Eliseyev A. The neutral point method for kernel-based combining disjoint training data in multi-modal pattern recognition. Proceedings of the 7th International Workshop on Multiple Classifier Systems, Prague, Czech Republic, May 23-25, 2007.

The Neutral Point Method for Kernel-Based Combination of Disjoint Training Data in Multi-modal Pattern Recognition

David Windridge[1], Vadim Mottl[2], Alexander Tatarchuk[2], and Andrey Eliseyev[3]

[1] Centre for Vision, Speech and Signal Processing, University of Surrey,
The Stag Hill, Guildford, GU2 7XH, UK
D.Windridge@surrey.ac.uk
[2] Computing Center of the Russian Academy of Sciences,
Vavilov St. 40, Moscow, 119991, Russia
vmottl@yandex.ru, aitech@yandex.ru
[3] Moscow Institute of Physics and Technology,
Institutsky Per. 9, Dolgoprudny, Moscow Region, 141700, Russia
andreyel@gmail.com

Abstract. Multiple modalities present potential difficulties for kernel-based pattern recognition in consequence of the lack of inter-modal kernel measures. This is particularly apparent when training sets for the differing modalities are disjoint. Thus, while it is always possible to consider the problem at the classifier fusion level, it is conceptually preferable to approach the matter from a kernel-based perspective. By interpreting the aggregate of disjoint training sets as an entire data set with missing inter-modality measurements to be filled in by appropriately chosen substitutes, we arrive at a novel kernel-based technique, the *neutral-point method*. On further theoretical analysis, it transpires that the method is, in structural terms, a kernel-based analog of the well-known sum rule combination scheme. We therefore expect the method to exhibit similar error-canceling behavior, and thus constitute a robust and conservative strategy for the treatment of kernel-based multi-modal data.

Keywords: Kernel-based pattern recognition; combining modalities; kernel fusion; classifier fusion.

1 Introduction

In data analysis and, in particular, pattern recognition, it is common practice to employ the term "modality" when speaking about a specific kind of mathematical computer-perceptible object representation. In terms of the measured modality, the hypothetical set of "all" real-world objects $\omega \in \Omega$ is represented by the output of the respective sensor $x(\omega) \in \mathbb{X}$ in the form of signals, images, or, in relatively rare simple cases, in the form of one-dimensional numerical features.

The essence of the training problem in supervised pattern recognition is extrapolation of the information contained in the finite training set of the accessible objects

M. Haindl, J. Kittler, and F. Roli (Eds.): MCS 2007, LNCS 4472, pp. 13–21, 2007.
© Springer-Verlag Berlin Heidelberg 2007

$\Omega^* = (X,Y) = \{x(\omega_j) \in \mathbb{X},\ y(\omega_j) \in \mathbb{Y} = \{1,...,m\},\ \omega_j \in \Omega^*\}$ onto the entire scale of the respective object representation $\hat{y}(x(\omega)): \mathbb{X} \to \mathbb{Y}$. The intention of increasing the generalization performance of the resulting recognition rule has led to the concept of multimodal systems, which combine several object representation modalities $\{x_i(\omega) \in \mathbb{X}_i,\ i=1,...,n\}$ into a unified recognition procedure $\hat{y}(x_1(\omega),...,x_n(\omega)):$ $\mathbb{X}_1 \times ... \times \mathbb{X}_n \to \mathbb{Y}$.

In the overview of multimodal biometrics given in [1] two principle levels of combining modalities are distinguished: the *signal level*, when, prior to training the classifier $\hat{y}(\omega)$, a unified representation of objects is formed $x(\omega) = \varphi(x_i(\omega), i=1,...,n)$ to combine all the particular modalities $\hat{y}(\omega) = \hat{y}(x(\omega))$, and the *classifier level*, when what is to be combined are the classifiers $\hat{y}(\omega) = \gamma[\hat{y}_i(x_i(\omega)), i=1,...,n]$, each trained individually by a single modality.

Until recently, most attention had been paid in the literature to principles of classifier fusion [2,3], because it was assumed that combining modalities of different character (real numbers and labels, for example) is not straightforward. However, recent achievements in the methodology of kernel fusion [4,5,6,7,8] have cleared the way for combining any number of modalities at the signal level.

The aim of this paper is to consider relationships between the two approaches to multimodal machine learning, kernel fusion and classifier fusion, under the specific assumption that the problem to be solved is that of two-class pattern recognition, and that, in addition, the kernel-based approach is applied within each modality.

Before closely scrutinizing the relationship between kernel and classifier fusion, we consider the specificity of a single modality-specific kernel-based classifier. As applied to the kernel-based approach, the principle of classifier fusion implies combining several recognition rules inferred from modality-specific data. In this paper, on the basis of the kernel fusion methodology considered in [8], we propose a unified view on the seemingly different principles of combining modalities at the signal and classifier level by, respectively, kernel and classifier fusion.

2   The Modality-Specific Kernel-Based Classifier

A two-argument symmetric function $K_i(x_i', x_i'') = K_i(x_i'', x_i')$ defined in the output scale of a particular sensor $\mathbb{X}_i = \{x_i(\omega),\ \omega \in \Omega\}$ is said to be kernel function in $\mathbb{X}_i$ if it forms positive semidefinite matrices $\left[K_i(x_i(\omega_j), x_i(\omega_l)); j,l=1,...,k\right]$ for all finite subsets of this set [9]. Any kernel $K_i(x_i', x_i'')$ embeds the scale of the respective sensor $\mathbb{X}_i$ into a hypothetical linear space with inner product $\tilde{\mathbb{X}}_i \supseteq \mathbb{X}_i$, in which the null element $\phi_i \in \tilde{\mathbb{X}}_i$ and linear operations $x_i' + x_i'': \tilde{\mathbb{X}}_i \times \tilde{\mathbb{X}}_i \to \tilde{\mathbb{X}}_i$ and $\alpha x_i: \mathbb{R} \times \tilde{\mathbb{X}}_i \to \tilde{\mathbb{X}}_i$ are defined in a special way. The role of the inner product is played by the kernel function $K_i(x_i', x_i'')$ [10] which will be linear with respect to its arguments $K_i(\alpha' x_i' + \alpha'' x_i'', x) = \alpha' K(x_i', x_i) + \alpha'' K(x_i'', x_i)$.

Thus, in terms of a single modality, a training set $\Omega_i^* = \{\omega_j, j=1,...,N_i\}$ is completely represented by the kernel matrix and class-indices of objects $y_j = y(\omega_j) = \pm 1$:

$$\Omega_i^* \Rightarrow \left\{ \mathbf{K}_i = \left[K_i\left(x_i(\omega_j), x_i(\omega_l)\right), \omega_j, \omega_l \in \Omega_i^* \right], y(\omega_j), \omega_j \in \Omega_i^* \right\}. \tag{1}$$

In addition, it is required to uphold the ability to compute the kernel values $K_i\left(x_i(\omega), x_i(\omega_j)\right)$ for any new real-world object $\omega \in \Omega$ and all the objects $\omega_j \in \Omega_i^*$ represented in the training set.

A commonly adopted kernel-based approach to the two-class pattern recognition problem is widely known under the name of Support Vector Machine (SVM) [9]. The main concept of this approach is that of the optimal discriminant hyperplane in the linear space $\tilde{\mathbb{X}}_i$ produced by the respective kernel $\hat{y}_i\left(x_i(\omega)\right) = K_i\left(\vartheta_i, x_i(\omega)\right) + b_i \gtrless 0$. In our terms, the discriminant hyperplane is defined by a hypothetical element of this linear space $\vartheta_i \in \tilde{\mathbb{X}}_i$ and by the threshold $b_i \in \mathbb{R}$. The SVM training criterion follows from the idea of maximizing the margin between the points of two classes in $\tilde{\mathbb{X}}_i$:

$$\begin{cases} K_i(\vartheta_i, \vartheta_i) + C \sum_{\omega_j \in \Omega_i^*} \delta_j \to \min\left(\vartheta_i \in \tilde{\mathbb{X}}_i, b \in \mathbb{R}, \delta_j \in \mathbb{R}\right), \\ y_j \left[K\left(\vartheta_i, x_i(\omega_j)\right) + b \right] \geq 1 - \delta_j, \delta_j \geq 0, \omega_j \in \Omega_i^*. \end{cases} \tag{2}$$

where $C > 0$ is sufficiently large coefficient. The dual form of this criterion is a quadratic programming problem with respect to the nonnegative Lagrange multipliers $\lambda_{i,j} \geq 0$ for the inequality constraints:

$$\begin{cases} \sum_{\omega_j \in \Omega_i^*} \lambda_{i,j} - (1/2) \sum_{\omega_j \in \Omega_i^*} \sum_{\omega_l \in \Omega_i^*} \left[y_j y_l K_i\left(x_i(\omega_j), x_i(\omega_l)\right) \right] \lambda_{i,j} \lambda_{i,l} \to \max, \\ \sum_{\omega_j \in \Omega_i^*} y_j \lambda_{i,j} = 0, \ 0 \leq \lambda_{i,j} \leq C/2, \omega_j \in \Omega_i^*. \end{cases} \tag{3}$$

The direction vector of the optimal discriminant hyperplane is the linear combination of the training-set objects with coefficients defined by the Lagrange multipliers found as the solution of this problem $\hat{\vartheta}_i = \sum_{\omega_j \in \Omega_i^*} y_j \hat{\lambda}_{i,j} \omega_j$. It must be kept in mind that the training-set objects occur in this linear combination as elements of the hypothetical linear space $\tilde{\mathbb{X}}_i \supseteq \mathbb{X}_i$ in accordance with the specific linear operations produced by the kernel $K_i(x_i', x_i'')$.

The objects $\omega_j \in \Omega_i^*$ whose Lagrange multipliers are positive in the solution of the dual problem $\hat{\lambda}_{i,j} > 0$ make the subset of support objects in the full training set:

$$\hat{\Omega}_i = \left\{ \omega_j \in \Omega_i^* : \hat{\lambda}_{i,j} > 0 \right\} \subseteq \Omega_i^*. \tag{4}$$

Only the support objects will form the direction vector of the optimal discriminant hyperplane

$$\hat{f}_i\left(x_i(\omega)\right)=\sum\nolimits_{j:\,\omega_j\in\hat{\Omega}_i}K_i\left(\hat{\vartheta}_i,x_i(\omega)\right)+\hat{b}_i\gtrless0\Rightarrow\hat{y}_i\left(x_i(\omega)\right)=\pm1\,,\;\;\hat{\vartheta}_i=\sum\nolimits_{\omega_j\in\hat{\Omega}_i}y_j\hat{\lambda}_{i,j}\omega_j\,, \quad (5)$$

and only the kernel matrix at the support objects will affect the recognition rule inferred from the training set of the respective modality:

$$\hat{f}_i\left(x_i(\omega)\right)=\sum\nolimits_{j:\,\omega_j\in\hat{\Omega}_i}y_j\hat{\lambda}_{i,j}K_i\left(x_i(\omega_j),x_i(\omega)\right)+\hat{b}_i\gtrless0,$$

$$\hat{b}_i=-\left(\sum\nolimits_{j:\,\omega_j\in\hat{\Omega}_i}\hat{\lambda}_{i,j}\sum\nolimits_{l:\,\omega_l\in\hat{\Omega}_i}y(\omega_l)\hat{\lambda}_{i,l}K_i\left(x_i(\omega_j),x_i(\omega_l)\right)\right)\Big/\sum\nolimits_{j:\,\omega_j\in\hat{\Omega}_i}\hat{\lambda}_{i,j}\right). \quad (6)$$

So, the result of training within the bounds of a single modality is completely represented by the subset of support objects and the positive values of Lagrange multipliers at them (4).

We introduce here a new notion, which will be especially important for the comparison of kernel fusion and classifier fusion. If a new object maps into a point strictly at the discriminant hyperplane $\hat{y}_i\left(x_i(\omega)\right)=0$ (6), it cannot be attributed to any one of the two classes. All these point will be said to be neutral points produced by the training set and denoted them by special symbol $\hat{x}_{\phi,i}$. It is obvious that there exists a continuum of neutral points for each modality $\tilde{\mathbb{X}}_{\phi,i}$ in the respective space $\tilde{\mathbb{X}}_i$:

$$\hat{x}_{\phi,i}\in\tilde{\mathbb{X}}_{\phi,i}\,,\;\;\tilde{\mathbb{X}}_{\phi,i}=\left\{x_i\in\tilde{\mathbb{X}}_i:K_i(\hat{\vartheta}_i,x_i)+\hat{b}_i=0\right\},\;\;\hat{b}_i=-K_i(\hat{\vartheta}_i,x_{\phi,i})\,. \quad (7)$$

3 Kernel Fusion: Combining Modalities at the Signal Level from a Full Training Set by Kernel Fusion

Let, at least, one kernel be defined in the output scale of each of several sensors $K_i(x_i',x_i'')$, $x_i',x_i''\in\mathbb{X}_i$, $i=1,...,n$. The union of all the modality-specific training sets $\Omega^*=\bigcup_{i=1}^n\Omega_i^*$ (1) will be called the unified training set. We shall say the unified training set Ω^* is *full* if each object $\omega_j\in\Omega^*$ is represented by all the modality-specific signals $x(\omega_j)=\left(x_i(\omega_j)\in\mathbb{X}_i,i=1,...,n\right)$, i.e., all the kernel-specific training sets coincide $\Omega_1^*=...=\Omega_n^*$.

A full training set Ω^* allows for immediate combination of several modalities by kernel fusion. All the known kernel fusion techniques are based on the idea of constructing an appropriate combined kernel (inner product) $K(x',x'')$, $x=(x_1,...,x_n)\in\tilde{\mathbb{X}}$, in the Cartesian product $\tilde{\mathbb{X}}=\tilde{\mathbb{X}}_1\times...\times\tilde{\mathbb{X}}_n=\left\{x=(x_i\in\tilde{\mathbb{X}}_i,i=1,...,n)\right\}$ of the linear spaces $\tilde{\mathbb{X}}_i\supseteq\mathbb{X}_i$ defined by the respective kernels. The sum of the initial kernels $K(x',x'')=\sum_{i=1}^n K_i(x_i',x_i'')$ will retain all the properties of inner product, i.e., be a kernel in $\tilde{\mathbb{X}}$. From this point of view, any choice of a point $\vartheta=(\vartheta_i\in\tilde{\mathbb{X}}_i,i=1,...,n)\in\tilde{\mathbb{X}}$ and real number $b\in\mathbb{R}$ yields a discriminant hyperplane with direction vector in the Cartesian product $\tilde{\mathbb{X}}$

$$\hat{f}(x(\omega)) = \hat{f}(x_i(\omega), i = 1,...,n) = K(\vartheta, x(\omega)) + b = \sum_{i=1}^{n} K_i(\vartheta_i, x_i(\omega)) + b \gtreqless 0, \qquad (8)$$

and produces, thereby, a kernel fusion technique.

It is apparent that if the norm $\sqrt{K_i(\vartheta_i, \vartheta_i)}$ of a component of the direction vector $\vartheta_i \in \tilde{\mathbb{X}}_i$ is small in its linear space, the respective kernel $K_i(x_i', x_i'')$ will little affect the recognition rule (8).

The straightforward application of the SVM training principle to the Cartesian product of the particular linear spaces $\tilde{\mathbb{X}} = \tilde{\mathbb{X}}_1 \times ... \times \tilde{\mathbb{X}}_n$ [9], namely, finding the optimal discriminant hyperplane in $\tilde{\mathbb{X}}$ with respect to the full training set Ω^*, results in the training criterion

$$\begin{cases} \sum_{i=1}^{n} K_i(\vartheta_i, \vartheta_i) + C \sum_{\omega_j \in \Omega^*} \delta_j \to \min(\vartheta_i \in \tilde{\mathbb{X}}_i, b \in \mathbb{R}, \delta_j \in \mathbb{R}), \\ y_j \left[\sum_{i=1}^{n} K_i(\vartheta_i, x_i(\omega_j)) + b \right] \geq 1 - \delta_j, \ \delta_j \geq 0, \ \omega_j \in \Omega^*. \end{cases} \qquad (9)$$

This optimization problem leads to the dual quadratic programming problem of the analogous structure as the usual SVM dual problem (3):

$$\begin{cases} \sum_{\omega_j \in \Omega^*} \lambda_j - (1/2) \sum_{\omega_j \in \Omega^*} \sum_{\omega_l \in \Omega^*} \left(y_j y_l \sum_{i=1}^{n} K_i(x_i(\omega_j), x_i(\omega_l)) \right) \lambda_j \lambda_l \to \max, \\ \sum_{\omega_j \in \Omega^*} y_j \lambda_j = 0, \ 0 \leq \lambda_j \leq C/2, \ \omega_j \in \Omega^*. \end{cases} \qquad (10)$$

The Lagrange multipliers obtained for the set of support objects

$$\hat{\Omega} = \left\{ \omega_j \in \Omega^* : \hat{\lambda}_j > 0 \right\} \subseteq \Omega^* \qquad (11)$$

yield the optimal recognition rule:

$$\hat{f}(x(\omega)) = \hat{y}(x_1(\omega),...,x_n(\omega)) = \sum_{\omega_j \in \hat{\Omega}} y_j \hat{\lambda}_j \sum_{i=1}^{n} K_i(x_i(\omega_j), x_i(\omega)) + \hat{b} \gtreqless 0,$$

$$\hat{b} = -\left(\sum_{\omega_j \in \hat{\Omega}} \hat{\lambda}_j \sum_{\omega_l \in \hat{\Omega}} y_l \hat{\lambda}_l \sum_{i=1}^{n} K_i(x_i(\omega_j), x_i(\omega_l)) \middle/ \sum_{\omega_j \in \hat{\Omega}} \hat{\lambda}_j \right). \qquad (12)$$

This is the simplest but not the only possible way of kernel fusion. The quasi-statistical approach to the signal-level modality combination considered in [8] covers the main kernel fusion principles known at present.

With the objective function in (9) as $\sum_{i=1}^{n} (1/r_i) K_i(\vartheta_i, \vartheta_i) + C \sum_{\omega_j \in \Omega^*} \delta_j \to$

$\min(\vartheta_i \in \tilde{\mathbb{X}}_i, r_i \in \mathbb{R}, b \in \mathbb{R}, \delta_j \in \mathbb{R})$ under additional constraint $\prod_{i=1}^{n} r_i = 1$, the training criterion displays a tendency to suppressing the weights at the "redundant" kernels $\hat{r}_i \to 0$ along with emphasizing $\hat{r}_i \gg 0$ the kernels which are "adequate" to the trainer's data, and, so, results in soft extraction of a relatively small number of most adequate kernels without full suppression of the others. Due to this property, this training technique is called in [8] the Relevance Kernel Machine (RKM).

If $\sum_{i=1}^{n} \sqrt{K_i(\vartheta_i, \vartheta_i)} + C \sum_{\omega_j \in \Omega^*} \delta_j \to \min(\vartheta_i \in \tilde{\mathbb{X}}_i, b \in \mathbb{R}, \delta_j \in \mathbb{R})$ is taken as the objective function in (9), the training technique selects a subset of support kernels

$\hat{I} \subseteq \{1,...,n\}$ with positive norms of the direction vectors $\left(K_i(\hat{\vartheta}_i,\hat{\vartheta}_i)>0, i\in\hat{I}\right)$ in contrast to the others which get completely suppressed $\left(K_i(\hat{\vartheta}_i,\hat{\vartheta}_i)=0, i\notin\hat{I}\right)$ [8]. Because only the support kernels $i\in\hat{I}$ participate in the recognition rule, this is a kind of Support Kernel Machine (SKM) first considered in [5].

All of these approaches to kernel fusion techniques are closely related to the problem of studying the relationship between kernel and classifier fusion as alternative strategies for combining pattern recognition modalities at, respectively, signal and classifier level. However, in this paper we restrict our consideration only to the simplest kernel fusion technique (9).

4   The Neutral Point Method of Combining Modalities from Disjoint Training Sets

It is common practice that particular modalities are employed by different expert groups, which hence derive their training sets independently of each other. If it is so, the training set $\Omega^*=\{\omega_j, j=1,...,N\}$ will consist of *disjoint* subsets $\Omega^*=\bigcup_{i=1}^{n}\Omega_i^*$, $\Omega_i^*\cap\Omega_l^*=\varnothing$, such that the output signals of only one modality-specific sensor $\left(x_i(\omega_j), \omega_j\in\Omega_i^*\right)$ are captured within the bounds of each of them.

With respect to this notation, the kernel fusion criterion (9) may be put in the following equivalent form:

$$\begin{cases}\sum_{i=1}^{n}\left(K_i(\vartheta_i,\vartheta_i)+C\sum_{\omega_j\in\Omega_i^*}\delta_j\right)\to\min\left(\vartheta_i\in\tilde{\mathbb{X}}_i, b\in\mathbb{R}, \delta_j\in\mathbb{R}\right),\\ \left[y_j\left(K_i(\vartheta_i,x_i(\omega_j))+\sum_{l=1,l\neq i}^{n}K_l(\vartheta_l,x_l(\omega_j))+b\right)\geq 1-\delta_j, \delta_j\geq 0, \omega_j\in\Omega_i^*\right], i=1,...,n.\end{cases} \quad (13)$$

Here, in each group of constraints at the training-set objects $\{\omega_j\in\Omega_i^*, i=1,...,n\}$, for any value of the abstract variable $\vartheta_i\in\mathbb{X}_i$, only one of n summands is defined, namely, $K_i\left(\vartheta_i,x_i(\omega_j)\right)$, whereas the other summands $K_l\left(\vartheta_l,x_l(\omega_j)\right)$ are not, because the sensor signals $x_l(\omega_j)$ are unknown for $l\neq i$ due to the assumption that the particular training sets are disjoint.

We hence propose a new method of combining modalities in supervised kernel-based pattern recognition in the case when the training sets for different modalities are disjoint. The idea consists in treating the problem (13) as that of learning with incomplete data and filling-up the unknown actual values of the sensor signals corresponding to other modalities $x_l(\omega_j)$, $l\neq i$, by one common value being the arbitrary neutral point $\hat{x}_{\phi,i}\in\tilde{\mathbb{X}}_{\phi,i}$ (7) of the i th linear space. After this substitution, the problem (13) takes the following form:

$$\begin{cases} \sum_{i=1}^n \left(K_i(\vartheta_i, \vartheta_i) + C\sum_{\omega_j \in \Omega_i^*} \delta_j \right) \to \min\left(\vartheta_i \in \tilde{\mathbb{X}}_i, b \in \mathbb{R}, \delta_j \in \mathbb{R} \right), \\ \left[y_j \left(K_i(\vartheta_i, x_i(\omega_j)) \right) + \sum_{l=1, l \neq i}^n K_l(\vartheta_l, \hat{x}_{\phi,l}) + b \right] \geq 1 - \delta_j, \delta_j \geq 0, \omega_j \in \Omega_i^* \right], i = 1,...,n. \end{cases} \quad (14)$$

Theorem. The solution of the optimization problem (13) is the totality of the optimal direction elements in the linear spaces of generalized features $\hat{\vartheta}_i \in \tilde{\mathbb{X}}_i$ (5) found as the solutions of the training problems (2) independently for each modality $i = 1,...,n$, along with the common threshold value equal to the sum of optimal thresholds for all modalities $\hat{b} = \sum_{i=1}^n \hat{b}_i$ (6).

Hence, replacement of the unknown actual values of sensor signals by the neutral points of the respective linear spaces leads to the discriminant function (5)

$$\hat{f}(x_i(\omega), i = 1,...,n) = \sum_{i=1}^n K_i(\hat{\vartheta}_i, x_i(\omega)) + \sum_{i=1}^n \hat{b}_i = \sum_{i=1}^n \left[K_i(\hat{\vartheta}_i, x_i(\omega)) + \hat{b}_i \right] \gtrless 0. \quad (15)$$

Here the expressions in brackets are nothing other than the discriminant functions built independently for each modality $\hat{f}_i(x_i(\omega))$, thus,

$$\hat{f}(x_i(\omega), i = 1,...,n) = \sum_{i=1}^n \hat{f}_i(x_i(\omega)). \quad (16)$$

So, the approach to filling-in the missing values of sensor signals we have adopted leads to the indicated recognition rule which, in structural terms, is a technique for combining particular classifiers, namely, by summation of particular discriminant functions. The neutral point method should therefore exhibit the error-canceling properties associated with classifier combination and should hence be a robust and safe approach to kernel-based classification of disjoint data sets.

An analogous technique of combining classifiers is known in the literature under the name of Sum Rule [2]. The distinction consists in that the known Sum Rule method is based on the assumption of the probabilistic output of the particular classifiers in the form of posterior class-membership probabilities $p_i^{(k)}(x_i(\omega))$, $\sum_{k=1}^m p_i^{(k)}(x_i(\omega)) = 1$. The combination principle consists in computing the unified posterior probabilities of classes by way of summing over the particular posterior probabilities: $p^{(k)}(x_i(\omega), i=1,...,n) = (1/n)\sum_{i=1}^n p_i^{(k)}(x_i(\omega))$. When there are only two classes $m = 2$, the posterior probabilities at the output of the i th classifier are completely determined by the posterior probability of one of the classes:

$$p(x_i(\omega), i = 1,...,n) = (1/2)\sum_{i=1}^n p_i(x_i(\omega)).$$

The analogy between our classifier fusion rule (16) and the Sum Rule is immediately apparent.

5 Discussion

At first inspection, it is hardly possible to encompass a generic way of combining modalities because of the vast variety of possible object representations. However, the kernel-fusion approach converts, in a natural way, different modalities into a unified mathematical language of inner products in linear spaces, which in fact makes such a comparison realistic. This is so even if the original modalities are not themselves vector or scalar quantities: the only scalar constraint is that of the kernel itself. This is hence particularly necessary in situations in which only relative distance measures are available, such as Genomics.

Thus in the simplest case, the sensor signals might have the form of scalar numerical features, i.e. be real numbers. What we have customarily done when learning in a multidimensional linear space, which is the Cartesian product of several real-valued axes, is thus nothing other than combining several modalities via a form of kernel fusion.

However, any purely kernel-based fusion method exhibits difficulties when the differences in modality are accompanied by differences in training set composition: in this case straightforward kernel-fusion will not suffice. This difficulty is also apparent for conventional classification: in fact it is clear that application of the classifier fusion principle is an inescapable necessity in the case of disjoint training subsets contained within disjoint modalities, since multiple decision confidences are the only quantities available for combining in a meaningful manner.

We have hence, by making certain conservative assumptions about the 'missing' kernel values, derived a *neutral point method* for addressing the above difficulty in a Kernel-based context. However, it transpires that the neutral point method has *itself* the exact structural form of a classifier combination scheme (in fact the Sum Rule decision scheme).

At its purest level, though, the principle of combining modalities with disjoint training sets via classifier fusion is based on the assumption that the modalities are *independent* (that is, for decision problems in which the individual modalities cannot be straightforwardly taken to define a composite Cartesian product space in which classification can take place). The principle of kernel-fusion, on the other hand, is not attached to this assumption: the fact that it becomes equivalent to one particular combination scheme under the neutral point assumption for missing data should not therefore be taken as significant for combination in general, but rather for the Sum Rule, *specifically.*

The fact that the Sum Rule combination scheme also exhibits ideal error-canceling properties [2] is thus a significant bonus, and a considerable further reason for advocating the neutral point method.

6 Conclusions

We have set out to address the difficulties that multiple modalities and disjoint training sets represent for kernel-based pattern recognition due to their absence of intramodal kernel information. Though possible to consider the problem at the classifier fusion level, we have motivated our work on the basis of the conceptual preferability of addressing the issue from a purely kernel-specific perspective. Hence, by interpreting the aggregate of disjoint training sets as complete data-sets with missing intermodality measurements that can be substituted by appropriately-chosen values, we have arrived at a novel classification technique, which we have named the *neutral-*

point method. We proceeded to theoretically demonstrate that the neutral-point method is a kernel-based analog of the well-known sum rule combination scheme. It is thus capable of error-cancellation, and gives strong backing for our assertion that the neutral-point choice of replacements for inter-modality measurements is a conservative and safe one.

Acknowledgments. This work is supported by the Russian Foundation for Basic Research, Grants 05-01-00679, 06-01-08042, 06-07-89249, and INTAS Grant 04-77-7347.

References

1. Ross A., Jain A.K. Multimodal biometrics: An overview. Proceedings of the 12th European Signal Processing Conference *(EUSIPCO), 2004.* Vienna, Austria, pp. 1221-1224.
2. Kittler J., Hatef M., Duin R., Matas J. On combining classifiers. IEEE Trans. on Pattern Analysis and Machine Intelligence, 1998, Vol. 20, No. 3, pp. 226-239.
3. Multiple Classifier Systems. Proceedings of the 1st - 6th International Workshops:Lecture Notes in Computer Science, Springer, 2001, 2002, 2003, 2004, 2005.
4. Lanckriet G.R.G., Cristianini N., Ghaoui L.E., Bartlett P., Jordan M.I. Learning the kernel matrix with semidefinite programming. J. Machine Learning Research, 5, 2004, pp. 27–72.
5. Bach F.R., Lankriet G.R.G., Jordan M.I. Multiple kernel learning, conic duality, and the SMO algorithm. Proceedings of the 21th International Conference on Machine Learning, Banff, Canada, 2004.
6. Sonnenburg S., Rätsch G., Schäfer C. A general and efficient multiple kernel learning algorithm. Proceedings of the 19th Annual Conference on Neural Information Processing Systems, Vancouver, Canada, December 5-8, 2005.
7. Mottl V., Krasotkina O., Seredin O., Muchnik I. Principles of multi-kernel data mining. Proceedings of the 4th International Conference on Machine Learning and Data Mining in Pattern Recognition, Leipzig, 2005, 52-61.
8. Mottl V., Tatarchuk A., Seredin O., Krasotkina O., Sulimova V. Combining pattern recognition modalities at the sensor level via kernel fusion. Proceedings of the 7th International Workshop on Multiple Classifier Systems, Prague, Czech Republic, May 23-25, 2007.
9. Vapnik V. *Statistical Learning Theory.* John-Wiley & Sons, Inc. 1998.
10. Mottl V. Metric spaces admitting linear operations and inner product. Doklady Mathematics, 2003, Vol. 67, No. 1, pp. 140–143.

Kernel Combination Versus Classifier Combination

Wan-Jui Lee[1], Sergey Verzakov[2], and Robert P.W. Duin[2]

[1] EE Department, National Sun Yat-Sen University, Kaohsiung, Taiwan
wrlee@water.ee.nsysu.edu.tw
[2] Information and Communication Theory Group, TU Delft, The Netherlands
serguei@edison.et.tudelft.nl, r.duin@ieee.org

Abstract. Combining classifiers is to join the strengths of different classifiers to improve the classification performance. Using rules to combine the outputs of different classifiers is the basic structure of classifier combination. Fusing models from different kernel machine classifiers is another strategy for combining models called kernel combination. Although classifier combination and kernel combination are very different strategies for combining classifier, they aim to reach the same goal by very similar fundamental concepts.

We propose here a compositional method for kernel combination. The new composed kernel matrix is an extension and union of the original kernel matrices. Generally, kernel combination approaches relied heavily on the training data and had to learn some weights to indicate the importance of each kernel. Our compositional method avoids learning any weight and the importance of the kernel functions are directly derived in the process of learning kernel machines. The performance of the proposed kernel combination procedure is illustrated by some experiments in comparison with classifier combining based on the same kernels.

1 Introduction

Traditional pattern recognition systems use a particular classification procedure to estimate the class of a given pattern. It has been observed that combining the decisions of different classifiers can be an efficient technique for improving the classification performance. If the combination function can take advantage of the strengths of the individual classifiers and avoid their weaknesses, the overall classification accuracy is expected to improve. Also, a larger stability for the classification system is highly anticipated. Many techniques have been proposed in last decade for combining classifiers [1].

A classifier combination system is usually composed of two phases, constructing individual classifiers and combining different classifiers. In the first phase, various models can be adopted to construct different classifiers, or the classifiers can be constructed on different features or from different sample datasets. In the second phase, the classifiers are combined by fixed or trained rules. This can be done on the basis of classifier outputs like posterior probabilities or using the crisp decisions (voting). Nevertheless, there are possibilities to combine the classifiers in an earlier stage in the classification system. In fact, the combination of models has attracted more and more attention recently, especially for kernel machines [2]. In kernel machine classifiers, different models can be built with different kernel functions. Combining models in kernel machine classifiers is thereby based on combining their kernels.

M. Haindl, J. Kittler, and F. Roli (Eds.): MCS 2007, LNCS 4472, pp. 22–31, 2007.
© Springer-Verlag Berlin Heidelberg 2007

The support vector machine (SVM) [2,3], motivated by the results of statistical learning theory, is one of the most popular kernel machines. Most of the kernel combination research is based on it. In SVM, the decision boundary for pattern recognition problems is represented by a small subset of training examples, called support vectors. Unlike the traditional methods that minimize the empirical training errors, support vector machines implement the structural risk minimization principle. By adopting this principle, SVM can find the optimal discriminant hyperplane minimizing the risk of an erroneous classification of unseen test samples. When input data cannot be linearly separated in the original space, they should be mapped into a high dimensional feature space, where a linear decision surface separating the training data can be designed. The computation does not need to be performed in the feature space since SVM depends on the direct application of the kernel function over the input data. Therefore, the kernel function is a key component of SVM for solving nonlinear problems, and the performance of SVM classifiers largely depends on the choice of the kernels.

However, the selection of kernel functions, the model and the parameters, is one of the most difficult problem of designing a kernel machine. Recently, an interesting development seeks to construct a good kernel from a series of kernels. The most simple way to combine kernels is by averaging them. But not each kernel should receive the same weight in the decision process, and therefore the main force of the kernel combination study is to determine the optimal weight for each kernel. The criterion for searching these weights is mainly based on Fisher's discriminant that maximizes the ratio of the between-class variance and the within-class variance. Optimization methods and heuristic approaches are also used for obtaining the weights. In [5], the weights of kernels are derived by optimizing the measure of data separation in the feature space by the semidefinite programming. Kernel target alignment is used to match the kernels with the data labels. Using boosting, a weighted combination of base kernels is generated in [4]. Some methods [6,7,8,9] try to find the best weights by maximizing a class separability criterion. All the approaches above rely heavily on the training data and some weights have to be learned before the combination of kernels to indicate the importance of each kernel.

In order to avoid learning any weight, we propose a compositional method for kernel combination. In this method, the new kernel matrix is composed of the original, different kernel matrices, by constructing a larger matrix in which the original ones are still present. Thereby, the properties of the original kernel functions can be preserved and the importance of these kernel functions are directly derived in the process of training support vector machines. Herewith, weights for individual objects with respect to the base kernels are found integrated in a single classifier optimization procedure. This procedure will thereby not overfit the training dataset as the weighted kernels methods may do due to the fact that they use the data twice: for optimising the weights as well as for training the classifier.

In this paper we experimentally study the differences of our kernel compositional method with other kernel combination methods, and the differences and influences of combining models and combining decisions for a classifier combination system. Some considerations for selecting more suitable strategies under different situations will be discussed.

The rest of the paper is organized as follows. In Section 2, some background of support vector machine is recapitulated. The construction of the discriminant hyperplane in the feature space and the effect of kernel functions is shown. In Section 3, our kernel composition method is presented. Simulation results for comparing kernel combination and classifier combination methods are given in Section 4. Finally, conclusions are summarized in Section 5.

2 Overview of Support Vector Machine

For convenience, we introduce the support vector classifier with d input variables x_{i1}, $x_{i2}, \ldots, x_{id}$ for 2-class problem with class labels $+1$ and -1 in this section. $\mathbf{x}_i$ and y_i represent i^{th} input datum (a vector) and its corresponding class label [2,3]. Extension to multi-class problems can be achieved by training multiple support vector machines.

2.1 Support Vector Machine

To control both training error and model complexity, the optimization problem of SVM is formalized as follows:

$$\text{minimize } \frac{1}{2} < \mathbf{w}, \mathbf{w} > + C \sum_{i=1}^{n} \xi_i,$$
$$\text{subject to } < \mathbf{w} \cdot \mathbf{x}_i > + b \geq +1 - \xi_i, \text{ for } y_i = +1$$
$$< \mathbf{w} \cdot \mathbf{x}_i > + b \leq -1 + \xi_i, \text{ for } y_i = -1$$
$$\xi_i \geq 0, \forall i. \tag{1}$$

By using Lagrange multiplier techniques, Eq.(1) could lead to the following dual optimization problem:

$$\text{maximize } \sum_{i=1}^{n} \alpha_i - \sum_{i=1}^{n} \sum_{j=1}^{n} \alpha_i \alpha_j y_i y_j < \mathbf{x}_i, \mathbf{x}_j >,$$
$$\text{subject to } \sum_{i=1}^{n} \alpha_i y_i = 0, \alpha_i \in [0, C]. \tag{2}$$

Using Lagrange multipliers, the optimal desired weight vector of the discriminant hyperplane is $\mathbf{w} = \sum_{i=1}^{n} \alpha_i y_i \mathbf{x}_i$. Therefore the best discriminant hyperplane can be derived as

$$f(\mathbf{x}) = < \sum_{i=1}^{n} \alpha_i y_i \mathbf{x}_i, \mathbf{x} > + b = (\sum_{i=1}^{n} \alpha_i y_i < \mathbf{x}_i, \mathbf{x} >) + b, \tag{3}$$

where b is the bias of the discriminant hyperplane.

2.2 Kernel Functions

In Eq.(3), the only way in which the data appears is in the form of dot products $< \mathbf{x}_i, \mathbf{x} >$. The discriminant hyperplane is thereby linear and can only solve a linearly separable classification problem. If the problem is nonlinear, instead of trying to fit a nonlinear model, the problem can be mapped to a new space by a nonlinear transformation using a suitably chosen kernel function. The linear model used in the new space corresponds to a nonlinear model in the original space. To make the above model nonlinear, consider a mapping $\phi(\mathbf{x})$ from the input space into some feature space as

$$\phi : \mathbb{R}^d \to \mathcal{H}. \tag{4}$$

The training algorithm only depends on the data through dot products in $\mathcal{H}$, i.e. on functions of the form $< \phi(\mathbf{x}_i), \phi(\mathbf{x}_j) >$. Suppose a kernel function K defined by

$$K(\mathbf{x}_i, \mathbf{x}_j) = < \phi(\mathbf{x}_i), \phi(\mathbf{x}_j) >, \tag{5}$$

is used in the training algorithm. Explicit knowledge of ϕ is thereby avoided. The dot product in the feature space can be expressed as a kernel function. Similar to Eq.(3) in linear problems, for a nonlinear problem, we will have the following discriminant function

$$f(\mathbf{x}) = \sum_{i=1}^{n} \alpha_i y_i K(\mathbf{x}_i, \mathbf{x}) + b. \tag{6}$$

In this paper, we will use the Gaussian radial basis function as the kernel function, and therefore

$$K(\mathbf{x}_i, \mathbf{x}_j) = e^{\left(-\frac{\|x_i - x_j\|^2}{\sigma^2}\right)}. \tag{7}$$

3   Composition of Kernel Matrices

Most kernel combination methods try to average out the kernel matrices in one way or another [5,4,6,7,8,9]. There is a risk, however, of losing information in the original kernel matrices. For example, if the dataset has varying local distributions, different kernels will be good for different areas. Averaging the kernel functions of such a dataset would lose some capability to describe these local distributions. In order to combine kernel matrices without losing any original information, we develop a kernel composition method which is an extension and aggregation of all the original kernel matrices.

Suppose the original kernel functions are $K_1, K_2, ...,$ and K_s and the feature functions of the original kernel functions are $\phi_1(\mathbf{x}), \phi_2(\mathbf{x})...,$ and $\phi_s(\mathbf{x})$. We would like to preserve and use all the feature functions to construct a new kernel function, so we should be able to compute inner products like $< \phi_p(\mathbf{x}), \phi_{p'}(\mathbf{x}') >$, where $\phi_p(\mathbf{x})$ and $\phi_{p'}(\mathbf{x}')$ are feature functions from different kernel spaces. We will show that this can be done if we can formulate $\phi_{\mathbf{p}}(\mathbf{x})$ as $K_p^{\frac{1}{2}}(\mathbf{x}, \mathbf{z})$ which is a function of $\mathbf{z}$ and belongs to the L_2 space. [1] Using the definition of inner products in the L_2 space, we define the compositional kernel function as

$$K_{p,p'}(\mathbf{x}, \mathbf{x}') \equiv < \phi_p(\mathbf{x}), \phi_{p'}(\mathbf{x}') > \equiv \int K_p^{\frac{1}{2}}(\mathbf{x}, \mathbf{z}) K_{p'}^{\frac{1}{2}}(\mathbf{x}', \mathbf{z}) d\mathbf{z}. \tag{8}$$

---

[1] $K_p^{\frac{1}{2}}(\mathbf{x}, \mathbf{z})$ can be computed based on eigenvalue decomposition: it has the same eigenfunctions as $K_p(\mathbf{x}, \mathbf{z})$ and its eigenvalues are the square roots of those of $K_p(\mathbf{x}, \mathbf{z})$.

Using the self-similarity property of Gaussian distributions, one can show that the square root of a radial basis kernel function is

$$K_p^{\frac{1}{2}}(\mathbf{x}, \mathbf{z}) = (\frac{4}{\pi \sigma_p{}^2})^{\frac{d}{4}} e^{(-2\frac{\|\mathbf{x}-\mathbf{z}\|^2}{\sigma_p{}^2})}, \qquad (9)$$

and the mixture of two kernel matrices can be derived as

$$K_{p,p'}(\mathbf{x}, \mathbf{x}') = (\frac{2\sigma_p\sigma_{p'}}{\sigma_p{}^2 + \sigma_{p'}{}^2})^{\frac{d}{2}} e^{(-2\frac{\|\mathbf{x}-\mathbf{x}'\|^2}{\sigma_p{}^2 + \sigma_{p'}{}^2})}. \qquad (10)$$

Clearly, $K_{p,p} \equiv K_p$. Consequently, the compositional kernel matrix K is of the form

$$K = \begin{pmatrix} K_{1,1} & K_{1,2} & \cdots & K_{1,s} \\ K_{2,1} & K_{2,2} & \cdots & K_{2,s} \\ \vdots & \vdots & \ddots & \vdots \\ K_{s,1} & K_{s,1} & \cdots & K_{s,s} \end{pmatrix}_{s \times n, s \times n}, \qquad (11)$$

where the original kernel matrices are on the diagonal. The other elements are mixtures of two different kernel matrices which are defined like $(K_{p,p'})_{i,j} = K_{p,p'}(\mathbf{x}_i, \mathbf{x}_j)$. It is obvious that entries of K are the inner products in L_2, and because of this K is positive semi-definite. The kernel matrix K is called the compositional kernel matrix. Also, the feature function $\phi(\mathbf{x})$ of the compositional kernel matrix can be defined as $\phi(\mathbf{x}) = [\phi_1(\mathbf{x}), \phi_2(\mathbf{x}), ..., \phi_s(\mathbf{x})]$. Note that the size of the compositional kernel matrix is $(s \times n) \times (s \times n)$ while the sizes of the original kernel matrices are $n \times n$. After the construction of the compositional kernel matrix, the support vector machine can proceed the learning of support vectors and their corresponding coefficients. Objects have to be replicated as the compositional kernel matrix is s times larger than the base kernels.

With the compositional kernel matrix, we can reformulate the optimization problem as follows:

$$\text{minimize } \frac{1}{2} <\mathbf{w}, \mathbf{w}> +C \sum_{i=1}^{s \times n} \xi_i,$$
$$\text{subject to } <\mathbf{w} \cdot \mathbf{x}_i> +b \geq +1 - \xi_i, \text{ for } y_i = +1$$
$$<\mathbf{w} \cdot \mathbf{x}_i> +b \leq -1 + \xi_i, \text{ for } y_i = -1$$
$$\xi_i \geq 0, \forall i. \qquad (12)$$

By using Lagrange multiplier techniques, Eq.(12) could lead to the following dual optimization problem:

$$\text{maximize } \sum_{i=1}^{s \times n} \alpha_i - (\sum_{i=1}^{n} \alpha_i y_i \phi_1(\mathbf{x}_i) + \cdots + \sum_{i=(s-1) \times n+1}^{s \times n} \alpha_i y_i \phi_s(\mathbf{x}_i))$$
$$(\sum_{j=1}^{n} \alpha_j y_j \phi_1(\mathbf{x}_j) + \cdots + \sum_{j=(s-1) \times n+1}^{s \times n} \alpha_j y_j \phi_s(\mathbf{x}_j)),$$
$$\text{subject to } \qquad \sum_{i=1}^{s \times n} \alpha_i y_i = 0, \alpha_i \in [0, C]. \qquad (13)$$

After calculating Lagrange multipliers, an optimal weight vector for the discriminant hyperplane can be found by $\mathbf{w} = \sum_{i=1}^{s \times n} \alpha_i y_i \mathbf{x}_i$. Therefore the best discriminant hyperplane can be derived as

$$
\begin{aligned}
f(\mathbf{x}) = \quad & (\sum_{i=1}^{n} \alpha_i y_i \phi_1(\mathbf{x}_i) + \cdots + \sum_{i=(s-1) \times n+1}^{s \times n} \alpha_i y_i \phi_s(\mathbf{x}_i)) \phi(\mathbf{x}) + s \times b \\
= \quad & \sum_{i=1}^{n} \alpha_i y_i (K_{1,1}(\mathbf{x}_i, \mathbf{x}) + K_{1,2}(\mathbf{x}_i, \mathbf{x}) + \cdots + K_{1,s}(\mathbf{x}_i, \mathbf{x})) + \cdots \\
+ \quad & \sum_{i=n \times (s-1)+1}^{s \times n} \alpha_i y_i (K_{s,1}(\mathbf{x}_i, \mathbf{x}) + K_{s,2}(\mathbf{x}_i, \mathbf{x}) + \cdots + K_{s,s}(\mathbf{x}_i, \mathbf{x})) \\
+ \quad & s \times b
\end{aligned}
\tag{14}
$$

where $s \times b$ is the bias of the discriminant hyperplane and $\mathbf{x}$ can be either a training or testing data pattern.

4 Experimental Results

In this section, we compare the experimental results obtained by our composition kernel combination method with those of another kernel combination and a classifier combination method. The kernel combination method is the weighted kernel for which the weights of the kernels are optimized by semidefinite programming [5]. The product rule is used to derive the classifier combiner. One synthetic dataset and three benchmark datasets [12] are used in the experiments. To test whether kernel combination methods are more capable of describing data with different local distributions than classifier combination methods, two of the four datasets used in the experiments are with different local distributions, and the other two datasets are regular real datasets. The single kernel and the combined kernel SVM classifiers in the experiments are implemented by LIBSVM [10] and the classifier combiners are built with the PRTOOLS [11]. In every experiment, several single kernel SVM classifiers are constructed, and kernel combination and classifier combination methods were used to combine these single classifiers. The sigma's of these single RBF kernels are assigned heuristically in the following way. The smallest sigma is the average distance of each data pattern to its nearest neighbor. The largest sigma is the average distance of each data pattern to its furthest neighbor. The other sigma's are determined by linear interpolation.

4.1 Experiment 1: Data with Varying Local Distributions

Banana and sonar datasets are used in experiment 1. The SVM parameter C is set to 1 in all experiments. The banana dataset is a synthetic 2-dimensional dataset with 400 data patterns in 2 classes, and it is rescaled in each dimension with

$$
x_{ij} = x_{ij} \times e^{(-\frac{x_{ij}}{16})}, \text{ for } i = 1, 2, ..., 400, \text{ and } j = 1, 2,
\tag{15}
$$

to have a variation of scales in the dataset. The sonar dataset contains information of 208 objects, 60 attributes, and two classes, rock and mine. The attributes represent the

energy within a particular frequency band integrated over a certain period of time. The
results are averaged over 20 experiments. For the rescaled banana dataset, 2 single kernel classifiers are built and different methods are used to combine these 2 classifiers
in each experiment. As for the sonar dataset, 4 single kernel classifiers are built and
combined in the experiments.

The results for all single kernel classifiers, kernel combination methods and classifier combination methods with rescaled banana dataset are in Figure 1. Moreover, the

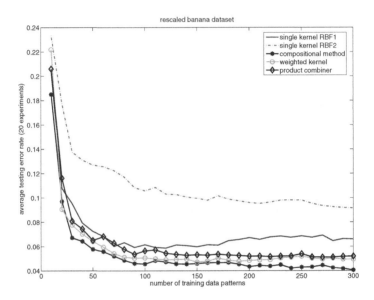

Fig. 1. Experiment results of rescaled banana dataset with our compositional method, weighted
kernel, product combiner and their comparisons with the single kernel classifiers. Standard deviations of the mean error results vary from 0.1112 (left) to 0.0088 (right).

experimental results of the sonar dataset are given in Figure 2. From Figure 1 and Figure 2, we can see that the compositional method performs better than the weighted kernel, especially when a smaller size of training dataset is given. This is because it avoids
the overtraining problem of the weighted kernel. Also, kernel combination methods outperform classifier combination methods when the dataset is composed of different local
distributions. A possible reason is that a combined model is more capable of adapting
to varying data distributions than can be realized by combining decision outputs.

4.2   Experiment 2: Benchmark Data

We use the glass and diabetes datasets in experiment 2. The glass dataset contains
214 instances, 9 features and 6 classes, and diabetes dataset is with 768 instances, 8
features and 2 classes. The SVM parameter C is set to 100 in all experiments. For
both datasets, 4 single kernel classifiers are built and different methods are used to
combine these 4 classifiers in each experiment, and the results are the averages of 20

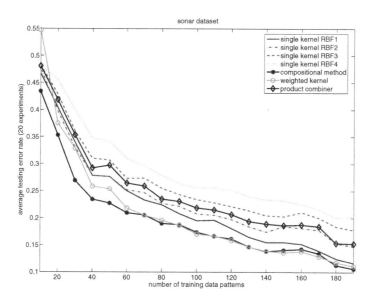

Fig. 2. Results of the sonar dataset for the proposed compositional method, weighted kernel, product combiner and their comparisons with the single kernel base classifiers. Standard deviations of the mean error results vary from 0.086 (left) to 0.038 (right).

Table 1. Diabetes dataset: number of support vectors generated with weighted kernel and our compositional method

method	number of training data patterns						
	10	50	100	150	200	250	300
	number of average support vectors (20 experiments)						
weighted kernel	9.7	40.3	65.7	88.2	111.4	133.4	153
compositional method	18.3	97.2	179.5	272.5	369.8	466.5	553.4

repeated experiments. The results of all single kernel classifiers, kernel combination methods and classifier combination methods with the glass dataset are shown in Figure 3. The results for the diabetes dataset are given in Figure 4, and the number of support vectors obtained with the kernel combination methods are given in Table 1. In Figure 3 and Figure 4, kernel combination methods and classier combination methods have similar performances if the number of training objects is large. When the size of the training set is small, kernel combination methods suffer more from overfitting, and therefore classier combination methods would be a better choice. Nevertheless, the compositional method performs better than all other methods. The number of support vectors, however, is about three times of those of the other kernel combination methods. This is related to the replication of the training set needed to apply the larger kernel matrix.

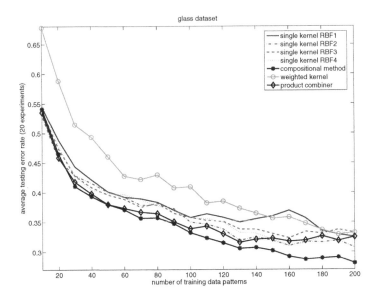

Fig. 3. Results for the glass dataset with the compositional method, weighted kernel, product combiner and their comparisons with the single kernel classifiers. Standard deviations of the mean error results vary from 0.13 (left) to 0.034 (right).

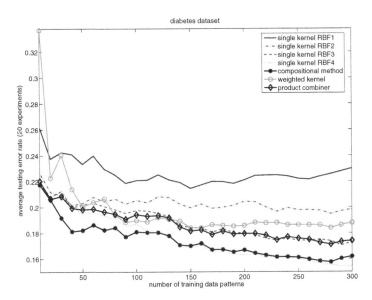

Fig. 4. Results of the diabetes dataset with the compositional method, weighted kernel, product combiner and their comparisons with the single kernel classifiers. Standard deviations of the mean error results vary from 0.092 (left) to 0.016 (right).

5   Conclusions

In this study we compared the performances of kernel combination and classifier combination methods for different types of data distribution. We also proposed a compositional kernel combination method to avoid the overfitting problem of the other kernel combination methods. When a dataset has a varying local data distributions, kernel combination methods are preferred. But classifier combination methods are more stable when the size of the training dataset is small. Nevertheless, the proposed compositional method is stable in all cases. If there is, however, a superior single kernel classifier, it will be very difficult to obtain a better classifier by classifier or kernel combining.

References

1. L. I. Kuncheva, *Combining Pattern Classifiers. Methods and Algorithms*, Wiley, 2004.
2. V. Vapnik, *The Nature of Statistical Learning Theory*, New York: Springer Verlag, 1995.
3. C. J. C. Burges, "A Tutorial on Support Vector Machines for Pattern Recognition," *Knowledge Discovery and Data Mining*, vol. 2, no. 2, pp. 1-43, 1998.
4. K. P. Bennett, M. Momma, and M. J. Embrechts, "MARK: A boosting algorithm for heterogeneous kernel models," in *Proc. 8th ACMSIGKDD Int. Conf. Knowledge Discovery and Data Mining*, pp. 24-31, 2002.
5. G. R. G. Lanckriet, N. Cristianini, P. Bartlett, L. E. Ghaoui, and M. I. Jordan, "Learning the kernel matrix with semidefinite programming," *Journal of Machine Learning Research*, vol. 5, pp. 27-72, 2004.
6. G. Fung, M. Dundar, J. Bi, and B. Rao, "A fast iterative algorithm for fisher discriminant using heterogeneous kernels," in *Proc. 21st Int. Conf. Machine Learning* , 2004.
7. I. M. de Diego, J. M. Moguerza, and A. Muoz, "Combining Kernel Information for Support Vector Classification," in *Proc. Multiple Classifier Systems*, pp. 102-111, 2004.
8. J. M. Moguerza, A. Muoz, and I. M. de Diego, "Improving Support Vector Classification via the Combination of Multiple Sources of Information," SSPR/SPR, pp. 592-600, 2004.
9. C. S. Ong, A. J. Smola, and R. C. Williamson, "Learning the kernel with hyperkernels," *Journal of Machine Learning Research*, pp. 1043-1071 , 2005.
10. C. C. Chang and C. J. Lin, *LIBSVM : a library for support vector machines*, [http://www.csie.ntu.edu.tw/ cjlin/libsvm], Taiwan, National Taiwan University, 2001.
11. R. P. W. Duin, P. Juszczak, P. Paclik, E. Pekalska, D. de Ridder, D. M. J. Tax, *PRTools4, A Matlab Toolbox for Pattern Recognition*, [http://www.prtools.org], the Netherlands, Delft University of Technology, ICT Group, 2004.
12. D. J. Newman, S. Hettich, C. L. Blake and C. J. Merz, *UCI Repository of Machine Learning Databases* , [http://www.ics.uci.edu/ mlearn/MLRepository.html], Irvine, CA: University of California, Department of Information and Computer Science, 1998.

Deriving the Kernel from Training Data

Stefano Merler, Giuseppe Jurman, and Cesare Furlanello

FBK-irst
I-38100 Povo, Trento, Italy
{merler,jurman,furlan}@itc.it

Abstract. In this paper we propose a strategy for constructing data–
driven kernels, automatically determined by the training examples. Basically, their associated Reproducing Kernel Hilbert Spaces arise from
finite sets of linearly independent functions, that can be interpreted as
weak classifiers or regressors, learned from training material. When working in the Tikhonov regularization framework, the unique free parameter
to be optimized is the regularizer, representing a trade-off between empirical error and smoothness of the solution. A generalization error bound
based on Rademacher complexity is provided, yielding the potential for
controlling overfitting.

1 Introduction

*It would be desirable to explore model selection methods that allow kernels to
be chosen in a more automatic way based on data.* This statement, taken from
[1], points out a key step when tackling a learning problem by a kernel method:
this would move toward one of the most important goals in the field of Machine
Learning, i.e., to provide learning systems as automatic as possible in order to
minimize the intervention of the human users. In general, recent kernel methods (for a detailed overview see [2]), e.g., Support Vector Machines (SVM) or
Regularization Networks, require only to choose the optimal kernel for the task
at hand, to select the eventual kernel parameters (for non-linear kernels) and to
optimize the regularization parameter. Although it might be possible to use prior
knowledge for developing an ad hoc kernel, in general there are not a priori jus-
tifications for the use of one kernel instead of another. This is usually dealt with
by user experience and literature knowledge, or by employing statistical model
selection techniques. However, as explained in [3], this step may affect the entire
learning process, since it is well known that kernels other than the standard
choices (Gaussian, polynomial) can improve the accuracy of the resulting solution in many tasks. The problem of individuating a suitable kernel for a certain
task has been addressed in several recent papers, where different techiques have
been proposed to define specific Reproducing Kernel Hilbert Spaces (RKHS) [4].
In particular, in [1] the authors propose a method for learning the kernel matrix
from data via semidefinite programming techniques, while in [5] the kernel is
chosen as a convex combination of basic kernels and in [6,7] new RKHS are built
on the top of a previously chosen RKHS. In this paper we propose a solution
bypassing the kernel choice by automatically building the kernel itself directly

M. Haindl, J. Kittler, and F. Roli (Eds.): MCS 2007, LNCS 4472, pp. 32–41, 2007.

by data. Basically, we construct a RKHS starting from a finite set of linearly independent functions, learned from training material. This solution is inspired by the work in [8], where a novel kernel for SVM, named Terminated Ramp kernel, is introduced by explicitly constructing the feature mapping starting from pure geometrical considerations. In particular, it has been shown that the solution is equivalent to a MCS obtained by minimizing training error and L_2 norm of the coefficients of the combination. Nevertheless, the approach proposed in this work has a much wider breath: in fact, its goal is to propose a general technique to generate data dependent kernel whatever the learning problem, where the Terminated Ramp kernel can be seen as an explaining example. In fact, the algorithm is introduced in the more general framework of the regularization theory, and thus it is not restricted only to Support Vector Machines; in particular, it is not even restricted to classification problems only. The shape of the kernel is now a metaparameter of the algorithm: the choice of the Terminated Ramp kernel is intended as an application example. Other classes of basis functions can be employed, e.g. splines, as well. Both splines and terminated ramp functions induce a nonparametric kernel: as a remarkable consequence, when working in the framework of Tikhonov regularization, the only free parameter to deal with remains the regularizer. This represents a trade-off parameter between empirical error and smoothness of the solution. A different approach have also been proposed in [9], where a method is introduced for modifying a preselected kernel in order to improve accuracy. More precisely, the training data are used for modifying a Gaussian kernel on the basis of the Riemannian geometrical structure of the space induced by the kernel itself. In our method, the kernel is completely induced by the training data, with no need for a preselected kernel function.

2   RKHS of Finite-Dimensional Classes

Let $F\colon X \to Y$ be an unknown function whose domain is a closed subset of $\mathbb{R}^n$ and $Y \subseteq \mathbb{R}$ ($Y = \{-1, 1\}$ for binary classification). Let $D = \{p_i \equiv (x_i, y_i)\}_{i=1}^N$ be a set of training examples, where $x_i \in X$ and $y_i \in Y$. For a given $\lambda \in (0, +\infty)$, an approximation of the unknown function F can be obtained by minimizing the Tikhonov regularization functional:

$$f_\lambda = \arg\min_{f \in H_K} \frac{1}{N} \sum_{i=1}^N V(y_i, f(x_i)) + \lambda \|f\|_{H_K}^2 \,, \tag{1}$$

where $V(y, z)$ is a loss function and $\|f\|_{H_K}$ is the norm of f in the RKHS H_K [10,11]. The parameter λ is called regularizer, and it represents a trade-off between the empirical risk minimization and the smoothness of the solution: increasing values of λ lead to smoother solutions. For binary classification purposes a suitable loss function is the hinge loss $V(y, f(x)) = \max\{0, 1 - yf(x)\}$, leading to SVM, while a typical choice for regression is the L_2 loss function $V(y, f(x)) = (y - f(x))^2$. Let $K\colon X \times X \to \mathbb{R}$ be a Mercer kernel, i.e., a continuous, symmetric and positive–definite function. Consider now the vector space

$H_0 = \{f(x) = \sum_{i=1}^{r} c_i K_{\bar{x}_i}(x) \mid c_i \in \mathbb{R}\}$, where in general the set $\{\bar{x}_i\}_{i=1}^{r}$ can be different from the training data set $\{x_i\}_{i=1}^{N}$. The vector space H_0 can be endowed with a scalar product by setting $\langle \sum_{i=1}^{r} c_i K(\bar{x}_i, x), \sum_{j=1}^{r} c'_j K(\bar{x}_j, x) \rangle_{H_0} = \sum_{i,j=1}^{r} c_i c'_j K(\bar{x}_i, \bar{x}_j)$. The completion H_K of H_0 is the RKHS. It is a Hilbert space satisfying the reproducing property $\langle f, K_{\bar{x}} \rangle_{H_K} = f(\bar{x})$. In regression problems, after having chosen a suitable Mercer kernel $K(x, x')$ and the regularizer $\lambda \in (0, +\infty)$, the solution $f_\lambda : X \to \mathbb{R}$ of problem (1) with the L_2 loss function is defined as $f_\lambda(x) = \sum_{i=1}^{N} c_i K_{x_i}(x)$. The coefficients $c = (c_1, \ldots, c_N)$ of the linear expansion above are the solution of the equation system $(N\lambda I + K)c = y$, whose components are the identity matrix I, the square positive–definite matrix K (the Gram matrix) with entries $K_{ij} = K(x_i, x_j)$ and the vector $y = (y_1, \ldots, y_N)$. As shown in [10] and [12], this can be proved by minimizing (1) and then by applying the reproducing property. In classification problems, the solution of problem (1) with the hinge loss function is given by $f_\lambda(x) = \sum_{i=1}^{N} c_i K_{x_i}(x)$, where $c_i = \frac{y_i \alpha_i}{2\lambda}$ and the α_i are the solution of the quadratic problem $\max_{\alpha \in \mathbb{R}^N} \sum_{i=1}^{N} \alpha_i - \frac{1}{4\lambda^2} \sum_{i,j=1}^{N} y_i y_j \alpha_i \alpha_j K(x_i, x_j)$, subject to $0 \le \alpha_i \le \frac{1}{N}$ for $i = 1, \ldots, N$, equivalent to the original formulation of SVM but for the constraint $\sum_{i=1}^{N} \alpha_i y_i = 0$ taking care of the global offset b in the solution (see [10] and [12] for details). The solution f_λ of problem (1) depends on the specific choice of the Mercer kernel K. Any given finite set of linearly independent functions $G_0 = \{k_1(x), \ldots, k_T(x)\}$ gives rise to a family of kernels inducing a RKHS (see [4] for details). In fact, let $G = \{f(x) = \sum_{t=1}^{T} a_t k_t(x) \mid a_t \in \mathbb{R}\}$ be the linear span of G_0. Any positive–definite $T \times T$ matrix A induces a scalar product on G by setting $\langle \sum_{t=1}^{T} a_t k_t(x), \sum_{s=1}^{T} a'_s k_s(x) \rangle = \sum_{s,t=1}^{T} a_s a'_t A_{st}$ and the induced norm is then $\|f\|^2 = \sum_{s,t=1}^{T} a_s a_t A_{st}$. It is immediately verified that the function $K(x, x') = \sum_{s,t=1}^{T} k_s(x) k_t(x') A_{st}^{-1}$ is the reproducing kernel of the class G_0 for the matrix A: define data-dependent kernel every kernel of the above shape where the functions k_j depend on data. In particular, when A is the identity matrix the resulting norm and kernel are respectively $\|f\|^2 = \sum_{t=1}^{T} a_t^2$ and $K(x, x') = \sum_{t=1}^{T} k_t(x) k_t(x')$. Although matrices A other than the identity, for instance diagonal, can be employed to take into account a priori knowledge, in what follows we assume $A = I$.

3   Specializing the Set G_0

3.1   Penalized Regression

The classical regularized nonparametric regression can be seen as an example of data–driven kernel method. In regularized nonparametric regression, the solution $f_\lambda(x)$ is obtained by minimizing the functional $\sum_{i=1}^{N} (y_i - f(x_i))^2 + \lambda J(f)$, where J is a suitable penalization term. This setup can be embedded in the data–driven kernel framework by looking for solutions of the form $f(x) = \sum_{t=1}^{T} \beta_t h_t(x)$, i.e. a linear combination of basis functions, with penalization $J(f) = \beta^T \Omega \beta$, for a suitable positive–definite block–diagonal $\Omega \in \mathcal{M}(T, \mathbb{R})$. In this case, we can define $G_0 = \{h_1, \ldots, h_T\}$, thus obtaining a solution f_λ with kernel $K(x, x') = \sum_{s,t=1}^{T} h_s(x) h_t(x') \Omega_{st}^{-1}$. A standard choice is to consider the union of spline basis functions for each coordinate function as the set of basis functions [13]. Therefore, this choice leads naturally to a data–driven kernel.

3.2 The Terminated Ramp Kernel

As a further example, we generalize the results obtained in [8], where a novel kernel for SVM, named terminated ramp kernel, is introduced by explicitly constructing the feature mapping starting from pure geometrical considerations. In particular, we rephrase such construction in terms of RKHS, obtaining a completely data–driven and therefore parameter–free kernel. The key step is the explicit definition of the set of functions G_0. For each pair of examples (p_i, p_j) with $y_i \neq y_j$ it is always possible to consider a function $k_{ij}(x) = k(x; p_i, p_j)$ such that $k_{ij}(x_i) = y_i$ and $k_{ij}(x_j) = y_j$. In fact, it is sufficient to consider the following generalization of the *terminated ramp function*[1]. Let $\langle w_{ij}, x \rangle + b_{ij}$ be a generic hyperplane. By emulating the idea underlying the SVM algorithm formulation, we impose that the weight vector w_{ij} is of the form $w_{ij} = \alpha_{ij}(y_i x_i + y_j x_j)$, corresponding to the expression of the weight vector of the maximal margin hyperplane parting p_i and p_j. The coefficient α_{ij} and the offset b_{ij} can therefore be computed by imposing that the hyperplane passes through the two points p_i and p_j. Finally, the terminated ramp function passing through p_i and p_j is obtained by applying a suitable squashing function $\sigma_{ij} \colon \mathbb{R} \to \mathbb{R}$ to the hyperplane: $k_{ij}(x) = \sigma_{ij}(\langle w_{ij}, x \rangle + b_{ij})$. The adopted shape for σ_{ij} is the piecewise-linear function $\sigma_{ij}(t) = \min t, y_{\max}$ for $t \geq 0$ and $\sigma_{ij}(t) = \max t, y_{\min}$ for $t < 0$, where $y_{\max} = \max\{y_i, y_j\}$ and $y_{\min} = \min\{y_i, y_j\}$. However, differently shaped squashing functions σ_{ij}, for instance differentiable, may be employed. Summarizing, the set of functions we adopt is $G_0 = \{1\} \cup \{k_{ij}(x) \mid 1 \leq i < j \leq N, \ y_i \neq y_j\}$, where the constant function 1 takes care of the global offset. The computational cost of a single terminated ramp function k_{ij} is $O(d)$, where d is the input dimension. Consequently the computation cost of evaluating the kernel is $O(|G_0|d)$, where $|G_0|$ is $O(N^2)$. In the following we propose an heuristic for reducing the number of terminated ramp functions without relevant loss of information. The idea is to consider, for each training data p_i, the k admissible nearest neighbours, that is the pairs $\{(p_i, p_{j_l})\}_{l=1,\ldots,k}$, where admissible means $y_i \neq y_{j_l}$, and to take into account only the terminated ramp functions determined by these pairs of training data. In regression, it is possible to relax the constraints of admissible output values from not identical to a certain degree of difference, i.e. by thresholding $(y_i - y_{j_l})^2 > \epsilon$. In Section 5 we analyze the accuracy as a function of k. In the regression case, the number of terminated ramp functions decreases from $\frac{N(N-1)}{2}$ to Nk. Note that k is not to be interpreted as a parameter of the model but it has to be preliminarily chosen according to the available computing power.

---

[1] The terminated ramp function $r \colon \mathbb{R} \to \mathbb{R}$ is defined in literature as follows: $r(t) = 0$ for $t \leq 0$, $r(t) = t$ for $0 < t < 1$ and $r(t) = 1$ for $t \geq 1$.

4   Generalization Error Bound

For $\gamma > 0$, we define $\epsilon_D^\gamma = \frac{1}{N}\sum_{i=1}^{N} I\left[y_i F(x_i) < \gamma\right]$, where $I[P]$ returns 1 if predicate P is true, 0 otherwise. ϵ_D^γ is the fraction of training examples in D classified with margin less than γ, ϵ_D^0 is the empirical error. In [8], an upper bound on the generalization error in the classification case was stated:

Proposition 1. Suppose $0 < \delta < 1/2$ and $0 < \gamma \leq 1$, then with probability at least $1 - \delta$ every SVM with the terminated ramp kernel has:

$$P[yf_\lambda(x) \leq 0] \leq \epsilon_D^\gamma + \sqrt{\frac{z}{N}\left(\frac{|G_0|^2 n_S^2 d}{4N^2\lambda^2\gamma^2} \log\left(\frac{|G_0|n_S}{2N\lambda\gamma}\right)\log^2 N + \log(1/\delta)\right)}$$

where n_S is the number of Suppor Vectors and z is a universal constant.

A similar bound, holding for any given data–driven kernel generated through the algorithm described in Section 2, can be derived in terms of Rademacher complexity [14]. We recall that for any function class $\mathcal{F}$, with probability at least $1-\delta$ every $f \in \mathcal{F}$ satisfies $P[yf(x) \leq 0] \leq \epsilon_D^0 + \hat{R}_N(\mathcal{F}) + \sqrt{\frac{9\log 2/\delta}{2N}}$, where $\hat{R}_N(\mathcal{F})$ is the empirical Rademacher complexity of the class $\mathcal{F}$. For kernel methods, i.e. $f(x) = \sum_{i=1}^{N} c_i K_{x_i}(x)$, the bound $\hat{R}_N(\mathcal{F}) \leq \frac{B}{N}\sqrt{\operatorname{tr}(K)} = \frac{B}{N}\sqrt{\sum_{i=1}^{N} K(x_i,x_i)}$ holds for a suitable B satisfying $c^T K c \leq B^2$, where $c = (c_1,\ldots,c_N)$ and K is the Gram matrix. Suppose that $\|k_t\|_\infty \leq 1$ for each $k_t \in G_0$. Then the following upper bound $\sum_{i,j=1}^{N} c_i c_j K(x_i,x_j) \leq \frac{|G_0|n_s^2}{4N^2\lambda^2} = B^2$ holds, where n_S is the number of Support Vectors. Summarizing, we obtain the following:

Proposition 2. Suppose $0 < \delta < 1$, then with probability at least $1 - \delta$ every data–driven kernel SVM has:

$$P[yf_\lambda(x) \leq 0] \leq \epsilon_D^0 + \sqrt{\frac{|G_0|^2 n_s^2}{4N^3\lambda^2}} + \sqrt{\frac{9\log 2/\delta}{2N}} \ ,$$

for any finite set G_0 of functions bounded between -1 and 1.

Proposition 1 (which holds only for squashed hyperplanes basis functions $k_{ij}(x)$) and Proposition 2 state that the generalization error is bounded by the sum of two terms. The former is related to the empirical error. The latter decreases with λ and, as for standard SVM, increases with the number of Support Vectors. It increases also with the number of basis functions. However, after having seen the data, it is always possible to choose a suitable value of λ making it independent from $|G_0|$. In general, the number of basis functions can be very large, as in the case of terminated ramp kernel. This makes always possible to lower the empirical error to zero. Nevertheless, the two propositions above guarantee that overfitting can be avoided by choosing a suitable λ: according to Eq. (1), the regularizer λ can be interpreted as a trade-off parameter between empirical error (which can be lowered to zero for $\lambda \to 0$) and smoothness of the solution (which can be increased by increasing λ). We underline again that λ is the only free parameter of the system.

5   Experiments

The introduced terminated ramp kernel (TR-K) has been applied in the framework of Regularization Networks in three regression problems on synthetic datasets to illustrate its behavior and to compare it with a classical solution obtained by Gaussian kernels (G-K). Moreover, a classification experiment on a proteomic data set is carried out comparing performances of TR-K and the linear kernel coupled with a feature selection process.

5.1   Experiment 1

The first problem consists in approximating the function $F(x) = \sin(\frac{\pi}{x})$. The training set D is built by selecting the relative minima and maxima of the function in the domain $[0.02, 0.7]$, i.e. $D = \{(\frac{2}{2k+1}, (-1)^k): 1 \leq k \leq 50, k \in \mathbb{N}\}$. The points in the dataset D share two key properties: they are the "important" points of the function F, that it, those where the sign of first derivative changes, and they are not uniformly distributed on the domain. This last property makes the approximation quite hard when employing G-K: in fact, for any choice of the bandwidth h, the function F can be approximated adequately only on a limited portion of domain. This is not anymore the case when TR-K is used, as displayed in Fig. 1: for instance, by setting $h = 10^{-6}$, both kernels are suitable for reconstructing F in the subset $[0.02, 0.1]$, while in $[0.1, 0.7]$ TR-K still works properly, but the solution obtained by G-K reduces to spikes on the training points. On a test set of 5000 points $(x_t, F(x_t))$ where the x_t are evenly spaced on $[0.02, 0.7]$, the resulting MSE is 0.049 for TR-K and 0.453 for G-K.

5.2   Experiment 2

The target function for experiment 2 is $F(x) = 4.26(e^{-|x|} - 4e^{-2|x|} + 3e^{-3|x|})$. The experiments consist in approximating the function F by TR-K and G-K when

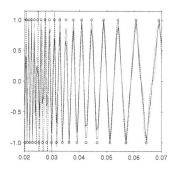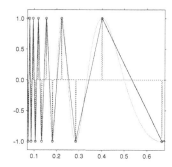

Fig. 1. Approximation of the function $F(x) = \sin(\pi/x)$ (dotted line) obtained by Gaussian kernel (dashed line) and terminated ramp kernel (solid line) in two different subsets of the domain. Circles represent training data.

Table 1. MSE $(\times 10^3)$ with standard deviation of experiment 2

σ	Test Set #1			Test Set #2		
	TR-K	G-K	p-value	TR-K	G-K	p-value
0.05	2.8 ± 1.9	4.6 ± 3.2	< 0.001	4.8 ± 1.5	6.8 ± 4.2	< 0.001
0.10	5.3 ± 2.6	8.4 ± 4.7	< 0.001	15.4 ± 2.6	18.2 ± 4.0	< 0.001
0.15	8.6 ± 3.3	11.9 ± 3.6	< 0.001	31.5 ± 3.4	34.7 ± 3.4	< 0.001
0.20	12.4 ± 4.0	18.5 ± 20.0	0.004	53.5 ± 5.0	60.4 ± 23.4	0.005
0.25	16.1 ± 5.8	19.2 ± 5.3	< 0.001	79.9 ± 5.9	82.8 ± 5.6	< 0.001
0.30	19.9 ± 6.5	23.2 ± 6.4	< 0.001	122.5 ± 7.0	126.2 ± 7.3	< 0.001
0.35	25.7 ± 16.9	30.8 ± 28.1	0.083	142.9 ± 16.4	147.1 ± 23.7	0.082
0.40	27.8 ± 13.4	32.2 ± 16.8	0.001	187.7 ± 13.6	191.8 ± 16.3	0.002
0.45	32.2 ± 14.9	37.7 ± 30.4	0.058	225.6 ± 14.9	230.7 ± 26.9	0.040
0.50	33.7 ± 14.7	37.5 ± 15.8	0.004	281.4 ± 16.3	283.1 ± 17.6	0.203

a Gaussian noise $\varepsilon \sim \mathcal{N}(0, \sigma^2)$ is injected into the training set D, for increasing values of the standard deviation $\sigma = 0.05t$, $t = 1, \ldots, 10$. For each value of σ, 100 training sets D have been built, each including 150 points $(x_i, F(x_i) + \varepsilon_i)_{1 \leq i \leq 150}$, where the x_i are uniformly sampled from $[-4, 4]$. To estimate the optimal value of the regularizer λ for both kernels (and optimal bandwidth h for the Gaussian one), we reserved 50 out of the 150 training points as validation set. The parameter λ was chosen among a list of 401 values $\lambda = 1.1^t$, for $-200 \leq t \leq 200$, while the 100 values of the Gaussian bandwidth h ranged between 0.001 and 10. The TestSet #1 consists in 1000 points $(x_i, F(x_i))$ without noise, while, for each value of σ, the TestSet #2 includes 1000 noisy points $(x_i, F(x_i) + \varepsilon_i)$, all with evenly spaced x_i. After the optimal parameters λ or (λ, h) (respectively for TR-K and G-K) have been chosen on the validation sets, we assessed performances on the two test sets by averaging over 100 replicated experiments. Results are reported in Table 1. The terminated ramp kernel (column TR-K) systematically shows a smaller MSE with respect to Gaussian kernel (column G-K). The difference is statistically significant in the majority of the cases (column p-value reports the p-values of significance t-tests between the MSE associated to the two kernels), especially in the low noise situations. As shown in Fig. 2a, whatever the noise level, in average the MSE on the test sets obtained by TR-K is very close to the validation error corresponding to the optimal value of λ. This indicates that overfitting can be avoided even though the empirical error can be arbitrarily lowered. Moreover, as expected, the optimal value of λ increases with the level of the injected noise. Fig. 2b could explain the shortcomings of G-K: in fact, the two approximations are in general quite similar, but TR-K behaves better in the framed region, where there is a gap in the training set. In the high noise level case, the two approximations are quite similar (Fig. 2c). Fig. 2d shows the MSE as a function of k (see Sec. 3.2) for three different values of the standard deviation σ of the injected noise. Whatever the noise, when more than 5 to 10 nearest neighbours are involved in the construction of the terminated ramp functions, the accuracy does not change significantly. Moreover, according to Propositions 1 and 2, the optimal value of λ (estimated on the validation sets) increases with k, and thus with $|G_0|$.

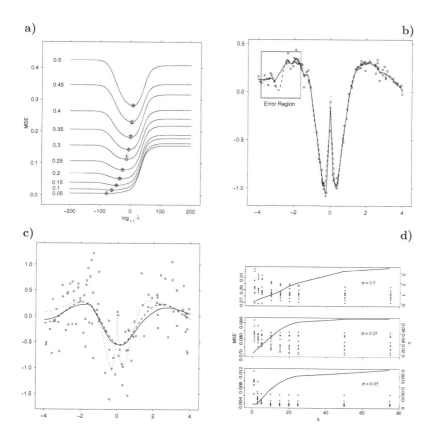

Fig. 2. a MSE curves of terminated ramp kernel for experiment 2 are reported as functions of the regularization parameter λ. MSE are averaged over 100 experiments and each curve refers to different values of σ. Circles identify the minimum of each curve, while crosses represents the MSE on the test set #2. **b** and **c** panels display the approximation of the function F (dotted line) obtained by Gaussian kernel (dashed line) and terminated ramp kernel (solid line) in two experiments with $\sigma = 0.05$ and $\sigma = 0.5$ respectively. Circles represent training data. **d** reduction by k-NN: circles represent MSE for different values of σ as functions of k (10 replicated experiments); solid lines represent the optimal values of the regularizer λ as a function of k.

5.3 Experiment 3

The setup for experiment 3 is identical to the previous one, but for the fact that the training points are evenly spaced and chosen in the domain $[0, 4]$, instead of uniformly sampled in $[-4, 4]$. In this case, G-K performs systematically better: unlike experiments 1 and 2, the distance between the abscissa of each two consecutive points is constant and, consequently, the choice of G-K is very likely to be the optimal one.

5.4   Experiment 4

In this classification task, the performances are compared of the Terminated Ramp kernel and the linear kernel when coupled with a feature ranking technique. In particular, two versions (the original and the non-recursive one) of the Recursive Feature Elimination algorithm (RFE) [15] are used. In the linear kernel, for each feature j, the square w_j^2 of the corresponding weight of the separating hyperplane can be used as a feature importance indicator, while, as shown is [8], a feature importance indicator for the TR kernel for feature j is the function $h_j = \sum_{t=1}^{T} |a_t| \frac{w_t^{(j)}}{\|w_t\|}$, where $w_t^{(j)}$ is the j-th component of the vector w_t. In this experiment, the use of TR-K with 1-RFE is compared to linear SVM with RFE and with 1-RFE on a proteomic dataset. The employed dataset was produced at Keck Laboratory at Yale by using a Micromass MALDI-L/R instrument. Detailed description of data and their preprocessing are included in [16]: 123 peaks are identified as describing features. The classification/ranking procedure is conducted whitin a complete validation framework as described in [17]. The whole dataset is split into $B = 400$ different training/test subsets, then the classification and the feature ranking procedure are performed on each of the training splits. The resulting test errors are then averaged over all the B splits. Moreover, the stability indicator for the produced set of B feature ranked lists is computed as described in [18] as measure of disarray (thus, the lower the better). The average test error for the original Ovarian Cancer dataset is reported in Fig. 3 together with the plot of the stability curves for the ranked lists produced by the three methods. Both the average test error and the stability indicator shows that the Terminated Ramp consistently displays the smallest misclassification rate for all feature subsets sizes; moreover, the B ranked lists emerging by the TR-K task are mutually much more similar than those produced by the experiments tackled by the linear kernel, both in the recursive and in the non-recursive feature ranking method.

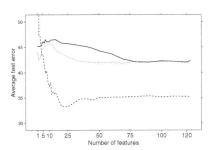 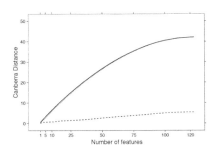

Fig. 3. Average test error and stability plot for the Ovarian cancer proteomic dataset. Dashed line represents TR/1-RFE, solid line represents Linear SVM/1-RFE and dotted line represents Linear SVM/RFE.

6   Conclusions

In this paper we propose a strategy for constructing a data–driven kernel, automatically determined by the training examples. We have shown two main examples of application of this procedure, namely penalized nonparametric regression and terminated ramp SVM. However, the general framework and the generalization error bound based on the Rademacher complexity are independent of the specific function class G_0. For instance, regularized ensembles can be built by defining G_0 as a set of different models, e.g., different versions of the same base model (like in Bagging) or different experts.

References

1. Lanckriet, G., Cristianini, N., Bartlett, P., El Ghaoui, L., Jordan, M.: Learning the Kernel Matrix with Semidefinite Programming. JMLR **5** (2004) 27–72
2. Shawe-Taylor, J., Cristianini, N.: Kernel Methods for Pattern Analysis. Cambridge University Press (2004)
3. Cristianini, N., Shawe-Taylor, J.: An Introduction to Support Vector Machines. Cambridge University Press (2000)
4. Aronszajn, N.: Theory of Reproducing Kernels. Trans. AMS **686** (1950) 337–404
5. Micchelli, C., Pontil, M.: Learning the Kernel Function via Regularization. JMLR **6** (2005) 1099–1125
6. Ong, C., Smola, A., Williamson, R.: Learning the Kernel with Hyperkernels. JMLR **6** (2005) 1043–1071
7. Rakotomamonjy, A., Canu, S.: Frames, Reproducing Kernels, Regularization and Learning. JMLR **6** (2005) 1485–1515
8. Merler, M., Jurman, G.: Terminated Ramp – Support Vector Machines: a nonparametric data dependent kernel. Neur. Net. **19**(10) (2006) 1597–1611
9. Amari, S., Wu, S.: Improving support vector machine classifiers by modifying kernel functions. Neur. Net. **12**(6) (1999) 783–789
10. Evgeniou, T., Pontil, M., Poggio, T.: Regularization Networks and Support Vector Machines. Adv. Comp. Math. **13** (2000) 1–50
11. Cucker, F., Smale, S.: On the Mathematical Fundations of Learning. Bull. AMS **39**(1) (2001) 1–49
12. Rifkin, R.: Everything old is new again: a fresh look at historical approaches in Machine Learning. PhD thesis, MIT (2002)
13. Hastie, T., Buja, A., Tibshirani, R.: Penalized Discriminant Analysis. Ann. Stat. **23** (1995) 73–102
14. Bartlett, P., Mendelson, S.: Rademacher and Gaussian Complexities: Risk Bounds and Structural Results. JMLR **3** (2002) 463–482
15. Guyon, I., Weston, J., Barnhill, S., Vapnik, V.: Gene Selection for Cancer Classification using Support Vector Machines. Mach. Lear. **46**(1/3) (2002) 389–422
16. Barla, A., Irler, B., Merler, S., Jurman, G., Paoli, S., Furlanello, C.: Proteome profiling without selection bias. In: Proc. CBMS 2006, IEEE (2006) 941–946
17. Furlanello, C., Serafini, M., Merler, S., Jurman, G.: Entropy-based gene ranking without selection bias for the predictive classification of microarray data. BMC Bioinf. **4** (2003) 54
18. Jurman, G., Merler, S., Barla, A., Paoli, S., Furlanello, C.: Algebraic stability indicators for ranked lists in molecular diagnostics. Submitted (2007)

On the Application of SVM-Ensembles Based on Adapted Random Subspace Sampling for Automatic Classification of NMR Data

Kai Lienemann, Thomas Plötz, and Gernot A. Fink

University of Dortmund, Intelligent Systems Group, Germany
{Kai.Lienemann,Thomas.Ploetz,Gernot.Fink}@udo.edu

Abstract. We present an approach for the automatic classification of Nuclear Magnetic Resonance Spectroscopy data of biofluids with respect to drug induced organ toxicities. Classification is realized by an Ensemble of Support Vector Machines, trained on different subspaces according to a modified version of Random Subspace Sampling. Features most likely leading to an improved classification accuracy are favored by the determination of subspaces, resulting in an improved classification accuracy of base classifiers within the Ensemble. An experimental evaluation based on a challenging, real task from pharmacology proves the increased classification accuracy of the proposed Ensemble creation approach compared to single SVM classification and classical Random Subspace Sampling.

1 Introduction

The reliable detection of drug induced adverse effects which might be considered toxic for particular organs or regions of organs is a major prerequisite for effective drug design in pharmacology. Within the research field of *Metabonomics* putative toxicities of particular pharmaceuticals are usually indicated by the change of concentrations of metabolites. For both qualitative and quantitative measurements of such changes the so-called ^1H *Nuclear Magnetic Resonance (NMR) Spectroscopy* of biofluids extracted from the treated organism has been proven very effective [1]. The process of NMR spectroscopy results in (high-dimensional) spectral data (cf. figure 1) where both positions and intensities of particular peaks convey the information about particular metabolites.

The process of spectra generation including the treatment of experimental animals is a very time and cost intensive task which usually results in rather small sample sets (typically only a few hundred spectra are available each containing several thousand measurement points). In addition to this the manual analysis of these complex data-sets is very tedious and its results are often of more or less subjective type. Thus, sophisticated methods for the automatic classification of NMR spectra dealing with both high dimensionality of the original data and small sample sets are required. Surprisingly, so far only very few, rather straightforward techniques have already been developed for the task of automatic analysis of NMR spectra.

M. Haindl, J. Kittler, and F. Roli (Eds.): MCS 2007, LNCS 4472, pp. 42–51, 2007.

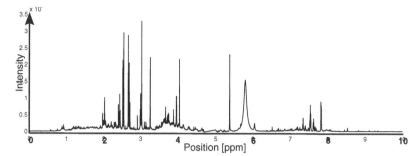

Fig. 1. Exemplary NMR spectrum consisting of approx. 130 000 measurements

In previous (internal) investigations we observed that the application of *Support Vector Machines (SVMs)* [2] performs best when aiming at the automatic classification of NMR spectra with respect to certain toxicity classes. However, for the application of an automatic analysis system in productive pharmacological environments its classification rate needs to be improved.

Generally, in order to process small but complex data sets recently approaches utilizing multiple classifiers have become popular. According to this, we propose a novel approach for generating SVM Ensembles based on iterative adapted Random Subspace Sampling (RSS) exploiting small but high-dimensional sample sets of NMR spectra. Contrary to standard RSS techniques our method is based on a dimension weighting scheme. According to SVM based classification results those feature vectors' components are favoured which are most informative with respect to the overall analysis. Based on a challenging task examining real pharmacological data the effectiveness of the new approach is demonstrated.

In the following section the state-of-the-art specifically for automatic classification of NMR spectra as well as for the general application of multiple classifier systems is briefly summarized. In section 3 the proposed approach of SVM Ensembles based on adapted Random Subspace Sampling is discussed. The results of the experimental evaluation are presented in section 4. The paper concludes with a discussion of perspectives and an outlook on future work.

2   Related Work

The determination of pharmaceutical adverse effects is an important prerequisite for drug design and its automation is highly desirable. However, according to the literature only few and more or less straightforward techniques have been developed addressing the automatic classification of NMR spectra.

In order to process (very) high-dimensional raw NMR spectral data, usually a basic initial abstraction procedure is applied. Therefore, small spectral regions are aggregated and the corresponding integral value is used for further processing. By means of this *bucketing* technique [3] "feature" vectors consisting of several hundred components (instead of thousands) are created.

The most prominent related work has been pursued within the COMET (*Consortium for Metabonomic Toxicity*) project [4] aiming at a system for complete analysis of (large amounts of non-public) NMR data including their automatic classification based on *CLOUDS* (*Classification of Unknowns by Density Superposition* [5]). Using CLOUDS toxicity classes are modeled by mixture densities of Gaussians (with predefined standard deviations) centered on the training samples used. Inspecting the related literature it is, unfortunately, not clear how the system performs for small sample sets as addressed by this paper.

For general classification tasks where only small sample sets are available the application of Support Vector Machines has been proven very effective. Classification is based on linear separation of data originating from different classes. Therefore, a discriminating hyperplane is constructed utilizing a subset of training vectors as support-points and a non-linear transformation into a high-dimensional feature space allowing for linear separation. For efficient evaluation usually kernel functions are applied avoiding the actual transformation into the high-dimensional space. Since linear separability (even in the high-dimensional space) cannot be guaranteed for all sample data the hyperplane's optimization is related to a so-called soft margin defined by *slack variables* [2].

In the last few years the application of multiple classifier systems has been proven effective for complex data sets. Therefore, different base classifiers are estimated either on modified sample sets or on alternative data representations. Both variations of the training data are derived from the original sample sets. Applying the set of classifiers to the original task results in multiple decisions which are aggregated in various ways in order to achieve a final classification. Compared to single classifiers substantial improvements in the overall classification performance of such *Classifier Ensembles* can be achieved [6].

The principle constraint for base classifiers used for Ensemble techniques is a classification accuracy of better than random – so-called *weak classifiers*. However, the Ensemble approach performs even better when *strong base classifiers* like SVMs are deployed (cf. e.g. [7]). Compared to single classifier approaches substantial improvements in classification performance can be obtained by Ensembles only when the underlying base classifiers contain substantial mutual diversity, i.e. modeling different characteristics of the training set.

As one approach for Ensemble creation utilizing a (limited) set of training data *Bagging* aggregates classifiers estimated on bootstrap replicates of all training samples [8]. Sample sets are derived (most likely) avoiding redundant or less informative samples for training and therefore possibly increasing the classification accuracy of the base classifiers. Alternatively, *Boosting* focuses on (re-)weighting of sample data for their consideration in the training procedure. During this iterative procedure the focus is concentrated on those samples which are harder to classify, i.e. causing classification errors.

Alternatively, base classifiers covering sub-spaces of the original feature space can be integrated into Ensemble approaches. Most prominently the *Random Subspace Sampling (RSS)* technique randomly selects subsets of feature components for base classifier training [9]. RSS reduces the effect of redundant or less informative dimensions and (most likely) alleviates the discrepancy between small sample-set sizes and high dimensionality.

3   SVM-Ensemble Based on Adapted RSS

The analysis of our first experiments addressing the automatic classification of NMR-spectra with respect to organ toxicities empirically proved the suitability of C-SVMs [2], explicitly controlling the sum of slack-variables in soft margin classification. Thus, they were chosen as starting point for our developments. Multiple SVM base-classifiers are integrated into an Ensemble aiming for improved classification of NMR-spectra when only small training sets are available.

Even when considering the bucket representation of NMR-spectra it is very unlikely that every particular dimension of the resulting (high-dimensional) feature vectors represents a similar amount of information for the overall classification process. In order to obtain reasonably diverse but relevant sample-sets for the estimation of the abovementioned base classifiers we propose the application of (improved) Random Subspace Sampling.

According to our practical experiences standard RSS, unfortunately, does not guarantee the selection of the most relevant feature components.[1] Thus, in our modified approach the random selection process is based on an underlying probability distribution assigning weights to every feature component. Exploiting this distribution multiple sub-spaces are derived from the original 203-dimensional NMR-bucket space by RSS. By means of the resulting sample-sets SVM base classifiers are trained and integrated into an Ensemble.

Since the optimal feature components' weights are not known in advance its probability distribution is learned in an iterative adaptation procedure. For this purpose, sub-spaces are created by applying adapted RSS, and SVMs are trained accordingly. During cross-validation these base classifiers are evaluated and according to the classification accuracies the weights of the feature components are either increased or decreased, thus, propagating the most relevant components.

In addition to the overview of the new approach given above and illustrated in figure 2, in the following, details regarding SVM training, adaptation of the actual weights, and the creation of the SVM Ensemble will be described.

3.1   Automated SVM Training

The classification accuracy of C-SVMs is mainly dependent on the choice of a feasible C value and possibly on additional kernel-specific parameters. A linear kernel is not parametrized, therefore reducing the complexity and time needed in the training phase. The C-parameter is optimized by grid search and the linear kernel is used in all further investigations. Choosing too small C-values leads to a low classification accuracy and can be improved by selecting larger values up to an asymptotic behavior (cf. e.g. [10]). This process motivates an automatic grid selection. A wide and coarse logarithmic grid is defined in a first phase and the evaluation starts at a reasonable small value, stopping if convergence in classification accuracy is reached (cf. figure 3). The best classification result γ_T is

---

[1] Since training / evaluation of SVM based Ensembles is rather time intensive the number of base classifiers, i.e. RSS guesses, is practically limited.

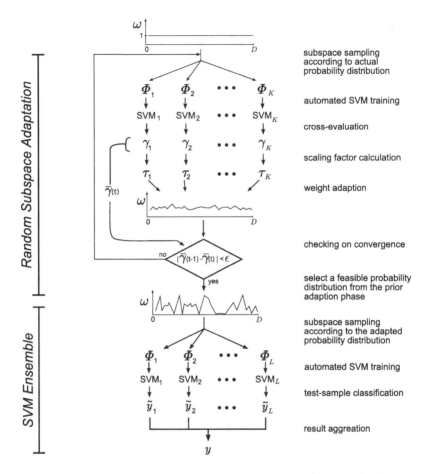

Fig. 2. Creation of SVM-Ensembles based on adapted RSS (see text for description)

determined and, based on this, the grid for the second phase is defined. Starting at the first value exceeding $\frac{\gamma_T}{2}$ up to the point of convergence, the solution space is divided into M steps equally spaced on a logarithmic scale (cf. figure 4). Increasing M results in a finer grid, but also in a longer training phase. The best parameter setting is chosen and used for the classification of test samples.

3.2 Modified Random Subspace Sampling

We propose a modification of Random Subspace Sampling (upper part of figure 2), specifically selecting the putatively most informative features with higher probability. Increased classification accuracy of SVMs trained on the resulting subspaces can be expected due to the explicit adaptation of the probability distribution "guiding" the underlying random process of RSS towards the selection of reasonable subsets.

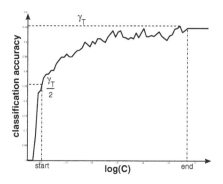

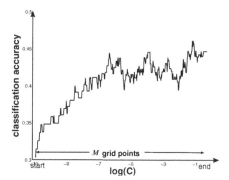

Fig. 3. Accuracy on a coarse, wide grid   **Fig. 4.** Accuracy on an optimized grid

Given a D-dimensional data set, all weights w_i for $i = 1, \ldots, D$ are initialized to one and the selection probability p_i for each feature is calculated according to these weights.

$$p_i = \frac{w_i}{\sum_{j=1}^{D} w_j} \quad i = 1, \ldots, D$$

Based on these probabilities K (most likely) different d-dimensional $(d < D)$ subspaces Φ_k for $k = 1, \ldots, K$ are determined based on the actual probability distribution and linear SVMs are trained on every subspace according to the algorithm described in section 3.1. All SVMs are sorted with respect to their classification accuracy, or an alternative evaluation measure, ranging from the best accuracy γ_B to the worst γ_W. A scaling factor τ_k is determined for each SVM, dependent on a free parameter ν and the corresponding classification accuracy γ_k.

$$\tau_k = \begin{cases} \frac{1}{\nu} + \left(\frac{2(\gamma_k - \gamma_W)}{\gamma_B - \gamma_W} \right) \left(1 - \frac{1}{\nu} \right) & \text{if } \frac{\gamma_k - \gamma_W}{\gamma_B - \gamma_W} < 0.5 \\ (2 - \nu) + \frac{(2\nu - 2)(\gamma_k - \gamma_W)}{\gamma_B - \gamma_W} & \text{otherwise} \end{cases} \quad k = 1, \ldots, K; \nu > 1$$

The values of every dimension are multiplied by the scaling factor of the SVMs, it was used within, reducing the weights of dimensions possibly leading to a lower classification accuracy and vice versa. The iterative reduction of probabilities corresponding to putatively less informative dimensions leads, after several iterations, to their de-facto exclusion from RSS due to a selection probability close to zero. Consequently, the classification accuracy of trained SVMs is increased, and, simultaneously, the diversity of selected subspaces is decreased (see below).

3.3   SVM-Ensemble

The overall principle of our proposed classification system corresponds to an Ensemble of L SVMs as (strong) base classifiers (lower part of figure 2) . Different SVMs are trained based on RSS, with an adapted random selection of dimensions for subspaces, and aggregating their classifications into a final decision. All SVMs within an Ensemble are trained on diverse subspaces Φ_l for $l = 1, \ldots, L$, determined according to a probability distribution of the prior adaptation process as described in section 3.2. Unlike an increasing classification accuracy, the diversity of SVMs built within the iterative adaptation process decreases and possibly converges to one final subspace. Therefore, the final probability distribution is apparently not the optimal choice in order to build an Ensemble of diverse base classifiers and an optimal intermediate result has to be selected. In addition to the classification accuracy, several measures of diversity (cf. [11], [12]) are possible and can be applied for the selection of a feasible probability distribution for building the SVM-Ensemble.

The selected probability distribution is used for the determination of an subspace for every base SVM and these are trained according to the algorithm described in section 3.1. A final classification y is achieved by aggregating the base classifier decisions $\tilde{y}_l$ by maximum vote. An improvement in the Ensemble accuracy is expected due to the improved base classifier's accuracy and their combination in an Ensemble.

4   Experimental Evaluation

In order to demonstrate the effectiveness of the new approach for SVM-Ensembles based on adapted Random Subspace Sampling as proposed in this paper an experimental evaluation based on real NMR sample sets has been pursued. In the following the data-sets used as well as the methodology applied, and the actual results are briefly summarized.

4.1   Data-Set and Methodology

The sample-set used for experimental evaluation consists of NMR-spectra analyzed in a real pharmacological task. Every spectrum originally consists of approximately 130 000 measurement points. By means of an initial bucketing step the dimensionality is reduced to 203. In summary, the data-set consists of 530 samples where every spectrum is assigned either to control (420 samples) or toxic (110), i.e. a two-class problem is considered.

For training, parameter optimization, and test the data-set was split into five disjoint sets by randomly selecting samples. Note that the actual random selection respected the imbalanced distribution of toxic and control spectra as mentioned above. By means of a five-fold cross-validation we ensured that every sample is once treated as test. In every of the five configurations possible three fifths are selected for training and one fifth for cross validation. The final classification rates are averaged over the results achieved on the five test sets (the particularly remaining fifths).

In order to avoid putative statistical artifacts all experiments related to random subspace sampling have been performed twenty times which (empirically) represents an upper limit for reasonable turn around times using current personal computers. The results reported correspond to averaging over all experiments.

Throughout the whole process of parameter training (SVM estimation, and adaptation of feature components' weights) we considered the *Matthews correlation coefficient (MC)* as optimization criterion:

$$MC = (TP \times TN - FP \times FN)((TP+FN)(TP+FP)(TN+FP)(TN+FN))^{-1/2}$$

with TP as number of true positive predictions, FP as number of false positives, TN as number of true negatives, and FN as number of false negatives, respectively. MC is normalized to $[-1\ldots 1]$. The larger MC the better the overall classification performance. The Matthews correlation coefficient was chosen because it is hardly sensitive to imbalanced data-sets. In addition to this, classification rates (overall (acc), and related to toxic (acc_T) and control (acc_C) samples) are reported which seems more informative for the actual Metabonomics task.

The experiments have been conducted using Matlab and the libSVM [13] interface, and our own Ensemble classification system.

4.2   Results

We first compared the SVM-Ensemble approach to single SVM classification in order to show the improvements already achieved by RSS SVM-Ensemble. In addition, the classification results achieved by our proposed method are discussed related to the single SVM and standard RSS approach.

The single SVM classifier and all further mentioned SVM base classifiers were trained according to the algorithm described in section 3.1 by cross-validation, as described in section 4.1, using $M = 300$ grid points in the second training phase. Random Subspace Sampling was performed by selecting 70 % of the original dimensionality randomly and the classification results of all base classifiers were aggregated according to the maximum vote decision rule. Under variation of L, the optimal number of base classifiers was assessed by cross-validation (cf. figure 7) and the classification results on the validation and test-set are shown in table 1. An increased MC can be achieved on the cross-validation set, but not on the test-set due to the reduced classification rate of toxic samples, which implies a better performance of the control samples.

The adaptation of prior probabilities for RSS was performed according to the algorithm described in section 3.2 using $K = 20$ SVMs in each iteration and scaling factor $\nu = 2$. The process of increasing accuracy and decreasing diversity is shown in figure 5, using the MC for accuracy determination and the Kohavi Walpert Variance, the Entropy Measure [11] and the Percentage Correct Diversity Measure (PCDM) [12] as possible rates for the determination of diversity. According to the MC and the Entropy Measure, a probability distribution is selected by scaling both measures to the range [0 - 1] and using the distribution from the iteration closest to the intersection point as demonstrated in figure 6. The cross-validation classification results of the RSS and adapted RSS SVM-Ensemble are illustrated in figure 7 under variation of L.

Table 1. Classification accuracy on the cross-validation and test-set

Method	cross-validation				test			
	MC	acc[%]	acc$_C$[%]	acc$_T$[%]	MC	acc[%]	acc$_C$[%]	acc$_T$[%]
single SVM	0.462	80.9	85.5	63.6	0.422	79.6	84.8	60.0
RSS(L=27)	0.537	86.1	**95.1**	51.5	0.404	82.4	**93.1**	41.4
adapted RSS (L=23)	**0.623**	**87.7**	92.6	**69.1**	**0.499**	**82.8**	87.7	**64.1**

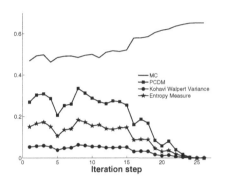 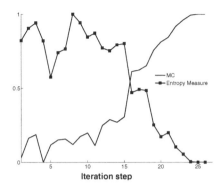

Fig. 5. MC vs. certain diversity measures   **Fig. 6.** MC and Entropy scaled to [0 - 1]

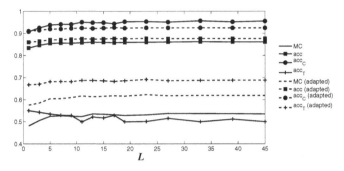

Fig. 7. Comparison of RSS and adapted RSS – Matthews correlation coefficient (MC), classification rate overall (acc) and regarding control (acc_C) and toxic (acc_T) samples

Our proposed method increases nearly all evaluation results compared to single SVM classification and RSS SVM-Ensemble. The high acc_C-values of the classical RSS approach results from the low classification rate of toxic samples, thus predicting most of the test samples as control. However, with the proposed method performance can be significantly increased for toxic samples, thus also yielding an overall improvement in the MC measure.

5   Discussion

We presented a modified Random Subspace Sampling approach for the construction of SVM-Ensembles. The random selection process is based on an underlying probability distribution, assigning high probabilities to features, regarded as most informative for classification by an prior adaptation phase. Within this adaptation phase several SVMs are trained, evaluated and the weights for every feature are modified, proportional to the relative classification accuracy. The improvement of the base classifiers classification accuracy by using an adapted probability distribution for subspace sampling leads to an overall improvement in accuracy of the Ensemble.

A further improvement in classification accuracy is expected by the use of alternative SVM kernel functions like the radial basis function or sigmoid kernel. But for an experimental evaluation an *efficient* SVM training has to be developed due to the more complex process of parameter optimization.

The bucketing procedure reduces the spectral dimensionality and serves as simple feature extraction method, but decreases the resolution and correspondence between features and single peaks. Reducing the size of integrated segments within the bucketing procedure facilitates the interpretation of weights achieved in the adaptation phase. If a correspondence of most informative dimensions to peaks of single metabolites could be achieved, (possibly) new biomarkers for the detection of organ toxicities could be discovered.

Acknowledgements

Parts of this work have been funded by a grant from Boehringer Ingelheim Pharma GmbH & Co. KG., Genomics group. The authors would like to thank the General Pharmacology Group of the company for providing the sample set.

References

1. Bales, J., et al.: Use of high resolution proton nuclear magnetic resonance spectroscopy for rapid multi-component analysis of urine. Clinical Chemistry **30** (1984) 426–432
2. Schölkopf, B., Smola, A.J.: Learning with Kernels. MIT Press, (2002)
3. Spraul, M., et al.: Automatic reduction of NMR spectroscopic data for statistical and pattern recognition classification of samples. Journal of pharmaceutical and biomedical analysis **12** (1994) 1215–1225
4. Lindon, J.C., et al.: Contemporary issues in toxicology the role of metabonomics in toxicology and its evaluation by the COMET project. Toxicology and Applied Pharmacology **187** (2003) 137–146
5. Ebbels, T., et al.: Toxicity classification from metabonomic data using a density superposition approach: CLOUDS. Analytica Chimica Acta **490** (2003) 109–122
6. Kittler, J., Hatef, M., Duin, R.P., Matas, J.: On combining classifiers. IEEE Transactions on Pattern Analysis and Machine Intelligence **20** (1998) 226–239
7. Kim, H.C., Pang, S., Je, H.M., Kim, D., Yang Bang, S.: Constructing support vector machine ensembles. Pattern Recognition **36** (2003) 2757–2767
8. Breiman, L.: Bagging predictors. Machine Learning **24** (1996) 123–140
9. Ho, T.K.: The random subspace method for constructing decision forests. IEEE Transactions on Pattern Analysis and Machine Intelligence **20** (1998) 832–844
10. Keerthi, S.S., Lin, C.J.: Asymptotic behaviors of support vector machines with gaussian kernel. Neural Computation **15** (2003) 1667–1689
11. Kuncheva, L.I., Whitaker, C.J.: Measures of diversity in classifier ensembles and their relationship with the ensemble accuracy. Machine Learning **51** (2003) 181–207
12. Banfield, R.E., et al.: A new ensemble diversity measure applied to thinning ensembles. In: Multiple Classifier Systems. Volume 2709 of LNCS. Springer (2003) 306–316
13. Chang, C.C., Lin, C.J.: LIBSVM: a library for support vector machines. (2001) Software available at `http://www.csie.ntu.edu.tw/~{}cjlin/libsvm`.

A New HMM-Based Ensemble Generation Method for Numeral Recognition

Albert Hung-Ren Ko, Robert Sabourin, and Alceu de Souza Britto Jr.

LIVIA, ETS, University of Quebec
1100 Notre-Dame West Street, Montreal, Quebec, H3C 1K3 Canada
PPGIA, Pontifical Catholic University of Parana
Rua Imaculada Conceicao, 1155, PR 80215-901, Curitiba, Brazil
albert@livia.etsmtl.ca, robert.sabourin@etsmtl.ca,
alceu@ppgia.pucpr.br

Abstract. A new scheme for the optimization of codebook sizes for HMMs and the generation of HMM ensembles is proposed in this paper. In a discrete HMM, the vector quantization procedure and the generated codebook are associated with performance degradation. By using a selected clustering validity index, we show that the optimization of HMM codebook size can be selected without training HMM classifiers. Moreover, the proposed scheme yields multiple optimized HMM classifiers, and each individual HMM is based on a different codebook size. By using these to construct an ensemble of HMM classifiers, this scheme can compensate for the degradation of a discrete HMM.

Keywords: Hidden Markov Models, Ensemble of Classifiers, Codebook Size, Clustering Validity Index, Pattern Recognition.

1 Introduction

The Hidden Markov Model (HMM) is one of the most popular classification methods for pattern sequence recognition, especially for speech recognition and handwritten pattern recognition problems [29, 30, 3, 34, 6]. The objective of the HMM is to model a series of observable signals, and it is this signal modeling ability that makes the use of HMM a better choice than other classification methods for recognition problems. As a stochastic process, HMM is constructed with a finite number of states and a set of transition functions between two states or over the same state [29, 3, 34]. Each state emits some observation(s), according to a codebook setting out corresponding emission probabilities. Such observations may be either discrete symbols or continuous signals. In a discrete HMM, a vector-quantization codebook is typically used to map the continuous input feature vector to the code word.

However, there are some parameters that need to be optimized in HMM, such as the number of states in the model [35], the structure of the observation emission [6], the structure of the state transition [14, 15, 1], the order of the state transition [29, 30, 6] and the optimization of the codebook size [29, 30]. HMM codebook size optimization is, in general, carried out by constructing a number of HMM classifiers and comparing their recognition rates on a validation data set. Given the extremely time-consuming

M. Haindl, J. Kittler, and F. Roli (Eds.): MCS 2007, LNCS 4472, pp. 52–61, 2007.

process of HMM training, HMM codebook size optimization remains a major problem. But, since discrete symbols in HMM are usually characterized as quantized vectors in its codebook by clustering, the fitness of the codebook is directly related to the fitness of the clustering, for which a number of clustering validity indices have been proposed [2, 27, 18, 19, 26]. This means that codebook size can actually be optimized by using clustering validity indices.

Another important issue in the research concerning the HMM is that the ensemble of the HMM (EoHMM) emerges as a promising scheme to improve HMM [10, 11, 12, 13, 14, 15, 1]. This is because an ensemble of classifiers (EoC) is known to be capable of performing better than its best single classifier [31, 25]. These classifiers can be generated by changing the training set, the input features or the parameters and architecture of the base classifiers [15]. The applicable ensemble creation methods include the Bagging, Boosting and Random Subspace methods. There may be other methods for the creation of HMM classifiers, based on the choice of features [13] for isolated handwritten images, and both column HMM classifiers and row HMM classifiers can be applied to enhance performance [4, 5]. The use of various topologies such as left-right HMM, semi-jump-in, semi-jump-out HMM [14], and circular HMM [1] can also be applied.

Because a data set usually consists of multiple levels of granularity [32, 7, 21], if clustering validity indices can give multiple optimized codebook sizes for HMM, then it is possible to construct EoHMMs based on different codebook sizes. This mechanism will give local optima of a selected clustering validity index. EoHMM are then selected by various objective functions and combined by different fusion functions. Because EoHMMs are constructed with multiple codebooks, the degradation associated with a single vector quantization procedure can be improved by multiple vector quantization procedures and by then classifier combination methods. The key questions that need to be addressed are the following:

1. Can the clustering validity index help in the selection of codebook sizes for optimizing HMM?
2. For HMM classifiers based on different codebook sizes selected by a clustering validity index, is the diversity among them strong enough to yield an EoHMM which performs well?

To answer these questions, we applied the selected index for EoHMM construction (Fig. 1). We used the HMM-based handwritten numeral recognizer in [4, 5]. It is important to note that HMM optimization is a very complex task, and there are still a great many issues associated with it. In this paper we only deal with the problem related to HMM codebook size optimization, and the analysis and the method presented therefore constitute only a small step towards a considerably improved understanding of HMM and EoHMM.

The paper is organized as follows. In the next section, we introduce the basic concepts of the used clustering index. Section 3 details the process of generation, selection and combination of HMM classifiers. In section 4, we report on experiments we carried out on the NIST SD19 handwritten numeral database. A discussion and a conclusion are presented in the final sections.

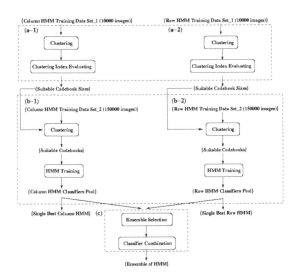

Fig. 1. The EoHMM classification system approach includes: (a) the adequate codebook sizes searching; (b) codebooks generation and HMM classifiers training (c) EoHMM selection and combination. Both (a) and (b) were carried out separately on column and row HMM classifiers.

2 Xie-Beni (XB) Index and Clustering Validity Indices

In general, an HMM codebook is generated from a vector quantization procedure, and each code word can be actually regarded as a centroid of a cluster in feature space. The fitness of the clustering depends on a number of different factors, such as clustering methods and the number of clusters. For an adequate HMM codebook, there should be a means to select a better clustering. A clustering validity index is a measure to evaluate the results of clustering algorithms and give an indication of a partitioning that best fits a data set, and a clustering validity index is independent of clustering algorithms and data sets. We used XB index as the clustering index in this experiment.

XB index [2, 27, 18, 19] was originally a fuzzy clustering validity index. For a fuzzy clustering scheme, suppose we have the data set $X = \{x_i, 1 \le i \le N\}$, where N is the number of samples and the centroids v_j of clusters $c_j, 1 \le j \le nc$, where nc is the total number of clusters. We seek to define the matrix of membership $U = u_{ij}$, where u_{ij} denotes the degree of membership of the sample x_i in the cluster c_j. To define the XB index, first one must define the sum of squared errors for fuzzy clustering. The sum of squared errors is defined as

$$J_m(U,V) = \sum_{i=1}^{N}\sum_{j=1}^{nc}(u_{ij})^m \|x_i - v_j\|^2 \tag{1}$$

where $1 \le m \le \infty$. In general, we use J_1 for the calculation. U is a partition matrix of fuzzy membership $U = u_{ij}$, and V is the set of cluster centroids $V = v_i$. In addition, the minimum inter cluster distance d_{min} must also be defined, as

$$d_{min} = min_{i,j} \|v_i - v_j\|$$ (2)

Supposing that we have N samples on the total data, XB index can be defined as

$$XB = \frac{J_m}{N \times (d_{min})^2}$$ (3)

XB index is designed to measure the fitness of fuzzy clustering, but it is also suitable for crisp clustering. The XB index has been mathematically justified in [36]. In order to obtain a group of potentially adequate codebook sizes, the clustering validity index used must have several local optima that can depict a data set at multiple levels of granularity [32, 7, 21]. This property is important because the best number of clusters depends on different hierarchical levels. An adequate clustering validity index should not only offer different clusterings, but also a reasonable distinction among them. When HMM classifiers are trained with the same features and with the same samples, the distinction among the codebooks is the only possibility that results in diversity among classifiers and boosts the EoHMM performance.

The XB index is found to have this desirable property in our problem (Fig. 2). The plot of XB index values versus the numbers of clusters gives local optima for codebook sizes and are thus adequate for the construction of an EoHMM. The selected codebook sizes are used again for the clustering on all samples. We perform the experiment on a benchmark database in the next section.

3   Experiments with EoHMMs

The experimental data was extracted from $NIST\ SD19$ as a 10-class handwritten numeral recognition problem. As a result, there is an HMM model for each class, and 10 HMM models for an HMM classifier. Five databases were used: the training set with 150000 samples ($hsf\_\{0-3\}$) was used to create 40 HMM classifiers, 20 of them being column HMM classifiers and other 20 being row HMM classifiers. For codebook size selection evaluated by clustering validity indices, due to the extremely large data set (150000 images are equivalent to 5048907 columns and 6825152 rows, with 47 features per column or per row), we use only the first 10000 images from the training data set to evaluate the quality of the clustering, and they are equal to 342910 columns and 461146 rows. Note that, at the clustering evaluation stage, we only examined the different numbers of clusters with the clustering validity index to select several suitable codebook sizes for an EoHMM. Then, the codebooks were generated with the whole training set, according to the previously selected codebook sizes. The training validation set of 15000 samples was used to stop HMM classifiers training once the optimum had been achieved. The optimization set containing 15000 samples ($hsf\_\{0-3\}$) was used for GA searching for ensemble selection. To avoid overfitting during GA searching, the selection set containing 15000 samples ($hsf\_\{0-3\}$) was used to select the best solution from the current population according to the defined objective function and then to store it in a separate archive after each generation. The selection set is also used for the final validation of HMM classifiers. Using the best solution from this archive, the test set containing 60089 samples ($hsf\_\{7\}$) was used to evaluate the accuracies of EoC.

Each column HMM used 47 features obtained from each column, and each row used 47 features obtained from each row. The features were extracted by the same means described in [4, 5], and K-Means was used for vector-quantization to generate codebooks for the HMM. The number of HMM states was optimized by the method described in [35]. The HMMs were trained by Baum-Welch algorithm [29, 30]. The benchmark HMM classifiers used 47 features, with the codebook size of 256 clusters [4, 5]. For benchmark column HMM, we have a recognition rate of 97.60%, and for benchmark row HMM the classification accuracy was about 96.76%, while the combination of the benchmark column HMM and the benchmark row HMM achieved a rate of 98.00%.

3.1 Behaviors of Clustering Validity Indices in HMM Features

To decide on suitable codebook sizes of HMM, we carried out clusterings on HMM features. Before we constructed the EoHMM, we performed K-Means clusterings with different numbers of clusters on HMM features, and showed the properties of clustering validity indices in this problem. Processing clusterings from 3 clusters to 2048 clusters for the clustering task, we showed the relationship between the XB index and the number of clusters for column HMM features, and many local minima can be observed (Fig. 2(a)). A similar tendency can be observed in row HMM features (Fig. 2(b)). This property, as we argued, is important to get multiple levels of granularity of the data set, and it offers codebook sizes for HMMs with the potential to perform well.

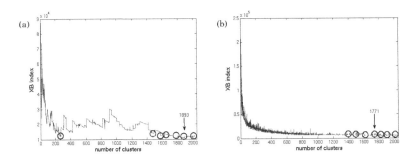

Fig. 2. The relationship between XB index and the number of clusters for: (a) HMM column features; (b) HMM row features. The circled areas indicate the places where the best 40 optima were found. The arrow indicates the smallest XB value with the respective number of clusters. Note that clusterings were carried out on the first 10000 images of the training data set.

3.2 Optimum Codebooks Selected by XB Index

Among all clusterings from 3 clusters to 2048 clusters, the best single column HMM achieved a classification accuracy of 98.42% with a codebook size of 1965, which is 0.82% better than the benchmark column HMM classifier; the best row HMM classifier had a recognition rate of 97.97%, with a codebook size of 1786, which is 1.21% better than the benchmark row HMM. Compared with the benchmark column HMM classifier (97.60%) and with the benchmark row HMM classifier (96.76%), codebooks selected by the XB index gave some improvement to performance. Note that performance is not necessarily proportional to the size of the codebooks. Based on these HMM classifiers, we then construct the EoHMMs.

3.3 Column-EoHMM and Row-EoHMM

We constructed three ensembles composed entirely of column HMM classifiers (COL-HMM), entirely of row HMM classifiers (ROW HMM) and of all HMM classifiers (ALL-HMM) (Table 1). The ensembles were then combined by the SUM rule [22, 38] and PCM-MAJ rule [24], since these two fusion functions have been shown to be very effective [22,24]. The ensemble of all HMM classifiers gave the best performance, given that the obvious diversity between the column HMM classifiers and the row HMM classifiers. With the PCM-MAJ rule, ALL-HMM performed 0.42% better than the single best HMM classifier, and achieved the best classification accuracy.

Table 1. Comparison of classification accuracies on test data set with two different fusion functions and on different types of EoHMMs. The number of classifiers is shown in parenthesis.

Fusion Functions → / EoHMM ↓	PCM-MAJ	SUM
COL-HMM (20)	**98.56 %**	98.55 %
ROW-HMM (20)	98.20 %	**98.26 %**
ALL-HMM (40)	**98.84 %**	98.78 %

3.4 Ensemble Selection

For evaluating classifier combinations, another approach is to go through the process of ensemble selection, because one of the most important requirements of EoCs is the presence of diverse classifiers in an ensemble. We tested the simple majority voting error (MVE) and the SUM rule, because of their reputation for being two of the best objective functions for selecting classifiers for ensembles [31]. We also tested 10 different compound diversity functions (CDFs) [23].

Table 2. Best Performances from 30 GA replications on the test data set. The numbers of classifiers are noted in parenthesis. The SUM was used as the fusion function in EoC.

Recognizers	Column HMM classifiers	Row HMM classifiers	Column & Row HMM classifiers
Benchmark	97.60 % (1 / -)	96.76 % (1 / -)	98.00 % (2 / SUM)
XB Selection	98.40 % (1 / -)	97.97 % (1 / -)	98.70 % (2 / SUM)
Classifier Pool	98.55 % (20 / SUM)	98.26 % (20 / SUM)	98.78 % (40 / SUM)
EoHMM Selection	-	-	**98.80 %** (16 / SUM)

These objective functions were evaluated by genetic algorithm (GA) searching. GA was set up with 128 individuals in the population and with 500 generations, which means 64, 000 ensembles were evaluated in each experiment. The mutation probability was set to 0.01, and the crossover probability to 50%. With various objective functions (MVE, SUM, 10 compound diversity functions [23]), and with 30 replications.

Table 3. Best Performances from 30 GA replications on the test data set. The numbers of classifiers are noted in parenthesis. The PCM-MAJ was used as the fusion function in EoC.

Recognizers	Column HMM classifiers	Row HMM classifiers	Column & Row HMM classifiers
Classifier Pool	98.56 % (20 / PCM-MAJ)	98.20 % (20 / PCM-MAJ)	98.84 % (40 / PCM-MAJ)
EoHMM Selection	-	-	**98.86 %** (16 / PCM-MAJ)

A threshold of 3 classifiers was applied as the minimum number of classifiers for an EoC during the whole searching process. The selected ensembles were then combined by two types of fusion functions: The SUM rule [22, 38] and the PCM-MAJ rule [23]. Among all objective functions, the best ensemble was selected by the CDF and composed of 16 HMM classifiers. The recognition rate achieved by the selected ensemble is 98.80% with the SUM rule, and 98.84% with the PCM-MAJ rule. For all replications of GA searching, the variances are smaller than 0.01%, which indicates that the GA searching gives quite stable results.

4   Discussion

In this work, we proposed to use the XB index in order to select various codebooks for the construction of Ensemble of HMMs. HMM classifiers constructed with codebook sizes selected by the XB index show a clear improvement compared with benchmark HMM classifiers, in both column HMM classifiers and row HMM classifiers [4,5]. With an improvement of 0.80% over the benchmark column HMM classifier and 1.21% over the benchmark row HMM classifier, the usefulness of the XB index in optimizing HMM is undeniable.

As a by-product, we can also use these HMM classifiers trained with different codebook sizes to construct an EoHMM. Considering that the best column HMM classifier already has a classification accuracy of 98.40% and the best row HMM classifier has a recognition rate of 97.97%, this improvement is significant. Such an improvement also indicates that the disadvantage of discrete HMM can be compensated by EoHMM based on various codebook sizes. We also note that, by combining column HMM classifiers and row HMM classifiers, the single best EoHMM of all the replications can have a classification accuracy of 98.86%. This is about 0.30% better than COL-HMM, thanks to the further diversity contributed by row features and column features (Table 2 & Table 3).

The proposed method also has a speed-up advantage over other EoHMM creation schemes. Suppose we need to construct M HMM classifiers for EoHMM, given S possible codebook sizes, the proposed scheme evaluates S clusterings using the XB index and then trains M HMM classifiers. For other ensemble creation methods, such as Bagging, Boosting, and Random Subspaces, we need to train $M * S$ HMM classifiers and then select among them for the best codebook size. This offers a significant speed-up in the optimization of the codebook sizes and a new ensemble creation method.

5   Conclusion

A fast codebook size optimization method for HMM and a new scheme of ensemble of discrete HMM were proposed in this paper. The codebook size was selected by evaluating the quality of clustering during the construction of codewords. Because the method does not require any HMM classifiers training, the proposed scheme offers a significant speed-up for codebook size optimization. In order to fairly evaluate clustering quality, we used a clustering validity index based on different predefined numbers of clusters.

Though a number of clustering validity indices were available, we used the XB index because it has the strong theoretical support [36] and has been shown effective in clustering [2, 27]. Moreover, the XB index demonstrated the property of discovering multiple levels of granularity in the data set, which would allow us to select adequate codebook sizes. In general, the HMM classifiers with codebook sizes selected by the XB index demonstrated an apparently better performance than benchmark HMM classifiers. As a by-product, we can construct an EoHMM trained with the full samples and full features based on different codebook sizes. Because the XB index gives multiple fit codebook sizes, these codebook sizes could result in more accurate and diverse HMM classifiers, and thus provide us with an EoHMM. The combination of column HMM classifiers and row HMM classifiers further improve the global performance of EoHMM.

To conclude, the result suggests that the new EoHMM scheme is applicable. The degradation associated with vector quantization in discrete HMM is compensated by the use of EoHMM without the need to deal with a number of optimization of parameters found in continuous HMM. EoHMM can also explore the advantage of the number of different ensemble combination methods proposed in the literature.

Future work is planned to further improve the performance of EoHMM by exploring the issue of the number of states that need to be optimized as well. With EoHMM based on different numbers of states, it will be possible to obtain further improvement without adding any parameters optimization problems, which will be of the great interest in the application of HMM. Furthermore, the codebook pruning will be also an interesting issue for the decrease of the computation cost for the construction of HMM classifiers.

Acknowledgment

This work was supported in part by grant OGP0106456 to Robert Sabourin from the NSERC of Canada.

References

1. Arica N. and Vural F.T.Y. (2000), "A shape descriptor based on circular Hidden Markov Model," *In 15th Intl. Conf. on Pattern Recognition (ICPR00)*
2. Bandyopadhyay S. and Maulik U. (2001), "Non-parametric Genetic Clustering : Comparison of Validity Indices," *IEEE Transactions on Systems, Man and Cybernetics Part-C*, vol. 31, no. 1, pp. 120-125
3. Bengio Y. (1999), "Markovian Models for Sequential Data", *Neural Computing Surveys*, vol. 2, pp. 129-162
4. Britto Jr. A (2001), "A Two-Stage HMM-Based Method for Recognizing Handwritten Numeral Strings," *Ph.D. Thesis*, Pontifical Catholic University of Paraná

5. Britto A.S., Sabourin R., Bortolozzi F. and Suen C.Y. (2003), "Recognition of Handwritten Numeral Strings Using a Two-Stage Hmm-Based Method", *International Journal on Document Analysis and Recognition (IJDAR 5)*, no. 2-3, pp. 102-117

6. Dietterich T. G. (2002), "Machine Learning for Sequential Data: A Review.", *In Structural, Syntactic, and Statistical Pattern Recognition*, Lecture Notes in Computer Science, vol. 2396, pp. 15-30, Springer-Verlag

7. Eppstein D. (1998), "Fast hierarchical clustering and other applications of dynamic closest pairs", *In Proceedings of the Ninth ACM-SIAM Symposium on Discrete Algorithms*, pp. 619–628

8. Guenter S. and Bunke H. (2005), "Off-line cursive handwriting recognition using multiple classifier systems - on the influence of vocabulary, ensemble, and training set size," *Optics and Lasers in Engineering*, vol. 43, pp. 437-454

9. Guenter S. and Bunke H. (2004), "Ensembles of classifiers derived from multiple prototypes and their application to handwriting recognition," *International Workshop on Multiple Classifier Systems (MCS 2004)*, pp. 314-323

10. Guenter S. and Bunke H. (2003), "Off-line Cursive Handwriting Recognition - On the Influence of Training Set and Vocabulary Size in Multiple Classifier Systems," *Proceedings of the 11th Conference of the International Graphonomics Society*

11. Guenter S. and Bunke H. (2002), "A new combination scheme for HMM-based classifiers and its application to handwriting recognition," *Proc. 16th Int. Conference on Pattern Recognition*, Vol. II, 332 - 337

12. Guenter S. and Bunke H. (2002), "Generating classifier ensembles from multiple prototypes and its application to handwriting recognition," *Proceedings of the 3rd International Workshop on Multiple Classifier Systems*, pp. 179 - 188

13. Guenter S. and Bunke H. (2002), "Creation of classifier ensembles for handwritten word recognition using feature selection algorithms," *Proc. 8th Int. Workshop on Frontiers in Handwriting Recognition*, pp. 183 - 188

14. Guenter S. and Bunke H. (2003), "Ensembles of Classifiers for Handwritten Word Recognition," *International Journal of Document Analysis and Recognition*, Volume 5, Number 4, 224 - 232

15. Guenter S. and Bunke H. (2003), "New Boosting Algorithms for Classification Problems with Large Number of Classes Applied to a Handwritten Word Recognition Task," *Proceedings of the 4th International Workshop on Multiple Classifier Systems*, pp. 326 - 335

16. Guenter S. and Bunke H. (2003), "Fast Feature Selection in an HMM-based Multiple Classifier System for Handwriting Recognition," *Pattern Recognition, Proceedings of the 25th DAGM Symposium*, pp. 289-296

17. Guenter S. and Bunke H. (2004), "Optimization of weights in a multiple classifier handwritten word recognition system using a genetic algorithm," *Electronic Letters of Computer Vision and Image Analysis*, vol. 3, no. 1, pp. 25 - 44

18. Halkidi M., Batistakis Y. and Vazirgiannis M. (2001), "On Clustering Validation Techniques," *Journal of Intelligent Information Systems*, vol. 17 , no. 2-3

19. Halkidi M., Batistakis Y. and Vazirgiannis M. (2002), "Clustering Validity Checking Methods: Part II," *SIGMOD Record*, vol. 31, no. 3, pp. 19-27

20. Huang X., Acero A. and Hon H. (2001), "Spoken Language Processing - a guide to theory, algorithm, and system development," *Prentice Hall PTR*

21. Johnson E. and Kargupta H. (1999), "Collective, hierarchical clustering from distributed, heterogeneous data", *In Large-Scale Parallel KDD Systems*, pp. 221–244

22. Kittler J., Hatef M., Duin R. P. W. and Matas J. (1998), "On Combining Classifiers," *IEEE Transactions on Pattern Analysis and Machine Intelligence*, vol. 20, no. 3, pp. 226–239

23. Ko, A., Sabourin, R., Britto Jr, A., "Combining Diversity and Classification Accuracy for Ensemble Selection in Random Subspaces" , *IEEE World Congress on Computational Intelligence (WCCI 2006) - International Joint Conference on Neural Networks (IJCNN 2006)*, 2006.
24. Ko, A., Sabourin, R., Britto Jr, A., "Evolving Ensemble of Classifiers in Random Subspace" , *Genetic and Evolutionary Computation Conference (GECCO 2006)*, 2006.
25. Kuncheva L. I., Skurichina M., and Duin R. P. W. (2002), "An Experimental Study on Diversity for Bagging and Boosting with Linear Classifiers," *International Journal of Information Fusion*, vol. 3, no. 2, pp. 245-258
26. Maulik U. and Bandyopadhyay S. (2002), "Performance Evaluation of Some Clustering Algorithms and Validity Indices," *IEEE Trans. Pattern Anal. Mach. Intell*, vol. 24, no. 12, pp. 1650-1654
27. Pakhira M.K., Bandyopadhyay S. and Maulik U. (2004), "Validity index for crisp and fuzzy clusters," *Pattern Recognition*, vol. 37, No. 3, pp. 487-501
28. Pekalska E., Skurichina M. and Duin R. P. W. (2004), "Combining Dissimilarity-Based One-Class Classifiers," *International Workshop on Multiple Classifier Systems (MCS 2004)*, pp. 122-133
29. Rabiner L. R. (1989), "A Tutorial on Hidden Markov Models and Selected Applications in Speech Recognition," *Proceedings of the IEEE*, 77(2):257 – 286
30. Rabiner L. R. and Juang B. H. (1993), "Fundamentals of Speech Recognition," *Prentice-Hall*
31. Ruta D. and Gabrys B. (2005), "Classifier Selection for Majority Voting," *International Journal of Information Fusion*, pp. 63-81
32. Seo J. and Shneiderman B. (2002), "Interactively Exploring Hierarchical Clustering Results," *IEEE Computer*, vol. 35, no. 7, pp. 80-86
33. Shipp C. A. and Kuncheva L.I. (2002), "Relationships between combination methods and measures of diversity in combining classifiers," *International Journal of Information Fusion*, vol.3, no. 2, pp. 135-148
34. Smyth P., Heckerman D., and Jordan M. I. (1997), "Probabilistic independence networks for hidden Markov probability models", *Neural Computation*, vol. 9, pp. 227–269
35. Wang X. (1994), "Durationally constrained training of HMM without explicit state durational", *Proceedings of the Institute of Phonetic Sciences 18*, pp. 111-130
36. Xie X.L. and Beni G. (1991), "A validity measure for fuzzy clustering",*IEEE Transactions of Pattern Analysis and Machine Intelligence* , pp. 841-847
37. Xu L., Krzyzak A., and Suen C. Y. (1992), "Methods of combining multiple classifiers and their applications to handwriting recognition," *IEEE Transactions on Systems, Man and Cybernetics*, vol. 22, no. 3, pp. 418-435
38. Xu L., Krzyzak A., and Suen C. Y. (1992), "Methods of combining multiple classifiers and their applications to handwriting recognition," *IEEE Transactions on Systems, Man and Cybernetics*, vol. 22, no. 3, pp. 418-435

Classifiers Fusion in Recognition of Wheat Varieties

Sarunas Raudys[1,2], Ömer Kaan Baykan[3], Ahmet Babalik[4],
Vitalij Denisov[2], and Antanas Andrius Bielskis[2]

[1] Institute of Mathematics and Informatics, Akademijos 4, Vilnius 08663, Lithuania
[2] Klaipeda University, H. Manto 84, Klaipeda 92294, Lithuania
[3] Department of Computer Engineering, Selcuk University 42075 Konya, Türkiye
[4] Department of Industrial Engineering, Selcuk University 42075 Konya, Türkiye
raudys@ktl.mii.lt,{obaykan,ababalik}@selcuk.edu.tr,
{vitalij,bielskis}@ik.ku.lt

Abstract. Five wheat varieties (Bezostaja, Çeşit1252, Dağdaş, Gerek, Kızıltan traded in Konya Exchange of Commerce, Turkey), characterized by nine geometric and three colour descriptive features have been classified by multiple classier system where pair-wise SLP or SV classifiers served as base experts. In addition to standard voting and Hastie and Tibshirani fusion rules, two new ones were suggested that allowed reducing the generalization error up to 5%. In classifying of kernel lots, we may obtain faultless grain recognition.

1 Introduction

Visual product classification is an important operation in food processing industry. Determination of wheat varieties is necessary process for growers, processors and consumers. Classification of wheat grains plays an important role in determining the market value of wheat varieties [1]. Final products which are bread, biscuit, macaroni quality are depending on use of specific wheat varieties. Accurate identification of that variety is crucial. Variety recognition of bulk wheat samples is necessary for standardizing wheat flour or pasta production quality. Identification process is also essential for breeders to predict yield and quality [2].

The size, shape and color of grain are heritable characters, so these characteristic can be used for wheat variety recognition. Classification is usually made by experts and trained inspectors through visual inspection which is tedious, labor-consuming and subjective. Recently, digital image processing techniques are commonly used in texture, shape analysis, type recognition and classification applications in grain industry in order to obtain quick and more reliable results. Computer based image analysis is a good alternative to visual identification [3].

The digital image analysis technique is applied to discriminate wheat classes which are Hard Red Winter (HRD) and Hard Red Spring (HRS) and varieties [4]. Using digital image processing techniques, geometrical properties for 31 bread wheat varieties were obtained and wheat kernels were classified by using statistical filter [1]. Digital image analysis algorithms were developed to classify bulk samples of Canada Western Red Spring (CWRS) wheat, Canada Western Amber Durum (CWAD) wheat, barley, oats, and rye using textural features extracted from different colors, and color features [5]. Grain shapes of 15 Indian Wheat varieties were investigated by using

M. Haindl, J. Kittler, and F. Roli (Eds.): MCS 2007, LNCS 4472, pp. 62–71, 2007.

digital image analysis [2]. In grain classification process, several methods such as statistical, fuzzy logic, artificial neural networks (ANN) etc. have been used. A method based on orthonormal transformations was proposed in order to discriminate digitized wheat cultivars. Bread and durum wheat cultivars were classified by using produced discriminate functions [6]. Healthy and defective cereal grains were classified by using statistical and neural network methods [7]. Classification performances of different neural network architectures were compared by using morphological features of CWRS wheat, CWAD wheat, barley, oats, and rye [8-11].

At the beginning, we applied image analysis methods mentioned above in order to extract descriptive features of five varieties of wheat kernels cultivated in Konya, Turkey (see Section 2.1) and performed classification experiments with standard multilayer perceptron (MLP). In dependence on the network architecture, the MLPs generalization errors varied between 10% and 12% [11]. This accuracy, however, was insufficient to use in practice for intelligent wheat kernel pricing.

In the ANN training, usually instead of minimization of classification error a mean square error is minimized. Moreover, in multi-class (say, K classes) situation, no particular attention is paid to obtain *classification rules that discriminate pairs of the classes* in a best possible way [12]. This factor is especially important in automatic classification of the wheat varieties. Therefore, in present paper we pay particular attention to support vector (SV) and single layer perceptron (SLP) based classifiers aimed to solve two-category problems. Here a problem arises how to design K category classifier from binary ones. Hsu and Lin [13] compared K "one-against-all" and $K(K-1)/2$ "one-against-one" decision making strategies and found that latter one is more preferable. Following their recommendations we consider *multiple classifier system based on utilization of one-against-one approach*. We investigate a wider assortment of the base experts and fusion rules. Utilization of specially designed MCS allowed minimizing generalization error of each single grain from 10% (Multilayer perceptron, MLP) up to 5% (MCS with SLPs used as base experts and kernel discriminant analysis used for fusion). Further increase in accuracy could be obtained if instead of classifying singe wheat kernels, we start classify lots of them: in classifying kernel lots of grains practically we may obtain faultless classification.

2   Material and Methods

In this study, kernel recognition is carried out for five wheat varieties. For each wheat variety 80 kernels were taken from various bulks raised in different regions of Konya, Turkey. Totally 400 kernels were taken. Healthy kernels of each variety were selected by experts at Konya Exchange of Commerce. Broken, damaged, shrinked, and very small kernels were excluded.

2.1   Image Acquisition and Analysis

Digital images of each wheat variety were obtained by using HP 5400 A4 desktop scanner with 1200*1200 dpi optical resolution. Eighty kernels of each wheat variety were placed at the scanner platform as seen in Figure 1. Digital images were obtained in 24 bit/pixel, 100 dpi resolution and tiff formats.

Digital color images obtained by a desktop scanner were transformed to gray level digital images. Noise was eliminated and edges were preserved by using a median filtering which is a non-linear filtering technique [14]. Gray level images were converted into binary images by using Otsu's methods. Segmentation algorithm was used in order to detect wheat kernels in the binary digital image and eliminate non kernel points by using morphological operations. Each wheat kernel was labeled after nine geometrical features: area, major axis, minor axis, perimeter, equivalent diameter, eccentricity, shape factor, roundness, and compactness and color information (R, G and B) were extracted from the digital images [1], [11]. Thus, the complete dataset for five varieties had numerical data for 12 characteristics on the 400 grains. Extracted features are shown Table 1.

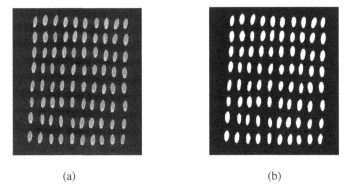

(a)   (b)

Fig. 1. a) wheat kernel images b) segmented images

Table 1. Wheat kernel features

Feature	Definition	Feature	Definition
A	Major axis	B	Minor axis
Perimeter	$\pi.\sqrt{(A^2 + B^2)/2}$	Eccentricity	$\sqrt{A^2 - B^2}/(2.A)$
Equivalent diameter	$4.Area/Perimeter$	Roundness	$4.Area/(pA^2)$
Shape factor	$4.\pi.Area/Perimeter^2$	Compactness	$\sqrt{4.Area\,p}/A$
Area	Pixels	R, G and B	$1/n\sum x_k$

2.2 Fuzzy Pre-processing

In an attempt to increase classification accuracy of MLP, we tested an option where fuzzy features were used instead of original ones enumerated in Table 1. At first, the dataset obtained from image analysis was normalized into [0, 1] range. Afterwards, a fuzzy pre-processing procedure was applied. For each feature, input membership functions and output membership functions were defined. These are selected as standard triangular membership functions used in fuzzy decision making [15]. Input and output range [0 1] are divided into 16 equal parts. After determining the membership functions, rules were constituted in a following way:

if *input* is in_j, then *output* is out_j, (j = 1, 2, ... , 17),

where in_j and out_j denote j-th input and output membership functions, respectively. Each feature value used as input value cuts two membership functions and forms two membership values. These membership values were determined for each of the feature values. The membership values were taken as a point to form output membership functions. Using rules base, on output membership functions, the output values were calculated by centroid defuzzification method [15]

$$output\_value = \int x\,\mu_{\text{out}}(x)dx / \int \mu_{\text{out}}(x)dx . \tag{1}$$

2.3 Training the Expert Classifiers

The pair-wise SLPs or SV classifiers served as base experts. Each time final allocation of unknown vector x to one of the pattern classes was performed by fusing the pair-wise decisions of K-1 base classifiers. To train SLPs perfectly for each pair of the classes we trained individual SLP in a special manner and stopped training on a right time moment. The main two requirements to profit from evolution of non-linear SLP classifier in two category situations is to move training data mean, $\hat{\mu}_{ij}$, of the pair of classes, Π_i and Π_j, into the centre of coordinates, and start training from the weight vector with zero components. To speed up training process and to reduce generalization error for each pair of the classes we performed whitening data transformation [16] $y = G_{ij}(x - \hat{\mu}_{ij})$, where $G_{ij} = \Lambda^{-1/2}\Phi^T$, and Λ, Φ^T are eigen-values and eigenvectors of pooled sample covariance matrix, $S = \Sigma N_i S_i / \Sigma N_i$, and S_i is sample estimate of covariance matrices of class, Π_i.

In finite training sample situation, we suggest using regularized estimate of the covariance matrix [16, 17], $S_{\text{regularized}} = S + \lambda\,I$, where I stands for $p{\times}p$ identity matrix, and λ is a regularization constant to be selected in experimental way. In this way, we improve sample size / dimensionality ratio (for more details about integration of statistical methods into SLP training see Chapter 5 in [16]). Important phase in SLP training is *determination of optimal number of iterations*. Actually, *determination of stopping moment in fact is determination of optimal complexity of the classifier*.

To determine "optimal" stopping moment we used artificially generated pseudo-validation set obtained from training vectors by means of a noise injection. A noise injection actually introduces *additional information that declares that a space between nearest vectors of a single pattern class is not empty, but instead is filled up with vectors of the same category*. This can be accomplished by adding random zero mean vectors to each training vector. Such procedure, however, distorts a geometry of data distribution. Colored k-NN noise injection was suggested to reduce data distortion [18]. To generate such noise, for each single training vector, x_{sl}, one finds its k nearest neighbors of the same pattern class and adds a noise only in a subspace formed by vector x_{sl} and the k neighboring training vectors, $x_{sl1}, x_{sl2}, ..., x_{slk}$. Random Gaussian, $N(0, \sigma_{\text{noise}}^2)$, noise is added ni_{nn} times along k lines connecting x_{sl} and x_{sl1}, $x_{sl2}, ..., x_{slk}$. Three parameters are required to realize noise injection procedure: 1) k, the number of neighbors, 2) ni_{nn}, the number of new, artificial vectors generated around each single training vector, x_{sl}, and 3) σ_{noise}, the noise standard deviation. A noise variance, σ^2_{noise}, has to be selected as a trade-off between a complexity of decision boundary and learning set size. When working with unknown data, one has to test several values of σ_{noise} and select the most suitable one. To speed up calculations we used "default" values: $k = 2$; $\sigma_{noise} = 1.0$ and $ni_{nn} = 25$.

To obtain the pair-wise support vector classifiers we used standard methods described in Chang and Lin Matlab package [19].

3 Multiple Classifier System for Making Final Classification

After obtaining $K(K-1)/2$ pair-wise classifications of each unknown vector, x, made by $K(K-1)/2$ SLPs or SV classifiers, we need to make a final categorization. Popular methods to combine outputs of the pair-wise classifications are voting and a method suggested by Hastie and Tibshirani [13, 20, 21]. Below we propose using two new alternative fusion methods. In both of them, we allocate vector x to class Π_z, if $K-1$ pair-wise classifiers out of $K(K-1)/2$ ones are allocating this vector to single pattern class, Π_z. Otherwise, we perform a second stage of decision making.

In *the first fusion algorithm*, we perform final categorization by the K-class net of SLPs. Here, both the pair-wise decisions and the fusion are performed by the hyperplanes. It could be a weakness of the method. In order to increase diversity of decision making procedure in initial and final classifications, in *the second fusion algorithm*, the final allocation of x is performed by local classification rule, the kernel discriminant analysis (KDA) [16, 17]. The latter procedure is similar to fusion rule of Giacinto *et al.* ([22] suggested in Multiple classifier systems framework (for recent review of fusion rules see e.g. [23]).

The K-class set of SLPs was considered above. In the KDA we perform classification according to nonparametric local estimates of conditional probability density functions of input vectors, $f_{KDA}(x| \lambda, \Pi_i)$, and q_i, prior probabilities of the classes $i = 1, 2, \ldots , K$, where λ is a smoothing parameter. In the experiments reported below, we used Gaussian kernel and performed classification according to the maximum of products $q_i \times f_{KDA}(x |\lambda, \Pi_i)$ $(i = 1, 2, \ldots , K)$. In order to have fair comparison of KDA based algorithm with other ones, we used default value, $\lambda = 1.0$. In order to obtain more reliable results, cross validation procedures were repeated 250 times. Reshuffling of the data vectors in each category was performed each time.

Classification of grain lots. In order to evaluate accuracy of a procedure to be used for intelligent pricing practically, we considered *two stage MCS where one classifies lots of the grain*. For example, if in classifying of the lot composed of 21 kernels randomly selected from a sackful of the grain, 16 kernels are recognized as belonging to class Π_1, three kernels – to class Π_3 and two – to class Π_5, then simple majority voting procedure will allocate this lot to class Π_1.

Below we will consider a modified, decision making procedure of second stage of multiple classifier system: we assign a lot of grains to class Π_K if *more than a half of the grains in the lot are recognized as belonging to this class*, Π_K. Otherwise decision making is assigned to trained inspectors. A question arises: how to evaluate probability of correct automatic decision making of this classification procedure.

Consider a situation where for testing we have n_{test} grains of class Π_K and n_{correct} grains have been classified correctly ($n_{\text{correct}} < n_{\text{test}}$). Let n_{lot} grains compose each single lot. In principle, we may form

$$k_{\text{lots}} = n_{\text{test}}!/(n_{\text{lot}}!(n_{\text{test}} - n_{\text{lot}})!) \tag{2}$$

such lots. Among k_{lots} of the lots, we could have

$$k_j = n_{\text{correct}}!/(j!(n_{\text{correct}} - j)!) \times (n_{\text{test}}\text{-}n_{\text{correct}})!/((n_{\text{lot}}\text{-}j)!(n_{\text{test}}\text{-}n_{\text{correct}}- n_{\text{lot}}+j)!) \tag{3}$$

lots where j grains in the lot are classified correctly and $n_{\text{lot}} - j$ grains are classified incorrectly ($j = 0, 1, \ldots, n_{\text{lot}}$). Note $k_{\text{lots}} = \sum_{j=0}^{n_{\text{lot}}} k_j$. According to the definition of our decision making procedure, we will perform correct lot allocation if in each single lot, a number of grains allocated to true pattern class exceeds $n_{\text{lot}}/2$. Therefore, a frequency of correct automatic decision making will be

$$P_{\text{correct}} = \sum_{j=n_{\text{lot}}/2+1}^{n_{\text{lot}}} k_j / k_{\text{lots}}. \tag{4}$$

In computerized intelligent wheat pricing, the combinatory analysis could also be used in order to develop criteria to judge about cleanliness of wheat varieties, a fraction of faulty, damaged, broken kernels, etc.

4   Results and Discussion

In present paper we concentrated on the *evolution* of the network of the pair-wise perceptrons in the situation where in final stage of learning process, the minimum empirical error or support vector (SV) classifiers could be obtained. We compared the best classifier obtained of SLP training and standard SV classifier. In evaluation of different variants of learning procedures we used two-fold cross validation technique. A half of vectors of each pattern class were selected for training. Remaining vectors were used for testing of the classification algorithms.

To determine optimal number of training epochs of K class SLP (KSLP) and two variants of pair-wise SLPs (pwSLP+KSLP and pwSLP+KDA) we used artificially generated validation set. This set was generated by means of colored noise injection as described above. Thus, in each of 500 experiments we used 200 training vectors and $25 \times 200 = 5,000$ 12-dimensional artificial vectors for validation. Average values of generalization errors evaluated in $2 \times 250 = 500$ runs of the experiments with randomly permuted data are presented in Table 2. In column "KSLP/*amb*/PW", we present performance estimates of two benchmark procedures:

1) average generalization error of K class net of SLPs,
2) a fraction, *amb*, of ambiguous vectors where K-1 perceptrons allocated the test vectors to more than to one pattern class,
3) average generalization error of the kernel discriminant analysis.

We have mentioned already that standard MLP was used as the third benchmark method. Its performance was notably lower as the best MCS. Therefore, no details are presented in Table 2. In subsequent four columns of Table 2 we present *averages* of generalization errors where pair-wise decisions of $K(K$-1$)/2$ SLP (on the left side of each column) or SV classifiers (on the right side) were fused by four different techniques: a) voting, b) Hastie-Tibshirani method, c) K class net of SLP or d) KDA as described above. The *best strategies* are marked in **bold**. Wheat variety confusion matrix in one single cross-validation experiment with SLP classification and KDA fusion rules is presented in Table 3. Average generalization error was 0.05 in this experiment. In Fig. 4 we present a histogram of distribution of generalization errors in 500 experiments with original (non-fuzzy) data, SLPs and KDA used for fusion.

Experimental investigations advocate that on average all four combinations of pair-wise classifications represented as MCSs outperform single stage classification algorithms, the K class net of SLPs, Kernel discriminant analysis and the MLPs. In all four pair-wise decision fusion methods, optimally stopped SLP as adaptive and more flexible method, outperformed MCS composed of maximal margin (support vector) classifiers. In all experiments, local fusion (KDA) of the pair-wise decisions outperformed the global fusion algorithms realized by the hyperplanes (K class net of SLPs, majority voting or H-T method).

The histogram gives an impression that in a situation where we have 200 vectors for training and 200 ones for testing, the results are highly variable. Assume true generalization error is 0.051 as indicated in the last column of Table 2. Standard deviation of cross validation error estimate, $\sqrt{0.051 \times 0.949 / 200} = 0.0156$, however, agrees with a spread of the distribution presented in the histogram: standard deviation of 500 generalization error values is even a little bit smaller, 0.013. Thus, rough

Table 2. Generalization errors (in %) in 500 experimental runs with different fusion strategies

Data set	$KSLP$/*amb*/KDA	SLP/ SVM + Voting	SLP/ SVM + H-T	SLP/ SVM + $KSLP$	SLP/ SVM + KDA
Original #$_{exp}$=500	9.8 / 0.050 /10.4	7.3 / 8.4	6.6 / 8.0	5.2 / 5.4	**5.09** / 5.32
Fuzzy #$_{exp}$= 500	10.6 / 0.049 /11.6	7.7 / 9.6	6.6 / 9.1	5.7 / 6.1	**5.32** / 5.83

Table 3. Confusion matrix of classification of the 200 test vectors with KDA used for fusion

Class	1	2	3	4	5
1	**40**	0	0	0	0
2	0	**37**	0	0	3
3	0	0	**39**	1	0
4	0	0	1	**39**	0
5	0	4	1	0	**35**

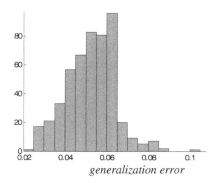

Fig. 4. A distribution of the generalization errors in 500 experiments with original data

evaluation using "3 sigma rule" is: that generalization error of the wheat varieties recognition method proposed is $0.051\pm3*0.0156/\sqrt{500}$, i.e. $5.0 - 5.2\%$.

Similar result could be obtained while using the same automatic decision making algorithm based of fuzzy features with 17 membership functions. Smaller number of membership functions resulted notably lower classification accuracy. Nevertheless, relatively high accuracy obtained with fuzzy features advocates that requirements to accuracy of feature extraction could be released. It means a speed of intelligent wheat kernel pricing could be increased at the expense of utilization of simpler and cheaper feature extraction hardware.

Equations (2), (3) and (4) derived in Section 3 allow evaluating the frequency of correct automatic decision making in classification of the lot of grains. Table 2 demonstrates that classification error in five category task is $P_{error} = 0.0509$. In our experiments, test set was compose of $n_{test} = 40$ kernels in each category. It means that in the set of $40\times5=200$ grains, on average ten kernels classified are classified incorrectly. In order to evaluate upper bound of classification performance in classification the lot of $n_{lot} = 21$ grains, let us consider unfavorable situation where only kernels of one class are classified incorrectly. It means that from 40 grains $n_{correct} = 30$ kernels will be classified correctly and 10 grains - incorrectly. Calculation according to Eq. (2), (3) and (4) gives: $P_{correct}^{upperbound} = 1.000$. In the 500 cross-validation experiments, where SLPs trained on original features served as base classifiers and KDA was used for fusion, a worst case was: 11 kernels of one wheat variety were misclassified. For such situation, $P_{correct}^{upperbound} = 0.9998$.

For *fuzzy features*, however, the worst case among 500 cross-validation experiments was when $n_{incorrect} = 15$ grains of one class were classified incorrectly. If $n_{lot} = 21$, then probability of correct decision making would be: $P_{correct}^{upperbound} = 0.958$, i.e. unsatisfactory. The probability of correct decision making could be increased if for the same fraction of incorrect classification of single grains, $P_{error} = 15/200$, the larger number of grains would be used to form the lot. For example, for $n_{test} = 120$ kernels of each category, $n_{incorrect} = 45$ and $n_{lot} = 75$ Equations (2), (3) and (4) result that probability of correct decision making would be: $P_{correct}^{upperbound} = 0.9999$, i.e. fairly good result. Classification of 120 grains is tedious and labor-consuming if classification would be performed by humans, however, this tack could be performed easily by automatic procedure.

We stress once more that all algorithms were compared in identical conditions. The artificially generated validation sets were used to determine stopping moments, single *a priori* fixed smoothing parameter value was used in KDA.

5 Concluding Remarks

Like SV machine, the binary single layer perceptron is very powerful classification technique. Here during development of training procedure we can obtain a variety of statistical classifiers [16]. In multi-class situation we suggest utilization the multiple classifer system where we perform decision making in two stages. At first, we classify unknown vector, x, by means of $K(K-1)/2$ single layer perceptrons optimally stopped for each pair of the pattern classes. Thus, for each pair of the classes we have the classifier of optimal complexity. We assign unknown vector to the i-th class if $K-1$ pair-wise dicriminant functions are classifying this vector to single class, Π_i. If the first stage classifiers disagree, for final allocation of vector x we suggest using local classification method, the kernel discriminant analysis.

In the wheat variety recognition task, the classification errors could be evaluated in terms of the money. So we are obliged to use perfect pair-wise classifiers. Utilization of suitable fusion rules is important as well. Testing performance of MCS based wheat varieties classification technique, 95% of correct allocations in recognition of each single grain and 99.99% in classification of the grain lots, is found to be satisfactory for wheat variety recognition of incoming wheat samples.

Supported by strong theoretical considerations about optimality of pair-wise decisions and diversity of base (pair-wise) classifiers and the KDA fusion rules, we have heavy arguments that two stage decision making strategy described above is promising and worth practical application and further investigation. In future analysis, more flexible fusion rules, small sample effects [24], specific points of the wheat lot classification could be investigated. No doubt, the experiments with larger number of wheat varieties and larger data sets should be conducted. A fraction of strange wheat variety, faulty, damaged and broken kernels and percentage of foreign materials at bulk wheat samples can be determined for purposes of intelligent pricing.

Acknowledgement. This study is supported by Scientific Research Projects Support Program (BAP) of Selcuk University.

References

1. Utku H, Köksel H, Use of statistical filters in the classification of wheat by image analysis. *J. of Food Engineering* 36 (1998), 385-394
2. Shouche S.P, Rastogi R, Bhagwat S.G., Sainis J.K, Shape analysis of grains of Indian wheat varieties. *Computers and Electronics in Agriculture* 33 (2001), 55–76
3. Dubey B.P., Bhagwat S.G., Shouche S.P., Sainis J.K., Potential of artificial neural network in varietal identification using morphometry of wheat grains. *Biosystems Engineering* 95 (2006), 61-67

4. Zayas I, Lai, F.S, Pomeranz Y, Discrimination between wheat classes and varieties by image analysis. *Cereal Chemistry* 63 (1986), 52-55

5. Majumdar S, Jayas D. S. Classification of bulk samples of cereal grains using machine vision. *J. Agric. Eng. Res.* 73 (1999), 35-47

6. Utku H, Application of the feature selection method to discriminate digitized wheat varieties. *J. of Food Engineering* 46 (2000), 211-216

7. Luo X, Jayas D.S, Symons S.J, Comparison of statistical and neural network methods for classifying creal grains using machine vision. *Transactions of the ASAE*, 42 (1999), 413-419

8. Paliwall J, Visen N. S, Jayas D. S, Evaluation of neural network Architectures for cereal grain classification using morphological features. *J. Agric. Eng. Res.* 79, 4 (2001), 361-370

9. Paliwall J, Visen N.S, Jayas D.S., White N.D.G., cereal grain and dockage identification using machine vision. *Biosystems Engineering* 85, 1 (2003), 51–57

10. Paliwall J, Visen N.S, Jayas D.S, White N.D.G, Comparison of a neural network and a non-parametric cassifier for grain kernel identification. *Biosystems Engineering* 85, 4 (2003), 405–413.

11. Babalık A, Baykan Ö.K, Botsali F.M, Determination of wheat kernel type by using image processing techniques and ANN. *Proc. of the Int. Conf. on Modeling and Simulation*, 1 (2006), 531-534, Konya/Turkey.

12. Raudys S, Denisov V., Belskis A. A pool of classifiers by SLP: A multi-class case. *Lecture Notes in Computer Science* 4142 (2006), 47 – 56.

13. Wu T.-F, Lin C.-J and Weng R.C.. Probability estimates for multi-class classification by pair-wise coupling. *J. of Machine Learning Research* 5 (2004), 975-1005.

14. Leemans V, Magein H And Destain M.F, Defects segmentation on golden delicious apples by using colour machine vision, *Comp. and Electronics in Agriculture* 20 (1998), 117-130.

15. Ross T.J, *Fuzzy Logic With Engineering Applications*, Mcgraw –Hill Inc, (1995) 136-138.

16. Raudys S. *Statistical and Neural Classifiers: An integrated approach to design*. Springer-Verlag, NY, 2001.

17. Duda R.O., Hart P.E. and Stork D.G. *Pattern Classification*. 2nd ed. Wiley, NY, 2000.

18. Skurichina M., Raudys S. and Duin R.P.W. K-NN directed noise injection in multilayer perceptron training, *IEEE Trans. on Neural Networks* 11 (2000), 504–511

19. Chang C.-C. and Lin C.-J.. *LIBSVM: a library for support vector machines*, 2001. Available at http://www.csie.ntu.edu.tw/~cjlin/libsvm

20. Hsu C. W. and Lin C. J. A comparison on methods for multi-class support vector machines. *IEEE Trans. on Neural Networks* 13 (2002), 415-425

21. Hastie T. and R. Tibshirani R. Classification by pair-wise coupling. *The Annals of Statistics* 26 (1998), 451-471

22. Giacinto G, Roli F. and Fumera G. Selection of classifiers based on multiple classifier behaviour. *Lecture Notes in Computer Science* 1876 (2000), 87–93

23. Raudys S. Trainable Fusion Rules. I. Large sample size case. *Neural Networks* 19 (2006), 1506-1516

24. Raudys S. Trainable Fusion Rules. II. Small sample-size effects. *Neural Networks*, 19 (2006), 1517-1527

Multiple Classifier Methods for Offline Handwritten Text Line Recognition

Roman Bertolami and Horst Bunke

Institute of Computer Science and Applied Mathematics
University of Bern, Neubrückstrasse 10, CH-3012 Bern, Switzerland
{bertolam,bunke}@iam.unibe.ch

Abstract. This paper investigates the use of multiple classifier methods for offline handwritten text line recognition. To obtain ensembles of recognisers we implement a random feature subspace method. The word sequences returned by the individual ensemble members are first aligned. Then the final word sequence is produced. For this purpose we use a voting method and two novel statistical combination methods. The conducted experiments show that the proposed multiple classifier methods have the potential to improve the recognition accuracy of single recognisers.

1 Introduction

After many years of research in the field of handwriting recognition there are still many open problems. Whereas good performance is achieved for isolated handwritten characters or digits, the recognition rate usually drops for word recognition. An even more difficult task is the recognition of unconstrained handwritten text lines. This problem is among the most challenging tasks in pattern recognition. There are large differences in individual writing style as well as in writing instruments, and the lexicon usually contains a huge amount of word classes to be distinguished (typically more than 10,000). Furthermore, the correct number of words in a text line is unknown in advance, which often leads to word segmentation errors. Therefore, a high recognition accuracy is difficult to achieve. In the literature recognition rates between 50% and 80% are reported, depending on the experimental setup [1,2,3,4].

In many different pattern recognition fields, ensemble methods have been successfully applied [5,6,7]. By the combination of the results of multiple classifiers, the recognition accuracy can often be improved compared to a single classifier system. In handwriting recognition, several ensemble methods have been presented for isolated digit [8,9], character [10], or word [11,12] recognition. However, the investigation of ensemble methods for unconstrained offline handwritten text line recognition has started only recently [13,14]. Additional synchronisation effort is required to combine multiple text line recognition systems because the number of words in the output returned by the individual recognisers might differ. In [13] a heuristic approach has been used to align and combine multiple handwritten text line recognisers. Positional information of the recognised

M. Haindl, J. Kittler, and F. Roli (Eds.): MCS 2007, LNCS 4472, pp. 72–81, 2007.
© Springer-Verlag Berlin Heidelberg 2007

words is exploited to reduce the search space of the alignment. In [14] multiple recognisers were built by specific integration of a statistical language model. Alignment and combination was done by means of the ROVER algorithm [15].

In this paper we further investigate ensemble methods for offline handwritten text line recognition. Our contribution is twofold. First, feature subspace methods are applied for the first time in offline handwritten text line recognition to generate individual ensemble members. Secondly, a novel statistical combination method is proposed.

The remaining part of the paper is organised as follows. Section 2 introduces the base recogniser and the ensemble generation procedure. Section 3 describes the combination methods, including an example. Experiments and results are discussed in Sect. 4 and conclusions are drawn in the last section of this paper.

2   Ensemble Generation

2.1   Hidden Markov Model Based Recogniser

The offline handwritten text line recogniser we use as the base recognition system is an enhanced version of the recognition system introduced in [16]. Improvements were made at the language model integration level as well as in the modeling of the characters. Additionally, the lexicon is not closed over the test set anymore.[1] The system can be divided into three major parts: preprocessing, hidden Markov model (HMM) based recognition, and postprocessing.

To reduce the impact of different writing styles, a handwritten text line image is normalised with respect to skew, slant, and baseline position in the preprocessing phase. After these normalisation steps, a handwritten text line is converted into a sequence of feature vectors. For this purpose a sliding window is used which is moved from left to right, one pixel at each step. Nine geometrical features are extracted at each position of the sliding window.

In the HMM based recognition phase each character is modelled with a linear HMM. The number of states is chosen individually for each character [4], and twelve Gaussian mixture components are used to model the output distribution in each state. The Baum-Welch algorithm is used for the training of the HMMs, whereas the recognition is performed by the Viterbi algorithm. A statistical language model supports the Viterbi decoding step. The integration of this language model is optimised on a validation set as described in [4].

A confidence measure c_w based on frame normalised likelihoods [17] is computed for each recognised word w. The confidence measure indicates how sure the recogniser is about its decision.

---

[1] The new setup is more realistic, because it makes less assumptions on the test data. However, we expect lower recognition rates under this new setup because it can happen that a word occurring in the test set is not present in the lexicon and therefore can not be recognised correctly.

2.2 Feature Subspace Methods

To get ensembles of text line recognition systems we apply the random feature subspace method [18]. Multiple recognisers are built on different subsets of features. These subsets are chosen randomly with a fixed size. The only constraint is that the same subset must not be used twice. We select 24 subsets each consisting of six (out of nine) features.

Next, 24 recognisers are trained on the subspaces.[2] The same topology is used for each recogniser. After training, the integration of the statistical language model is optimised individually for each recogniser on a validation set.

Instead of using all 24 recognisers in one large ensemble we apply an ensemble member selection strategy. On a validation set, we apply a greedy forward search to find the optimised ensemble [14]. First, the individual subspace recogniser which performs best is selected as an ensemble member. Then, we tentatively add each other ensemble member and measure the performance of the resulting new ensembles. The best performing ensemble is selected for continuation. Iteratively, we add the best remaining subspace recogniser to the ensemble. This method is also known as overproduce-and-select [6].

3 Combination of Word Sequences

3.1 ROVER Combination

The *Recogniser Output Voting Error Reduction* (ROVER) system [15] was developed in the field of continuous speech recognition. It became a standard tool for the combination of multiple continuous speech recognisers. The algorithm consists of two phases. First, there is an alignment phase, followed by a voting phase.

ROVER applies an incremental algorithm to align multiple sequences of words delivered by the individual ensemble members. At the beginning, the first and the second word sequence are aligned in a single Word Transition Network (WTN). This WTN is aligned with the next recognised word sequence and so on. Null transition arcs ε are inserted in the WTN if the length of the input sequences differ. The final WTN, including each of the n recognised word sequences, does not guarantee an optimal alignment but in practice the sub-optimal algorithm often provides an adequate solution for the trade-off between computational costs and alignment accuracy.

An example of multiple sequence alignment using ROVER is shown in Fig. 1. Given the image of the handwritten text *the mouth-organ*, the recognisers R_1, R_2, and R_3 produce three different results. In the first step the results of R_1 and R_2 are aligned in a single WTN. Subsequently, the result of R_3 is aligned with this WTN.

Once the alignment is complete, the best scoring word sequence is extracted from the WTN by voting. For this purpose, a decision is made individually for

---

[2] As the training of our HMM recognisers is computationally very demanding, it is not possible to experiment with larger ensembles.

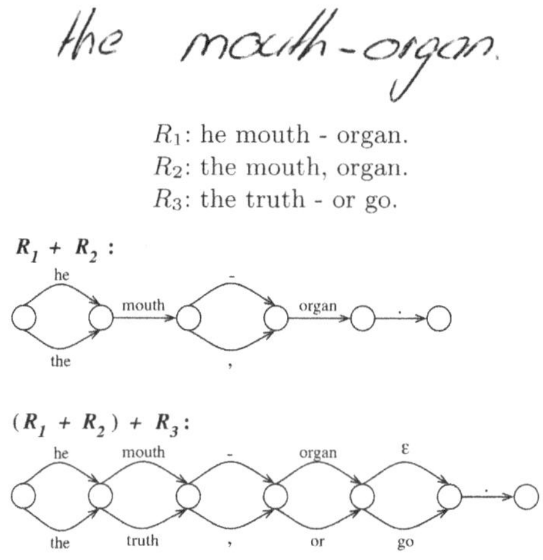
the mouth-organ.
R_1: he mouth - organ.
R_2: the mouth, organ.
R_3: the truth - or go.
$R_1 + R_2$:
he
mouth
-
organ
.
the
,
$(R_1 + R_2) + R_3$:
he
mouth
-
organ
ε
.
the
truth
,
or
go

Fig. 1. Example of an iterative alignment of multiple recognition results

each segment of the WTN. The decision depends on the size n of the ensemble, of alternatives present in the WTN, on the number of occurrences m_w of a word w in the current segment of the WTN, and on the confidence measure c_w of w. This confidence measure is defined as the maximum confidence measure among all occurrences of w at the current position in the WTN. For each possible word class w, the score s_w is calculated as follows:

$$s_w = \lambda \frac{m_w}{n} + (1 - \lambda)c_w \tag{1}$$

Paramter λ weights the influence of the confidence score c_w against the number of occurences m_w. The optimised value of λ is found by probing various values on a validation set. Additionally, because the null transition arcs ε don't have confidence measures, a global confidence measure c_ε has to be determined experimentally. Finally, the word w with the highest score s_w is returned as the final result for each segment (we refer to [15] for more details about ROVER).

3.2 Statistical Decision

Various statistical decision strategies have been proposed in the literature to combine the results of the individual members of a multiple classifier system [8,19,20]. However, if the number of classes is large most of these methods are not feasible because there is usually not enough training data available to estimate the required probabilities sufficiently well. In contrast, the statistical decision method proposed in this paper is able to handle an arbitrarily large number of classes. It considers not the class label itself, but which recognisers output a particular class label. The decision method is used as an extension to the

ROVER combination scheme. It uses the same alignment module, but applies the novel decision method instead of the voting procedure based on Eq. 1 to find the final decision.

Once the alignment is complete, we apply the statistical decision method to each segment of the WTN. A feature vector X_w is extracted for each word class w that occurs in the considered segment. The feature vector contains the confidence measures c_w of the recognisers that output w:

$$X_w = (x_{w,C_1}, \ldots, x_{w,C_n}) \tag{2}$$

where

$$x_{w,C_i} = \begin{cases} c_w & \text{if classifier } C_i \text{ outputs } w \\ 0 & \text{else} \end{cases} \tag{3}$$

The feature vector X_w is used as input to a Multi-Layer Perceptron (MLP). The MLP consists of l input neurons, one hidden layer, and two output neurons. One of the output neurons represents the score for w being correct, whereas the other output neuron represents the score for w being incorrect under input X_w. The score for correctness is used to estimate the probability $p(w = correct|X_w)$.

The final word class $\hat{w}$ is calculated by

$$\hat{w} = \underset{w}{argmax}\, p(w = correct|X_w). \tag{4}$$

A simplified version of this method uses binary feature vectors as input of the MLP. These feature vectors indicate whether a word is present in the output of a specific recogniser or not. For this purpose, Eq. 3 is rewritten as follows:

$$x_{w,C_i} = \begin{cases} 1 & \text{if classifier } C_i \text{ outputs } w \\ 0 & \text{else} \end{cases} \tag{5}$$

Note, that in contrast to the ROVER combination scheme and the statistical decision method using the confidence measure c_w, the binary decision method does not require the recognisers to output confidence values. Thus, it is more generally applicable.

An example of the binary version of the statistical decision method is given in Fig. 2. The scanned image of the handwritten text *leave in the autumn* is shown in (a). In this example three different recognisers R_1, R_2, R_3 are used. The outputs of these recognisers are aligned in a WTN as shown in (b). Next, a binary feature vector is built for each word that occurs in a segment according to Eq. 5. The resulting feature vectors are listed in (c). For each of these vectors the MLP calculates the score for a correct decision (d). The final combination result shown in (e) is then derived according to Eq. 4.

a) Input image of handwritten text:

$$leave\ in\ the\ autumn$$

(b) WTN including the aligned recognition results of R_1, R_2, R_3:

	Segment 1	Segment 2	Segment 3	Segment 4
R_1:	leave	is	the	autumn
R_2:	leave	in	that	autumn
R_3:	leave	is	that	august

(c) Input feature vectors:

Segment 1: $X_{leave} = (1, 1, 1)$
Segment 2: $X_{is} = (1, 0, 1)$ $X_{in} = (0, 1, 0)$
Segment 3: $X_{the} = (1, 0, 0)$ $X_{that} = (0, 1, 1)$
Segment 4: $X_{autumn} = (1, 1, 0)$ $X_{august} = (0, 0, 1)$

(d) Estimated probabilities for the correctness of a decision:

Segment 1: $p(correct|X_{leave}) = 0.9$
Segment 2: $p(correct|X_{is}) = 0.5$ $p(correct|X_{in}) = 0.7$
Segment 3: $p(correct|X_{the}) = 0.7$ $p(correct|X_{that}) = 0.3$
Segment 4: $p(correct|X_{autumn}) = 0.6$ $p(correct|X_{august}) = 0.2$

(e) Combination result:

$$leave\ in\ the\ autumn$$

Fig. 2. Example of the statistical decision procedure using binary feature vectors

4   Experiments and Results

All experiment reported in this section are conducted on handwritten text lines from the IAM[3] database [21] and make use of the HMM based recogniser described in Sect. 2.1.

4.1   Experimental Setup

A writer independent task is considered. Thus, none of the writers in the test set is represented in the training or validation set of the system. The training set consists of 6161 text lines written by 283 writers; 56 writers have contributed 920 text lines to the validation set, whereas the test set contains 2781 text lines by 161 writers.

The statistical language model is based on three different corpora, the LOB corpus [22], the Brown corpus [23], and the Wellington corpus [24]. A bigram language model is built for each of the corpora. These bigram models are then combined linearly with optimised mixture weights [25].

---

[3] The IAM database is publicly available for download at
http://www.iam.unibe.ch/~fki/iamDB

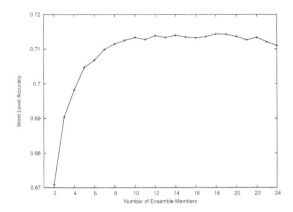

Fig. 3. Validation of the number of ensemble member using the ROVER combination method

The underlying lexicon consists of the 20,000 most frequent words that occur in the corpora. The lexicon has not been closed over the test set, i.e. there may be words in the test set that do not occur among the 20,000 most frequent words included in the lexicon. This scenario is more realistic than a closed lexicon because the texts in the test set are usually unknown in advance.

For computational reasons, the selection of ensemble members is accomplished with a greedy forward search on the validation set using the ROVER combination algorithm only. Figure 3 shows the result of this validation procedure. The best performing ensemble has $n = 18$ members. The same ensemble is then used to test the three combination methods, i.e. ROVER, statistical decision with confidence measures, and statistical decision with binary vectors.

The MLPs used by the statistical decision methods are trained and optimised on the validation set. We train the weights of the MLP with a standard back-propagation algorithm. During the validation phase the number of hidden neurons as well as the number of training iterations are optimised by means of minimising the mean square error on the validation set. 820 text lines are used for training. The remaining 100 text lines are used for validation.

4.2 Results

Finally, we measure the performance of the optimised systems on the test set. As a reference system we train and optimise a single base recogniser which uses all nine features. This base recogniser achieves a word recognition accuracy of 64.48%. The ROVER algorithm attains an accuracy of 65.29% and the novel statistical decision method with confidence measures achieves an accuracy of 65.31%. The simplified version that uses only binary input features for the MLP slightly improves this accuracy to 65.35%. Compared to the base recogniser, all improvements are statistically significant, whereas the difference between

Table 1. Recognition accuracies measured on test and validation set

	Validation	Test
Reference System	69.94%	64.48%
ROVER	71.44%	65.29%
Statistical with Confidence	71.52%	65.31%
Statistical with Binary	71.90%	65.35%

ROVER and the statistical decision methods is not statistically significant. The significance is computed at the text line level with a significance level of 5%. The results of the different methods on the validation and on the test set are summarised in Tab. 1.

One advantage of ensemble methods is that we usually get more stable results than with a single recogniser. This observation is confirmed in our experiments. For each system we measure the standard deviation of the recognition accurracies among the individual text lines in the test set (Tab. 2). As expected the standard deviation of the single recogniser is higher than the standard deviation among results of the ensemble methods.

Table 2. Standard deviation of the recognition accuracies of the text lines in the test set. The standard deviation decreases if ensemble methods are applied indicating that the results become more stable.

	Standard Deviation
Reference System	26.7%
ROVER	25.1%
Statistical with Confidence	25.1%
Statistical with Binary	25.0%

5   Conclusions

In this paper we have investigated the use of multiple classifier methods for offline handwritten text line recognition. The ensembles are created by means of the random feature subspace procedure. Three methods, one previously known and two novel ones, are evaluated to combine the results of the ensemble members.

The handwritten text line recognisers are based on hidden Markov models using a mixture of Gaussians and an individual number of states for each basic model. A large lexicon of 20,000 word classes is used, and a statistical language model trained on three different corpora supports the recognition step. To generate the ensemble members we implement a random feature subset method. Six out of nine features are randomly chosen to build the subsets. A greedy forward search is applied to select the ensemble members.

The ROVER framework is used to combine the results of the ensemble member. First, an iterative algorithm is applied to align the results in a word transition network. Secondly, we extract the best scoring transcription from the network to get the final result. Additionally, we use a novel statistical decision methods as an extension to ROVER. A feature vector is calculated for each occurring word class based on the outputs of the ensemble members. Using this feature vector, a Multi-Layer Perceptron estimates the probability that an output class is the correct decision. The novel statistical decision method is able to deal with an arbitrarily large number of classes (in our case 20,000 word classes).

Experiments have been conducted on a large set of text lines from the IAM database. In terms of word level accuracy the ensemble methods significantly outperform the baseline system. The statistical decision methods perform slightly better than the ROVER decision method. Additionally, we show that the variance can be reduced by the ensemble methods, which indicates that the results become more stable.

Acknowledgement

This research was supported by the Swiss National Science Foundation (Nr. 200020-19124/1). Additional funding was provided by the Swiss National Science Foundation NCCR program "Interactive Multimodal Information Management (IM)2" in the Individual Project "Visual/video processing". The authors thank Dr. Matthias Zimmermann for providing the statistical language model.

References

1. Kim, G., Govindaraju, V., Srihari, S.: Architecture for handwritten text recognition systems. In Lee, S.W., ed.: Advances in Handwriting Recognition, World Scientific Publ. Co. (1999) 163–172
2. Senior, A., Robinson, A.: An off-line cursive handwriting recognition system. IEEE Transactions on Pattern Analysis and Machine Intelligence **20**(3) (1998) 309–321
3. Vinciarelli, A., Bengio, S., Bunke, H.: Offline recognition of unconstrained handwritten texts using HMMs and statistical language models. IEEE Transactions on Pattern Analysis and Machine Intelligence **26**(6) (2004) 709–720
4. Zimmermann, M., Chappelier, J.C., Bunke, H.: Offline grammar-based recognition of handwritten sentences. IEEE Transactions on Pattern Analysis and Machine Intelligence **28**(5) (2006) 818–821
5. Rahman, A., Fairhurst, M.: Multiple classifier decision combination strategies for character recognition: A review. International Journal on Document Analysis and Recognition **5**(4) (2003) 166–194
6. Kuncheva, L.I.: Combining Pattern Classifiers: Methods and Algorithms. John Wiley & Sons Inc (2004)
7. Oza, N., Polikar, R., Kittler, J., Roli, F., eds.: Multiple Classifier Systems, 6th International Workshop, Springer LNCS 3541 (2005)
8. Huang, Y.S. Suen, C.: A method of combining multiple experts for the recognition of unconstrained handwritten numerals. IEEE Transactions on Pattern Analysis and Machine Intelligence **17**(1) (1995) 90–94
9. Oliveira, L.S., Morita, M., Sabourin, R.: Feature selection for ensembles applied to handwriting recognition. International Journal on Document Analysis and Recognition **8**(4) (2006) 262 – 279

10. Sirlantzkis, K., Fairhurst, M., Hoque, M.: Genetic algorithm for multiple classifier configuration: A case study in character recognition. In: 2nd International Workshop on Multiple Classifier Systems, Cambridge, England. (2001) 99–108
11. Gader, P., Mohamed, M., Keller, J.: Fusion of handwritten word classifiers. Pattern Recognition Letters **17** (1996) 577–584
12. Günter, S., Bunke, H.: Multiple classifier systems in off-line handwritten word recognition - on the influence of training set and vocabulary size. International Journal of Pattern Recognition and Artificial Intelligence **18**(7) (2004) 1303–1320
13. Marti, U.V., Bunke, H.: Use of positional information in sequence alignment for multiple classifier combination. In: 2nd International Workshop on Multiple Classifier Systems, Cambridge, England. (2001) 388 – 398
14. Bertolami, R., Bunke, H.: Ensemble methods for handwritten text line recognition systems. In: International Conference on Systems, Man and Cybernetics, Hawaii, USA. (2005) 2334–2339
15. Fiscus, J.: A post-processing system to yield reduced word error rates: Recognizer output voting error reduction. In: IEEE Workshop on Automatic Speech Recognition and Understanding, Santa Barbara. (1997) 347–352
16. Marti, U.V., Bunke, H.: Using a statistical language model to improve the performance of an HMM-based cursive handwriting recognition system. International Journal of Pattern Recognition and Artificial Intelligence **15** (2001) 65–90
17. Brakensiek, A., Rigoll, G.: Handwritten address recognition using hidden Markov models. In Dengel, A., Junker, M., Weisbecker, A., eds.: Reading and Learning, Springer (2004) 103–122
18. Ho, T.K.: The random space method for constructing decision forests. IEEE Transactions on Pattern Analysis and Machine Intelligence **20**(8) (1998) 832–844
19. Xu, L., Krzyzak, A., Suen, C.Y.: Methods of combining multiple classifiers and their applications to handwriting recognition. IEEE Transactions on Systems, Man, and Cybernetics **22**(3) (1992) 418–435
20. Raudys, S.: Trainable fusion rules. i. large sample size case. Neural Networks **19**(10) (1006) 1506–1516
21. Marti, U.V., Bunke, H.: The IAM-database: an English sentence database for offline handwriting recognition. International Journal on Document Analysis and Recognition **5** (2002) 39 – 46
22. Johansson, S., Atwell, E., Garside, R., Leech, G.: The Tagged LOB Corpus, User's Manual. Norwegian Computing Center for the Humanities, Bergen, Norway. (1986)
23. Francis, W.N., Kucera, H.: Brown corpus manual, Manual of Information to accompany A Standard Corpus of Present-Day Edited American English, for use with Digital Computers. Department of Linguistics, Brown University, Providence, USA (1979)
24. Bauer, L.: Manual of Information to Accompany The Wellington Corpus of Written New Zealand English. Department of Linguistics, Victoria University, Wellington, New Zealand (1993)
25. Goodman, J.: A bit of progress in language modeling. Technical Report MSR-TR-2001-72, Microsoft Research (2001)

Applying Data Fusion Methods to Passage Retrieval in QAS

Hans Ulrich Christensen and Daniel Ortiz-Arroyo

Computer Science Department
Aalborg University Esbjerg
Niels Bohrs Vej 8, 6700 Denmark
huc1405@student.aaue.dk, do@cs.aaue.dk

Abstract. This paper investigates the use of diverse data fusion methods to improve the performance of the passage retrieval component in a question answering system. Our results obtained with 13 data fusion methods and 8 passage retrieval systems show that data fusion techniques are capable of improving the performance of a passage retrieval system by 6.43% and 11.32% in terms of the mean reciprocal rank and coverage measures respectively.

Keywords: Data Fusion, Question Answering Systems, Passage Retrieval.

1 Introduction

A *Question Answering System (QAS)* is one type of information retrieval (IR) system that attempts to find exact answers to user's questions expressed in natural language. In an *Open-Domain Question Answering System (ODQAS)*, questions are not restricted to certain topics and answers have to be found in an unstructured document collection. *Passage Retrieval (PR)*, one component of a QAS, extracts text segments from a group of retrieved documents and ranks these passages in decreasing order of computed likelihood for containing the correct answer. Typically, such text segments are referred to as *candidate passages*.

Data Fusion applied to Information Retrieval (IR Data Fusion) is the intelligent combination of a variety of IR system's opinions on a document's relevance to the user's information need represented in a query. If the combined relevance estimate of a document is more accurate than any of the individual IR system's estimates, performance will be improved. The findings of several recent studies on the application of Data Fusion to IR report improvements in performance [3] [5] [16]. Using Data Fusion techniques, a QAS will be able to provide correct answers to more questions.

This paper is organized as follows. Section 2 briefly describes related work on the application of IR Data Fusion methods to a QAS. Section 3 describes the IR Data Fusion methods investigated. Section 4 investigates which normalization schema performs best for IR Data Fusion applied to PR in a QAS. Section 5 describes the evaluation of the Data Fusion methods and the results achieved. Finally, section 6 presents conclusions and future work.

M. Haindl, J. Kittler, and F. Roli (Eds.): MCS 2007, LNCS 4472, pp. 82–92, 2007.

2   Related Work

Although several studies have investigated the application of Data Fusion to QA systems and in general achieved promising results—e.g. Harabagui et al. [4] report a consistent improvements in terms of precision as high as 20%—only few have investigated the potentially beneficial application of Data Fusion to the task of PR within a QAS. Our contribution in this regard is methodological i.e. we explore experimentally diverse techniques to fuse effectively an ensemble of PR systems to improve the overall performance of a QAS.

The internal Data Fusion experiment carried out by Unsunier et al. reported in [18] achieves a consistent improvement in Coverage@n ranging as high as 119% at Coverage@1. However, the machine learning techniques they employed are based on the learned features of answering passages; hence requiring an extra training step.

As part of their evaluation of a number of PR systems, Tellex et. al. [17] experimentally fuse three PR systems achieving a 6% increase in performance in terms of Mean Reciprocal Rank (MRR). Several other IR studies on the application of Data Fusion for document retrieval (e.g. Lee [9] and Montague [12]) have reported important improvements in performance but on ad-hoc document retrieval systems and not specifically in PR for QAS. Contrarily to these previous approaches, the methodology presented in this paper explores what is the best way to fuse the ranking evaluations produced by diverse PR systems.

3   Descriptions of the Fusion Methods

This section describes with some detail the IR Data Fusion methods we applied to Passage Retrieval. Table 1 shows the IR Data Fusion methods grouped according to Montague's classification scheme [12], which is based on two characteristics of the input: (1) *whether similarity scores are available or ranks only* and (2) *whether training data are available or not.* Typically, training data are judged search results, which are then used for learning IR system specific performance weights. Accordingly, this schema consists of four classes of Fusion methods: *ranks only (RO)*, *relevance scores (RS)*, *ranks and training data (R+W)*, and *relevance scores and training data (RS+W)*.

Intuitively, the more information a Fusion method uses for fusing n search results, the better it performs on average. Therefore, we expect an improved performance in RS+W Fusion methods followed by RO+W, RS, and finally RO Fusion method, which we expect to perform worst.

3.1   Data Fusion Methods Based on Ranks Only

Based on Social Choice Theory, Montague and Aslam [13] proposed an adapted version of the Condorcet voting method: the *Condorcet-fuse method*, which they found to be just as effective as the CombMNZ Fusion method. The Condorcet-fuse method is a generalization of the Condorcet election process, where the winner of an election is the candidate that beats or ties with every other candidate in

	Availabilty of training data	
	No training data available	**Training data available**
Only passage ranks available	Condorcet-Fuse Borda-Fuse Tellex et al. algorithm	Weighted Condorcet-Fuse Weighted Borda-Fuse
Relevance scores available	CombMNZ MEOWA	Linear Combination Weighted MEOWA

Availabilty of relevance scores

Fig. 1. Classification of the 9 IR Data Fusion methods

a pair-wise comparison, such that the result is a ranked list of documents rather than a single winner. This is accomplished by first executing the Condorcet election process for all pairs of IR systems constructing a graph, where documents are nodes and a directed edge $x \rightarrow y$ means that x has received at least as many votes as y and thus must be ranked higher. Then, traversing all nodes of the graph yields the Fused ranking, where the first node is the highest ranked document. While the Condorcet-fuse voting method has a time complexity of $O(n^2 * k)$, n being the number of documents and k the number of IR systems, Montague and Aslam [13] propose an efficient implementation of Condorcet-fuse using a modified QuickSort method.

In [1], Montague and Aslam also introduce a novel voting Fusion method to the problem of Data Fusion in IR: *Borda-Fuse*, which is an adaptation of the Borda Count election process, where voters give candidates a certain amount of points and the winner is the one who makes more points. Evaluation showed that in two of the five tests using TREC test data, Borda-fuse performed better than the best component IR system in the election [1].

Tellex and colleagues [17] propose a simple yet effective method for fusing the search results of multiple PR in a QAS systems. The method combines a passages rank and a simple vote: the total number of passages retrieved by all component PR systems with a specific document ID into a fused relevance score. Application of the Fusion methods to the 3 best performing passage retrieval methods of the PRISE IR system showed that it was able to improve the Mean Reciprocal Rank by 6% [17]. The method calculates a score for each passage as follows.

$$score(a, r) = \frac{1}{r} + docScore(docID(a, r)) \tag{1}$$

Interestingly, Tellex et al.'s method re-ranks the set of top n candidate passages retrieved by all component PR systems and thus does not fuse identical passages thereby avoiding the difficulty of identifying identical passages.

Based on the observation that frequently when Tellex et al.'s Fusion method boosted low ranked passages, those passages in fact were non-relevant, we propose in this paper a new Fusion method called *Tellex modified*, where the union of top m passages retrieved by all component PR systems is re-ranked. However, although we restricted Tellex et al.'s Fusion method from including passages at lower ranks, the document counts are still computed for the top 300 passages retrieved by all component PR systems.

3.2   Data Fusion Methods Based on Relevance Scores

Fox and Shaw [6] introduce and evaluate the 6 simple Fusion methods of table 1.

Table 1. The six Fusion Methods introduced by Fox and Shaw (adapted from [6])

CombMAX	$r_f(d_i) = \max\limits_{\forall s_j \in S} \left(r_{s_j}(d_i) \right)$
CombMIN	$r_f(d_i) = \min\limits_{\forall s_j \in S} \left(r_{s_j}(d_i) \right)$
CombSUM	$r_f(d_i) = \sum\limits_{\forall s_j \in S} \left(r_{s_j}(d_i) \right)$
CombANZ	$r_f(d_i) = CombSUM/t$
CombMNZ	$r_f(d_i) = CombSUM * t$
CombMED	$r_f(d_i) = \begin{cases} r_{s_{(n+1)/2}}(d_i) & \text{if } n \text{ is odd} \\ (r_{s_n}(d_i) + r_{s_{(n+1)}}(d_i))/2 & \text{if } n \text{ is even} \end{cases}, r_{s_0}(d_i) \geq \dots r_{sn}(d_i)$

In table 1, $r_f(d_i)$ is the fused rank of the document d_i, $r_{s_j}(d_i)$ document d_i's rank at the IR system $s_j \in S$, the set of IR systems to be fused, and t the number of IR systems retrieving d_i.

Out of the six "comb"-methods, Fox and Shaw provide evidence that CombSUM followed by CombMNZ performs best. They argue that this is because both methods utilize information about *ranking* (since highly ranked documents are preferred) and *voting* (because documents found by multiple systems are preferred). Later Lee [10] found that CombMNZ in fact performs relatively better. Although these variation in effectiveness may be explained by differences in document collections and query sets, it seems reasonable to assume that in general CombMNZ is superior to CombSUM since more recent Fusion experiments supports this observation.

3.3   Data Fusion Methods Based on Ranks and Training Data

A *weighted Data Fusion method* takes into account a component PR system's ability to provide answering passages. This way, important component PR systems have a greater influence on the Fused relevance score.

As suggested by Aslam and Montague [1], Borda-fuse can be extended to a weighted variant: *Weighted Borda-fuse* by multiplying the points, which a PR system S_i assigns to a candidate passage with a system weight α_i. This is equally true for passages, which a PR system retrieves and those not retrieved, which are given an average score. This way, the relevance assessments of a PR system considered good at providing candidate passages is preferred. Experimental comparison with CombMNZ Fusion method, where non-optimized weights were used, showed that weighted Condorcet Fuse was able to achieve the same level of performance. Thus, by using improved performance weights, Weighted Borda-fuse has the potential of outperforming CombMNZ [13].

Just like Borda-fuse, Condorcet-fuse can be easily extended to take importance weights into account. In *weighted Condorcet-fuse*, rather than crisp votes, each component PR system gives an importance weighted vote. However, this time the importance weights are used in the binary candidate elections, where the sum of weights rather than votes is compared giving preference to the highest sum. Comparison with the CombMNZ Fusion method showed than weighted Condorcet Fuse performed best on three of four TREC data sets [13].

3.4 Data Fusion Methods Based on Relevance Scores and Training Data

Vogt and Cottrell's *Linear combination* (LC) Data Fusion method combines the relevance scores and training data of two or more component IR systems into a combined relevance score per document [19]. In LC, training data are used for calculating *importance weights* based on standard IR metrics thus reflecting the overall ability of an IR system to provide relevant documents. Given both relevance scores and performance weights the aggregated relevance score is calculated using equation 2.

$$s_{LC}(d) = \sum_{\forall s_i \in S} \alpha_i * s_i(d) \tag{2}$$

where $S_{LC}(d)$ is the fused relevance score assigned to the document d, s_i is the ith PR system's of the set of PR systems to be combined S relevance score, and a_i the importance weight assigned to the ith PR systems. In LC, if an IR system does not retrieve a particular document, then the IR systems is assumed to consider it non-relevant. Accordingly, such a document is assigned a relevance score of 0. Although simple, in various experiments LC has performed well often outperforming the base-line system with a margin of 5% to 10%.

Recently, a number of researchers have investigated the application of the *Ordered-Weighted Averaging (OWA)* class of Fuzzy logic averaging operators to Data Fusion. A desirable property of OWA is that the degree of ANDness can be adjusted by changing the OWA weights.

$$OWA(\boldsymbol{v_i}, \boldsymbol{a_i}) = \sum_{i=1}^{n} v_i * a_i \tag{3}$$

where $\boldsymbol{v}$ is a vector of OWA weights $(v_1, v_2, ...v_n)$ with $\sum v_i = 1$ sorted is descending order and $\boldsymbol{a}$ a vector of Fuzzy satisfaction degrees $(a_1, a_2, ...a_n)$, $a_i \in [0, 1]$. Diaz et al. investigated the use of the OWA class of Fuzzy averaging operator to ad-hoc IR. They found OWA to outperform Borda-fuse when at least 8 IR systems are combined [3]. In [11] it is reported the use of an adapted version of the weighted maximum entropy OWA (MEOWA) operator as a weighted classifier combination method. It was found that the adapted weighted MEOWA operator improved performance measured by the F_1 measure with 6.51% compared to the best performing classifier [11] in the ensemble.

4   Normalization of Relevance Scores

In general, in Data Fusion applied to IR normalization of relevance scores is necessary since different IR systems use different scales for relevance scores. For example, one IR system might chose to use positive real values and another IR system values in the Unit Interval. Two well-known normalization schemes are shift-scale normalization and shift-sum normalization of equations 4 and 5.

$$score^n_{s_k}(d_i) = \frac{score_{s_k}(d_i) - \min\limits_{j=1}^{m} score_{s_k}(d_j)}{\max\limits_{j=1}^{m} score_{s_k}(d_j) - \min\limits_{j=1}^{m} score_{s_k}(d_j)} \tag{4}$$

$$score^n_{s_k}(d_i) = \frac{score_{s_k}(d_i) - \min\limits_{j=1}^{m} score_{s_k}(d_j)}{\sum\limits_{j=1}^{m} score_{s_k}(d_j) - \min\limits_{j=1}^{m} score_{s_k}(d_j)} \tag{5}$$

where $score_{s_k}(d_i)$ is the unnormalized score of document d_i retrieved by the IR system s_k, $score^n_{s_k}(d_i)$ is the normalized score, and m the number of documents retrieved by the IR system in question.

In order to determine which of the 3 normalization schemes including "no normalization" performs best for Data Fusion applied to PR, we performed an experiment, where the three Data Fusion methods utilizing relevance-scores: CombMNZ, CombSUM and MEOWA are tested with all 238 unique combination of the 8 PR systems: FuzzyPRS [2], JIRS TW and JIRS DM [7], LucenePRS, LucenePRS+FuzzyPRS, Terrier in expC2 [14], and Zettair [1] applied to two QA test sets: CLEF03 and TREC11. Accordingly, $2 * 3 * 238 = 1,428$ runs have to be performed. Performance is measured using the three standard QA metrics: Mean Reciprocal Rank (MRR), Coverage@20, and Redundancy@20.

In summary we found that (1) using no normalization consistently performed worse measured by both Coverage@20 and Redundancy@20 indicating the necessity of using a normalization scheme in PR Data Fusion, and (2) applied to PR Data Fusion, in terms of MRR and Coverage@20 shift-max normalization in general performs better than shift-sum normalization.

---

[1] Zettair and Lucene are popular open source search engines.

5   Evaluation

Using the methodology employed by Aslam and Montague [1] and Tellex et al. [17], we performed two experiments to investigate the capability of a number of Fusion methods' to improve the performance of the PR module in a QA system to provide an answer to 5 questions. In both experiments we used the same IR Data Fusion methods, component PR systems, QA test data and performance metrics described in subsection 1.

The first experiment, which we denote as *brute-force*, was designed to explore a number of PR systems' ability to improve performance no matter the number and performances of the component PR systems combined. Ideally, a Fusion method will be able to consistently improve the performance of the best performing component PR system. Each of the Fusion methods was tested with all different component PR system subsets of sizes $\{2, 3, 4, 5, 6\}$.

In the second experiment - denoted as *best-to-worst* - we investigated the Fusion methods' ability to improve performance by using knowledge of the past performances of the PR systems. The $i \in \{1, 2, 3, 4, 5, 6\}$ best performing PR systems were combined. Since the top 1 to top 6 PR systems amount to 6 different sets of PR systems, 6 runs with each of the Data Fusion methods had to be performed.

5.1   Methodology

Besides the 9 Data Fusion methods described in section 3, we applied subclass weighting to weighted Condorcet-Fuse, weighted Borda-Fuse, LC and weighted MEOWA (IWMEOWA). Thus, the total number of different Data Fusion methods with which we experimented was 13.

As importance weights we used the performance weights computed using the TREC11 and CLEF03 test data. Evaluation of 7 different performance weights found that max-normalized MRR (nMRR) to perform best.

While the two Fusion experiments were being performed, we found it necessary to exclude Condorcet-fuse with question type weights because it consistently worsened performance.

In our experiments we used the following 8 component PR systems: JIRS [7] using the Distance Model, FuzzyPRS [2], JIRS using the Simple Model, FuzzyPRS, FuzzyPRS+LucenePRS, LucenePRS, Swish-e, Terrier PL2 [14] using In expC2 probabilistic model, and Zettair. A *component PR system* must a) be able to automatically process a question set and b) for each question produce a search result, which contains the information on relevance score, document ID and passage text in the required syntax.

As test data we used TREC12's set of 495 questions and the corpus called AQUAINT consisting of $1,033,461$ documents of English news text and CLEF04's 180 question and the AgenciaEFE corpus of $454,045$ Spanish newswire documents. To answer questions automatically for TREC12 we used

Ken Litkowsky's regular expression patterns of correct answers[2] and for CLEF4 we used the pattern supplied with JIRS[3] The TREC12 question set was reduced to 380, since 115 questions do not have a recognizable pattern.

As evaluation metrics we used MRR, Coverage, and Redundancy. *Mean Reciprocal Rank (MRR)* is defined at the average of the reciprocal value of the first hit to each question within the top 5 candidate passages:

$$MRR = \frac{1}{|Q|} \sum_{i=1}^{|Q|} RR_i \qquad (6)$$

where $RR_i = \frac{1}{r_i}$ if $r_i \leq 5$ or 0 otherwise and Q is the set of questions and r_i the rank of the first answering passage in response to a particular question. As is done in the JIRS system [8], we measure coverage on the first top 20 passages. *Coverage* is defined as the proportion of questions for which an answer can be found within the n top-ranked passages:

$$cov(Q, D, n) \equiv \frac{|\{q \in Q | R_{D,q,n} \cap A_{D,q} \neq \emptyset\}|}{|Q|} \qquad (7)$$

being Q the question set, D the passage collection, $A_{D,q}$ the subset of D which contains correct answers for $q \in Q$, $R_{D,q,n}$ the n top ranked passages. *Redundancy* is defined the average number, per question, of the top n passages, which contain a correct answer [15].

$$Redundancy(Q, P, n) \equiv \frac{\sum_{q \in Q} |R_{P,q,n} \cap A_{P,q}|}{|Q|} \qquad (8)$$

where Q is the set of questions, $R_{P,q,n}$ the n top ranked passages and $A_{P,q}$ the subset of passages P containing correct answers to $q \in Q$.

5.2   Results

When the Data Fusion methods were applied to PR, using 2 different sets of test data (TREC12 and CLEF04), we were able to improve performance measured by a maximum of 6.43% in terms of MRR and by 11.32% in terms of Coverage@20. These results were obtained by fusing 4 PR system and using our modified version of Tellex et. al.'s [17] Fusion method as shown in table 2.

In general we were not able to improve performance when using Redundancy@20. Somewhat surprisingly, the modified Tellex Fusion method neither requires relevance scores of passages nor importance weights of the PR systems to be fused.

We also obtained the results of the brute-force approach employing both TREC12 and CLEF04 as test data. Comparing the performance results achieved

---

[2] Ken Litkowsky's patterns are available from the TREC website:
http://trec.nist.gov.
[3] Patterns of correct answers to CLEF QA test data are available from JIRS' website:
http://jirs.dsic.upv.es/.

Table 2. The MRR and Coverage@20 of Modified Tellex compared to the 2nd best Fusion methods tested with a) TREC12 (top) and b) CLEF04 (bottom) QA test data

Performance metric	MRR					Coverage@20				
Number of PR4QA systems combined	2	3	4	5	6	2	3	4	5	6
Avg. of best component PR4QA systems	0,2999	0,3093	0,3160	0,3208	0,3242	0,5903	0,6066	0,6168	0,6233	0,6274
Modified Tellex (best)	0,3165	0,3291	0,3363	0,3411	0,3444	0,6420	0,6752	0,6870	0,6937	0,6959
Relative performance in %	5,54	6,41	6,43	6,33	6,25	8,77	11,32	11,39	11,30	10,91
LC	0,2999	0,3159	0,3269	0,3322	0,3353	0,6130	0,6357	0,6508	0,6586	0,6644
Relative performance in %	0,00	2,15	3,46	3,55	3,43	3,85	4,79	5,51	5,66	5,89

Performance metric	MRR					Coverage@20				
Number of PR4QA systems combined	2	3	4	5	6	2	3	4	5	6
Avg. of best component PR4QA systems	0,3522	0,3620	0,3691	0,3745	0,3787	0,5903	0,6066	0,6168	0,6233	0,6274
Modified Tellex (best)	0,3567	0,3666	0,3712	0,3759	0,3785	0,6224	0,6575	0,6727	0,6806	0,6845
Relative performance in %	1,28	1,26	0,59	0,39	-0,03	5,45	8,40	9,07	9,19	9,10
LC w. question class weights	0,3497	0,3616	0,3695	0,3765	0,3847					
LC						0,6153	0,6420	0,6547	0,6639	0,6708
Relative performance in %	-0,70	-0,11	0,12	0,54	1,60	4,24	5,83	6,15	6,52	6,92

in terms of MRR and Coverage@20 metrics when applying the Fusion methods to both TREC12 and CLEF04 test data revealed that in general only the modified version of Tellex et al.'s [17] method was able to improve performance in terms of these metrics.

For each of the 4 classes of Fusion methods we calculated the average and maximum of the results achieved when all Fusion methods were applied to both test sets. We found that the class of Fusion methods, which only takes a ranked list of candidate passages as input, performed best, contrarily to our expectation that Fusion methods utilizing more information on relevance perform better.

We used a historical MRR metric computed using CLEF03 and TREC11 sets of test data to rank the individual PR systems according to their performances, since we found this metric to perform best. We found that all three performance metrics were consistently either improved or remained the same compared to the results of the brute-force experiments for both TREC12 and CLEF04 test data. Although the results did not reveal a Fusion method, which consistently benefited the most from fusing the i best performing PR systems, the results indicated that the combination of the top 2 PR was able to achieve the highest improvements.

We tested both the unweighted and weighted versions of Condorcet-fuse yielding a total of 4 Fusion methods. While both Fusion methods consistently improved performance for the TREC11 QA test set by a small margin, they fail doing so when applied to CLEF04 QA test data, where performance measured as MRR degrades by a maximum of 3.56% thus indicating a need for more advanced weighting schemes i.e. applying machine learning techniques.

Finally, we tested IWMEOWA, Condorcet-fuse and Linear Combination with both types of weighting resulting in 6 different Fusion methods applied to both TREC12 and CLEF04 test data. We found that using weights per question type instead of overall importance weights did not consistently provide additional performance improvements.

6   Conclusions and Future work

This paper investigated the application of a total of 13 Data Fusion methods to Passage Retrieval in a QAS, eight of these utilize importance weights and importance weight per subclass of questions. Using 2 sets of QA test data, we found that the data fusion mechanisms were able to improve MRR by a maximum of 6.43% and Coverage@20 by 11.32%. These results were obtained by fusing 4 PR in a QAS systems with our proposed modification to Tellex et. al.'s method [17]. Contrarily to our initial expectations, based on the performance improvements obtained by the use of importance weights in voting systems applied in information retrieval systems and [3] patent classification [11], our experiments indicate that importance weights did not yield significant improvements in performance. The reason for this may be that we used a too simplistic approach to obtain the performance weights employed in our experiments and that the proposed question classification scheme does not generalize well with new questions.

As future work we plan to apply machine learning techniques and advanced question classification schemes to Data Fusion of PR systems in a QAS to improve performance even further.

References

1. J. Aslam and M. Montague. Models for metasearch. *The 24th Annual ACM Conference on Research and Development in Information Retrieval (SIGIR 01), New Orleans, LA*, 2001.
2. H. U. Christensen. Exploring the use of fuzzy logic in passage retrieval for question answering, March 2006. Preliminary master's thesis report available online: http://hufnc.1go.dk/MidtermReport.pdf.
3. E. D. Diaz, A. De, and V. Raghavan. A comprehensive owa-based framework for result merging in metasearch. *Proceedings of Rough Sets, Fuzzy Sets, Data Mining, and Granular Computing: 10th International Conference, RSFDGrC 2005, Regina, Canada*, 2005.
4. Harabagiu et al. Employing two question answering systems in trec-2005. *In proceedings of The Fourteenth Text REtrieval Conference (TREC 2005)*, 2005.
5. W. Fan, M. Gordon, and P. Pathak. On linear mixture of expert approaches to information retrieval. *Decision Support Systems*, 42:975–987, 2006.
6. E. A. Fox and J. A. Shaw. Combination of multiple searches. *In The Second Text REtrieval Conference (TREC-2), Gaithersburg, MD, USA*, pages 243–249, March 1994.
7. J. Gómez-Soriano and M Montes y Gómez. Jirs—the mother of all the passage retrieval systems for multilingual question answering? http://www.dsic.upv.es/workshops/euindia05/slides/jgomez.pdf.
8. J. Gómez-Soriano, M. Montes y Gómez, E. Arnal, L. Villase nor Pineda, and P. Rosso. Language independent passage retrieval for question answering. *Fourth Mexican International Conference on Artificial Intelligence MICAI 2005*, Lecture Notes in Artificial Intelligence, Springer-Verlag, November 2005. Monterrey, Mexico.
9. J. H. Lee. Combining multiple evidence from different properties of weighting schemes. *In proceedings of the 18th annual international ACM SIGIR conference on Research and development in information retrieval*, July 1995.

10. J. H. Lee. Analyses of multiple evidence combination. *In: Belkin NJ, Narasimhalu AD and Willett P, eds. SIGIR 97: Proceedings of the Twentieth Annual International ACM-SIGIR Conference on Research and Development in Information Retrieval*, pages 267–276, July 1997.

11. H. Mathiassen and D. Ortiz-Arroyo. Automatic classification of patents using classifier combinations. In *Proceedings of IDEAL 2006, 7th International Conference on Intelligent Data Engineering and Automated Learning LNCS Vol. 4224*, pages 1039–1047, September 20-23rd 2006.

12. M. Montague. *Metasearch: Data fusion for document retrieval*. PhD thesis, Dartmouth College, 2002.

13. M. Montague and J. Aslam. Condorcet fusion for improved retrieval. *The 11th Annual ACM Conference on Information and Knowledge Management (CIKM 02), Tysons Corner, VA.*, July 2002.

14. I. Ounis, G. Amati, V. Plachouras, B. He, C. Macdonald, and D. Johnson. Terrier information retrieval platform. In *Proceedings of the 27th European Conference on IR Research (ECIR 2005)*, volume 3408 of Lecture Notes in Computer Science, pages 517–519. Springer, 2005.

15. I. Roberts and R. Gaizauskas. Evaluating passage retrieval approaches for question answering. *In Advances in Information Retrieval: Proceedings of the 26th European Conference on Information Retrieval (ECIR04), number 2997 in LNCS*, Lecture Notes in Computer Science, Springer-Verlag:72–84, 2004.

16. A. Spoerri. How the overlap between the search results of different retrieval systems correlates with document relevance. *In Grove, Andrew, Eds. Proceedings 68th Annual Meeting of the American Society for Information Science and Technology (ASIST) 42*, 2005.

17. S. Tellex, B. Katz, J. Lin, G. Marton, and A. Fernandes. Quantitative evaluation of passage retrieval algorithms for question answering. *In Proceedings of the 26th Annual International ACM SIGIR Conference on Research and Development in Information Retrieval (SIGIR 2003)*, July 2003.

18. N. Unsunier, M. Amini, and P. Gallinari. Boosting weak ranking functions to enhance passage retrieval for question answering. *In IR4QA workshop of SIGIR 2004*, 2004.

19. C. C. Vogt and G. W. Cottrell. Fusion via a linear combination of scores. *Information Retrieval*, 1(1):151–173, October 1999.

A Co-training Approach for Time Series Prediction with Missing Data

Tawfik A. Mohamed[1], Neamat El Gayar[2], and Amir F. Atiya[3]

[1] Faculty of Computers and Information, Cairo University, Giza, Egypt
tawfik_fci@yahoo.com
[2] Faculty of Computers and Information, Cairo University, Giza, Egypt
hmg@link.net
[3] Dept Computer Engineering, Cairo University, Giza, Egypt
amir@alumni.caltech.edu

Abstract. In this paper we consider the problem of missing data in time series analysis. We propose a semi-supervised co-training method to handle the problem of missing data. We transform the time series data to set of labeled and unlabeled data. Different predictors are used to predict the unlabelled data and the most confident labeled patterns are used to retrain the predictors further to and enhance the overall prediction accuracy. By labeling the unknown patterns the missing data is compensated for. Experiments were conducted on different time series data and with varying percentage of missing data using a uniform distribution. We used KNN base predictors and Fuzzy Inductive Reasoning (FIR) base predictors and compared their performance using different confidence measures. Results reveal the effectiveness of the co-training method to compensate for the missing values and to improve prediction. The FIR model together with the "similarity" confidence measures obtained in most cases the best results in our study.

Keywords: Time series prediction, missing data, co-training, semi-supervised learning, k-nearest neighbor , fuzzy inductive reasoning, ensemble prediction.

1 Introduction

Missing values, encountered typically in real world data sets, negatively affects the performance of regression or classification models. Most developed regression or classification algorithms assume the data is complete. The designer, often not knowing how to deal with the missing inputs or features, takes the easy route and simply deletes the corrupted training patterns. This however is detrimental to classification/ regression performance as it wastes a lot of useful data. The problem of handling missing values has been studied extensively in the statistics literature [2].

Time series forecasting is a certain domain of application for statistical regression and machine learning models whereby the temporal structure and ordering of the data is utilized in some way. To our knowledge, Limited work has been done to deal with missing data in time series [1]. Recently, some approaches have

M. Haindl, J. Kittler, and F. Roli (Eds.): MCS 2007, LNCS 4472, pp. 93–102, 2007.

been introduced in the literature on how to deal with missing data in benchmark artificial time series with a limited number of missing points. Among the successful models used for this particular problem were using recurrent neural networks, Kalman smoothers, ensemble models, fuzzy logic systems and genetic optimization [3], [4], [5], [6], [7]. The objective of our research is to look at the problem of missing data in time series as a problem of semi-supervised learning. Semi-supervised learning deals with learning using a labeled and an unlabeled data set [8]. The unlabeled data are considered incomplete or "missing" because they do not have class labels. Most semi-supervised learning techniques deal with classification problems.

In this paper we mainly focus on one class of semi-supervised learning techniques which is the co-training algorithm. A co-training approach to semi-supervised classification was proposed by Blum and Mitchell in 1998 [9]. Further variations of the co-training algorithm are proposed in [10], [11], [12], [13]. It is noteworthy that previous research mainly focuses on classification while regression remains almost untouched. This is because most classifiers can output a confidence measure to its classification. A big problem in regression, however, is the difficulty to calculate the confidence of the estimation of a regressor. Zhou et al. [14] proposed a co-training style semi-supervised regression algorithm named COREG. This algorithm mainly employs two K-Nearest Neighbor (KNN) regressors. The labeling confidence is calculated through consulting the influence of the labeling of unlabeled examples on the labeled examples.

In our study we extend the semi-supervised regression problem to be applied for improving the accuracy of time series prediction with missing data. In particular, we first reformulate the problem of missing data in time series into the problem of semi-supervised learning ; by transforming time series data set into a set of labeled and unlabeled data. We extend the co-training algorithm in [14] to be applied to an ensemble of predictors. We also use K-Nearest Neighbors (KNN) [15] and Fuzzy Inductive Reasoning (FIR) [7] method as base predictors and with different measures of confidence.

The proposed model was tested on different data sets with varying percentages of missing data. Experiments show that the proposed approach can effectively increase the accuracy of the time series prediction model even if missing data exist in a substantial ratio. The paper is organized as follows; Section 2 formulates the problem of time series prediction into a problem of semi-supervised learning. Section 3 describes the used co-training algorithm. Section 4, discusses the base learners and the confidence measures. Section 5, describes the used data sets, and outlines details of the experiments conducted. In Section 6, results are summarized and discussed. Finally, the paper is concluded in Section 7.

2   Semi-supervised Approach to the Problem of Missing Data

Semi-supervised techniques deal with using a set L of labeled data and a set U of unlabelled data for learning. In this section we describe how to generate L and

U for time series data with missing values. These data sets will be used to apply the co-training algorithm as described in section 3 to enhance the prediction accuracy.

A time series is a sequence of vectors, y_t , $t = 0, 1, \ldots$, where t represents elapsed time. We will consider here only sequences of scalars as we primarily deal with univariate time series. Theoretically, y may be a value, which varies continuously with t, such as a temperature. In practice, for any given physical system, y will be sampled to give a series of discrete data points, equally spaced in time. The rate at which samples are taken dictates the maximum resolution of the model. The prediction of time series signals is based on their past values. Therefore, it is necessary to obtain a data record. Hence, future values of a time series y_t can be predicted as a function of past values $y_{t-1}, y_{t-2}, \ldots, y_{t-n}$.

The problem of time series prediction now becomes a problem of system identification. The unknown system (model) to be identified is the function f (.) with input variables are the past values of the time series. We can convert time series to a set of patterns or observations with inputs and output. The output is concatenated to the n past knowledge on the series to form a $(n + 1)$-dimensional vector of the following form:

$$V = [y_{t-n}, \ldots, y_{t-2}, y_{t-1}, y_t] \ . \tag{1}$$

By sliding a window of size n over the whole time series one would obtain a set of patterns relating past values with the predicted value. As follows is an example for a window size of 5. The resulting vectors $V_1, V_2, \ldots, V_i$ represent the available knowledge in the time series that can be used for training.

Now if the time series contains missing values then not all vectors $V_1, V_2, \ldots, V_i$

$$V_i = [y_i, y_{i+1}, y_{i+2}, y_{i+3}, y_{i+4}] \tag{2}$$

can be used for training. To link now the training to the semi-supervised learning, the labeled data set L (i.e. the complete data set that can be used for training) consists of all observations V_i that contain no missing values either in their input values $y_{t-n}, \ldots, y_{t-1}$ or in their output value y_t. On the other hand, the unlabelled data U contains only those observations where the missing value appears only in the output part y_t. Observations that have missing values in any of the input entries compose incomplete data that can be added later to either L or U as their their entries are filled later with learning as will be described in the next section.

3   Co-training for Time Series with Missing Data

Figure 1 shows the main steps of our proposed technique to use co-training in handling missing data in the time series. As described in section 2 the time series data are converted into observations that are divided into a set of labeled and unlabeled data. K different predictor models are chosen. In our implementation we use homogenous predictors that are guaranteed to be diverse through initializing them with different parameters. All predictors are initially trained with the same labeled training data L. A random pool U' is chosen from U and all predictors produce an estimation for all the unlabelled patterns in U'. Every predictor chooses the most confident u_i it can find an estimate for among all patterns of U' and augments it to the labeled set of any other predictor. The incremental data set produced by any predictor i (Π_i) contains new estimation for the label u_i in addition to any new labeled pattern that resulted from estimating u_i given the original data. The algorithm in Figure 1 guarantees that if an unlabelled data is estimated by most confidence among one predictor that it will be removed from U' so that other predictors should look for other $u's$ to label. Every predictor $Pred_i$ is then retrained with the new data set L_i:

$$L_i = L_i \bigcup \Pi_j \quad s.t \, i \neq j \,. \tag{3}$$

This indicates that each predictor is retrained with the augmented data that is a result of the labeling of another predictor. In our implementation we simply choose $j = i + 1$ and for $i = K$, $j = 1$. The retaining process is repeated by exploring other patterns from U until L_i stops increasing or until there are no more unlabelled patterns. The final output of the predictors are then tested on a given test data by calculating the error of the average output of the predictors.

4   Base Predictors and Confidence Measures

To be able to effectively implement the co-training algorithm following factors should be taken into account:

1. the choice of a predictor that is easily retrainable.
2. guranteeing diversity of the predictor ensemble.
3. the possibility to estimate the confidence of the prediction.

Here we introduce our suggestion of using *KNN* and *FIR* base learners and how the confidence can be calculated in each case. *KNN* classifiers belong to the family of instance-based learning algorithms and are popular for their simplicity to use and implementation, robustness to noisy data and their wide applicability in a lot of appealing applications [16]. In *KNN* we get the k nearest neighbors of the input using any distance measure and the output is the average of the k outputs [15]. *KNN* is a lazy learning method which does not hold a separate training phase, the refinement (i.e retraining) of the KNN learners can be efficiently realized [14].

Herrera [7] proposed using *Fuzzy Inductive Reasoning* in modeling time series prediction models. Fuzzy Inductive Reasoning (*FIR*) generate a qualitative input-output model of a system from training data. *FIR* is an additive learning method which can adapt its learning to newly labeled patterns. This is unlike other models like neural networks that must learn again from scratch if a new labeled pattern is added to the original labeled pattern. For this reason *FIR* base predictor was also found to be suitable for the co-training model proposed.

- **Given:**
  1. $Y = y_1, y_2, y_3, \ldots y_L$ time series data of length L containing missing data
  2. L, a set of labeled data from Y .
  3. U, a set of unlabeled data from Y .
  4. K different prediction models $pred_1, pred_2, \ldots, pred_i, ..pred_K$
- Creat a pool U' by choosing u examples at random from U
- for each predictor $pred_i$ let $L_i = L$
- **Repeat**
  1. For each predictor $pred_i$ while size(U') > 0:
     - Retrain $pred_i$ with L_i
     - Use $pred_i$ to label all examples from U'
     - Find the most confident predicted unlabeled pattern u_i from U' and its confidence value c_i
     - If $c_i \geq 0$ then
       * Delete u_i from U'
       * Replace the corresponding missing value of the unlabeled pattern u_i with the label of u_i
       * Find the new labeled pattern(s) Π_i due to this replacement
       * Modify U due to this replacement
       Else
       * $\Pi_i = \{\}$
  2. Augment Labeled data set L_i for each predictor $pred_i$:
     $L_i = L_i \cup \Pi_j$ s.t $j \neq i$
  3. Replenish U' by randomly picking new examples from U

  Until there is no change in all L_i
- Output:
  - Ensemble of all predictors

Fig. 1. Co-training for time series with missing data

Diversity among the pool of the predictors for co-training is very important. Here, the diversity among the learners is achieved through utilizing different distance metrics. In fact, a key issue of *KNN* learner and *FIR* learners is how to determine the distances between different instances. The *Minkowsky* distance shown in Eq. 4 is usually used for this purpose. Note that different concrete distance metrics can be generated through setting different values to the distance order, p. Therefore, the vicinities identified for a given instance may be different using the Minkowsky distance with different orders. Thus, the predictors $pred_1$, $pred_2$, $\ldots$, $pred_i$, $\ldots$, $pred_K$ can be diverse through initializing them with different p values. Such a setting can also bring another profit, that is, since it is usually difficult to decide which p value is better for the concerned task, the functions of these learners may be somewhat complementary [14].

$$D_p\left(X_r, X_q\right) \equiv \left(\sum |x_{r,l} - x_{q,l}|^p\right)^{\frac{1}{p}} . \tag{4}$$

A basic step of the co-training algorithm is to find the most confident predicted unlabeled pattern u_i from U' and its confidence value c_i.(refer to step 1 in Figure 1). Intuitively, the most confident estimation of a missing value should be such that the error of the predictor on the original set of labeled examples should decrease the most, if the most confidently estimated missing value is added to time series. Hence the confidence of the estimation can be calculated as the difference between the root mean square error (RMSE) of the predictor trained on the original labeled data and the predictor after it has been trained with the augmented data set. This method is applicable to any base predictor but can be computationally expensive. We will refer to it as the "error confidence measure" as it depends on the calculation of the RMSE. On the other hand, the *FIR* model [6] provides for a confidence measure called "similarity confidence" that is directly computable from the output of the *FIR* model.

5   Data and Experiments

Experiments were conducted on three different data sets. Figure 2 depicts the data sets used. The first data set is the CATS benchmark data set [17]. This artificial time series is given with 5,000 points of data. Results on this data set with 100 missing points is reported in [18]. The second data set is the River Nile flow data set. This data set consists of 3653 data points and reports the readings of the average daily flow volume for each ten-day period at the Dongola station, located in Northern Sudan (south of the High Dam) at the Nile river [19]. The last data set is the I-Frames time series data which is obtained from a repository of downloadable MPEG-4 video traces maintained by the Technical University of Berlin [20]. The time series represents the size of the I-frames portion of the MPEG-4 encoding. It is available for high-,medium-, or low-quality encoded video sequences. For our experiments we used 7499 data points of high-quality traces.

The time series are normalized to [0,1] and the window length used to divide time series data to set of patterns "labeled patterns and unlabeled patterns" is equal 5 "4 inputs+ 1 output". For each time series the first 75% of data are used in training and the last 25% of data are used for testing. Different percentage of missing data using uniform distribution (10%, 20%, 30%, 40%, 50% and 60%) was imposed on the original data. For each percentage, runs were repeated 10 times for different positions of the missing data.

For the co-training using *KNN* learners we used 2 predictor with distance orders set to p=2 and p=5, and with k=5. We used the "error confidence" for the calculation of the confidence. The size of U' was chosen to be ≤ 100. Improvement due to using Co-Training over using the case deletion method, i.e. method when incomplete data is discarded from learning is calculated on test data. Similarly, experiments were conducted for two *FIR* predictors and confidence was calculated using "error confidence"' and "similarity confidence". The following section presents the results.

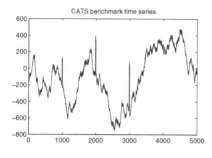
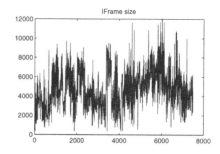

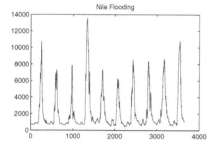

Fig. 2. Time series data sets

6   Results and Discussion

Tabels 1, 2 and 3 summarize the results on the CATS Benchmark data set, the Nile flow data set and the I-frame data set, respectively. For each data set, the tables list the improvement in the accuracy of the prediction gained by applying the co-training algorithm over the case deletion method. Results are presented for using the KNN and FIR predictors in a co-training framework using different confidence measures. In particular, the results using "error confidence" (*COT-ERROR*) is presented for the KNN, while for the FIR both results using "error confidence" (*COT-ERROR*) and "similarity confidence" (*COT-SIMILAR*) are presented. The improvement in the prediction is calculated for different percentages of the missing data.

Table 1. Summary of results for the CATS benchmark data

	CATS Benchmark					
	KNN Base Predictor					
	Percentage of Missing Data					
	10%	20%	30%	40%	50%	60%
COT-ERROR	5.88%	6.4%	9.9%	22.8%	17%	22.8%
	FIR Base Predictor					
COT-ERROR	0.16%	-1.7%	1.1%	-0.07%	-0.06%	0.03%
COT-SIMILAR	2%	-3.6%	-2.7%	-1.5%	18%	20%

Table 2. Summary of results for the Nile flow data

Nile flooding						
KNN Base Predictor						
_	Percentage of Missing Data					
	10%	20%	30%	40%	50%	60%
COT-ERROR	5%	11.3%	4.4%	19.3%	30.6%	15.5%
FIR Base Predictor						
COT-ERROR	0.5%	2.1%	2.1%	2.8%	2.6%	1.1%
COT-SIMILAR	3.7%	3.2%	10.6%	8.2%	25%	40%

Table 3. Summary of results for the Iframe data

Iframe size						
KNN Base Predictor						
	Percentage of Missing Data					
	10%	20%	30%	40%	50%	60%
COT-ERROR	1.8%	0.9%	1.7%	-0.8%	-10.8%	-1.7%
FIR Base Predictor						
COT-ERROR	1.7%	1.3%	1.4%	3.5%	0.7%	-0.7%
COT-SIMILAR	2.6%	6.8%	10%	8.7%	6%	12%

Examining the results of the tables it can be seen that for the CATS benchmark data co-training with _KNN_ predictors with "error confidence" seems to produce the most consistent improvements in the prediction accuracy among the tested models for all values of the missing percentages. The co-training with FIR and "similarity Confidence" produces also good improvements for higher percentages of missing data. For the Nile flow data similar results are observed while the _FIR_ and "similarity Confidence" performed consistently well for all percentage of missing data and outperformed the _KNN_ predictors with "error confidence" considerably at 60% missing ratio. It is noticeable that on this data set the co-training algorithm was always able to improve prediction. For the Iframe data, the _FIR_ and "similarity Confidence" produced a consistently better improvement in prediction.

7   Conclusions and Future Work

In this work we have introduced a new approach to handle missing data in time series prediction using co-training. First the problem of missing data in time series is formulated as a semi-supervised learning problem. Then, the co-training algorithm which was basically designed for classification and only recently for regression, is modified to be applied for the time series prediction problem. We have suggested the use of different base learners and their ensemble and different confidence measures. Experiments were conducted on three time data sets with different characteristics. Results show that in most cases the proposed co-training approach can effectively increase the accuracy of the time series prediction model even if missing data exist in a substantial ratio. The FIR model together with the "similarity confidence" measure obtained a most consistent improvement in the prediction accuracy and achieved the best results in our study.

Currently we are in the process of extending our experiments to multiple predictors, different data sets and different base predictors. We are also investigating the effect of different distributions of missing data, in particular when missing values appear in chunks; as this is realistic in many real world applications; like applications in which a sensor fails suddenly and several consecutive readings are lost.

Acknowledgments. This work was supported by the Egyptian Ministry of Communications & Information Technology's Center of Excellence . The second author was partially supported by the DFG (German Research Society) grants SCHW 623/3-2 and SCHW 623/4-2.

References

1. Tresp, V., Hofmann, R.: Missing and Noisy Data in Nonlinear Time-Series Prediction, Neural Networks for Signal Processing, IEEE Signal Processing Society, New York, (1995), 1-10
2. Peter J. Brockwell, P.J and Davis, R.A.: Introduction to Time Series and Forecasting, Second Edition, Springer Texts in Stat. Springer-Verlag, (2002)
3. Lendasse, A. et al.: Vector quantization: a weighted version for timeseriesecasting, Future Generation Computer Systems, Vol 21, (2005), 1056-1067
4. Cai, X., Zhang, N., Venayagamoorthy, G., Wunsch, D.: Time Series Prediction with Recurrent Neural Networks Using a Hybrid PSO-EA Algorithm, IJCNN04, Budapest, (2004)
5. Nguyen, H. H., Chan, C. W., Wilson, M.: Prediction Oil Well Production Using Multi- Neural Networks, Electrical and Computer Engineering, IEEE CCECE, (2002)
6. Liu, X., Kwan, B. W., Foo, S. Y.: Time Series Prediction Based on Fuzzy Principles, Department of Electrical & Computer Engineering FAMU-FSU College of Engineering, Florida State University, (2005)
7. Herrera, J. L.:Time Series Prediction Using Inductive Technique, Ph.D, " instituto de organizacioa y control de sistemas industrials, (1999)
8. Zhu, X.: Semi-supervised learning literature survey, Technical report, Computer Sciences TR 1530, Univ. Wisconsin, Madison, USA, Jan. (2006)
9. Blum A., Mitchell T.: Combining labeled and unlabeled data with co-training, Proc. of the Workshop on Computational Learning Theory,(1998), pp. 92-100
10. Zhou, Y., Goldman, S.: Democratic Co-Learning, Proceedings of the 16th IEEE International Conference on Tools with Artificial Intelligence (ICTAI 2004), (2004) pp 594-602
11. Soliman, M., El Gayar, N.: A Co-training Approach for Semi-Supervised Multiple Classifiers, ICGST International Journal on Artificial Intelligence and Machine Learning, ICGSTAIML, Volume (6), Special Issue on Multiple Classifier Systems, May (2006) , pp 9-16.

12. El Gayar, N., Shaban, S.A., Hamdy, S.: Face Recognition with co-training and ensemble driven learning; WSEAS Transactions on Computers, Vol. 6, No. 3, March (2007), pp . 507- 513
13. Didaci, L., Roli, F: Using Co-training and Self-training in Semi-supervised Multiple Classifier Systems, Lecture Notes in Computer Science, Springer Verlag, Vol. 4109, (2006), pp. 522-530
14. Zhou, Z.H., Li, M. : Semi-supervised regression with co-training, International Joint Conference on Artificial Intelligence (IJCAI) (2005)
15. Dasarthy, B.V.: Nearest Neighbor Norms: NN Pattern Classification Techniques. IEEE Computer Society Press, Los Alamitos, CA, (1991)
16. Duda, R.O., Hart, P.E. and D.G. Stork, Pattern Classification, 2nd ed., New York: John Wiley and Sons, (2001)
17. http: //www.cis.hut.fi/ lendasse/competition/data.txt
18. Lendasse, A. et al.,: Time Series Prediction Competition: The CATS Benchmark, IJCNN'2004 proceedings, Budapest (Hungary), 25-29 July (2004), IEEE, pp. 1615-1620
19. Atiya A. F., El-Shoura S. M., Shaheen, S. I., El-Sherif, M. S.: A Comparison Between Neural-Network Forecasting TechniquesCase Study: River Flow Forecasting, IEEE Transactions on Neural Networks, Vol. 10, No. 2, March (1999)
20. Fitzek, F. H. P., Reisslein, M.: MPEG-4 and H:263 video traces for network performance evaluation, IEEE Network, Vol. 15, No. 6, , November/December (2001), pp 40-54

An Improved Random Subspace Method and Its Application to EEG Signal Classification

Shiliang Sun

Department of Computer Science and Technology,
East China Normal University, Shanghai, 200062, China
shiliangsun@gmail.com

Abstract. Ensemble learning is one of the principal current directions in the research of machine learning. In this paper, subspace ensembles for classification are explored which constitute an ensemble classifier system by manipulating different feature subspaces. Starting with the nature of ensemble efficacy, we probe into the microcosmic meaning of ensemble diversity, and propose to use region partitioning and region weighting to implement effective subspace ensembles. An improved random subspace method that integrates this mechanism is presented. Individual classifiers possessing eminent performance on a partitioned region reflected by high neighborhood accuracies, are deemed to contribute largely to this region, and are assigned large weights in determining the labels of instances in this area. The robustness and effectiveness of the proposed method is shown empirically with the base classifier of linear support vector machines on the classification problem of EEG signals.

Keywords: ensemble learning, ensemble diversity, random subspace, EEG signal classification.

1 Introduction

Feature selection that seeks the single feature subset that is most germane for a certain task is a traditional yet challenging problem in the research of machine learning and pattern recognition. Although it has some apparent advantages, such as reducing the measurement and storage demands, decreasing training and utilizing time, and getting rid of the curse of dimensionality [1], from a more comprehensive view, it may pretermit some realistic considerations.

Suppose there are many experts intending to solve one and the same pattern classification task all by themselves. The first phase they confront will be feature extraction. In the event that they all have rich prior knowledge about the pattern, the features extracted by different experts would be consistent to a large extent and these features are probably closely related to the classification task as well. On the other hand, if they are provided with poor knowledge about the pattern, the feature sets obtained may differ from one another greatly, which is the case especially for newly emerging research topics in the fields of machine learning and data mining. At this time, they often have recourse to some kind of criterion

M. Haindl, J. Kittler, and F. Roli (Eds.): MCS 2007, LNCS 4472, pp. 103–112, 2007.

to search for important features from the original ones, and consequently realize the objective of feature selection.

Actually, whatever the true scenario is, as a result, the experts are likely to adopt different feature sets to train classifiers and carry out later classification. And each individual feature set can have some kind of performance guarantee (because it is obtained by an expert). The traditional feature selection ideology overlooks the existence of different feature subsets for the same pattern, and the feasibility of improving performance by feature ensembles. It is promising to achieve high performance under the condition that classification outcomes from different experts are combined, since each outcome may contain partial information for the classification task.

Feature selection can be roughly divided into two categories. One is to look for features in a transformed space, like principal component analysis and Fisher discriminant analysis [2]. The other is to select features in the original space, such as the various filter and wrapper methods [1,3]. This paper analyzes how to effectively combine different feature subsets to improve classification performance, namely subspace ensembles methods. In principle, the feature subsets can be drawn randomly or selected elaborately from the original feature space or a transformed space. Because it makes no difference in our following analysis, here the style of random selection from the original space is adopted.

The paper proceeds as follows. In Section 2, we review the historical efforts other researchers made on the rationality of ensemble learning, and give our own insights on ensemble diversity. Based on this discussion, in Section 3 we present our approach for improving the random subspace ensemble [4]. As an application of the proposed method, Section 4 reports experimental results on performance of classifying electroencephalogram (EEG) signals. Finally, after discussing related work in Section 5, we give concluding remarks and future research directions in Section 6.

2   Ensemble Diversity

2.1   Historical Achievements

In recent years, it is widely acknowledged that an effective ensemble learning system should consist of individuals that are not only highly accurate, but are diverse as well, that is, a right balance should hold between diversity and individual performance [5,6,7,8,9,10]. The diversity here means complementariness, namely, data misclassified by some individual classifiers can be correctly classified by others so that their voted performance tends to outperform any individual classifier. In other words, individual classifiers make errors on different regions of the input space [11]. As subspace ensembles reside in the category of ensemble learning systems, diversity is an equally essential rule for subspace ensembles to conform to. Study on the meaning of diversity for ensemble learning does make sense to supervise the design of subspace ensemble methods.

The concept of diversity plays an important role in explaining the efficacy of ensemble learning. According to the taxonomy given by Kuncheva and Whitaker, the diversity measures for classification ensembles can be divided into two categories, pairwise measures and non-pairwise measures [9]. Pairwise diversity measures calculate the average of a particular (dis)similarity metric between all possible pairs of individual classifiers in an ensemble, with examples such as Q statistic and correlation coefficient. Non-pairwise measures often calculate a statistic using the notion of entropy or using (dis)similarity metrics between individual classifiers and the averaged classifier, such as entropy measure and coincident failure diversity [9]. Kuncheva and Whitaker [9] recommend the pairwise Q statistic where classifiers are compared as a function of correctness or incorrectness with regard to a validation set based on the principle that it is understandable and relatively easy to implement [12]. Readers can refer to [9,13] for a survey on all kinds of diversity measures.

For regression ensembles with the objective error criterion of mean squared error, the regression diversity can be exactly quantified in terms of the ambiguity decomposition [8] and the bias-variance-covariance decomposition [14]. However, for classification ensembles, there are no such straight theories and the meaning of diversity is not exactly comprehended especially when individual classifiers output non-ordinal discrete labels [13]. Sometimes people cannot help but evaluate the contribution of diversity to ensemble classification empirically. For instance, Dieterich [15] provides an empirical verification from the relationship between the diversity and accuracy of individual classifiers for the effectiveness of bagging, boosting and randomization methods. Opitz [11] and Tsymbal et al. [16] also show the rationality of ensemble feature selection for classification making use of the notion of diversity.

2.2   Region Partitioning and Region Weighting

The above endeavor contributed to the research of diversity greatly, but the precise meaning of diversity is still not fully solved. Here we investigate the validity of ensemble learning from the microcosmic essence of ensemble diversity, and propose to use the idea of region partitioning and region weighting to improve the ensemble performance. We provide the following example to show the conception and intuition of region partitioning and region weighting.

Fig. 1 gives a schematic diagram of region partitioning for classification ensembles. The data distributions belong to two different classes, which are respectively denoted by two elliptical curves. Linear classifiers are trained to implement classification, two of which (classifier 1 and classifier 2) are shown in the figure. The regions misclassified by classifier 1 and classifier 2 are respectively marked with horizontal bars and vertical bars. Obviously, for a test sample to be classified, if it drops into the area of horizontal bars, it is classifier 2 instead of classifier 1 that should take over the classification task. On the contrary, if it drops into the area of vertical bars, classifier 1 should be adopted for classification. On condition that the sample falls into blank regions, both classifiers can be used since either of them exhibits ascendant performance on these regions. An ensemble able to manipulate individual classifiers based on their performance on different regions

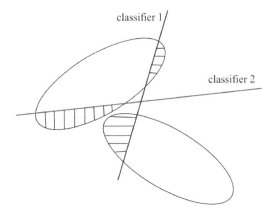

Fig. 1. A schematic diagram of region partitioning for classification ensembles. Classifiers 1 and 2 divide the whole decision space into two parts respectively.

would be meritorious, and implicitly expresses the idea of region partitioning and region weighting.

The aim of region partitioning is to find the salient regions that are helpful in guiding ensemble learning. In this paper, region partitioning is carried out according to the performance distribution of each individual classifier on its decision space. Individual classifiers are taken into account with different importance weights based on their accuracies on the partitioned regions. This idea of region weighting with respect to partitioned regions is different from the accustomed weighting approach in ensemble leaning where the weight is proportional to the total accuracy of an individual classifier. The principle of region partitioning and region weighting indicates the essence of ensemble diversity from a microcosmic aspect.

3   The Improved Random Subspace Method

The random subspace ensemble method, recently proposed by Ho [4], constructs individual classifiers by means of the random selection for feature subsets, and has shown its effectiveness on a lot of classification problems. In the random subspace method, feature subsets are picked at random with replacement from the original feature space, and individual classifiers are created only based on those attributes in the chosen feature subsets using the whole training set. The outputs from all individual classifies are combined by uniform majority voting to give the final prediction.

Based on the above microcosmic interpretation for ensemble diversity, we present the improved random subspace method to enhance the original random subspace method. For subspace ensembles, we deem that each individual (subspace) classifier also has its own salient regions in its corresponding subspace. On how to perform region partitioning and region weighting for each subspace classifier, the idea of local neighborhood accuracy is adopted.

For a test sample, if an individual classifier in subspace ensembles performs well in its adjacent area, then the classifier has high confidence on its outputs in this region, and should maintain a large weight in determining the label of the sample. To be specific, in this paper we apply k nearest neighbors with the metric of Euclidean distance to evaluate the confidence of each individual classifier on its output about the test sample, although other techniques such as the notion of window functions used in nonparametric density estimation [2] are also applicable. If an individual classifier classifies the k nearest neighbors of the test sample with a higher accuracy, then the classifier contributes more in determining its label, and vice versa.

Suppose M individual classifiers $\{C_m(\cdot)\}$ $(m = 1, ..., M)$ are constructed from M feature subspaces, whereas every feature subspace is formed by features taken from the original feature space. Define the label set as $\{\omega_i\}$ $(i = 1, ..., L)$. For a new test sample x, we first seek its k nearest neighbors from the training set in each subspace respectively. Then, calculate the correctly classified number of these k samples using every individual classifier. The number is defined as the weight value $W_m(x)$ of the individual classifier $C_m(\cdot)$ with respect to the test sample x. In succession, the output from each individual classifier is obtained, which is represented as a binary function:

$$\Theta_m(x \in \omega_i) = \begin{cases} 1, & \text{for } C_m(x) = \omega_i \\ 0, & \text{otherwise .} \end{cases} \tag{1}$$

Finally, all the binary function outputs and weight outputs from individual classifiers in subspace ensembles for x are combined using the rule of majority voting [17] to give the final predicted label $\Omega_{ens}(x)$ as follows,

$$\Omega_{ens}(x) = \arg\max_{\omega_i} \sum_{m=1}^{M} W_m(x)\Theta_m(x \in \omega_i) . \tag{2}$$

The detailed flow diagram for the improved random subspace method is given in Table 1.

4   Case Study

In this section, we do a preliminary case study with a linear base classifier, i.e. SVM, to evaluate the performance of the improved random subspace method. The data used for analysis are EEG (electroencephalogram) signals generated when users are operating brain-computer interfaces [18]. The original random subspace method is employed for a comparison. As Ho [4] showed that using half of the feature components usually yielded good accuracy, in the experiments we fix the size of feature subsets as 50% of the number of original attributes. Since the ensembles involve random sampling and hence are random algorithms, we run each ensemble 5 times, and average the results over 5 rounds.

Table 1. The improved random subspace method

Inputs: $\{F_m\}_{m=1}^M$ is an ensemble feature set comprising M feature subsets. C is an appointed base classifier. S is a training set. k is the number of nearest neighbors. x is a test sample.
Output: The predicted label of x.
Procedure:
1): Train M individual classifiers $\{C_m(\cdot)\}$ based on feature sets $\{F_m\}_{m=1}^M$, and obtain their outcomes for each sample in the training set.
2): Find the k nearest neighbors of x in each subspace, calculate their right classified number by the corresponding individual classifier, and give their weights $\{W_m(x)\}$.
3): Get the outcomes of $\{C_m(x)\}$ for the test sample x.
4): Combine all the outputs by majority voting using (1) and (2), and give the final predicted label for x.

4.1 Data Sets

The EEG signals used are recorded from three normal subjects (denoted by S1, S2, S3 respectively) during three mental imagery tasks for operating a potential BCI. The tasks are imagination of repetitive self-paced left hand movements (class ω_1), imagination of repetitive self-paced right hand movements (class ω_2) and generation of different words beginning with the same random letter (class ω_3) [19]. The classification task is to classify the signals as corresponding to one of the three possible tasks. Through feature extraction, an EEG sample becomes a 96-dimensional vector [20].

In the paper we use these 96-dimensional data as input, and the numbers of samples in four recording sessions for S1, S2, and S3 are 3488/3472/3568/3504, 3472/3456/3472/3472, and 3424/3424/3440/3488 respectively [20]. For assessment, nine data sets are constructed each with separate training set and test set from the data of the above subjects S1, S2, and S3. Namely, the first three data sets are formed using the data of four sessions from S1, and so on, for a total of nine data sets. Specifically, data sets 1, 2, 3 are respectively composed of sessions $1 \sim 2$, $2 \sim 3$, $3 \sim 4$ of S1. For each data set, the former session serves as a training set, and the latter session serves as a test set. Data sets 4 to 9 are formed similarly with data from subjects S2 and S3.

4.2 Results

First, the ensemble sizes for the random subspace (RS) and the improved random subspace (IRS) methods are both taken as 25, since it has been shown that for many ensemble problems, the biggest profit in accuracy is already made with this number of individual classifiers [16,21]. Then, to investigate the influence of the ensemble size to the performance of these two ensemble methods, we also conduct experiments using ensemble size 100 under the same configuration.

Table 2 gives the test results. In Table 2, IRS-k means the improved random subspace method with k as the number of nearest neighbors for a test sample as indicated in Table 1. Different k parameters (3, 5, and 7) are adopted to comprehensively understand the behavior of the improved random subspace method. Note that since the present classification problem involves three classes, the expected accuracy rate by random guess will be 33.33%.

Table 2. Test set accuracy rates (%) of two ensemble classification methods RS and IRS with ensemble sizes 25 and 100

Size	Method	Data set								
		1	2	3	4	5	6	7	8	9
25	RS	64.98	72.22	66.22	49.31	57.04	62.98	47.59	34.41	42.04
	IRS-3	66.13	73.18	69.26	48.99	57.40	63.28	48.69	35.41	42.99
	IRS-5	66.01	73.14	69.13	48.91	57.54	63.26	48.71	35.26	42.84
	IRS-7	65.88	73.14	69.05	49.00	57.46	63.28	48.67	35.05	42.82
100	RS	65.03	72.11	65.65	49.22	57.55	63.39	47.58	34.46	42.37
	IRS-3	66.24	73.14	69.14	49.06	57.72	63.61	48.93	35.39	43.31
	IRS-5	66.19	73.18	69.04	49.09	57.88	63.61	48.74	35.45	43.00
	IRS-7	66.09	73.08	68.94	49.18	57.76	63.49	48.92	35.33	43.00

4.3   Comparison

To provide a more clear performance comparison for the random subspace and the improved random subspace methods, from Table 2 win-loss-tie scores are calculated between these two ensemble methods, which are given in Table 3. A comparison in bold means the performance difference between the corresponding algorithms is statistically significant at the 95% confidence level evaluated by the one-tailed paired t-test. For example, when ensemble size is 25, the value between IRS-3 (56.15) and RS being **8-1-0** means that the win-loss-tie score between these two methods is 8-1-0, and there exist statistically significant differences. As an auxiliary comparison, the averaged accuracy rates are also listed after the corresponding method. The last column in Table 3 reports the relative improvements of the averaged accuracy rates in the same row.

From Table 3, we draw the conclusion that the performance of the improved random subspace method is superior to that of the original random subspace method, at least on the used EEG signal data. As we can see that under the same ensemble size the accuracy rate of the improved random subspace method is statistically significantly better than that of random subspace method, and its mean performance improvement with respect to different ensemble sizes is also larger than that of the random subspace method. Further, the robustness of the improved random subspace method is also manifested because the accuracies with different k values (3, 5, and 7) are quite similar.

Table 3. A win-loss-tie comparison between RS and IRS, and their own mean performance improvements with different ensemble sizes

Size 25	Size 100	Improvement
RS	RS	
RS(55.20)	RS (55.26)	0.11%
IRS-3 (56.15) **8-1-0**	IRS-3 (56.28) **8-1-0**	0.23%
IRS-5 (56.09) **8-1-0**	IRS-5 (56.24) **8-1-0**	0.27%
IRS-7 (56.04) **8-1-0**	IRS-7 (56.20) **8-1-0**	0.29%

5   Related Work

There are some methods related to but different from our approach in nature, several of which are discussed below.

In the neural network context, the mixtures of experts [22] train gating networks to determine the mixture coefficients of different expert networks. All the expert networks and gating networks are assumed to be generalized linear models. The gating networks give mixture coefficients depending on the input sample.

Ortega [23] develops an approach for combining knowledge from a variety of individual classifiers. This approach involves learning a "referee" for each individual classifier, which characterizes the situations where each individual classifier is able to make correct predictions. For future samples, the referees are first consulted to select one or more individual classifiers whose predictions are then returned.

The meta decision trees [24] adopt the idea of ordinary decision trees to combine multiple classifiers. Their leaves specify which individual classifier should be used. The input for meta decision trees is derived from the class probability distributions predicted by the individual classifiers for a specific sample.

Considering the problem of dynamic classifier selection, Woods et al. [25] select one single best classifier evaluated from the neighboring region of a test sample to carry out classification. In their experiments, five classifiers of different types are used for switch. If possible, each classifier would be optimized by elaborate feature and parameter selection. In other words, they uses the switch of few strong classifiers.

6   Conclusion

In this paper, we investigate the exact microcosmic meaning of ensemble diversity, and propose to use region partitioning and region weighting by neighborhood accuracy to implement effective subspace ensembles. Experimental results indicate that the proposed improved random subspace method outperforms the random subspace method, and is robust on the choice of the number of nearest neighbors. Furthermore, to carry out a comprehensive evaluation, we run the random subspace and the improved random subspace methods with different ensemble sizes as well. And the results show that the performance improvement of the improved random subspace method is larger than that of the random subspace method.

In the future, several research directions can be further investigated. For example, study the performance of the improved random subspace method with other base classifiers (e.g. decision trees), and take into account the distances between nearest neighbors and test samples to amend the calculation of weights.

References

1. Guyon, I., Elisseeff, A.: An Introduction to Variable and Feature Selection. J. Mach. Learn. Res., Vol. 3 (2003) 1157–1182
2. Duda, R.O., Hart, P.E., Stork, D.G.: Pattern Classification, 2nd ed. John Wiley & Sons, New York (2000)
3. Kohavi, F., John, G.: Wrappers for Feature Subset Selection. Artif. Intell., Vol. 97 (1997) 273–324
4. Ho, T.: The Random Subspace Method for Constructing Decision Forests. IEEE Trans. Pattern Anal. Mach. Intell., Vol. 20 (1998) 832–844
5. Breiman, L.: Random Forests. Mach. Learn., Vol. 45 (2001) 5–32
6. Brown, G., Wyatt, J., Tiňo, P.: Managing Diversity in Regression Ensembles. J. Mach. Learn. Res. Vol. 6 (2005) 1621–1650
7. Hansen, L., Salamon, P., Neural Network Ensembles. IEEE Trans. Pattern Anal. Mach. Intell., Vol. 12 (1990) 993–1001
8. Krogh, A., Vedelsby, J.: Neural Network Ensembles, Cross Validation, and Active Learning. In: G. Tesauro, D. Touretzky, T. Leen, ed., Advances in Neural Information Processing Systems, Vol. 7. MIT, Cambridge (1995) 231–238
9. Kuncheva, L., Whitaker, C.: Measures of Diversity in Classifier Ensembles and Their Relationship with the Ensemble Accuracy. Mach. Learn., Vol. 51 (2003) 181–207
10. Saranh, A., Demirekler, M.: On Output Independence and Complementariness in Rank-Based Multiple Classifier Decision Systems. Pattern Recogn., Vol. 34 (2001) 2319–2330
11. Opitz, D.: Feature Selection for Ensembles. Proc. of the Sixteenth National Conference on Artificial Intelligence (1999) 379–384
12. Banfield, R., Hall, L., Bowyer, K., Kegelmeyer, W.: Ensemble Diversity Measures and Their Application to Thinning. Information Fusion, Vol. 6 (2005) 49–62
13. Brown, G., Wyatt, J., Harris, R., Yao, X.: Diversity Creation Methods: a Survey and Categorisation. Information Fusion, Vol. 6 (2005) 5–20
14. Ueda, N., Nakano, R.: Generalization Error of Ensemble Estimators. Proc. of the International Conference on Neural Networks (1996) 90–95
15. Dietterich, T.: An Experimental Comparison of Three Methods for Constructing Ensembles of Decision Trees: Bagging, Boosting, and Randomization. Mach. Learn., Vol. 40 (2000) 139–157
16. Tsymbal, A., Pechenizkiy, M., Cunningham, P.: Diversity in Search Strategies for Ensemble Feature Selection. Information Fusion, Vol. 6 (2005) 83–98
17. Kittler, J., Hatef, M., Duin, R., Matas, J.: On Combining Classifiers. IEEE Trans. Pattern Anal. Mach. Intell., Vol. 20 (1998) 226–239

18. Nicolelis, M.A.L.: Actions from Thoughts. Nature, Vol. 409 (2001) 403–407
19. Millán, J.R.: On the Need for On-Line Learning in Brain-Computer Interfaces. Proc. 2004 Int. Joint Conf. Neural Networks, Vol. 4 (2004) 2877–2882
20. Chiappa, S., Millán, J.R.: Data set V <mental imagery, multi-class>. [Online]. Available: http://ida.first.fraunhofer.de/projects/bci/competition_iii/desc_V.html (2005)
21. Bauer, E., Kohavi, R.: An Empirical Comparison of Voting Classification Algorithms: Bagging, Boosting, and Variants. Mach. Learn., Vol. 36 (1999) 105–139
22. Jordan, M.I., Jacobs, R.A.: Hierarchical Mixtures of Experts and the EM Algorithm. Neural Comput., Vol. 6 (1994) 181–214
23. Ortega, J.: Making the Most of What You've Got: Using Models and Data to Improve Prediction Accuracy. Ph.D. Thesis, Vanderbilt Univeristy, Nashville, TN (1996)
24. Todorovski, L., Džeroski, S.: Combining Classifiers with Meta Decision Trees. Mach. Learn., Vol. 50 (2003) 223–249
25. Woods, K., Kegelmeyer, W.P., Bowyer, K.: Combination of Multiple Classifiers using Local Accuracy Estimates. IEEE Trans. Pattern Anal. Mach. Intell., Vol. 19 (1997) 405–410

Ensemble Learning Methods for Classifying EEG Signals

Shiliang Sun

Department of Computer Science and Technology,
East China Normal University, Shanghai, 200062, China
shiliangsun@gmail.com

Abstract. Bagging, boosting and random subspace are three popular
ensemble learning methods, which have already shown effectiveness in
many practical classification problems. For electroencephalogram (EEG)
signal classification arising in recent brain-computer interface (BCI) research, however, there are almost no reports investigating their feasibili-
ties. This paper systematically evaluates the performance of these three
ensemble methods for their new application on EEG signal classification.
Experiments are conducted on three BCI subjects with k-nearest neighbor and decision tree as base classifiers. Several valuable conclusions are
derived about the feasibility and performance of ensemble methods for
classifying EEG signals.

Keywords: EEG signal classification, ensemble learning, bagging,
boosting, random subspace.

1 Introduction

The research motivation of the current brain-computer interfaces (BCIs) is mainly
to provide those motor-disabled but cognition-intact patients a communication
and control channel directly between the brain and external devices, without the
participation of peripheral nerves and muscles [1,2]. During the last decade, it has
evoked a wide interest among different fields such as neuroscience, biomedical engineering, clinical rehabilitation and computer science [1,2,3,4,5]. Each discipline
therein makes contributions to BCI research with a different emphasis, and the
developments of BCI technology benefit from this interdisciplinary cooperation.

Classification methods, which convert electrophysiological input from users
into their intents which can then correspond to external device commands, are a
core component in the BCI system [5]. In the current paper, we concentrate on
the problem of classifying electroencephalogram (EEG) signals (brain activities
taken from the scalp of the head) for underlying applications in a BCI.

Many single classifiers have already been assessed for EEG signal
classification, such as neural networks, Fisher discriminant analysis, support
vector machines, hidden Markov models, Bayesian classifiers, and source analysis [6,7,8,9,10,11,12]. However, as one of the principal current directions in machine learning, ensemble learning has not yet been paid enough attention during

M. Haindl, J. Kittler, and F. Roli (Eds.): MCS 2007, LNCS 4472, pp. 113–120, 2007.
© Springer-Verlag Berlin Heidelberg 2007

the previous study of BCIs [13]. As far as we know, there are almost no results systematically reported on EEG signal classification using ensemble methods. As a consequence, people do not know whether ensemble methods are effective for EEG signal discrimination, or even if so, to what extent. Simultaneously, comparisons among different ensemble methods for classifying EEG signals, although they are needed to guide decisions about which one to choose, are still lacking.

This paper tries to complete this study empirically. Three well-known and popular ensemble learning methods bagging [14], boosting [15] and random subspace [16] are adopted to carry out EEG signal classification. Although they have demonstrated effectiveness in a variety of application problems, it is not straightforward to judge generally which is the best [17]. For a specific task, e.g. the considered problem of EEG signal classification, however, it is possible to give an evaluation of their relative performance.

The remainder of this paper is organized as follows. In Section 2, we explain briefly the base classifiers and ensemble classification methods used for classifying EEG signals. Then in Section 3 we report experimental results of EEG signal classification on three representative BCI users/subjects, analyze the results and try to provide an explanation of why some ensemble methods are good or not. Finally we give concluding remarks and the future work plan in Section 4.

2   Base Classifiers and Ensemble Classification Methods

Two kinds of classifiers k-nearest-neighbor and C4.5 decision tree are espoused as base classifiers for evaluating ensemble classification methods. In this section, after giving a simple note for the mentioned base classifiers, we also briefly review the three ensemble classification methods bagging, boosting and random subspace.

2.1   Base Classifiers

K-Nearest-Neighbor (KNN). The KNN classifier assigning the label of a test sample with the majority label of its k nearest neighbors in the training set is a classical classification rule [18]. To evaluate the performance of ensemble methods, in this paper we simply set the value of k as 5, i.e. the 5-nearest-neighbor rule is adopted.

C4.5 Decision Tree. The C4.5 algorithm is the most popular in a series of tree-growing methods for classification, e.g. CART, ID3 [18]. It is also a prevalent base classifier for evaluating ensemble methods. In this paper, the Weka software for C4.5 with the default configuration is used [19].

2.2   Ensemble Classification Methods

Bagging. The Bagging predictor introduced by Breiman is a popular ensemble learning approach which integrates the bootstrap sampling technique to manipulate the selection of training data [14]. Every time it selects T samples at random with replacement from the original training set consisting of T samples to learn an individual classifier. Prediction of a test sample by an ensemble is given through uniform majority voting of all individual classifiers. Theoretically, it is shown that if bootstrap can induce significant differences in the constructed individual classifiers, the accuracy of bagging will grow to a large extent [14].

Boosting (AdaBoost). The AdaBoost family of algorithms proposed by Freund and Shapire, which is also known as boosting, is another kind of powerful ensemble method [15]. The basic idea is to explicitly alter the distribution of training data (weights of each training sample) fed to every individual classifier. Initially the distribution is uniform for all the training samples. During the boosting procedure, the distribution is adjusted after completing the training of each classifier. For misclassified samples the weights are increased, while decreased for correctly classified samples. The final ensemble is constructed by combining all individual classifiers according to their own accuracies. Among the many variants for the boosting algorithm, here we employ the AdaBoost.M1 algorithm [15].

Random Subspace (RanSub). The random subspace ensemble method proposed by Ho, utilizes the random selection of feature subspaces to construct individual classifiers, and has shown efficacy on many classification problems [16]. This method can take advantage of high dimensionality, and is an effective countermeasure for the traditional problem of the curse of dimensionality [16]. Its merit can be attributed to the high ensemble diversity, which compensates for the possible deficiency of accuracies in member classifiers [20]. In random subspace, feature subspaces are picked at random from the original feature space, and individual classifiers are created only based on those attributes in the chosen feature subspaces. The outputs from all individual classifies are combined by uniform majority voting to form the final prediction. As Ho shows that using half of the feature components usually yields good accuracies, in our experiment we also fix the size of feature subspaces as half the number of original attributes [16].

3 Experiment and Discussion

3.1 Data Processing and Experimental Results

The data set for analysis contains EEG recordings taken from three normal subjects (denoted by Sj1, Sj2, Sj3 respectively) during three mental imagery tasks for operating a potential BCI. The tasks are imagination of repetitive self-paced left hand movements (class C_1), imagination of repetitive self-paced right hand movements (class C_2) and generation of different words beginning with the same random letter (class C_3) [21,22]. For a certain subject, there are four non-feedback sessions recorded on the same day, each lasting four minutes or so with breaks of 5-10 minutes in between. The subjects perform a given task for about 15 seconds and then switch randomly to the next task at the operator's request. The classification task is to give outputs indicating which mental task the subjects are performing.

The sampling rate for the raw EEG potential signals is 512Hz. The signals are first spatially filtered by means of a surface Laplacian [21]. Then, every 62.5 ms the power spectral density in the band 8-30 Hz is estimated using the last second of data with a frequency resolution of 2 Hz for the eight centro-parietal channels C3, Cz, C4, CP1, CP2, P3, Pz, and P4. The scalp locations of the eight electrodes as shown in Fig. 1 are closely related to the considered mental imagery tasks. Resultantly, an EEG sample is a 96-dimensional vector. In the paper we use these 96-dimensional data as input, and the numbers of samples in the four sessions for Sj1, Sj2, and Sj3 are respectively 3488/3472/3568/3504, 3472/3456/3472/3472, and 3424/3424/3440/3488 [22]. It was shown that subjects Sj1, Sj2, and Sj3 represent three different levels of mental consistency, which are respectively consistent, scarcely consistent, and inconsistent [11]. Therefore the data are representative and in this paper they are employed to evaluate algorithms.

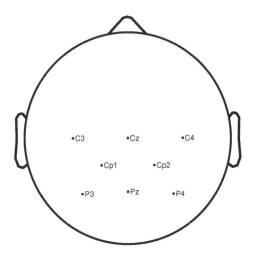

Fig. 1. The top view of the locations for the eight electrodes where spectral features are extracted

For the purpose of assessment, nine data sets are constructed each with separate training set and test set from the data of the above subjects Sj1, Sj2, and Sj3. The first three data sets are formed using the data of four sessions from Sj1, and so on, for a total of nine data sets. Specifically, data sets 1, 2, 3 are respectively composed of sessions $1 \sim 2$, $2 \sim 3$, $3 \sim 4$ of Sj1. For each data set, the former session serves as a training set, and the latter session serves as a test set. Data sets 4 to 9 are formed with a similar style from subjects Sj2 and Sj3.

The ensemble sizes for bagging, boosting and random subspace are all taken as 25, since it has been shown that for many ensemble problems, the biggest profit in accuracy is already made with this number of individual classifiers [20,23].

Since the ensembles involve random sampling, we run each ensemble 5 times, and average the results over 5 rounds.

The experimental results of ensembles with different base classifiers for these nine data sets are shown in Table 1, where 'single' means an individual base classifier trained using all the intact training data. Note that since the present classification problem involves three classes, the error rate by completely random classification would be 33.33%.

Table 1. Test set accuracy rates (%) of ensemble classification methods with base classifiers KNN and C4.5

Method		Data set								
		1	2	3	4	5	6	7	8	9
KNN	Single	64.63	68.33	65.27	45.78	54.23	57.49	43.55	37.24	41.00
	Bagging	63.97	68.29	65.16	46.15	54.58	57.94	44.04	36.99	40.96
	AdaBoost	62.59	66.55	62.62	44.40	53.92	55.65	43.55	37.02	40.83
	RanSub	67.86	72.95	72.79	46.81	56.47	60.74	46.91	38.37	44.25
C4.5	Single	56.74	63.54	59.45	49.45	50.84	52.59	41.41	39.53	37.93
	Bagging	66.95	72.34	70.79	52.60	58.45	59.56	47.77	38.58	39.75
	AdaBoost	65.94	71.61	69.17	51.44	57.06	57.93	46.17	39.40	40.71
	RanSub	66.39	73.22	72.41	49.40	56.85	60.62	47.21	38.55	40.58

3.2   Comparison and Discussion

Further to provide a general view of the performance of different ensemble classification methods ('Single' can be regarded as a special ensemble), based on Table 1 a win-loss-tie comparison is constructed between every two ensemble methods, as given in Table 2. A comparison in bold means the performance difference between two algorithms is statistically significant at the 95% confidence level evaluated by the one-tailed paired t-test. For example, when KNN is used as base classifiers, the value between RanSub and Single is **9-0-0** which means that the win-loss-tie score between these two methods is 9-0-0, and there exist statistically significant differences. As an auxiliary comparison, the averaged accuracy rates for each method are also listed in the second column.

From Table 2, we draw several conclusions about the performance of different ensemble methods for EEG signal classification as follows. Because the ensemble performance depends on the selection of base classifiers to a large extent and the parameters of each base classifier are not tuned to their full potential, here we don't assess the relative performance of ensemble methods across different base classifiers.

Besides, with respect to the effectiveness of ensemble classification methods, it is widely acknowledged that an effective ensemble classification system should consist of individuals that are not only highly accurate, but are diverse as

Table 2. A win-loss-tie comparison between different ensemble methods

		Single	Bagging	AdaBoost
KNN	Single (53.06)			
	Bagging (53.12)	4-5-0		
	AdaBoost(51.90)	**0-8-1**	**1-8-0**	
	RanSub (56.35)	**9-0-0**	**9-0-0**	**9-0-0**
C4.5	Single (50.16)			
	Bagging (56.31)	**8-1-0**		
	AdaBoost(55.49)	**8-1-0**	**2-7-0**	
	RanSub (56.14)	**7-2-0**	4-5-0	5-4-0

well [24]. In deriving the following conclusions and discussions, this rule will be used as a guide.

1) For KNN, only random subspace brings significant performance improvements compared to a single classifier. The bagging ensemble does almost not change the performance, while boosting deteriorates the performance.

The stability of KNN with respect to changes of training sets can accounts for this phenomenon. KNN is a stable classifier [25], while ensemble methods constructed through subsampling the training examples (e.g. bagging and boosting) don't work well for stable classifiers [13]. Because high stability means low diversity among individual classifiers, which is harmful to the performance of ensemble methods. However, KNN benefits random subspace, since random subspace carries out classification in subspaces of much lower dimensionality and this can diminish the negative influence of noises for the precise determination of neighbors. The neighbors can be calculated more accurately in a space of low dimensionality. Thus the performance of individual classifiers would rise, which can favor the final accuracy of ensemble methods.

2) For C4.5, all the three ensemble methods make great performance improvements compared to a single classifier. Bagging is the best, while boosting brings comparatively small improvement. The performance of random subspace is in-between of them.

Since C4.5 decision tree is an unstable classifier [13,25], the diversity among individual classifiers in ensemble methods is high. Thus the three ensemble methods tend to improve the classification performance.

3) The performance of ensemble methods differs among different base classifiers. Depending on the selection of base classifiers, the performance of an ensemble method can outperform that of a single classifier or suffer a reverse. Generally speaking, ensemble learning for EEG signal classification is effective, though different ensemble methods would display different performance, and even some combination of base classifiers and ensemble methods would deteriorate the performance.

4 Conclusion

Three ensemble learning methods, bagging, boosting and random subspace are assessed in the context of EEG signal classification for underlying applications in BCIs with the base classifiers KNN and C4.5. The effectiveness of ensemble methods over a single base classifier is shown empirically. Experimental results also indicate that the capability of ensemble methods is subject to the type of base classifiers. These findings are helpful in guiding the choice of classification algorithms for future BCI applications.

As the focus of the paper is to evaluate the performance of ensemble learning methods, it is beyond the scope of the current research to find the best parameter configuration for each subject and even on-line methods to further improve the classification performance. These issues would be investigated in the future.

Acknowledgments. The author would like to thank IDIAP Research Institute of Switzerland for making the data set publicly available for academic analysis.

References

1. Nicolelis, M.A.L.: Actions from Thoughts. Nature, Vol. 409 (2001) 403–407
2. Wolpaw, J.R., Birbaumer, N., McFarland, D.J., Pfurtscheller, G., Vaughan, T.M.: Brain-Computer Interfaces for Communication and Control. Clin. Neurophysiol., Vol. 113 (2002) 767–791
3. Ebrahimi, T., Vesin, J.M., Garcia, G.,: Brain-Computer Interface in Multimedia Communication. IEEE Signal Proc. Mag., Vol. 20 (2003) 14–24
4. Wolpaw, J.R., Birbaumer, N., Heetderks, W.J., McFarland, D.J., Peckham, P.H., Schalk, G., Donchin, E., Quatrano, L.A., Robinson, C.J., Vaughan, T.M.: Brain-Computer Interface Technology: a Review of the First International Meeting. IEEE Trans. Rehab. Eng., Vol. 8 (2000) 164–173
5. Vaughan, T.M.: Guest Editorial Brain-Computer Interface Technology: a Review of the Second International Meeting. IEEE Trans. Neural Syst. Rehabil. Eng., Vol. 11 (2003) 94–109
6. Garrett, D., Peterson, D.A., Anderson, C.W., Thaut, M.H.: Comparion of Linear, Nonlinear, and Feature Selection Methods for EEG Signal Classification. IEEE Trans. Neural Syst. Rehabil. Eng., Vol. 11 (2003) 141–144
7. Müller, K.-R., Anderson, C.W., Birch, G. E.: Linear and Nonlinear Methods for Brain-Computer Interfaces. IEEE Trans. Neural Syst. Rehabil. Eng., Vol. 11 (2003) 165–169
8. Obermaier, B., Munteanu, C., Rosa, A., Pfurtscheller, G.: Asymmetric Hemisphere Modeling in an Offline Brain-Computer Interface. IEEE Trans. Syst. Man Cybern. Part C-Appl. Rev., Vol. 31 (2001) 536–540
9. Millán, J.R., Renkens, F., Mouriño, J., Gerstner, W.: Brain-Actuated Interaction. Artif. Intell., Vol. 159 (2004) 241–259
10. Sun, S., Zhang, C.: Learning On-Line Classification via Decorrelated LMS Algorithm: Application to Brain-Computer Interfaces. Lect. Notes Comput. Sc., Vol. 3735 (2005) 215–226
11. Sun, S., Zhang, C.: Adaptive Feature Extraction for EEG Signal Classification. Medical & Biological Engineering & Computing, Vol. 44 (2006) 931–935

12. Kamousi, B., Liu, Z., He, B.: Classification of Motor Imagery Tasks for Brain-Computor Interface Applications by Means of Two Equivalent Dipoles Analysis. IEEE Trans. Neural Syst. Rehabil. Eng., Vol. 13 (2005) 166–171

13. Dietterich, T.G.: Machine Learning Research - Four Current Directions. AI Mag., Vol. 18 (1997) 97–136

14. Breiman, L.: Bagging predictors. Mach. Learn., Vol. 24 (1996) 123–140

15. Freund, Y., Shapire, R.E.: A Decision-Theoretic Generalization of On-Line Learning and an Application to Boosting. J. Comput. Syst. Sci., Vol. 55 (1997) 119–139

16. Ho, T. K.: The Random Subspace Method for Constructing Decision Forests. IEEE Trans. Pattern Anal. Mach. Intell., Vol. 20 (1998) 832–844

17. Dietterich, T.G.: An Experiemental Comparison of Three Methods for Constructing Ensembles of Decision Trees: Bagging, Boosting, and Randomization. Mach. Learn., Vol. 40 (2000) 139–157

18. Duda, R.O., Hart, P.E., Stork, D.G.: Pattern Classification. John Wiley & Sons, New York (2000)

19. Witten, I.H., Frank, E.: Data Mining: Practical Machine Learning Tools and Techniques, 2nd ed. Morgan Kaufmann, San Francisco (2005)

20. Tsymbal, A., Pechenizkiy, M. and Cunningham, P.: Diversity in Search Strategies for Ensemble Feature Selection. Information Fusion, Vol. 6 (2005) 83–98

21. Millán, J.R.: On the Need for On-Line Learning in Brain-Computer Interfaces. Proc. 2004 Int. Joint Conf. Neural Networks, Vol. 4 (2004) 2877–2882

22. Chiappa, S., Millán, J.R.: Data set V <mental imagery, multi-class>. [Online]. Available: http://ida.first.fraunhofer.de/projects/bci/competition_iii/desc_V.html, 2005

23. Bauer, E., Kohavi, R.: An Empirical Comparison of Voting Classification Algorithms: Bagging, Boosting, and Variants. Mach. Learn., Vol. 36 (1999) 105–139

24. Breiman, L.: Random Forests. Mach. Learn., Vol. 45 (2001) 5–32

25. Breiman, L.: Heuristics of Instability and Stabilization in Model Selection. Ann. Stat., Vol. 24 (1996) 2350–2383

Confidence Based Gating of Colour Features for Face Authentication

Mohammad T. Sadeghi[1], Samaneh Khoshrou[1], and Josef Kittler[2]

[1] Signal Processing Research Lab., Department of Electronics
University of Yazd, Yazd, Iran
[2] Centre for Vision, Speech and Signal Processing
School of Electronics and Physical Sciences
University of Surrey, Guildford GU2 7XH, UK
{M.Sadeghi,J.Kittler}@surrey.ac.uk

Abstract. We address the problem of fusing colour information for face authentication. The performance of a face verification system in different colour spaces is experimentally studied first. The verification process is based on the normalised correlation measure within the LDA feature space. The confidence level of the measurement made is then calculated for each colour subspace. Confidence measures are used within the framework of a gating process in order to select a subset of colour space classifiers. The selected classifiers are finally combined using the voting rule for decision making. Using the proposed method, the performance of the verification system is considerably improved as compared to the intensity space. The proposed colour fusion scheme also outperforms the best colour space in different conditions.

1 Introduction

Recently, in a number of studies, it has been demonstrated that colour information can improve the performance of the face recognition and verification systems. A brief history of different methods of involving colour features in the face verification systems can be found in [10] where a systematic evaluation of signal, feature and decision level fusion of data derived from a multispectral face image has been studied. The authors focused on face verification using the Normalised Correlation and Gradient Direction metrics in Linear Discriminant Analysis (LDA) spaces associated with the respective R,G, B colour channels. The results demonstrated that the most beneficial fusion methods are the decision level and feature level fusion but the decision level fusion was computationally the simplest. In [6] the underlying physical process of image formation has been analysed and it has been shown that by adopting the intensity image, intensity normalised green and opponent colour channels we can separate the imaging effects of object shape and object albedo, and create complementary image data channels that lead to face experts with an enhanced degree of diversity. It has been demonstrated that the fusion of these experts will result in significant improvements in performance over the system in which the face

M. Haindl, J. Kittler, and F. Roli (Eds.): MCS 2007, LNCS 4472, pp. 121–130, 2007.

experts work with the raw R,G,B channel data or other colour spaces such as H, S, V.

However, as the image formation process is very complicated, some of the simplifying assumptions may not be valid in practical situations. Our experimental studies show that, in different conditions different colour spaces can lead to a better performance. Even in the same imaging conditions (lighting conditions etc.), the use of different colour spaces could be beneficial to represent the skin colour efficiently. Therefore, the main idea behind the current study is to involve as many colour spaces as possible in the verification process and then select the best set of colour spaces by training or dynamically. In the latter case, the best subset of the colour based classifiers is selected by gating of the colour space experts based on confidence measures derived for each colour space. Classifiers with an acceptable level of confidence value are combined for decision making. The proposed method is in principle similar to the approach presented by Zhou *et. al* for ensembling neural networks [14]. Surprisingly good results are obtained using the proposed method. The paper is organised as follows. In the next section different colour spaces adopted in different machine vision applications are reviewed. The face verification process is briefly discussed in Section 3. The proposed method of colour space selection is described in Section 4. The experimental set up is detailed in Section 5. Section 6 presents the results of the experiments. Finally, in Section 7 the paper is drawn to conclusion.

2   Colour Spaces

For computer displays, it is most common to describe colour as a set of three primary colours: Red, Green and Blue. However, it has been demonstrated that in different applications using different colour spaces could be beneficial. In this section some of the most important colour spaces are reviewed. Considering the R, G, B system as the primary colour space, we can classify the other colour spaces into two main categories: Linear and Nonlinear transformation of the R, G,B values.

2.1   Linear Combination of R,G,B

CMY-based colour space is commonly used in colour printing systems. The name CMY refers to cyan, magenta and yellow. The RGB values can be converted to CMY values using:

$$C = 255 - R, \quad M = 255 - G, \quad Y = 255 - B \tag{1}$$

There are several CIE-based colour spaces, but all are derived from the fundamental XYZ space:

$$\begin{bmatrix} X \\ Y \\ Z \end{bmatrix} = \begin{bmatrix} 0.41 & 0.36 & 0.18 \\ 0.21 & 0.72 & 0.07 \\ 0.02 & 0.02 & 0.95 \end{bmatrix} \begin{bmatrix} R \\ G \\ B \end{bmatrix} \tag{2}$$

A number of different colour spaces including YUV, YIQ, YES and YC_bC_r are based on separating luminance from chrominance (lightness from colour). These spaces are useful in compression and other image processing applications. Their formal definition can be found in [2].

$I1I2I3$ or Ohta's features [7] were first introduced for segmentation as optimised colour features and are shown in equations:

$$I1 = \frac{R + G + B}{3.0}, \quad I2 = R - B, \quad I3 = 2G - R - B \tag{3}$$

LEF Colour Space defines a colour model that combines the additivity of the RGB model with the intuitiveness of the hue-saturation-luminance models by applying a linear transformation to the RGB cube [8].

2.2   Nonlinear Combination of R,G,B

The chromaticities for the normalised RGB are obtained by normalising the RGB values with the intensity value, I:

$$r = R/I, \quad g = G/I, \quad b = B/I \tag{4}$$

where $I = (R + G + B)/3$. Similar equations are used for normalising the XYZ values. The result is a 2D space known as the CIE chromaticity diagram. The opponent chromaticity space is also defined as

$$rg = r - g, \quad yb = r + g - 2b \tag{5}$$

Kawato and Ohya [5] have used the ab space which is derived from NCC rg-chromaticities as:

$$a = r + g/2, \quad b = \sqrt{3}/(2g) \tag{6}$$

In [13], two colour spaces namely $P1$ and $P2$ have been defined by circulating the r, g and b values in equation 5. Log-opponent (or Log-opponent chromaticity) space has been applied to image indexing in [1]. The space is presented by equations:

$$Ln_{rg} = \ln(R/G) = \ln R - \ln G$$
$$Lnyb = ln(\frac{R.G}{B^2}) = \ln R + \ln G - 2\ln B \tag{7}$$

TSL (Tint - Saturation - Lightness) colour space is also derived from NCC rg-chromaticities [12].

$l1l2l3$ colour space as presented in [4] has been adopted for colour-based object recognition. Many people find HS-spaces (HSV, HSB, HSI, HSL) intuitive for colour definition. For more information about the relevant equations used in this study, the reader is referred to [3].

3   Face Verification Process

The face verification process consists of three main stages: face image acquisition, feature extraction, and finally decision making. The first stage involves sensing and image preprocessing the result of which is a geometrically registered and photometrically normalised face image. Briefly, the output of a physical sensor (camera) is analysed by a face detector and once a face instance is detected, the position of the eyes is determined. This information allows the face part of the image to be extracted at a given aspect ratio and resampled to a pre-specified resolution. The extracted face image is finally photometrically normalised to compensate for illumination changes.

The raw colour camera channel outputs, R, G and B are converted according to the desired image representation spaces. In this study different colour spaces reviewed in the previous section were considered.

In the second stage of the face verification process the face image data is projected into a feature space. The final stage of the face verification process involves matching and decision making. Basically the features extracted for a face image to be verified, $\mathbf{x}$, are compared with a stored template, $\boldsymbol{\mu}_i$, that was acquired on enrolment. In [11], it was demonstrated that the Gradient Direction (GD) metric or Normalised Correlation (NC) function in the Linear Discriminant Analysis (LDA) feature space works effectively in the face verification systems. In this study we adopted the NC measure in the LDA space. The score, s, output by the matching process is then compared to a threshold in order to decide whether the claim is genuine or impostor. If this final stage of processing is applied to different colour spaces separately, we end up with a number of scores, $s_k = s(\mathbf{x}_k)$, $k = 1, 2, \ldots, N$ which then have to be fused to obtain the final decision. The adopted fusion method is studied in the next section.

4   Confidence Based Gating of Scores

One of the most exciting research directions in the field of pattern recognition and computer vision is classifier fusion. Multiple expert fusion aims to make use of many different classifier designs to improve the classification performance. In the case considered here, as different colour spaces could be more efficient in different conditions, it seems reasonable to expect that a better performance could be obtained by combining classifiers which are based on different colour spaces. In the previous study [9], we proposed a colour space selection algorithm based on the sequential search methods of feature selection. The proposed method works effectively for selecting an optimum subset of colour subspaces. One of the most important features of the proposed method is that the colour subspaces are selected adaptively based on the overall quality of the image data used in the enrolment and test stages. The main idea behind the current study is to select the most discriminative colour features not only based on the overall quality of the training and test data but also based on the characteristics of each test image individually. We expect that by dynamically selecting the experts using the respective colour subspaces, the performance of the verification system is improved.

In order to select the colour features for each test data individually, a confidence level is defined for each measurement. Suppose that for a test sample, x, s_i refer to the ith colour space score. Let $p_e(s)$ denote probability of error. Then, if $p_e(s_i) < p_e(s_j)$ for all $j \neq i$, we can say that the colour space i has the highest confidence level, i.e.

$$CL(s_i) = 1 - p_e(s_i) \tag{8}$$

Moreover,

$$p_e(s) = p_e(s|C)p_e(C) + p_e(s|I)p_e(I) \tag{9}$$

where $p_e(s|C)/p_e(s|I)$ refer to the probability of error when x is classified as client/impostor and $p_e(C)$ and $p_e(I)$ refer to the probability of client and impostor errors respectively.

In the evaluation step, in addition to the threshold(s), the probability density functions of the distances corresponding to the miss-classified samples, $P_e(s|C)$ and $P_e(s|I)$, can be estimated. These functions are determined for all subspaces individually. In this study a simple unimodal exponential function was used for modelling the density functions. $p_e(C)$ and $p_e(I)$ are in fact the False Rejection and False Acceptance error in the evaluation step. Then, in the test step, the error probabilities of the measured distances are calculated using Equation 9 for all spaces. The CL values of Equation 8 are considered as the confidence levels of the measurements made. The final decision is made using the scores corresponding to the measurements with an acceptable level of confidence. The confidence level threshold is adaptively determined in the evaluation step. The adopted threshold is then used in the test stage.

5   Experimental Design

The aim of the experiments is to show that by fusing the sensory data used by component experts, the performance of the multiple classifier system improves considerably. We use the XM2VTS database [1] and its associated experimental protocols for this purpose.

The XM2VTS database is a multi-modal database consisting of face images, video sequences and speech recordings taken of 295 subjects at one month intervals. The database is primarily intended for research and development of personal identity verification systems where it is reasonable to assume that the client will be cooperative. Since the data acquisition was distributed over a long period of time, significant variability of appearance of clients, e.g. changes of hair style, facial hair, shape and presence or absence of glasses, is present in the recordings.

The XM2VTS database contains 4 sessions. Two shots at each session, with and without glasses, were acquired for people regularly wearing glasses.

---

[1] http://www.ee.surrey.ac.uk/Research/VSSP/xm2vtsdb/

For the task of personal verification, a standard protocol for performance assessment has been defined. The so called Lausanne protocol splits randomly all subjects into a client and impostor groups. The client group contains 200 subjects, the impostor group is divided into 25 evaluation impostors and 70 test impostors. Eight images from 4 sessions are used.

From these sets consisting of face images, training set, evaluation set and test set are built. There exist two configurations that differ by a selection of particular shots of people into the training, evaluation and test sets. The training set is used to construct client models. The evaluation set is selected to produce client and impostor access scores, which are used to find a threshold that determines if a person is accepted or not. According to the Lausanne protocol the threshold is set to satisfy certain performance levels (error rates) on the evaluation set. In this study, the threshold have been determined based on the Equal Error Rate criterion, i.e. by the operating point where the false rejection rate (FRR) is equal to the false acceptance rate (FAR). False acceptance is the case where an impostor, claiming the identity of a client, is accepted. False rejection is the case where a client, claiming his true identity, is rejected. The evaluation set is also used in fusion experiments (classifier combination) for training. The sequential search algorithms pick the best colour spaces using this set of data.

Finally the test set is selected to simulate realistic authentication tests where impostor's identity is unknown to the system. The performance measures of a verification system are the False Acceptance rate and the False Rejection rate.

The original resolution of the image data is 720×576. The experiments were performed with a relatively low resolution face images, namely 64×49. The results reported in this article have been obtained by applying a geometric face registration based on manually annotated eyes positions. Histogram equalisation was used to normalise the registered face photometrically.

6   Experimental Results

Table 1 shows the performance of the face verification system using the individual colour spaces considering the first configuration of the Lausanne protocol. The values in the table indicate the FAR and FRR in both evaluation and test stages. As we expect, the best performance is obtained neither in the original RGB spaces nor in the intensity space. Some other colour spaces such as U in the YUV space or opponent chromaticities individually can lead to better results. Table 2 shows some results of the same experiments considering the second XM2VTS configuration.

In the next step, the proposed confidence based gating approach was used in order to find an optimum subset of colour spaces. Suppose that we found the colour spaces with the higher confidence level, the question is how to fuse the selected classifiers. In this study we fused the classifiers using the simple voting rule. The other important issue is how to select an appropriate threshold on the confidence level. We adopted two different methods of gating. In the first group of experiments, we wanted to optimise the number of colour subspaces. Figures 1(a)

Table 1. Identity verification results using different colour spaces (configuration 1)

subspace	R	G	B	I	H	Sat	Val	r	g
FAR Eval.	1.94	1.91	2	2.18	2.1	1.72	2.05	1.8125	1.62
FRR Eval.	2.33	2.17	1.667	1.83	1.667	1.83	2.1667	2	1.33
FAR Test	2.13	1.92	2.24	2.24	2.027	1.78	2.34	1.96	1.62
FRR Test	2	1.75	1.5	1.25	0.5	1.25	2	0.75	1
subspace	b	T(TSL)	S(TSL)	L(TSL)	V(YUV)	rg	U(YUV)	Cr	I2
FAR Eval.	1.782	1.425	1.28	2.04	2.38	1.32	2.25	1.56	2.16
FRR Eval.	1.667	1.67	1.33	2.33	2.33	1.67	1.67	2	2.33
FAR Test	1.817	1.258	1.51	2.062	2.36	1.467	2.08	1.94	2.12
FRR Test	1.25	1	1.75	1.5	0.75	1.25	0	1.5	0.75
subspace	I3	E(LEF)	F(LEF)	X(CIE)	Y(CIE)	Z(CIE)	Y(YES)	E(YES)	S(YES)
FAR Eval.	1.577	2.235	1.49	2.39	2.35	2.08	2.03	2.16	1.95
FRR Eval.	1.83	2	1.67	1.83	1.83	1.83	2.33	1.83	2
FAR Test	1.59	2.36	1.37	2.51	2.43	2.34	2.04	2.033	1.79
FRR Test	0.75	0.5	0.5	1.25	1.5	1.75	1.5	0.75	0.25
subspace	I(YIQ)	Q(YIQ)	a(ab)	b(ab)	Lnrg	Lnyb	l1	l2	l3
FAR Eval.	2.13	1.81	1.76	1.58	1.3	1.69	2.41	2.19	1.71
FRR Eval.	2.17	1.833	1.833	1.5	1.67	1.5	1.833	2.5	1.67
FAR Test	2.4	1.7	1.87	1.628	1.4027	1.7973	2.09	2.25	1.58
FRR Test	1.5	0.75	1.5	1	1.75	1.25	1	1.25	1.5
subspace	L(HSL)	Xn	Yn	Zn	C(CMY)	M(CMY)	Y(CMY)	bg	
FAR Eval.	2.13	1.79	1.6	1.65	2.22	1.92	2.032	1.47	
FRR Eval.	2.33	1.83	1.5	1.667	2.5	2.17	1.67	1.67	
FAR Test	2.23	1.892	1.65	1.6902	2.46	1.92	2.28	1.15	
FRR Test	1	1	0.5	1.25	2	1.75	1.5	0.75	

Table 2. Identity verification results using some of the colour spaces (configuration 2)

subspace	R	G	B	I	H	S	V	r	g	b	U	Yn	bg	F(LEF)
FAR Eval.	1.19	1.40	1.295	1.225	1.26	1.03	1.003	1.51	0.75	1.00	0.87	0.89	0.82	0.87
FRR Eval.	1.5	1	1.25	1.25	1.25	1.25	1.25	1.25	0.75	1.25	1	1	1	1
FAR Test	1.57	1.82	1.93	1.79	1.15	1.46	1.31	2.16	0.77	1.80	1.06	1.12	1.03	1.24
FRR Test	1.5	1.25	1.5	1.5	0.5	1	1.75	1.25	0.5	0.75	1	0.5	0.75	1.25

and (b) show the error rate versus the number of colour spaces (with the highest CL values) in the evaluation step considering the first and second experimental configurations of the database. As one can see, the optimum number of colour spaces is around 29 for the first and 11 for the second configuration. Therefore, in the test step, the first 29 (or 11) colour spaces were used for decision making. The first rows of tables 3 and 4 show the relevant results. Figures 1(c) and (d) also show the error rate versus the number of colour spaces for the test step. In the second gating method, in the evaluation step an optimum threshold is determined. The colour subspaces with a confidence level higher than the threshold

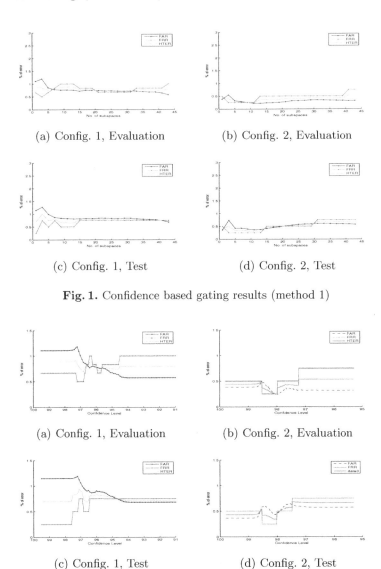

(a) Config. 1, Evaluation   (b) Config. 2, Evaluation

(c) Config. 1, Test   (d) Config. 2, Test

Fig. 1. Confidence based gating results (method 1)

(a) Config. 1, Evaluation   (b) Config. 2, Evaluation

(c) Config. 1, Test   (d) Config. 2, Test

Fig. 2. Confidence based gating results (method 2)

can participate in the voting process. Figure 2 contains the associated results. The upper plots demonstrate that the optimum threshold for the confidence level is around 96.8% and 98.4% for the first and second configurations respectively. The second rows of tables 3 and 4 show the relevant results. Apparently, both methods considerably improve the performance of the face verification system compared to the intensity space and even the best subspaces in each protocols. As we mentioned in the previous study [9] a sequential search approach which is in principle similar to the "plus L and take away R" algorithm was applied to

Table 3. Verification results using the proposed colour fusion methods (config. 1)

	Evaluation			Test		
	FAR	FRR	TER	FAR	FRR	TER
Gating (Method 1)	0.71	0.66	1.37	0.83	0.75	1.58
Gating (Method 2)	0.87	0.5	1.37	0.95	0.5	1.45
Plus 2 Take away 1	0.48	0.5	0.98	0.55	1	1.55

Table 4. Verification results using the proposed colour fusion methods (config. 2)

	Evaluation			Test		
	FAR	FRR	TER	FAR	FRR	TER
Gating(Method 1)	0.22	0.25	0.47	0.36	0.25	0.61
Gating(Method 2)	0.23	0.25	0.48	0.43	0.25	0.68
Plus 2 Take away 1	0.19	0.25	0.44	0.27	0.25	0.52

find an optimum subset of the colour spaces. The third rows of tables 3 and 4 demonstrate the associated results. As one can see, the results are comparable with the results using the proposed method. One of the main characteristics of the XM2VTS database is that the image data has been collected in the controlled conditions. The comparison of the proposed methods using images collected in different scenarios is a matter of interest in the future studies.

7   Conclusions

We addressed the problem of fusing colour information for face authentication. In a face verification system which is based on the normalised correlation measure in the LDA face space. A confidence base gating approach was proposed in order to find an optimum subset of the colour spaces for each test data individually. Using the proposed method, the performance of the verification system was considerably improved as compared to the intensity space. The proposed colour fusion scheme also consistently outperforms the best colour space in different conditions.

Acknowledgements. The financial support from Iran Telecommunication Research Centre is gratefully acknowledged. A partial support from the EU Network of Excellence Biosecure and from the EPSRC Grant GR/S98528/01 is also gratefully acknowledged.

References

1. J. Berens and G. Finlayson. Log-opponent chromaticity coding of colour space. In *Proceedings of the Fourth IEEE International Conference on Pattern Recognition*, pages 1206–1211, 2000.

2. P. Colantoni et al. Color space transformations. Technical report, http://www.raduga-ryazan.ru/files/doc/colorspacetransform95.pdf.

3. J. Foley, A. van Dam, S. Feiner, and J. Hughes. *Computer graphics: principles and practice (2nd ed.)*. Addison-Wesley Longman Publishing Co., Inc., Boston, MA, USA, 1996.

4. T. Gevers and A. Smeulders. Colour based object recognition. In *ICIAP (1)*, pages 319–326, 1997.

5. S. Kawato and J. Ohya. Real-time detection of nodding and head-shaking by directly detecting and tracking the "between-eyes". In *Proceedings of the Fourth IEEE International Conference on Automatic Face and Gesture Recognition*, pages 40–45, 2000.

6. J. Kittler and M. Sadeghi. Physics-based decorrelation of image data for decision level fusion in face verification. In *the Fifth Workshop on Multiple Classifier Systems (MCS 2004)*, pages 354–363, Cagliari, Italy, June 2004.

7. Y. Ohta, T. Kanade, and T. Sakai. Colour information for region segmentation. *Computer Graphics and Image Processing*, 13(3):222 – 241, July 1980.

8. N. Rudaz, R. Hersch, and V. Ostromoukhov. Specifying colour differences in a linear colour space (LEF). In *Proceedings of the IS&T/SID Colour Imaging Conference: Colour Science, Systems and Applications, Arizona, USA*, pages 197–202, 1997.

9. M. Sadeghi, S. Khoshrou, and J. Kittler. Colour feature selection for face authentication. Accepted for publication in Proceedings of the International Conference on Machine Vision Applications, MVA'07, Japan, 2007.

10. M. Sadeghi and J. Kittler. A comparative study of data fusion strategies in face verification. In *the 12th European Signal Processing Conference*, Vienna, Austria, 6-10 September 2004.

11. M. Sadeghi and J. Kittler. Decision making in the LDA space: Generalised gradient direction metric. In *the 6th International Conference on Automatic Face and Gesture Recognition*, pages 248–253, Seoul, Korea, May 2004.

12. J. Terrillon, M. Shirazi, H. Fukamachi, and S. Akamatsu. Comparative performance of different skin chrominance models and chrominance spaces for the automatic detection of human faces in colour images. In *Proceedings of the Fourth IEEE International Conference on Automatic Face and Gesture Recognition*, page 54, USA, 2000.

13. C. Vertan, M. Cuic, and N. Boujemaa. On the introduction of a chrominance spectrum and its applications. In *Proceedings of the First International Conference on Colour in Graphics and Image Processing*, pages 214–218, 1-4 Oct. 2000.

14. Z-H. Zho, J. Wu, , and W. Tang. Ensembling neural networks: Many could be better than all. *Artificial Intelligence, 2002, 137(1-2): 239-263*, 137(1-2):239–263, 2002.

View-Based Eigenspaces with Mixture of Experts for View-Independent Face Recognition

Reza Ebrahimpour[1,3], Ehsanollah Kabir[2], and Mohammad Reza Yousefi[3]

[1] School of Cognitive Sciences, Institute for Studies on Theoretical Physics and Mathematics,
Niavaran, Tehran, P.O. Box 19395-5746, Iran
ebrahimpour@ipm.ir
[2] Department of Electrical Engineering, Tarbiat Modarres University, Tehran,
P.O. Box 14115-143, Iran
kabir@modares.ac.ir
[3] Department of Electrical Engineering, Shahid Rajaee University, Tehran, Iran
m.r.yousefi@srttu.edu

Abstract. We propose a new model for view-independent face recognition, which lies under the category of multi-view approaches. We use the so-called "mixture of experts", ME, in which, the problem space is divided into several subspaces for the experts, and the outputs of experts are combined by a gating network. In the proposed model, instead of allowing ME to partition the face space automatically, the ME is directed to adapt to a particular partitioning corresponding to predetermined views. In this model, view-dependent representations are used to direct the experts towards a specific area of face space. The experimental results support our claim that directing the mixture of experts to a predetermined partitioning of face space is a more beneficial way of using conventional ME for view-independent face recognition.

1 Introduction

Recognizing faces from novel viewing directions is a challenging task in computer vision, which the human visual system performs efficiently. The major issue in view-independent face recognition is the ability to identify a familiar face from different viewing directions, from which the face was not seen in the past.

There are different methods for handling pose variations in face recognition. These methods are divided into the following three major groups: (a) the invariant features methods, (b) the 3D model-based methods, and (c) the multiview methods [1,2].

Invariant features methods attempt to extract features that do not change when faces are seen from novel views, such as geometric invariants [3,4]. A drawback of these methods is the unfeasibility of finding sufficient number of invariant features for reliable recognition. In addition, there are many informative features that are intrinsically view-dependent and are not used in these methods.

The 3D model-based methods focus on constructing a prototypical view (frontal view) from a 3D model which is extracted from the input image. A recent survey of approaches to 3D face recognition is provided in [5]. Such methods work well for

M. Haindl, J. Kittler, and F. Roli (Eds.): MCS 2007, LNCS 4472, pp. 131–140, 2007.

small rotation angles, but they fail when the angle is large causing some important features to be invisible [2].

Most proposed methods are based on using a number of multiview samples. In multiview methods, an adequate number of different views of a face are used to deal with the pose problem [1]. An example is the work by Beymer [6], which models faces with templates from 15 views, sampling different poses from the viewing sphere. The recognizer consists of two main stages, a geometrical alignment stage where the input is registered with the model views and a correlation stage for matching.

Under the category of multiview methods, there are other works in which the attempt is made to propose representation schemes that are robust to changes in viewpoint. Of such methods, the most famous one is the single-view eigenspaces. The concept of single-view eigenspace was first introduced in [7], based on the Principal Component Analysis, PCA, (originally proposed in [8] and popularized by [9]). They use the face images in five common poses to build five single-view eigenspaces. For a test face, the distance to each single-view eigenspace is calculated and the pose class with the minimum distance is recognized. The single-view eigenspaces has also been used in [10] with three projection spaces of frontal, half profile and profile. The alternative solution for view-independent recognition with PCA technique is the global eigenspace. The global eigenspace is created from all face images in different poses. This method has been used in [11] to simultaneously perform object pose estimation and recognition.

In this paper, we propose a model for view-independent face recognition, based on "mixture of experts" (ME), in which the outputs of several classifiers (experts) are integrated by a gating network. The gating network decides which of the experts should be used for each input image. In our model, instead of allowing the mixture network to self-partition the face space, we define particular subspaces and, attempt, in some ways, to direct the experts towards them. The proposed model makes use of view-based eigenspaces in the representation layer of each expert and helps the experts to specialize in a predetermined view of face. The gating network with a global eigenspace (made by all the training images) in its input layer learns to find the pose of the input face image and so directs more error information (feedback) to the expert that performs best. Eventually, expert 1 "specializes" in one view of face, expert 2 specializes in another view of the face, and so on.

The rest of this paper is organized as follows. In section 2, the principles of the combining methodology, on which our proposed model is based, are briefly described. In section 3, the proposed model, mixture of view-based experts, is introduced, followed by descriptions on their training process and the experimental results. Section 4 presents a discussion on the function and performance of the proposed mixture of view-based experts. And finally, Section 5 draws conclusion and summarizes the paper.

2   Mixture of Experts (ME)

From a computational point of view, according to the principle of divide and conquer, a complex computational task is solved by dividing it into a number of computationally simple tasks and then combining the solutions to those tasks. In supervised learning, computational simplicity is achieved by distributing the learning task among a number of experts, which in turn divides the input space into a set of subspaces. The combination of experts is said to constitute a combination of classifiers.

Mixture of experts is the most famous method in the category of dynamic structures of classifier combining, in which the input signal is directly involved in actuating the mechanism that integrates the outputs of the individual experts into an overall output [12].

Consider a *modular neural network* (Fig. 1) in which the learning process proceeds by fusing self–organized and supervised forms of learning. The experts are technically performing supervised learning in that their individual outputs are combined to model the

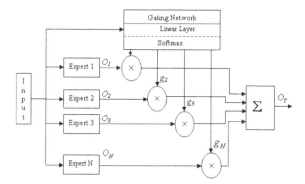

Fig. 1. The mixture of experts is composed of expert networks and a gating network. The experts compete to learn the training patterns and the gating network mediates the competition. The gating network is simultaneously trained to combine the experts' outputs.

desired response. There is, however, a sense in which the experts are also performing self–organized learning; that is they self–organize to find a good partitioning of the input space so that each expert does well at modeling its own subspace, and as a whole group they model the input space well. The learning algorithm of the mixture structure is described in [13].

However, in our models, in order to improve the performance of the expert networks, and consequently the whole network performance, we use our revised version of ME in which MLPs are used as the expert and gating networks. The details of the learning rules of ME with MLPs are described in our previous work [14].

3   Proposed Model: Mixture of View-Based Experts

Our proposed model is designed to achieve view-independent face recognition with a mixture of view-based experts (Fig. 2). In this model, the face space (spanning from right to left profile along the horizontal plane) is divided into five predetermined views (namely -90°, -45°, 0°, +45° and +90° views) and each expert is trained to recognize faces of a specific view at an individual level (view-based experts). These experts have the ability to recognize faces close to their specific views. This property enables the model to use a combination of two or more experts in order to recognize

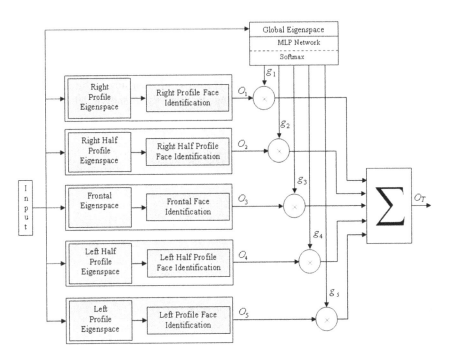

Fig. 2. Sketch of the mixture of view-based experts. This model consists of expert networks which have specialization over a specific pose and a gating network which mediates between experts by finding the pose of the input face image. Expert modules obtain specialization according to the view-dependent representation placed in their input layer. The experts are able to recognize faces close to their corresponding views. Combining the outputs of two or more experts by the gating network leads to the recognition of faces in intermediate unseen views.

faces in intermediate unseen views. In this model the gating network contains a global eigenspace in its representation layer which is different from that of experts; so it differs from the conventional ME which employs a same representation layer for both experts and gating network. Thus, the first layer of the gating network with the global PCA mapping, reveals information on the view of the input face image, and in the second layer, the MLP network, according to the information of the previous layer, inhibits or excites one or more experts to produce the final output. The third layer, softmax function, preserves the rank order of its input values, and is a differentiable generalization of the "winner-takes-all" operation of picking the maximum value.

3.1 View-Based Experts

Each of the five view-based experts of the network structure shown Fig. 2 is composed of two sub-layers: representation and identification (Fig. 3).

To approach a representation layer with a view-based eigenspace, for a given set of M individuals under C different views, we build a view-based set of C distinct eigenspaces, each capturing the variation of the M individuals in a common view. The view-based eigenspace is essentially an extension of the eigenface technique to multiple sets of eigenvectors, one for each combination of orientation. One can view this architecture as a set of parallel observers, each trying to explain the image data with their set of eigenvectors [7,15]. As shown in Fig. 3, each of those view-based eigenspaces is added to the representation layer of each expert network. Therefore, each expert network obtains expertise over the view according to which the eigenspace of its representation layer is made.

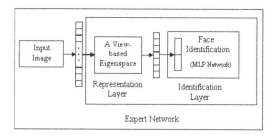

Fig. 3. An expert network is composed of two sub-layers: representation and identification. In the representation layer, PCA mapping is carried out and in the identification layer an MLP network performs the identification task.

3.2 Network Training

In our experiments, the network's task is to recognize the faces of intermediate unseen views as individuals. We use a subset of the PIE database which consists of 10 identities with 9 different images of 9 different poses spaced evenly from -90 to +90 with 22.5° steps. Faces with ±45, ±90 and 0° rotations are used to train and those with ±67.5 and ±22.5° rotations are used to test the networks. Fig. 4 shows examples of images used for training and testing the networks.

As in PIE database there is just one sample of each pose for each identity, we face the "small sample size" problem, which exists in high-dimensional pattern recognition tasks, where the number of available samples is smaller than the dimensionality of the samples. Numerous techniques have been developed to attack this problem; for a detailed discussion of these methods see Ref [16], however we try to solve it with the basic idea of synthesizing multiple new face images which imitate the corrupted images for recognition. The imitation is done by a noise model [17] with three noise parameters controlling the degree of contrast, brightness and Gaussian blur, respectively. An example of synthesized images is shown in Fig. 5, where, by changing the values of noise parameters, 14 corrupted images corresponding to one sample image are imitated, which essentially improves the representative of the given sample.

To form a view-based eigenspace, for instance for the right half profile eigenspace, face images of that view including the synthesized images are used. Therefore, we have 150 (15×10, 10 identities and 15 images for each training view of each identity) images for each view, which by using the efficient technique for PCA described in [8], we make a view-based eigenspace formed by the 50 eigenvectors of that training view's covariance matrix.

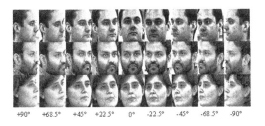

+90°   +68.5°   +45°   +22.5°   0°   -22.5°   -45°   -68.5°   -90°

Fig. 4. Examples of face images, taken from the PIE database, used to train and test our proposed model. Faces with ±90°, ±45° and 0° rotations are used to train, and faces in intermediate views (with ±68.5° and ±22.5° rotations) are used test the ability of our models to perform view-independent face recognition.

In the training phase, each input image is projected into the five view-based eigenspaces and is then fed into its corresponding identification layer of experts. At the same time, the input image is projected into the global eigenspace which is placed in the input layer of the gating network. Rest of the training process is done according to the training rules mentioned in section 3-2. It should be mentioned that after searching for network parameter settings which maximize the expertise of each expert in its corresponding view and also lets the gating network to select the experts that are performing the best at recognizing the input image, we found the optimum values of 0.01 and 0.05 for η_e and η_g, respectively.

Fig. 5. Synthesizing new images. The single image at the top is the original, the images in the middle row are generated by changing the contrast and brightness of the original image, and the images in the lower row are generated by applying Gaussian blur.

3.3 Experimental Results

To evaluate the performance of mixture of view-based experts and also exhibit the advantage of using view-based eigenspaces, we compare it with the ME which has a global PCA transform in its input layer. As mentioned before, in our experiment, the networks' task is to recognize the faces of intermediate unseen views as individuals. For similar network topologies for the gating and experts in both mixture of view-based experts and ME, we experiment them on the test set described in the previous subsection. The results of this experiment is reported in Table 1, where for a variety

Table 1. Recognition rates of different topologies of mixture of view-based experts and ME. In each column, for fixed values of hidden neurons of gating network and expert networks, recognition rate, averaged over ten training runs with different random initial weights, is reported.

No. of hidden neurons of gating network		16	18	20	22	24	26
No. of hidden neurons of experts		45	50	55	60	65	70
Recognition rate (%)	ME with Global Eigenspace [14]	71.02	71.48	75.53	**77.14**	73.54	69.12
	Proposed Model	78.53	76.57	**80.51**	78.58	76.50	77.22

of the number of hidden neurons, for gating and expert networks, the performance on the test set in terms of recognition rate, which is the average of 10 training runs with different initial random weights, is listed. As shown in Table 1, mixture of view-based experts outperforms ME with a much better recognition rate. The best result of this experiment for mixture of view-based experts is 86.45%, and for ME is 78.26%, with 22 and 60 hidden neurons in proposed model and 20 and 55 hidden neurons in ME, for the gating and experts, respectively.

4 Discussion

As shown in Table 1, mixture of view-based experts achieves higher recognition rate in comparison with ME. In this subsection we examine the role of expertise and specialization of experts in the prominence of proposed model. In order to attain a better understanding of the function of experts in mixture of view-based experts, we performed an additional experiment involving unseen face images in similar views as the training samples which were synthesized by the technique described in subsection 4-2 and were not used in the training phase of networks. The experiment was carried out with 750 face images of -90°, -45°, 0°, 45° and 90° rotations and we observed the performance of each expert in the proposed model and ME. Fig. 6 summarizes the division of labor performed by each expert of mixture of view-based experts and ME over 10 runs with $\eta_e = 0.01$ and $\eta_g = 0.05$. The bars denote the recognition rate of each of five experts, broken down by input face pose class, and the error bars denote standard error. Note that in Fig. 6.b the most left bar in each group corresponds

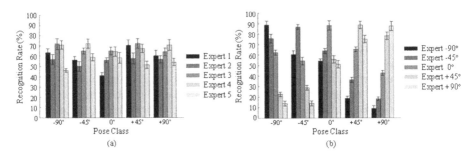

Fig. 6. Recognition rates of ME and mixture of view-based experts, averaged over ten training runs on unseen synthesized images of training views broken down by pose class. Bars denote the recognition rate of experts. (a) Modules of ME structures are not biased to prefer one class of pose to another as they recognize input images about to the same extent irrespective of their pose class. (b) Experts of the proposed model demonstrate expertise over their view of specialization as they well recognize faces of their corresponding pose and for faces of other pose classes their performance decreases dramatically. See Discussion for details.

to -90° expert and the next one to -45° expert and so on. Clearly, considering Fig. 6.a, for any input face image, irrespective of its pose, the experts reveal almost the same recognition rate. In Fig. 6.b, there is strong expertise in experts in their corresponding pose class which is noticeably greater than that of ME. As, for instance, the performance of -45° expert, shown by the second bar in each bar group, is greater for faces with -45° rotation, whereas it degrades dramatically for faces of other pose classes. Therefore, regarding the better performance and the existence of expertise in mixture of view-based experts, in comparison with ME, shown in Table 1and Fig. 6a and b respectively, we conclude that to achieve view-independent face recognition with mixture structure, it is more beneficial to quantize and aggregate the face space with respect to pose and then direct each expert towards learning its corresponding pose class, instead of allowing the ME to self partition it, like what is done in its conventional style. In other words, dividing the face space with respect to pose is a helpful solution that ME itself cannot reach, but when it is directed towards such solution by means of view-based eigenspaces, the model exhibits robustness to variations in pose in terms of high recognition rate for faces of novel views.

5   Conclusion

We have presented a computational model, based on mixture of experts, to perform view-independent face recognition. Our studies lend support to our claim that there is a better way of training a ME for view-independent face recognition when we do not rely on ME to partition the face space. The basic idea was to partition the face space with respect to pose and direct each expert towards a predefined subspace. In our model we used view-dependent representations to direct expert towards their corresponding views of face.

Note that we do not argue that mixture of experts should always be trained in such ways. There might be several applications that the problem space partitioning by ME itself is more fitting the task at hand. But in view-independent face recognition, where faces of a common view are similar insofar as they form a remarkably homogenous category, we observed that our method of partitioning the face space reveals better performance than the conventional ME with self-partitioning of space.

Using mixture structures with view-based experts in view-independent face recognition appears to be a promising avenue for future research. In future work, we plan to explore more complicated representation mechanisms for experts to lead to specialization in supervised computational models that are more biologically plausible. As another route to increasing our experts' specialization, we will also make effort to incorporate different methods of teacher-directed learning.

References

1. Du, S. and, Ward, R.K.: Face Recognition Under Pose Variations. Journal of the Franklin Institute **343** (2006) 596-613.
2. Zhao, W., Chellappa, R., Rosenfeld, A. and, Phillips, P.J.: Face Recognition: A Literature Survey. ACM Computing Surveys (2003) 399-458.
3. Cootes, T.F., Edwards, J.F. and, Taylor, C.J.: Active appearance models. IEEE Transactions Pattern Analysis and Machine Intelligence **23**(6) (2001) 681-685.
4. Wiskott, L., Fellous, J.M. and, Von Der Malsburg, C.: Face recognition by elastic bunch graph matching. IEEE Transactions Pattern Analysis and Machine Intelligence **19** (1997) 775-779.
5. Bowyer, K.W., Chang, K. and, Flynn, P.: A survey of approaches and challenges in 3D and multi-modal 3D + 2D face recognition. Computer Vision and Image Understanding **101**(1) (2006) 1-15.
6. Beymer, D.J. Face recognition under varying pose. Technical Report 1461, MIT AI Lab, Massachusetts Institute of Technology, Cambridge, MA, 1993.
7. Pentland, A., Moghaddam, B. and, Starner, T.: View-based and Modular Eigenspaces for face recognition. In: Proceedings of the International Conference on Computer Vision and Pattern Recognition (1994) 84-91.
8. Kirby, M. and, Sirovich, L. Application of the KL procedure for the characterization of human faces. IEEE Transactions Pattern Analysis and Machine Intelligence **12**(1) (1990) 103-108.
9. Turk, M. and, Pentland. A.: Eigenfaces for recognition. Journal of Cognitive Neuroscience **3**(1) (1991) 71-86.
10. Sehad, A., Hocini, H., Hadid, A., Djeddi, M. and, Ameur, S.: Face Recognition under Varying Views. Lecture Notes in Computer Sience **1811** (2000) 258-267.
11. Murase, H. and, Nayar, S.K.: Visual learning and recognition of 3-D objects from appearance. International Journal of Computer Vision **14** (1995) 5-24.
12. Haykin, S. Neural Networks: A Comprehensive Foundation. USA: Prentice Hall (1999)
13. Jacobs, R., Jordan M., Nowlan, S., and Hinton, G.: Adaptive mixtures of local experts. Neural Computation, **3** (1991) 79 – 87.
14. Ebrahimpour, R., Kabir, E., and Yousefi, M.R.: Teacher-directed learning with mixture of experts for view-independent face recognition. Lecture Notes in Computer Science **4362** (2007) 601-611.

15. Shakhnarovich, G. and Moghaddam, B.: Face Recognition in Subspaces. Handbook of Face Recognition, (2004).
16. Tan, X., Chen, S., Zhou, Z.-H. and Zhang, F.: Face recognition from a single image per person: A survey. Pattern Recognition **39** (2006) 1725-1745.
17. Phillips, J.P. and Newton, E.M.: Meta-analysis of face recognition algorithms. Proceedings of the Fifth IEEE International Conference on Automatic Face and Gesture Recognition, Washington, DC (2002) 235 - 241.

Fusion of Support Vector Classifiers for Parallel Gabor Methods Applied to Face Verification

Ángel Serrano[1], Isaac Martín de Diego[1], Cristina Conde[1], Enrique Cabello[1], Li Bai[2], and Linlin Shen[2]

[1] Face Recognition & Artificial Vision Group, Universidad Rey Juan Carlos,
Camino del Molino, s/n, Fuenlabrada, E-28943, Madrid, Spain
{angel.serrano,isaac.martin,cristina.conde,
enrique.cabello}@urjc.es
http://frav.escet.urjc.es/
[2] School of Computer Science & IT, University of Nottingham, Jubilee Campus,
Nottingham, NG8 1BB, United Kingdom
{bai,lls}@cs.nott.ac.uk

Abstract. In this paper we present a fusion technique for Support Vector Machine (SVM) scores, obtained after a dimension reduction with Bilateral-projection-based Two-Dimensional Principal Component Analysis (B2DPCA) for Gabor features. We apply this new algorithm to face verification. Several experiments have been performed with the public domain FRAV2D face database (109 subjects). A total of 40 wavelets (5 frequencies and 8 orientations) have been used. Each set of wavelet-convolved images is considered in parallel for the B2DPCA and the SVM classification. A final fusion is performed combining the SVM scores for the 40 wavelets with a raw average. The proposed algorithm outperforms the standard dimension reduction techniques, such as Principal Component Analysis (PCA) and B2DPCA.

Keywords: Biometrics, Face Verification, Gabor Wavelet, Principal Component Analysis, Bilateral 2D Principal Component Analysis, Parallel Gabor Principal Component Analysis, Support Vector Machine.

1 Introduction

Since the last decade, face biometrics applications have been found to be feasible, as well as user-friendly and privacy-respectful methods. One of the working modes of these systems is the so-called face verification, where a user claims an identity, in the same way as a person does when writing his/her PIN number at an automated teller machine. The user's biometric data are compared to his/her corresponding biometric template in order to verify whether or not the person is who he/she claims to be. Therefore face verification is a 1-to-1 problem, much easy to tackle compared to face identification (1-to-N problem).

The huge amount of biometric data makes it mandatory to perform a dimension reduction prior to any processing. Turk and Pentland presented the now classical Principal Component Analysis method (PCA), which maximizes the variance over the data, after converting the images into column vectors [1]. There have been several

M. Haindl, J. Kittler, and F. Roli (Eds.): MCS 2007, LNCS 4472, pp. 141–150, 2007.

modifications and improvements of this method. For instance, in [2] the so-called 2DPCA was proposed, which keeps the 2D information in the images, as every pixel is correlated to its neighbours. In fact, this method is equivalent to perform a PCA over the rows of the image [3]. Although 2DPCA outperforms PCA in recognition rates, it usually needs more projection coefficients. A Bilateral-projection-based Two-Dimensional Principal Component Analysis (B2DPCA) was developed as an alternative to 2DPCA [3]. One of the challenges to achieve with B2DPCA was to remove the necessity of more coefficients to represent an image in 2DPCA than in PCA. Furthermore, these authors demonstrated the superiority of this method over the conventional PCA for face recognition.

Gabor wavelets [4] are a useful technique because of their resemblance to the sensibility of visual cortex in mammals. Their good results when applied to face recognition and their robustness to changes of illumination make these wavelets a powerful tool in biometrics systems.

In previous works different strategies have been used to combine Gabor wavelets with dimension reduction methods. For example, in [5] the values of the convolutions were computed only over a set of fiducial points (eyes, nose and mouth) and then fed to a PCA algorithm. Others [6][7][8][9] compute an augmented feature vector via the Gabor feature fusion for all the orientations and scales, and then they perform a downsampling process to reduce the huge dimensionality of the resulting vector. These methods compute all the possible convolutions to build a unique feature vector to be fed into a classifier, such as SVM. Up to now, B2DPCA has not been previously combined with Gabor wavelets.

In this paper we propose a new fusion algorithm for Support Vector Machines (SVM) scores [10] obtained after a dimension reduction with B2DPCA for Gabor features. Recently, we have developed a fusion method based on a dimension reduction with PCA [11]. We would like to evaluate the benefits obtained when different, and more powerful, dimension reduction methods are employed. We compare our methods with B2DPCA and standard PCA.

The remainder of this paper is organized as follows. In Section 2, we present the face database used in this work. In Section 3, we explain the design of our experiments, and we detail the proposed method. In Section 4, we present and discuss our results. Section 5 summarizes the conclusions.

2 FRAV2D Face Database

We have employed a complete facial images database, the public domain FRAV2D Face Database [12]. It contains 109 subjects, mainly 18 to 40 years old. There are 32 images per subject, which is more than the number of images per subject used in other usual databases for face verification. It was collected in a year's time with volunteers (students and lecturers) at the Universidad Rey Juan Carlos in Madrid (Spain). Each image is a 240×340 colour picture obtained with a CCD video-camera. The face of the subject occupies most of the image.

Fig. 1. Examples of images from the FRAV2D Database (from left to right: frontal view with diffuse illumination, gestures, occlusion, and frontal view with zenithal illumination)

The images were obtained in a unique session per person. The subject had to sit down on a stool at a fixed distance to the camera, although he or she was asked to stand up and sit down again between two shots. Only one parameter was changed between two pictures.

The images were taken under several controlled conditions of pose and illumination. The distribution of images is as follows: 12 frontal views with neutral expression (diffuse light from two focuses was used), 4 images with a 15° turn with respect to the camera axis, 4 images with a 30° turn with respect to the camera axis, 4 images performing different face gestures, such as smiles, expression of surprise, etc., 4 images with occluded faces features (the subject is looking at the camera occluding the left part of his/her face with his/her left hand), and 4 images with zenithal instead of diffuse illumination.

In order to apply face normalization in size and orientation, the position of the eyes was found in every image. A window of size 128×128 pixels containing the most meaningful part of the face was selected in every image, with the eyes located in the same position. For the images with occlusions, only the right eye is visible. In this case, the image was cropped so that the right eye is located at the same position as in the other images, but no correction in size and orientation was applied. Finally the images were stored in equalized grey scale and histogram equalization was performed to correct variations in illumination. That is the information to be analyzed (Figure 1).

3   Design of the Experiments

In this section, we describe the experiments that have been considered using the FRAV2D face database. First, the database was divided into a gallery set with 2 frontal images with neutral expression and diffuse illumination per subject and a unique test set, with 2 disjoint frontal images different to the previous ones. A second experiment design was considered with a gallery set with 4 frontal images with neutral expression and diffuse illumination per subject and 4 different test sets, all of them with 4 images per subject: a disjoint set of frontal images with neutral expression diffuse illumination, images with gestures (such as smiles or winks), images with the left part of the face occluded, and a set of frontal images with neutral expression, but with zenithal illumination.

We have performed a dimension reduction process with four different methods: PCA, B2DPCA, Parallel Gabor PCA and Parallel Gabor B2DPCA, the latter being first proposed in this paper. After that, the obtained projection coefficients have been used to train a set of SVM classifiers. Finally, the images in the test sets were projected onto the corresponding reduced frameworks and their projections were fed into the SVMs in order to perform the classification process devoted to face verification.

In the following subsections, let A_i be the i-th image of size $h{\times}w$ in the face database and let A_i' be the column vector of size $hw{\times}1$ computed by the transpose of the concatenation of all the rows in A_i.

3.1 Principal Component Analysis (PCA)

First, we consider a classical dimension reduction method, the standard PCA [1]. The basic idea is to consider only the d highest eigenvalues of the covariance matrix obtained from the images A_i. The corresponding d eigenvectors are concatenated to create the projection matrix P, of size $hw{\times}d$. The projection coefficients for the image A_i are calculated as follows:

$$C_i = A_i'^{\,T} P , \qquad (1)$$

where T is the transpose operator. C_i is a row vector of size $1{\times}d$ that contains the projections of the image A_i onto the framework of the most significant eigenvectors. As this dimensionality d is much lower than the total amount of pixels in the image (hw), there is an important dimension reduction.

After computing the projection matrix for the gallery database, the projection coefficients for each image are calculated. An independent Support Vector Machine (SVM) classifier was trained for each person in the database. For each subject, we considered his/her images as genuine and everybody else's as impostors. Therefore each SVM was prepared to verify the identity of one subject in the database.

All the images in the test set were projected onto the PCA framework and their coefficients were fed to the previously trained SVMs. With the resulting scores, a unique receiver operating characteristic curve (ROC) was computed and the corresponding equal error rate (EER), for which the false acceptance rate equals the false rejection rate, was derived in order to characterize the verification process performance (see Figure 3-a for a summary of the PCA-based classification algorithm).

3.2 Bilateral 2D Principal Component Analysis (B2DPCA)

Kong et al. [3] suggested a generalization of the 2DPCA method, that consists on performing a 2D principal component analysis using two projection matrices, P_L and P_R, which multiply every 2D image from both sides, left and right respectively:

$$C_i = P_L^{\,T} A_i P_R . \qquad (2)$$

The size of P_L is $h{\times}l$ and the size of P_R is $w{\times}r$. Therefore the projection coefficients C_i form a matrix of size $l{\times}r$. Both matrices P_L and P_R are computed with a very fast-convergent iterative process [3], based on the minimization of the approximation error between the original images and their projection in the B2DPCA framework.

In our experiments, we considered l equal to r, so that the projections C_i are square matrices. We then transformed these projections matrices into 1D vectors via row

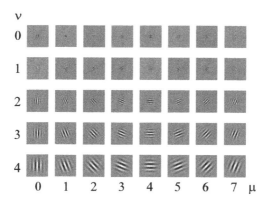

Fig. 2. Real part of the set of 40 Gabor wavelets ordered by frequency (ν) and orientation (μ)

concatenation and transposition in order to train a SVM classifier. An overall ROC curve and the corresponding EER were computed using the resulting SVM scores (see Figure 3-a for a summary of the B2DPCA-based classification algorithm).

3.3 Parallel Gabor Methods

Following notation in [13], Gabor wavelets can be defined as the product of a complex wave and a Gaussian envelope (Figure 2):

$$\psi_{\mu\nu}(\vec{r}) = \frac{k_\nu^2}{\sigma^2}\exp\left(-\frac{k_\nu^2\|\vec{r}\|^2}{2\sigma^2}\right)\left[\exp\left(i\vec{k}_{\mu\nu}\cdot\vec{r}\right)-\exp\left(-\frac{\sigma^2}{2}\right)\right] \quad , \tag{3}$$

where $\vec{r} = (x, y)$, the σ parameter is equal to 2π, the wave vector is defined as $\vec{k}_{\mu\nu} = k_\nu\left(\cos\varphi_\mu, \sin\varphi_\mu\right)$ with a module equal to to $k_\nu = 2^{(-(\nu+2)/2)}\pi$ and an orientation $\varphi_\mu = \mu\pi/8$ radians. Usual values of μ and ν are $0 \le \mu \le 7$ (that represents 8 orientations) and $0 \le \nu \le 4$ (5 frequencies), respectively.

The convolution of an image A_i with a wavelet $\varphi_{\mu\nu}$ is a complex matrix of size $h \times w$. It is usual to consider only the magnitude in further computations, instead of the complex value of the convolution. In [11] it was shown that the convolution with a set of Gabor wavelets can be performed in parallel. In this scenario, the face database is convolved with the first wavelet and the results are fed to a dimension reduction algorithm, such as a PCA or a B2DPCA, and then to a classifier, such as SVM. After computing the corresponding classification scores, the whole process is repeated with the following wavelet. Once the 40 Gabor wavelets have been used independently, a final classifier fusion is performed by considering the average of the scores obtained from the SVM for each wavelet. This process can be divided in the following steps (Figure 3-b):

1. The first phase consists on the convolution of the images in the gallery database set with the wavelet of orientation μ and frequency ν. Therefore we generate an alternative gallery database, where each image has been obtained after a convolution with a certain Gabor wavelet.

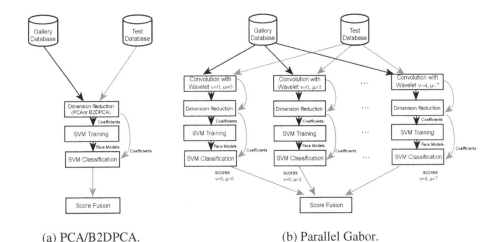

(a) PCA/B2DPCA.   (b) Parallel Gabor.

Fig. 3. A schematic view of the PCA/B2DPCA (a), and Parallel Gabor (b) methods. In both cases, the black arrows correspond to the training phase, where the gallery database is used to train the SVMs and to generate the face model for each subject. The grey arrows correspond to the test phase, where the test database is used to perform the SVM classification and the fusion of the scores.

2. Then, a dimension reduction process is applied. We propose to use a B2DPCA or a standard PCA.
3. With the projection coefficients computed in the previous step, a set of SVM classifiers are trained, one per each subject in the database. For a certain person, the coefficients of his/her images are considered as genuine values, while those of the remainder subjects are used as fake values. Each SVM yields a face model for every subject in the database.
4. Next, the images in the test database set, which are different to those in the gallery database, are convolved with the wavelet of orientation μ and frequency ν. These convolutions are then projected onto the eigenvector framework (PCA or B2DPCA) and the resulting coefficients are evaluated into the set of the previously trained SVMs.
5. Every classifier produces a set of numerical scores: the more positive, the more confident is the acceptance, and the more negative, the more confident is the rejection. For intermediate values, the classifier is not able to verify the identity of the subject. We compute the scores obtained for all subjects in the test set considering each SVM face model. The resulting scores for all the SVMs are then concatenated to a unique score vector, to be used in the final score fusion.
6. After repeating the steps 1–5 for each Gabor wavelet (considering every orientation μ and every frequency ν), we obtain 40 score vectors. Then we perform the fusion of scores by averaging them element-wise. Finally, a unique ROC curve and the corresponding EER can be computed.

4   Results and Discussion

4.1   Influence of the Strategy for the Fusion of Scores for Parallel Gabor Methods

First of all, we consider the 2-image training and 2-image test experiment (only frontal views with neutral expression and diffuse illumination). We compared the Parallel Gabor PCA method with the Parallel Gabor B2DPCA. For every Gabor wavelet, there is a set of scores obtained from the SVM classification of the test database (step 5 in the Section 3.3).

We have considered three different strategies for the fusion of the scores of these 40 sets: an element-wise average of the scores (from now on called "raw average"), a previous normalization of the scores into the range 0–1, followed by an element-wise average as before ("normalized average") and a previous standardization of the scores, transforming them into zero mean and unit variance and then an element-wise average as before ("standardized average").

The results obtained for the test database are presented in Table 1. The raw average strategy yields the best results in both Parallel Gabor methods compared to the normalized average and the standardized average. Parallel Gabor B2DPCA improves Parallel Gabor PCA (EER equal to 0.14% vs. 0.15%), but it needs a bigger dimensionality for the projection coefficients (22×22 vs. 185).

Table 1. Best equal error rate and corresponding dimensionality for the Parallel Gabor Methods for the 2-image training and 2-image test experiment, considering three types of fusion of scores

	Parallel Gabor PCA			Parallel Gabor B2DPCA		
	Raw average	Normalized average	Standardized average	Raw average	Normalized average	Standardized average
EER (%)	0.15	0.18	0.19	0.14	0.16	0.18
Dimension	185	205	205	22×22	20×20	18×18

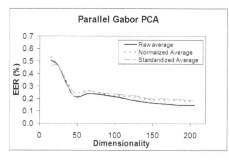
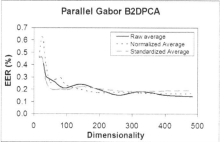

Fig. 4. Evolution of the EER for Parallel Gabor PCA and Parallel Gabor B2DPCA, with a raw average of the scores (continuous line), a normalization of scores to the range 0–1 plus an average (dashed line) and a standardization of scores to zero mean and unit variance plus an average (long dashed line)

Figure 4 shows the evolution of the EER for both Parallel Gabor methods, with the three strategies of fusion of scores. For Parallel Gabor PCA, the raw average always produces the lowest error. However, for Parallel Gabor B2DPCA, the raw average and the normalized average alternate to yield the lowest error, depending on the dimensionality considered. As a comparison, the best EER for PCA in this experiment was 2.98% (dimensionality 150), for B2DPCA it was 2.01% (dimensionality 18×18).

4.2 Comparison of the Parallel Gabor Methods

The previous experiment showed that the best EER for both Parallel Gabor methods was obtained with the raw average of the scores. Therefore, this will be the fusing strategy considered in the 4-image training and 4-image test experiment. In this case, four different test sets were considered: frontal image with diffuse illumination, gestures, occlusions and frontal image with zenithal illumination.

Table 2. EER (%) obtained when the test set contains (a) frontal images with diffuse illumination, (b) images with gestures, (c) images with occlusions and (d) frontal images with zenithal illumination

	Dimension	PCA	Parallel Gabor PCA	Dimension	B2DPCA	Parallel Gabor B2DPCA
	20	1.80	0.23	4×4	2.74	0.23
(a)	50	0.69	0.0064	7×7	0.67	0.030
	100	0.46	*0.0021*	10×10	0.46	*0.0021*
	150	0.46	*0.0021*	12×12	0.46	*0.0021*
	20	12.98	7.80	4×4	15.83	8.90
(b)	50	9.40	5.73	7×7	10.76	5.68
	100	8.03	5.15	10×10	8.38	5.28
	150	7.34	*4.94*	12×12	8.72	5.06
	20	41.51	30.73	4×4	47.25	31.48
(c)	50	37.39	24.06	7×7	39.91	25.26
	100	33.79	23.41	10×10	36.38	23.40
	150	32.34	23.10	12×12	36.99	*22.71*
	20	5.28	1.83	4×4	9.19	2.98
(d)	50	3.07	0.46	7×7	2.73	0.69
	100	2.06	*0.23*	10×10	2.30	0.34
	150	1.84	*0.23*	12×12	1.83	*0.23*

Table 2 shows the evolution of the EER for selected dimensions for the four test sets and the four methods considered here. For images with gestures, the best results are obtained for Parallel Gabor PCA. For images with occlusions, Parallel Gabor B2DPCA is the method that produces the lowest error. For the remainder test sets (frontal images with diffuse illumination and zenithal illumination, respectively), both algorithms draw with the same EER. As a summary, the results obtained for Parallel Gabor B2DPCA were similar to those for Parallel Gabor PCA. Therefore, these methods seem to be robust regarding the dimension reduction technique.

5 Conclusions

In this paper, we presented a new method for the fusion of SVM classifiers obtained from Parallel Gabor B2DPCA for face verification applications. Up to now, B2DPCA had not been previously combined with Gabor wavelets. We developed two experiments with the public domain FRAV2D face database.

In the first one (2-image-per-person training and 2-image-per-person test), the best results were obtained when an element-wise average of the SVM scores was applied. In this case, the Parallel Gabor B2DPCA obtained a better error than the Parallel Gabor PCA (0.14 % vs. 0.15 %).

In the second experiment (4-image-per-person training and 4-image-per-person tests), the Parallel Gabor Methods obtained similar results, outperforming the standard dimension reduction techniques (PCA and B2DPCA). Although further experiments are needed to draw definitive conclusions, the Parallel Gabor Methods proposed here seem to be robust regarding the dimension reduction technique.

As future work, we will enlarge the battery of tests to take into account other dimension reduction methods. Other combination of information techniques for SVM will be used [14]. We will also consider the analysis of other public face databases to evaluate our methods.

Acknowledgments. A part of this work has been carried out at the University of Nottingham (United Kingdom), with financial support of the Universidad Rey Juan Carlos of Madrid (Spain). Special thanks have to be given to Ian Dryden, from the School of Mathematics of the University of Nottingham, for his interesting discussions.

References

1. Turk, M., Pentland, A.: Eigenfaces for Recognition. Journal of Cognitive Neuroscience, Vol. 3, Issue 1 (1991) 71–86.
2. Yang, J., Zhang, D., Frangi, A., Yang, J.-Y.: Two-Dimensional PCA: A new approach to appearance-based face representation and recognition. IEEE Transactions on Pattern Analysis and Machine Intelligence, Vol. 26, No. 1 (2004) 131–137.
3. Kong, H., Wang, L., Teoh, E. K., Li, X., Wang, J.-G., Venkateswarlu, R.: Generalized 2D principal component analysis for face image representation and recognition. Neural Networks, Vol. 18, Issues 5–6 (2005) 585–594.
4. Daugman, J.G.: Uncertainty relation for resolution in space, spatial-frequency and orientation optimized by two-dimensional visual cortical filters. Journal of the Optical Society of America A: Optics Image Science and Vision, Vol. 2, Issue 7 (1985) 1160–1169.
5. Chung, K.-C., Kee, S.C., Kim, S.R.: Face Recognition using Principal Component Analysis of Gabor Filter Responses. International Workshop on Recognition, Analysis and Tracking of Faces and Gestures in Real-Time Systems (1999) 53–57.
6. Liu, C.J., Wechsler, H.: Gabor feature based classification using the enhanced Fisher linear discriminant model for face recognition. IEEE Transactions on Image Processing, Vol. 11, Issue 4 (2002) 467–476.

7. Shen, L., Bai, L.: Face recognition based on Gabor features using kernel methods. 6th IEEE Conference on Face and Gesture Recognition (2004) 170–175.
8. Fan, W., Wang, Y., Liu, W., Tan, T.: Combining Null Space-Based Gabor Features for Face Recognition. 17th International Conference on Pattern Recognition ICPR'04, Vol. 1, (2004) 330–333.
9. Qin, J., He, Z.-S.: A SVM face recognition method based on Gabor-featured key points. 4th International Conference on Machine Learning and Cybernetics, Vol. 8 (2005) 5144–5149.
10. Vapnik, V.N.: The Nature of Statistical Learning Theory, Springer Verlag (1995).
11. Serrano, Á., Conde, C., Martín de Diego, I., Cabello, E., Bai, L., Shen, L.: Parallel Gabor PCA with fusion of SVM scores for face verification. 2nd International Conference on Computer Vision Theory and Applications (2007), accepted for publication.
12. FRAV Database, http://frav.escet.urjc.es/databases/FRAV2D/
13. Wiskott, L., Fellous, J.M., Kruger, N., von der Malsburg, C.: Face recognition by Elastic Bunch Graph Matching. IEEE Transactions on Pattern Analysis and Machine Intelligence, Vol. 19, Issue 7 (1997) 775–779.
14. Martín de Diego, I., Muñoz, A., M Moguerza, J.: On the Combination of Kernels for Support Vector Classifiers. Submitted.

Serial Fusion of Fingerprint and Face Matchers

Gian Luca Marcialis and Fabio Roli

Department of Electrical and Electronic Engineering – University of Cagliari
Piazza d'Armi – I-01923 Cagliari Italy
{marcialis,roli}@diee.unica.it

Abstract. The serial fusion of multiple biometric traits for personal identity verification has been poorly investigated so far. However, this approach exhibits some potential advantages, for example, the possibility of reducing the verification time for genuine users and the requested degree of user cooperation. Moreover, the use of multiple biometrics can discourage fraudulent attempts to deceive the system. In this paper, some preliminary results on a novel approach to multi-modal serial fusion are reported, with comparative results against the commonly used parallel fusion of face and fingerprint matchers.

1 Introduction

In the last years, fusion of multiple biometric matchers has been widely investigated [1-5]. The commonly adopted approach is the so-called score-level parallel fusion. In other words, the matching scores obtained from different matchers are combined in parallel, and the acceptance threshold is evaluated on the new score interval.

It has been widely shown that the multi-modal fusion allows obtaining more robust results [5-6] against environmental conditions changes and, in the case of multi-sensor or multiple biometrics fusion, has the potential advantage of discouraging fraudulent attempts to deceive the system. Accordingly, among the others, the fusion of multiple biometrics obtained a notable interest both in academic and industrial communities.

On the other hand, it can be noted that such a multi-modal approach increases the system invasiveness and requires a higher cooperation degree from the users, due to the systematic use of more than one biometric. In the following we refer to these approaches as "parallel" approaches. Although some genuine users could be accepted by using only one biometric trait, the average verification time of parallel fusion is always equal to that of the slowest biometric, both in terms of cooperation required and matching time. Therefore, it has been recently argued that a different fusion scheme, based on the serial processing of multiple biometrics, could be a better trade-off [5, 7]. In these serial systems, the user submits only one trait (the first one in the processing chain), and the system requires further submissions or novel biometrics if there is not enough evidence for classifying the subject as genuine user or impostor. To the best of our knowledge, only the system proposed in [7] is based on this concept, and it uses the Wald test for deciding the subject classification or requiring

M. Haindl, J. Kittler, and F. Roli (Eds.): MCS 2007, LNCS 4472, pp. 151–160, 2007.

further biometrics. This method generalizes the Neyman-Pearson approach proposed in [8].

In this paper, we propose a simple approach to the serial fusion of face and fingerprint matchers. This approach generalizes the processing architecture commonly used in biometric systems for personal identity verification. Preliminary experiments with two biometrics, namely, face and fingerprint traits, are reported on well-known benchmark data sets. We also report some comparative results against the commonly used parallel fusion based on score averaging.

The paper is organized as follows. Section 2 describes the proposed system. Section 3 describes the individual matchers adopted. Section 4 reports the experiments. Section 5 draws some preliminary conclusions.

2   The Proposed Serial Fusion Architecture

In personal verification systems, based, for example, on fingerprints, the person to be authenticated submits to the system her/his fingerprint and identity. The system matches the input fingerprint with the one associated to the given identity and stored in its database. A degree of similarity, named score, is computed. The score usually range in [0,1] interval. If the score is higher than a certain value (the so called acceptance threshold), the claimed identity is accepted and the person is classified as a genuine user. Otherwise, she/he is classified as an impostor and the access to the required resource is denied. It is worth remarking that the score is the similarity degree between the input biometric and the related template.

Given a certain acceptance threshold value, the performance of the matcher is assessed in terms of false acceptance rate (FAR) as the percentage of accepted impostors, and false rejection rate (FRR) as the percentage of rejected genuine users. FAR and FRR derive from the score distributions of impostors and genuine users, respectively, as follows:

$$FAR(s^*) = \int_{s^*}^{1} p(s \mid impostor)ds \tag{1}$$

$$FRR(s^*) = \int_{0}^{s^*} p(s \mid genuine)ds \tag{2}$$

Where s^* is the given acceptance threshold.

With reference to the above verification scheme, we propose the two-stage serial architecture depicted in Figure 1. According to this figure, the subject submits to the system the first biometric which is processed and matched against the related template. If the resulting score is more than a predefined upper threshold, she/he is accepted as a genuine user. If the score is less than a predefined lower threshold, she/he is rejected as an impostor. Otherwise, the system requires a second biometric.

On the basis of it the subject is finally accepted or rejected. It is easy to see that this scheme can be extended to more than two biometrics.

The rationale behind this triple thresholds approach is similar to that related to the "reject option" introduced in other works [9-10]. We exemplified it in Figure 2. Since the matching score is a similarity value, we can consider three regions: in the first one it is low enough to classify the subject as an impostor, in the second one it is high enough to include the subject in the genuine users class, the third one is an "uncertainty region". In this region, the error functions, that is, FAR and FRR, are overlapped, thus it is very difficult to assess the reliability of the matcher decision. On the other hand, the subject can be classified at once if the related matching score is high (or low) enough.

The crucial issue in this architecture is how to set the lower and upper acceptance thresholds. In the following we give a possible solution which derives from practical considerations. But it is worth remarking that such solution is not the best one, and other solutions can be given as well (e.g. by defining some formal "optimality concept"), for example depending on the operative environment (the security degree that would be achieved), thus obtaining different ROC curves. In order to easily set the lower and upper acceptance thresholds, the first stage matcher should reject or "not classify" all impostors, thus requiring the second biometric for all them. On the other hand, the first stage matcher should accept all genuine users, or, at most, "not classify" them. It is crucial that the first stage matcher rejects no genuine users before allowing them to being accepted by the second stage matcher.

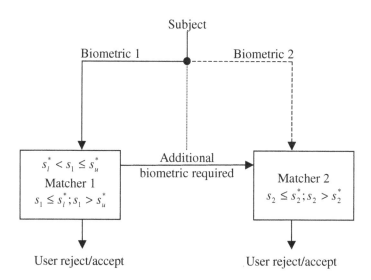

Fig. 1. The proposed serial scheme to serial person verification. The subject submits the biometric 1 which is used to classify him on the basis of lower and upper thresholds s_l^* and s_u^*. If the score falls into the $(s_l^*, s_u^*]$ interval, an additional biometric ("biometric 2") is required and the subject is finally classified.

Accordingly, we set the lower threshold to the zeroFRR operational point, which assures that genuine users are not rejected with 0% error probability (FRR=0%), and the upper threshold to the zeroFAR operational point, which assures that impostor are not accepted with 0% error probability (FAR=0%). This is pointed out in Figure 2, where the "uncertainty region" corresponds to the $(s_l^*, s_u^*]$ interval set between zeroFRR and zeroFAR operational points.

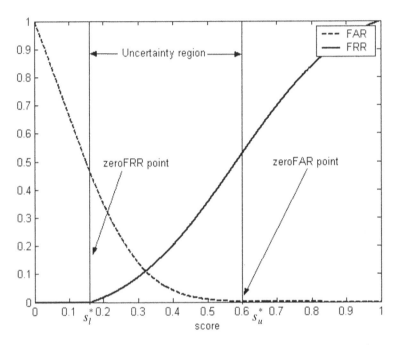

Fig. 2. FAR and FRR for each score value. The subject classification can be devoted to a secondary matcher in the uncertainty region. In the figure we pointed with s_l^* and s_u^* two possible lower and upper acceptance thresholds.

3   Face and Fingerprint Matchers

The face matcher we used in our experiments is based on the Linear Discriminant Analysis transformation. The Linear Discriminant Analysis (also called Fisher Discriminant Analysis) is defined by the transformation [11]:

$$y = W_{LDA}^t x \tag{3}$$

Where x is the original face image, and y the transformed pattern. The columns of W_{LDA} matrix are the eigenvectors of $S_w^{-1} S_b$, where S_w is the *within-class scatter matrix*, and S_b is the *between-class scatter matrix*. It is possible to show that this choice maximizes the ratio $\det(S_b)/\det(S_w)$.

These matrices are computed as follows:

$$S_w = \sum_{j=1}^{c}\sum_{i=1}^{n_j}(x_i^j - m_j)\cdot(x_i^j - m_j)^t \ , \quad m_j = \frac{1}{n_j}\sum_{i=1}^{n_j}x_i^j \tag{4}$$

Where x_i^j is the *i*-th pattern of *j*-th class (subject), and n_j is the number of patterns for the *j*-th class.

$$S_b = \sum_{j=1}^{c}(m_j - m)\cdot(m_j - m)^t \ , \quad m = \frac{1}{n}\sum_{i=1}^{n}x_i \tag{5}$$

The eigenvectors of LDA are called "fisherfaces" and the components of the transformed space are the most discriminant features. Since the LDA transformation cannot be computed if the inequality $n >= d + c$ does not hold, where n is the number of samples, d is the original space dimensionality, c is the number of classes, we first performed a transformation of the face space to an intermediate feature space with reduced dimensionality $d_{intermediate} << d$. In particular, the PCA transform has been used to generate such intermediate space according to the Belhumeur et al.'s idea [11]. The matching score between two face image transformed in the LDA space is given by the normalized cosine function of the two patterns as follows:

$$score = 0.5 \cdot (\cos(t, y)+1) \tag{6}$$

Where y is the input face image and t is the template face image.

The fingerprint matcher is based on the well-known String algorithm [12]. The String algorithm uses the minutiae-points as a string of features. The so-called "minutiae" points correspond to the bifurcations and the terminations of the ridge lines. In this paper, minutiae have been extracted from the skeletonised fingerprint images obtained by the commonly used enhancement, binarization and post-processing phases. Two fingerprints are compared by the respective set of minutiae points, so generating a matching score. This score is proportional to the number of minutiae couples of the two fingerprints which can be considered as "aligned". Briefly, let X be the template minutiae set. Let T be the input minutiae set. For each minutia $x \in X$, the following algorithm is performed. For each $t \in T$, x is aligned to t. After this alignment, x and t match perfectly. Let $A(x, t) = \{(x_i,t_i), x_i \in X, t_i \in T : aligned(x_i,t_i)= true\}$ be the set of other couples of aligned minutiae. x_i and t_i are considered as aligned on the basis of a pre-defined "minutiae distance" not exceeding a certain fixed threshold. At the end of these loops, the value $\max_{x,t}\{|A(x,t)|\}$ is converted to the matching score by the formula:

$$score = \frac{\left(\max\{|A(x,t)|\}\right)^2}{|X|\cdot|T|} \tag{7}$$

4 Experimental Results

4.1 Data Sets

We performed experiments by using a "chimerical" data set made up of face images coming from the AR data set and fingerprint images coming from the FVC2000-DB2 data set. It is worth noting that composing artificial data sets is reasonable in this case because no correlation has been shown between face and fingerprint images of the same subject.

Therefore, we created our multi-modal data set by combining the AR face data set [13] and the FVC-2000 DB2 data set [14].

The AR data set is characterised by pictures taken under strictly controlled conditions. No restrictions on wear (clothes, glasses, etc.), make-up, hair style, etc. were imposed to participants. Each person participated in two sessions, separated by two weeks (14 days) time. The same pictures were taken in both sessions. Each session is made up of seven images under different environmental conditions. We selected 100 subjects (50 males and 50 females) and considered the first session to compute the parameters of the LDA transformation and the templates of each subject (the average vector was computed). We manually cropped faces and, after histogram stretching and equalization, resized them at 80x80 pixels. The FVC2000 data sets are made up of 800 fingerprint images. The number of subjects is 100. The DB2 data set has been obtained by acquiring fingerprints with a capacitive sensor (256x364 pixel per image). The capacitive acquisition source exhibit the following characteristics. Briefly, it evaluates the capacitance between the silicon-based acquisition surface and the finger skin, being this capacitance different from ridges to valleys. Further details about this acquisition principle can be found in [15].

Examples of face and fingerprint images from FVC2000-DB2 data set are shown in Figure 3(b).

| (a) | (b) |

Fig. 3. (a) Example of face images from the AR data set. (b) Example of fingerprint images from the FVC2000-DB2 data set.

The first fingerprint impression of each subject has been considered as the template, which was coupled with the related face template.

The remaining seven fingerprint impressions were randomly coupled with the seven face images of the AR second session. The so obtained 700 couples of fingerprints and faces were used as "evaluation set".

We further subdivided the evaluation set as follows: two couples were used as gallery set, in order to compute the thresholds of the serial model. The rest of the data was used as probe set, i.e., to test the algorithms in presence of novel patterns. Accordingly, we obtained:

- 200 genuine matching scores couples and 19,800 impostor matching scores couples in the gallery set;
- 500 genuine matching scores couples and 49,500 impostor matching scores couples in the probe set.

In order to obtain significant results from the artificial multi-modal data set, we permutated three times the subjects each other (e.g. fingerprints of subject i were couple with faces of subject j) and five times the impressions each others (e.g. the face impression h was coupled with the fingerprint impression k). Therefore, the performance evaluation is related to the mean of fifteen different coupling of faces and fingerprints.

Performances were assessed and compared in terms of the Receiver Operating Characteristic curves (ROC), which plot the percentage of false acceptances (FAR) and false rejections (FRR) in function of a given set of threshold values.

4.2 Results

Figure 4 shows the ROC curves of the individual matcher on the gallery set. In particular, zeroFAR values for the face and fingerprint matchers are 52.1% and 20.5%, and zeroFRR values are 38.7% and 35.7%, respectively. They point out that the fingerprint matcher performs much better than the face one. Accordingly, the fingerprint matcher should be considered at the first stage, because the percentage of subjects to be accepted by using the second matcher is reduced.

By applying to the probe set the thresholds computed on the gallery, we obtained the ROC curves shown in Figure 5. In this Figure, we show the performance of the

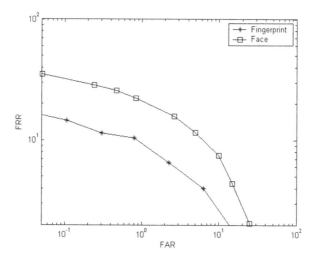

Fig. 4. ROC curves of the individual matchers on the gallery set

best individual matcher, the serial fusion using the face or fingerprint matcher at the first stage, and the parallel system obtained by averaging face and fingerprint matches scores. Figure 5 shows that the serial systems significantly improve the performance with respect to the best individual one.

On average, the serial systems exhibit a performance similar to that of the parallel fusion (similar results has been obtained by multiplying matching scores in parallel fusion). However, in order to appreciate the obtained performance, it should be considered the percentage of subjects accepted by the first stage matcher. These values are reported in Table 1 and are related to the probe set. In particular, 74.8% of genuine users are accepted when using the fingerprint trait at the first stage, whilst this value is 46.6% when using the face trait at the first stage (second column, third and fourth rows of Table 1). This has a favourable impact (1) on the acceptability of this system, because only one biometric is required to the most of genuine users; (2) on the verification time, especially if the first matcher is the fastest one. As an example, in our experiments the verification time of face and fingerprint matchers is 0.1 sec and 3.0 sec, respectively. By considering the face matcher at the first stage, the average verification time of genuine users is reduced to 1.5 sec. The parallel system verification time is obviously 3.0 sec, thus the verification time reduction is about 50%.

On the other hand, it is easy to see that only 1.0% of impostors are wrongly accepted (third column, third and fourth rows of Table 1). This clearly means that they are rejected at the first stage or are constrained to submit the second biometric.

Therefore, the proposed system fitted quite well the trade-off between performance, verification time and acceptability, which are practical requirement of notable applicative relevance in the design of personal verification systems.

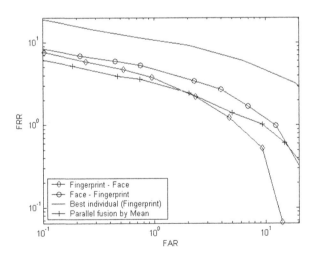

Fig. 5. ROC curves on the probe set of the best individual matcher, the serial fusion of face and fingerprint matchers (Fingerprint-Face and Face-Fingerprint) and the parallel fusion by matching scores averaging

Table 1. Genuine users ed impostors of the probe set accepted by the first stage matcher. The third and fourth rows are related to the face matcher and the fingerprint matcher at the first stage, respectively.

	First stage matcher – Accepted patterns	
	Genuine users	**Impostors**
Face-Fingerprint	46.6%	1.0%
Fingerprint-Face	74.8%	1.0%

5 Conclusions

Despite of its potential advantages, the serial fusion of multiple matchers has been poorly investigated so far. In this paper, we proposed a serial approach for fusion of multiple matchers, and investigated, in particular, the case of face and fingerprint matchers.

Reported results on well-known benchmark data sets showed that the proposed system performed similarly to commonly used parallel fusion approaches. Moreover, the percentage of subject accepted by the first stage matcher showed that it is possible to reduce the cooperation degree and the average verification time of genuine users, which favourably impacted on the acceptability of multimodal systems.

The proposed system can be easily extended to more than two biometrics, but some issues are still open, among the others, if the parallel fusion of overall matching scores at the last stage could be useful for further improving performances, and how to decide the collocation of each matcher into the processing chain (in particular, which matcher has to be inserted at the first stage?), especially by considering different evaluation parameters, as the performance and the average verification time.

Acknowledgments

This work was partially supported by the Italian Ministry of University and Scientific Research (MIUR) in the framework of the research project on Multi-modal Biometric and Pattern Recognition Systems for Video Surveillance and Security in Computer Systems.

References

[1] L. Hong and A.K. Jain, Integrating faces and fingerprints for person identification, *IEEE Transactions on Pattern Analysis and Machine Intelligence*, 20 (12) 1295-1307, 1998.
[2] A. Ross and A.K. Jain, Information Fusion in Biometrics, *Pattern Recognition Letters*, 24 (13) 2115-2125, 2003.
[3] P. Verlinde, P. Druyts, G. Chollet, M. Acheroy, M., A multi-level data fusion approach for gradually upgrading the performances of identity verification systems, *Sensor Fusion: Architectures, Algorithms and Application III*, B. Dasarathy Ed., vol.3719, pp.14-25, Orlando, FL, USA, SPIE Press, 1999.

[4] G.L. Marcialis and F. Roli, Fingerprint verification by fusion of optical and capacitive sensors, *Pattern Recognition Letters*, 25 (11) 1315-1322, 2004.

[5] A. Ross, K. Nandakumar, A.K. Jain, *Handbook of multibiometrics*, Springer, 2006.

[6] G.L. Marcialis and F. Roli, Decision-level fusion of PCA and LDA-based face recognition algorithms, *International Journal of Image and Graphics*, 6 (2) 293-311, 2006.

[7] K. Takabashi, M. Mimura, Y. Isobe, Y. Seto, A secure and user-friendly multi-modal biometric system, *Biometric Technology for Human Identification*, A.K. Jain, N.K. Ratha (Eds.), Proceedings of the SPIE, Vol. 5404, pp. 12-19, 2004.

[8] S. Prabhakar and A.K. Jain, Decision-level fusion in fingerprint verification, *Pattern Recognition*, 35 (4) 861-874, 2002.

[9] P. Pudil, J. Novovicova, S. Blaha, J. Kittler, Multistage Pattern Recognition with Reject Option. Proc. 11th IAPR-ICPR international conference, vol. 2, pp. 92-95, 1992.

[10] C. Sansone, M. Vento, Signature verification: increasing performance by a multi-stage system, *Pattern Analysis and Applications*, 3 169-181, 2000.

[11] P.N. Belhumeur, J.P. Hespanha, D.J. Kriegman, Eigenfaces vs. Fisherfaces: Recognition Using Class Specific Linear Projection, *IEEE Transactions on Pattern Analysis and Machine Intelligence*, 19 (7) 711-720, 1997.

[12] A.K. Jain, L. Hong, R. Bolle, On-line fingerprint verification, *IEEE Transactions on Pattern Analysis and Machine Intelligence*, 19 (4) 302-314, 1997.

[13] A. Martinez and R. Benavente, The AR Face Database, CVC Technical Report #24, 1998.

[14] D. Maio, D. Maltoni, R. Cappelli, J.L. Wayman, A.K. Jain, FVC-2000: Fingerprint Verification Competition, *IEEE Transactions on Pattern Analysis and Machine Intelligence*, 24 (3) 402-41, 2002.

[15] X. Xia, and L. O'Gorman, Innovations in fingerprint capture devices, *Pattern Recognition*, 36 (2) 361-369, 2003.

Boosting Lite – Handling Larger Datasets and Slower Base Classifiers

Lawrence O. Hall[1], Robert E. Banfield[1], Kevin W. Bowyer[2],
and W. Philip Kegelmeyer[3]

[1] Department of Computer Science & Engineering
University of South Florida
Tampa, Florida 33620-5399
{hall,rbanfiel}@csee.usf.edu
[2] Computer Science & Engineering
384 Fitzpatrick Hall, Notre Dame, IN 46556
[3] Sandia National Labs
Computational Sciences and Math Research Department
PO Box 969, MS 9159
wpk@sandia.gov

Abstract. In this paper, we examine ensemble algorithms (Boosting Lite and Ivoting) that provide accuracy approximating a single classifier, but which require significantly fewer training examples. Such algorithms allow ensemble methods to operate on very large data sets or use very slow learning algorithms. Boosting Lite is compared with Ivoting, standard boosting, and building a single classifier. Comparisons are done on 11 data sets to which other approaches have been applied. We find that ensembles of support vector machines can attain higher accuracy with less data than ensembles of decision trees. We find that Ivoting may result in higher accuracy ensembles on some data sets, however Boosting Lite is generally able to indicate when boosting will increase overall accuracy.

Keywords: classifier ensembles, boosting, support vector machines, decision trees.

1 Introduction

A boosted ensemble of classifiers is typically created to get higher accuracy for a particular type of base classifier on a particular data set. Here, we are going to instead examine how boosting may be used to deal with data sets that have a large number of examples and/or learning algorithms that are very time-consuming. In [1], Pavlov et. al. examined several methods for speeding up the learning process for support vector machines. One of those methods used boosting on a small subset of the data and reported good accuracies and significantly decreased learning times.

In this paper, we present a learning algorithm along the same lines as in [1], that we call Boosting Lite. The idea is to build the classifiers in the ensemble with

M. Haindl, J. Kittler, and F. Roli (Eds.): MCS 2007, LNCS 4472, pp. 161–170, 2007.

small subsets of the available training data. The goal is to obtain approximately the same accuracy that you would get with a boosted ensemble or from a single classifier. Obviously, building each classifier with a small subset of the data will be much faster than using all the data. Hence, we look for a time savings and therefore the ability to better scale to large data sets.

In [2] Ivoting was shown to provide boosting-like results using a subset of the overall training data. This idea was further explored in a distributed system context in [3] where the accuracy was shown to be comparable to that of boosting. The Boosting Lite approach is much closer to standard boosting than is Ivoting. We will compare it to Ivoting results using eleven data sets. Also, for three data sets we compare Boosting Lite with SVMs as the base classifier.

2   Related Work

This work is motivated in part by the Boost-SMO algorithm introduced in [4] and again briefly discussed in [1]. Using linear support vector machines (SVM), between 1% and 90% of the training data was used in the creation of a boosted ensemble. The authors do not indicate how large any individual ensemble was, but indicate it was typically from 10 to 15 classifiers. They do indicate that they stopped when a specified maximum ensemble size was reached or the error of the current SVM was within ϵ of 0.5. Their version of a boosting algorithm was modified from standard boosting described in [5]. It was unclear whether a subset was initially selected or new subsets were selected from all the data for each classifier. From a personal communication [6], we found that a new subset of size x% was selected from all the re-weighted training data for each new classifier. On four data sets, they were able to show that it was possible to obtain the same accuracy as using an SVM-SMO model built on all the data by using as little as 2-5% of the data to train each classifier. The training time was from 3 to 400 times faster. However, the factor of 400 time result used 1% Boost-SMO which did not produce an ensemble classifier that was as accurate as using all the data (it was 0.6% less accurate in that case).

The Boost-SMO algorithm was not adapted for use with any other base classifier. The utility of an adaptation to decision trees is explored here. Work on Ivoting [2,3], which is a boosting-like approach that has been applied to decision trees, suggests that the adaptation may be useful. Ivoting works as follows. An example is randomly selected from the full data set with all examples having the same probability of being selected. If it is incorrectly classified by the classifiers in the existing ensemble that do not have it in its training set, then it goes into the training set for the next classifier. Otherwise, it goes into the training set with probability $\frac{e(k)}{1-e(k)}$, where e(k) is the error estimate at stage k.

The sizes of the training sets in the original work [2] were one of 100, 200, 400 or 800 examples. Experiments used five data sets that ranged from 2000 examples to 43,500 examples. So, relatively small subsets, from roughly 1.8% to 40% of the data, were used for each training set. Boost-SMO used a percentage of the total training data size. At 5% of the data, which resulted in good accuracy, training sets would range from 100 to 2175 examples, which is slightly larger than used in [2].

A distributed version of Ivoting called DIvoting has also been introduced [3]. Accuracies were found to approximate Adaboost accuracies in many cases. That is, they were even higher than for a single classifier in many cases. Further, DIvoting also showed significant reductions in the time required to build an Adaboost-equivalent ensemble. Still, DIvoting was not faster than building a single decision tree. Decision trees typically require $O(fn \log n)$ time to build a single tree, where n is the number of training samples and f is the number of features. So the time to build an ensemble of size e, each using only $1/k$th of the data, is $O(ef\frac{n}{k} \log(\frac{n}{k}))$. So it scales up linearly with e, but scales down faster than linearly with k. As a result, it is *possible* to build an ensemble of decision trees on $1/k$th of the data more quickly than a single tree on all the data, but it is unlikely unless there is a very large amount of data.

In this paper, we focus on what can be accomplished on a single processor. The previous work raises the question of whether an adaptation of Adaboost.M1W [7], which has been shown to be a highly accurate boosting algorithm for more than two classes, can be effectively applied to small subsets of data for other types of classifiers. In particular, we will look at decision trees. We will compare with Ivoting results in terms of accuracy and whether speedups are possible for decision trees. We will compare with SVMs on 3 data sets, also. The other question that we are investigating is whether Ivoting might be effective in providing fast training for support vector machines.

We compare Boosting Lite experimentally on 11 datasets to (a) regular Adaboost and to (b) a single classifier trained on all the training data, using decision trees. We compare Boosting Lite using decision trees to Boost-SMO using SVMs [1,4] on three data sets by using new experimental numbers for Boosting Lite generated for this paper and published numbers for Boost-SMO on three datasets. We compare Boosting Lite using decision trees to Ivoting [2,3] using decision trees on 7 datasets using new experimental numbers for Boosting Lite generated for this paper and published numbers or approximate numbers from a graph for Ivoting [3].

3   Boosting Lite

The algorithm we are naming Boosting Lite is based on Adaboost.M1W [7]. The differences in implementation are as follows. While all the training data is weighted, only a specified x% of it is chosen for the kth training set. The examples are chosen probabilistically based on their weights, with replacement. So, it is possible for an example to appear in the training set more than one time. The algorithm is shown in Figure 1.

We grow the ensemble until a specified number of classifiers have been added or until the next classifier does not meet the standard boosting criterion for being added to the ensemble. Each of the classifiers in the ensemble is built on

Let I("statement") = 1 iff "statement" is true, and 0 otherwise.
Let x_i be the ith example and c_i denote the class of that example.

Input: Let $L = \{(x_1, c_1), \ldots, (x_n, c_n) : x_i \in X \text{ and } c_i \in C\}$ with $2 \leq |C| \leq n$ and $|X| = n$.
Let h be a classifier that takes in an x_i and generates a class in C.
Let T be the number of boosting rounds

Initialize: $D_i(i) = \frac{1}{n}$.
For $t = 1, \ldots, T$:

- Train a classifier h_t with a subset of size $S << n$ randomly sampled according to the weighted distribution, D_t, where h_t should minimize the weighted error rate:
  $\epsilon_t = \sum_i D_t(i) I(h_t(x_i) \neq c_i)$.

- Set $\alpha_t = \ln(\frac{(|C|-1)(1-\epsilon_t)}{\epsilon_t})$.
- Update D: $D_{t+1}(i) = D_t(i) e^{-\alpha_t I(h_t(x_i)=c_i)} / Z_t$
  where Z_t is a normalization factor (chosen so that D_{t+1} is a distribution)

Output: Set the final classifier $H(x)$: $H(x) = \arg\max_{c \in C} f(x, c) = \arg\max_{c \in C}(\sum_{t=1}^{T} \alpha_t I(h_t(x) = c))$

Fig. 1. Boosting Lite algorithm (a modified version of AdaBoost.M1W)

a rather small subset of the original data set. This enables each classifier to be built more quickly and creates the potential to scale to very large data sets.

The algorithm was applied with the OpenDT [8] decision tree learning algorithm, which is essentially a public domain re-implementation of C4.5 release 8 [9] without pruning, with the RainForest algorithm for evaluating attributes [10] and using the median method for handling missing values. The single tree results come from C4.5 with default pruning (CF=0.25).

4   Data Sets

For comparison purposes we have used all but one of the data sets on which Ivote and SMO-Boost were evaluated in [1,4]. The Reuters data set was not used because we could not re-create the train/test data partitions. The data sets were used with the training and testing sub-divisions from [1,2,3] for comparison. We also include two other data sets which have a good number of examples, **pendigits** and **krk**. Table 1 shows the names of the data sets and their characteristics. They come primarily from the UCI repository [11] and statlog project [12].

The training set sizes range from a modest 4335 examples to 209,529 examples in 315 dimensions. For the **krk** data set that was not previously partitioned into a training and test set, we did a tenfold cross validation to get an average accuracy and time.

Table 1. Description of data sets attributes and size

Data Set	# attributes	# Train ex.	# Test ex.	# classes
adult	14	30162	1560	2
digit	256	7291	2007	10
dna	60	2000	1186	3
forest cover	54	98884	396257	2
Jones	315	209529	17731	3
krk	6	28056	0	18
letter	16	15000	5000	26
pendigits	16	7494	3498	10
shuttle	9	43500	14500	7
satimage	36	4335	2000	6
web	294	31932	4886	2

5   Experimental Results

There were three data sets, **adult, forest cover** and **web,** used in both the
SVM experiments and our experiments. The support vector machine was used
with sequential minimal optimization training (SMO) and 1% of the data. The
first column of Table 2 shows the accuracy from a single tree, and the next three
show the accuracy of ensembles of 100 boosted trees using 1%, 5%, and 100% of
the data. We calculate the difference in accuracy between a single support vector
machine classifier and the boosted SVM ensemble, as well as the single decision
tree accuracy and the 1% Boosting Lite ensemble. The gap between the two
differences is given in the fifth column (BL - SVM). A positive number means
the SVM ensemble is closer to the accuracy of a single SVM than the decision
tree ensemble is to a single tree. For both types of classifier, the ensembles
are less accurate than the single classifier. For each dataset, the difference in
accuracy between an ensemble of decision trees and a single tree is more than
for the ensemble of support vector machines and a single support vector machine.
This suggests that support vector machines may be used to create an accurate
ensemble classifier from less examples than are needed for a decision tree. This
result is particularly striking for the **forest cover** data set where there is over an
11% difference between a single tree and an ensemble of boosted decision trees
built with 1% of the data. For support vector machines, the difference between
the ensemble and a single support vector machine was only 1%.

However, there are two caveats that arise when examining results from these
three data sets. As can be seen in Table 2, boosting does not increase the accuracy
for two of the three data sets when using all the data, at least for decision tree
classifiers. This suggests that more data sets and more experiments are necessary.
The data sets need to be evaluated to determine if they do in fact benefit from
boosting.

It has been shown, for a relatively small number of data sets, that Ivoting can
result in accuracies that are very close to the accuracy of a boosted ensemble for
CART trees [2] and C4.5 trees [3]. Seven of those data sets are included in this

Table 2. Boosting Lite (BL) on decision trees compared with SVM's. The last column compares the gap in ensemble accuracy and single classifier accuracy with a positive number meaning the gap was lower for the SVM's.

Data Set	Single tree	BL-1%	BL-5%	Boosting	BL - SVM
adult	85.97	83.71	84.26	84.56	1.36
forest cover	76.91	65.58	75.06	81.58	10.16
web	76.16	75.1126	75.5014	74.5395	0.41

study. The best accuracy with Ivoting (as reported in the literature) came with a bite-size (training set size) of 800 examples, [2]. In Table 3, we show the results for a single tree and ensembles of size 100 created with 1, 5, and 100% of the data, as well as the accuracy for an Ivoted ensemble and the most comparable accuracy from Boosting Lite. The Ivote results are all from the CART decision tree classifier using bites of 800 examples with three exceptions. The **forest cover, pendigits**, and **Jones** results come from a C4.5 classifier and the **Jones** bite size is 818 [3]. We do not show the Ivote results for **krk** because one cannot obtain good accuracy when subsets are used, as discussed below.

Table 3. Boosting Lite (BL) on decision trees compared with Ivoting

Data Set	Single tree	BL-1%	BL-5%	Boosting	BL Comp	Ivote (800)
digit	86.85	89.44	92.68	94.37	94.22	94.5
dna	92.66	88.11	94.8567	94.941	95.62	96.2
forest cover	76.91	65.58	75.06	81.58	65.57	73.9
Jones	52.78	61.29	62.04	66.97	61.29	64.2
krk	80.73	45.90	69.66	89.17	-	-
letter	81.02	79.96	93.96	97.12	95.88	96.2
pendigits	92.11	94.68	97.03	97.43	96.91	96.97
shuttle	99.95	99.99	99.99	99.99	99.99	99.99
satimage	85.35	82.25	88.05	90.85	90.35	91.3

For Boosting Lite, the results come from a percentage of the training data which is comparable to that of bites with 800 examples and up to 500 trees in the ensemble. In each case, we set the number of trees for Boosting Lite to be equal to the number of iterations Ivoting required to converge to a stable accuracy [2,3]. With the exception of the two data sets with the same type of decision tree classifier, it is not possible to directly compare accuracies. However, we can look at how well the ensemble built with less data per tree did in approximating the accuracy of an ensemble built with all of the data available for each tree. For the **shuttle** data set all types of boosted classifiers are highly accurate. Boosting Lite is within 0.5% in accuracy for the **satellite** and **digit** data sets and exceeds the accuracy of the full ensemble for the **dna** data set.

For the **forest cover, Jones**, and **letter** data sets, a Boosting Lite ensemble results in a classifier that is at least 1% less accurate and as much as 16%

less accurate than Adaboost.M1W on all the data. Ivote (100 trees) is also less accurate than a fully boosted classifier on each of these data sets. However, it is almost equivalent to the results from the boosted CART ensemble for the **letter** data set. It is only 3% less accurate for **forest cover** and 2.7% less accurate for the **Jones** data set. Ivoting is using just over 0.5% of the data for the **forest cover** results and about 0.4% of the data for the **Jones** results. For both **forest cover** and **Jones**, Ivoting results in a higher accuracy ensemble classifier than Boosting Lite even though it uses less than half as much data.

The results with the **pendigits** data set do show a 3% accuracy difference between boosting at 1% and boosting with the full data set. Using 5% of the data results in an ensemble within about 0.4% of the boosted ensemble with all the data. **krk** involves a chess endgame and suffers significant accuracy degradations in a tenfold cross validation with less than 10% of the training data available and up to 500 trees. With 10% of the data available for each tree in the ensemble, it reaches 80.9% accuracy with 200 trees. The nature of this domain likely causes the requirement for more data.

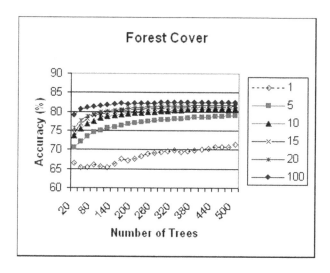

Fig. 2. Boosting Lite and Boosting accuracies on the **forest cover** data

To get an idea of the differences in classifier accuracy for different percentages of the training data and as more trees are added to a Boosting Lite ensemble, we show results for the **forest cover** data set in Figure 2. This data set shows greater differences for different sized training sets than most. The shape of the curves for 5% and greater is typical. It is also the largest data set with most of the data reserved for testing. You can see that with 1% of the data the ensemble never reaches the accuracy of boosting with all the data. With 5% the accuracy gets close and for 15% and 20% the accuracies are very close.

6   Discussion

A question that we were originally interested in was whether there was any possibility of speeding up decision tree construction for large data sets using Boosting Lite. OpenDT uses the RainForest algorithm [10] to avoid sorting data at internal nodes, making it quite a bit faster than older decision tree building algorithms such as C4.5. To look at timing, we took the time required to build a single tree in OpenDT and the time required to prune a C4.5 tree built on the same data and added the two times. This became the time to build a single tree. This can be compared with the time required to build 100 trees using 1% of the data. For more trees and/or more data, there is no time reduction from using the Boosting Lite approach. In fact even with 1% of the data, only for the **web**, **Jones** and **digit** data sets were there any speedups. In these cases, the speedups are 6.7, 1.3 and 1.4 times respectively. However, in general there is a slowdown for the data sets used here under the conditions described. Interestingly, the accuracies were higher than those obtained with a single tree for the **Jones** and **digit** data sets for which speedups were observed. The accuracy on the third (**web**) was higher than boosting with all the data, but 1% lower than a single decision tree.

Boosting Lite on 5% of the data provides accuracies which are greater than those obtained from one tree for all data sets where boosting results in a more accurate ensemble with two exceptions (**krk** and **forest cover**). The **krk** data set would probably not induce a data miner to try using subsets because the search space for chess is known to be large. So, Boosting Lite at 5% could be used to predict whether boosting will help on a data set.

The results indicate that while Boosting Lite is closer to classical boosting in operation than Ivoting, Ivoting seems often more accurate. Ivoting selects examples for the next training set randomly, but primarily admits them to the training set based on error from classifiers that do **not** have them in their training data set (this error rate is often called out of bag error). Ivoting's higher accuracy in some cases seems to indicate that using out of bag accuracy allows for better selection of training examples for the boosted classifiers. Given that Boosting Lite provides significant time savings for support vector machines, this raises the question of whether Ivoting might generally provide more accurate ensembles and maintain the time savings for slower classifiers like support vector machines and potentially neural networks.

7   Summary

In this paper we examined a variant of boosting that was originally introduced for speeding up support vector machine learning and adapted it to decision trees. We found that it appears that, when boosted, support vector machines can learn accurate models from smaller subsamples than decision trees. Boosting with subsampled data using decision trees as the base classifier was faster for 3 of 11 data sets than building a single tree on all the data. In order to have any chance of speeding up the learning on these data sets, the number of trees needed to be limited to 100 and the training set for each tree needed to be limited to 1% of the total training data set size. This is a function of the speed of decision trees and indicates that benefits require larger training sets than used here. Still, Boosting Lite on 5% of the data could be used to predict whether boosting with all the data will help on a data set.

For two of the three data sets used in the support vector machine work [4,1], we found that boosting with decision trees and all of the training data did not result in an increase in accuracy compared to a single decision tree. This result is somewhat anomalous, and suggests that further investigation on a broader range of datasets is needed. Also, we compared with an alternative boosting approach using subsamples, Ivoting. Ivoting was often able to result in a more accurate ensemble. This is likely due to using an error estimate from only trees which were not built with a potential training example in the selection process of examples for succeeding training data sets. Applying Ivoting to SVMs with large data sets has the potential to build accurate classifiers quickly, and it is an area for future research.

Acknowledgments. This research was partially supported by the Department of Energy through the ASCI PPPE Data Discovery Program, Contract number: DE-AC04-76DO00789.

References

1. D. Pavlov, D. Chudova, and P. Smyth. Towards scalable support vector machines using squashing. In *Proceedings of the Sixth ACM SIGKDD International Conference on Knowledge Discovery and Data Mining*, pages 295–299, 2000.
2. L. Breiman. Pasting bites together for prediction in large data sets. *Machine Learning*, 36(1,2):85–103, 1999.
3. N. V. Chawla, L. O. Hall, K. W. Bowyer, and W. P. Kegelmeyer. Learning ensembles from bites: A scalable and accurate approach. *Journal of Machine Learning Research*, 5:421–451, 2004.
4. D. Pavlov, J. Mao, and B. Dom. Scaling-up support vector machines using boosting algorithm. In *15th International Conference on Pattern Recognition*, volume 2, pages 219–222, 2000.
5. R. Schapire. A brief introduction to boosting. In *Proc. of the Sixteenth Intl. Joint Conf. on Artificial Intelligence*, 1999.
6. Dmitry Pavlov. Personal communication, 2006.
7. Gunther Eibl and Karl-Peter Pfeiffer. How to make AdaBoost.M1 work for weak classifiers by changing only one line of the code. In *Machine Learning: Proceedings of the Thirteenth European Conference*, pages 109–120, 2002.
8. Robert Banfield. *OpenDT*, 2005. http://opendt.sourceforge.net/.
9. J. R. Quinlan. *C4.5: programs for machine learning*. Morgan Kaufmann, 1993.
10. J. Gehrke, R. Ramakrishnan, and V. Ganti. Rainforest: A framework for fast decision tree construction of large datasets. *Journal of Data Mining and Knowledge Discovery*, 4(2-3):127–162, 2000.

11. C.J. Merz and P.M. Murphy. *UCI Repository of Machine Learning Databases.* Univ. of CA., Dept. of CIS, Irvine, CA. http://www.ics.uci.edu/~mlearn/MLRepository.html.

12. D. Michie, D. J. Spiegelhalter, and C. C. Taylor. Machine learning, neural and statistical classification, 1994. ftp://ftp.ncc.up.pt/pub/statlog/.

Information Theoretic Combination of Classifiers with Application to AdaBoost

Julien Meynet and Jean-Philippe Thiran

Signal Processing Institute
Ecole Polytechnique Fédérale de Lausanne (EPFL)
CH-1015 Lausanne, Switzerland
julien.meynet@epfl.ch, jp.thiran@epfl.ch
http://itswww.epfl.ch

Abstract. Combining several classifiers has proved to be an efficient machine learning technique. We propose a new measure of the goodness of an ensemble of classifiers in an information theoretic framework. It measures a trade-off between diversty and individual classifier accuracy. This technique can be directly used for the selection of an ensemble in a pool of classifiers. We also propose a variant of AdaBoost for directly training the classifiers by taking into account this new information theoretic measure.

Keywords: classifier combination, information theory, diversity, AdaBoost.

1 Introduction

In many pattern recognition tasks, combining the decisions of several classifiers has shown to be an effective technique for improving the classification performances. For example, training a classifier can become very complex when a large number of features or examples are needed. Such a problem can be addressed by splitting it into lower complexity problems and combine the individual decisions. Dietterich gives in [1] three main reasons why an ensemble of classifier may be a better choice than a monolithic classifier. First, when the same learning accuracies can be achieved by several classifiers, a good solution is to average all their decisions rather than just picking one of them randomly. Then, many learning techniques use local searches to converge toward a solution, with the risk of staying stacked in local optima. Running several searches and combining the solutions can improve the performances. Finally, from a representational point of view, it is possible that the class of functions chosen for learning the classifier does not contain the optimal solution. Combining several functions of this class allows to reach solutions outside of this class. In [2], Freund and Shapire also discuss why averaging classifiers can avoid overfitting.

Many techniques have been proposed in the past few years for combining classifiers. On the first hand, the classifiers can be either trained on different sample subsets or different feature sets or use various learning algorithms. On the second hand, the combination itself can be performed according to two strategies: non trainable combiners (majority vote, probability rules: sum, product, mean, median, etc.) and trainable combiners (weighted majority vote, classifier as combiner, etc...). More detailed surveys on classifier combination can be found in [3] and [4].

M. Haindl, J. Kittler, and F. Roli (Eds.): MCS 2007, LNCS 4472, pp. 171–179, 2007.

The use of an ensemble is only justified if it is better than its best individual member. To fulfill this requirement, classifiers need to commit errors on different new data. This concept defines the notion of diversity between classifiers. Diversity and its relevance in building good ensembles of classifiers will be discussed throughout this paper. An overview of the different diversity measures is given in [5].

In this paper, we introduce an information theoretic framework to define a new measure of the goodness of an ensemble. It is based on the trade-off between the individual accuracies and the diversity between the classifiers. The remaining of the paper is structured as follows: Section 2 gives a short introduction to information theoretic classification. Then section 3 introduces the combination of classifiers in this information theoretic framework. Some experiments and results will be exposed in section 4 and finally some conclusions will be drawn.

2 Information Theoretic Classification

Information theoretic classification was first introduced by Principe et al. in [6]. We summarize its concept here: the classification problem is formulated through the following first order Markov chain:

$$C \rightarrow \hat{C} \rightarrow E, \tag{1}$$

where C represents the true class labels defined over the set Ω_c, $\hat{C}$ models the classification steps through the decided class labels and E is the error random variable taking values into $\{1, 0\}$. The probability of making an error during the classification process is thus:

$$P_e = P(E = 1) = P(\hat{C} \neq C). \tag{2}$$

Fano's inequality [7] gives a lower bound on this probability of error:

$$P_e \geq \frac{H_S(C|\hat{C}) - 1}{\log |\Omega_c|} = \frac{H_S(C) - I_S(C; \hat{C}) - 1}{\log |\Omega_c|}, \tag{3}$$

where $H_S(C) = - \sum_{k \in \Omega_c} p(C_k) \log p(C_k)$ is Shannon's entropy [8] of C, $I_S(C; \hat{C}) = \sum_{k,j \in \Omega_c^2} p(C_k, \hat{C}_j) \log \frac{p(C_k, \hat{C}_j)}{p(C_k)p(\hat{C}_j)}$ is Shannon's Mutual Information (MI) between C and $\hat{C}$ and $|\Omega_c|$ is the number of classes.

From this lower bound Erdogmus et al. [9] also derived an upper bound using Jensen's inequality described in [8]:

$$\frac{H_S(C) - I_\alpha(C; \hat{C}) - h_S(P_e)}{\log |\Omega_c| - 1} \leq P_e \leq \frac{H_S(C) - I_\beta(C; \hat{C}) - h_S(P_e)}{\min_k H_S(C|e, \hat{c}_k)}, \tag{4}$$

where $h_S(P_e) = -P_e \log P_e - (1 - P_e) \log (1 - P_e)$ is the binary Shannon's entropy and $I_\alpha(C; \hat{C})$ represents Renyi's definition of the mutual information with $\alpha \in \mathbb{R}^+ \setminus \{1\}$. The tightest bounds are obtained when the Renyi's entropy coefficients (α, β) tend to 1 in which case Renyi's definitions correspond to Shannon's ones. As the number of classes $|\Omega_c|$ is fixed, $H_S(C)$ does not depend on the classification process, bounds in Eq. 4 point out that maximizing the MI between the two random variables C and $\hat{C}$ will tend to minimize the probability Pe of making an error.

This formulation of the classification problem has been extended to feature extraction (Fisher et al. [10], Hild et al. [11]) and processing of multimodal signals (Butz et al. [12]). Sindhwani et al. [13] also proposed a feature selection technique for support vector machines and neural networks based on similar information theoretic considerations. In the next section we will extend these properties to the framework of multiple classifiers.

3 Information Theoretic Classifier Combination

In this work, we present a new classifier combination scheme using this information theoretic framework. Let us consider that we already have a team of given classifiers. The goal is to find the best combination of members in the sense that it will maximize $I_{C,\hat{C}}$.

For simplification and without loss of generality, let us consider a two class problem with labels $\{-1, 1\}$ and three classifiers to be combined. We denote by $\hat{C}_i$, $i \in \{1, 2, 3\}$ the random variables representing the output labels of the classifier i, $I_{C,\hat{C}_i}$, the MI between individual classifier i and the true labels and finally $I_{i,j} = I_{\hat{C}_i,\hat{C}_j}$, $i, j \in 1, 2, 3$, $j \geq i$ the MI between two distinct classifiers. The quantity to be maximized is:

$$I_{C,\hat{C}} = \sum_{k=-1,1} \sum_{j=-1,1} P_{C,\hat{C}}(k,j) \log \frac{P_{C,\hat{C}}(k,j)}{P_C(k)P_{\hat{C}}(j)}. \tag{5}$$

In order to be able to derive analytical properties about the combination process, we need to find probability relationships between the classifiers. The complexity of this task is that these probabilities depend on the combination rule that is used to combine the decisions of the ensemble members. In this work we restrict the combination rule to majority voting. It is not an heavy restriction though, as despite its simplicity, majority vote has proved to be an efficient rule for many multiple classifiers systems. Moreover, majority vote can easily be extended to weighted majority vote which is widely used in the multiple classifiers community. For example, AdaBoost [15] performs a weighted majority vote of weak classifiers.

Considering a majority voting scheme, the probability $P_{\hat{C}}(i)$ that the final decision is i is related to each voter classifier:

$$P_{\hat{C}}(i) \leq P_{\hat{C}_1,\hat{C}_2}(i) + P_{\hat{C}_1,\hat{C}_3}(i) + P_{\hat{C}_2,\hat{C}_3}(i). \tag{6}$$

A second usefull property is given by the lemma described in [16]: The probability of a group of odd size N with any competence structure $(p_1, p_2, \ldots, p_N)$, where $p_i > 0.5$ for each i to reach the correct decision, when utilizing the simple majority rule, is larger than the probability $p = \frac{1}{N} \sum_{i=1}^{N} p_i$ of a random group member to do so.

It is an extension of a the Condorcet Jury theorem (1785). See [3] for details. In our case this theorem leads to:

$$P_{C,\hat{C}}(i) \geq \frac{1}{3}(P_{C,\hat{C}_1}(i) + P_{C,\hat{C}_2}(i) + P_{C,\hat{C}_3}(i)). \tag{7}$$

Note that majority voting improves over the average accuracy but not necessarily over the best classifier.

Now considering these bounds (Eq. 6 and Eq. 7) in each term of the mutual information in Eq. 5, it follows that: minimizing the MI between each pair of classifier $I_{\hat{C}_i,\hat{C}_j}, i \neq j$ and maximizing the MI between each single classifier and the true class labels $I_{C,\hat{C}_i}$ will maximize $I_{C,\hat{C}}$.

As introduced in section 2, $I_{C,\hat{C}_i}$ represents the accuracy of classifier i, while $I_{\hat{C}_i,\hat{C}_j}$ measures the similarity between the two classifiers i and j. Moreover, minimizing $I_{\hat{C}_i,\hat{C}_j}$, means maximizing the diversity between the two classifiers. In other words, for obtaining a good ensemble, we need classifiers that are individually accurate but that make errors on different examples.

In the remaining of the paper we will refer to similarity or diversity, note that these two terms represent inverse quantities.

It is important to note that this is a sufficient condition for maximazing $I(C, \hat{C})$, but it is not a necessary condition. For example, it is possible to have an ensemble with high accuracy but very low diversity between classifiers. This will be discussed experimentally in section 4.

3.1 Diversity

Diversity seems to be a key element for obtaining effective ensembles of classifiers. In the literature there exists different measures of diversity. They can be splitted into pairwise and non pairwise diversities. The most widespread are the Q statistic [17], Double fault [18] and the Disagreement Measure [19]. More details about diversity and how to create diversity in ensemble are given in [20]. Conceptually, forcing diversity between classifiers can improve the classification performances by encouraging the complementarity of the classifiers. However, Kuncheva reported in [3] that the improvement over the best individual accuracy by forcing diversity is negligible. In fact directly maximizing diversity between classifiers will force to decrease the individual classifiers accuracies. The two extreme cases would be to build random classifiers with very large diversities but poor accuracies, or train very accurate classifiers with very low diversity but in this case the combination becomes useless. The goal is thus to find a good trade-off between average individual accuracy and diversity between members.

3.2 Information Theoretic Score

In this work, we evaluate experimentally the dependency between our information theoretic measures of accuracy and diversity.

Outputs of two classifiers (C_1, C_2) with equal accuracies are iteratively simulated. We report in Fig. 1 the similarity between output labels $I(C_1; C_2)$ for each trial as a function of the average individual accuracy $\frac{I(C;C_1)+I(C;C_2)}{2}$.

According to Fig. 1, we simply approximate the similarity between two classifiers by a second order polynomial of the average individual accuracies. Fig. 2 gives a graphical interpretation of this behavior. A classifier is represented by a vector. Its projection onto the horizontal axis measures its individual accuracy while the difference between vertical projections of two vectors measures the diversity between them. The dashed

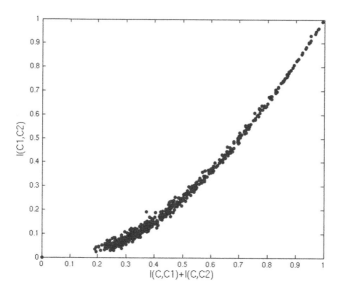

Fig. 1. The similarity of 2 classifiers $I(C_1; C_2)$ function of the average individual accuracy $\frac{I(C_2;C)+I(C_1;C)}{2}$. The 2 classifiers have the same individual accuracy.

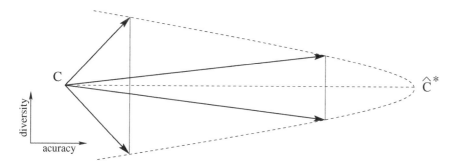

Fig. 2. Graphical representation of Accuracy/diversity dilemma

line represents the maximal diversity allowed between two classifiers with identical accuracy. It appears that two poor classifiers can have large diversity while two accurate classifiers cannot be so diverse.

In the following, we will consider two terms based on the mutual information between classifiers: the average accuracy of the K classifiers:

$$ITA = \frac{\sum_{i=1}^{K} I(C; C_i)}{K}, \tag{8}$$

and the diversity between the classifiers:

$$ITD = \frac{\binom{K}{2}}{\sum_{i=1}^{K-1} \sum_{j=i+1}^{K} I(C_i; C_j)}. \tag{9}$$

Taking into account the second order approximation of the similarity between the classifiers and the average accuracy, we propose the Information Theoretic Score (ITS) as:

$$ITS = (1 + ITA)^3.(1 + ITD). \tag{10}$$

This model is a choice and other similar modeling could be chosen. The next section tries to validate this definition in the context of overproduction and selection of classifiers.

4   Experiments and Results

4.1   Overproduction and Selection

The information theoretic score defined above gives a measure of the goodness of an ensemble. A first natural approach for taking advantage of this score is thus to over-produce classifiers and then select the ensemble that maximizes the ITS. We consider a 2 class toy problem using the Banana dataset available in the Matlab Pattern Recognition Toolbox [21]. We generate 1000 training examples for both classes and we split this training set into 15 smaller subsets by random sampling. We then train one classifier with each subset. A first experiment (Fig. 3(a)) consists in training 15 Support Vector Machines (SVMs) with radial basis kernels (the parameters being evaluated by cross-validation). The 455 possible combinations of three classifiers (triplets) are exhaustively tested. For each triplet, we measure the ITS, the ensemble accuracy on a large test set and the we also compute the average individual accuracy of the three classifiers. This mean is represented by the grey level of the circles in Fig. 3(a). In the second experiment, three different learning algorithm are used. We trained 5 SVMs, 5 linear classifiers and 5 K-nearest neighbors (KNN) and again ITS is measured for each triplet. Results are reported in Fig. 3(b).

As expected, the triplets of classifiers with low ITA (dark circles) lead to low classification accuracy. When the three individual classifiers are accurate (light circles in Fig. 3(a) and Fig. 3(b)), the final classification is generally accurate. However, in both configuration, the lightest points (which means the 3 best classifiers combined together) do not give necessarily the best combination. This phenomenon is more visible in the case of 15-SVMs as they only have slight differences in their individual accuracies. In any case, the ensembles with high ITS are very accurate. These experiments show that, at least in toy problems, the ITS can overcome the limitations of diversity as presented in section 3.1. Howerver, in these experiments, the relation between the size of the training sets and the complexity of the classifiers may play an important role [14]. This will be studied in a further work.

4.2   Modified AdaBoost

In many problems, it is not trivial to train a pool of relevant classifiers such that a good combination can be extracted. Moreover the number of possible ensembles to be tested varies dramatically with the number of classifiers in the pool and the number of classifier wanted in the ensemble. We thus propose here to directly learn an ensemble of

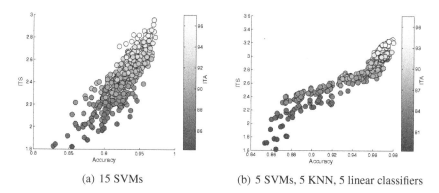

(a) 15 SVMs   (b) 5 SVMs, 5 KNN, 5 linear classifiers

Fig. 3. Combination accuracy and ITS for each triplet of classifiers. (a) 15 SVMs with RBF kernels and (b) 5 SVMs with RBF kernels, 5 KNN classifiers and 5 linear classifiers. The color of the circle is proportional the the average accuracy of the ensembles.

classifiers with high ITS. One of the drawbacks of the information theoretic approach is that the objective function to be optimized is not differentiable. In this paper we propose a technique for building classifiers ensembles by boosting.

AdaBoost [15] is a learning algorithm which iteratively builds a linear combination of some basic functions (*weak classifiers*) by greedily minimizing the risk based on the exponential loss,

$$L(y, f(\mathbf{x})) = \exp\left(-y f(\mathbf{x})\right). \tag{11}$$

The final decision function has the form

$$f_T(\mathbf{x}) = \text{sign}\left(\beta_0 + \sum_{k=1}^{T} \beta_k h_k(\mathbf{x})\right), \tag{12}$$

with $h_k : \mathbb{R}^n \to \{\pm 1\}$ being the weak classifiers. Training in the case of AdaBoost comes to finding the weak classifiers and their corresponding weights. For a detailed description of the algorithm see [15]. There are a number of theoretical and practical advantages in using AdaBoost, of importance here being the fact that by suitably choosing the weak classifiers, one may perform a feature selection implicitly when training the classifier. Another important feature of AdaBoost is that it converges towards a large margin classifier with positive impact on its generalization properties. However, in the presence of high levels of noise, AdaBoost, like the majority of classifiers, may overfit the training set.

We propose a modified version of it that selects weak classifiers that maximizes a weighted ITS instead of picking the weak classifier that minimize the weighted training error. The convergence properties of AdaBoost are not affected by the change as far as the weighted training error of each selected classifier remains at least slightly better than random guessing. We test this algorithm in a face class modeling application. We consider a two class problem with 19×19 pixels face and non face images (see [22]). We use slightly more than 3700 faces for training and roughly 4300 for testing. Non face

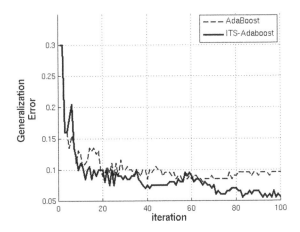

Fig. 4. Comparison between AdaBoost and its modified version based on the ITS criterion

images were selected by bootstrapping on randomly selected images. We used 5000 images for training and 10000 for testing. Simple decision stumps are used as weak classifiers. Fig. 4 gives a comparison between default AdaBoost and the ITS-AdaBoost proposed here. It turns out that the generalization is improved compared to AdaBoost (even if the training convergence is slower). It can be explained by the fact that we explicitly add more diversity at each iteration.

5 Conclusions

This paper presents a new ensemble learning technique in an information theoretic framework. It provides a tool for measuring the goodness of an ensemble by taking into account a trade-off between individual accuracy and diversity. This information theoretic criterion has been used in two learning strategies. Selection of overproduced classifiers, and modified version of AdaBoost. These techniques have been tested in the face class modeling context showing the improvements brought by this information theoretic approach.

Acknowledgments

This work is supported by the Swiss National Science Foundation through the National Center of Competence in Research on "Interactive Multimodal Information Management (IM2)".

References

1. Thomas G. Dietterich, "Ensemble methods in machine learning," *Lecture Notes in Computer Science*, vol. 1857, pp. 1–15, 2000.
2. Y. Freund, Y. Mansour, and R. Schapire, "Why averaging classifiers can protect against overfitting," in *In Proceedings of the Eighth International Workshop on Artificial Intelligence and Statistics*, 2001.

3. Ludmila I. Kuncheva, *Combining Pattern Classifiers Methods and Algorithms*, John Wiley, New York,, New York, NY, USA, 2004.
4. Josef Kittler, Mohamad Hatef, Robert P. W. Duin, and Jiri Matas, "On combining classifiers," *IEEE Trans. Pattern Anal. Mach. Intell.*, vol. 20, no. 3, pp. 226–239, 1998.
5. L. Kuncheva and C. Whitaker, "Measures of diversity in classifier ensembles," *Machine Learning*, vol. 51, no. 2, pp. 181 – 207, 2003.
6. J.C. Principe, D. Xu, and J.W. Fisher, "Learning from examples with information theoretic criteria," *J. VLSI Signal Process. Syst.*, vol. 26, pp. 61 – 77, 2000.
7. R.M. Fano, *Transmission of Information: A Statistical Theory of Communication*, MIT Press, Wiley, Cambridge, 1961.
8. T. Cover and J. Thomas, *Elements of Information Theory*, John Wiley and Sons, Inc., New York, 1991.
9. Deniz Erdogmus and Jose C. Principe, "Lower and upper bounds for misclassification probability based on renyi's information," *Journal of VLSI Signal Processing*, vol. 37, pp. 305–317, 2004.
10. J. Fisher, III and J. Principe, "A methodology for information theoretic feature extraction," in *IEEE International Conference on Neural Networks (IJCNN'98)*, Anchorage, AK, 1998, vol. 3, pp. 1712–1716.
11. Kenneth E. Hild II, Deniz Erdogmus, Kari Torkkola, and Jose C. Principe, "Feature extraction using information-theoretic learning," *IEEE Trans. Pattern Anal. Mach. Intell*, vol. 28, no. 9, pp. 1385–1392, 2006.
12. Torsten Butz and Jean-Philippe Thiran, "From error probability to information theoretic (multi-modal) signal processing," *Signal Processing*, vol. 85, no. 5, pp. 875–902, 2005.
13. Vikas Sindhwani, Subrata Rakshit, Dipti Deodhare, Deniz Erdogmus, Jose C. Principe, and Partha Niyogim, "Feature selection in mlps and svms based on maximum output information," *IEEE Transactions On Neural Networks,*, vol. 15, pp. 937–949, 2004.
14. Sarunas Raudys, "Trainable fusion rules. II Small sample-size effects," *Neural Networks*, vol. 19, no. 10, pp. 1517–1527, 2006.
15. Yoav Freund and Robert E. Schapire, "A decision-theoretic generalization of on-line learning and an application to boosting," *J. Comput. Syst. Sci.*, vol. 55, no. 1, pp. 119–139, 1997.
16. L. Shapley and B. Grofman, "Optimizing group judgemental accuracy in the presence of interdependencies," *Public Choice*, vol. 43, pp. 329–343, 1984.
17. G. Yule, "On the association of attributes in statistics.," *Biometrika*, vol. 2, pp. 121–134, 1903.
18. Giorgio Giacinto and Fabio Roli, "Design of effective neural network ensembles for image classification purposes," *Image Vision Comput*, vol. 19, no. 9-10, 2001.
19. D. Skalak, "The sources of increased accuracy for two proposed boosting algorithms," in *AAAI '96 Workshop on Integrating Multiple Learned Models for Improving and Scaling Machine Learning Algorithms*, 1996.
20. G. Brown, J. Wyatt, R. Harris, and X. Yao, "Diversity creation methods: A survey and categorisation," *Journal of Information Fusion*, vol. 6, no. 1, pp. 5–20, March 2005.
21. R.P.W. Duin, P. Juszczak, P. Paclik, E. Pekalska, D. de Ridder, and D.M.J. Tax, "Prtools4, a matlab toolbox for pattern recognition," *Delft University of Technology*, 2004.
22. J. Meynet, V. Popovici, M. Sorci, and J. Thiran, "Combining svms for face class modeling," in *13th European Signal Processing Conference - EUSIPCO, Antalya, Turkey*, 2005.

Interactive Boosting for Image Classification

Yijuan Lu[1], Qi Tian[1], and Thomas S. Huang[2]

[1] Department of Computer Science, University of Texas at San Antonio, TX, USA
{lyijuan,qitian}@cs.utsa.edu
[2] Beckman Institute, University of Illinois at Urbana-Champaign, Urbana, IL,USA
huang@ifp.uiuc.edu

Abstract. Traditional boosting method like adaboost, boosts a weak learning algorithm by updating the sample weights (the relative importance of the training samples) iteratively. In this paper, we propose to integrate feature re-weighting into boosting scheme, which not only weights the samples but also weights the feature elements iteratively. To avoid overfitting problem caused by feature re-weighting on a small training data set, we also incorporate relevance feedback into boosting and propose an interactive boosting called i.Boosting. It merges adaboost, feature re-weighting and relevance feedback into one framework and exploits the favorable attributes of these methods. In this paper, i.Boosting is implemented using Adaptive Discriminant Analysis (ADA) as base classifiers. It not only enhances but also combines a set of ADA classifiers into a more powerful one. A feature re-weighting method for ADA is also proposed and integrated in i.Boosting. Extensive experiments on UCI benchmark data sets, three facial image data sets and COREL color image data sets show the superior performance of i.Boosting over AdaBoost and other state-of-the-art projection-based classifiers.

Keywords: Relevance Feedback, Adaboost, Feature Re-weighting, Multiple Classifiers.

1 Introduction

Recent years have witnessed an explosion of digital images generated from different areas such as commerce, academia and medical institutes. The dramatic increase of images demands efficient indexing and retrieval methods, especially for a large image database. In image retrieval, an image is represented by its image feature vector as a data point in a high-dimensional space. Its dimension ranges from tens to hundreds. However, traditional statistical approaches have difficulties in modeling data directly in such a high dimensional space. Hence, dimension reduction technique plays a critical role in alleviating the high dimensionality problem.

A good dimension reduction method can map the high dimensional data space to a low dimensional space without loss of much useful information. However, any single dimension reduction method cannot find the optimal projection. Traditional techniques, such as Principal Component Analysis (PCA) [1] and Linear Discriminant Analysis (LDA) [2], cannot work well when the data distribution cannot be modeled

M. Haindl, J. Kittler, and F. Roli (Eds.): MCS 2007, LNCS 4472, pp. 180–189, 2007.
© Springer-Verlag Berlin Heidelberg 2007

as Gaussian or mixture of Gaussians. A better solution is to boost a set of projections and corresponding classifiers first using boosting algorithms. Then combine these boosted classifiers using fusion in the projected space [3].

Here, boosting algorithms are designed to construct a "strong" classifier from a "weak" learning algorithm and present the superior result given by a thresholded linear combination of the weak classifiers. AdaBoost [4] is often regarded as the generic boosting algorithm. The basic idea of AdaBoost is to iteratively re-weight the training samples based on the outputs of some weak learners. Misclassified samples will receive higher weights in the next iteration. This forces the classifier to focus more on the incorrectly classified examples.

However, during this procedure, only weights of samples are updated. It doesn't update any feature element weight, which is important and very useful especially for image databases using high dimensional image features [5]. In this paper, we incorporate feature re-weighting into boosting and propose a new feature re-weighting approach for Adaptive Discriminant Analysis (ADA) [3]. In addition, considering feature re-weighting on small training data set tends to bias to the training set and causes overfitting, we integrate user feedback into boosting scheme and propose a novel interactive boosting framework (i.Boosting). i.Boosting not only weights the samples, but also weights the feature elements iteratively. Besides, in i.Boosting, relevance feedback provides boosting with more misclassification information. And better than simple relevance feedback, Adaboost forces classifiers to pay more attention to wrongfully predicted samples in user feedback.

In this paper, i.Boosting is implemented using ADA as base classifiers. It not only enhances but also combines multiple ADA classifiers into a more powerful one. Extensive experiments on the UCI benchmark data sets, three facial image data sets and COREL color image data sets show that the superior performance of i.Boosting.

In section 2, feature re-weighting and relevance feedback techniques will be briefly described. Interactive boosting scheme and i.Boosting with ADA are illustrated in section 3. Experimental results and conclusions will be given in section 4 and 5 respectively.

2 Feature Re-weighting and Relevance Feedback

2.1 Classic Feature Re-weighting

In image database, each image $i \in I$ is represented by its M features $f_i = [f_{i1}, f_{i2}, \cdots f_{iM}]^T$. Let the feature of query image q be $f_q = [f_{q1}, f_{q2}, \cdots f_{qm}]^T$, the Euclidean distance between query image and the image in the database is

$$d = (f_i - f_q)^T W(f_i - f_q)$$

W is the feature weighting matrix indicating the importance of each component of features. After relevance feedback, the user provides the relevance of each image to the query and the feature weights can be updated to make similar images close to each other and dissimilar images far away from each other. Traditional feature re-weighting methods are based on distance metric, e.g., generalized Euclidean distance [5]. In this paper, we apply a dynamic feature re-weighting method before dimension reduction in order to obtain a better projection after each iteration in relevance feedback.

2.2 Adaptive Discriminant Analysis

In our paper, we use Adaptive Discriminant Analysis (ADA) [3] as our dimension reduction method. It can provide an accurate model of the complex distribution for positive and negative samples by finding an optimal projection in the following way:

$$W_{ADA} = \arg\max_{W} \frac{|W^T[\lambda S_{P->N} + (1-\lambda)S_{N->P}]W|}{|W^T[\eta S_P + (1-\eta)S_N]W|} \tag{1}$$

in which

$$S_{N->P} = (f_N f_N^T) \cdot * \sum_{i \in Negative}(x_i - m_P)(x_i - m_P)^T \tag{2}$$

$$S_{P->N} = (f_P f_P^T) \cdot * \sum_{j \in Positive}(x_j - m_N)(x_j - m_N)^T \tag{3}$$

$$S_P = (f_P f_P^T) \cdot * \sum_{j \in Positive}(x_j - m_P)(x_j - m_P)^T \tag{4}$$

$$S_N = (f_N f_N^T) \cdot * \sum_{i \in Negative}(x_i - m_N)(x_i - m_N)^T \tag{5}$$

The m_P and m_N are the means of positive and negative samples, respectively. f_P and f_N are feature element weights of positive and negative samples, respectively. $\cdot *$ stands for Hadamard product operation. S_P (or S_N) is the within-class scatter matrix for the positive (or negative) examples. $S_{N \to P}$ (or $S_{P \to N}$) is the between-class scatter matrix from the negative (or positive) examples to the centroid of the positive (or negative) examples. The two parameters $\lambda \in (0,1), \eta \in (0,1)$ control the bias between positive and negative samples. Proper setting of parameters may fit the real distribution of data better than LDA and PCA [3].

However, to find an optimal setting, exhaustive searching in 2D parameter (λ, η) space is needed and computationally expensive. Boosting can alleviate this problem by enhancing and combing a set of weak ADA classifiers into a more powerful one. (An ADA classifier is denoted as ADA projection and a base classifier in the projected space)

For each weak ADA classifier, to find a better projection, the ratio of $\frac{trace(\lambda S_{P->N} + (1-\lambda)S_{N->P})}{trace(\eta S_P + (1-\eta)S_N)}$ need to be maximized. Intuitively, it is to minimize the "within-class scatter" and maximize the "between-class scatter". Therefore, the criterion can be redefined to maximize

$$\begin{aligned} & trace(\lambda S_{P->N} + (1-\lambda)S_{N->P}) - trace(\eta S_P + (1-\eta)S_N) \\ & = trace(\lambda S_{P->N} - \eta S_P) + trace((1-\lambda)S_{N->P} - (1-\eta)S_N) \end{aligned} \tag{6}$$

Hence, re-weighting scheme for ADA is to update f_P by maximizing $trace(\lambda S_{P->N} - \eta S_P)$ and update f_N by maximizing $trace((1-\lambda)S_{N->P} - (1-\eta)S_N)$ based on (2), (3), (4), and (5).

2.3 Relevance Feedback

To efficiently incorporate user feedback and enhance the retrieval accuracy, relevance feedback can also be integrated in the boosting.

Relevance Feedback was initially developed in document retrieval [6] and widely applied in content-based image retrieval (CBIR) [7, 8]. A challenge in CBIR is the *semantic gap* between the high-level semantics in human mind and the low-level computed features (such as color, texture, and shape). In order to bridge the gap between low-level features and high-level semantics, relevance feedback is introduced.

The basic idea of relevance feedback is to get human in the loop. At first, computer processing provides initial retrieval results. Users are then asked to evaluate the current retrieval results according to degrees that are relevant or irrelevant to his/her request. The system then applies the user's feedback to update the training examples to improve performance for the next round. This learning process can be applied iteratively if the user desires. Relevance Feedback algorithms have been shown to provide dramatic performance improvement in image retrieval systems [8].

3   Interactive Boosting

3.1 Methodology

Motivated by the strength and success of adaboost, dynamic feature re-weighting and Relevance Feedback, we propose an interactive boosting framework called i.Boosting. It can integrate user relevance feedback, adaboost (sample re-weighting) and

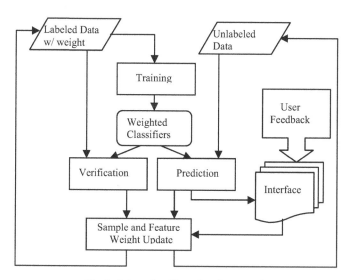

Fig. 1. Interactive Boosting framework

feature re-weighting in the loop of boosting and better bridge the gap between semantic concept and image features. Figure 1 gives an illustration of the basic idea of the interactive boosting framework.

3.2   Interactive Boosting in ADA

Based on the framework described in section 3.1, the brief algorithm below shows how the i.Boosting is implemented with multiple ADA classifiers.

Algorithm: i.Boosting with ADA as weak classifiers

Input: Labeled Sample Set X and label Y, Unlabeled Sample Set U
   Feature vector D and Feature element d
   K ADA classifiers with different (λ, η)
   M: The dimension of feature (feature size), p: positive samples, n: negative samples
   T: The total number of runs

Initialization: sample weight $w_{k,t=1}(x) = 1/|X|$ and feature weight $f_{p,t=1}(d) = 1, f_{n,t=1}(d) = 1$

Boosting
   For each classifier $k = 1,\ldots,K$ do
       For $t = 1,\ldots,T$
           • Train each ADA classifier on labeled samples with weights. Note that
             $$\sum_{x \in X} w_{k,t}(x) = 1, \ \sum_{d \in D} f_{p,t}(d) = \sum_{d \in D} f_{n,t}(d) = M$$
           • Get the probability-rated prediction on labeled and unlabeled sample.
           • Compute the weights of classifiers based on its classification error rate $\varepsilon_{k,t}$ on
             labeled samples $\alpha_{k,t} = \dfrac{1}{2}\ln(\dfrac{1-\varepsilon_{k,t}}{\varepsilon_{k,t}})$
           • Present samples from the unlabeled data set with their predicted labels to user
           • Obtain user feedback on the ground truth labels
           • Construct new labeled training set by adding data and corresponding labels obtained
             from user feedback
           • Update   the   weight   of   all   training   samples
             $$w_{k,t+1}(x) = w_{k,t}(x)\exp(-\alpha_{k,t} \cdot h_{k,t}(x) \cdot y)$$
           • Compute the new $|\lambda S_{P \to N} - \eta S_P|$ and $|(1-\lambda)S_{N \to P} - (1-\eta)S_N|$ in eq. (6)
           • Update the weight of features $f_{p,t}(d), f_{n,t}(d)$ accordingly
       End for t
   End for each classifier
The final prediction $H(x) = sign(\sum_{k,t} \alpha_{k,t} h_{k,t}(x))$, using sum rule to combine multiple classifiers

---

4   Experiments and Analysis

In this section, we experimentally evaluate the performance of the interactive boosting on benchmark dataset, image and face classification. The test data sets include UCI benchmark data sets, COREL image data set and three popular face image data sets, which cover a wide range of data in computer vision applications. In order to comprehensively evaluate the performance of our proposed method, we compare it with AdaBoost, ADA with Relevance Feedback and other state-of-the-art projection techniques. In all experiments, our boosted ADA is trained on 36 ADA classifiers with (λ, η) evenly sampled from 0 to 1 with step size of 0.2. Bayesian classifier is used on the projected data for all projection-based methods. In order to have statistical analysis of our scheme, we perform a pseudo relevance feedback. At each relevance feedback, 5 images are fed to the system automatically based on their ground truth labels. In all experiments, average prediction error rate of 50 runs is reported.

4.1 Interactive Boosting on UCI Data Set

First, we tested the effectiveness of the proposed i.Boosting on benchmark data sets from UCI repository. For comparison purpose, four independent experiments are designed and implemented to compare i.Boosting with other related variants.

Due to the limited space, we only show the results on SPECTF heart databases, which describe diagnosing of cardiac Single Proton Emission Computed Tomography (SPECT) images. Similar results are obtained on other data sets. This SPECTF data set contains 267 instances (patients) and totally 43 attributes. Each of the patients is classified into two categories: normal and abnormal. The sizes of the training set and testing set are 80 and 187, respectively. The average error rate across five iterations is plotted in Fig. 2, where the x-axis denotes the iteration number (between 0 to 5). 0 stands for the starting status before iterations begin.

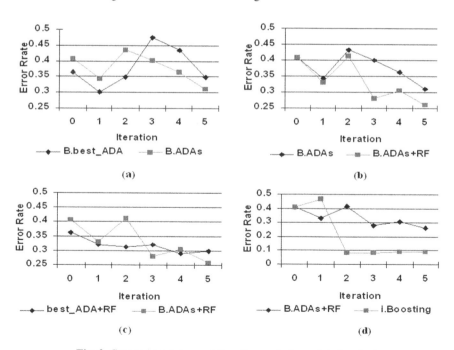

Fig. 2. Comparison between i.Boosting and other related variants

a) boosting single ADA classifier vs boosting multiple ADA classifiers
In this experiment, we compare a boosted single best ADA classifier (B.best_ADA) with boosted multiple ADA classifiers (B.ADAs). The boosted multiple ADA classifiers are trained on 36 ADA classifiers with (λ, η) evenly sampled from 0 to 1 with step size of 0.2. The single best ADA is the best one chosen from these 36 classifiers. Showed in Fig. 2 (a), as iteration goes on, the error rates of the B.best_ADA classifier and B.ADAs decrease. Although B.ADAs starts with a set of weak classifiers, after three iterations $(T=3)$, it outperforms the B.best_ADA. It verifies that AdaBoost provides a general way of combining and enhancing a set of ADA classifiers in the parametric space.

b) boosting multiple ADA classifiers with and without relevance feedback
Secondly, we evaluate the effect of integrating user feedback into boosting scheme. From Fig.2 (b), we can find the performance improvement of using AdaBoost alone (B. ADAs) is less than that of boosted ADAs with relevance feedback (B.ADAs+RF). The performance of B.ADAs+RF is consistently better than that of B.ADAs (w/o relevance feedback) by up to 30.4% on SPECTF heart set. Obviously, the reason is that user feedback and human judgement could be accumulated iteratively to facilitate learning process.

c) single ADA classifier+RF (w/o boosting) vs boosting multiple ADA classifiers+RF
The third experiment is designed to verify if the performance improvement of B.ADAs+RF is introduced by relevance feedback only. Hence, we compare the single best ADA classifier with only relevance feedback (best_ADA+RF) and boosted multiple ADA classifiers with relevance feedback (B.ADAs+RF). From the experimental result in Fig. 2 (c), we can conclude that: 1) B.ADAs+RF and Relevance Feedback only starts with similar performance in iteration 1; 2) After several iterations, simple relevance feedback gain less performance improvement than B.ADAs+RF. In conclusion, B.ADAs+RF has obvious advantage over the simple relevance feedback method in that the classifiers are trained to pay more attention to wrongfully predicted samples in user feedback through a reinforcement training process.

d) boosting multiple ADA classifiers+RF(w/o feature re-weighting) vs i.Boosting
The last experiment is to evaluate the performance of feature re-weighting in interactive boosting. In Fig. 2 (d), we can find after two iterations, the i.Boosting performed much better than B.ADAs+RF (without feature re-weighting). Besides, i.Boosting becomes much steadier after several iterations. It is clear that our method i.Boosting boosts not only a set of weak classifiers but also the individual features.

4.2   Interactive Boosting for Image Classification

In order to evaluate interactive boosting for image classification, we test i.Boosting on COREL image databases. This database contains 1386 color images, which are categorized into 14 classes. Each class contains 99 images. Each image is represented by 37 feature components including color moments [9], wavelet-based texture [10] and water-filling edge-based structure features [11]. For simplicity, we randomly pick

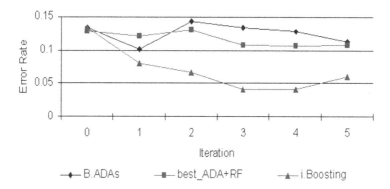

Fig. 3. i.Boosting on COREL data set

up two classes of images for classification. One-third of the images are used for training while the rest are used for testing.

The experimental result showed in Fig. 3 is consistent with the results on the UCI data set. i.Boosting, boosted multiple ADA classifiers (without relevance feedback) and the best ADA classifier with relevance feedback start with similar performance in iteration 1. But as iteration goes on, i.Boosting gains much better performance improvement than the other two. It demonstrates that interactive boosting exploits the favorable attributes of adaboost, feature re-weighting and relevance feedback well.

4.3 Interactive Boosting for Face Classification

To evaluate interactive boosting for face classification, we tested i.Boosting on three well-known face image databases with change of illumination, expression and head pose, respectively. The Harvard Face image database contains images from 10 individuals, each providing total 66 images, which are classified into 10 sets based on increasingly changed illumination condition [12]. The AT&T Face Image database [13] consists of grayscale images of 40 persons. Each person has 10 images with different expressions, open or closed eyes, smiling or non-smiling and wearing glasses or no glasses. The UMIST Face Database [14] consists of 564 images of 20 people, which covers a range of poses from profile to frontal views. Figure 4 gives some example images from the databases. Sixty image features are extracted to represent these images including histogram, wavelet-based texture and water-filling edge-based structure features.

For each database, we randomly chose one person's face images as positive and the rest face images of others are considered as negative. For comparison purpose, 6 state-of-the-art projection-based techniques: Eigenface [12], LDA, BDA [15], DEM [16], KDEM [16], ADA [3] are tested on the same databases. To be consistent, the results for these techniques are obtained after 5 iterations of relevance feedback.

The results are listed Table 1 with the smallest error rate in bold. It is clear that i.Boosting performs best in 4 out of 5 tests and second to the best ADA in one test. It is clear that i.Boosting provides more robustness to the changes of illumination, expression and pose than other techniques.

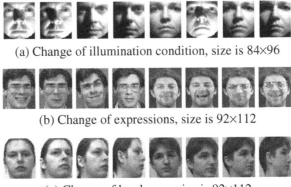

(a) Change of illumination condition, size is 84×96

(b) Change of expressions, size is 92×112

(c) Change of head pose, size is 92×112

Fig. 4. Example Face images from three facial databases

Table 1. Comparison of i.Boosting with state-of-the-art techniques on three different face databases

	Error Rate (%)	Harvard Dataset			ATT Dataset	UMIST Dataset
		Subset 1	Subset 2	Subset 3		
Methods	Eigenface	6.33	9.1	4.16	0.31	3.81
	LDA	15.06	15.17	15.33	2.07	0.51
	BDA	1.42	4.0	1.43	0.83	1.36
	DEM	14.96	15.18	15.26	3.35	1.28
	KDEM	11.21	13.33	11.18	1.67	2.64
	Best single ADA	0.33	**2.7**	0.84	0.04	0.17
	i.Boosting	**0.16**	3.0	**0.58**	**0.02**	**0.11**

5   Conclusion and Future Work

In this paper, we propose a novel interactive boosting framework to integrate feature re-weighting and relevance feedback into standard boosting scheme. Compared to the traditional boosting scheme, the proposed method updates both sample weights and feature weights iteratively. It obtains more performance improvement from the relevance feedback by putting human in the loop to facilitate learning process. It has obvious advantage over the simple relevance feedback method in that the classifiers are trained to pay more attention to wrongfully predicted samples in user feedback through a reinforcement training process. All experimental results show the superior performance of the proposed interactive boosting framework.

Our future work includes testing different user feedback schemes such as active learning techniques [17] in the interactive boosting. Different base classifiers and their corresponding feature re-weighting schemes will be implemented. We will also evaluate the performance difference among different boosting and fusion schemes.

Acknowledgement

This work was supported in part by Army Research Office (ARO) grant under W911NF-05-1-0404, by Department of Homeland Security (DHS) and by the San Antonio Life Science Institute (SALSI).

References

1. Jolliffe, I. T.: Principal Component Analysis. 2nd edition, New-York: Springer-Verlag (2002)
2. Duda, R., Hart, P., and Stork, D.: Pattern Classification. 2nd edition, John Wiley & Sons, Inc., (2001)
3. Yu, J. and Tian, Q.: Adaptive Discriminant Projection for Content-based Image Retrieval. Proc. of Intl. Conf. on Pattern Recognition, Hong Kong, August (2006)
4. Freund, Y. and Schapire, R.: A short introduction to boosting. Journal of Japanese Society for Artificial Intelligence, 14(5) (1999) 771-780
5. Wu, Y. and Zhang, A.: A Feature Re-weighting Approach For Relevance Feedback In Image Retrieval. IEEE International Conference of Image Processing (2002)
6. Salton, G. and McGill, M. J.: Introduction to modern information retrieval. New York: McGraw-Hill Book Company(1992)
7. Rui, Y., Huang, T. S., Ortega, M. and Mehrotra, S.: Relevance feedback: a power tool in interactive content-based image retrieval. IEEE Trans Circuits and Systems for Video Tech., vol. 8, no. 5, (1998) 644-655
8. Zhou, X., and Huang, T. S.: Relevance feedback in image retrieval: a comprehensive review. ACM Multimedia Systems Journal, special issue on CBIR, 8(6) (2003) 536-544
9. Stricker, M., Orengo, M.: Similarity ofcolor images, Proceedings of SPIE Storage and Retrieval for Image and Video Databases, San Diego, CA (1995)
10. Smith, J.R., Chang, S.F.: Transform features for texture classi.cation and discrimination in large image database, Proceedings ofIEEE International Conference on Image Processing, Austin, TX (1994)
11. Zhou, X.S., Rui, Y., Huang, T.S.: Water-.lling algorithm: a novel way for image feature extraction based on edge maps, in: Proceedings ofIEEE International Conference on Image Processing, Kobe, Japan (1999)
12. Belhumeur, P., Hespanha, J., and Kriegman, D.: Eigenfaces vs. Fisherfaces: recognition using class specific linear projection. IEEE Trans. PAMI, Vol. 19, No. 7, July (1997)
13. Rowley, H. A., Baluja, S., and Kanade, T.: Neural network-based face detection. IEEE Trans. PAMI, Vol. 20 (1998)
14. Samaria, F. and Harter, A.: Parameterisation of a stochastic model for human face identification. IEEE Workshop on Applications of Computer Vision, Sarasota FL, December (1994)
15. Zhou, X. and Huang, T. S.: Small sample learning during multimedia retrieval using biasMap IEEE CVPR (2001)
16. Tian, Q., Wu, Y., Yu, J., and Huang, T.S.: Self-supervised learning based on discriminative nonlinear features for image classification. Pattern Recognition, Special Issue on Image Understanding for Digital Photographs, Vol. 38 (2005)
17. Tong, S. and Chang, E.: Support vector machine active learning for image retrieval. Proc. of ACM Int'l. Conf. Multimedia, (2001) 107-118

Group-Induced Vector Spaces

Manuele Bicego[1,*], Elżbieta Pękalska[2], and Robert P.W. Duin[3]

[1] DEIR, University of Sassari, Italy
bicego@uniss.it
[2] School of Computer Science, University of Manchester, UK
[3] Delft University of Technology, The Netherlands

Abstract. The strength of classifier combination lies either in a suitable averaging over multiple experts/sources or in a beneficial integration of complementary approaches. In this paper we focus on the latter and propose the use of group-induced vector spaces (GIVSs) as a way to combine unsupervised learning with classification. In such an integrated approach, the data is first modelled by a number of groups, found by a clustering procedure. Then, a proximity function is used to measure the (dis)similarity of an object to each group. A GIVS is defined by mapping an object to a vector of proximity scores, computed with respect to the given groups. In this study, we focus on a particular aspect of using GIVSs in a mode of building a trained combiner, namely the integration of generative and discriminative methods. First, in the generative step, we model the groups by simple generative models, building the GIVS space. The classification problem is then mapped in the resulting vector space, where a discriminative classifier is trained. Our experiments show that the integrated approach leads to comparable or better results than the generative methods in the original feature spaces.

1 Introduction

Practice in Multiple Classifier Systems as well as life experience show that a proper integration of complementary expertise leads to a better understanding of the problem and, usually, to better solutions. In this paper, we combine the complementary views of unsupervised and supervised learning. One possible approach is to discover the data structure and to apply different classifiers (or their combinations) depending on the position of objects in a vector space or groups they belongs to. Given a set of classifiers, this can be realized in local neighborhoods, e.g. by a dynamic classifier selection, as discussed in [15,2].

Here, we propose a simpler strategy that builds a group-induced vector space (GIVS) from the information of group structure. The main idea is to create such a representation space for the addressed problem such that it is successfully employed by discriminative approaches also for very small sample size problems or for non-vectorial data. Therefore, we characterize the problem in terms of (overlapping) groups determined by a clustering procedure. In principle, groups

---

* Corresponding author: via Torre Tonda, 34 - 07100 Sassari, Italy. Tel: +39 79 2017321 - Fax: +39 079 2017312.

M. Haindl, J. Kittler, and F. Roli (Eds.): MCS 2007, LNCS 4472, pp. 190–199, 2007.

can also be obtained by using label information. Nevertheless, the use of labels should be avoided, since this prevents the risk of overtraining (re-using the same information). Additionally, groups may also have different scales (both large and small groups are permitted) or be detected on different levels of a hierarchical clustering. Given such (possibly multiple-view) groups, a proximity function is needed that measures similarity of an object to each group. This is defined in agreement with the underlying grouping criterion or the property of the clustering technique, such as the Euclidean distance to the class centre if the K-means clustering is used or log-likelihood in case of the EM-clustering. In a GIVS, an object is mapped to a proximity vector, such that each proximity score reflects a similarity of an object to a group. The construction of this vector space is a fusion of weak proximity scores which encode in multiple views the grouping tendencies in the data. A statistical classifier trained in GIVS combines the weak clustering evidences towards a good solution. Note, however, that such a classifier should be simple in order to avoid overtraining, as the final result is a trained combiner [4]. A similar idea was also used for image classification in [9].

In general, our approach bears some resemblance to mixtures of local models. This includes local PCA models utilising either 'hard' [8] or 'soft' [6] assignments in in the partitioning phase, or probabilistic models based on local probabilistic PCA [14] or mixture of Gaussians [11]. All but first techniques couple both the partitioning and local model building into a EM approach. As a result, the model parameters and the mixing weights are optimized simultaneously. There are two main differences between such mixtures of local models and our approach. First, we derive a sequentially trained combiner which optimizes both unsupervised and supervised stages separetely. Secondly, the models are flexible: both local and global, possibly weak and overlapping and they may be derived by any clustering procedure, including these without the probabilistic character.

Another related approach is a network of locally tuned RBF units proposed in [12]. It first uses an unsupervised learning, such as K-means to determine cluster centers. These are then taken as RBF centers (of a hidden layer), whose widths are estimated by some nearest-neighbor heuristics. The output layer is a weighted linear combination of the RBFs. In the supervised setting, it is optimized by a gradient descent method. While it seems ad-hoc, its good performance may now be better understood in the light of our proposal, as explained below.

In this paper, we focus on a particular aspect of the proposed approach related to the integration of generative and discriminative methods, two complementary learning paradigms [7,13]. Generative methods model class probability density functions, while discriminative methods directly define the class boundaries. Generative techniques better characterize data, while discriminative techniques usually lead to a high performance. The combination of their strengths by the use of GIVSs seems to be a way for improvement. Here we study to what extent the simple generative modeling of groups in case of vectorial problems is beneficial for building GIVSs and training discriminative classifiers there.

The paper is organised as follows. Section 2 describes the proposed methodology, while Sections 3 and 4 explain the experimental set-up and analyze the results. The findings are summarized in Section 5.

2   Proposed Methodology

This section describes our integrated framework for combing grouping evidence with supervised learning. The starting point is a C-class classification problem, defined by a training set $\mathcal{X} = \{\mathbf{x}_1, \mathbf{x}_2, ..., \mathbf{x}_N\}$ with the associated labels $\{y_1, y_2, ..., y_N\}$, and a test set $\mathcal{Z} = \{\mathbf{z}_1, \mathbf{z}_2, ..., \mathbf{z}_M\}$. The group-induced vector space (GIVS) classification methodology is defined via the following steps:

1. **Grouping**: choose or detect groups inside the training set. This can be achieved either by employing the label information (e.g. groups are chosen as the original classes) or not. Although the latter choice prevents possible overtraining from the repetitive usage of labels, both *Supervised grouping* and *Unsupervised grouping* have been used. In the latter case, the groups are determined by a clustering technique and are assumed to represent natural clusters inside the training set. Any clustering methodology can be used here, such as the simple K-means or the complex mode-seeking. Note that clusters may overlap, which means that examples belong to multiple clusters. In addition, we also define the *Fused Unsupervised Grouping* strategy, which collects sets of groups obtained by the Unsupervised Grouping for a growing number of clusters from 2 to F. The training set is therefore used multiple times, each time to find a particular number of groups.

   In general, the result of a supervised or unsupervised grouping process is a group structure $\mathcal{G}$ describing the training set with K groups, $G_1, G_2, \ldots, G_K$. Of course, $K = C$ in Supervised grouping, while $K = 2 + \ldots + (F-1) + F = \frac{(2+F)(F-1)}{2}$, in Fused Unsupervised Grouping.

2. **Group characterization:** in this step, a set of generative one-class models (such as Gaussian probability densities) are built based on the group structure $\mathcal{G}$ in order to model or describe the elements inside the groups. It is important to emphasize that each model is trained following a one-class paradigm, i.e. without any knowledge of the remaining training examples. As a result, a set of models $\{M_k\}$ describes the group structure $\mathcal{G}$. In our experimental study, we used very simple models, namely Gaussian probability density models with diagonal or spherical covariance matrices.

3. **Building Group-Induced Vector Spaces:** in this step the GIVS is constructed by representing each object by its distance or similarity to each group G_k. Formally, each object $\mathbf{x}_i$ is mapped to the Group-Induced Vector Space by the following function:

$$givs_K(\mathbf{x}_i)\colon \mathbf{x}_i \longrightarrow [f(\mathbf{x}_i, M_1),\ f(\mathbf{x}_i, M_2),\ \ldots,\ f(\mathbf{x}_i, M_K)]^T,\qquad(1)$$

where $f(\mathbf{x}_i, M_k)$ is a function measuring the relation between the vector $\mathbf{x}_i$ and the model M_k of the group G_k. For instance, this is the probability that $\mathbf{x}_i$ belongs to the model. In our experiments, we either used the Euclidean distance between $\mathbf{x}_i$ and the mean of G_k in case M_k is a spherical Gaussian model or the log-likelihood when M_k is the a diagonal Gaussian model. The training set $\mathcal{X}$ and the test set $\mathcal{Z}$ are then mapped to this new space with the $givs_K(\cdot)$ function. Depending on the grouping used, the resulting spaces are called *Supervised GIVS*, *Unsupervised GIVS* or *Fused Unsupervised GIVS*, while their dimensions equal to C, K and $\frac{(2+F)(F-1)}{2}$, correspondingly.

4. **Classification in the GIVS**: the classification problem is solved in the new feature space, in which the training set is

$$\mathcal{GIVS}(\mathcal{X}) = \{givs_K(\mathbf{x}_1), givs_K(\mathbf{x}_2), ..., givs_K(\mathbf{x}_N)\}$$

with the associated labels $\{y_1, y_2, ..., y_N\}$ and the test set is

$$\mathcal{GIVS}(\mathcal{Z}) = \{givs_K(\mathbf{z}_1), givs_K(\mathbf{z}_2), ..., givs_K(\mathbf{z}_M)\}.$$

Any vector-based classification strategy can be used in the GIVS, such as the KNN (k-nearest neighbor) or SVM (support vector machine).

An important feature of our approach is its applicability to problems in which a direct feature space cannot easily be extracted. Examples include problems dealing with sequences, strings, structures or graphs, i.e. problems in which a vector space is not directly obtainable, and discriminative approaches are not easily employable. In such cases, the usual option is to apply generative approaches. The generative models make use of the specific properties of the non-vectorial representations, but they loose at the same time as the discriminative approaches typically have a higher discrimination power. In this sense, the strategy proposed here is a method of combining generative and discriminative strategies, a very challenging research task [7,10]. Generative models are used to characterize groups, while the classification is performed in the corresponding GIVS by discriminative techniques.

3 Experimental Evaluation

This section presents our results. They are obtained by testing different variants of the combined generative-discriminative approach applied to several classification problems. In particular, the general scheme outlined in Section 2 has been instantiated by the following choices:

1. **Grouping:** in the supervised case, groups are defined by the given classes, hence their cardinality equals C, the number of classes. In the unsupervised cases (standard and fused), a traditional Gaussian Mixture Model (GMM) for clustering is adopted assuming diagonal covariance matrices. The number of clusters K varies from 2 to 15. Also F varies from 2 to 15, leading to fused vector spaces of the dimension in the range of 2 to $119 = 2 + ... + 14 + 15$.
2. **Group characterization:** two simple models are applied here: a Gaussian model with a diagonal covariance matrix and a spherical Gaussian model.
3. **Building Group-Induced Vector Spaces:** the proximity measure $f(\mathbf{x}_i, M_k)$ is defined differently for the two models:

   (a) Diagonal Covariance Gaussian:

   $$f(\mathbf{x}_i, M_k) = \log \mathcal{N}(\mathbf{x}_i \mid \boldsymbol{\mu}_k, \boldsymbol{\Sigma}_k) \tag{2}$$

i.e. the log-likelihood expressing the confidence that $\mathbf{x}_i$ belongs to the Gaussian model M_k defined by the mean vector $\boldsymbol{\mu}_k$ and the covariance matrix $\boldsymbol{\Sigma}_k$. In general, it is the negative square Mahalanobis distance, which now simplifies to the negative normalized (per feature) square Euclidean distance due to a diagonal covariance matrix. This choice is motivated by the traditional use of log-likelihood models in the literature. The logarithmic transformation is usually applied to probability estimates. It often simplifies the corresponding expression (when based on the exponent function) and, more importantly, emphasizes the differences in small probabilities, leading to better numerical accuracies.

(b) Spherical Gaussian:

$$f(\mathbf{x}_i, M_k) = ||\mathbf{x}_i - \boldsymbol{\mu}_k||_2, \tag{3}$$

i.e. the Euclidean distance of $\mathbf{x}_i$ to the mean of the Gaussian group M_k, which is a natural choice for spherical clusters.

4. **Classification in the GIVS**: here we choose two simple discriminative classifiers, the K-nearest Neighbor (KNN), with K optimized by the leave-one-out error on the training set, and the Logistic Linear classifier (LogLC) [3]. The idea is that we can reduce the complexity of the classifier while increasing the discrimination power and the complexity of the vector space.

Different versions of the proposed combining scheme are tested on several well-known data sets from the UCI Repository [5]. These are: *Banana, Ecoli, Liver, Diabetes, Breast* (Wisconsin Breast Cancer), *Glass, Wine* and *Ionosphere* data. The classification accuracy is computed by using the hold-out technique [3]. Here, the data set is randomly split into two equal and non-overlapping parts, one used for training and the other for testing. The training set is first normalized (to a unit variance) and then the KNN and LogLC are trained in supervised and unsupervised GIVSs. The classifiers are then tested on the normalized test set. This process is repeated 20 times and the results are averaged out. These average performances are shown in Table 1, for which the average standard deviations are less than 0.8%. This suggests that the proposed scheme is robust against data partitioning and initialisations of GMM. Concerning the (Fused) Unsupervised GIVS, only the best results in the testing set over the different values of K and F are shown. A brief discussion on how to choose these values is presented in the next section.

We compare our combined scheme to the corresponding generative classification methods; see Table 2. In case of the diagonal covariance Gaussian model, the standard maximum-a-posterior (MAP) approach was used, while for the spherical Gaussian model, the minimum distance approach was used. Since we deal with vectorial data sets, we also compare our approach to some standard discriminative classifiers trained in the original features spaces; see Table 2.

4   Analysis of the Results

Several observations can be made while studying the results from Tables 1 and 2:

Table 1. Average classification accuracies of the proposed generative-discriminative integration schemes on different data sets

Group Model	Diagonal Gaussian		Spherical Gaussian	
Measure	Log PDF		Euclidean distance	
Classifier	KNN	LogLC	KNN	LogLC
Banana, 2 classes (150-150), 2 features				
Supervised GIVS	86.07%	79.30%	91.92%	92.57%
Unsupervised GIVS	97.58%	84.10%	98.07%	97.12%
Fused Unsup. GIVS	97.72%	84.10%	98.08%	95.43%
Ecoli, 3 classes (143-77-52), 5 features				
Supervised GIVS	92.34%	93.36%	92.45%	92.55%
Unsupervised GIVS	90.15%	92.55%	92.81%	93.36%
Fused Unsup. GIVS	89.71%	91.02%	92.96%	92.37%
Liver, 2 classes (145-200), 6 features				
Supervised GIVS	55.78%	59.08%	56.79%	59.42%
Unsupervised GIVS	58.82%	70.12%	57.86%	65.03%
Fused Unsup. GIVS	59.51%	70.12%	57.17%	66.27%
Diabetes, 2 classes (500-268), 8 features				
Supervised GIVS	74.49%	75.59%	64.83%	67.98%
Unsupervised GIVS	67.94%	77.37%	73.16%	76.91%
Fused Unsup. GIVS	66.28%	77.43%	72.46%	76.64%
Breast, 2 classes (444-239), 9 features				
Supervised GIVS	95.42%	96.52%	70.13%	69.37%
Unsupervised GIVS	95.38%	96.52%	96.45%	96.71%
Fused Unsup. GIVS	95.28%	96.52%	96.48%	96.58%
Glass, 4 classes (70-76-17-51), 9 features				
Supervised GIVS	61.81%	61.62%	62.64%	62.64%
Unsupervised GIVS	60.42%	62.13%	68.98%	65.14%
Fused Unsup. GIVS	60.69%	61.11%	68.52%	64.91%
Wine, 3 classes (59-71-48), 13 features				
Supervised GIVS	92.33%	93.50%	70.00%	46.61%
Unsupervised GIVS	90.94%	92.78%	94.83%	95.39%
Fused Unsup. GIVS	90.83%	94.11%	94.94%	94.72%
Ionosphere, 2 classes (225-126), 32 features				
Supervised GIVS	88.81%	89.77%	38.78%	87.41%
Unsupervised GIVS	87.93%	90.43%	92.39%	92.64%
Fused Unsup. GIVS	87.53%	91.11%	92.67%	90.77%

1. Classifiers trained in the GIVS perform almost always evidently better than the corresponding generative approaches. There are two exceptions, the *Ecoli* and the *Wine* data, where there is no significant improvement. This can however be easily explained by the fact that in the original feature vector spaces the classes are well described by normal distributions. The original models are therefore well suited, hence well performing. The other examples indicate that our integrated method is able to recover from situations in which generative models are improper either due to wrong assumptions (such as independently distributed features or Gaussian models for non-Gaussian

Table 2. Average classification accuracies of the standard discriminative and generative methods on different data sets

Data	Generative methods		Discriminative methods		
	Diag-Gauss (MAP)	Sph-Gauss (Min-dist)	KNN	LogLC	SVM
Banana	80.02%	92.05%	97.53%	85.68%	97.99%
Ecoli	92.45%	92.04%	94.22%	94.33%	94.99%
Liver	53.41%	59.28%	61.25%	68.02%	64.65%
Diabetes	75.22%	67.71%	74.19%	76.55%	77.01%
Breast	95.89%	60.37%	96.54%	96.52%	96.86%
Glass	47.41%	47.27%	69.06%	63.11%	67.36%
Wine	94.83%	95.67%	95.40%	96.93%	97.65%
Ionosphere	80.00%	89.01%	85.31%	75.97%	93.22%

classes), or due to estimation errors (e.g. for an unfavourable sample size or feature size). Our results show that in spite of a wrong model, discriminative classifiers built in the group-induced spaces lead to good results. In brief, our sequential generative-discriminative combination, being a trained combining classification scheme, can recover from initially unsuitable models.

2. When comparing the proposed integrated scheme to the discriminative approaches in the original feature spaces we can observe that they give almost comparable results, except for the *Liver* and *Ionosphere* data (except SVM). In these problems, the corresponding GIVSs are highly discriminative; the classifiers trained there outperform the classifiers in the original feature spaces. The *Liver* problem is very challenging and it seems that by using the clustering mechanism, the method is able to capture important groups in the original space to build a discriminative GIVS. With respect to the *Ionosphere* set, we should mention that this is a high-dimensional problem (32 dimensions), in which discriminative approaches could suffer from the curse of dimensionality (actually SVM, which is less sensitive to this problem, performs well on these data). By using the GIVS, we can reduce the dimension to a moderate size, significantly improving the results.

3. By analysing the GIVS approach in depth, we can observe that the Unsupervised GIVS almost always leads to better (or at least equal) results than the Supervised GIVS. If the classes cannot be characterized by normal distributions and we fit each class with a single Gaussian, then the resulting model is very poor. However, natural clusters can be discovered if we fit several ($> C$) Gaussian models to the complete data, neglecting the label information. The more-complex geometry of the classes can be revealed in this way. This fact is illustrated in Fig. 1. Different groups are shown in subplot (b). Some of them span both classes and capture the real geometry of the problem.

Concerning the Fused Unsupervised approach, there is no substantial improvement over the simple Unsupervised GIVS scheme. The logical explanation is that the dimension of the Fused GIVS is very high and the classifiers trained there suffer from the curse of dimensionality. Surely, a more clever fusion strategy is necessary, which is currently under investigation.

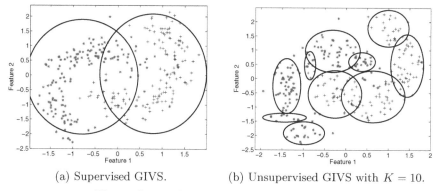

(a) Supervised GIVS.   (b) Unsupervised GIVS with $K = 10$.

Fig. 1. Groups determined for the Banana data

4. With respect to the clustering technique, GMM seems to be a reasonable choice, since we use Gaussian models. Moreover, typically this technique is quite accurate and permits overlapping clusters. Some experiments with K-means and other methodologies were also performed, but the obtained results were comparable.

5. The two group models (Diagonal Covariance Gaussian and Spherical Gaussian) show different behaviours depending on the data characteristics. In general, the former leads to better results in low-dimensional feature spaces, while it is outperformed by the latter in high-dimensional spaces. See Table 1 to compare the results of the high-dimensional *Wine* and *Ionosphere* data with respect to the other ones. The Diagonal Covariance Gaussian models describe the groups in a more flexible way than the spherical Gaussian models are capable to, but they need sufficient data to determine their $2d$ parameters in the d-dimensional space. When the dimension of the feature space grows, simpler models are preferred to avoid bad estimates.

Finally, we emphasize that the used models should relatively be simple to prevent overtraining. In the current set-up we use the same training data twice: to build the GIVS and to train the classifier. So, we can only benefit from the sequential integration if the models are weak (such that we do not adjust to the data noise) and the final classifier is simple. The use of a complex model in the first stage can lead to overfitting of the complete classification strategy. To justify this in practice, we performed the same experiments with a model based on Parzen windows, hardly obtaining any improvements over the generative approach.

Number of groups for Unsupervised GIVS. To apply the Unsupervised (Fused) GIVS, we have to a priori set K (or F), the number of groups. Different values of K were evaluated in our experiments; we only present the overall best results. Since K is a free parameter, it should be chosen based on the training set only. Our experiments suggest, however, that the choice of perfect K is not crucial, providing that K is *sufficiently* large. In Fig. 2 we plot the average classification accuracy reached in the Unsupervised GIVS as a function of K (only the best classifier in the GIVS space is considered). The results are shown for the

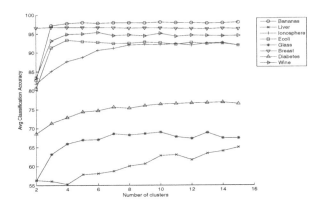

Fig. 2. Classification accuracy of the best discriminative method in the Unsupervised GIVS based on the spherical Gaussian model as a function of the number of clusters. The results are shown for several data sets.

non-Gaussian data sets and the spherical Gaussian model. We can observe that in almost all cases the performance increases with the growing number of clusters up to a certain number after which there is no further improvement. The value of K should also not be too large in order to prevent a decreasing performance due to the high dimension. Nevertheless, this peaking behavior was not present in the range we examined. Moreover, we could observe that for difficult problems (such as *Liver*, *Ionosphere* and *Diabetes*) the performance increase is slow, asking for a large number of clusters in order to reach a satisfactory accuracy.

A possible solution to the direct computation of K is to determine the best value using the leave-one-out error on the training set (as typically done in several other classification contexts). Another approach is to link this value to the dimension of the problem, in terms of the cardinality of objects and classes, and the number of features.

5   Summary

In this paper, we propose a general strategy to integrate the strengths of unsupervised learning, which encodes data structure, and supervised learning. This is realized via group-induced vector spaces in which statistical classifiers are trained. In our experiments we deal with simple vectorial data and focus on combination of generative and discriminative approaches. Generative techniques (here, simple Gaussian models) are used to describe the data structure, while discriminative techniques (here, the KNN and logistic classifier) combine weak grouping evidences in a classification setting.

We find out that such an integrated generative-discriminative approach outperforms the generative techniques and leads to better results than the discriminative techniques in high-dimensional spaces (*Ionosphere* data) or in the case of highly-overlapping problems (*Liver* data). The stability of our scheme relies on the power of combining weak models: multiple (overlapping) clusters cover the data and their evidence is accumulated by a simple final combiner. In such a case, the discussed method will be robust against structure shifts in future data.

It is important to emphasize that the discussed approach is more general than the discriminative methods, applicable in vector spaces only. Now, we can also deal with non-vectorial structures, for which typically only generative models are fitted, as discriminative techniques are lacking. Since many powerful descriptive models are available (such as hidden Markov models), the advantage of the proposed integration lies in its wide applicability to almost any vectorial and non-vectorial classification problem. Future work will include the study of non-vectorial structures.

Finally, we also note that another possible employment of our approach is in the semi-supervised classification context [1]. Additional unlabeled data could efficiently be exploited in order to create an accurate and representative feature space, where a discriminant classifier may be trained using labels.

References

1. I. Cohen, F. Cozman, N. Sebe, M. Cirelo, and T. Huang. Semisupervised learning of classifiers: Theory, algorithms, and their application to human-computer interaction. *IEEE Trans. Pattern Analysis Machine Intell.*, 26(12):1553–1567, 2004.
2. L. Didaci, G. Giacinto, F. Roli, and G.L. Marcialis. A study on the performances of dynamic classifier selection based on local accuracy estimation. *Pattern Recognition*, 38(11):2188–2191, 2005.
3. R.O. Duda, P.E. Hart, and D.G. Stork. *Pattern Classification*. Wiley., 2001.
4. R.P.W. Duin. The combining classifier: To train or not to train? In *International Conference on Pattern Recognition*, volume II, pages 765–770, Canada, 2002.
5. S. Hettich, C.L. Blake, and C.J. Merz. UCI repository of ML databases, 1998. http://www.ics.uci.edu/~mlearn/MLRepository.html.
6. G. Hinton, M. Revow, and P. Dayan. Recognizing handwritten digits using mixtures of linear models. In *Neural Inf. Proc. Syst.*, pages 1015–1022, 1995.
7. T.S. Jaakkola and D. Haussler. Exploiting generative models in discriminative classifiers. In *Neural Inf. Proc. Syst.*, 1999.
8. M. Kambhatla and T.K. Leen. Dimension reduction by local principal component analysis. *Neural Computation*, 9:443–482, 1997.
9. C. Lai, D.M.J. Tax, R.P.W. Duin, E. Pękalska, and P. Paclík. A study on combining image representations for image classification and retrieval. *International Journal of Pattern Recognition and Artificial Intelligence*, 18(5):867–890, 2004.
10. M. Layton and M. Gales. Augmented statistical models: Exploiting generative models in discriminative classifiers. In *Neural Inf. Proc. Syst.*, 2005.
11. G. McLachlan and D. Peel. *Finite Mixture Models*. John Wiley & Sons, Inc., 2000.
12. J.E. Moody and C. Darken. Fast learning in networks of locally-tuned processing units. *Neural Computation*, 1:281–294, 1989.
13. A. Ng and M. Jordan. On discriminative vs generative classifiers: A comparison of logistic regression and naive Bayes. In *Neural Inf. Proc. Syst.*, 2002.
14. M.E. Tipping and C. Bishop. Mixtures of probabilistic principal component analyzers. *Neural Computation*, 11:443–482, 1999.
15. K. Woods, W.P. Kegelmeyer, and K. Bower. Combination of multiple classifiers using local accuracy estimates. *IEEE Trans. on Pattern Recognition and Machine Intelligence*, 19(4):405–409, 1997.

Selecting Diversifying Heuristics for Cluster Ensembles

Stefan T. Hadjitodorov[1] and Ludmila I. Kuncheva[2]

[1] CLBME, Bulgarian Academy of Sciences, 1113 Sofia, Bulgaria
sthadj@argo.bas.bg
[2] School of Computer Science, University of Wales, Bangor, UK
l.i.kuncheva@bangor.ac.uk.

Abstract. Cluster ensembles are deemed to be better than single clustering algorithms for discovering complex or noisy structures in data. Various heuristics for constructing such ensembles have been examined in the literature, e.g., random feature selection, weak clusterers, random projections, etc. Typically, one heuristic is picked at a time to construct the ensemble. To increase diversity of the ensemble, several heuristics may be applied together. However, not any combination may be beneficial. Here we apply a standard genetic algorithm (GA) to select from 7 standard heuristics for k-means cluster ensembles. The ensemble size is also encoded in the chromosome. In this way the data is forced to guide the selection of heuristics as well as the ensemble size. Eighteen moderate-size datasets were used: 4 artificial and 14 real. The results resonate with our previous findings in that high diversity is not necessarily a prerequisite for high accuracy of the ensemble. No particular combination of heuristics appeared to be consistently chosen across all datasets, which justifies the existing variety of cluster ensembles. Among the most often selected heuristics were random feature extraction, random feature selection and random number of clusters assigned for each ensemble member. Based on the experiments, we recommend that the current practice of using one or two heuristics for building k-means cluster ensembles should be revised in favour of using 3-5 heuristics.[1]

Keywords: Pattern recognition; multiple classifier systems; cluster ensembles; genetic algorithms; diversifying heuristics.

1 Introduction

Selecting a good clustering algorithm is more difficult than selecting a good classifier. The difficulty comes from the fact that in clustering there is no supervision, i.e., data have no labels against which to match the partition obtained through the clustering algorithm. Therefore, instead of running the risk of picking an unsuitable clustering algorithm, a cluster ensemble can be used [13]. The

---

[1] This work was supported by research grant # 15035 under the European Joint Project scheme, Royal Society, UK.

M. Haindl, J. Kittler, and F. Roli (Eds.): MCS 2007, LNCS 4472, pp. 200–209, 2007.

presumption is that even a basic off-the-shelf cluster ensemble will outperform a randomly chosen clustering algorithm. The question then becomes whether we can guide the selection of a cluster ensemble.

Here we are interested in *cluster ensembles*. Various heuristics have been proposed for building diverse cluster ensembles. Usually these heuristics are applied one at a time or at most two. The large majority of the publications on cluster ensembles are devoted to finding a combination method (called sometimes a consensus function), for example [1, 3, 5, 11, 15, 6, 14, 10], while few papers look into comparisons between different diversifying heuristics e.g., [8]. In this study we propose to evaluate combinations of such heuristics by a standard genetic algorithm. Our hypothesis is that better cluster ensembles could be created using more than one diversifying heuristics at the same time. The objective is to find out which diversifying heuristics and combinations thereof are being selected more frequently by a data-guided GA.

Our application is focused on a class of datasets whose common characteristics are: (1) small number of true classes (often overlapping), which may or may not correspond to coherent clusters; (2) moderate number of observations (up to few hundred); (3) moderate number of features (typically 5 to 30). Such data sets are collected, for example, in clinical medicine for pilot research studies. In the experiments reported in Section 4 we have used, among others, six such benchmark data sets from the UCI Machine Learning Repository [2].

The rest of the paper is organized as follows. Section 2 lists the heuristics for building diverse cluster ensembles and explains the main ensemble algorithm. Section 3 describes briefly the genetic algorithm. The choice of data sets and the experimental set-up are detailed in Section 4, where we also present and discuss the results. Section 5 concludes the study.

2   Cluster Ensembles

We investigate the effect of various design heuristics on the ensemble accuracy. These heuristics are necessary in order to make sure that the individual clusterers produce different, yet sensible, partitions of the data.

2.1   Cluster Ensembles

Let $P_1, \ldots, P_L$ be a set of partitions of a data set $\mathbf{Z}$, each one obtained from applying a clustering algorithm, or a 'clusterer'. The aim is to find a resultant partition P^* which best represents the structure of $\mathbf{Z}$. We implemented the pairwise approach [4] because it has been a popular choice despite its comparatively large computational complexity. The generic version of the pairwise cluster ensemble algorithm is outlined below.

1. Given is a data set $\mathbf{Z}$ with N elements. Pick the ensemble size L and the number of clusters c. Usually c is larger than the suspected number of clusters so there is "overproduction" of clusters.
2. Generate L partitions of $\mathbf{Z}$ with c clusters in each partition.

3. Form a co-association matrix for each partition, $M^{(k)} = \left\{ m_{ij}^{(k)} \right\}$, of size $N \times N$, $k = 1, \ldots, L$, where $m_{ij}^{(k)} = 1$, if $\mathbf{z}_i$ and $\mathbf{z}_j$ are in the same cluster in partition k, and $m_{ij}^{(k)} = 0$ otherwise.

4. Form a final co-association matrix $\mathbf{M}$ (consensus matrix) from $M^{(k)}$, $k = 1, \ldots, L$, and derive the final clustering using this matrix. A typical choice for $\mathbf{M}$ is the average of the individual matrices $M^{(k)}$.

The consensus matrix $\mathbf{M}$ can be regarded as a similarity matrix between the points of $\mathbf{Z}$. Therefore, it can be used with any clustering algorithm which operates directly upon a similarity matrix. Viewed in this context, cluster ensemble is a type of *stacked clustering* whereby we can generate layers of similarity matrices and apply clustering algorithms on them. Extensive experimentation have singled out hypergraph methods (HGPA, CSPA and MCLA [13]) and average linkage as the best consensus functions. In a previous study we found that better results were obtained if we used $\mathbf{M}$ as a new feature space and ran k-means on it [9].

The randomisation heuristics come into play in Step 2 where the individual partitions are formed.

Cluster validation presents a difficult problem with no trivial solution. Here we assume that this problem has been solved and the "true" number of clusters is available. This assumption, restrictive as it is, is not unusual for studies like ours. The focus of this paper is the relative merit of heuristics and combinations of heuristics compared to one another. We may well pre-set the best possible scenario where the number of clusters is given as this setup will not disadvantage any of the heuristics.

The most widely used indices to estimate similarity between partitions are Rand, Jaccard, adjusted Rand, correlation, mutual information and entropy. When the number of obtained clusters is the same as the number of known groups in the data, the apparent accuracy of the cluster ensemble (classification accuracy) has been used as the most intuitive measure. To calculate classification accuracy, each cluster is labeled with the class most represented within and the proportion of correctly labeled objects from the whole of Z is evaluated. This re-labeling of the clusters guarantees the best classification accuracy.

3   The Genetic Algorithm for Selecting Diversifying Heuristics

Genetic algorithms (GA) are a popular optimization technique [7]. They provide a form of guided random search whereby the solution is evolved within a "population" through subsequent iterations called generations. Each population consists of "chromosomes" which describe the individuals. In our case, an individual will be a cluster ensemble encoded as a 12-bit binary string. The first seven bits encode the heuristics as explained in the next section. A value of 1 means that the respective heuristic is chosen for the ensemble. Bits 8 to 12 encode the ensemble size in the following way. These bits are assigned "weights" as [5, 10, 20, 50, 100]. The ensemble size, L, is the sum of the weights of the selected bits (values 1). For example, [0,0,1,0,1] means $L = 120$. The fitness function used to evaluate the merit of a chromosome is the classification accuracy of the respective ensemble (the accuracy of the resultant partition P^*). Interestingly, in this implementation, the same chromosome may get different fitness values if evaluated twice. This is because only the structure of the ensemble is determined within the chromosome. The fitness depends upon various random parameters according to the heuristics in the chromosome. In other words, slightly different phenotypes may correspond to the same genotype. In order to eliminate part of this randomness, we take as the fitness of a chromosome, the average of five evaluation runs.

We use the standard GA with choices as shown below

1. Pick the parameters of the GA:
   (a) Population size m (even).
   (b) Maximum number of generations T_{max}.
   (c) Mutation probability P_m.
2. Generate a random population of m chromosomes and calculate their fitness values.
3. For $i = 1 : T_{max}$,
   (a) Assuming that the whole population is the mating set, select $m/2$ couples of parents from the current population (repetitions are allowed).
   (b) Perform (one-point) crossover to generate m offspring chromosomes.
   (c) Mutate the offspring according to the mutation probability.
   (d) Calculate the fitness values of the mutated offspring.
   (e) Pool the offspring and the current population and select as the next population the m chromosomes with the highest fitness.
4. End i.

The limit number of generations, population size and mutation probability are parameters of this GA model. We assume that the whole population is allowed to reproduce, the crossover probability is set to 1.0, and since elitist selection is used the generation gap is not fixed. This drives the model closer to a random search with main emphasis being on exploration.

4 The Experiment

4.1 Data Sets

Figure 1 shows four artificial data sets: difficult-doughnut, easy-doughnut, four-gauss and two-spirals. The first three datasets were generated in 2-D (as plotted) and then 10 more dimensions of uniform random noise were appended to each data set. A total of 100 points were generated from each distribution.[2]

---

[2] Matlab code for generating these data sets is available at
    http://www.informatics.bangor.ac.uk/~kuncheva/activities/patrec1.html

Easy doughnut Difficult doughnut   Four gauss   Two spirals

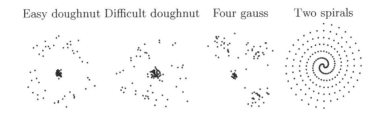

Fig. 1. The four artificial data sets used in this study. The first three data sets were generated with 10 additional noise features.

Three benchmark biological datasets were used: crabs [12], iris and soybean-small from UCI [2]. The parameters of all data sets are summarized in Table 1. The eleven medical data sets in this study come from two sources. The datasets breast, heart, liver, lymph, pima diabetes and thyroid are from UCI while the other five data sets are now available at .http://www.informatics.bangor.ac.uk/.kuncheva/activities/patrec1.html

These data sets are

> contractions (98 objects, 9 features, 2 classses)
> weaning (151 objects, 17 features, 2 classes)
> respiratory (85 objects, 17 features, 2 classes)
> laryngeal (213 objects, 16 features, 2 classes)
> voice-3 (238objects, 10 features ,3 classes)

4.2 Experimental Protocol

All real data sets except iris and soybean-small were standardized (all features were transformed to have mean 0 and standard deviation 1). The standardization was deemed necessary because the data contained mixed variables and variables measured in very different scales.

All ensembles used k-means, started from a random initialization, as the base clusterer. The following heuristics were encoded as the first 7 bits of the chromosome in the GA.

1. Different samples. We used subsampling of size randomly chosen between the number of clusters and the total number of objects.
2. Weak clustering algorithm. k-means is stopped after the second iteration.
3. Random projections (feature extraction). We form d random projections where d is the number of relevant principal components obtained from the correlation matrix of the data (eigenvalues greater than 1).
4. Feature selection. A non-empty random subset of the original feature set is picked. Each feature has a chance of 0.5 to be included in the set.
5. Label noise. Here we used 5% label noise.
6. Random number of clusters. If this heuristic is selected, the number of over-produced clusters, c, is picked from the range from 2 to 22.

7. Hybrid ensembles. This heuristic offers another possibility for incorporating diversity in a non-uniform way. The hybridization is not done over different clustering methods but consists in giving each clusterer in the ensemble the freedom to apply different heuristics. The example below illustrates this hybridization.

The seven heuristics are represented as the first 7 of the 12 bits of the chromosome while the last 5 bits encode the ensemble size. For example, an ensemble represented by chromosome

| 0 | 0 | 1 | 1 | 0 | 1 | 0 | 1 | 0 | 0 | 1 | 0 |

will consist of 55 (5+50) clusterers. Each of them will be built using k-means with random feature selection (heuristic 4) followed by random linear feature extractions (heuristic 3)[3] and a randomly chosen number of overproduced clusters between 2 and 22 (heuristic 6). Consider now the following chromosome, corresponding to a hybrid ensemble

| 0 | 0 | 1 | 1 | 0 | 1 | **1** | 1 | 0 | 0 | 1 | 0 |

In this case, each of the 55 clusterers will have a chance to select any combination of the three heuristics (3, 4 and 6) or none of them. This means that the hybridization opens up a second possibility for further "refined" selection of the already selected heuristics.

If none of the first 7 bits of the chromosome is switched to 1, only random initialization of k-means is applied. If none of the last 5 bits of the chromosome is switched to 1, a default value of $L = 5$ is assigned.

The GA parameters were chosen as follows: population size $m = 10$; maximum number of generations $T_{max} = 30$ and mutation probability $P_m = 0.15$.

4.3   Results

Table 1 displays the data characteristics, the end results from the GA and the corresponding accuracies. N denotes the number of objects in the data set, n is the number of features, c is the number of clusters, L is the ensemble size and Acc is the classification accuracy of the ensemble. Shown for each data set is the best chromosome in the last (30th) generation. The classification accuracy Acc is an average of 5 runs of the ensemble. In the last column we show the classification accuracy obtained by Greene et al. [8].

Our hypothesis is that the improved ensemble accuracy is owed to the selection of appropriate heuristics. Figure 2 shows the proportion of times each of the 7 heuristics has been selected. The large error bars give the means and the 95% confidence intervals of the respective proportions calculated within the last population of the GA. As there are 18 data sets, and each population contains 10

---

[3] The order in which we apply heuristics 3 and 4 is immaterial. We have chosen to apply 4 before 3 for computational convenience.

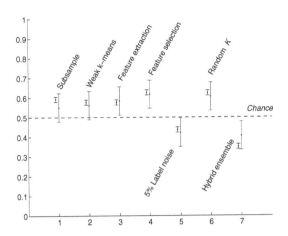

Fig. 2. Mean proportions of individual occurrences of the 7 heuristics with 95% confidence intervals for the mean. The large intervals are derived from the last population of the GA; the small intervals are derived from the whole run of the GA.

Table 1. Data characteristics and the end results from the GA

				Heuristics									
Dataset	N	n	c	1	2	3	4	5	6	7	L	Acc	[8]
difficult doughnut	100	12	2	0	0	0	1	0	1	0	65	0.982	
easy doughnut	100	12	2	0	0	0	1	0	1	1	60	1.000	
four gauss	100	12	4	1	1	1	1	1	0	0	130	0.982	
spirals-2	194	2	2	0	1	1	0	0	1	0	120	0.551	(1.000)
crabs	200	7	2	1	1	1	1	1	0	0	165	0.625	
iris	150	4	3	1	0	1	1	1	1	0	165	0.933	(0.893)
soybean-small	47	35	4	1	0	0	1	1	0	0	170	0.915	
breast	277	9	2	0	1	1	0	1	1	1	10	0.718	(0.762)
heart	270	13	2	1	1	0	1	1	0	0	150	0.829	(0.600)
liver	345	6	2	1	1	1	0	1	0	1	120	0.602	(0.585)
lymph	148	18	4	1	0	1	0	0	1	1	110	0.488	(0.615)
pima diabetes	768	8	2	1	1	0	1	0	1	0	185	0.698	(0.675)
thyroid	215	5	3	1	0	1	0	1	1	1	170	0.889	(0.793)
contractions	98	27	2	1	0	1	1	0	0	0	65	0.845	
intubation	302	17	2	0	0	1	0	0	0	1	170	0.772	
laryngeal	213	16	2	0	0	1	1	0	0	1	55	0.822	
respiratory	85	17	2	1	1	0	1	0	1	0	155	0.948	
voice-3	238	10	3	0	1	1	1	0	0	0	5	0.771	

chromosomes, the proportions are calculated from 180 chromosomes. For reference, we plot the probability of being selected by chance (0.5) with a dashed line. According to the confidence intervals, heuristics 3, 4 and 6 are selected more often than chance whereas label noise (heuristic 5) and hybrid ensembles (heuristic 7) are suppressed. The short error bars show the mean and the 95% confidence

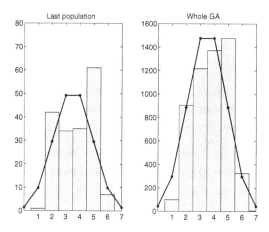

Fig. 3. Histograms of the number of selected heuristics. The overlaid polygon is the theoretical binomial distribution for $n = 7$ and $p = 0.5$.

intervals of the proportions calculated from the whole run of the GA (30 generations). Thus each proportion is evaluated on $30 \times 10 \times 18 = 5400$ chromosomes. The heuristics which are picked more often than chance are Subsample, Weak k-means, Feature extraction, Feature selection and Random c.

Shown in Figure 3 are the histograms of the number of selected heuristics for an ensemble. The left plot is obtained from the last populations for the 18 data sets, and the right plot is obtained from the whole run of the GA. If each heuristic was selected independently and completely by chance, the number of selected heuristics would follow a binomial distribution with parameters $n = 7$ and $p = 0.5$. The polygon for the binomial distribution is overlaid in the two plots. To check whether the obtained distribution differs from binomial, we carried out a χ^2 test. With significance $p < 10^{-9}$, both obtained distributions are different from binomial distribution.

Table 2. Combinations of heuristics with largest frequency of occurrence for a specified number of selected heuristics

# selected	Heuristics 1 2 3 4 5 6 7	Frequency	Proportion	95% CI
7	1 1 1 1 1 1 1	6	0.011	0.0020–0.0200
6	1 1 1 1 1 1 0	143	0.0265	0.0222–0.0308
5	1 1 1 1 0 1 0	302	0.0559	0.0498–0.0620
4	1 1 1 0 0 1 0	262	0.0485	0.0428–0.0542
3	0 0 1 1 0 0 1	131	0.0243	0.0202–0.0284
2	0 0 0 1 0 1 0	194	0.0359	0.0310–0.0409
1	0 0 0 1 0 0 0	56	0.0104	0.0077–0.0131

The most notable difference from the binomial probability is observed for 5 heuristics selected together. Five heuristics have been selected in 33.89% of the ensembles in the last populations of the GA and in 27.35% of the ensembles within the whole run. The next largest difference is for 2 selected heuristics in the last population (23.33%).

Table 2 shows which combinations of heuristics have been encountered most frequently when different number of heuristics have been selected. For example, for five selected heuristics, heuristics 1, 2, 3, 4, and 6 appeared in 302 out of 1477 chromosomes. The last column of the table shows the 95% confidence interval for the mean (averaged on 5400 cases). Knowing that the chance for selecting a particular combination is $\frac{1}{2^7} = 0.0078$, the chances of selecting the combinations shown in the table are significantly larger than chance ($\alpha = 0.05$) for 2 to 6 selected heuristics. The probability of selecting all 7 heuristics is significantly below chance while the probability for selecting only heuristic 4 is not significantly higher than chance.

No combination of heuristics appeared together consistently. A glance at the correlation matrix using the whole run of the GA reveals that correlations between pairs of heuristics are weak, varying between -0.2598 (feature extraction and feature selection) and 0.2456 (weak k-means and label noise). Therefore, we can think of the diversifying heuristics as fairly independent.

5   Conclusions

We restricted our study to datasets which one may acquire from pilot studies in biomedical domain, e.g., pilot clinical trials. Such data sets have small number of classes (we assume that they correspond to clusters), moderate number of observations (up to few hundred) and moderate number of features (typically 5 to 30). Our collection for this study consisted of 18 such data sets, among which artificial, real, benchmark and new medical data. Using a GA to select combination of heuristics as well as ensemble size we found that: (1) More than 1 heuristic is better. The collection of heuristics being chosen most often by the GA was {Subsample, Weak k-means, Feature extraction, Feature selection and Random c} and (2) Too many is not necessarily good. Ensembles with more than 5 heuristics appeared to be too random to be useful.

We also observed that ensemble sizes of 100+ fared better than smaller ensemble for the type of problems in this study. However, it seems that the accuracy for ensemble sizes beyond 100 starts to level off and ensembles of 2000 clusterers may only offer marginal improvement at the expense of a large increase of the computational cost.

Our experimental results indicated low dependency between heuristics. This was partly expected because the heuristics come from different ways of handling the data and setting the clustering procedures. The independence shows that each heuristic has a specific niche and should not be lightly ignored. This study was focused on selection of heuristics assuming that the "correct" number of clusters is known. Evaluating the number of clusters is a challenging problem of its own, worthy of a separate study.

References

1. H. Ayad, O. Basir, and M. Kamel. A probabilistic model using information theoretic measures for cluster ensembles. In *Proc. 5th International Workshop on Multiple Classifier Systems, MCS04*, pages 144–153, Cagliari, Italy, 2004.
2. C. L. Blake and C. J. Merz. UCI repository of machine learning databases, 1998. http://www.ics.uci.edu/~mlearn/MLRepository.html.
3. X. Z. Fern and C. E. Brodley. Solving cluster ensemble problems by bipartite graph partitioning. In *Proc. 21th International Conference on Machine Learning, ICML*, Banff, Canada, 2004.
4. A. Fred. Finding consistent clusters in data partitions. In F. Roli and J. Kittler, editors, *Proc. 2nd International Workshop on Multiple Classifier Systems, MCS'01*, volume 2096 of *Lecture Notes in Computer Science*, pages 309–318, Cambridge, UK, 2001. Springer-Verlag.
5. A. N. L. Fred and A. K. Jain. Combining multiple clusterungs using evidence accumulation. *IEEE Transactions on Pattern Analysis and Machine Intelligence*, 27(6):835–850, 2005.
6. J. Ghosh. Multiclassifier systems: Back to the future. In F. Roli and J. Kittler, editors, *Proc. 3d International Workshop on Multiple Classifier Systems, MCS'02*, volume 2364 of *Lecture Notes in Computer Science*, pages 1–15, Cagliari, Italy, 2002. Springer-Verlag.
7. D. Goldberg. *Genetic Algorithms in Search, Optimization and Machine Learning*. Addison-Wesley, NY, 1989.
8. D. Greene, A. Tsymbal, N. Bolshakova, and P. Cunningham. Ensemble clustering in medical diagnostics. Technical Report TCD-CS-2004-12, Department of Computer Science, Trinity College, Dublin, Ireland, 2004.
9. L. I. Kuncheva, S. T. Hadjitodorov, and L. P. Todorova. Experimental comparison of cluster ensemble methods. In *Proc. FUSION*, Florence, Italy, 2006.
10. B. Minaei, A. Topchy, and W. Punch. Ensembles of partitions via data resampling. In *Proceedings of the International Conference on Information Technology: Coding and Computing, ITCC04*, Las Vegas, 2004.
11. S. Monti, P. Tamayo, J. Mesirov, and T. Golub. Consensus clustering: A resampling based method for class discovery and visualization of gene expression microarray data. *Machine Learning*, 52:91–118, 2003.
12. B. D. Ripley. *Pattern Recognition and Neural Networks*. University Press, Cambridge, 1996.
13. A. Strehl and J. Ghosh. Cluster ensembles - A knowledge reuse framework for combining multiple partitions. *Journal of Machine Learning Research*, 3:583–618, 2002.
14. A. Topchy, B. Minaei, A. K. Jain, and W. Punch. Adaptive clustering ensembles. In *Proceedings of ICPR, 2004, Cambridge, UK*, 2004.
15. A. Weingessel, E. Dimitriadou, and K. Hornik. An ensemble method for clustering, 2003. Working paper, http://www.ci.tuwien.ac.at/Conferences/DSC-2003/.

Unsupervised Texture Segmentation Using Multiple Segmenters Strategy

Michal Haindl and Stanislav Mikeš

Institute of Information Theory and Automation
Academy of Sciences CR, Prague, Czech Republic
{haindl,xaos}@utia.cas.cz

Abstract. A novel unsupervised multi-spectral multiple-segmenter texture segmentation method with unknown number of classes is presented. The unsupervised segmenter is based on a combination of several unsupervised segmentation results, each in different resolution, using the sum rule. Multi-spectral texture mosaics are locally represented by four causal multi-spectral random field models recursively evaluated for each pixel. The single-resolution segmentation part of the algorithm is based on the underlying Gaussian mixture model and starts with an over segmented initial estimation which is adaptively modified until the optimal number of homogeneous texture segments is reached.

The performance of the presented method is extensively tested on the Prague segmentation benchmark using the commonest segmentation criteria and compares favourably with several alternative texture segmentation methods.

1 Introduction

Segmentation is the fundamental process which affects the overall performance of any automated image analysis system. Image regions, homogeneous with respect to some usually textural or colour measure, which result from a segmentation algorithm are analysed in subsequent interpretation steps. Texture-based image segmentation is area of intense research activity in recent years and many algorithms were published in consequence of all this effort. These methods are usually categorized [1] as region-based, boundary-based, or as a hybrid of the two. Different published methods are difficult to compare because of lack of a comprehensive analysis together with accessible experimental data, however available results indicate that the ill-defined texture segmentation problem is still far from being satisfactorily solved. Spatial interaction models and especially Markov random fields-based models are increasingly popular for texture representation [2], [1], [3], etc. Several researchers dealt with the difficult problem of unsupervised segmentation using these models see for example [4], [5], [6], [7] or [8],[9].

The concept of decision fusion [10] for high-performance pattern recognition is well known and widely accepted in the area of supervised classification where (often very diverse) classification technologies, each providing complementary

M. Haindl, J. Kittler, and F. Roli (Eds.): MCS 2007, LNCS 4472, pp. 210–219, 2007.

sources of information about class membership, can be integrated to provide more accurate, robust and reliable classification decisions than the single classifier applications. It is also noted [11] that a single classifier with a single feature set and a single generalized classification strategy often does not comprehensively capture the large degree of variability and complexity encountered in many application domains while multiple decision combination can help to alleviate many of these problems by acquiring multiple-source information through multiple features extracted from multiple processes.

Similar advantages can also be expected for the unsupervised segmentation applications. However, a direct unsupervised application of the supervised classifiers fusion idea is complicated with unknown number of data hidden classes and consequently a different number of segmented regions in segmentation results to be fused. This paper exploits above advantages by combining several unsupervised segmenters of the same type but with different feature sets.

2   Combination of Multiple Segmenters

The proposed method combines segmentation results from different resolution. We assume to down-sample input image Y into M different resolutions $Y^{(m)} = \downarrow^{\iota_m} Y$ with sampling factors ι_m $m = 1, \ldots, M$ identical for both directions and $Y^{(1)} = Y$. Local texture for each pixel $Y_r^{(m)}$ is represented the 3D simultaneous causal autoregressive random field model (CAR) parameter space Θ_r (4) and modelled by the Gaussian mixture model (5),(6).

2.1   Single-Resolution Texture Model

Static smooth multi-spectral textures require three dimensional models for adequate representation. We assume that single multi-spectral textures can be locally modelled using a 3D simultaneous causal autoregressive random field model (CAR). This model can be expressed as a stationary causal uncorrelated noise driven 3D autoregressive process [12]:

$$Y_r = \gamma X_r + e_r \ , \tag{1}$$

where $\gamma = [A_1, \ldots, A_\eta]$ is the $d \times d\eta$ parameter matrix, d is the number of spectral bands, I_r^c is a causal neighborhood index set with $\eta = card(I_r^c)$ and e_r is a white Gaussian noise vector with zero mean and a constant but unknown covariance, X_r is a corresponding vector of the contextual neighbours Y_{r-s} and $r, r-1, \ldots$ is a chosen direction of movement on the image index lattice I. The selection of an appropriate CAR model support (I_r^c) is important to obtain good texture representation but less important for segmentation. The optimal neighbourhood as well as the Bayesian parameters estimation of a CAR model can be found analytically under few additional and acceptable assumptions using the Bayesian approach ([12]). The recursive Bayesian parameter estimation of the CAR model is [12]:

$$\hat{\gamma}_{r-1}^T = \hat{\gamma}_{r-2}^T + \frac{V_{x(r-2)}^{-1} X_{r-1} (Y_{r-1} - \hat{\gamma}_{r-2} X_{r-1})^T}{(1 + X_{r-1}^T V_{x(r-2)}^{-1} X_{r-1})} \, , \tag{2}$$

where $V_{x(r-1)} = \sum_{k=1}^{r-1} X_k X_k^T + V_{x(0)}$. Local texture for each pixel is represented by four parametric vectors. Each vector contains local estimations of the CAR model parameters. These models have identical contextual neighbourhood I_r^c but they differ in their major movement direction (top-down, bottom-up, rightward, leftward), i.e.,

$$\tilde{\gamma}_r^T = \{\hat{\gamma}_r^t, \hat{\gamma}_r^b, \hat{\gamma}_r^r, \hat{\gamma}_r^l\}^T \, . \tag{3}$$

The parametric space $\tilde{\gamma}$ is subsequently smooth out, rearranged into a vector and its dimensionality is reduced using the Karhunen-Loeve feature extraction ($\bar{\gamma}$). Finally we add the average local spectral values ζ_r to the resulting feature vector (Θ_r).

2.2 Mixture Based Segmentation

Multi-spectral texture segmentation is done by clustering in the CAR parameter space Θ defined on the lattice I where

$$\Theta_r = [\bar{\gamma}_r, \zeta_r]^T \tag{4}$$

is the modified parameter vector (3) computed for the lattice location r. We assume that this parametric space can be represented using the Gaussian mixture model (GM) with diagonal covariance matrices due to the previous CAR parametric space decorrelation. The Gaussian mixture model for CAR parametric representation is as follows:

$$p(\Theta_r) = \sum_{i=1}^{K} p_i \, p(\Theta_r \mid \nu_i, \Sigma_i) \, , \tag{5}$$

$$p(\Theta_r \mid \nu_i, \Sigma_i) = \frac{|\Sigma_i|^{-\frac{1}{2}}}{(2\pi)^{\frac{d}{2}}} e^{-\frac{(\Theta_r - \nu_i)^T \Sigma_i^{-1} (\Theta_r - \nu_i)}{2}} \, . \tag{6}$$

The mixture model equations (5),(6) are solved using a modified EM algorithm. The algorithm is initialized using ν_i, Σ_i statistics estimated from the corresponding rectangular subimages obtained by regular division of the input texture mosaic. An alternative initialization can be random choice of these statistics. For each possible couple of rectangles the Kullback Leibler divergence

$$D\left(p(\Theta_r \mid \nu_i, \Sigma_i) \,\|\, p(\Theta_r \mid \nu_j, \Sigma_j)\right) =$$
$$\int_\Omega p(\Theta_r \mid \nu_i, \Sigma_i) \, \log\left(\frac{p(\Theta_r \mid \nu_i, \Sigma_i)}{p(\Theta_r \mid \nu_j, \Sigma_j)}\right) d\Theta_r \tag{7}$$

is evaluated and the most similar rectangles, i.e.,

$$\{i, j\} = \arg\min_{k,l} D\left(p(\Theta_r \mid \nu_l, \Sigma_l) \,\|\, p(\Theta_r \mid \nu_k, \Sigma_k)\right)$$

are merged together in each step. This initialization results in K_{ini} subimages and recomputed statistics ν_i, Σ_i. $K_{ini} > K$ where K is the optimal number of textured segments to be found by the algorithm. Two steps of the EM algorithm are repeating after initialization. The components with smaller weights than a fixed threshold $(p_j < \frac{0.1}{K_{ini}})$ are eliminated. For every pair of components we estimate their Kullback Leibler divergence (7). From the most similar couple, the component with the weight smaller than the threshold is merged to its stronger partner and all statistics are actualized using the EM algorithm. The algorithm stops when either the likelihood function has negligible increase $(\mathcal{L}_t - \mathcal{L}_{t-1} < 0.05)$ or the maximum iteration number threshold is reached.

2.3   Resulting Mixture Probabilities

Resulting mixture model probabilities are mapped to the original fine resolution image space for all $m = 1, \ldots, M$ mixture submodels, i.e.,

$$p(\Theta_r^{(m)}) = \sum_{i=1}^{K^{(m)}} p_i^{(m)} p(\Theta_r^{(m)} \mid \nu_i^{(m)}, \Sigma_i^{(m)}) \ , \tag{8}$$

$$p(\Theta_r^{(m)} \mid \nu_i^{(m)}, \Sigma_i^{(m)}) = \frac{|\Sigma_i^{(m)}|^{-\frac{1}{2}}}{(2\pi)^{\frac{d}{2}}} e^{-\frac{(\Theta_r^{(m)} - \nu_i^{(m)})^T (\Sigma_i^{(m)})^{-1} (\Theta_r^{(m)} - \nu_i^{(m)})}{2}} \ . \tag{9}$$

The M cooperating segmenters deliver their class response in the form of conditional probabilities. Each segmenter produces a preference list based on the mixture component probabilities of a particular pixel belonging a particular class, together with a set of confidence measurement values generated in the original decision-making process.

Single-resolution segmentation results cannot be combined without knowledge of the mutual correspondence between regions in all different-resolution segmentation probabilistic mixture component maps $(K^1 \times \sum_{m=2}^{M} K^m$ combinations). Mutual assignments of two probabilistic maps are solved by using the Munkre's assignment algorithm which finds the minimal cost assignment

$$g : A \mapsto B, \ \sum_{\alpha \in A} f(\alpha, g(\alpha))$$

between sets $A, B, |A| = |B| = n$ given the cost function $f(\alpha, \beta), \alpha \in A, \beta \in B$. α corresponds to the fine resolution probabilistic maps, β corresponds to downsampled probabilistic maps and $f(\alpha, \beta)$ is the Kullback Leibler divergence between probabilistic maps. The algorithm has polynomial complexity instead of exponential for the exhaustive search.

The parametric vectors representing texture mosaic pixels are assigned to the clusters based on our modification of the sum rule according to the highest component probabilities, i.e., Y_r is assigned to the cluster ω_{j*} if

$$\pi_{r,j*} = max_j \sum_{s \in I_r} w_s \left(\sum_{m=1}^{M} p(\Theta_{r-s}^{(m)} \mid \nu_j^{(m)}, \Sigma_j^{(m)}) \right) ,$$

where w_s are fixed distance-based weights, I_r is a rectangular neighbourhood and $\pi_{r,j*} > \pi_{thre}$ (otherwise the pixel is unclassified). The area of single cluster blobs is evaluated in the post-processing thematic map filtration step. Regions with similar statistics are merged. Thematic map blobs with area smaller than a given threshold are attached to its neighbour with the highest similarity value.

3 Experimental Results

The algorithm was tested on natural colour textures mosaics from the Prague Texture Segmentation Data-Generator and Benchmark [13]. The benchmark test mosaics layouts and each cell texture membership are randomly generated and filled with colour textures from the large (more than 1000 high resolution colour textures) Prague colour texture database. The benchmark ranks segmentation algorithms according to a chosen criterion. There are implemented three groups of criteria – region-based [14], pixel-wise [15] and consistency measures [16]. The region-based [14] performance criteria mutually compare ground truth (GT) image regions with the corresponding machine segmented regions (MS). They are the correct, oversegmentation, undersegmentation, missed and noise criteria, i.e., *correct* > 75% GT (ground truth) region pixels are correctly assigned, *oversegmentation* > 75% GT pixels are assigned to a union of regions, *undersegmentation* > 75% pixels from a classified region belong to a union of GT regions, missed (GT in none of the previous categories) and noise (MS in none of the previous categories). The pixel-wise criteria group contains the most frequented classification criteria such as the omission and commission errors, class accuracy, recall, precision, etc. Finally the last criteria set incorporates the global and local consistency errors [16].

Tab.1 compares the overall benchmark performance of the proposed algorithm CAR3D-multi ($M = 3, \iota_1 = 1, \iota_2 = 1.5, \iota_3 = 2$, segmentation time 14 min/img on the Athlon 2GHz processor) with the Blobworld [17] (30 min/img), JSEG [18] (30 s/img), Edison [19] (10 s/img), TFR/KLD [20] and our previously published method GMRF [8] (55 min/img), CAR3D [9] (7 min/img), respectively. These results demonstrate very good pixel-wise and correct region segmentation properties of our method while the undersegmentation results are slightly worse and oversegmentation results are only average. For all the pixel-wise criteria or the consistency measures our method is among the best ones. The table demonstrates improvement of the presented multi-segmenters method over the single-segmenter version published earlier [9] in most benchmark criteria. Figs.1,2 show four selected 512×512 experimental benchmark mosaics created from four to eleven natural colour textures. The last three or four rows on these figures demonstrate comparative results from the six alternative algorithms. Hard natural textures were chosen rather than synthesized (for example using Markov random field models) ones because they are expected to be more difficult for the underlying segmentation model. The third row on Fig.1 demonstrates robust behaviour of our CAR3D-multi algorithm but also infrequent algorithm failures producing the oversegmented thematic map for some textures. Such failures can

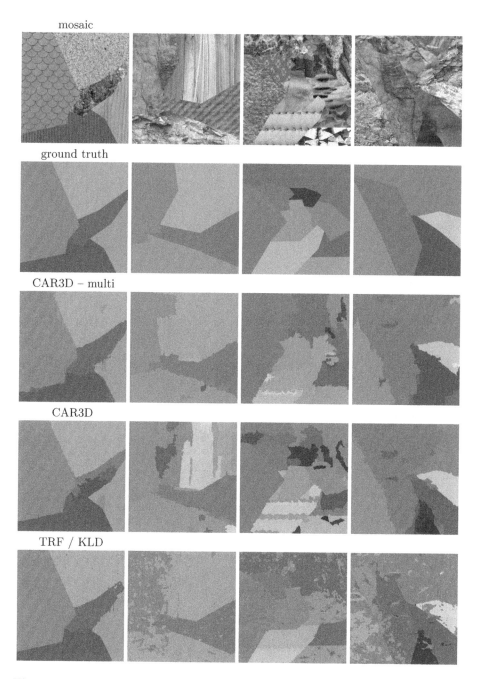

Fig. 1. Selected experimental texture mosaics, ground truth from the benchmark and the corresponding segmentation results

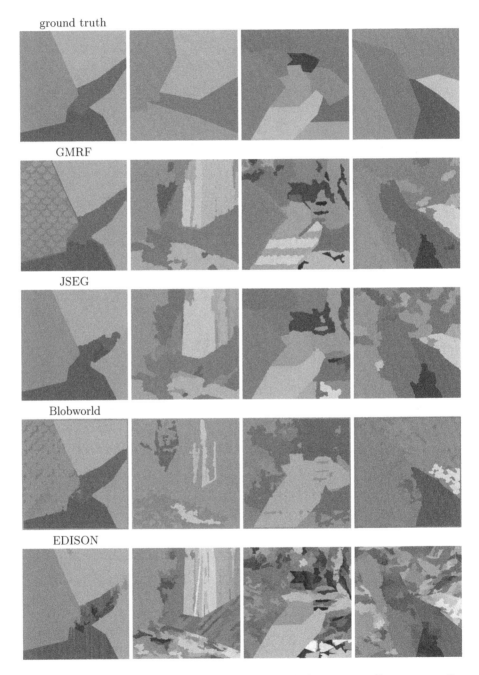

Fig. 2. Selected ground truth from the benchmark and the corresponding segmentation results

Table 1. Benchmark criteria ($\times 100$): CS = correct segmentation; OS = over-segmentation; US = under-segmentation; ME = missed error; NE = noise error; O = omission error; C = commission error; CA = class accuracy; CO = recall - correct assignment; CC = precision - object accuracy; I. = type I error; II. = type II error; EA = mean class accuracy estimate; MS = mapping score; RM = root mean square proportion estimation error; CI = comparison index; GCE = Global Consistency Error; LCE = Local Consistency Error;

	Benchmark – Colour						
	TFR/KLD	CAR3D-multi	CAR3D	GMRF	JSEG	Blobworld	EDISON
CS	51.25	43.45	37.42	31.93	27.47	21.01	12.68
OS	5.84	53.19	59.53	53.27	38.62	7.33	86.91
US	7.16	20.28	8.86	11.24	5.04	9.30	0.00
ME	31.64	9.91	12.54	14.97	35.00	59.55	2.48
NE	31.38	10.51	13.14	16.91	35.50	61.68	4.68
O	23.60	30.24	35.19	36.49	38.19	43.96	68.45
C	22.42	16.03	11.85	12.18	13.35	31.38	0.86
CA	67.45	61.73	59.46	57.91	55.29	46.23	31.19
CO	76.40	69.76	64.81	63.51	61.81	56.04	31.55
CC	81.12	85.89	91.79	89.26	87.70	73.62	98.09
I.	23.60	30.24	35.19	36.49	38.19	43.96	68.45
II.	4.09	4.57	3.39	3.14	3.66	6.72	0.24
EA	75.80	70.86	69.60	68.41	66.74	58.37	41.29
MS	65.19	61.75	58.89	57.42	55.14	40.36	31.13
RM	6.87	4.69	4.66	4.56	4.62	7.52	3.09
CI	77.21	73.58	73.15	71.80	70.27	61.31	50.29
GCE	20.35	15.38	12.13	16.03	18.45	31.16	3.55
LCE	14.36	8.12	6.69	7.31	11.64	23.19	3.44

be reduced by a more elaborate postprocessing step. The GMRF [8], JSEG [18], Blobworld [17] and Edison [19], algorithms on these data performed mostly worse as can be seen in their corresponding rows on Figs.1,2 some areas are underseg-mented while other parts of the mosaics are oversegmented. Fig.1 illustrates also the improvement of the multi-segmenters version of the algorithm at the cost of slight increase of computational complexity. This result can be further improved by more sophisticated postprocessing.

4   Conclusions

We proposed novel multi-segmenter efficient and robust method for unsupervised texture segmentation with unknown number of classes based on the underlying CAR and GM texture models. Although the algorithm uses the random field type model it is relatively fast because it uses efficient recursive parameter esti-mation of the model and therefore is much faster than the usual Markov chain Monte Carlo estimation approach. Usual handicap of segmentation methods is their lot of application dependent parameters to be experimentally estimated.

Our method requires only a contextual neighbourhood selection and two additional thresholds. The algorithm's performance is demonstrated on the extensive benchmark tests on natural texture mosaics. It performs favorably compared with six alternative segmentation algorithms. These test results are encouraging and we proceed with more elaborate postprocessing and some modification of the texture representation model.

Acknowledgements

This research was supported by the EC project no. FP6-507752 MUSCLE, grants No.A2075302, 1ET400750407 of the Grant Agency of the Academy of Sciences CR and partially by the MŠMT grants 1M0572 DAR, 2C06019.

References

1. Reed, T.R., du Buf, J.M.H.: A review of recent texture segmentation and feature extraction techniques. CVGIP–Image Understanding **57** (1993) 359–372
2. Kashyap, R.: Image models. In T.Y. Young, K.F., ed.: Handbook of Pattern Recognition and Image Processing. Academic Press, New York (1986)
3. Haindl, M.: Texture synthesis. CWI Quarterly **4** (1991) 305–331
4. Panjwani, D., Healey, G.: Markov random field models for unsupervised segmentation of textured color images. IEEE Transactions on Pattern Analysis and Machine Intelligence **17** (1995) 939–954
5. Manjunath, B., Chellapa, R.: Unsupervised texture segmentation using markov random field models. IEEE Transactions on Pattern Analysis and Machine Intelligence **13** (1991) 478–482
6. Andrey, P., Tarroux, P.: Unsupervised segmentation of markov random field modeled textured images using selectionist relaxation. IEEE Transactions on Pattern Analysis and Machine Intelligence **20** (1998) 252–262
7. Haindl, M.: Texture segmentation using recursive markov random field parameter estimation. In Bjarne, K., Peter, J., eds.: Proceedings of the 11th Scandinavian Conference on Image Analysis, Lyngby, Denmark, Pattern Recognition Society of Denmark (1999) 771–776
8. Haindl, M., Mikeš, S.: Model-based texture segmentation. Lecture Notes in Computer Science (2004) 306 – 313
9. Haindl, M., Mikeš, S.: Unsupervised texture segmentation using multispectral modelling approach. In Tang, Y., Wang, S., Yeung, D., Yan, H., Lorette, G., eds.: Proceedings of the 18th International Conference on Pattern Recognition, ICPR 2006. Volume II., Los Alamitos, IEEE Computer Society (2006) 203–206
10. Kittler, J., Hojjatoleslami, A., Windeatt, T.: Weighting factors in multiple expert fusion. In: Proc. BMVC, BMVA, BMVA (1997) 41–50
11. Rahman, A., Fairhust, M.: Multiple classifier decision combination strategies for character recognition: A review. Int. Journal on Document Analysis and Recognition (2003) 166–194
12. Haindl, M., Šimberová, S.: A Multispectral Image Line Reconstruction Method. In: Theory & Applications of Image Analysis. World Scientific Publishing Co., Singapore (1992) 306–315

13. Mikeš, S., Haindl, M.: Prague texture segmentation data generator and benchmark. ERCIM News (2006) 67–68
14. Hoover, A., Jean-Baptiste, G., Jiang, X., Flynn, P.J., Bunke, H., Goldgof, D.B., Bowyer, K., Eggert, D.W., Fitzgibbon, A., Fisher, R.B.: An experimental comparison of range image segmentation algorithms. IEEE Transaction on Pattern Analysis and Machine Intelligence **18** (1996) 673–689
15. Martin, D., Fowlkes, C., Malik, J.: Learning to detect natural image bounderies using brightness and texture. IEEE Transactions on Pattern Analysis and Machine Intelligence **26** (2004) 1–19
16. Martin, D., Fowlkes, C., Tal, D., Malik, J.: A database of human segmented natural images and its application to evaluating segmentation algorithms and measuring ecological statistics. In: Proc. 8th Int. Conf. Computer Vision. Volume 2. (2001) 416–423
17. Carson, C., Thomas, M., Belongie, S., Hellerstein, J.M., Malik, J.: Blobworld: A system for region-based image indexing and retrieval. In: Third International Conference on Visual Information Systems, Springer (1999)
18. Deng, Y., Manjunath, B.: Unsupervised segmentation of color-texture regions in images and video. IEEE Transactions on Pattern Analysis and Machine Intelligence **23** (2001) 800–810
19. Christoudias, C., Georgescu, B., Meer, P.: Synergism in low level vision. In Kasturi, R., Laurendeau, D., Suen, C., eds.: Proceedings of the 16th International Conference on Pattern Recognition. Volume 4., Los Alamitos, IEEE Computer Society (2002) 150–155
20. Scarpa, G., Haindl, M.: Unsupervised texture segmentation by spectral-spatial-independent clustering. In Tang, Y., Wang, S., Yeung, D., Yan, H., Lorette, G., eds.: Proceedings of the 18th International Conference on Pattern Recognition, ICPR 2006. Volume II., Los Alamitos, IEEE Computer Society (2006) 151–154

Classifier Ensembles for Vector Space Embedding of Graphs

Kaspar Riesen and Horst Bunke

Department of Computer Science, University of Bern,
Neubrückstrasse 10, CH-3012 Bern, Switzerland
{riesen,bunke}@iam.unibe.ch

Abstract. Classifier ensembles aim at a more accurate classification than single classifiers. Different approaches to building classifier ensembles have been proposed in the statistical pattern recognition literature. However, in structural pattern recognition, classifier ensembles have been rarely used. In this paper we introduce a general methodology for creating structural classifier ensembles. Our representation formalism is based on graphs and includes strings and trees as special cases. In the proposed approach we make use of graph embedding in real vector spaces by means of prototype selection. Since we use randomized prototype selection, it is possible to generate n different vector sets out of the same underlying graph set. Thus, one can train an individual base classifier for each vector set und combine the results of the classifiers in an appropriate way. We use extended support vector machines for classification and combine them by means of three different methods. In experiments on semi-artificial and real data we show that it is possible to outperform the classification accuracy obtained by single classifier systems in the original graph domain as well as in the embedding vector spaces.

1 Introduction

The key idea in multiple classifier systems is to combine several classifiers such that the resulting combined system achieves a higher classification accuracy than the original classifiers individually [1]. In the case of statistical patterns, that is, patterns represented by feature vectors, a large number of methods for the creation and combination of classifiers have been developed over the past few years. Bagging, for instance, creates classifiers by randomly selecting the set of training examples to be used for each classifier [2]. A similar idea is that of random feature subset selection [3]. In this method, one randomly selects the features (dimensions) to be used for each feature vector to create a group of classifiers. A third prominent example of classifier creation methods is boosting, where classifiers are created sequentially out of a single base classifier by giving successively higher weights to those training samples that have been misclassified [4].

Structural pattern recognition is characterized by the use of symbolic data structures, such as strings, trees, or graphs, for pattern representation. Such representations have a number of advantages over feature vectors used in the statistical

M. Haindl, J. Kittler, and F. Roli (Eds.): MCS 2007, LNCS 4472, pp. 220–230, 2007.

approach. For example, a string may consist of an arbitrary number of symbols. This is in contrast to a feature vector where one is confined to always using the same number of features, regardless of the size or the complexity of the individual patterns to be represented. Furthermore, if one uses graphs, structural relationships between individual pattern components can be conveniently represented. There is no direct way to represent such relations in a feature vector. In fact, there are many applications in pattern recognition and related areas, including computational biology and chemistry, where such representations are essential [5].

One disadvantage of the structural approach is that the space of strings, trees or graphs has very little mathematical structure. This means that elementary operations, such as computing the average, the covariance, or the product of two object representations, do not exist. Therefore, up to a few exceptions [6,7,8], mostly classifiers of the nearest neighbor type have been applied to structural pattern representations. Consequently, there has been little work on multiple classifier systems based on structural pattern representations. A pioneering paper is [9] where it was shown that by the use of statistical and structural classifiers in a multiple classifier system the accuracy of a fingerprint recognition system can be improved. In [10] an approach has been proposed where several graph representations of the same pattern are derived and merged into a single representation format. Then the single graph resulting from the merging operation is input to a nearest neighbor classifier based on graph edit distance. In [11], random node selection on graphs has been used in order to derive ensembles of graph-based classifiers. But still, only classifiers of the nearest neighbor type are applied in this work.

In the current paper we propose a new method that is based on two fundamental ideas. The first idea is the embedding of graphs into the n-dimensional real space by means of prototype selection and edit distance computation. Such a procedure has been originally proposed in [12] in order to embed feature vectors in a dissimilarity space. In subsequent work a similar procedure has been used for the embedding of strings and graphs [13,14]. By means of this procedure any set of graphs can be mapped to a set of feature vectors. Consequently, any pattern recognition method that has ever been developed for feature vector representations becomes applicable to graphs. The second fundamental idea in this paper is based on the observation that mapping a population of graphs into a vector space is controlled by a set of prototypes. One possible procedure to actually get these prototypes is by random selection from the given training set of graph. Obviously, if we repeat the process of random selection a number of times, we can derive different graph sets that all can be used in order to train a classifier. As a result, we get a classifier ensemble for structural input data. The classifier we adopted for the work described in this paper is Support Vector Machine (SVM). However, any other type of classifier can be used as well.

2 Graph Embedding in Real Vector Spaces

In [15] an approach to graph embedding in vector spaces has been introduced. This method is based on algebraic graph theory and utilizes spectral matrix decomposition. Another approach for graph embedding has been proposed in [16]. It makes use of the relationship between the Laplace-Beltrami operator and the graph Laplacian to embed a graph onto a Riemannian manifold. Our embedding method makes explicitly use of graph edit distance [17,18]. The key idea of graph edit distance is to define the dissimilarity, or distance, of graphs by the amount of distortion that is needed to transform one graph into another. A sequence of edit operations that transforms a graph g_1 into another graph g_2 is called an *edit path* between g_1 and g_2. Costs are assigned to each edit path, representing the strength of the distortions of this edit sequence. Consequently, the *edit distance* of two graphs is defined as the minimum cost, taken over all edit paths between two graphs under consideration. Typically, the edit distance is used to classify an input graph by computing its distance to a number of training graphs and feeding the resulting distance values into a nearest-neighbor classifier. In our approach we make use of edit distances to construct a vectorial description of a given graph. Our method was originally developed for the problem of embedding sets of feature vectors in a dissimilarity space [12,19]. The embedding of strings and graphs has been studied in [13,14]. Assume we have a labeled set of training graphs, $T = \{g_1, \ldots, g_t\}$, and a dissimilarity measure $d(g_i, g_j)$. After having selected a set $P = \{p_1, \ldots, p_m\}$ of $m < t$ prototypes from T, i.e. $P \subseteq T$, we compute the dissimilarity of a graph $g \in T$ to each prototype $p \in P$. This leads to m dissimilarities, $d_1 = d(g, p_1), \ldots, d_m = d(g, p_m)$, which can be interpreted as an m-dimensional vector $(d_1, \ldots, d_m)$. In this way we can transform any graph from the training set, as well as any other graph from a validation or testing set, into a vector of real numbers. Note that whenever a graph from the training set, which has been choosen as a prototype before, is transformed into a vector $\mathbf{x} = (x_1, \ldots, x_m)$ one of the vector components is zero.

Different methods for selecting the m prototypes needed for embedding have been proposed in the literature [12,13,14]. The intention of all methods is the same, that is, finding a selection of m prototypes that lead to a good performance

---

Algorithm 1. Generating n prototype sets out of one graph set.

Input:	Training graphs $T = \{g_1, \ldots, g_t\}$, number of required prototype sets n, and dimensionality of the resulting feature vectors m
Output:	Set $PROTO$ consisting of n different prototype sets of size m each

```
 1: initialize TABU to the empty set {}
 2: initialize PROTO to the empty set {}
 3: for i = {1, . . . , n} do
 4:     P_i = {}
 5:     for j = {1, . . . , m} do
 6:         if |TABU| == t then
 7:             reset TABU to the empty set {}
 8:         else
 9:             select p randomly out of T \ TABU
10:             P_i = P_i ∪ {p}
11:             TABU = TABU ∪ {p}
12:         end if
13:     end for
14:     PROTO = PROTO ∪ {P_i}
15: end for
16: return PROTO
```

of the resulting classifier in the vector space. Since in this paper we want to generate not only one, but a number of vector sets out of the same graph set, we make use of the random method described in Algorithm 1. Output of this procedure is a set consisting of n different prototype sets of size m each. To build such a set, the method described in Alg. 1 randomly picks n times m graphs from the training set T. After picking a graph from T, the selected graph becomes temporarily unavailable for further selection. Once all training graphs from T have been selected, all training graphs become available again. This procedure is very interesting in that it naturally lends itself to a method for the automatic generation of classifier ensembles.

3   Extended Support Vector Machine

In Sect. 2 we have introduced a general methodology for embedding graphs in real vector spaces. Clearly, one can build arbitrarily many different vector sets out of the same graph set. Assume a given graph set has been embedded n times with different prototypes. Hence, we have n different vector sets available all representing the same graphs. Obviously, it is possible to train a classifier on each vector set seperately. Therefore, we obtain n classifers $L_1, \ldots, L_n$ whose results can be combined to one output. In the following we assume that we deal with a problem involving k different classes $\{C_1, \ldots, C_k\}$. As any classifier combination method necessarily depends on the type of the n underlying classifiers, we distinguish three types of classifiers:

- **Type-1 classifiers:** Output of these classifiers is exactly one class C_i.
- **Type-2 classifers:** Output is a ranking list, i.e. an ordered list $(C_{i1}, \ldots, C_{ik})$ including all classes, where C_{i1} is the class with the highest and C_{ik} the class with the lowest plausibility.
- **Type-3 classifiers:** Output is a plausibility value $p(C_i)$ for each class C_i. This plausibility value corresponds with the probability that a test element under consideration belongs to the respective class. Thus, each classifer L_j outputs a vector of size k, $\{(p_j(C_1), \ldots, p_j(C_k))\}_{1 \leqslant j \leqslant n}$.

Pattern classification by means of support vector machines (SVMs) has become very popular recently [20,21]. The basic idea of SVM is to seperate classes of patterns by hyperplanes. Intuitively, one would choose a hyperplane such that its distance to the closest pattern of either class is maximal. Such hyperplanes are expected to perform best on an independent test set. SVMs are able to find such optimal hyperplanes. Originally, SVMs have been developed to handle two class problems. To generalize SVM to problems with more than two classes one can use the *1-to-1* method. In this approach all pairs of classes $(C_i, C_j)_{1 \leqslant i < j \leqslant k}$ are considered seperately, and for each pair an individual SVM is trained. This leads to $k(k-1)/2$ different SVMs. An unseen test element is assigned to the class C_i that occurs the most frequently among the $k(k-1)/2$ SVM decisions. Output of a traditional SVM is one class and thus SVMs are typically type-1 classifiers. Since we want to use not only combiners depending on type-1 but also on type-2 and type-3 classifers, one has to generalize SVM appropriately. The first generalization, which leads to a type-2 classifier, is simple and straightforward. Instead of returning only the most frequent class C_i among the $k(k-1)/2$ SVM decisions, one can extend the i-th SVM to return an ordered list $(C_{i1}, \ldots, C_{ik})$. C_{i1} stands for the most frequent class and C_{ik} represents the class that has won the fewest SVM decisions. To get a type-3 classifier out of a standard SVM one can use the information about the distance f of a test sample to the hyperplane of the current SVM. These distances f are used to obtain pairwise class probabilities by feeding them into a *sigmoid* function:

$$r_{ij} = \frac{1}{1+exp(\alpha f + \beta)},$$

where α and β are parameters that have to be estimated. To obtain one probability $p(C_i)$ per class out of the r_{ij} values one has to to solve an optimization problem. The probabilistic SVM resulting from this procedure is described in more detail in [22,23].

4   Classifier Ensembles

Let us summarize the whole procedure discussed so far. Starting point are patterns given by graph-based representations. With random prototype selection and graph edit distance computation, we embed these graphs in real vector spaces. Since we use randomized prototype selection, this step leads to n different vectorial descriptions of the same graph set. Based on these n vector sets one can train n different SVMs. Hence, from an unknown test pattern, we get n different classification results. Output of i-th SVM is either a single class C_{i1} (type-1 classifier), a vector with all possible classes $(C_{i1}, \ldots, C_{ik})$ ordered by the frequency of all SVM decisions (type-2 classifier), or a list with plausibility values $(p_j(C_1), \ldots, p_j(C_k))$, where $p_j(C_i)$ is derived from the distances of the test elements to the hyperplanes of the individual SVMs (type-3 classifier). Based on these three different output formats of the n SVMs, one can use different combination strategies to obtain the final result. In this work we use a *Voting* algorithm for type-1 SVMs, a ranking sum method for type-2 SVMs (*Borda count*) and *Bayes' combination* using the plausibility values obtained by type-3 SVMs.

- **Voting:** The class C_{i1} output by classifier L_i $(1 \leq i \leq n)$ is regarded as one vote for $C_{i1} \in \{C_1, \ldots, C_k\}$. The class that receives the plurality of the votes is choosen by the combiner. This method is often termed *plurality voting* [1]. Of course, one can use more restrictive voting methods with rejection (e.g. *majority voting* [1]).
- **Borda Count:** Assume that each classifier L_i outputs an ordered list including all classes $\{C_j\}_{1 \leq j \leq k}$. To combine the results of type-2 classifiers one can introduce rank functions $r_i(C_{ij})$ for each classifer L_i. Function $r_i(C_{ij})$ delivers the position of the class C_{ij} in the ordered list given by classifier L_i, i.e. $r_i(C_{ij}) = j$. Hence, for each class $\{C_i\}_{1 \leq i \leq k}$ the sum of all ranks can

be computed, $R(C_i) = \sum_{j=1}^{n} r_j(C_i)$. Subsequently, the combiner chooses the class $\{C_i\}_{1 \leq i \leq k}$ with the minimum value of $R(C_i)$. This combination method is known as *Borda count*.

- **Bayes' Combination:** In this approach the individual plausibility values $\{p_j(C_i)\}_{1 \leq j \leq n}$ are combined to get one plausibility value P_i per C_i. Common strategies to combine the plausibility values are given below [24]:
  - $P_i = \max(p_1(C_i), \ldots, p_n(C_i))$
  - $P_i = \min(p_1(C_i), \ldots, p_n(C_i))$
  - $P_i = \frac{1}{n} \sum_{j=1}^{n} p_j(C_i)$
  - $P_i = \prod_{j=1}^{n} p_j(C_i)$

  Regardless which of these formulas is used, the ensemble eventually chooses the class C_i with the maximum value of the corresponding P_i. In the present paper we use the last approach based on the product, which is known as *Bayes' combination*.

A crucial question is how many classifiers should be included in an ensemble. With Alg. 1 we have the possibility to build n vector sets, and thus we have n classifiers available. To determine the size of the final ensemble we propose a sequential floating search selection according to Algorithm 2 [25]. First the best individual classifier in terms of classification accuracy is added to the ensemble in line 2. Then, the best fitting classifier, i.e. the classifier that complements the ensemble generated so far the best, is added incrementally (line 5 and 6). After each forward step a number of backward steps are applied as long as the resulting subsets are better than the evaluated ones at that level (line 11 and 12). Obviously, this procedure generates n subsets of the classfier set $L = \{L_1, \ldots, L_n\}$ with size 1 to n. The best performing subset, i.e. the ensemble E_i with the lowest classification error on an independent validation set is used as the final ensemble (line 19). This strategy is also known as *overproduce-and-select* [1].

5 Experimental Results

The purpose of the experiments described in this section is to compare the classification accuracy of the ensembles obtained by the proposed method with two reference systems. The first reference system is a traditional nearest-neighbor classifier in the graph domain, while a single SVM in the vector domain is used as the second reference system. The first reference system, the nearest-neighbor classifier, has proved to be suitable for the classification task in graph domains for many different applications. Basically, this classifier assigns the label of the nearest neighbor in a training set in terms of edit distance to an unknown test-element. Note that as of today – up to few exceptions, e.g. [6] – there exist no other classifiers for general graphs that can be directly applied in the graph domain. The second reference system is obtained through picking the best individual classfier L_i out of L, i.e. the classifier that leads to the best classification accuracy on the validation set. In each of our experiments we make use of three

---

Algorithm 2. Determine the best performing classifier ensemble.

Input: A set of n classifiers $L = \{L_1, \ldots, L_n\}$ sorted in order of their
          individual classification accuracy. (L_1 has the highest and L_n
          the lowest classification accuracy)
Output: The best performing classifier ensemble E_{max}

1: Initialize n empty ensembles $E = \{E_1, \ldots, E_n\}$
2: add the best individual classifier to the ensemble: $E_1 = \{L_1\}$
3: intitalize $k := 1$
4: **while** $k < n$ **do**
5:     $L^+ = argmax_{L_i \in L \setminus E_k} accuracy(E_k \cup \{L_i\})$
6:     add the classifier L^+ to the ensemble: $E_{k+1} = E_k \cup \{L^+\}$
7:     $k := k + 1$
8:     initialize $removed := false$
9:     **repeat**
10:        $removed := false$
11:        $L^- = argmax_{L_i \in E_k} accuracy(E_k \setminus \{L_i\})$
12:        **if** $accuracy(E_k \setminus \{L_i\}) > accuracy(E_{k-1})$ **then**
13:            $E_{k-1} = E_k \setminus \{L_i\}$
14:            $k := k - 1$
15:            $removed = true$
16:        **end if**
17:    **until** $removed = false$
18: **end while**
19: **return** the best performing ensemble $E_{max} = argmax_{E_i \in E} accuracy(E_i)$

---

disjoint graph sets, the *validation set*, the *test set* and the *training set*. The validation set is used to determine optimal parameter values for multiple graph embeddings and classification. The embedding parameters to be validated consist of the number of prototypes, i.e. the dimensionality of the resulting feature vector spaces, and the best performing ensemble, i.e. the best combination of ensemble members in terms of classification accuracy (see Alg. 1 and Alg. 2). Parameters for classification consist of different parameters for the SVM and depend on the kernel function [21,26]. The parameter values and the ensemble that result in the lowest classification error on the validation set are then applied to the independent test set.

5.1   Letter Database

The first database used in the experiments consists of graphs representing distorted letter drawings. In this experiment we consider the 15 capital letters of the Roman alphabet that consists of straight lines only (*A, E, F, ...*). For each class, a prototype line drawing is manually constructed. To obtain aribtrarily large sample sets of drawings with arbitrarily strong distortions, distortion operators are applied to the prototype line drawings. This results in randomly shifted, removed, and added lines. These drawings are then converted into graphs in a simple manner by representing lines by edges and ending points of lines by nodes. Each node is labeled with a two-dimensional attribute giving its position. The graph database used in our experiments consists of a training set, a validation set, and a test set, each of size 750 for each of a total of five different distortion levels. The results of the experiments on the letter database are given in Table 1. First of all, the single SVM classifier in the vector domain improves the classification accuracy compared to the reference system in the graph domain on all distortion levels. Note that two out of five improvements are statistically significant. Similar results have been reported in [14]. Despite these good results, the ensemble methods obtains further improvements. Especially on distortion levels 0.3, 0.5, 0.7 and 0.9, the ensemble methods achieve better results. Note that 8 out of 12 improvements compared to the single SVM are statistically significant. Compared to the first reference system, there are even 11 statistically significantly improvements. Only at distortion level 0.1 the single SVM is superior to the voting and Borda count method. The optimal parameters for this experiment, found on the validation set, are 150 prototypes per embedding and 12 ensemble members on average for voting, 13 ensemble members on average for Borda count and an ensemble of size 8 on average for Bayes' combiner.

Table 1. Letter Database: Classification accuracy in the graph and vector space

	Ref. Systems		Classifier Ensembles		
Distortion	k-NN (graph)	single SVM	Plurality Voting	Borda Count	Bayes' Combiner
0.1	98.27	98.53	98.27	98.13	98.67
0.3	97.60	98.00	98.27	98.53 ⊚	98.67 ⊚
0.5	94.00	96.53 ∘	97.07 ∘	96.93 ∘	97.07 ∘
0.7	94.27	94.53	96.00 ⊚	95.87 ⊚	96.00 ⊚
0.9	90.13	93.33 ∘	94.27 ⊚	94.40 ⊚	94.53 ⊚

∘ Statistically significant improvement over the first reference system (Z-test, $\alpha = 0.05$)
⊚ Statistically significant improvement over both reference systems (Z-test, $\alpha = 0.05$)

5.2   Real World Data

For a more thorough evaluation of the proposed methods we additonally use three real world data sets. First we apply the proposed method to the problem of image classification. Images are converted in graphs by segmenting them into regions, eliminating regions that are irrelevant for classification, and representing the remaining regions by nodes and the adjacency of regions by edges [27]. The Le Saux image database consists of five classes (*city, countryside, people, streets, snowy*) and is split into a training set, a validation set and a test set of size 54 each. The classification accuracies obtained by the different methods are given in the first row of Table 2. Although the single SVM improves the accuracy by 5.6%, this improvement is not statistically significant. The further improved result achieved by the Borda count method – which actually corresponds to an improvement by 7.4% – obtains no statistical significance, either. Neither are the superior results of the reference systems compared to the other ensemble methods statistically significant. All this is due to the small size of the Le Saux database. We used 20 prototypes for embedding and 27 (voting), 7 (Borda count) and 31 (Bayes' combiner) ensemble members for classification. The second real world dataset is given by the NIST-4 fingerprint database [28]. We construct graphs from fingerprint images by extracting characteristic regions in fingerprints and converting the results into attributed graphs [29]. We use a validation set of size 300 and a test and training set of size 500 each. In this experiment we address

Table 2. Fingerprint-, Image- and Molecules Database: Classification accuracy in the graph and vector space

	Ref. Systems		Classifier Ensembles		
Database	k-NN (graph)	single SVM	Plurality Voting	Borda Count	Bayes' Combiner
Le Saux	57.4	63.0	61.1	64.8	55.6
NIST-4	82.6	84.8 ○	85.2 ○	85.0 ○	84.8 ○
Molecules	97.1	98.1 ○	98.3 ⊚	98.3 ⊚	97.7

○ Statistically significant improvement over the first reference system (Z-test, $\alpha = 0.05$)
⊚ Statistically significant improvement over both reference systems (Z-test, $\alpha = 0.05$)

the 4-class problem (*arch, left-loop, right-loop, whorl*). The single SVM and all ensemble methods achieve statistically significantly better results than the first reference system. However, there is no significant difference between the single SVM and the proposed classifier ensembles. Nevertheless, note that the ensemble obtains two improvements and one equal result compared to the second reference system. On this data set a configuration with 100 prototypes for embedding and 11 (voting and Borda count) and 2 (Bayes' combiner) ensemble members obtains the best result on the validation set and is therefore used on the test set.

Finally, we apply the proposed method of graph embedding and subsequent SVM classification to the problem of molecule classification. To this end, we construct graphs from the AIDS Antiviral Screen Database of Active Compounds [30]. Our molecule database consists of two classes (*active, inactive*), which represent molecules with activity against HIV or not. We use a validation set of size 250, a test set of size 1500 and training set of size 250. Thus, there are 2000 elements totally (1600 inactive elements and 400 active elements). The molecules are converted into graphs in a straightforward manner by representing atoms as nodes and the covalent bonds as edges. Nodes are labeled with the corresponding chemical symbol and edges by the valence of the linkage. Although the accuracy of the reference system in the graph domain is quite high, it can be statistically significantly improved by the single SVM. The voting and the Borda count methods outperform the reference system in the graph domain, too. Actually, the good result achieved in vector domain by a single SVM can be further improved by these ensemble methods with statistical significance. We used 150 prototypes for embedding, and 14 (voting and Borda count) and 23 (Bayes' combiner) ensemble members for classification.

6 Conclusions

While many methods for building classifier ensembles based on feature vector representations of the underlying data have been proposed, little work has been done for structural representations. In this paper we propose a general approach to graph based classifier ensembles. Our approach makes use of graph embedding in real vector spaces. The key idea is to map graphs to the m-dimensional real space by means of graph edit distance and prototype selection. To this end, we discuss a randomized prototype selector with the objective of finding n different prototype sets. With these sets, one can map a set of graphs n times to different vector sets, such that we obtain n different vector sets all representing the same graph set, i.e. the same pattern elements. For each vector set an individual SVM is trained and thus one gets n different classifiers. Hence, a number of methods become available for combining the results of individual ensemble members. The proposed methods were tested on a number of graph datasets with different characteristics, comming from various application domains. From the results of our experiments, one can conclude that the classification accuracy can be enhanced by most ensemble methods on almost all data sets.

Acknowledgements

This work has been supported by the Swiss National Science Foundation (Project 200021-113198/1). Furthermore, we would like to thank R. Duin and E. Pekalska for valuable discussions and hints regarding the embedding method. Finally, we thank B. Le Saux for making the Le Saux database available to us.

References

1. L. Kuncheva. Combining Pattern Classifiers: Methods and Algorithms. John Wiley, 2004.
2. L. Breiman. Bagging predictors. Machine Learning, 24:123–140, 1996.
3. T.K. Ho. The random subspace method for constructing decision forests. IEEE Trans. on Pattern Analysis ans Machine Intelligence, 20(8):832–844, 1998.
4. Y. Freund and R.E. Shapire. A decision theoretic generalization of online learning and application to boosting. Journal of Computer and Systems Sciences, 55:119–139, 1997.
5. D. Conte, P. Foggia, C. Sansone, and M. Vento. Thirty years of graph matching in pattern recognition. Int. Journal of Pattern Recognition and Artificial Intelligence, 18(3):265–298, 2004.
6. M. Bianchini, M. Gori, L. Sarti, and F. Scarselli. Recursive processing of cyclic graphs. IEEE Transactions on Neural Networks, 17(1):10–18, January 2006.
7. M. Neuhaus and H. Bunke. Edit distance based kernel functions for structural pattern classification. In Pattern Recognition, pages 1852 – 1863, 2006.
8. T. Gärtner, J. Lloyd, and P. Flach. Kernels and distances for structured data. Machine Learning, 57(3):205–232, 2004.
9. G.L. Marcialis, F. Roli, and A. Serrau. Fusion of statistical and structural fingerprint classifiers. In J. Kittler and M.S. Nixon, editors, 4th Int. Conf. Audio- and Video-Based Biometric Person Authentication, LNCS 2688, pages 310–317. Springer, 2003.
10. M. Neuhaus and H. Bunke. Graph-based multiple classifier systems – a data level fusion approach. Lecture Notes in Computer Science, 3617:479–487, 2005.
11. A. Schenker, H. Bunke, M. Last, and A. Kandel. Building graph-based classifier ensembles by random node selection. In F. Roli, J. Kittler, and T. Windeatt, editors, Proc. 5th Int. Workshop on Multiple Classifier Systems, LNCS 3077, pages 214–222. Springer, 2004.
12. E. Pekalska, R. Duin, and P. Paclik. Prototype selection for dissimilarity-based classifiers. Pattern Recognition, 39(2):189–208, 2006.

13. B. Spillmann, M. Neuhaus, H. Bunke, E. Pekalska, and R. Duin. Transforming strings to vector spaces using prototype selection. In Proc. 11.th int. Workshop on Strucural and Syntactic Pattern Recognition, LNCS 4109, pages 287–296. Springer, 2006.

14. K. Riesen, M. Neuhaus, and H. Bunke. Graph embedding in vector spaces by means of prototype selection. Submitted.

15. R.C. Wilson, E.R. Hancock, and B. Luo. Pattern vectors from algebraic graph theory. IEEE Trans. on Pattern Analysis ans Machine Intelligence, 27(7):1112–1124, 2005.

16. A. Robles-Kelly and E.R. Hancock. A riemannian approach to graph embedding. Pattern Recognition, 40:1024–1056, 2007.

17. A. Sanfeliu and K.S. Fu. A distance measure between attributed relational graphs for pattern recognition. IEEE Transactions on Systems, Man, and Cybernetics (Part B), 13(3):353–363, 1983.

18. H. Bunke and G. Allermann. Inexact graph matching for structural pattern recognition. Pattern Recognition Letters, 1:245–253, 1983.

19. R. Duin and E. Pekalska. The Dissimilarity Representations for Pattern Recognition: Foundations and Applications. World Scientific, 2005.

20. C. Burges. A tutorial on support vector machines for pattern recognition. Data Mining and Knowledge Discovery, 2(2):121–167, 1998.

21. J. Shawe-Taylor and N. Cristianini. Kernel Methods for Pattern Analysis. Cambridge University Press, 2004.

22. C.C. Chang and C.J. Lin. LIBSVM: A Library for Support Vector Machines, 2001. Software available at http://www.csie.ntu.edu.tw/~cjlin/libsvm.

23. C.F.J. Wu, C.J. Lin, and R.C. Weng. Probability estimates for multi-class classification by pairwise coupling. Journal of Machine Learning Research, 5:975–1005, 2004.

24. J. Kittler, M. Hatef, R. Duin, and J. Matas. On combining classifiers. IEEE Trans. on Pattern Analysis ans Machine Intelligence, 20(3):226–239, 1998.

25. P. Pudil, J. Novovicova, and J. Kittler. Floating search methods in feature-selection. PRL, 15(11):1119–1125, November 1994.

26. B. Schölkopf and A. Smola. Learning with Kernels. MIT Press, 2002.

27. B. Le Saux and H. Bunke. Feature selection for graph-based image classifiers. In Proc. 2nd Iberian Conf. on Pattern Recognition and Image Analysis, LNCS 3523, pages 147–154. Springer, 2005.

28. C.I. Watson and C.L. Wilson. NIST special database 4, fingerprint database. National Institute of Standards and Technology, March 1992.

29. M. Neuhaus and H. Bunke. A graph matching based approach to fingerprint classification using directional variance. In Proc. 5th Int. Conf. on Audio- and Video-Based Biometric Person Authentication, LNCS 3546, pages 191–200. Springer, 2005.

30. Development Therapeutics Program DTP. Aids antiviral screen, 2004. http://dtp.nci.nih.gov/docs/aids/aids_data.html.

Cascading for Nominal Data

Jesús Maudes, Juan J. Rodríguez, and César García-Osorio

Escuela Politécnica Superior – Lenguajes y Sistemas Informáticos
Universidad de Burgos
Av. Cantabria s/n, 09006, Burgos, Spain
{jmaudes,jjrodriguez,cgosorio}@ubu.es

Abstract. In pattern recognition many methods need numbers as inputs. Using nominal datasets with these methods requires to transform such data into numerical. Usually, this transformation consists in encoding nominal attributes into a group of binary attributes (one for each possible nominal value). This approach, however, can be enhanced for certain methods (e.g., those requiring linear separable data representations). In this paper, different alternatives are evaluated for enhancing SVM (Support Vector Machine) accuracy with nominal data. Some of these approaches convert nominal into continuous attributes using distance metrics (i.e., VDM (Value Difference Metric)). Other approaches combine the SVM with other classifier which could work directly with nominal data (i.e., a Decision Tree). An experimental validation over 27 datasets shows that Cascading with an SVM at Level-2 and a Decision Tree at Level-1 is a very interesting solution in comparison with other combinations of these base classifiers, and when compared to VDM.

Keywords: Ensembles, Nominal Data, Cascade Generalization, Support Vector Machines, Decision Trees.

1 Introduction

Data can be classified into numerical and qualitative. Qualitative data can only take values from a finite, pre-defined set. If no order is assumed between such values, the data is referred to as Nominal or Categorical.

In pattern recognition many methods require numerical inputs, so there is a mismatch when they are applied to nominal data. One approach for adapting nominal data to numerical methods is to transform each nominal feature into n binary features (NBF [5]), where n is the number of possible values the nominal feature can take. Following this method, a nominal value is translated into a group of binary attributes, where all values are zero, except the one corresponding to the attribute indicating such nominal value.

Fig. 1 shows six samples having two attributes A and B, and a class C, translated into binary. Both attributes can take only the following three values: (a1, a2, a3) and (b1, b2, b3), respectively. As shown in the example, this transformation can lead to a non-linear separable representation of data that is not suitable for applying a linear learner.

M. Haindl, J. Kittler, and F. Roli (Eds.): MCS 2007, LNCS 4472, pp. 231–240, 2007.

Two approaches will be analyzed in this paper to deal with nominal data. The first consists in using another numerical representation of nominal data (i.e., VDM [11], [3]), and the second, in constructing new input dimensions that improve classification task. These new input dimensions are calculated as the output from another classifier that can deal directly with nominal data without any conversion (i.e., a Decision Tree). We will test this approach by firstly using SVM as linear classifier and secondly using different ways of combining Decision Trees and SVMs.

This paper is structured as follows. Section 2 describes VDM metric for conversion of nominal attributes into numerical data. Section 3 presents Cascading and describes how it can be used with nominal data. Section 4 extends Cascading scheme to similar approaches. Section 5 contains experimental validation. Section 6 discusses experimental results. Finally, Section 7 concludes.

2   VDM

An alternative approach to binary conversion is transforming symbolic values into numeric continuous values. VDM (Value Difference Metric) for measuring distances between symbolic features values is presented in [11]. Dutch [3] uses VDM to transform symbolic features into numeric, and then the converted data is applied to a classifier.

In [3] VDM is tested using FSM networks and k-NN classifiers, and better or similar results are obtained with VDM conversion than with raw data.

VDM replaces each nominal value x of an attribute A with a probability vector $v=(v_1,..., v_c)$, where c is the number of classes and $v_i=P(class=c_i|A=x)$. Thus, VDM can significantly augment input dimensionality in multiclass problems. Nominal to binary conversion also increases input dimensionality, but, in this case, the increment is due to the cardinality of the nominal attribute domains.

3   Cascading for Nominal Attributes Transformation

Cascade Generalization (also known as *Cascading*) [4] is an architecture for designing classification algorithms. Cascading is commonly used at two levels. *Level-1* is trained with the raw dataset, whereas *Level-2* uses all the original features from the dataset plus the output of the Level-1 classifier as its inputs. Level-1 outputs are vectors representing a conditional probability distribution $(p_1, ... , p_c)$, where p_i is the Level-1 classifier estimated probability that the input data belongs to class i, and c is the number of classes in the dataset. Cascading can be extended to n levels.

Training one classifier with the output of another classifier uses to lead to overfitting. However, Cascading is not degraded by overfitting because the Level-2 classifier also uses the original samples as input features. Moreover, the more Level-1 and Level-2 classifiers differ, the better Cascading works. In [4] some ideas are presented for selecting both classifiers, which are subsequently commented on in Section 6.

As we have seen, nominal to binary conversion can result in a data representations that are not linearly separable. Cascading is presented as a solution to avoid this problem, because the input space is augmented with new features that transform the non-linearly separable data representation into another that is likely to avoid the problem.

Samples	Samples Binarized
(a1, b1, c1) (a1, b2, c2) (a2, b2, c1) (a3, b1, c2) (a3, b3, c1) (a2, b3, c2)	(1, 0, 0, 1, 0, 0, c1) (1, 0, 0, 0, 1, 0, c2) (0, 1, 0, 0, 1, 0, c1) (0, 0, 1, 1, 0, 0, c2) (0, 0, 1, 0, 0, 1, c1) (0, 1, 0, 0, 0, 1, c2)

Class c1 points	Class c2 points	Sum of c1 inequations
$x1+x4+k>0$	$x1+x5+k<0$	$x1+x2+x3+x4+x5+x6+2k>0$
$x2+x5+k>0$	$x3+x4+k<0$	**Sum of c2 inequations**
$x3+x6+k>0$	$x2+x6+k<0$	$x1+x2+x3+x4+x5+x6+2k<0$
		=>**incompatibility => non linear separability**

Fig. 1. Nominal data conversion into binary can lead to non linear separable regions. The figure shows an example where getting an hyperplane of coefficients xi and constant k, to separate class c1 points from class c2 points is impossible.

In our approach, these new features are calculated by a Level-1 classifier, which can deal directly with nominal data (i.e., a Decision Tree). Thereby avoiding any mismatch between the nominal data and the Level-1 classification method.

On the other hand, Level-2 input consists of the nominal to binary converted attributes plus the Level-1 classifier output. Accordingly, VDM input dimensionality grows as the number of nominal attributes rises, whereas the Cascading Level-1 output only adds c new dimensions (where c is the number of classes). However, Level-2 input dimensionality is also high, because of the nominal to binary conversion.

4 Stacking and Grading for Nominal Data

Using a Level-1 Decision Tree for constructing continuous features for another method at Level-2 can be achieved using other similar approaches.

Stacked Generalization, also known as *Stacking* [13] also uses two levels (and can use more). Although levels are numbered in a different way in [13], for the sake of simplicity we still assume that Level-1 is used as the base classifier and Level-2 as the classifier that receives Level-1 output as input. Stacking uses to work with more than one base classifier, and those base classifiers use to be different.

Let b the number of base classifiers and c the number of classes. n disjoint partitions (or *folders*) from training data are used for training nxb initial base classifiers. So each input is used for testing exactly b times (once through the n folders corresponding to the b base classifiers that we wish to obtain). Then, the Level-2 classifiers are trained with a new dataset of cxb dimensionality plus the class attribute. For each original instance such cxb features are obtained using the c probability estimations from the b classifiers that used the latter instance for testing. Finally, the nxb classifiers are discarded, and a new set of Level-1 b base classifiers is calculated, this time using the whole training set. Overfitting is therefore avoided, because Level-1 and Level-2 classifiers are different, and because cross-validation means the Level-2 classifier training set differs from the Level-1 classifiers training set.

Grading [10] is another two-level method that uses n *partitions* like Stacking. In [10] levels are also numbered in a different way, but again we will still keep our numeration. Just as in Stacking, the set of *nxb* base classifiers are calculated before-hand, but are tested this time with cross validation. The output of each base learner is a binary attribute that signifies whether the prediction in question is correct or not (*graded prediction*). Subsequently, *b* Level-2 classifiers (all of the same type) are calculated, each one being trained with the original features plus the graded predictions obtained from one group of *n* base classifiers. Graded predictions are used as Level-2 class. Finally, the *nxb* base classifiers are discarded, and *b* new base classifiers are calculated using the whole training set. The final prediction is made by Level-2 classifiers using a voting rule.

Stacking and Grading can be used for nominal data in the same way we have used Cascading (i.e., a single Decision Tree at Level-1). Note that Stacking and Grading require computing the discarded base classifiers, so they are computationally more expensive than Cascading even when only one Level-1 classifier is required.

On the other hand, Stacking Level-2 classifiers do not use nominal to binary converted data, so the Level-2 input dimension is not increased and is always equal to the number of classes when only one Level-1 classifier is used. However, the Grading Level-2 input dimension increases because its Level-2 classifier takes both the graded prediction and the nominal to binary converted attributes as their input values, as they do in Cascading.

Obviously, Stacking and Grading were not devised for only one base classifier, but we have tested them in order to compare Cascading with other combinations of "one" SVM with "one" Decision Tree.

5 Experimental Validation

The validation was performed by implementing generalized Cascading and VDM algorithms in Java within WEKA [12]. We tested Cascading with a Decision Tree in Level-1, and with an SVM in Level-2 against the following methods, using 27 datasets:

1. A Decision Tree. WEKA J.48 is an implementation of the C4.5 Release 8 Quinlan Decision Tree [9]. This implementation was also applied in all methods that use a Decision Tree as their Level-1 or Level-2 method.
2. SMO [8], an implementation of SVM provided by WEKA. Linear kernel was used. This implementation was also used in all methods that required an SVM as their Level-1 or Level-2 method.
3. J.48 with VDM and SMO with VDM. In both cases, nominal features were replaced by VDM output.
4. WEKA Stacking implementation, with ten folders using J.48 as Level-1 and SMO as Level-2 and vice versa.
5. WEKA Grading implementation, with ten folders using J.48 as Level-1 and SMO as Level-2 and vice versa.
6. Finally, we inverted our initial Cascading scheme, that is: SMO in Level-1 and J.48 in Level-2.

A 10x10 fold cross validation was applied. The *corrected resampled t-test statistic* from [7] was used (significance level 5%) for comparing the methods. The 100 (10x10) results for each method and dataset are considered as the input for the test.

Table 1 shows the used datasets. Most of them are from the UCI repository [1], and the rest are from Statlib. All datasets selected have no numerical or ordinal attributes[1]. The only modifications made on datasets were: (i) ID attributes have been removed (i.e., in *Molecular biology promoters* and *Splice* datasets). (ii) In *Monks-1* and *Monks-2*, only training set is considered, because testing set is a subset of the training set. (iii) In *Monks-3* and *Spect*, a union is made of both training and testing sets.

Table 1. Datasets used in Experimental Validation. #E = Number of instances, #A = Number of attributes included class, #C = Number of classes. (U)=>From UCI, (S)=>From Statlib.

Dataset	#E	#A	#C	Dataset	#E	#A	#C
Audiology (U)	226	70	24	Postop. patient (U)	90	9	3
Boxing1 (S)	120	4	2	Primary tumor (U)	339	18	21
Boxing2 (S)	132	4	2	Solar flare 1 C (U)	323	11	3
Breast cancer (U)	286	10	2	Solar flare 1 M (U)	323	11	4
Car (U)	1728	7	4	Solar flare 1 X (U)	323	11	2
Dmft (S)	797	5	6	Solar flare 2 C (U)	1066	11	8
Fraud (S)	42	12	2	Solar flare 2 M (U)	1066	11	6
Kr-vs-kp (U)	3196	37	2	Solar flare 2 X (U)	1066	11	3
Mol Biol Prmtrs (U)	106	58	2	Soybean (U)	683	36	19
Monks-1 (U)	432	7	2	Spect (U)	267	23	2
Monks-2 (U)	432	7	2	Splice (U)	3190	61	3
Monks-3 (U)	438	7	2	Tic-tac-toe (U)	958	10	2
Mushroom (U)	8124	23	2	Vote (U)	435	17	2
Nursery (U)	12960	9	5				

Accuracy results are shown in Tables 2 and 3. Bold font has been used to mark the best method for each dataset. A "•" or a "○", respectively, indicate a significant loss or win with respect to the proposed Cascading configuration (Level-2=SMO, Level-1=J.48). Hence, our method has only 5 significative losses and 55 significative wins when compared with all methods over the 27 datasets. In both tables the last row computes the significative wins, ties and losses for each method tested in comparison to Cascading Level-2=SMO, Level-1=J.48.

Table 2 shows that only VDM+J.48 accuracy is comparable to the Cascading configuration, but VDM+SMO only wins once. Table 3 shows Stacking and Grading accuracies. Significant wins and losses against Cascading Level-2=SMO, Level-1=J.48 are marked in the same way. Neither of the two latter methods shows any significative wins.

Table 4 ranks the methods using the difference between significative wins and losses, comparing each method with all the others. It shows that Cascading Level-2=SMO,

---

[1] Some attributes from these datasets are in fact ordinal, but for convenience we have treated them as nominal, just as they appear on the Weka web site. Retrieved 3 March 2007 from http://www.cs.waikato.ac.nz/ml/weka/.

Level-1=J.48 is the best option. There is an important gap between this method and the second method in the ranking. Regarding SMO enhancement, Cascading Level-2=SMO, Level-1=J.48 seems to work much better than VDM+SMO. Third place for Cascading Level-2=J.48 Level-1=SMO, is discussed in the next section.

Table 2. Accuracy of SVM and J.48 alone or combined using Cascading or VDM. Significative wins and losses with respect to the 1st method (i.e., Cascading level2=SMO, level1=J.48) are marked "○" and "●" respectively. The final row row details significant wins, ties and losses against that method.

Dataset	Cascading Level2=SMO Level1=J.48	Cascading Level2=J.48 Level1=SMO	J.48	SMO	SMO + VDM	J.48 + VDM
Audiology	**82.65**	79.13	77.26●	80,77	80.15	76.73●
Boxing1	83.67	81.58	**87.00**	81,58	83.25	81.08
Boxing2	80.44	**82.34**	80.44	**82,34**	80.89	79.91
Breast C.	74.14	69.83●	**74.28**	69,52●	69.05●	70.88
Car	95.14	95.57	92.22●	93,62●	86.74●	**97.30**○
Dmft	19.81	19.17	19.60	**21,14**	19.71	20.06
Fraud	73.60	76.10	63.05	76.10	75.00	**86.40**○
Kr-vs-kp	**99.44**	98.78●	**99.44**	95,79●	94.09●	99.36
Molc. B. P.	91.42	91.01	79.04●	91,01	**93.13**	76.22●
Monks-1	96.60	**99.35**	96.60	74,86●	75.00●	76.28●
Monks-2	67.14	67.14	67.14	67,14	67.14	**90.07**○
Monks-3	**98.63**	**98.63**	**98.63**	96,12●	95.89●	**98.63**
Mushroom	**100.00**	**100.00**	**100.00**	**100.00**	**100.00**	**100.00**
Nursery	98.29	96.71●	97.18●	93,08●	91.80●	**99.42**○
Postop. P	67.22	68.67	69.78	67,33	69.89	69.33
Primary T.	44.31	43.31	41.39	**47.09**	44.67	41.22
Solar f1-C	88.95	**89.30**	88.95	88.49	88.74	88.15
Solar f1-M	89.67	89.92	89.98	89.70	**90.10**	89.61
Solar f1-X	**97.84**	**97.84**	**97.84**	**97.84**	**97.84**	**97.84**
Solar f2-C	82.91	**82.93**	**82.93**	82.91	**82.93**	82.89
Solar f2-M	**96.62**	**96.62**	**96.62**	**96.62**	**96.62**	**96.62**
Solar f2-X	**99.53**	**99.53**	**99.53**	**99.53**	**99.53**	**99.53**
Soybean	94.13	91.17●	91.78●	93,10	**94.36**	92.77
Spect	81.62	83.68	81.35	83,61	79.30	81.69
Splice	93.55	92.93	94.17	92,88	**96.07**○	94.28
Tic-tac-toe	97.35	**98.33**	85.28●	**98,33**	69.11●	94.28●
Vote	**96.69**	95.88	96.57	95,77	95.75	96.57
wins/ties/losses		**0/23/4**	**0/21/6**	**0/21/6**	**1/19/7**	**4/19/4**

According to [2], a better way to rank the methods is doing a ranking for each dataset. A number is assigned to each method and dataset corresponding to its ranking position in such dataset. If there were ties, average ranks are assigned. Then, for each method, the average ranking is calculated over all datasets, as in first column of Table 5. The methods are then ordered increasingly using these values. Once again,

Cascading Level-2=SMO Level-1=J.48 is shown as the best method. Regarding SMO enhancement, once again Cascading Level-2=SMO Level-1=J.48 works much better than VDM+SMO.

In both rankings we can see that the most computationally expensive options (i.e., Stacking and Grading) perform worse even than J.48 on their own.

Table 3. Accuracy of Stacking and Grading. Significative wins and losses against Cascading level2=SMO, level1=J.48 are marked with "○" and "●" respectively. The final row details significant wins, ties and losses against such method.

Dataset	Stacking Level2=SMO Level1=J.48	Stacking Level2=J.48 Level1= SMO	Grading Level2=SMO Level1=J.48	Grading Level2=J.48 Level1=SMO
Audiology	73.98●	72.70●	70.72●	77.52●
Boxing1	86.58	81.67	85.17	81.67
Boxing2	80.67	**82.34**	79.14	**82.34**
Breast C.	72.02	68.83●	73.23	69.20●
Car	92.47●	93.58●	92.06●	93.67●
Dmft	19.81	17.72	19.46	**21.14**
Fraud	66.10	70.70	64.90	76.40
Kr-vs-kp	**99.44**	95.78●	**99.44**	96.81●
Molc. B. P.	30.29●	91.01	72.56●	91.01
Monks-1	96.60	75.00●	96.60	81.79●
Monks-2	67.14	67.14	67.14	67.14
Monks-3	**98.63**	96.12●	**98.63**	98.10
Mushroom	**100.00**	**100.00**	**100.00**	**100.00**
Nursery	97.18●	93.12●	97.18●	93.05●
Postop. P	**71.11**	**71.11**	**71.11**	67.67
Primary T.	40.27	36.20●	32.93●	46.29
Solar f1-C	88.86	88.86	80.86	88.49
Solar f1-M	**90.10**	90.07	**90.10**	89.83
Solar f1-X	**97.84**	**97.84**	**97.84**	**97.84**
Solar f2-C	**82.93**	82.86	**82.93**	82.91
Solar f2-M	**96.62**	**96.62**	**96.62**	**96.62**
Solar f2-X	**99.53**	**99.53**	**99.53**	**99.53**
Soybean	91.77●	89.53●	90.29●	93.01
Spect	79.42	83.45	81.58	**83.83**
Splice	94.15	93.10	94.17	92.87
Tic-tac-toe	85.77●	**98.33**	85.28●	**98.33**
Vote	96.57	95.77	96.57	95.77
Wins/ties/losses	**0/21/6**	**0/18 /9**	**0/20/7**	**0/21/6**

Finally, Cascading and Stacking get better results when J.48 is used in Level-1 than when SMO is used in this level. That might confirm our hypothesis that it is better using methods that can deal directly with nominal data in Level-1. However, this idea does not work with Grading, perhaps because Grading is more influenced by Level-2, so it may perform better if the method at that level works well with nominal data.

6 Discussion

Results using Cascading to improve SMO with a method that deals directly with nominal attributes (Level-2=SMO, Level-1=J.48) are better than using VDM (VDM+SMO). VDM estimates probabilities of how related are symbolic values to classes, as does J.48 in Level-1 does. An important difference between both methods is that VDM builds c new attributes for each nominal attribute (c = number of classes), whereas J.48 always constructs c features independently of the number of nominal attributes. Thus, it seems that Cascading Level-1=J.48 performs better and is more accurate, even though it calculates fewer attributes.

Table 4. Difference between significatives wins and losses ranking

Wins-Losses	Wins	Losses	Method
50	55	5	Casc. Level-2=SMO, Level-1=J.48
36	56	20	VDM+J.48
15	39	24	Casc. Level-2=J.48, Level-1=SMO
8	33	25	J.48
-2	30	32	Grading Level-2=J.48, Level-1=SMO
-11	26	37	Stacking Level-2=SMO, Level-1=J.48
-11	26	37	SMO
-19	25	44	Grading Level-2=SMO, Level-1=J.48
-31	24	55	VDM+SMO
-35	15	50	Stacking Level-2 J.48, Level-1=SMO

Table 5. Methods ranked by their average ranking over all datasets

Average Ranking	Method
4.52	Cascading Level-2=SMO, Level-1=J.48
4.98	Cascading Level-2=J.48, Level-1=SMO
5.07	J.48
5.13	Stacking Level-2=SMO, Level-1=J.48
5.54	Grading Level-2=J.48, Level-1=SMO
5.67	VDM+SMO
5.67	VDM+J.48
5.80	Grading Level-2=SMO, Level-1=J.48
5.80	SMO
6.48	Stacking Level-2=J.48, Level-1=SMO

If we have two instances with the same symbolic value for some nominal feature, but belonging to a different class, VDM will calculate the same probability vector for both of them. In our opinion, however, it is preferable that different values would be provided to aid the classification task, for example taking into account the values of the rest of attributes of the instance, as Level-1 J.48 does. This issue is of especial interest wherever linear separability is required.

Another interesting question related to our experimental results, is that they are apparently contradictory to [4], in which a strategy to choose an appropriate algorithm for each Cascading level is provided, based on the following three points:

- *"Combine classifiers with different behavior from a Bias-Variance analysis.*
- *At low level use algorithms with low variance.*
- *At high level use algorithms with low bias".*

Variance and *Bias* are terms from a loss function to measure an algorithm error [6]. Bias measures the average guess of the learning algorithm (low Bias means high accuracy), whereas Variance measures how this learning can vary from one dataset to another. Thus an unstable algorithm such as a Neural Network or a Decision Tree has a high variance, whereas the variance of a more stable one, such as SVM or Boosting, will be lower. Increasing Variance commonly leads to decreasing Bias and vice versa (for example tuning some parameters of some classifiers). So, the application of Cascading with the above rules is an attempt at combining learners, one with low bias and other with low variance, to arrive at a new one with lower values in both measures.

. Note that [4] prefers low variance at low level and low bias at high level, because by *"selecting learners with low bias for high level, we are able to fit more complex decision surfaces, taking into account the 'stable' surfaces drawn by the low level learners".* [4] provides an experimental validation over 26 UCI datasets to show it, but in this experiment nominal and continuous attributes are mixed in the datasets.

However, those *'stable surfaces'* can be drawn in a inappropriate way when data is nominal, especially if the method at the low level can not deal directly with nominal data and needs some kind of conversion, as for example SVM. Moreover, SVM used in this paper validation is a linear classifier, and feeding it with nominal data converted into binary it can degrade its performance, because the data transformed in this way might show a non-linearly separable representation.

7 Conclusions

Certain classification methods require their input data to be numerical (e.g., linear classifiers). This means that some kind of conversion is required when nominal data is applied to them. Usually, such conversion is implemented using a nominal to binary translation. We have illustrated that this approach can easily lead to non-linear separability, such that an enhancement is required if we want to use nominal data with linear classifiers.

Conversion of nominal data into continuous data can avoid this problem. We have tested this idea using VDM. Another solution is Cascading Level-2=Linear Classifier, Level-1=Decision Tree (or any other method that can deal with nominal data directly). Level-1 output is concatenated to binaries features from nominal to binary conversion, augmenting Level-2 input dimensionality, but working towards enhanced linear separability. This approach was tested for Level-2=SVM and Level-1=Decision Tree. We also have tested these two classifiers combined with Stacking and Grading. We attempted to invert the position of SVM and J.48 to confirm the importance of applying a classifier that can work with nominal data without conversion into Level-1.

The experimental validation shows that VDM for enhancing an SMO is worse than Cascading, perhaps because Cascading constructs the probability vector based on the Level-1 output, and takes account of all dataset attributes, whereas VDM only takes account of the attribute to be converted and the class. Cascading also shows better results than other methods, including Stacking and Grading, which require greater computation time. It is worth noting that both for Cascading and for Stacking, it is better to put the method that does not need to convert nominal data at Level-1. However, experimental results show that VDM+J.48 is an interesting choice, so our next work is to test Cascading using VDM.

References

1. Blake, C.L., Merz, C.J.: UCI Repository of Machine Learning Databases. http://www.ics.uci.edu/mlearn/MLRepository.html.
2. Demsar, J.: Statistical Comparisons of Classifiers over Multiple Data Sets. Journal of Machine Learning Research, 7, (2006) 1–30.
3. Duch W., Grudzinski K., Stawski G.: Symbolic Features in Neural Networks. Proc. 5th Conference on Neural Networks and Soft Computing, Zakopane, (2000) 180-185.
4. Gama, J., Brazdil, P.: Cascade Generalization. Machine Learning, 41(3). (2000) 315-343.
5. Grabczewski K., Jankowski, N.: Transformations of Symbolic Data for Continuous Data Oriented Models. In Artificial Neural Networks and Neural Information Processing, ICANN/ICONIP 2003. Springer, Vol. 2714 (2003) 359-366.
6. Kohavi, R., Wolpert, D. H.: Bias Plus Variance Decomposition for Zero-One Loss Functions. In L. Saitta (Ed.), Machine Learning, Procs 13th International Conference. Morgan Kaufmann (1996) 275-283.
7. Nadeau C., Bengio Y.: Inference for the Generalization Error. Machine Learning, 52 (2003) 239-281.
8. Platt, J.: Fast Training of Support Vector Machines using Sequential Minimal Optimization. In: B. Schoelkopf, C. Burges, and A. Smola, (eds.). Advances in Kernel Methods. MIT Press. (1998).
9. Quinlan, R.: C4.5: Programs for Machine Learning. Morgan Kaufmann Publishers, San Mateo, CA. (1993).
10. Seewald, A.K., Fuernkranz J.: An Evaluation of Grading Classifiers. In: Hoffmann F. et al. (eds.). Advances in Intelligent Data Analysis, 4th International Conference, IDA 2001, Proceedings, Springer, Berlin/Heidelberg/New York/Tokyo (2001) 115-124.
11. Stanfill C., Waltz D.: Toward Memory-Based Reasoning. Communication of the ACM, 29, (1986) 1213-1229.
12. Witten H., Frank E.: Data Mining: Practical Machine Learning Tools and Techniques. Morgan Kaufmann, 2nd edn., (2005). http://www.cs.waikato.ac.nz/ml/weka.
13. Wolpert, D.: Stacked Generalization. Neural networks. Vol. 5 (1992) 241-260.

A Combination of Sample Subsets and Feature Subsets in One-Against-Other Classifiers

Mineichi Kudo[1,*], Satoshi Shirai[1], and Hiroshi Tenmoto[2]

[1] Division of Computer Science
Graduate School of Information Science and Technology
Hokkaido University, Sapporo 060-0814, Japan
mine@main.ist.hokudai.ac.jp
http://prml.main.ist.hokudai.ac.jp
[2] Department of Information Engineering
Kushiro National College of Technology
Otanoshike Nishi 2-32-1, Kushiro, Hokkaido 084-0916, Japan
tenmo@kushiro-ct.ac.jp

Abstract. We investigated a "sample-feature-subset" approach which is a kind of extension of bagging and the random subspace method. In the procedure, we collect some subsets of training samples in each class and then remove the redundant features from those subsets. As a result, those subsets are represented in different feature spaces. We constructed one-against-other classifiers as the component classifiers by feeding those subsets to a base classifier and then combined them in majority voting. Some experimental results showed that this approach outperformed the random subspace method.

1 Introduction

Recently, classifier fusion is gathering much attention in pattern recognition. The main stream is divided into two sub-streams: one is bagging [1] or boosting [2] that utilizes several subsets of training samples, and the other is the random subspace method [3] that utilizes several subsets of features (spaces), For classifier fusion/combination, several important facts have been already obtained in references [4,5,6] such as 1) negatively correlated (component) classifiers much contribute to the improvement of the combined classifier, 2) even positively correlated (component) classifiers work in some cases, 3) randomly selected feature subsets contribute in other cases, 4) the effectiveness of such a random subspace method depends on to what degree redundant features exist, and, as a result, 5) the effectiveness of bagging, boosting and the random subspace method depend on problems and the ways of combination as well as the base classifiers.

In this paper, we extend these frameworks to a general one in which some subsets of the training samples are collected in different feature spaces, that is, a "sample-feature-subset" approach. We investigate the possibility of such

---

* Corresponding author.

M. Haindl, J. Kittler, and F. Roli (Eds.): MCS 2007, LNCS 4472, pp. 241–250, 2007.

an approach in some experiments. In this approach, we select some subsets of the training sample set in one class at a time. Then, for each subset of a class, we select a feature subset, taking into account all the samples belonging to the other classes. These subsets can overlap each other and feature subset selection is optional. In this sense, it can be seen as a variant of bagging where random sampling with replacement is made (although duplication of a sample is out of consideration). While, it is also an extension of the random subspace method where random selection of features is made, while features are selected systematically in the proposed method.

2   Majority Vote in One-Against-Other Classifiers

First, let us consider the error rate when we make ready C one-against-other classifiers Φ_i $(i = 1, 2, \ldots, C)$ for C classes of $\{\omega_1, \omega_2, \ldots, \omega_C\}$. We assume that each of $\Phi_i(x)$ outputs 1 for showing that x is assigned to class ω_i and -1 for not-assigned to class ω_i. Let us denote the error rate of Φ_i by

$$e_i = \text{Prob}(x \in \omega_i \to \omega_j(j \neq i)) + \text{Prob}(x \in \omega_j(j \neq i) \to \omega_i))$$
$$= e_i^n + e_i^p,$$

where e_i^n is called the "negative error" and e_i^p is called the "positive error."

With these C classifiers, we can construct a total classifier Φ in several ways. The simplest one is as follows:

$$\Phi(x) = \arg\max_i \Phi_i(x).$$

In this Φ, a sample x is assigned to class ω_i if $\Phi_i(x) = 1$ for only one i and is rejected otherwise. In this paper, we mainly consider another form:

$$\Phi(x) = \arg\max_i \left(\Phi_i(x) - \frac{1}{C-1} \sum_{j \neq i} \Phi_j(x) \right).$$

This is a majority vote. The first term means a vote to class ω_i from class ω_i and the second term means votes to class ω_i from the other classes. It is meant that a *negative vote* from class $\omega_j(j \neq i)$ is distributed to the other $C-1$ classes evenly. This Φ is equivalent to the simplest one in assignment because

$$\Phi_i(x) - \frac{1}{C-1} \sum_{j \neq i} \Phi_j(x) \geq \Phi_k(x) - \frac{1}{C-1} \sum_{j \neq k} \Phi_j(x)$$
$$\Longleftrightarrow \frac{C}{C-1}(\Phi_i(x) - \Phi_k(x)) \geq 0 \Longleftrightarrow \Phi_i(x) - \Phi_k(x) \geq 0. \tag{1}$$

The difference is that the latter Φ can distinguish two kinds of rejection in value: (1) "no-vote" rejection with all (-1)'s or "totally ambiguous vote" rejection with all 1's ($\max_i \Phi_i(x) = 0$) and (2) "ambiguous vote" rejection, that is, multiple assignment to more than one class but not all classes ($0 < \max_i \Phi_i(x) < 2$).

The error rate e of Φ is upper-bounded by

$$e \le \sum_{i=i}^{C} e_i.$$

This is because that an error occurs only when at least one component classifier Φ_i mistakes. Therefore, designing better one-against-other classifiers derives designing of a better total classifier.

Let us examine this error in detail. Here, by R_i let us denote the class region determined by Φ_i such that $R_i = \{x \mid \Phi_i(x) = 1\}$. Then, the universe U is partitioned into R_i and $\overline{R_i}$, where the over-line shows the complementary set. Here, the error e of the total classifier is written as

$$e = \sum_{i} \sum_{j \ne i} \mathrm{Prob}(x \in w_i \to w_j).$$

This equation can be expressed in two ways:

$$e = \sum_{i} \mathrm{Prob}(x \in w_i \to w_j (j \ne i)), \qquad (2)$$

and

$$e = \sum_{i} \mathrm{Prob}(x \in w_j (j \ne i) \to w_i). \qquad (3)$$

These two different expressions mean, respectively,

$$e = \sum_{i} e_i^n, \qquad (4)$$

and

$$e = \sum_{i} e_i^p. \qquad (5)$$

However, these equations do not always hold. Eqs. (2) and (4) hold if the *negative* class (mis)assignment is necessarily possible and Eqs. (3) and (5) hold if the *positive* class (mis)assignment is necessarily possible.

In general, we can show that

$$e = \sum_{i} e_i^n + \mathrm{Prob}(x \in \bigcap_{i} R_i),$$

$$= \sum_{i} e_i^p + \mathrm{Prob}(x \in \overline{\bigcup_{i} R_i}).$$

As special cases, we can see that

Case I: If $\bigcap_i R_i = \emptyset$, then $e = \sum_i e_i^n$. This is the case that every class regions do not share a common part of the universe, in other words, no totally ambiguous region exists. In the word of classifiers, the condition holds when $\Phi_i(x) = 1$ $(i = 1, \ldots, C)$ never happens for every x.

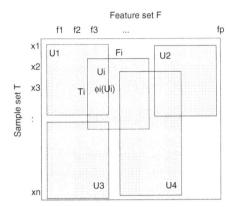

Fig. 1. Several subsets of an information table

Case II: If $\overline{\bigcup_i R_i} = \emptyset$, that is, $\bigcup_i R_i = U$, then $e = \sum_i e_i^p$. This is the case that no-vote reject region exists. The condition holds when $\Phi_i(x) = -1 \ (i = 1, \ldots, C)$ never happens for every x.

Case III: If both Case I and Case II hold at the same time, then $e = \sum_i e_i^n = \sum_i e_i^p$. This is the most desirable case. The condition holds when above two extreme votes never happens for every x.

Among these cases, Case I is most probable. Then, for large $C(> 2)$, a guideline to improve the total classifier is to suppress the negative error of each component classifier, that is, to widen the class region as long as the totally ambiguous region $\bigcap_i R_i$ is not produced. If we remove some redundant features, a region secured in the original feature space is widen. Thus, such a feature selection depending on each class region would be effective.

3   Subsets Both in Sample Set and Feature Set

In general, multiple classifiers can be generated from different subsets of training samples such as being seen in bagging (boosting is its weighted version), or from different subsets of features such as being seen in the random subspace method. We can consider both at once (Fig. 1). Here, a subset $U_i = T_i \times F_i$ of the product space $T \times F$, where T is the training sample (index) space and F is the feature (index) space, gives one piece of information for designing a (component) classifier ϕ_i. Here, we implicitly assume a "measurement" function x behind such as

$$x : T \times F \to D$$
$$(i, j) \mapsto x_{ij} \in D_j,$$

where x_{ij} is the value of ith training sample in jth measurement and the range D can change according to index j. It should be noted that some subsets can overlap in training sample subsets or feature subsets or both. More general formulation is possible by thinking different probabilities on $T \times F$, but we limit ourselves to this "hard" layout in this paper.

Then we can have any number of classifiers we want. The problem is how to choose such subsets. What we know for classifier combination is that it is better to make ϕ_i's be independent in the output or more hopefully be negatively correlated. However, in general, it is difficult to achieve this. Indeed, classifiers with higher correct recognition rates are naturally more (positively) correlated. This is the reason why combination of classifiers is most effective for weak learners (classifiers with a little better performance than the chance level). Nevertheless, it would be promising to make the component classifiers approach to be independent by adopting both independent training sample subsets and independent feature subsets.

In this paper, therefore, we choose some subsets U_i from the viewpoints: 1) feature selection is effective for situations in which the dimensionality p is relatively large to the number n of training samples and 2) effective features can depend on the local area, that is, different feature subsets can be most effective for different parts of training samples.

4   Subset Selection by Subclass Method

For choosing several subsets over training samples and features, we use the subclass method [7]. When the subclass method is applied to the training samples with correct class labels, some hyper-rectangle regions are found in each class. The characteristics is told in two-fold: 1) each hyper-rectangle region of a class does not include any *negative sample* belonging to the other classes (exclusiveness), and 2) such hyper-rectangle regions are maximal among hyper-rectangle regions keeping exclusiveness (maximalness). Precisely speaking, each hyper-rectangle is uniquely determined by a subset of *positive samples* and the hyper-rectangles are chosen so as to exclude the negative samples and to occupy as large space as possible. Some hyper-rectangles are gathered so as to cover all the positive training samples.

In this paper, we pay attention to a smaller feature subset provided that each of the hyper-rectangles keeps exclusive in the narrowed feature space. We remove redundant features from each hyper-rectangle as long as it still excludes the negative samples. This is carried out in a greedy manner. Such an operation corresponds to removing the both edges in the corresponding axis of the hyper-rectangle in order. Such a feature selection technique is already proposed [8].

In summary, first we find several subsets T_i (hyper-rectangles in the full feature set F) of training samples in a certain class by the subclass method, and then choose only necessary feature subset F_i by removing redundant features. As a result, we have $U_i = T_i \times F_i$ (a hyper-rectangle in F_i). An example is shown in Fig. 2. In Fig. 2, a family of subclasses (hyper-rectangles) are chosen first in each class, then the redundant features are removed from all the subclasses.

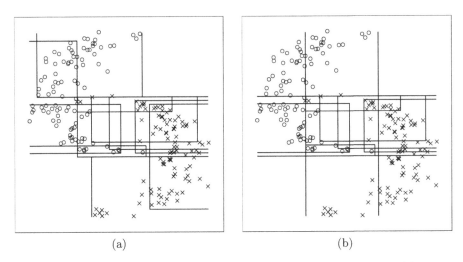

(a)   (b)

Fig. 2. Selected subsets by subclass method: (a) original rectangles and (b) feature-selected rectangles

In Fig. 2, we see that some rectangles infinitely expand their edges to either direction (axis).

Through this procedure, we have a set of subsets $U_i = T_i \times F_i$ having the following properties: 1) every training sample is included in at least one subset (one hyper-rectangle), 2) each hyper-rectangle can be regarded as a classifier that distinguishes a part of the positive samples from all the negative samples, and 3) different subsets are represented in different feature spaces. Let us denote $U_i \in \omega_k$ to make clear to which class U_i belongs. With the training sample set S_k of class ω_k, it is noted that $T_i \subseteq S_k$ and $F_i \subseteq F$ for $U_i (= T_i \times F_i) \in \omega_k$.

Now we can construct ϕ_i from $U_i \in \omega_k$. By ϕ_j^k, let us denote the jth classifier of class ω_k. For designing ϕ_j^k, we use a pair of *positive sample set* $P_j^k = T_i (\subseteq S_k)$ for some i and and the *negative sample set* $N_j^k = \bigcup_{l \neq k} S_l$ both in subspace $F_j^k = F_i$. Let classifiers ϕ_j^k be consistent with (P_j^k, N_j^k) in space F_j^k for every j and k (partly consistent with (S_k, N_j^k)). Then, if we use Φ such as

$$\Phi(x) = \arg\max_k \left(\max_j \phi_j^k(x) \right),$$

then the total classifier Φ is consistent with a whole training sample set $T = \bigcup_i S_i$. The set of the hyper-rectangles found by the subclass method may be used as ϕ_j^k in this way.

As a result, we have the same number of *one-against-other* classifiers as the number of the subsets obtained.

5   Combination of Subsets

We have the component classifiers such as

$$\phi_1^1, \phi_2^1, \ldots, \phi_{n_1}^1, \phi_1^2, \ldots, \phi_{n_2}^2, \ldots, \phi_1^C, \ldots, \phi_{n_C}^C.$$

Then, the total classifier in a majority vote becomes

$$\Phi(x) = \arg\max_k \left(\sum_{i=1}^{n_k} \phi_i^k(x) - \frac{1}{C-1} \sum_{l \neq k} \sum_{j=1}^{n_l} \phi_j^l(x) \right). \tag{6}$$

This means that $\Phi_k = \sum_{i=1}^{n_k} \phi_i^k(x)$. It should be noted that this Φ is not always consistent with the training samples even if all the ϕ_i^k's are partly consistent. This is because, when we compare the votes to two classes ω_i and ω_k, with (1), we have

$$\Phi_i(x) > \Phi_k(x) \iff \sum_{j=1}^{n_i} \phi_j^i(x) > \sum_{j=1}^{n_k} \phi_j^k(x).$$

Thus, for $x \in \omega_i$, if $(n_i + n_k)/2 \ (> n_i/2)$ component classifiers $\phi_j^i(x)$ output -1, then $\Phi_i(x) < \Phi_k(x)$ can happen. It does not happen if over half of component classifiers $\phi_j^i(x)$ of ω_i always output 1, then Φ is consistent with all the training samples. To make Φ be consistent, we may replace Φ_k with $\Phi_k = \frac{1}{n_k} \sum_{i=1}^{n_k} \phi_i^k(x)$.

6   Experiments

6.1   Conditions

We found T_i's by the randomized subclass method [9]. Then, some features were removed to obtain F_i. Last, we constructed ϕ_i's with a base classifier on the basis of (P_j^k, N_j^k) for $T_i \in \omega_k$. In the following experiments, we chose the nearest neighbor classifier as the base classifier. It is noted that the nearest neighbor classifier is consistent with the given training samples. For comparison, the hyper-rectangles are also directly chosen as the component classifiers ϕ_i.

Used datasets are three of one artificial and two real-world ones taken from UCI machine learning database [10]. The first dataset is chosen to show the effectiveness of using different feature subsets depending on some parts of samples. The remaining two datasets are chosen because the random subspace method succeeded to improve the classification performance for these datasets.

In the random subspace method, the features were randomly selected. The number of selected features was about a half $\lceil p/2 \rceil$ of the original number p of features. The number m of component classifiers were chosen to $m = 100$, according to reference [3]. To verify another possibility, we also used $m = 1,000$.

For calculation of the classification rate, the real-world datasets were randomly split into two disjoint halves: one for training and another for testing, and vice versa. In reporting, the two results are distinguished as "1st" and "2nd."

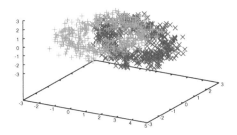

Fig. 3. Torus dataset in the first three dimensions.

The classification methods are six in total: **1-NN** (the nearest neighbor method), **Subclass without feature selection** (the hyper-rectangle rule in the original feature space), **Subclass with feature selection** (the hyper-rectangle rule in the selected feature space), **RSubspace** (the random subspace method) with randomly chosen **100 feature subsets**, **RSubspace** with randomly chosen **1,000 feature subsets**, and **SFsubset** (the proposed method with the selected sample-feature subsets).

The used datasets are follows:

Torus data (artificial). First, to confirm the effectiveness of feature selection, we used Torus data. Two rings belonging to distinct classes are orthogonally placed in an untouched manner in the first three dimensions (Fig. 3). That is, locally only one or two features are enough for classifying these classes. More seven features are introduced to make the problem be more practical. They obey all the standard Gaussian in common to two classes. The number n of training samples was changed as $n = 200, 1000, 2000$ (halves for two classes).

Vehicle data (real-world). The task is to classify a given silhouette to one of four types of vehicle, using 18 features extracted from the silhouette. The number of training samples is 946.

Letter data (real-world). The task is to identify each of black-and-white rectangular pixel displays as one of the 26 capital letters in the English alphabet. The features are 16 primitive numerical attributes including statistical moments and edge counts. The number of training samples is 20,000 in total.

6.2 Results

The results are summarized in Table 1. We notice several interesting facts:

1. **Effectiveness of feature selection:** Compare two groups of {**1-NN, Subclass without feature selection**} without feature selection and {**Subclass with feature selection, RSubspace, SFsubset**} with feature selection. In Torus, the advantage of selecting features is clear when it is contaminated with 7 noise features. In the uncontaminated (pure) case, such advantage is not seen. This means that hyper-rectangles were not appropriate for capturing such a ring structure, so that appropriate subsets were not chosen. Nevertheless, when

the size of training samples is large ($n = 2,000$), the proposed **SFsubset** succeeds to improve **1-NN** (from 99.03% to 99.35%). While, **RSubspace** is rather inferior to **1-NN** in the uncontaminated case. In Vehicle, **Subclass without feature selection** is the best. This implies that such hyper-rectangles fit the true class region, but failed to choose good feature subsets. This may be because almost all features contribute to classification evenly. In Letter, both **RSubspace** and **SFsubset** were effective. In this dataset, we can imagine that different groups of "letters" are distinguished from the remaining groups in different features.

2. **Effectiveness of sample selection:** Compare two groups of {**1-NN, RSubspace**} without sample selection and {**Subclass, SFsubset**} with sample selection. In Vehicle, the advantage of sample subset selection is remarkable.

3. **Effectiveness of sample-feature selection:** Compare **RSubspace** and **SFsubset**. Except for one case, **SFsubset** is superior to **RSubspace**. This implies that sophisticated selection of feature subsets can be better than random selection of feature subsets. In Torus in the contaminated smallest-sample case ($n = 200$), **RSubspace** is better. This implies that **SFsubset** depends on the subsets chosen by the hyper-rectangles but the hyper-rectangles were not appropriate for this case.

Table 1. Experimental results

Name	Method and Recognition rate (%)					
	1-NN	Subclass	Subclass	RSubspace	RSubspace	SFsubset
Feature Selection	No	No	Auto	A half	A half	Auto
Sample Selection	No	Auto	Auto	No	No	Auto
Base Classifier	Itself	Hyp.-rect.	Hyp.-rect.	1-NN	1-NN	1-NN
# Component Clfs.	1	Auto	Auto	100	1000	Auto
Combination	No	Eq. (6)	Eq. (6)	Eq. (6)	Eq. (6)	Eq. (6)
(pure, p=3)						
Torus (n=200)	**97.11**	96.65	95.25	93.69	93.69	96.86
Torus (n=1000)	98.51	**98.62**	98.54	94.79	94.79	98.26
Torus (n=2000)	99.03	98.92	98.90	95.19	95.19	**99.35**
(contaminated, p=10)						
Torus (n=200)	84.11	90.85	91.24	90.98	**92.78**	87.82
Torus (n=1000)	89.98	97.57	**97.76**	93.51	95.33	97.27
Torus (n=2000)	91.04	98.05	98.25	94.54	96.07	**98.59**
(p=18, n=423)						
Vehicle(1st)	51.30	**62.65**	61.70	54.85	55.79	56.26
Vehicle(2nd)	47.99	**56.26**	55.56	52.01	53.66	53.66
(p=16,n=10,000)						
Letter (1st)	94.17	89.29	89.28	94.57	94.59	**94.72**
Letter (2nd)	94.07	89.74	89.21	94.18	94.14	**94.62**

7 Conclusion

We investigated the effectiveness of a "sample-feature-subset" approach in which some parts of information are taken from a given information table. Each subset is consisting of a subset of the training samples represented in a subset of features. It differs from the random subspace method in the choice of feature subsets; the random subspace method chooses them randomly while the proposed approach chooses them depending on the pre-chosen subsets of samples. It also differs from bagging or boosting in the choice of sample subsets; the first two choose the subsets of training samples independently of classes while our approach chooses some subsets class by class, so that one subset produces a one-against-other classifier of a certain class.

Through experiments, we confirmed that such a "sample-feature-subset" framework can be better than the random subspace method. We have not yet compared it with bagging and boosting. It would be necessary in the future in order to obtain deeper understanding about the best way to choose such subsets. In this paper, we used the subclass method for choosing the subsets of training samples and constructed one-against-other classifiers so as to be partly consistent with the training samples. It is possible to use other ways such as co-clustering in which the training samples are clustered one class at a time. This work is in the beginning stage and the results showed only the possibility of such an approach. It is worth discussing about other ways to choose such subsets and the other ways to generate the component classifiers with different base classifiers.

References

1. L. Breiman. Bagging predictors. *Machine Learning Journal*, 24(2):123–140, 1996.
2. Y. Freund and R. E. Shapire. Experiments with a new boosting algorithm. In *13th International Conference on Machine Learning*, pages 148–156, 1996.
3. T. K. Ho. The random subspace method for constructing decision forests. *IEEE Transactions on Pattern Analysis and Machine Intelligence*, 20(8):832–844, 1998.
4. N. Ueda and R. Nakano. Analysis of generalization error on ensemble learning. *IEICE*, J80-D-II(9):2512–2521, 1997 (in Japanese).
5. M. Skurichina and R. P. W. Duin. Bagging, boosting and the random subspace method for linear classifiers. *Pattern Analysis and Applications*, 5:121–135, 2002.
6. S. B. Oh. On the relationship between majority vote accuracy and dependency in muliple classifier systems. *Pattern Recognition Letters*, 24:359–363, 2003.
7. M. Kudo and M. Shimbo. Optimal subclasses with dichotomous variables for feature selection and discrimination. *IEEE Trans. Systems, Man, and Cybern.*, 19:1194–1199, 1989.
8. M. Kudo and M. Shimbo. Feature selection based on the structural indices of categories. *Pattern Recognition*, 26:891–901, 1993.
9. M. Kudo, S. Yanagi, and M. Shimbo. Construction of class regions by a randomized algorithm: A randomized subclass method. *Pattern Recognition*, 29:581–588, 1996.
10. C.L. Blake and C.J. Merz. UCI repository of machine learning databases [http://www.ics.uci.edu/~mlearn/mlrepository.html], 1998.

Random Feature Subset Selection for Ensemble Based Classification of Data with Missing Features

Joseph DePasquale and Robi Polikar[*]

Signal Processing and Pattern Recognition Laboratory, Electrical and Computer Engineering, Rowan University, 201 Mullica Hill Rd, Glassboro, NJ 08028 USA
depasq63@students.rowan.edu, polikar@rowan.edu

Abstract. We report on our recent progress in developing an ensemble of classifiers based algorithm for addressing the missing feature problem. Inspired in part by the random subspace method, and in part by an AdaBoost type distribution update rule for creating a sequence of classifiers, the proposed algorithm generates an ensemble of classifiers, each trained on a different subset of the available features. Then, an instance with missing features is classified using only those classifiers whose training dataset did not include the currently missing features. Within this framework, we experiment with several bootstrap sampling strategies each using a slightly different distribution update rule. We also analyze the effect of the algorithm's primary free parameter (the number of features used to train each classifier) on its performance. We show that the algorithm is able to accommodate data with up to 30% missing features, with little or no significant performance drop.

1 Introduction

One of the most frustrating problems encountered in field implementation of an automated decision making system is to get caught unprepared for partial loss of data. Unless it was designed to be robust against such a potential loss, there is nothing a classifier can do when faced with processing a data instance with missing components. The partial loss of field data need not even be catastrophic: e.g. if a single sensor malfunctions (loss of one feature) during data collection, the entire data cannot be processed by such classifiers. This problem is hardly rare: bad sensors, failed pixels, malfunctioning equipment, signal saturation, data corruption, etc. are all familiar scenarios in practical applications.

The missing feature problem has been well researched. The oldest, and perhaps most commonly used solution is to substitute a meaningful estimate of the missing value, such as the k-nearest neighbors of the missing value [1]. However, such *data imputation* techniques require that the training data be sufficiently dense for the estimate to be a faithful representative of the missing value. Such a requirement, however, is rarely met in practice, even for datasets with modest number of features. Other approaches with sound theoretical underpinnings are also available that provide

---

[*] Corresponding author.

M. Haindl, J. Kittler, and F. Roli (Eds.): MCS 2007, LNCS 4472, pp. 251–260, 2007.

precise performance guarantees under certain conditions. These are typically probabilistic approaches, based on density estimation. Therefore, they require that certain a priori knowledge regarding the underlying data distributions be known or estimated, which also requires a sufficiently dense database. Such knowledge is often vague or non-existent, and inaccurate choices may lead to inferior performance, particularly for large datasets. Classical Bayesian estimation and expectation maximization based techniques fall into this category [2].

Other approaches use neuro-fuzzy algorithms, which provide, perhaps, a more natural setting for dealing with the missing data. In such approaches, unknown values of the data are either estimated, or a classification is made using the existing features, by calculating the fuzzy membership of the data point to its nearest neighbors, clusters, or hyperboxes. The parameters of the clusters and hyperboxes are determined from the existing data points. Algorithms based on general fuzzy min-max neural networks [3], or ARTMAP and fuzzy c-means clustering [4] are examples of this approach.

More recently, ensemble based approaches have been proposed to address the missing feature problem. For example, Melville *et al.* show that the algorithm DECO-RATE, which generates artificial data (with no missing values) from existing data (with missing values) is quite robust to missing data [5]. On the other hand, Juszczak and Duin [6] propose combining an ensemble of one-class classifiers trained on a single feature. This approach is capable of handling any combination of missing features, with the fewest number of classifiers possible. The approach can be very effective so long as single features can reasonably estimate the underlying decision boundaries, which is not always plausible.

We have previously proposed an alternative approach, Learn^{++}.MF, that trains multi-class classifiers using a random subset of the feature space, where the number of features is a free parameter of the algorithm. Any instance missing a feature is then classified as the majority vote of those classifiers whose training data did not include the missing features. This approach essentially combines the random feature selection in random subspace methods [7], with the distribution update rule of AdaBoost inspired Learn^{++} [8]. The original algorithm built on this premise was crude, but could handle up to 10% missing data using a specific feature distribution update rule [9]. In this contribution, we formalize the algorithm, and extend our work by i) analyzing the effect of different update rules; ii) analyzing the effect of the algorithm's primary free parameter, the number of features used in each subset; and iii) evaluating the algorithm with up to 30% missing features. These analyses provide us with informative clues on how such parameters should be selected, and under which conditions the algorithm can be expected to perform well.

2   Learn^{++}.MF

Ensemble of classifies hints at a trivially intuitive approach for the missing feature problem that can guarantee a reasonable performance for any number and any combination of missing features: simply create one (or more) classifier(s) with every possible combination of the available features, and use those classifiers whose training features did not include the missing ones. This exhaustive approach is of course becomes practically impossible even for a modest number of features, as the number of classifiers grows exponentially with the number of features. However, the probability of a particular feature combination being missing also diminishes exponentially as the number of features increase. Therefore, trying to account for every possible combination is hardly an effective use of computing resources. On the other hand, Juszczak and Duin's approach, training one class-classifiers trained with each feature separately, sits on the other end of the spectrum, and offers the fewest number of classifiers that can handle any feature combination (at a cost of potential performance drop due to single feature training).

Learn^{++}.MF, recognizing the inefficiency of trying to accommodate every feature combination as well as the difficulty of obtaining a good classifier using a single feature, offers a compromise: it trains an ensemble of classifiers with a random subset of the features, where the number of features is a free parameter of the algorithm. It also uses an iterative distribution update rule so that feature combinations not previously accounted for are more likely to be selected next (see, however, the effect of using different update rules in Section 3).Doing so, Learn^{++}.MF can achieve classification performances with little or no loss (compared to a fully intact data) even when large portions of data are missing.

The pseudocode of the algorithm is given in Figure 1. The inputs to the algorithm are the training data, a supervised classification algorithm, a sentinel value *sen* to represent missing values, the number of classifiers to be generated, T, and the number of features (*nof*) to be used to train each classifier. The algorithm maintains a distribution D over the features to determine which features should be more likely to be selected next. This distribution is initialized to be uniform so that each feature has equal probability of being selected to train the first classifier. During the tth iteration, the algorithm draws a random bootstrap sample of *nof* features according to then current feature distribution D_t. The indices of these features are then placed in a list, called $F_{selection}(t)$. This list allows the algorithm to keep track of which features have been used for each classifier, so that appropriate classifiers can be called during testing depending on the then available set of features. Classifier C_t, is trained using the features in $F_{selection}(t)$.

The distribution D_t is then updated by reducing the weights of those features that have just been used. This gives other features a better chance to be selected into the next feature subset. T such classifiers are iteratively generated, each using a different subset of *nof* features. In this current version, we do not check the performance of each classifier, since the distribution update rule is applied to features, and not to actual training data instances (as in AdaBoost). Interleaving two distribution update rules, one on features and one on training data, is however being considered as future work.

During testing, a given instance z_i is first checked for its missing features $M(i)$, which were previously flagged with a sentinel. The algorithm then cross-checks the features in $M(i)$ against those available in $F_{selection}(t)$ for each classifier C_t. Classifiers whose feature lists do not include any of those in $M(i)$ are then combined using majority voting.

Inputs:
- Sentinel value *sen*.   • **BaseClassifier** and the number of classifiers, T.
- Training data set $S=\{(\mathbf{x}_i, \mathbf{y}_i) \mid i=1,\ldots,N\}$ with N instances with f features, each.
- Number of features used to train each classifier, *nof*.

Initialize $D_1(j) = 1/f, \forall j, j = 1, \cdots, f$ (1)

Do for $t = 1, 2,\ldots, T$:
1. Normalize D_t so that it is a proper distribution.
2. Draw a bootstrap sample of *nof* features from D_t to be placed in $F_{selection}(t)$
3. Call **BaseClassifier** to generate classifier C_t using features in $F_{selection}(t)$
4. Update the distribution D_t using a suitable update rule

Validation / Testing

Given test data $Z=\{\mathbf{z}_i\}$, i=1,\ldots,M

Do for $i = 1,2,\ldots,M$:
$$M(i) = \left\{\arg(\mathbf{z}_i(j) == sen)\right\}, \; \forall j, j = 1, \cdots, f.$$ (2)

$$\mathcal{E}(\mathbf{z}_i) = \arg\max_{y \in Y} \sum_{t:C_t(\mathbf{z}_i)=y} \left[\!\!\left[\left(M(i) \cap F_{selection}(t)\right) = \varnothing \right]\!\!\right]$$ (3)

Fig. 1. Pseudocode of the Learn^{++}.MF algorithm

The original distribution update rule we had previously used simply reduced the distribuion weight of each feature by a factor f, where f is the total number of features. While such a distribution update rule certainly makes intuitive sense, it is possible to devise other rules as well. For example, is $1/f$ the correct scaling factor to reduce the feature weights? How about $1/nof$, since the actual number of features used by each classifier is *nof*? Or f/nof, as the ratio of the two? Or does it really matter to have a database specific update rule? How about using a strict bootstrap sampling from a uniform distribution? The different distribution update rules can all be represented as in Equation (4), where the parameter β is one of $1/f$, $1/nof$ or n/nof.

$$D_{t+1}\left(F_{selection}(t)\right) = \beta * D_t\left(F_{selection}(t)\right)$$ (4)

The algorithm was implemented with the above mentioned update rules, which was also compared to uniform sampling. Furthermore, note that the primary free parameter of Learn^{++}.MF is the number of features *nof* used to train each classifier (and to a lesser extend, the number of classifiers T to be generated). In order to determine the effect of *nof* on algorithm behavior, several values of *nof* were also evaluated for each database tested.

3 Experiemental Results

We present the implementation results on three datasets: Wisconsin Breast Cancer and Wine databases from UCI [10], and the real-world volatile organic compound

(VOC) identification database. The wine database was selected for its similarity to the VOC database in terms of its feature size. This allows to check for repeatability on datasets of similar size. Missing features were simulated by removing a certain percetange (% missing features – PMF) of values from the entire dataset and replace them with a sentinel. PMF was varied from 0 to 30%. All results are averages of 10 indepent trials, each randomly splitting the training and test data into two equal partitions.

Table 1 shows the total number of features f, the different values of nof, and the total number of classifiers generated (T) for each database. Note that for each chosen value of nof, the ensemble can accommodate up to f-nof features missing at a time. Hence a classifier trained with, say 3 of 12 features, can accommodate *any and all* of 1 through 9-way combination of the remaining 9 features being missing. This is how Learn[++].MF avoids using prohibitively large number of classifiers.

Table 1. Number of features (nof) and classifiers (T) used for each dataset

Dataset	f	nof_1	nof_2	nof_3	nof_4	Nof_4	T
VOC	12	3	4	5	6	---	200
WBC	30	10	12	14	16	---	1000
WINE	13	3	4	5	6	7	200

3.1 VOC Database

The VOC database consists of the responses of 12 quartz crystal microbalances type chemical sensors to 12 volatile organic compounds (VOC), including toluene, xylene, hexane, octane, methanol, tricholoroethylene (TCE), among others. Figure 2 illustrates the performance of the algorithm in four rows, one for each distribution update rule of nof/f, $1/nof$, $1/f$, and *uniform selection* respectively. For each update rule, we provide two plots, classifier performance with respect to percent missing features (PMF), and the percent instances processed (PIP – explained below) with respect to PMF. Performances for different values of nof are indicated using different line styles on each plot.

From the ensemble performance plots (on the left of Fig. 2), we make the following observations. First and foremost, as expected, there is a general decline in the ensemble classification performance as the percentage of missing features increase. However, this decline is very mild, the worst case being from 96% to 93%. In most cases, the differences are not even statistically significant. Hence, the algorithm can easily handle as much as 30% (perhaps even higher, but not tested yet) of missing data with little or no performance drop. Second, algorithm seems to do better with the first two distribution update rules, however, the differences were only significant for certain nof values.

The performance plots tell only half of the story, however. We also need to consider the amount of data that can be processed by the algorithm, on which nof has a

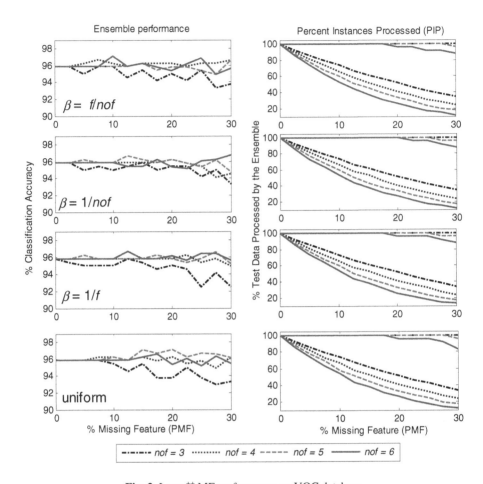

Fig. 2. Learn[++].MF performance on VOC database

dramatic impact, which is even more pronounced on higher dimensional data. As previously mentioned, Learn[++].MF does not guarantee that all possible combinations of features can be accommodated as missing data. Since features are selected at random, there may be certain feature combinations not represented by any of the classifiers trained in the ensemble. Instances with those exact feature combinations cannot be processed by any of the classifiers in the ensemble, and hence cannot be processed. Learn[++].MF attempts to minimize the number of such instances. The plots on the right side of Figure 2 provide a graphical representation of this issue, as it plots percentage of instances that can be processed, for different PMF values. Note that two sets of plots are given: the group of curves showing an exponentially decaying characteristic on the lower side of the plot represent the average PIP if we were to use a single classifier, averaged over 10 trials. The group of curves on the upper side of the plot show the PIP when the Learn[++].MF ensemble is used. Notice that a substantially larger percentage of instances can be processed by the ensemble.

More interesting to notice, however, is the impact of the *nof* parameter on PIP. The figure indicates that the smaller the *nof*, the larger the PIP. In fact, for *nof*=3 and *nof*=4, PIP was 100% even for with 30% of the data missing. For *nof*=6, PIP was 100% for up to 20% missing data, but dropped to 85% - 87% for 30% missing data. This observation makes sense: when a large number of features are used for training, then so many features are required at the time of testing, and hence fewer missing features can be accommodated.

3.2 Wine Database

The wine database consists of 13 features of various chemical analysis results to predict three types of wine origins. This database was used due to its similarity in size to the VOC database (both in terms of number of features, and total data size), and same number of classifiers (200) was generated. This allows us to test for the repeatability of the algorithm's performance behaviors and trends over different datasets of similar size. The results, formatted similar to that of VOC dataset are illustrated in Figure 3.

Tested using five different values of *nof*, the algorithm shows very similar performance and behavior trends on this database, as it did for the VOC database. Specifically, we note that the ensemble performance is far more resistant to missing features when fewer *nof* values are used. For example, when only 3 or 4 features are used, there is no statistically significant performance drop even when 30% of data are missing, particularly for the first two distribution update rules of *f/nof* and 1/*nof*. There is some performance drop when larger values of *nof* are used, however, these are very modest. We also see similar behavior with the percentage of data that can be processed. The ensemble can process 100% of the data for *nof*=3 and *nof*=4, even when 30% of the data are missing. For *nof*=7, PIP drops to about 80% when 30% of the data are missing. In all cases, however, the algorithm – on average – is capable of processing substantially larger portion of the data than a single classifier can process alone. Finally, we do observe that the algorithm performs marginally better using the *f/nof* and 1/*nof* update rules than the original 1/*f* and the uniform distribution; however, the differences are rarely statistically significant.

3.3 WBC Database

The WBC database includes 30 features used as a diagnostic biomarker for distinguishing between benign and malignant tumors. Many of the trends observed for the VOC and Wine data can also be seen on this database, which has a larger feature size. Specifically, we observe in Figure 4 that the algorithm can accommodate up to 30% missing features with practically no loss of performance for *nof*=10, and only about

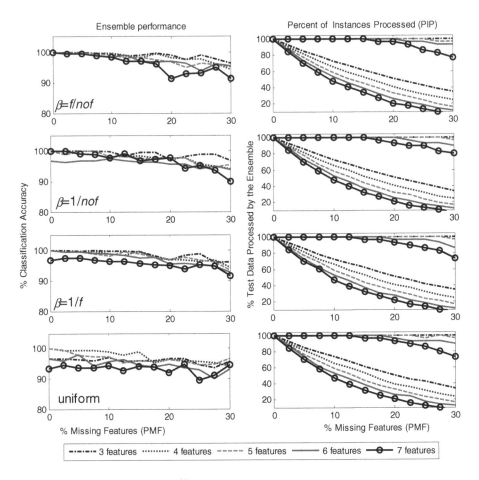

Fig. 3. Learn[++].MF performance on WINE database

7% loss for *nof*=16. Hence the selection of *nof* once again shows its impact: there is less of a performance drop for larger PMF values, when fewer features are used for training.

In other words, using fewer features during training, if adequate to model the data, generates an ensemble that is more resistant to missing data.

The PIP plots also display a now familiar trend: using fewer features in training not only gives better performance (as seen on performance plots), but also allows the ensemble to classify a larger percentage of instances as amount of missing data increases. Furthermore, while the drop in PIP is negligible up to 15% missing data for all values of *nof*, the differences becomes more substantial at higher PMF values, due to larger feature size of this database. In fact, with *nof*=16 features, the PIP displays a steep drop from 100% for a PMF of 15% to about 35% for a PMF of 30%. On the other hand, when fewer features are used for training, for example *nof*=10, PIP barely drops a couple percentage points even for 30% missing data.

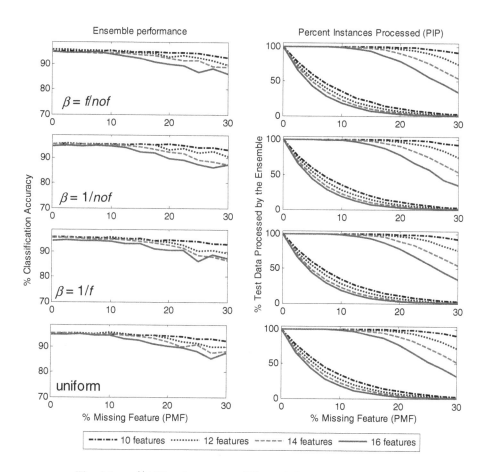

Fig. 4. Learn^{++}.MF performance on Wisconsin breast cancer database

4 Conclusions

In this paper, we described an ensemble based algorithm to address the missing feature problem in classification applications. The approach consists of generating a large number of classifiers using different subsets of the features, and then using only those classifiers whose training features did not include the missing features in the test instance. We observe that the algorithm works rather well with as much as 30% of the data missing.

The newer distribution update rules *f/nof* and *1/nof* do add some performance gain to the algorithm, though the impact of the update rule was at best modest. The impact of the number of features used to train the classifiers, however, is quite dramatic: using fewer features to train the individual classifiers provides a better performance *and* can process a higher portion of the data, particularly when larger percentage of data is missing. PIP can be increased by increasing classifier count, T, if computational resources allow to do so. Of course, larger feature sets also require larger number of classifiers to be generated, however reduced dimensionality in using feature subspaces allow faster training of each classifier, and offsets some of the computational burden of the algorithm. Based on our empirical observations, the number of classifiers required for good performance is typically on the order of 20-30 per dimensionality (feature) of the original data.

Notice that we have only considered the case of test data having missing features; however, the very nature of the algorithm also allows training with missing data. The random feature subsets would then be drawn from the available features only. Finally, we should add that the algorithm makes an implicit assumption: there is redundancy in the features that is distributed randomly. Of course, the identity of the redundant features are unknown to us, since otherwise, they would not have been part of the data. This is not an overly restricting assumption, as it is met by many real-world applications. It is those applications for which this algorithm is expected to perform well.

Acknowledgments. This material is based upon work supported by the National Science Foundation under Grant No. ECS-0239090.

References

1. Morin, R.L., Raeside, D.E.: A reappraisal of distance-weighted k-nearest neighbor classification for pattern recognition with missing data. IEEE Trans. Systems, Man and Cybernetics 11 (1981) 241-243.
2. Dempster, A., Laird N., Rubin, D.R.: Maximum-likelihood from incomplete data via the EM algorithm (with discussion), Jour. of the Royal Statistical. Society, Series B, (1997) 1-38.
3. Gabrys, B.: Neuro-Fuzzy Approach to Processing Inputs with Missing Values in Pattern Recognition Problems, International Journal of Approximate Reasoning 30 (2002) 149-179.
4. Lim, C., Leong, J., Kuan, M.: A Hybrid Neural Network System for Pattern Classification Tasks with Missing Features. IEEE Transactions on Pattern Analysis and Machine Intelligence 27, (2005) 648-653
5. Melville, P., Shah, N., Mihalkova L., and Mooney R.: Experiments on ensembles with missing and noisy data, MCS 2004, Lecture Notes in Computer Science, 3077, (2004) 293-302.
6. Juszczak P. and Duin, R.P.W: Combining One-Class Classifiers to Classify Missing Data, MCS2004, Lecture Notes in Computer Science 3077 (2004) 92-101.
7. Ho, T.K.: The Random Subspace Method for Constructing Decision Forests, IEEE Transactions on Pattern Analysis and Machine Intelligence 20 (1998) 832-844.
8. Polikar, R., Udpa, L., Udpa, S., Honavar, V.: Learn++: An incremental learning algorithm for supervised neural networks. IEEE Transactions on System, Man and Cybernetics (C), 31 (2001) 497-508.
9. Krause S., Polikar, R.: An Ensemble of Classifiers Approach for the Missing Feature Problem, Int. Joint Conf. on Neural Networks 1 (2003) 553-556
10. Blake, C.L., Merz, C.J: UCI Machine Learning Repository," [Online Document], Accessed: 25 Nov 2006. http://www.ics.uci.edu/~mlearn/MLRepository.html

Feature Subspace Ensembles:
A Parallel Classifier Combination Scheme Using Feature Selection

Hugo Silva[1] and Ana Fred[2]

[1] Instituto de Telecomunicações, Lisbon, Portugal
hugo.silva@lx.it.pt
[2] Instituto de Telecomunicações,
Instituto Superior Técnico, Lisbon, Portugal
afred@lx.it.pt

Abstract. In feature selection (FS), different strategies usually lead to different results. Even the same strategy may do so in distinct feature selection contexts. We propose a feature subspace ensemble method, consisting on the parallel combination of decisions from multiple classifiers. Each classifier is designed using variations of the feature representation space, obtained by means of FS. With the proposed approach, relevant discriminative information contained in features neglected in a single run of a FS method, may be recovered by the application of multiple FS runs or algorithms, and contribute to the decision through the classifier combination process. Experimental results on benchmark data show that the proposed feature subspace ensembles method consistently leads to improved classification performance.

1 Introduction

In classification systems, patterns are usually represented by d-dimensional measurement vectors, known as feature representation spaces (FRS). In many application domains, the dimension d of these spaces is very high, and the curse of dimensionality problem often arises: *the ratio between the number of patterns and the data dimensionality is very small.* Furthermore, some dimensions of the FRS may not possess relevant pattern discriminative information, and classifiers are often affected by irrelevant, or even misleading features [1][2].

Feature analysis is therefore an important step in pattern classification systems design, and two different approaches exist: *feature selection* (FS), which consists of determining a subspace of the original FRS containing only the features with most relevant discriminative information; and *feature extraction*, which consists of constructing a different FRS based on the discriminative information provided by the original one. Although a feature extraction method (Principal Component Analysis (PCA)) is illustrated in benchmark results for comparison purposes, our work focuses on FS methods.

A wide range of FS methods with different frameworks is available [3][4][5][6], usually based on the optimization of some feature subspace evaluation criteria.

M. Haindl, J. Kittler, and F. Roli (Eds.): MCS 2007, LNCS 4472, pp. 261–270, 2007.

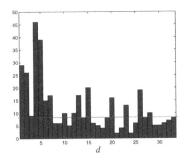

Fig. 1. Illustrative feature histogram for 50 runs of a FS algorithm on the Ionosphere benchmark data set. The horizontal axis corresponds to each of the dimensions of the FRS; the vertical axis corresponds to the number of times a given dimension d was selected. An horizontal line indicates the mean subspace size.

Typically, through FS some features from the original FRS are discarded or neglected. Nevertheless, FS originates some problems: (a) *multiplicity of feature selection contexts (FSCs)[1]., and consequent diversity of the solutions;* (b) *overfitting of the feature subspaces to a particular FSC;* (c) *suboptimality of most FS methods;* (d) *relevance of the discriminative information contained in neglected features, when a single feature subspace is used.* Figure 1 illustrates a feature histogram for 50 runs of a FS algorithm. As we can observe, all of the original FRS is covered, yet some of the features were more frequently selected than others. For the same FS method, different FSCs originated a great diversity of feature subspaces.

In [7], a technique to address the last problem is suggested. Instead of using a single classifier and feature subspace, the combined decisions of multiple classifiers, designed on sequentially selected feature subspaces is used. The method evolves from an initial step where a suboptimal feature subspace is selected; in each subsequent step it iterates by selecting a suboptimal feature subspace from the features that were neglected in the previous step, until all features of the original FRS are included in a particular feature subspace. However, this approach may present some difficulties, mainly due to the fact that irrelevant or misleading features are forced to be taken into account for classification purposes.

We propose a *feature subspace ensemble approach* (FSE), in which a parallel classifier combination scheme is used to combine the individual decisions of multiple classifiers, designed using variations of the FRS obtained by means of FS. Without forcing the full coverage of the original FRS, our approach attempts to recover relevant discriminative information contained in neglected features (e.g., by a single run of a FS method), by application of multiple FS runs or algorithms. The resulting feature subspaces are used to design multiple classifiers, contributing to the global decision through the classifier combination process.

The rest of the paper is organized as follows: Section 2 presents notation and definitions used throughout the rest of the paper. Section 3 describes the FSE

---

[1] The concept of feature selection context (FSC) is later defined in Section 2.

method. Section 4 presents results of the application of the method to benchmark data sets. Finally, Section 5 summarizes results and draws the main conclusions.

2 Notation and Definitions

Let $X = \{x_1, \cdots, x_n\}$ denote a set of n patterns, represented in a d-dimensional FRS enumerated by $F = \{f_1, \cdots, f_d\}$. An individual classifier C_r, performs a mapping of F into c decision regions, corresponding to a set $W = \{w_1, \cdots, w_c\}$ of c categories or classes. According to the adopted decision rule, classifying a given pattern $x_i \in X$ within the set W, has an associated error which is typically used to measure the classifier performance.

As introduced in Section 1, FS consists of analyzing the original FRS, F, with the purpose of determining which features $f_j \in F$ are relevant, and which can potentially be discarded according to some feature subspace evaluation criteria J. Let $F_r^* \subset F$ denote a subspace of F containing its most relevant features according to the criteria J_r.

In general, different FS strategies lead to different feature subspaces F_r^*. Even the same strategy may do so, if some variation of the criteria J, or the training data Y_r is considered. We define a *feature selection context* (FSC), $S_r(A_r, J_r, Y_r)$ as the training conditions that lead to a given feature subspace F_r^*. These comprehend the feature selection algorithm A_r, the feature subspace evaluation criteria J_r, and the training data Y_r, through which F_r^* is determined.

3 Feature Subspace Ensembles

FS is an important step in classification systems design to rule out potentially irrelevant or misleading features. As described in Section 2, FS provides a great diversity of solutions due to the multiplicity of available FSCs. Generally, a variation S_r of the FSC leads to a different subspace F_r^*.

Without any superiority evidence among multiple solutions determined by FS, it is not clear why a subspace F_a^* obtained in a given FSC, S_a, should be considered over a subspace F_b^* obtained in a different FSC, S_b [8]. Furthermore, through FS some features from the original FRS may be neglected for several reasons (e.g., stopping criteria in state space search based FS methods, character of the training data, among others); an overview of the problems resulting from this fact was provided in Section 1.

In this section, we propose a more effective method, based on classifier combination rules [2][9]. Unlike other methods [7], our feature subspace ensemble (FSE) approach does not force the full coverage of the original FRS, F, which may stand as a problem if F contains irrelevant or misleading features. Instead, relevant discriminative information contained in neglected features $f_j \in F$ is expectedly recovered by application of FS in different FSCs. From this process multiple feature subspaces F_r^* are determined, contributing to the classifier decision through parallel classifier combination strategies [2][10].

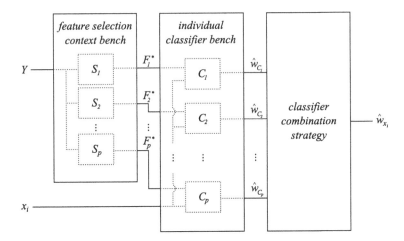

Fig. 2. Feature subspace ensemble (FSE) system. A bench of classifiers is trained using individual feature subspaces F_r^* obtained for some variation S_r of the FSC. Each classifier C_r produces an individual decision $\hat{w}_{C_r}$. In the end, all decisions are combined using a classifier combination strategy to produce a global decision $\hat{w}_{x_i}$.

3.1   Ensemble Strategy

Our feature subspace ensemble approach consists of designing multiple classifiers using variations F_r^* of the FRS, obtained by means of FS. The classification of a given pattern $x_i \in X$ is performed by combining the individual decisions of each classifier.

Instead of using a single classifier C_r and a single feature subspace F_r^*, a set $\mathcal{F}^* = \{F_1^*, \cdots, F_p^*\}$ of p feature subspaces is considered, each selected in a given feature selection context S_r ($0 < r \leq p$). Using each subspace $F_r^* \in \mathcal{F}^*$, a classifier $C_r \in \mathcal{C}$ is designed, and a set $\mathcal{C} = \{C_1, \cdots, C_p\}$ of p classifiers is obtained. A global decision is produced by applying a classifier combination method to the ensemble $\mathcal{C}$.

Figure 2 depicts a block diagram for a FSE system. Using a set of training patterns Y, a feature selection context bench $\mathcal{S} = \{S_1^*, \cdots, S_p^*\}$, of p feature selection contexts produces a feature subspace ensemble $\mathcal{F}^* = \{F_1^*, \cdots, F_p^*\}$. Each resulting feature sub-space $F_r^* \in \mathcal{F}^*$ is used to train a classifier $C_r \in \mathcal{C}$. The classification of a given pattern x_i is performed by a two stage process of p individual decisions $\hat{w}_{C_1}, \ldots, \hat{w}_{C_p}$ (produced by each classifier $C_r \in \mathcal{C}$), and their combination in order to produce a global decision $\hat{w}_{x_i}$. This way, the discriminative content of each particular subspace F_r^* contributes to the global decision as a result of the classifier combination strategy.

Several classifier combination methods have been studied and proposed over the years, with the purpose of improving the classification performance, presenting positive results [2][10][11][9]. A range of classifier design methods has also been used, some also exploring variations of the FRS [7][12]. Our focus is not the optimization of the process but instead to further enhance how different subspaces, when used to design individual classifiers, can improve the recognition rate.

3.2   Improved Classification Performance

On one hand classifier combination strategies are prone to improve the overall classification performance. As previously stated, the decision produced by a given classifier $C_r \in \mathcal{C}$ may be inadequate due to a particularly inappropriate or misleading FSC.

In such case, using a classifier combination strategy, the remaining decisions are likely to overcome it, thus improving or at least not degrading the classification performance. On the other hand, one of the purposes of feature selection is also the improvement the classifier recognition rate [3].

Feature subspace ensembles benefit from both the contribution of classifier combination methods and feature selection. The advantages result from a mixture of these two in the sense that, from feature subspace selection better individual decision ability is to be expected, and if such is not achieved (e.g., due to the feature selection context), the remaining decisions from classifier ensembles will most likely overcome the misleading decisions.

3.3   Illustrative Feature Subspace Ensemble Strategy Implementation

In this section we illustrate the FSE strategy by proposing an instantiation of it using specific FS and classifier combination strategies. Results with the proposed framework are presented in Section 4. We adopt a wrapper feature selection framework [6], since in these methods, the feature subspace evaluation criteria J is the classification performance of a decision rule. For the particular feature selection context of each FS run, the feature subspace that optimizes the recognition rate is selected. A heuristic sequential forward search (SFS) method [13], which has proven to produce adequate results when compared to more sophisticated strategies [14][8], is hereafter used.

SFS starts from an empty feature set $F_{t=0}^*$; at each step F_{t+1}^* all possible super-spaces containing the most relevant feature subspace according to J in the previous step, F_t^*, and one from the remaining features $f_j \in F \setminus F_t^*$ are formed and evaluated by J. The search evolves until a stopping criteria is met, for which we adopted the degradation of J; that is, if none of the super-spaces formed at a given step F_{t+1}^* improves J, the search stops and the subspace F_t^* is considered the best for the particular FSC.

We use the k-NN rule classifier with an Euclidean neighborhood metric [2]. A 1-NN neighborhood was adopted, since it is a particular case of the k-NN rule where $\hat{w}_{x_i}$ for a given pattern x_i is assigned as the category of the closest pattern from the training set Y. For all ensemble classifiers, the 1-NN method is used in the FSC and also for performance evaluation, and a simple majority voting strategy was chosen as classifier combination rule [15][16][17].

Thus, for a given run, indexed by r, our feature selection context S_r is: (a) SFS wrapper feature selection algorithm A_r; (b) 1-NN classification performance (on a validation set), feature subspace evaluation criteria J_r; and (c) a randomly selected training set Y_r.

4   Experimental Results

The performance of the feature subspace ensemble method was evaluated on benchmark data from the UCI machine learning repository. The characterization of the data sets we used is provided in Table 1.

Table 1. Benchmark data summary

	id	# classes	# features	# patterns
Breast Cancer	1	2	9	683
House Votes	2	2	16	232
Ionosphere	3	2	34	351
Iris	4	3	4	150
Pima	5	2	8	768
SAT	6	6	36	2000
Wine	7	3	13	178
Yeast Cell Cycle	8	5	17	384

4.1   Methodology

All data sets were preprocessed to ensure the removal of patterns containing missing values, and nominal values were converted to discrete numerical values. 50 data selection runs were performed for each data set; in each run r two sets X_r and Y_r of randomly selected patterns are selected, and a feature subspace F_r^* is determined. Each set exclusively contains 50% of the available patterns.

To compute the results with the FSE method, we adopted the illustrative framework of Section 3.3. In the FS phase, to compute J_r, we used Y_r as training set for the classifier and X_r as validation set. In the classification performance evaluation phase, the classifier is designed using the feature subspace F_r^*; X_r is used as training, and Y_r is used as testing set. Note that for classification performance evaluation purposes the testing data is unseen by the classifier.

In each classification performance evaluation run a FSE of size $p = 24$ is created, containing 24 randomly selected feature subspaces from the previously determined during data selection. We evaluated the classification performance using F (that is, without FS), SFS selected, and randomly selected feature representation spaces. For random feature subspace selection, we used the mean feature subspace size and standard deviation interval obtained with SFS, and randomly selected from F a random number of features within that interval.

Principal component analysis (PCA), a feature extraction method, was also evaluated for comparison purposes. For this case, in each data selection run we applied the PCA algorithm to Y_r, and sequentially selected the $k < d$ principal components with best classification performance using X_r as validation set.

4.2   Results

Figure 3(a) illustrates the results presented in Table 2 of the average classification error (and standard deviation), for both individual classifier designed in an

Table 2. Mean classification error. *individual*: classifier design using an individual feature subspace; *ensemble*: feature subspace ensemble method; *all*: no feature selection; *sfs*: wrapper sequential forward search; *rnd*: random feature selection; *pca*: principal component analysis.

	individual				ensemble		
	all	sfs	rnd	pca	all	sfs	rnd
Breast	4.36	4.35	4.85	**3.11**	4.36	**3.24**	3.25
Cancer	(0.89)	(1.15)	(1.27)	**(0.60)**	(0.89)	(0.82)	**(0.76)**
House	9.22	8.90	27.24	**7.84**	9.22	**5.14**	26.84
Votes	**(1.79)**	(6.74)	(11.95)	**(1.79)**	(1.79)	**(1.64)**	(9.00)
Ionosphere	14.70	11.48	14.69	**9.36**	14.70	**6.30**	7.73
	(2.10)	(2.59)	(2.17)	**(2.06)**	(2.10)	**(1.67)**	(1.73)
Iris	5.17	6.23	10.96	**3.55**	5.17	**4.64**	6.45
	(1.94)	(3.16)	(9.85)	**(1.84)**	(1.94)	**(1.85)**	(2.21)
Pima	33.15	31.47	36.05	**31.30**	33.15	**27.55**	29.09
	(2.19)	(2.13)	(3.22)	**(1.24)**	(2.19)	**(1.57)**	(1.70)
SAT	12.58	12.97	13.34	**11.70**	12.56	**11.29**	11.91
	(0.87)	(0.81)	(0.96)	**(0.73)**	(0.87)	**(0.74)**	(0.85)
Wine	28.11	**10.00**	23.31	27.50	28.11	**5.82**	8.96
	(3.70)	(6.29)	(9.56)	(3.85)	(3.70)	**(2.09)**	(4.58)
Yeast Cell	28.39	29.22	30.70	**27.60**	28.39	**25.61**	26.90
Cycle	(2.24)	(3.01)	(2.43)	**(2.07)**	(2.24)	(1.98)	**(1.93)**

individual FRS (labeled with the i prefix), and the feature subspace ensemble methods (labeled with the e prefix), computed according to the methodology described in Section 4.1. Figure 3(b) illustrates the average feature subspace size for each method.

When compared to the individual feature subspace classifier case, feature subspace ensembles consistently led to improved classification performance, in terms of error rates, with lower variability (Figure 3(a)), with both SFS and randomly selected feature subspaces. In most cases, feature subspace ensembles using FS outperform PCA, holding comparable results when improvements are not achieved.

Furthermore, from the SFS feature subspace selection process, a reduction of the original representation space F is also achieved (Figure 3(b)), providing more compact models. In general, the dimension d of feature subspaces selected through SFS is lower than the number of principal components that provided better classification performance using PCA. Feature subspace ensembles fulfill two of the main objectives of feature selection: (a) *improvement of the classification performance*; and (b) *dimensionality reduction*[3].

These experimental results corroborate what was stated in Section 3: *feature subspace ensembles benefit from both classifier combination strategies and feature subspace selection*. This is due to the fact that, if a feature selection context or classifier training process (particularly unsuited), misleads the classifier decision, the remaining decisions will likely overcome it, improving, or at least not degrading the results.

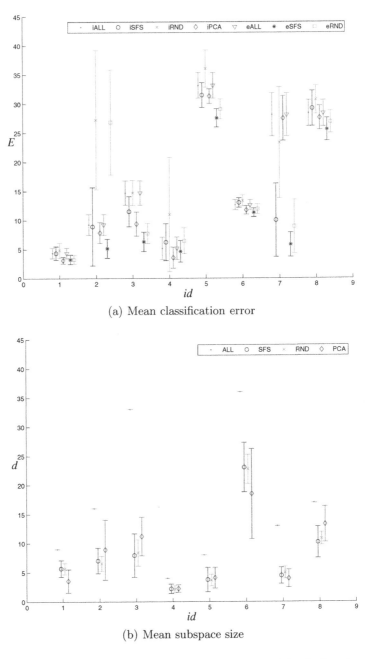

(a) Mean classification error

(b) Mean subspace size

Fig. 3. Mean classification error E, and mean subspace size d, for the benchmark data listed in Table 1. *id*: data set order number; *all*: no feature selection; *sfs*: wrapper sequential forward search; *rnd*: random feature selection; *pca*: principal component analysis; the *i* prefix labels the curves for individual classifier and subspace cases, and the *e* labels the curves for the feature subspace ensemble method.

5   Conclusions

Feature selection techniques, while of great importance for data dimensionality reduction and improved classification accuracy, present several difficulties. These include: (a) *non uniqueness of an optimal solution*; *non-optimality of most FS methods*; *great diversity of feature spaces produced*; and *omission of potentially relevant features*.

In this paper we addressed the above mentioned problems by proposing the association of FS and classifier combination under a feature subspace ensemble approach (FSE). The concept of feature selection context was introduced, and the general FSE approach was defined. Also, we presented an illustrative instantiation of the FSE method using the heuristic sequential forward search (SFS) method, 1-NN classifier and the majority voting classifier combination rule. We applied the technique to 8 data sets from the UCI repository, in a comparative study between the original space (that is, without FS), SFS, random feature selection, and PCA, feature representation spaces (FRS).

Experimental results have shown, that the proposed FSE method consistently leads to improved classification performance (in terms of error rates), when compared to the corresponding average results for an individual classifier designed using a single feature representation space. Furthermore, while the PCA method performed better in all data sets, when compared the remaining individual FRS classification cases, it was consistently outperformed by the proposed FSE method. Ongoing work comprises the extension of the method to other FS and feature extraction methods, as well as the exploration of combination techniques involving multiple FS methods and a more extensive validation of results.

Acknowledgments

This work was partially supported by the Portuguese Foundation for Science and Technology (FCT), Portuguese Ministry of Science and Technology, and FEDER, under grant POSI/EEA-SRI/61924/2004, and by the Institute for Systems and Technologies of Information, Control and Communication (INSTICC) and the Instituto de Telecomunicações (IT), Pólo de Lisboa, under grant P260.

References

1. Heijden, V., Duin, R., Ridder, D., Tax, D.: Classification, parameter estimation and state estimation - an engineering approach using MATLAB. John Wiley & Sons Inc (2004)
2. Duda, R., Hart, P., Stork, D.: Pattern classification, 2nd edition. John Wiley & Sons Inc (2001)
3. Guyon, I., Elisseeff, A.: An introduction to variable and feature selection. Journal of Machine Learning Research **3** (2003) 1157–1182
4. Kudo, M., Sklansky, J.: Comparison of algorithms that select features for pattern classifiers. Pattern Recognition **33** (2000) 25–41

5. Jain, A., Zongker, D.: Feature selection: Evaluation , application, and small sample performance. IEEE Transactions on Pattern Analysis and Machine Intelligence **19**(2) (1997) 153–158

6. Kohavi, R., John, G.: Wrappers for feature subset selection. Artificial Intelligence **97**(1-2) (1997) 273–324

7. Skurichina, M., Duin, R.: Combining feature subsets in feature selection. Multiple Classifier Systems **3541** (2005) 165–175

8. Reunanen, J.: Overfitting in making comparisons between variable selection methods. Journal of Machine Learning Research **3** (2003) 1371–1382

9. Kittler, J., Hatef, M., Duin, R., Matas, J.: On combining classifiers. IEEE Transactions on Pattern Analysis and Machine Intelligence **20** (1998) 226–239

10. Duin, R., Tax, D.: Experiments with classifier combining rules. In: Proceedings 1st International Workshop of Multiple Classifier System. Volume 1857., Springer-Verlag (2000)

11. Lam, L.: Classifier combinations: Implementation and theoretical issues. Lecture notes in computer science **1857** (2000) 78–86

12. Grimaldi, M., Cunningham, P., Kokaram, A.: An evaluation of alternative feature selection strategies and ensemble techniques for classifying music (May 2003)

13. Russell, S., Norvig, P.: Artificial Intelligence: A Modern Approach (2nd Edition). Prentice Hall (December 2002)

14. Silva, H.: Feature selection in pattern recognition systems. Master's thesis, Universidade Técnica de Lisboa, Instituto Superior Técnico (2007)

15. Tax, D., Duin, R.: Using two-class classifiers for multiclass classification. In: International Conference on Pattern Recognition, Quebec, Canada (2002)

16. Fred, A.: Finding consistent clusters in data partitions. In: MCS '01: Proceedings of the Second International Workshop on Multiple Classifier Systems, London, UK, Springer-Verlag (2001) 309–318

17. Lam, L., Suen, S.: Application of majority voting to pattern recognition: An analysis of its behavior and performance. IEEE Transactions on Systems, Man, and Cybernetics **27** (1997) 553–568

Stopping Criteria for Ensemble-Based Feature Selection

Terry Windeatt and Matthew Prior

Centre for Vision, Speech and Signal Proc (CVSSP)
University of Surrey, Guildford, Surrey, United Kingdom GU2 7XH
{t.windeatt,m.prior}@surrey.ac.uk

Abstract. Selecting the optimal number of features in a classifier ensemble normally requires a validation set or cross-validation techniques. In this paper, feature ranking is combined with Recursive Feature Elimination (RFE), which is an effective technique for eliminating irrelevant features when the feature dimension is large. Stopping criteria are based on out-of-bootstrap (OOB) estimate and class separability, both computed on the training set thereby obviating the need for validation. Multi-class problems are solved using the Error-Correcting Output Coding (ECOC) method. Experimental investigation on natural benchmark data demonstrates the effectiveness of these stopping criteria.

Keywords: RFE, ECOC, Multiple Classifiers, feature selection.

1 Introduction

Tuning classifier parameters normally requires a validation set or cross-validation techniques. However, there is no guarantee that a pseudo-test set is representative, and for many problems there is insufficient data to rely on this approach. For a classifier ensemble, there is the additional difficulty that base classifier optimality with respect to generalisation does not necessarily imply ensemble optimality (Section 2). The class separability measure defined in Section 2.1 was proposed in [1] for tuning base classifier parameters. It was shown that the optimal number of training epochs of a MLP (Multilayer Perceptron) base classifier was generally different from the number for the optimal classifier ensemble. In this paper the ensemble OOB (Out-of-Bootstrap) estimate is used to select the optimal number of features for classifier ensemble. Although the OOB estimate has been documented previously for model selection, there has not been any systematic study of its use in feature selection, as described in this paper.

Consider the situation for which patterns consist of a large number of features, many of which are suspected to be irrelevant to the classification problem at hand. To reduce dimensionality, a decision needs to be taken whether to select or extract features. One of the most popular general purpose feature extraction techniques is Principal Component Analysis (PCA), which is a mapping or projection on to the principal directions and is an effective method of feature space reduction. It is particularly important to reduce the number of features for small sample size problems (Section 3). In general, feature extraction techniques make use of all the

M. Haindl, J. Kittler, and F. Roli (Eds.): MCS 2007, LNCS 4472, pp. 271–281, 2007.

original features when mapping to new features. However, over-fitting may result if the dimension space is high. Furthermore, it may not be successful due to complex class distributions [2]. Finally, feature extraction methods are difficult to interpret in terms of the importance of original features.

In this paper, feature ranking is combined with Recursive Feature Elimination (RFE Section 3). The focus of the paper is on stopping criteria for feature selection rather than on feature ranking methods. A simple ranking strategy is chosen in Section 3 to demonstrate the effectiveness of the stopping criteria. There have been many improvements to feature ranking strategies in recent years, motivated by the need to handle large number of features, as required in certain data mining and bio-informatics applications. The basic approaches in feature subset selection can be found in [3] from Pattern Recognition perspective, and in [11] from machine learning perspective. Although the motivation for the approach described in this paper is that it should scale up to handle hundreds and thousands of features, in Section 4 the experimental evidence is presented for datasets up to 100 features.

2   Ensemble Techniques

In this paper, we assume a simple parallel MCS architecture with homogenous two-class base classifiers. For the two-class case, the combining rule is majority vote while for multi-class the decision rule is defined in equation (7). Injecting randomness into the MCS framework has been found to be a good strategy for improving generalisation performance. Random perturbations have been shown to be useful for patterns (Bootstrapping), features (Random Subspace Method RSM [4]), Class Labels (Error-Correcting Output Coding: ECOC) as well as in base classifiers themselves. Of these four types of random perturbation methods, all are used in this paper except RSM. Bootstrapping is a popular ensemble technique and implies that if μ training patterns are randomly sampled with replacement, $(1-1/\mu))^{\mu} \cong 37\%$ are removed with remaining patterns occurring one or more times. The OOB estimate uses the patterns left out. The individual base classifier OOB should be distinguished from the ensemble OOB. For the ensemble OOB, all training patterns contribute to the estimate, but the only participating classifiers for each pattern are those that have not been used with that pattern for training (that is, approximately thirty-seven percent of classifiers).

Selecting parameters for MCS design should ideally be carried out using only the training set, but this is difficult and may result in a biased choice. Model selection from training data is known to require a built-in assumption, since realistic learning problems are in general ill-posed. The only assumption in this paper is that base classifier complexity and number of features are varied over a suitable range. Since each base classifier sees only approximately sixty three percent of the training set, OOB gives a biased estimate of the absolute value of generalization error [5]. In this paper, the estimate of the absolute value is not important, and it is shown experimentally in Section 4 that the reduced number of training patterns does not lead to an inaccurate estimate of the optimal values of generalization error. Note also that the OOB estimate does not require any assumptions regarding underlying probability distributions.

2.1 Diversity and Class Separability

Diversity measures have received much attention recently since it is recognized that diversity among base classifiers is a necessary condition for improvement in ensemble performance. However, there is no general agreement about how to quantify the notion of diversity among a set of classifiers. Diversity measures can be categorised into two types [6], pair-wise and non-pair-wise. In order to apply pair-wise measures to finding overall diversity of a set of classifiers it is necessary to average over the set. Non-pair-wise measures attempt to measure diversity of a set of classifiers directly, based for example on variance, entropy or proportion of classifiers that fail on randomly selected patterns. The main difficulty with diversity measures is the so-called accuracy-diversity dilemma. As base classifiers approach the highest levels of accuracy, diversity must decrease so that it is expected that there will be a trade-off between diversity and accuracy. The Diversity/Accuracy Dilemma leads us to expect that ensemble performance may not be optimized when each individual classifier is optimized [7].

Normally class separability measures rely on a Gaussian assumption and refer to the ability to predict separation of patterns into classes using original features. In [1] a class separability measure is proposed for MCS that is based on a binary feature representation, in which each pattern is represented by its binary MCS classifier decisions. It is restricted to two-class problems and the measure is computed from the binary-to-binary mapping. The problem with applying conventional class separability measures is that the implicit Gaussian assumption is not appropriate for this mapping.

Let there be μ patterns with the label ω_m given to each pattern x_m where $m = 1,\dots \mu$. In an MCS framework, the mth pattern may be represented by the B-dimensional vector formed from the B base classifier decisions given by

$$x_m = (\xi_{m1}, \xi_{m2}, \dots, \xi_{mB}) \qquad \xi_{mi}, \omega_m \in \{0,1\}, \quad i = 1\dots B \qquad (1)$$

In equation (1) $\omega_m = f(x_m)$ where f is the unknown binary-to-to binary mapping from classifier decisions to target label. Following [6], the notation in equation (1) is modified so that the classifier decision is 1 if it agrees with the target label and 0 otherwise

$$x_m = (y_{m1}, y_{m2}, \dots, y_{mB}) \qquad y_{mi}, \omega_m = \in \{0,1\}, \ y_{mi} = 1 \ iff \ \xi_{mi} = \omega_m \qquad (2)$$

Pairwise diversity measures, such as Q statistic, Correlation Coefficient, Double Fault and Disagreement measures [6] take no account of class assigned to a pattern. In contrast, class separability [8] is computed between classifier decisions (equation (2)) over pairs of patterns of opposite class, using four counts defined by logical AND ($\wedge$) operator

$$\tilde{N}_{mn}^{ab} = \sum_{j=1}^{B} \psi_{mj}^{a} \wedge \psi_{nj}^{b}, \quad \omega_m \neq \omega_n \quad a,b \in \{0,1\}, \ \psi^1 = y, \psi^0 = \bar{y} \qquad (3)$$

The nth pattern for a two-class problem is assigned

$$\sigma'_n = \frac{1}{\tilde{K}_\sigma} \left(\frac{\tilde{N}_n^{11}}{\sum_{m=1}^{\mu} \tilde{N}_m^{11}} - \frac{\tilde{N}_n^{00}}{\sum_{m=1}^{\mu} \tilde{N}_m^{00}} \right) \tag{4}$$

where $\quad \tilde{K}_\sigma = \left(\dfrac{\tilde{N}_n^{11}}{\sum_{m=1}^{\mu} \tilde{N}_m^{11}} + \dfrac{\tilde{N}_n^{00}}{\sum_{m=1}^{\mu} \tilde{N}_m^{00}} \right), \tilde{N}_n^{ab} = \sum_{m=1}^{\mu} \tilde{N}_{mn}^{ab}$

The motivation for σ'_n comes from estimation of the first order spectral coefficients [1] of the binary-to-binary mapping defined in equation (1). Each pattern is compared with all patterns of the other class, and the number of jointly correctly ($\tilde{N}_n^{11}$) and incorrectly ($\tilde{N}_n^{00}$) classified patterns are counted. Note that a classifier that correctly classifies one pattern but incorrectly classifies the other does not contribute. The two terms in equation (4) represent the relative positive and negative evidence that the pattern comes from the target class. We sum over patterns with positive coefficient to produce a single number between –1 and +1 that represents the separability of a set of patterns

$$\sigma' = \sum_{n=1}^{\mu} \sigma'_n, \sigma'_n > 0 \tag{5}$$

In our experiments in Section 4 we use the Q diversity measure, as recommended in [6]. Diversity Q_{ij} between ith and jth classifiers is defined as

$$Q_{ij} = \frac{N_{ij}^{11} N_{ij}^{00} - N_{ij}^{01} N_{ij}^{10}}{N_{ij}^{11} N_{ij}^{00} + N_{ij}^{01} N_{ij}^{10}} \tag{6}$$

where $N_{ij}^{ab} = \sum_{m=1}^{\mu} \psi_{mj}^{a} \wedge \psi_{mj}^{b}$ with a,b, Ψ defined in equation (3). The mean is taken

over B base classifiers $\quad Q = \dfrac{2}{B(B-1)} \sum_{i=1}^{B-1} \sum_{j=i+1}^{B} Q_{ij} \,.$

2.2 Error-Correcting Output Coding ECOC

To solve a multi-class problem in the ECOC [9] framework we need a set of codes to decompose the original problem, a suitable two-class base classifier, and a decision-making framework. For a K-class problem, each row of the $K \times B$ binary ECOC matrix Z acts as a code word for each class. Each of the B columns of Z partitions the training data into two super-classes according to the value of the corresponding binary element.

To classify pattern x_m, it is applied to the B trained base classifiers forming vector $[x_{m1}, x_{m2}, ..., x_{mB}]$ where x_{mj} is the soft output of the jth base classifier. The L^1 norm distance L_i (where   i = 1…. K) between output vector and code word for each class is computed

$$L_i = \sum_{j=1}^{b} \left| Z_{ij} - x_{mj} \right| \qquad (7)$$

and x_m is assigned to the class corresponding to closest code word. For the OOB estimate, the decision rule in equation (7) is modified. Training pattern x_m is classified using only those classifiers that are in the set OOB_m, defined as the set of classifiers for which x_m is OOB.   The summation in equation (7) is therefore modified to $\sum_{j \in OOB_m}$. In this paper, a random code matrix with near equal split of classes (approximately equal number of 1's in each column) is chosen. Issues surrounding various coding and decoding strategies were discussed in [9].

3 Feature Ranking

The aim of feature selection is to find a feature subset from the original set of features such that an induction algorithm that is run on data containing only those features generates a classifier that has the highest possible accuracy [10]. Typically, an exhaustive search is computationally prohibitive, and the problem is known to be NP-hard [10], so that a greedy search scheme is required. For problems with hundreds or thousands of features, classical feature selection schemes are not greedy enough, and filter, wrapper and embedded approaches have been developed [11]. One-dimensional feature ranking methods consider each feature in isolation and rank the features according to a scoring function, but are disadvantaged by implicit orthogonality assumptions [11]. They are very efficient but in general have been shown to be inferior to multi-dimensional methods [11] that consider all features simultaneously.

The issue of feature relevance, redundancy and irrelevance has been explicitly addressed in many papers. As noted in [12] it is possible to think up examples for which two features may appear irrelevant in isolation but be relevant when considered together. Also adding redundant features can provide the desirable effect of noise reduction. It thus appears necessary to do more than consider individual features by themselves as with one-dimensional methods.

The most important problem arises from the relatively small number of patterns relative to the number of features. In Pattern Recognition this is known as the small sample size problem, that is when the number of patterns is less than or of comparable size to the number of features [2]. It means that there is a risk of the classifier over-fitting the data, and thereby capturing unwanted idiosyncrasies.

Feature ranking problems have received much attention in the literature. However, there has been relatively little work devoted to handling feature ranking explicitly in the context of MCS. Most previous work has focused on determining feature subsets to combine, but differ in the way the subsets are chosen. The Random Subspace Method (RSM) [4] is the best known method, and it was shown that a random choice of feature subset, (allowing a single feature to be in more than one subset), improves performance for high-dimensional problems. In [2], forward feature and random (without replacement) selection methods are used to sequentially determine disjoint optimal subsets. In [13], feature subsets are chosen based on how well a feature correlates with a particular class. Ranking subsets of randomly chosen features before combining was reported in [14].

Recursive Feature Elimination (RFE) [15] is a simple algorithm for eliminating irrelevant features and operates recursively as follows:

1) Rank the features according to a suitable feature ranking method

2) Identify and remove the r least ranked features

If $r>1$, which is usually desirable from an efficiency viewpoint, a feature subset ranking is obtained. The main advantage of RFE is that the only requirement to be successful is that at each recursion the least ranked subset does not contain a strongly relevant feature [12].

In this paper, we use modulus of neural network weights w for feature ranking, given by

$$w_i = \sum_j \left| W_{ij}^1 * W_j^2 \right| \qquad O = \sum_j S(\sum_i x_i W_{ij}^1) * W_j^2 \qquad (8)$$

where O is the output of single output single hidden-layer MLP (sigmoid activation function S), i,j are the input and hidden node indices, x_i is input feature, W^1 is the first layer weight matrix and W^2 is the output weight vector [16]. The product of weights strategy in equation (8) has been found in general not to give a reliable feature ranking [17]. However, when used with RFE it is only required to find the least relevant features. We have not experimented with any more sophisticated strategies based on sensitivity analysis [18].

4 Experimental Evidence

Natural two-class and multi-class benchmark problems have been selected from [19] and [20] and are shown in Table 1. For datasets with missing values the scheme suggested in [19] is used. All experiments use random training/testing splits, and the results are reported as mean over ten runs. Unless otherwise specified, two-class problems are split 20/80 and use 100 base classifiers. Multi-class problems are also split 20/80 but use 200 base classifiers, one for each two-class decomposition, as described in Section 2.2. To test the RFE strategy described in Section 3, the original features are normalized to mean 0 std 1 and the number of features increased to one hundred by adding noisy features (Gaussian std 0.25).

The purpose of the initial experiment is to determine generalization performance as the number of hidden nodes and number of training epochs of MLP base classifiers are systematically varied. Each node-epoch combination is repeated ten times with the same number of nodes and epochs used for each MLP. All other parameters of the base classifier MLPs are fixed at the same values over all runs. The number of hidden nodes is varied over 2-16 and number of training epochs over 1-69 (log scale). Random perturbation of the MLP base classifiers is caused by different starting weights on each run, combined with bootstrapping (Section 2). The experiment is performed with one hundred single hidden-layer MLP base classifiers, using the Levenberg-Marquardt training algorithm with default parameters.

Table 1. Benchmark Datasets showing numbers of patterns, classes, continuous and discrete features

DATASET	#pat	#class	#con	#dis
cancer	699	2	0	9
card	690	2	6	9
credita	690	2	3	11
dermatology	366	6	1	33
diabetes	768	2	8	0
ecoli	336	8	5	2
glass	214	6	9	0
heart	920	2	5	30
iris	150	3	4	0
ion	351	2	31	3
segment	2310	7	19	0
soybean	683	19	0	35
vehicle	846	4	18	0
vote	435	2	0	16
vowel	990	11	10	1
wave	3000	3	21	0
yeast	1484	10	7	1

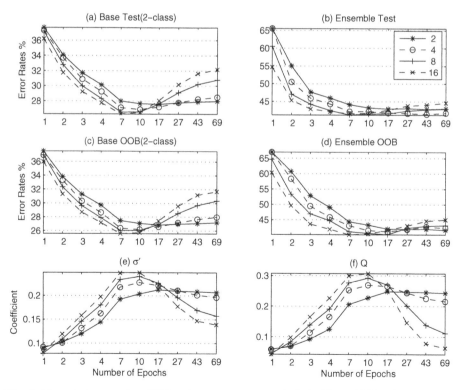

Fig. 1. Mean test error rates, OOB estimates, measures σ', Q for Yeast 20/80 with [2,4,8,16] nodes

A typical set of curves for various node-epoch combinations (*Yeast* 20/80) is shown in Figure 1, with (a) (b) showing base classifier and ensemble test error rates, (c) (d) the base classifier and ensemble OOB estimates and (e) (f) the measures σ', Q defined in equations (5) and (6). It may be seen that σ' and base classifier OOB are good predictors of base classifier test error rates as base classifier complexity is varied. The correlation between σ' and test error was thoroughly investigated in [7], showing high values of correlation that were significant (95 % confidence when compared with random chance). In [7] it was also shown that bootstrapping did not significantly change the ensemble error rates, actually improving them slightly on average. The class separability measure σ' shows that the base classifier test error rates are optimized when the number of epochs is chosen to maximize class separability. Furthermore, at the optimal number of epochs Figure 1 (f) shows that diversity is minimized. It appears that MLP base classifiers starting from random weights increase correlation (reduce diversity) as complexity is increased and peaks as the classifier starts to over-fit the data. A possible explanation of increasing diversity with over-fitting is that classifiers produce different fits of those patterns in

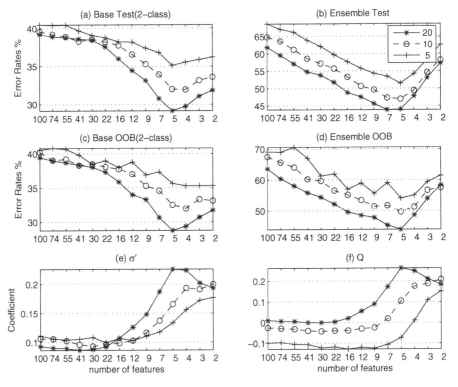

Fig. 2. Mean test error rates, OOB estimates, measures σ', Q for RFE, Yeast with [20/80 10/90 5/95] train/test split

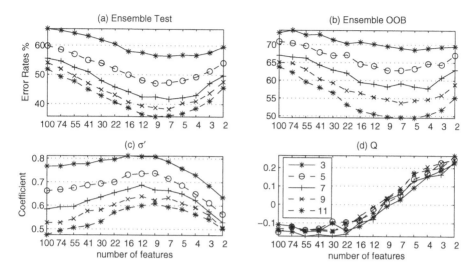

Fig. 3. Mean ensemble test error rate, ensemble OOB estimate, measures σ', Q over ten multi-class 20/80 datasets with [3 5 7 9 11] base classifiers

the region where classes are overlapped [7]. Note also from Figure **1** that the ensemble is more resistant to over-fitting than base classifier, and the ensemble OOB accurately predicts this trend. This experiment was performed for all the datasets, and in general the ensemble test error was found to be more resistant to over-fitting for both two-class and multi-class datasets. Based on these results 8 hidden nodes was chosen, with 7 epochs for two-class and 20 epochs for multi-class data.

Figure **2** shows RFE for Yeast 20/80, 10/90, 5/95 with noisy features added to make a total of one hundred features. The recursive step size is chosen using a logarithmic scale to start at 100 and finish at 2 features with minimum step size of 1. Both base classifier OOB and σ' are seen to correlate well with base classifier test error. Similarly, ensemble OOB achieves minimum error at the same number of features as ensemble test error. Note from Figure **2** (b) (d) that the OOB estimate is generally a poor indicator of absolute value of generalization error.

To determine the effect of RFE on a range of two-class and multi-class problems, RFE was applied to the datasets shown in Table 1. The RFE curves (not shown) appeared similar to Figure 2 achieving a minimum at the number of features predicted by OOB. The mean ensemble test error rate over all features and all datasets was 13.9 % for seven two-class problems and 18.2% for ten multi-class. For comparison, using original features (Table 1) the mean error rate was 14.1 % for two-class and 17.8 % for multi-class, demonstrating that the RFE strategy effectively eliminates irrelevant features.

A potential problem with bootstrapping is that each base classifier sees only approximately 63% training patterns. To determine the effect of the reduced sample size, the RFE experiment was repeated without bootstrapping. The number of features at which the OOB and the test error started to rise did not change. For seven two-class problems, the mean best error rate was 13.4 % for two-class and 18.2% for multi-class.

Finally the effect of a reduced number of base classifiers [3 5 7 9 11] on multi-class problems is shown in Figure 3, which is the mean over ten datasets. It may be seen that the ensemble OOB estimate is not a reliable indicator as number of classifiers is reduced, but the peak value of σ' is still a good predictor of when to stop eliminating features. The base classifier OOB (not shown) is also unreliable due to too few classifiers.

5 Conclusion

It is shown in this paper that the number of features may be selected using an out-of-bootstrap (OOB) error estimate. The base classifier OOB estimate achieves a minimum when the estimate of class separability reaches a maximum. The method is extended to multi-class problems using ECOC, and is seen to be less sensitive to over-fitting when the number of features is reduced below the optimal number. The modulus of neural network weights provide a good feature ranking criterion, but for large number of features it is better to combine wth RFE to recursively remove irrelevant features. Further work is aimed at testing the proposed method on higher dimensional datasets and comparing results from different feature ranking strategies [12] [11].

References

[1] Windeatt T., Vote Counting Measures for Ensemble Classifiers, *Pattern Recognition* 36(12), 2003, 2743-2756.
[2] Skuruchina M. and Duin R. P. W., Combining feature subsets in feature selection, *Proc. 6th Int. Workshop Multiple Classifier Systems*, Editors: N. Oza, R. Polikar, F. Roli, J. Kittler, Seaside, Calif. USA, June, 2005, Lecture notes in computer science, Springer-Verlag, 165-174..
[3] Fukunaga K., Statistical Pattern Recognition, Academic Press, 1990
[4] Ho T. K., The random subspace method for constructing decision forests, *IEEE Trans. Pattern Analysis and Machine Intelligence*, 20(8) 1998, 832-844.
[5] Bylander T, Estimating generalisation error two-class datasets using out-of-bag estimate, *Machine Learning* 48, 2002,287-297.
[6] Kuncheva L. I. and Whitaker C. J., Measures of diversity in classifier ensembles, *Machine Learning* 51, 2003, 181-207.
[7] Windeatt T., Accuracy/Diversity and ensemble classifier design, *IEEE Trans. Neural Networks*, 17(5), 2006, 1194-1211.
[8] Windeatt T. Diversity Measures for Multiple Classifier System Analysis and Design, *Information Fusion*, 6 (1), 2004, 21-36
[9] Windeatt T. Ghaderi R., Coding and Decoding Strategies for Multi-class Learning Problems, *Information Fusion*, 4(1), 2003, 11-21.
[10] Kohavi R. and John G. H., Wrappers for feature subset selection, *Artificial Intelligence Journal*, special issue on relevance, 97 (1-2), 1997, 273-324.

[11] Guyon I. and Elisseeff A. An introduction to variable and feature selection, *Journal of Machine Learning Research* 3, 2003, 1157-1182.

[12] Yu L. and Liu H., Efficient feature selection via analysis of relevance and redundancy, *Journal of Machine Learning Research* 5, 2004, 1205-1224.

[13] Oza N., and Tumer K., Input Decimation ensembles: decorrelation through dimensionality reduction, *Proc. 2nd Int. Workshop Multiple Classifier Systems*, Editors: J. Kittler, F. Roli, , Cambridge, UK, July, 2001, Lecture notes in computer science, Springer-Verlag, 238-247.

[14] Bryll R., Gutierrez-Osuna R. and Quek F. Attribute bagging: improving accuracy of classifier ensembles by using random feature subsets, *Pattern Recognition* 36, 2003, 1291-1302.

[15] Guyon I., Weston J., Barnhill S. and Vapnik V., Gene selection for cancer classification using support vector machines, *Machine Learning* 46(1-3), 2002, 389-422.

[16] Hsu C. Huang H. and Schuschel D., The ANNIGMA-wrapper approach to fast feature selection for neural nets, *IEEE Trans. System, Man and Cybernetics-Part B:Cybernetics* 32(2), 2002, 207-212.

[17] Wang W., Jones P. and Partridge D. Assessing the impact of input features in a feedforward neural network, Neural Computing and Applications 9, 2000, 101-112.

[18] Montana J. J. and Palmer A., Numeric Sensitivity analysis applied to feedforward neural networks, Neural Computing and Applications 12, 2003, 119-125.

[19] Prechelt L., Proben1: A set of neural network Benchmark Problems and Benchmarking Rules, *Tech Report 21/94*, Univ. Karlsruhe, Germany, 1994.

[20] Merz C. J., Murphy P. M., UCI repository of machine learning databases, 1998, http://www.ics.uci.edu/~mlearn/MLRepository.html

On Rejecting Unreliably Classified Patterns

Pasquale Foggia[1], Gennaro Percannella[2], Carlo Sansone[1], and Mario Vento[2]

[1] Dipartimento di Informatica e Sistemistica,
Università degli Studi di Napoli Federico II,
Via Claudio, 21 I-80125 Napoli, Italy
{foggiapa,carlosan}@unina.it
[2] Dipartimento di Ingegneria dell'Informazione e di Ingegneria Elettrica,
Università di Salerno, Via Ponte Don Melillo, 1 I-84084 Fisciano (SA), Italy
{pergen,mvento}@unisa.it

Abstract. In this paper we propose to face the rejection problem as a new classification problem. In order to do that, we introduce a trainable classifier, that we call *reject classifier*, to distinguish it from the classifier to which the reject option is applied (termed *primary classifier*). This idea yields a reject option that is largely independent of the approach used for the primary classifier, working also for systems providing as their only output the guess class.

The whole classification system can be seen as a serial multiple classifier system: given an input patter x, the primary classifier limits to two the number of possible classes (i.e., its guess class and the reject class), while the reject classifier attributes x to one out of these two classes.

The proposed reject method has been tested on three different publicly available databases. We also compared it with other reject rules and the results demonstrated the effectiveness of the proposed approach.

1 Introduction

It has been a long time since Pattern Recognition researchers understood the importance, in many mission-critical applications of classification techniques, of providing the classifier with a *reject option*, that is the possibility of refusing to assign the examined pattern to any class, possibly prompting for a further investigation by another system or by a human supervisor. The first work trying to cast the reject problem in a formal, theoretically sound framework is a paper by Chow [1] published 50 years ago. After half a century of experience with rejection in classification, is there any room left for improvements?

In our opinion there some points that have not yet been solved in a satisfactory way by the reject methods proposed so far. A first issue regards the overly restrictive assumptions on the classifier outputs. The first reject rule still in use, the Chow's rule [2], is based on the hypothesis that the classifier provides a good estimate of the *a posteriori* probability of each class. While this hypothesis is acceptable when a very large training set is available, this is not the case in many important applications. It should be considered that the post-probability

M. Haindl, J. Kittler, and F. Roli (Eds.): MCS 2007, LNCS 4472, pp. 282–291, 2007.
© Springer-Verlag Berlin Heidelberg 2007

estimation is a more general, (and so more difficult) problem than the bare classification. Hence, a training set that is large enough to train a decision function to perform a good classification, could be not adequate for obtaining a good post-probability estimate. In these cases, Chow's rule could yield a bad rejection performance.

Some researchers have tried to overcome this limitation by estimating the expected value of the Bayesian risk as the average cost of the reject decisions obtained by thresholding the classifier output. The underlying assumption is that the output is a measure related to the a posteriori probability (and so is applicable only to *type 3* classifiers of the taxonomy by Xu et al. [3]), although it is not necessarily a direct estimate. While this assumption is more commonly met in practical applications, it still rules out a significant number of classifiers that have proved to be effective in some contexts, such as decision trees and structural classifiers, and also parallel multiple classifier systems (MCS), such as those based on majority voting [3]. Note that in case of MCS, the evaluation of the post-probabilities is anyhow much more difficult [5]; in fact, even in the hypothesis that each base classifier provides a very good estimate of the post-probabilities, the evaluation of the post-probabilities after the combination can be correctly achieved only if the classifiers can be assumed independent or the dependencies among the experts can be statistically characterized.

A second issue is concerned with the lack of generality about the classification technique. Several authors, trying to improve the performance of the reject option over the Chow's rule and its derivatives, have resorted to methods specifically tailored to a particular classifier or multiple classifier system. In [4] a maximum margin classifier with reject option is proposed. This led to a Support Vector Machine (SVM) whose rejection region is determined during the training phase, that is, a SVM with an embedded reject option. With regard to MCS, a reject rule devised for *Naive* Bayes combining rule is proposed in [5], while a particular combining scheme with reject option is proposed in [6], where the Behavior Knowledge Space (BKS) is presented. The computation of the reject threshold is performed in such a way to make the classification, error and reject rates of the system as much as possible close to preassigned values. Since this is made by using the BKS, this approach cannot be easily extended to other MCS architectures. While such techniques can indeed improve the reject performance, the drawback is that the whole system becomes tied to a single classification technique and is not easy to switch to a more profitable classifier when it should become available.

Now let us consider a third important issue, i.e. the difficulty in leveraging the different amounts of information available in different applications of a same technique. Classifier technology has (since long time) evolved toward the use of systems based on some more or less complex forms of training or learning. Such systems have the distinctive advantage of being able to adapt, either automatically or with the help of some hand-tuning of their parameters, to the quite diverse amount of information available for a given application. For instance, using a neural network one can choose a small number of neurons, to control the over-specialization behavior, if the training set is small and not satisfactorily representative of the pattern variability; on the other hand one can use more neurons, to follow more closely the boundaries between the classes and improve classification performance, if an adequate training set is available. The same classifier can be adapted to very different problems by choosing the appropriate balancing between its behaviors. Unfortunately, this degree of flexibility is lost when we consider the current reject systems. The information used to perform the reject decision is hard-wired into the system itself, and cannot be adapted, or tuned, to better fit the information at hand except by switching to an entirely different reject rule.

So, summing up our objectives, we want to develop a reject method that makes little or no assumption on the structure of the classifier and of its outputs, and can adapt to some degree to the training information available in the application at hand. Our proposed solution is to face the rejection problem as a new classification problem. In other words, we introduce a trainable classifier that we call *reject classifier*, to distinguish it from the classifier to which the reject option is applied (termed *primary classifier*). As we will show, this idea can yield a reject option that is largely independent of the approach used for the primary classifier, working also for *type 1* systems (i.e. systems yielding as their only output the attributed class). Furthermore, the use of a reject classifier entails the same adaptability of the reject system to suit the available information. Note that the whole classification system can be seen as a serial multiple classifier system: the primary classifier reduces to two the number of possible classes (the guess class and the reject class) for each input pattern x, while the reject classifier attributes x to one out of these two classes.

The rest of the paper is organized as follows: in Section 2, we will present in detail the proposed method. Then, an experimental comparative evaluation on some publicly available databases is reported in Section 3. Finally, some conclusions are drawn.

2   The Proposed Method

As discussed in the introduction, we propose the use of a two-stage system. In Figure 1, an architectural overview of our system is depicted.

The first block is the *primary classifier*, that is the object of the reject system. We assume that the input of this classifier is a vector of n real-valued features; while this assumption does not hold for all conceivable classifiers (for instance consider graph-based classifiers), it is applicable to a very broad range of classification techniques. Furthermore, it is the only restriction that our method imposes on the primary classifier. As the output of the primary classifier, the reject system requires the index of the attributed class; in other words, it assumes a *type 1* classifier. Since this information can be derived also from classifiers yielding more information in their output (e.g. classifiers producing a ranking, or a measure, or a probability), the *type 1* assumption poses no restriction on the primary classifier. The input feature vector, together with the primary classifier

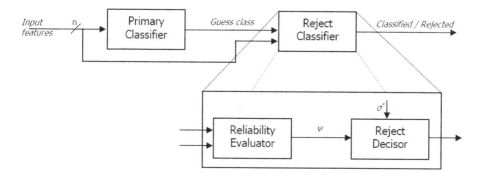

Fig. 1. Architecture of the proposed reject system

guess, forms the input of the *reject classifier*. This is made up of two blocks: the goal of the first one, the *reliability evaluator*, is to provide a measure of the reliability ψ of the classification operated by the first stage. This is indeed a real-valued quantity, with 0 meaning "completely unreliable" and 1 meaning "absolutely trustworthy". However, we do not assume that this quantity is a probability, to avoid putting unnecessary complexity in the reliability evaluator.

The reliability evaluator does not output directly a reject decision. If this would have been the case, it would have to be trained taking into account also the costs associated to errors, rejects and correct classifications, in order to minimize the Bayesian risk. While this is conceptually possible, it would have required the development of a non-standard, more complex classifier, instead of a simpler and better understood one. Another alternative would have been to train the reject classifier so as to output a reject decision by minimizing the error probability. While this approach could give good results in some applications, it would not take into account the different, application-dependent costs, yielding in general a larger expected cost for the proposed answers. As a consequence, the output of the reliability evaluator has to be thresholded by a *reject decisor* in order to obtain the final decision. The determination of the optimal threshold, say σ^*, is discussed in subsection 2.1.

For the training of the reliability evaluator we have chosen a supervised approach. Namely, the reliability classifier is trained on a *reliability-training set* for which the true class of the patterns is known. The desired output is set to 0 for patterns to which the primary classifier assigns the wrong class, and to 1 for correctly classified patterns. Our method relies on the generalization ability of the reliability evaluator to interpolate intermediate values for patterns that are across regions with good classification results and regions poorly classified.

Notice that, while the task of the reject classifier is itself a full classification task, it is expected to be simpler than the one faced by the primary classifier. This can be figured by simply considering that both classifiers operate on the same input space, but while the reject classifier has to face a two classes problem (reliable or unreliable patterns), the primary classifier usually has to discriminate among two or more classes. This means that even in the cases in which the training set is not adequately representative for obtaining a good classifier or a good estimate of the *a posteriori* class probabilities, it is still possible that the patterns suffice to train a properly working reliability classifier.

2.1 Optimal Values of the Reject Threshold

The rationale of the method used in this paper for fixing the reject threshold has been presented in [5]. For the sake of completeness, in the following we will briefly review it; moreover, we will introduce the function used in Section 3 for comparing different reject rules.

To this regard, it is assumed that an effectiveness function P, taking into account the requirements of the particular application, evaluates the quality of the classification in terms of correct recognition, misclassification and rejection rates. Under this assumption the optimal reject threshold value, determining the best trade-off between reject rate and misclassification rate, is the one for which the function P reaches its absolute maximum. The requirements of a given application domain are specified by attributing costs to misclassifications, rejects and correct classifications. The cost of an error can be a function of the guess and of the actual class [7]. To operatively define the function P, let us refer to a general classification problem. Suppose that the patterns to be classified can be assigned to one of $N+1$ classes, labeled with $0, 1, ..., N$. Labels $1, ..., N$ denote the actual classes, while 0 is a fictitious class collecting the rejected patterns. For each actual class i, let us call R_{ii} the percentage of patterns correctly classified, R_{ij} the percentage of patterns erroneously assigned to the class j (with $j \neq i$) and R_{i0} the percentage of rejected patterns.

For the same class i, let R_{ii}^0 and R_{ij}^0 respectively indicate the percentages of patterns correctly classified and of patterns erroneously assigned to the class j, when the classifier is used at 0-reject. If we assume for P a linear dependence on R_{ii}, R_{ij} and R_{i0}, its expression is given by:

$$P = \sum_{i=1}^{N} C_{ii}(R_{ii} - R_{ii}^0) - \sum_{i=1}^{N} \sum_{j=1, j \neq i}^{N} C_{ij}(R_{ij} - R_{ij}^0) - \sum_{i=1}^{N} C_{i0} R_{i0} \qquad (1)$$

In other words, P measures the actual effectiveness improvement when the reject option is introduced, with respect to the performance of the classifier at 0-reject. The term C_{ij} denotes the cost of assigning to the class j a pattern belonging to the class i. Note that, if $j = 0$, this is the cost of rejecting a pattern coming from the class i, while, if $j = i$, C_{ij} actually represents the gain associated to a correct classification. Obviously, in order that a rejection be convenient, for each class i, the following relation must hold:

$$C_{ij} \geq C_{i0} \quad \forall j \neq 0, j \neq i \qquad (2)$$

Since R_{ii}, R_{ij} and R_{i0} depend on the value of the reject threshold σ, P is also a function of σ. Starting from the results presented in [5], it is possible to show that the following relation holds:

$$P(\sigma) = \sum_{i=1}^{N} \sum_{j=1, j \neq i}^{N} (C_{ij} - C_{i0}) \int_{0}^{\sigma} D_{ij}(\psi) d(\psi) - \sum_{i=1}^{N} (C_{ii} + C_{i0}) \int_{0}^{\sigma} D_{ii}(\psi) d(\psi)$$

(3)

where $D_{ii}(\psi)$ and $D_{ij}(\psi)$ (with $j \neq i$) are, respectively, the occurrence density curves of correctly classified and misclassified patterns for the class i as a function of the value of σ. In other words, $D_{ij}(\psi) d(\psi)$ is the fraction of patterns of the class i assigned to class j with a reliability in the interval $[\psi, \psi + d\psi]$.

The optimal value σ^* of the reject threshold σ is the one for which the function P gets its maximum value. In practice, the functions $D_{ij}(\psi)$ are not available in their analytical form and therefore, for evaluating σ^*, they should be experimentally determined in tabular form on a set of labeled patterns, adequately representative of the target domain. The value of σ^* can be then determined by means of an exhaustive search among the tabulated values of $P(\sigma)$.

3   Experimental Results

The aim of the performed tests is to compare our method with the other classical reject approaches on real data. In particular, we considered the Chow's rule [1,2] and the reject rule proposed by Foggia et al. in [5]. According to the method in [5], the reliability of the classification can be expressed as a function $\psi = \psi(\psi_a, \psi_b)$, where ψ_a and ψ_b account for two different situations which can give rise to unreliable classifications: (a) there is no class whose output value is sufficiently high to judge the classification reliable; (b) there is not a clear overwhelming class. To combine the reliability parameters, we considered the operators (ψ_{max}, ψ_{min}, ψ_{med}, ψ_{sym}) used in [5].

We have considered three different databases coming from the UCI Machine Learning Repository [8]. The first database (*letter*) contains the 26 capital letters in the English alphabet: the character images were based on 20 different fonts, randomly distorted. The second database (*pendigits*) contains handwritten digits obtained by means of a digitizing tablet. The third database (*spam*) refers to the problem of determining whether a given email is spam or not. The characteristics of the considered databases are summarized in Table 1, where we have reported the number of the classes and the size of the training, validation and test sets. It is worth noting that while in the *pendigits* and the *letter* databases the patterns

Table 1. Characteristics of the employed databases

Data set	letter	pendigits	spam
# classes	26	10	2
# training patterns	5985	3748	1381
# validation patterns	5999	3747	1380
# test patterns	8016	3498	1840

Table 2. Recognition rates obtained by each primary classifier on the test sets of the considered databases

Classifier	Rec. rate (*letter*)	Rec. rate (*pendigits*)	Rec. rate (*spam*)
MLP10 (10 hidden neurons)	73.13%	90.19%	92.83%
MLP40 (40 hidden neurons)	82.31%	92.82%	93.10%
MLP80 (80 hidden neurons)	86.40%	93.05%	93.21%
NN	92.18%	97.20%	86.30%

are uniformly distributed within the classes, in the spam database the non-spam patterns outnumber the spam patterns (2788 non-spam vs 1813 spam). We partitioned the databases in the training, validation and test sets preserving the original class distribution.

In order to assess the effectiveness of the proposed method with respect to different paradigms for primary classification, in our experimentation we considered a statistical classifier, a Nearest Neighbor (*NN*), and a neural network, a Multi-Layer Perceptron (*MLP*). The employed MLP has a single hidden layer. Learning has been performed with the standard Back-Propagation algorithm, with a constant learning rate equal to 0.5. The sigmoidal activation function was chosen for all the neurons. Tests were carried out employing 10, 40 and 80 neurons in the hidden layer. The validation set was used to avoid overtraining. The training set has been also used as the reference set of the NN classifier.

The recognition rates obtained by each primary classifier on the considered databases are shown in Table 2. It is interesting to note the high variability of the performance obtained by the selected primary classifiers: this allows us to assess the performance of the proposed method in different situations.

As stated in the previous Section, the rationale of our method does not depend on the particular technique used for the reliability evaluation. In particular, in this work we have experimented the use of a Support Vector Machine (SVM) approach. More precisely, since the goal of the reliability evaluator is to provide a real-valued measure, we have adopted a variant of SVM known as Support Vector Regression (ϵ-SVR). The ϵ-SVR has been trained by using the validation sets as reliability-training sets. With regard to the choice of the ϵ-SVR parameters, we performed a grid search to obtain their optimal values. The validation sets were also used to calculate the optimal value of the reject thresholds for the reject decisor and the rule proposed in [5].

In order to compare the proposed reject rule with respect to the rules in [2] and [5], we employed the effectiveness improvement index P defined in eq. (1). The values of ψ_a and ψ_b needed by the reject rule described in [5] have been calculated, for each classifier, as proposed in [9]. The Chow's rule, instead, has been applied after estimating the a posteriori probability of each class as suggested in [10] (for the MLP) and in [3] (for the NN classifier).

Table 3. Performance of the considered reject methods. Each cell of the table shows the number of occurrences where a given method obtained the highest value of P, over the 40 devised configurations for each database.

Reject method	letter	pendigits	spam
chow	3	5	15
min	4	1	17
med	2	9	17
max	3	0	16
sym	1	0	15
svr	31	26	26

We assumed that the three considered recognition tasks do not require to distinguish among the possible kinds of errors ($C_{ii} = C_c$, $C_{ij} = C_e$, $C_{i0} = C_r$, $\forall i, \forall j \neq i$). So, it is possible to define a *normalized cost* as the ratio $C_n = (C_e - C_r)/(C_c + C_r)$. In particular, for our tests, we considered $C_e \in \{2.5, 3, 4, 5, 6, 7, 8, 10, 12, 14\}$ and set $C_c = 1$ and $C_r = 2$.

In Table 3, we reported the performance of the selected approaches. Each cell of the table shows the total number of occurrences where a given method obtained the highest value of P over the 40 tests resulting from the ten C_n values combined with the four primary classifiers considered. In the figure the names *chow, min, med, max, sym* and *svr* stand for the Chow's rule, the reject rule in [5] using ψ_{min}, ψ_{med}, ψ_{max} and ψ_{sym}, and the proposed reject classifier, respectively. It is worth noting that the sum of the values on each column of the Table 3 is not constant (and equal to the total number of tests for each database, i.e. 40) as it would be expected; this is ascribable to the fact that, in the cases in which n different algorithms have obtained the same best score, we declared n winners. From the results presented in Table 3, it can be seen that the proposed approach performs significantly better than the others. This behavior is more evident when the number of the classes of the primary classifier is higher than that of the reject classifier. In order to provide a more quantitative insight of the experimental results, in Figure 2 we have reported the performance of the considered reject approaches as a function of C_n on the three used databases. The performance is expressed in terms of P averaged on the four employed classifiers (MLP10, MLP40, MLP80, NN). For the sake of clarity, among all the combining operators proposed in [5], we reported only the results obtained by using ψ_{med}, since it provided in most cases the highest value of P. It is worth noting that, as it could be expected, the improvements provided by the use of reject option are more evident in the case of the *letter* database; in fact, the average recognition rate obtained by the primary classifiers on this database is about 10% lower with respect to the results obtained on the *pendigits* and the *spam* databases. From the results reported in Figure 2, it is possible to note that the proposed reject system performs better than all the other rules on the *letter* and the *spam* databases for all costs configurations; differently, on the *pendigits*

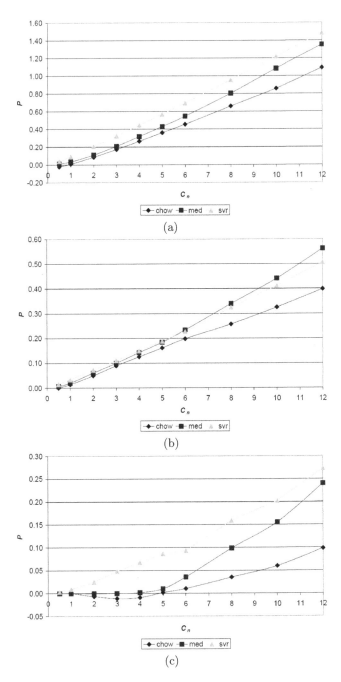

Fig. 2. Trends of P versus C_n in case of *(a) letter, (b) pendigits, (c) spam* database. In each case P is averaged on the four employed classifiers (MLP10, MLP40, MLP80, NN).

database the proposed method provides slightly higher performance only for low values of C_n, while the rule in [5] is to be preferred in case of high values of C_n.

4   Conclusions

The reject methods proposed so far make restrictive assumptions on the outputs provided by the classifier to which the reject option is applied. Moreover, they lack of generality regarding the choice of classification technique. In order to overcome these limitations, in this paper we developed a reject method that makes little or no assumption on the structure of the classifier and of its outputs, and can adapt to some degree to the training information available in the application at hand. We compared our proposal with other less general but well-known reject rules on three standard databases. Obtained results demonstrated the effectiveness of the proposed method.

References

1. C.K. Chow: An optimum character recognition system using decision functions, IRE Trans. Electron. Comput., **6** (1957) 247–254.
2. C.K. Chow: On optimum recognition error and reject tradeoff. IEEE Trans. on Information Theory, **16** (1970) 41-46.
3. L. Xu, A. Krzyzak, C.Y. Suen: Method of combining multiple classifiers and their application to handwritten numeral recognition, IEEE Trans. Syst. Man Cybernetics **22** (3) (1992) 418–435.
4. G. Fumera and F. Roli: Support vector machines with embedded reject option. In: Lee S, Verri A (eds) Pattern recognition with support vector machines. Lecture Notes in Computer Science, vol 2388. Springer, Berlin Heidelberg New York, pp 68-82, 2002.
5. P. Foggia, C. Sansone, F. Tortorella, M. Vento: Multiclassification: reject criteria for the Bayesian combiner, Pattern Recognition **32** (1999) 1435–1447.
6. Y.S. Huang and C.Y. Suen: A method of combining multiple experts for the recognition of unconstrained handwritten numerals, IEEE Trans. Pattern Anal. Mach Intelligence, **17** (1995) 90–94.
7. C. Sansone, F. Tortorella, M. Vento: A Classification Reliability-driven reject rule for Milti-Expert Systems, International Journal of Pattern Recognition and Artificial Intelligence **15**(6) (2001) 885–904.
8. C. Blake, E. Keogh and C. J. Merz, UCI Repository of machine learning databases, http://www.ics.uci.edu/~mlearn/MLRepository.html. University of California, Department of Information and Computer Science, Irvine, CA, 1998.
9. L.P. Cordella, P. Foggia, C. Sansone, F. Tortorella, M. Vento, Reliability Parameters to Improve Combination Strategies in Multi-Expert Systems, Pattern Analysis and Applications, Springer, vol. 2, no. 3, pp. 205-214, 1999
10. J. Kittler, M. Hatef, R.P.W. Duin, J. Matas, On Combining Classifiers. In *IEEE Trans. on Pattern Analysis and Machine Intell.*, 20(3), pp. 226-239, March 1998.

Bayesian Analysis of Linear Combiners

Battista Biggio, Giorgio Fumera, and Fabio Roli

Dept. of Electrical and Electronic Eng., Univ. of Cagliari
Piazza d'Armi, 09123 Cagliari, Italy
{bat,fumera,roli}@diee.unica.it

Abstract. A new theoretical framework for the analysis of linear combiners is presented in this paper. This framework extends the scope of previous analytical models, and provides some new theoretical results which improve the understanding of linear combiners operation. In particular, we show that the analytical model developed in seminal works by Tumer and Ghosh is included in this framework.

1 Introduction

One of the main open problems in the field of multiple classifier systems is the lack of a general theoretical framework which can give a unifying view of the large number of classifier combining rules and ensemble construction methods proposed so far in the literature [6]. With regard to combining rules, some theoretical results, with limited scope, are currently available for the majority voting and the linear combination of classifiers outputs. In particular, a theoretical framework for linear combiners, which are the focus of this paper, has been developed in seminal works by Tumer and Ghosh [8,9], and was then exploited and extended in [1] and [2]. Theoretical analysis of linear combiners were also reported in [3,5,4]. The framework by Tumer and Ghosh was the first to provide useful insights into the behaviour of the linear combination by simple averaging, and some practical guidelines to the design of linearly combined classifier ensembles [8,9]. Fumera and Roli extended these results to the weighted average combining rule [2], and derived some guidelines for the choice between simple and weighted averaging. Although the theoretical predictions of the model by Tumer and Ghosh are derived under very strict and unrealistic assumptions, the authors noted that they were confirmed with good accuracy on many real data sets [2]. This raised an issue about the scope of the model by Tumer and Ghosh.

The work presented in this paper is a by-product of an attempt to provide an explanation to the above issue. We found that the theoretical analysis of the misclassification probability of individual and linearly combined classifiers given by Tumer and Ghosh can be developed under a new theoretical framework, which is presented in Sect. 2. The new theoretical framework has a broader scope than the one by Tumer and Ghosh, and includes it as a particular case, as explained in Sect. 3. We finally show in Sect. 4 that our framework provides some more insights into the operation of linear combiners, and also provides a partial answer to the open issue mentioned above about the prediction capability of Tumer and

M. Haindl, J. Kittler, and F. Roli (Eds.): MCS 2007, LNCS 4472, pp. 292–301, 2007.

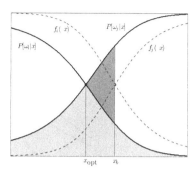

Fig. 1. True posteriors (solid lines) around the ideal boundary x_{opt} between ω_i and ω_j, and estimated posteriors (dashed lines) leading to the boundary x_b, and to an added error (dark gray area) over Bayes error (light gray area)

Ghosh model. We believe that the results presented in this paper can be a further step towards a more general framework for multiple classifier systems.

2   A Bayesian Framework for Generalization Error Analysis

Consider a given C-class classification problem, and a classifier which provides estimates $f_k(x), k = 1, \ldots, C$, of the a posteriori probabilities $\mathbb{P}[\omega_k|x]$, where x denotes a feature vector. The $f_k(x)$'s are considered random variables (their randomness depends for instance on the random choice of the training set). If Bayes decision rule is applied to the estimated posteriors, x is assigned to the class ω_i such that $i = \arg \max_k f_k(x)$, and non optimal decisions are taken if $\arg \max_k f_k(x) \neq \arg \max_k \mathbb{P}[\omega_k|x]$. This causes an additional misclassification probability (named *added error* in [8,9]) over Bayes error. In the following we consider the case of a one-dimensional feature space: all the results can be extended to multi-dimensional feature spaces as described in detail in [7].

The framework by Tumer and Ghosh is based on analyzing the added error in a region of the feature space around an ideal boundary x_{opt} between two classes ω_i and ω_j, in the case in which the estimation errors lead to a boundary x_b between the *same* classes, which can be shifted from the ideal one. An example is given in Fig. 1. In this case, it is easy to see that the added error is given by

$$e_{\mathrm{add}}(x_b) = \int_{x_{\mathrm{opt}}}^{x_b} \left(\mathbb{P}[\omega_j|x] - \mathbb{P}[\omega_i|x] \right) \mathbb{P}[x] \mathrm{d}x. \qquad (1)$$

Note that it depends on the posteriors of classes ω_i and ω_j only.

Our aim is instead to analyze the added error under more general conditions, namely in a region of the feature space around *any* given estimated boundary x_b between two classes ω_i and ω_j, without making any assumption on the true

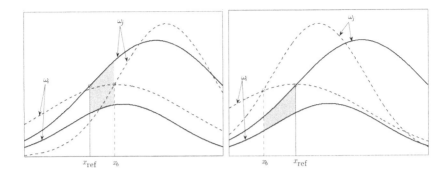

Fig. 2. Two possible realizations of the estimates of the posteriors of classes ω_i and ω_j (dashed lines), leading to an estimated class boundary x_b. The true posteriors are shown as solid lines. The difference $\Delta e_{\text{add}}(x_{\text{ref}}, x_b)$ (x_{ref} is the same in both plots) corresponds to the gray areas: it is positive in the left and negative in the right.

posteriors or on the presence of ideal boundaries in such region. To this aim, consider a given interval $[x_1, x_2]$ which contains an estimated boundary x_b. Assuming without loss of generality that $f_i(x_b) > f_j(x_b)$ for $x < x_b$, so that x is assigned to ω_i, if $x < x_b$, the added error in $[x_1, x_2]$ can be written as a function of x_b, as $e_{\text{add}}(x_b) = \int_{x_1}^{x_b}(\mathbb{P}[\omega(x)|x] - \mathbb{P}[\omega_i|x])\mathbb{P}[x]dx + \int_{x_b}^{x_2}(\mathbb{P}[\omega(x)|x] - \mathbb{P}[\omega_j|x])\mathbb{P}[x]dx$, where $\omega(x) = \arg\max_{\omega_k}\mathbb{P}[\omega_k|x]$. Note that $e_{\text{add}}(x_b)$ depends on the maximum of the posteriors in each x, which does not necessarily coincide with the posterior of ω_i or ω_j, contrary to the case considered by Tumer and Ghosh. To the purpose of our analysis, namely the comparison between the added error of individual classifiers and of their linear combination, it is convenient to remove the above dependence on $\mathbb{P}[\omega(x)|x]$. This can be achieved by considering any fixed reference point $x_{\text{ref}} \in [x_1, x_2]$, and by rewriting $e_{\text{add}}(x_b)$ as $e_{\text{add}}(x_{\text{ref}}) + [e_{\text{add}}(x_b) - e_{\text{add}}(x_{\text{ref}})]$, where $e_{\text{add}}(x_{\text{ref}})$ is the added error that one would get if the estimated boundary x_b lay in x_{ref}. The term between square brackets is the difference between the added error when the estimated boundary lies in a point x_b, and $e_{\text{add}}(x_{\text{ref}})$, and will be denoted as $\Delta e_{\text{add}}(x_{\text{ref}}, x_b)$. It is easy to see that

$$\Delta e_{\text{add}}(x_{\text{ref}}, x_b) = \int_{x_{\text{ref}}}^{x_b} (\mathbb{P}[\omega_j|x] - \mathbb{P}[\omega_i|x])\,\mathbb{P}[x]dx \ . \tag{2}$$

An example is given in Fig. 2. Note now that $\Delta e_{\text{add}}(x_{\text{ref}}, x_b)$ depends on the posteriors of ω_i or ω_j only, contrary to both $e_{\text{add}}(x_{\text{ref}})$ and $e_{\text{add}}(x_b)$. The main idea behind our framework is to express the added error of each individual classifier, as well as the one of the linear combiner, using the same reference point x_{ref}, as the sum of $e_{\text{add}}(x_{\text{ref}})$, which is a constant term *identical* for each classifier, and the term $\Delta e_{\text{add}}(x_{\text{ref}}, \cdot)$, which can be different for each classifier. This allows to evaluate the reduction of the added error which can be attained by the linear combination by comparing the latter term only.

We now formalize the main assumption on which our model is based. It is analogous to the main assumption of Tumer and Ghosh model reported in Sect. 3, although it was not explicitly phrased in this form in [8,9].

Assumption 1. *Each realization of the random variables $f_k(x), k = 1, \ldots, C$, leads to an estimated boundary x_b between ω_i and ω_j in the considered interval $[x_1, x_2]$ of the feature space. No other estimated class boundary lies in $[x_1, x_2]$.*

As a consequence, x_b is a random variable whose distribution depends on the distribution of the $f_k(x)$'s.

2.1   Added Error of a Single Classifier

Following the approach in [8,9], we start our analysis by writing the estimates $f_k(x)$ as $\mathbb{P}[\omega_k|x] + \varepsilon_k(x)$, where $\varepsilon_k(x)$ denotes the estimation error. An estimated boundary x_b between two classes ω_i and ω_j is characterized by $f_i(x_b) = f_j(x_b) > f_k(x_b), k \neq i, j$. We will denote with b the offset $x_b - x_{\text{ref}}$. As in [8,9], if b is small enough with respect to the changes in the posteriors and in $\mathbb{P}[x]$, a first order approximations of the posteriors and a zero order approximation of $\mathbb{P}[x]$ can be made around the reference point x_{ref}: $\mathbb{P}[\omega_k|x_{\text{ref}}+b] \simeq \mathbb{P}[\omega_k|x_{\text{ref}}]+b\mathbb{P}'[\omega_k|x_{\text{ref}}], k = i, j$, e $\mathbb{P}[x_{\text{ref}} + b] \simeq \mathbb{P}[x_{\text{ref}}]$. Substituting in Eq. 2 we obtain

$$\Delta e_{\text{add}}(x_{\text{ref}}, x_b) = \frac{\mathbb{P}[x_{\text{ref}}]t}{2}\left(\frac{2u}{t}b + b^2\right) \ , \tag{3}$$

where

$$u = \mathbb{P}[\omega_j|x_{\text{ref}}] - \mathbb{P}[\omega_i|x_{\text{ref}}], \ t = \mathbb{P}'[\omega_j|x_{\text{ref}}] - \mathbb{P}'[\omega_i|x_{\text{ref}}] \ . \tag{4}$$

The expected value of $\Delta e_{\text{add}}(x_{\text{ref}}, x_b)$ with respect to b is then

$$\Delta E_{\text{add}} = \mathbb{E}[\Delta e_{\text{add}}(x_{\text{ref}}, x_b)] = \frac{\mathbb{P}[x_{\text{ref}}]t}{2}\left[\frac{2u}{t}\beta_b + \beta_b^2 + \sigma_b^2\right] \ , \tag{5}$$

where β_b and σ_b^2 denote the expected value and the variance of b.

It is also possible to express b as a function of the estimation errors: this allows to rewrite Eq. 5 in a form which will be useful to compare the expected added error of an individual classifier with the one of linearly combined classifiers. From $f_i(x_b) = f_j(x_b)$, rewriting $f_k(x), k = i, j$, as $\mathbb{P}[\omega_k|x] + \varepsilon_k(x)$, and using the first order approximation of the posteriors, we obtain

$$b = \frac{\varepsilon_i(x_b) - \varepsilon_j(x_b)}{t} - \frac{u}{t} \ . \tag{6}$$

Assuming as in [8,9] that the estimation errors on different classes $\varepsilon_i(x)$ and $\varepsilon_j(x)$ are uncorrelated, from Eq. 6 we obtain

$$\beta_b = \frac{\beta_i - \beta_j}{t} - \frac{u}{t}, \ \sigma_b^2 = \frac{\sigma_i^2 + \sigma_j^2}{t^2} \ , \tag{7}$$

where β_k and $\sigma_k^2, k = i, j$, denote the expected value (named *bias* in [8,9]) and the variance of $\varepsilon_k(x_b)$. Substituting the above expression of β_b into Eq. 5 we obtain

$$\Delta E_{\text{add}} = \frac{\mathbb{P}[x_{\text{ref}}]t}{2} \left[-\frac{u^2}{t^2} + \frac{1}{t^2}(\beta_i - \beta_j)^2 + \frac{1}{t^2}(\sigma_i^2 + \sigma_j^2) \right] . \tag{8}$$

The expected added error in $[x_1, x_2]$ is then given by

$$E_{\text{add}} = e_{\text{add}}(x_{\text{ref}}) + \Delta E_{\text{add}} . \tag{9}$$

It is easy to see that the expected added error is the sum of three terms: a constant term $e_{\text{add}}(x_{\text{ref}}) - \frac{\mathbb{P}[x_{\text{ref}}]u^2}{2t}$, whose value depends only on the choice of the reference point x_{ref}; a term depending on the bias of estimation errors, and the other on their variance.

2.2   Added Error of Linearly Combined Classifiers

Consider now a linear combination of the posteriors estimates provided by an ensemble of N classifiers, $f_k^n(x), k = 1, \ldots, C; n = 1, \ldots, N$, using positive weights w_n which sum up to 1, as in [2]:

$$f_k^{\text{ave}}(x) = \sum_{n=1}^{N} w_n f_k^n(x) = \mathbb{P}[\omega_k | x] + \varepsilon_k^{\text{ave}}(x) = \mathbb{P}[\omega_k | x] + \sum_{n=1}^{N} w_n \varepsilon_k^n(x) . \tag{10}$$

To proceed with our analysis, we extend the assumption 1 to the estimates of each individual classifier, and of their linear combination. Now, as in Sect. 2.1, we rewrite the added error $e_{\text{add}}^{\text{ave}}(x_{b^{\text{ave}}})$ in $[x_1, x_2]$ as $e_{\text{add}}^{\text{ave}}(x_{\text{ref}}) + [e_{\text{add}}^{\text{ave}}(x_{b^{\text{ave}}}) - e_{\text{add}}^{\text{ave}}(x_{\text{ref}})]$, using the same reference point x_{ref} as in each individual classifier. With the same approximations, assumptions and steps as in Sect. 2.1, we obtain:

$$b^{\text{ave}} = \frac{\varepsilon_i^{\text{ave}}(x_{b^{\text{ave}}}) - \varepsilon_j^{\text{ave}}(x_{b^{\text{ave}}})}{t} - \frac{u}{t} , \tag{11}$$

while the expected value of $\Delta e_{\text{add}}^{\text{ave}}(x_{\text{ref}}, x_{b^{\text{ave}}})$ is

$$\Delta E_{\text{add}}^{\text{ave}} = \frac{\mathbb{P}[x_{\text{ref}}]t}{2} \left\{ -\frac{u^2}{t^2} + \frac{1}{t^2}(\beta_i^{\text{ave}} - \beta_j^{\text{ave}})^2 + \frac{1}{t^2} \left[(\sigma_i^{\text{ave}})^2 + (\sigma_j^{\text{ave}})^2 \right] \right\} , \tag{12}$$

where

$$\beta_k^{\text{ave}} = \sum_{n=1}^{N} w_n \beta_k^n, \ (\sigma_k^{\text{ave}})^2 = \sum_{n=1}^{N} w_n^2 (\sigma_k^n)^2 + \sum_{n=1}^{N} w_n^2 \sum_{m \neq n} \rho_k^{mn} \sigma_k^m \sigma_k^n, k = i, j , \tag{13}$$

ρ_k^{mn} denotes the correlation coefficient between $\epsilon_k^m(x)$ and $\varepsilon_k^n(x)$, and σ_k^m is the standard deviation of $\varepsilon_k^m(x)$. Finally, the expected added error in $[x_1, x_2]$ is

$$E_{\text{add}}^{\text{ave}} = e_{\text{add}}(x_{\text{ref}}) + \Delta E_{\text{add}}^{\text{ave}}. \tag{14}$$

Eqs. 14,12 show that the expected added error of the linear combiner, as the one of individual classifiers (see Eqs. 9 and 8), is given by the *same* constant term $e_{\text{add}}(x_{\text{ref}}) - \frac{\mathbb{P}[x_{\text{ref}}]u^2}{2t}$, plus a bias term and a variance term. The error reduction attainable by the linear combination can thus be evaluated taking into account only the bias and variance terms.

In the next Section we will point out the different scopes of the two frameworks in their capability of modeling the added error, and show that Tumer and Ghosh framework is included in ours. In Sect. 4 we will then compare the predictions about the behaviour of linear combiners which can be obtained from the two frameworks.

3   Comparison with Tumer and Ghosh Framework

As explained in Sect. 2, Tumer and Ghosh framework differs from ours since it evaluates the added error in an interval of the feature space containing an *ideal* boundary x_{opt} between two classes ω_i and ω_j, which is characterized by $\mathbb{P}[\omega_i|x_{\text{opt}}] = \mathbb{P}[\omega_j|x_{\text{opt}}] > \mathbb{P}[\omega_k|x_{\text{opt}}], k \neq i, j$. The main assumption of Tumer and Ghosh framework can be phrased as follows.

Assumption 2. *Each realization of the random variables* $f_k^n(x), k = 1, \ldots, C; n = 1, \ldots, N$, *leads to an estimated boundary between* ω_i *e* ω_j, *in a given interval* $[x_1, x_2]$ *which contains an ideal boundary* x_{opt} *between the same classes, both for each individual classifier and for their linear combination. Furthermore, there are no other estimated or ideal class boundaries in the considered interval.*

This is more restrictive than assumption 1 of our framework, which does not require the presence of such an ideal boundary, and thus allows to model the added error only for a subset of cases which can be modeled by our framework. Under assumption 2, the added error in $[x_1, x_2]$ is given by Eq. 1. Denoting the offset $x_b - x_{\text{opt}}$ with b, making a first order approximation of the posteriors and a zero order approximation of $\mathbb{P}[x]$ around x_{opt}, and assuming that the estimation errors on different classes are uncorrelated as in Sect. 2, it turns out [8,9] that

$$b^n = \frac{\varepsilon_i(x_{b^n}) - \varepsilon_j(x_{b^n})}{t}, \quad b^{\text{ave}} = \frac{\varepsilon_i(x_{b^{\text{ave}}}) - \varepsilon_j(x_{b^{\text{ave}}})}{t}, \tag{15}$$

while the expected added error in $[x_1, x_2]$ is

$$E_{\text{add}}^n = \frac{\mathbb{P}[x_{\text{opt}}]t}{2} \left\{ \frac{1}{t^2}(\beta_i^n - \beta_j^n)^2 + \frac{1}{t^2}\left[(\sigma_i^n)^2 + (\sigma_j^n)^2\right] \right\},$$
$$E_{\text{add}}^{\text{ave}} = \frac{\mathbb{P}[x_{\text{opt}}]t}{2} \left\{ \frac{1}{t^2}(\beta_i^{\text{ave}} - \beta_j^{\text{ave}})^2 + \frac{1}{t^2}\left[(\sigma_i^{\text{ave}})^2 + (\sigma_j^{\text{ave}})^2\right] \right\}, \tag{16}$$

where t, $\varepsilon_k^{\text{ave}}(x)$, β_k and $\sigma_k^2, k = i, j$, are defined exactly as in Sect. 2. It is worth noting that the two expressions of the expected added error are the sum of a bias and a variance term formally identical to the ones derived from our model (see Eqs. 13 and 8 for an individual classifier, and 13, 12 for a linear combiner): the only difference is that our model leads to a further constant additive term

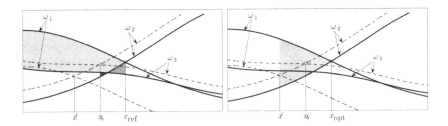

Fig. 3. True (solid lines) and estimated posteriors (dashed lines) for a three-class problem, leading to an ideal boundary x_{opt} between ω_1 and ω_2, and to an estimated boundary x_b between ω_3 and ω_2. The added error corresponds to the light gray plus the dark gray area in the left panel, while it would be erroneously evaluated by Tumer and Ghosh framework as the gray area in the right panel (see text for a complete explanation).

due to the fact that in our model the reference point x_{ref} needs not to coincide with an ideal boundary x_{opt} (which could even not exist in $[x_1, x_2]$).

We now show that Tumer and Ghosh framework is included in ours, in the sense that, under the more restrictive assumption 2, they both lead to the same expression of the expected added error in the considered interval, provided that the reference point x_{ref} is chosen equal to the ideal boundary x_{opt} between ω_i and ω_j. To this aim, it is sufficient to note that in this case the term $u = \mathbb{P}[\omega_j|x_{opt}] - \mathbb{P}[\omega_i|x_{opt}]$ is null, since the true posteriors are equal in the ideal boundary x_{opt}, and the term $e_{add}(x_{opt})$ is null as well, since, when the estimated boundary coincides with the ideal one ($x_b = x_{opt}$), the added error vanishes. It immediately follows that the expressions of b and of the expected added error given by the two frameworks are identical.

We finally point out that there are cases in which the added error can be correctly modeled by our framework only. This happens when assumption 1 holds while 2 does not, namely when there is no ideal boundary between ω_i and ω_j in the considered interval, or equivalently when the effect of the estimation errors on the posteriors is not a shift of an ideal class boundary. It is worth noting that these are cases of practical interest: as pointed out in [6], in complex pattern recognition problems it is likely that estimation errors cause different effects besides the shift of ideal boundaries. To clear up this point, we consider an example taken from [6] for a three-class problem, which is illustrated in Fig. 3, left. In the considered interval there is an ideal boundary x_{opt} between ω_1 and ω_2, while estimation errors lead to a boundary x_b between ω_3 and ω_2. Note that there is also a point x' such that $f_1(x') = f_2(x')$, which however is not an estimated boundary between ω_1 and ω_2. The true added error corresponds to the light gray area in Fig. 3, left. Tumer and Ghosh framework would erroneously model it with reference to the point x', as the grey area in Fig. 3, right. Consider instead $x_{ref} = x_{opt}$ as the reference point for our framework, for the sake of simplicity (any other point could be used as well). Our framework correctly models the added error as the sum of $e_{add}(x_{ref})$, namely the one corresponding to $x_b = x_{ref}$

(the sum of the light gray and of the intermediate gray areas in Fig. 3, left), and of $\Delta e_{\mathrm{add}}(x_{\mathrm{ref}}, x_b)$ (the dark gray area minus the intermediate gray area), which results in the sum of the light and dark gray areas in Fig. 3, left.

To sum up, our model has a broader scope than the one by Tumer and Ghosh, since it allows to model the added error under more general conditions. As a result, one may expect that our framework gives more accurate predictions on the behaviour of linear combiners, which in turn could provide better guidelines for their design. This issue is discussed in the next Section.

4   Analysis of Simple and Weighted Averaging

In [8,9] the model by Tumer and Ghosh was exploited to evaluate the reduction of the added error attainable by the simple average combining rule (from now on, SA) with respect to individual classifiers. Some further results were pointed out in [2]. The main results were the following:

1. SA reduces the variance component of the expected added error by an amount which depends on the correlation between estimation errors ρ_k^{mn} of the different classifiers (see Eqs. 16 and 13); for negatively correlated errors, the variance component can be reduced up to zero.
2. SA guarantees at least a bias component not greater than the maximum one exhibited by the individual classifiers.

These results suggested in [8,9] that the design of individual classifiers should focus on obtaining low bias and correlation, while the variance can be reduced by averaging classifiers.

What does the model presented in Sect. 2 add to the above results? Note first that in our model the bias and variance components of the expected added error, in Eqs. 8 ($\frac{\mathbb{P}[x_{\mathrm{ref}}]t}{2}[\frac{1}{t^2}(\beta_i - \beta_j)^2 + \frac{1}{t^2}(\sigma_i^2 + \sigma_j^2)]$) and 12 ($\frac{\mathbb{P}[x_{\mathrm{ref}}]t}{2}\{\frac{1}{t^2}(\beta_i^{\mathrm{ave}} - \beta_j^{\mathrm{ave}})^2 + \frac{1}{t^2}[(\sigma_i^{\mathrm{ave}})^2 + (\sigma_j^{\mathrm{ave}})^2]\}$), can be either positive or negative depending on the sign of the term t given by Eq. 4, while t is always positive in Tumer and Ghosh model. If $t > 0$, the bias and variance components of the two models are identical, and thus the above results provided by Tumer and Ghosh model hold also for ours. Instead, if $t < 0$, the bias and variance components derived from our model are *negative*. This implies that the expected added error of the SA can even be higher than the one of each individual classifier, and anyway it can never be lower than that of the best individual classifier. Furthermore, the reduction in the expected added error increases for increasing correlation between the estimation errors. Therefore, in presence of different estimated boundaries characterized by both positive and negative values of the corresponding t, the net effect of SA will be determined by the counterbalance of the two behaviours above. In other words, the advantage of SA over individual classifiers could be lower than the one predicted by Tumer and Ghosh model.

A further exploitation of Tumer and Ghosh model was carried out in [2], to compare the behaviour of the SA with that of the weighted average (from now on, WA) combining rule. An analytical comparison was possible only under the simplest case of unbiased and uncorrelated errors. The main theoretical results derived in [2] can be summarized as follows:

1. SA is the optimal linear combining rule, only if the individual classifiers exhibit the same misclassification rate.
2. WA can always perform at worst as the best classifier of the ensemble.
3. The improvement in misclassification rate which can be attained by WA over SA depends on the *error range* of the ensemble, namely on the misclassification rates of the best and worst individual classifiers: the broader the error range, the higher the improvement; being equal the error range, the improvement strongly depends on the degree of performance *imbalance*, namely on the distribution of the misclassification rates of the other individual classifiers. In particular, for classifiers exhibiting a narrow error range (say, below 0.05), the advantage of WA over SA is quite small (say, below 0.01).

This suggested in [2] some new simple guidelines for the choice between SA and WA in real applications. Basically, it could be worth using WA only if the individual classifiers exhibit a broad error range (say, above 5%), unless the weights can be estimated with high reliability; otherwise the small ideal advantage can be canceled out by weight estimations from small and noisy data sets. Although the assumption of unbiased and uncorrelated errors, as well as the main assumption of Tumer and Ghosh model (being the effect of estimation errors the shift of ideal boundaries) are likely to be violated in practice, it turned out that the derived predictions about the behaviour of SA and WA, and thus the validity of the above guidelines, were confirmed by experimental results on real data sets reported in [2]. It was left as an open problem to understand why theoretical predictions derived under assumptions which were apparently very restrictive were confirmed on real data sets. A partial answer can be given thanks to the new model described in this paper. By carrying out the same analysis described in detail in [2] for the case of unbiased and uncorrelated errors, it turns out that our model gives the *same* predictions above about the behaviour of WA and SA, for the case in which $t > 0$. Moreover, for $t < 0$ *only* prediction 2 above changes: in this case WA performs at best (instead of at worst) as the best individual classifier. This is thus an indication that the predictions derived from Tumer and Ghosh model were confirmed on real data sets since they actually hold under more general conditions. We point out that experimental results analogous to [2] (not reported here due to space limits) were obtained on six more real data sets taken from the UCI repository, namely Optdigits, DNA, Ionosphere, Satellite, Satimage and Segmentation.

5   Conclusions

In this paper we presented a new theoretical framework for the analysis of the reduction in misclassification probability which can be attained by linearly combining an ensemble of classifiers which provide estimates of the a posteriori probabilities. Our framework has a broader scope than the one developed in works by Tumer and Ghosh, and includes it as a particular case. It allows to analyze the added error around any class boundary provided by the estimated posteriors, not only around boundaries which are shifted from ideal ones as in [8, 9]. This gives a more general understanding of the operation of linear combiners. In particular, this allowed us to point out some behaviours of linear combiners (technically, the cases in which the term t is negative) which were not contemplated by Tumer and Ghosh model. Nevertheless, we found that many of the predictions of our model, in particular the ones from which practical guidelines for the design of linear combiners can be derived, are nearly identical to the predictions derived from the previous model: this gives a partial explanation to an open issue pointed out in [2], raised by the fact that theoretical prediction derived by Tumer and Ghosh model under strict and unrealistic assumptions turned out to be experimentally confirmed on real data sets.

To sum up, the main contribution of this paper is the development of a theoretical framework which allows a more general understanding of linear combiners. We are also investigating whether the ideas behind the theoretical frameworks considered in this work could suggest new theoretical models for other combining rules, which would be a useful step towards a more general framework for multiple classifier systems.

Acknowledgment. The authors would like to thank Gavin Brown for his valuable comments and suggestions on this work.

References

1. Alexandre, L.A., Campilho, A.C. Kamel, M.: Combining Independent and Unbiased Classifiers Using Weighted Average. In: Proc. 15th Int'l Conf. on Pattern Recognition, Vol. 2. IEEE Press (2000) 495–498
2. Fumera, G., Roli, F.: A Theoretical and Experimental Analysis of Linear Combiners for Multiple Classifier Systems. IEEE Trans. Pattern Analysis Machine Intelligence **27** (2005) 942–956
3. Kittler, J., Hatef, M., Duin, R.P.W., Matas, J.: On combining classifiers. IEEE Trans. Pattern Analysis Machine Intelligence **20** (1998) 226–239
4. Kittler, J., Alkoot, F. M.: Sum versus Vote Fusion in Multiple Classifier Systems. IEEE Trans. Pattern Analysis Machine Intelligence **25** (2003) 110–115
5. Kuncheva, L.I.: A theoretical study on six classifier fusion strategies. IEEE Trans. Pattern Analysis Machine Intelligence **24** 281–286
6. Kuncheva, L.I.: Combining Pattern Classifiers: Methods and Algorithms. Hoboken, N.J., Wiley (2004)
7. Tumer, K.: Linear and order statistics combiners for reliable pattern classification. PhD dissertation, The University of Texas, Austin (1996)
8. Tumer, K., Ghosh, J.: Analysis of Decision Boundaries in Linearly Combined Neural Classifiers. Pattern Recognition **29** (1996) 341–348
9. Tumer, K., Ghosh, J.: Linear and order statistics combiners for pattern classification. In: Sharkey, A.J.C. (ed.): Combining Artificial Neural Nets. Springer (1999) 127–155

Applying Pairwise Fusion Matrix on Fusion Functions for Classifier Combination

Albert Hung-Ren Ko, Robert Sabourin, and Alceu de Souza Britto Jr.

LIVIA, ETS, University of Quebec
1100 Notre-Dame West Street, Montreal, Quebec, H3C 1K3 Canada
PPGIA, Pontifical Catholic University of Parana
Rua Imaculada Conceicao, 1155, PR 80215-901, Curitiba, Brazil
albert@livia.etsmtl.ca, robert.sabourin@etsmtl.ca,
alceu@ppgia.pucpr.br

Abstract. We propose a new classifier combination scheme for the ensemble of classifiers. The Pairwise Fusion Matrix (PFM) constructs confusion matrices based on classifier pairs and thus offers the estimated probability of each class based on each classifier pair. These probability outputs can then be combined and the final outputs of the ensemble of classifiers is reached using various fusion functions. The advantage of this approach is the flexibility of the choice of the fusion functions, and the experiments suggest that the PFM combined with the majority voting outperforms the simple majority voting scheme on most of problems.

Keywords: Fusion Function, Combining Classifiers, Diversity, Confusion Matrix, Pattern Recognition, Majority Voting, Ensemble of Learning Machines.

1 Introduction

Different classifiers usually make different errors on different samples, which means that we can arrive at an ensemble that makes more accurate decisions by combining classifiers [10, 14, 8, 18, 4, 19]. For this purpose, diverse classifiers are grouped together into what is known as an Ensemble of Classifiers (EoC). There are two problems in optimizing the performance of an EoC: first, how classifiers are selected, given a pool of different classifiers, to construct the best ensemble; and second, given all the selected classifiers, choosing the best rule to combine their outputs. These problems are fundamentally different, and should be solved separately to reduce the complexity involved in optimizing EoCs; the former focuses on ensemble selection [10, 14, 6, 13] and the latter on ensemble combination, i.e. the choice of fusion functions [15, 8, 13].

Several important factors must be considered for an EoC: (a) find a pertinent objective function for selecting the classifiers; (b) use a pertinent searching algorithm to apply this criterion; and (c) use a adequate fusion function to combine classifier outputs. Diversity measures are designed as objective functions for ensemble selection [10, 5, 3, 6], but their performances are not convincing. On the other hand, some different fusion functions have been suggested for combining classifiers [15, 14, 6, 17, 9, 8, 18, 13], but they are either based on strong assumptions [1, 11], such as simple fusion functions,

M. Haindl, J. Kittler, and F. Roli (Eds.): MCS 2007, LNCS 4472, pp. 302–311, 2007.

or required a large data set, such as trained fusion functions [14, 6, 17, 9]. Given insufficient training samples, simple fusion functions may outperform some trained fusion functions [11]. Here are the key questions that need to be addressed:

1. Can a trained fusion function be effective without large training samples?
2. Can we take the interaction among classifiers into account in combining classifiers?

To answer these questions, we propose a method for combining classifiers. With the same fashion, pairwise fusion matrix (PFM) transforms an EoC into an ensemble of classifier pairs. With the prospect of using classifier pairs, PFM can obtain useful probabilities for classifier combination, transform the crisp class label outputs into class probability outputs and reduce the number of samples needed for ensemble training.

The paper is organized as follows. In section 2, the traditional fusion functions for crisp class outputs are discussed, and the proposed pairwise fusion matrix is presented in section 3. Experimental results of both ensemble selection and classifier combination are compared in section 4. Discussion and conclusion are presented in the remaining sections.

2   Fusion Functions for Crisp Output Classifier Combination

2.1   Traditional Fusion Functions

Several simple fusion functions for combining classifiers have been proposed, such as Maximum Rule (MAX), Minimum Rule (MIN), Sum Rule (SUM), Product Rule (PRO) and simple Majority Voting Rule (MAJ) [8, 18, 1, 7]. These directly compare the outputs from all individual classifiers in an ensemble, and do not require any further training. Some related theoretical studies are presented in [8, 18]. These simple fusion functions are straightforward. Since they are relatively simple and do not explore the relationships between classifiers or those between classes, they are suboptimal [1], and, as stated in [16], these fusion functions rely on the very restrictive assumption of the independence of estimates. To address this shortcoming, other, more sophisticated strategies have been proposed which use more available information in combining classifiers [14, 6, 17, 9], such as Naive Bayes (NB) [14, 18], Decision Templates (DT) [9], Behavior-Knowledge Space (BKS) and Wernecke's method (WER) [17].

Nevertheless, if classifiers only give crisp label outputs, then a lot of these fusion functions are useless, because they require the class probability outputs. Traditional class combination schemes such as MAX, MIN, SUM and PRO cannot apply on classifiers with only crisp label outputs, and some trained fusion functions such as DT have the same drawback. Only few fusion functions such as MAJ, NB, BKS or WER can be used here. We give a short introdution on these fusion functions:

1. Simple Majority Voting Rule (MAJ)
   This rule does not require the *a posteriori* outputs for each class, and each classifier gives only one crisp class output as a vote for that class. Then, the ensemble output is assigned to the class with the maximum number of votes among all classes. For any sample $x \in X$, for a group of L classifiers in a T-class problem, we denote the

decision of label outputs from classifier $f(i)$ is $c(i), 1 \leq c(i) \leq T$, and we write $d_{i,t} = 1$ for $c(i) = t, 1 \leq t \leq T$ and zero otherwise. Consequently, we calculate the discriminant function for class $l, 1 \leq l \leq T$ as:

$$g(l|x) = \sum_{i=1}^{L} d_{i,l} \qquad (1)$$

And the class is selected as the one with the maximum value of $g(l|x)$:

$$k = \arg \max_{l=1}^{T} g(l|x) \qquad (2)$$

2. Naive Bayes (NB)

   Among these methods, the simplest is based on the assumption that all classifiers are mutually independent. Under this precondition, for a group of L classifiers in a T-class problem, we can calculate the probability $P(l|c(i), x)$ of the class label being $l, 1 \leq l \leq T$ if classifier $f(i)$ gives the class label output $c(i)$ on a sample x. Then we can use these estimated probabilities for classifying samples in the test set X:

$$\tilde{P}(l|x) \propto \prod_{i=1}^{L} P(l|c(i), x) \qquad (3)$$

$$k = \arg \max_{l=1}^{T} \tilde{P}(l|x) \qquad (4)$$

   This is the so-called naive nayes (NB) combination [14, 18]. However, it is very unlikely that all classifiers in an ensemble will be mutually independent.

3. Behavior-Knowledge Space (BKS) and Wernecke's method (WER)

   Some authors propose constructing a complex BKS table [17] in order to have full access to the information on classifier behavior. Given N samples and L classifiers in a T-class problem, the ideal goal is to obtain the probability $P(l|c(1), \cdots, c(i), \cdots, c(L), x)$ for the whole data X, where l is a possible class label for a sample $1 \leq l \leq T$, and $c(i)$ is the decision of classifier $f(i)$ over the sample, with L classifiers $1 \leq i \leq L$. Each probability can be located in a cell of a look-up table (BKS table), and then be used by multinomial combination, such as direct comparison of these probabilities in the BKS table, known as the Behavior-Knowledge Space (BKS), or considering a 95% confidence interval of the probabilities in the BKS table, known as Wernecke's method (WER) [17]. For BKS, the class is assigned by simply comparing the values in each cell in BKS table:

$$k = \arg \max_{l=1}^{T} P(l|c(1), \cdots, c(i), \cdots, c(L), x) \qquad (5)$$

In reality, however, this probability could be impossible to obtain. With L classifiers in a T-class problem, there are $T \times T^L$ different situations for this group of classifiers, and it is not difficult to see that the number of samples N is unlikely to be sufficient for T^{L+1} different situations, i.e. in general, $N \ll T^{L+1}$. As a result, obtaining any idea of this probability is also unlikely, and thus it is usually impossible to proceed with BKS or WER, except on low class dimensions with a very small number of classifiers in an ensemble and a very large number of samples. Given the strict limit on the size of the training data set, some authors suggest that BKS tends to overfit, as well as being too self-assured [9].

We notice that these methods for combining classifiers have their own disadvantages, even though they are applicable on classifiers with only crisp class outputs. Above all, we observe that most trained fusion functions tend to explore more information from the training set. For this reason, most classifier combination strategies need to take the interaction between classifiers and between classes into consideration. If these elements are ignored, as with NB, then the performance cannot be satisfactory. If these elements are fully explored, as with BKS or WER, given the complicated behavior of classifiers in an ensemble, especially in a high class dimension and with a large number of classifiers, the number of samples can scarcely be sufficient, and the probabilities obtained will usually be unreliable.

Herein lies the problem with training ensembles for combining classifiers. The fact that an ensemble acts in an extremely large space means that we need to use a method which is both effective and accurate. Given this dilemma, we propose a method which considers an ensemble of classifier pairs rather than an EoC. The proposed pairwise fusion matrix (PFM) transformation is a practical solution and is applicable on all existent fusion functions. First, PFM transforms a group classifiers with only crisp label outputs into an ensemble of classifier-pairs with class probability outputs. As a result, it is possible to apply fusion functions such as MAX, MIN, SUM or PRO. Second, PFM takes into account the pairwise interaction between classifiers on their class label outputs, and thus offers a more reliable class probability estimation. We detail this transformation and its use in combining classifiers in the next section.

3   Pairwise Fusion Matrix Transformation (PFM)

The dilemma of EoCs is that, given a limited number of samples, we need to take into account the interaction among classifiers. PFM makes use of pairwise estimation to solve this problem. If we only take classifier pairs into account, we need only calculate the probability $P(l|c(i), c(j), x)$, where $c(i)$ and $c(j)$ are the decisions of classifier $f(i)$ and classifier $f(j)$ over a sample x respectively. For $P(l|c(i), c(j), x)$, given T classes there are only $T \times T^2 = T^3$ different situations, and if the number of samples N is large enough, i.e. $N \gg T^3$, we can obtain a reliable estimation of this probability. This probability can be approximated by calculating PFM:

$$P(l|c(i), c(j)) = N(x \in l, c(i), c(j))/N(c(i), c(j)) \tag{6}$$

where $N(c(i), c(j))$ is the total number of samples on which classifier $f(i)$ gives crisp output $c(i)$, and classifier $f(j)$ gives crisp output $c(j)$, while $N(x \in l, c(i), c(j))$ is the number of samples the real class label of which is l, $1 \leq l \leq T$. The probability $P(l|c(i), c(j), x)$ is, in fact, the concept of a 3-dimensional confusion matrix, where the decision of classifier $c(i)$, the decision of classifier $c(j)$ and the real class label of samples represent each dimension. For any sample x with a class label k, PFM provides a pairwise matrix of classifier $f(i)$ and classifier $f(j)$, with the probability of how likely it will be classified as class $c(i)$ by $f(i)$ and as class $c(j)$ by $f(j)$. For any sample x classified as class l by classifier $f(i)$, PFM provides a partial confusion matrix between classifier $f(j)$ and the real class labels of samples. All the confusion matrices of classifier $f(j)$ can be derived quickly from any pairwise confusion matrices concerning $f(j)$:

$$P(l|c(j), x) = \sum_{i=1}^{T} P(l|c(i), c(j), x) \qquad (7)$$

where $c(i)$ constitutes the class label outputs of classifier $f(i)$. In other words, it is a cube of T^3 cells with N samples filled in; since L classifiers mean $\frac{L \times (L-1)}{2}$ classifier pairs, we can obtain $\frac{L \times (L-1)}{2}$ pairwise confusion matrices (PFM).

The probabilities from these pairwise confusion matrices offer several advantages over the traditional ensemble combination strategies: (a) they do not require the class probability outputs of each sample but only the class label outputs of each sample from individual classifiers; (b) they transform the simple class label outputs into the class probability outputs; and (c) they take into account of the interaction between classifiers. Note that the use of pairwise confusion matrices is a transformation, not an actual classifier combination scheme. Based on these pairwise class probabilities, we can apply other different classifier combination rules. We give two examples of the application of PFMs in general fusion functions:

1. Pairwise Fusion Matrix using Sum Rule (PFM-SUM)
   Assign x → k   if

$$\frac{2}{L \times (L-1)} \sum_{i,j=1, i>j}^{L} P(k|c(i), c(j), x) = \qquad (8)$$

$$\max_{l=1}^{T} \frac{2}{L \times (L-1)} \sum_{i,j=1, i>j}^{L} P(l|c(i), c(j), x) \qquad (9)$$

2. Pairwise Fusion Matrix using Majority Voting Rule (PFM-MAJ)
   This rule is similar to the simple MAJ rule, but uses the pairwise probability $P(l|c(i), c(j), x)$ from the classifier pair $f(i)$ and $f(j)$ instead of the simple probability $P_i(l|x)$ from a single classifier $f(i)$ considering class l.

Other fusion functions, such as DT or NB, will require further training, but are applicable as well. To prove that PFMs are applicable, we carry out the experiments on classifier combination without ensemble selection in the next section.

4   Experiments on Fusion Functions

To ensure that the PFM is useful for combining classifiers, we tested it on problems extracted from a UCI machine learning repository. There are several requirements for the selection of pattern recognition problems. First, the databases must have a large feature dimension for the Random Subspace method. Second, to avoid the dimensional curse during training, each database must have sufficient samples of its feature dimension. Third, to avoid identical samples being trained in Random Subspace, only databases without symbolic features are used. Fourth, to simplify the problem, we do not use databases with missing features. In accordance with the requirements listed above, we carried out our experiments on 7 databases selected from the UCI data repository (see Table 1). Among available samples, in general, 50% are used as a training data set, and 50% are used as a test data set, except for the Image Segmentation dataset, whose training data set and test data set have been defined on UCI data repository. Of the training data set, 70% are used for classifier training and 30% are used for validation. Ensemble-training (including BKS, NB and PFM) used the entire available training data set. The cardinality of Random Subspace is set under the condition that all classifiers have recognition rates more than 50%.

Table 1. UCI data for ensembles of classifiers

Database	Classes	Training Samples	Test Samples	Features	Random Subspace Cardinality
Ionosphere	2	175	175	34	20
Liver-Disorders	2	172	172	6	4
Pima-Diabetes	2	384	384	8	4
Wisconsin Breast-Cancer	2	284	284	30	5
Wine	3	88	88	13	6
Image Segmentation	7	210	2100	19	4
Letter Recognition	26	10000	10000	16	12

The three different classification algorithms used in our experiments are K-Nearest Neighbors Classifiers (KNN), Parzen Windows Classifiers (PWC) and Quadratic Discriminant Classifiers (QDC) [2]. For each of 7 databases and for each of 3 classification algorithms, 10 classifiers were generated as the pool of classifiers. Among these, each classifier has a 50% chance of being selected from this pool to construct ensembles, ensembles were thus constructed by different numbers of classifiers, and at least three classifiers are required for an ensemble. As a result, all ensembles were constructed from $3 \sim 8$ classifiers. 30 ensembles had been generated for each database, for each ensemble generation method and for each classification algorithm. Note that each ensemble can have different number of classifiers. In total, we evaluated $30 \times 7 \times 3 = 630$ ensembles. We then combined these ensembles with 5 different fusion functions (Table $2 \sim 4$).

In previous studies, BKS has been shown to be comparatively accurate when an ensemble of 3 classifiers is involved [14], but the BKS could be outperformed by most of the other fusion functions when more classifiers are involved [9]. In our study, the BKS apparently performs very well in 2- and 3-class problems. But when the class dimension is larger than 6, due to huge data size and limited computer memory we could not construct the BKS table.

We also observe that PFM-MAJ offers quite stable performance, in general better than that offered by the simple MAJ rule. The t-statistic test shows that the significance level is at 2.78%, so there is little chance for simple MAJ to perform as well as PFM-MAJ. Interestingly, we note that the difference in performance between PFM-MAJ and simple MAJ is somehow related to classifier diversity. It is not difficult to understand

Table 2. Comparison of recognition rates of different fusion functions with Random Subspace on UCI machine learning problems with KNN classifiers. All numbers are in percents (%), the standard variances are indicated in parenthesis.

Fusion Functions →	MAJ	NB	BKS	PFM -MAJ	PFM -SUM
Ionosphere	78.28 (0.03)	82.04 (0.01)	**92.44 (-)**	80.58 (0.02)	77.80 (0.02)
Liver-Disorders	68.68 (0.04)	68.08 (0.07)	**82.81 (0.03)**	69.21 (0.06)	69.07 (0.05)
Pima-Diabetes	96.52 (0.01)	97.27 (-)	95.35 (0.01)	**97.40 (-)**	96.15 (0.01)
Wisconsin Breast-Cancer	92.51 (0.01)	92.37 (0.01)	89.51 (0.06)	**93.12 (0.01)**	92.44 (0.01)
Wine	76.82 (0.16)	84.47 (0.31)	**92.73 (0.20)**	85.27 (0.33)	84.81(0.23)
Image Segmentation	77.10 (0.14)	**87.43 (0.08)**	-	86.02 (0.15)	82.28 (0.15)
Letter Recogntion	81.64 (0.03)	89.31 (0.04)	-	**89.38 (0.02)**	83.51 (0.02)

Table 3. Comparison of recognition rates of different fusion functions with Random Subspace on UCI machine learning problems with PARZEN classifiers. All numbers are in percents (%), the standard variances are indicated in parenthesis.

Fusion Functions →	MAJ	NB	BKS	PFM -MAJ	PFM -SUM
Ionosphere	79.79 (0.01)	80.11 (0.01)	**93.76 (-)**	82.54 (0.02)	79.23 (0.01)
Liver-Disorders	62.89 (0.06)	51.50 (0.15)	**81.60 (0.02)**	65.23 (0.03)	64.61 (0.02)
Pima-Diabetes	71.45 (0.05)	34.90 (-)	**78.64 (0.07)**	72.59 (0.04)	70.03 (0.05)
Wisconsin Breast-Cancer	92.25 (-)	92.16 (-)	90.85 (0.04)	**92.64 (-)**	92.29 (0.01)
Wine	80.72 (0.26)	87.08 (0.36)	**92.54 (0.17)**	87.80 (0.39)	84.96 (0.28)
Image Segmentation	77.29 (0.26)	84.15 (0.41)	-	**85.21 (0.20)**	82.28 (0.19)
Letter Recogntion	88.41 (0.02)	**93.81 (0.03)**	-	93.72 (0.01)	89.43 (0.01)

Table 4. Comparison of recognition rates of different fusion functions with Random Subspace on UCI machine learning problems with QDC classifiers. All numbers are in percents (%), the standard variances are indicated in parenthesis.

Fusion Functions →	MAJ	NB	BKS	PFM -MAJ	PFM -SUM
Ionosphere	86.11 (0.10)	82.28 (0.03)	**92.14 (0.01)**	86.16 (0.03)	86.24 (0.02)
Liver-Disorders	60.12 (0.03)	50.00 (-)	**79.23 (0.01)**	61.39 (0.05)	61.20 (0.04)
Pima-Diabetes	68.84 (0.03)	48.52 (2.89)	**79.06 (0.04)**	71.02 (0.08)	68.71 (0.04)
Wisconsin Breast-Cancer	95.87 (0.01)	96.51 (0.01)	96.15 (0.01)	**96.76 (0.01)**	95.88 (0.01)
Wine	95.72 (0.02)	98.33 (0.01)	**99.02 (0.01)**	97.84 (0.01)	96.70 (0.02)
Image Segmentation	73.33 (1.13)	22.76 (8.17)	-	**84.70 (0.23)**	84.37 (0.16)
Letter Recogntion	82.66 (0.02)	89.05 (0.04)	-	**90.14 (0.01)**	83.73 (0.01)

that this property is in some way influenced by the types of classifiers used in experiments, because different classification algorithms lead to different levels of diversity among classifiers.

5   Discussion

For EoCs, the ideal is to obtain the probability $P(l|c(1), \cdots, c(i), \cdots, c(L), x)$ for the whole data set X, where l is the possible class label, and $c(1), \cdots, c(i), \cdots, c(L)$

are decisions of individual classifiers $f(1), \cdots, f(i), \cdots, f(L)$ respectively. But, in reality, this approach might not work owing to the limitation with respect to the number of samples. Instead of estimating $P(l|c(1), \cdots, c(i), \cdots, c(L), x)$, the proposed PFM deals with the probability $P(l|c(i), c(j), x)$ from pairwise confusion matrices on an evaluated class l, and thus is much more applicable, while at the same time taking into account classifier interaction.

When no class probability outputs are provided, most simple fusion functions, such as MAX, MIN, SUM and PRO, cannot be applied. The only available simple fusion function is the simple MAJ. For trained fusion functions, DT requires the class probability outputs from classifiers, and to deal with a problem involving crisp class label outputs, only NB or BKS, WER are applicable. However, for high-class dimension problems and large-size ensembles, there is no way to use BKS or WER. On all selected UCI machine learning problems, PFM-MAJ almost always outperforms simple MAJ as a fusion function for combining classifiers. Moreover, the difference in performance between PFM-MAJ and simple MAJ is to some extent correlated with the diversity of ensembles, especially when KNN is used in Random Subspace.

6   Conclusion

In this paper, we use pairwise fusion matrix for classifier combination, which transforms crisp class label outputs into class probability outputs and thus takes into account the interaction of classifiers in a pairwise manner. To conclude, the proposed method has some significant advantages:

1. PFM offers a somewhat performance boosting for ensembles.
2. PFM can apply on all kinds of existent fusion functions.
3. Because of its pairwise nature, it does not need too many samples for training compared with BKS or WER.

The experiment reveals that the performance of PFM is promising. Intuitively, PFM can also be used for other trained fusion functions, such as NB or DT. This will require another training data set, but we are interested in investigating the potential use of PFM in improving the performance of trained fusion functions.

The key element that makes an ensemble of classifier pairs outperform an EoC is that the use of PFM takes the interaction into consideration. The pairwise manner may still be sub-optimal, but, if the class dimension is low and we have few classifiers and a large number of samples, PFM can be upgraded to the third degree, i.e. we can obtain the probabilities of any class label l by calculating $P(l|c(i), c(j), c(h), x)$ based on three classifier outputs $c(i), c(j), c(h)$. This would require the construction of 4-dimensional confusion matrices and allow us to interpret the interaction of three classifiers at the same time. Another possible improvement scheme would be the use of PFM-MAJ as an objective function for ensemble selection. In the same way that simple MAJ is used for ensemble selection (i.e. MVE) and for classifier combination, one can also apply PFM-MAJ for both ensemble selection and classifier combination.

Given that this exploratory work has been accomplished evaluating millions of ensembles, but with a restricted number of classification algorithms, and in a limited number of problems, it will be advisable to carry out more experiments on classifier combination as well as ensemble selection, with more pattern recognition problems and more classification methods.

Acknowledgment

This work was supported in part by grant OGP0106456 to Robert Sabourin from the NSERC of Canada.

References

1. R. P. W. Duin, "The Combining Classifier: To Train or Not to Train?" *16th International Conference on Pattern Recognition (ICPR)*, vol. 2, pp. 20765, 2002
2. R.P.W. Duin, "Pattern Recognition Toolbox for Matlab 5.0+," available free at: ftp://ftp.ph.tn.tudelft.nl/pub/bob/prtools
3. G. Giacinto and F. Roli, "Design of effective neural network ensembles for image classification purposes," *Image and Vision Computing*, vol. 19, no. 9-10, pp. 699-707, 2001
4. L. K. Hansen, C. Liisberg and P. Salamon, "The error-reject tradeoff," *Open Systems and Information Dynamics*, vol. 4, pp. 159-184, 1997
5. T. K. Ho, "The random space method for constructing decision forests," *IEEE Transactions on Pattern Analysis and Machine Intelligence*, vol. 20, no. 8, pp. 832-844, 1998
6. Y. S. Huang and C.Y. Suen, "A method of combining multiple experts for the recognition of unconstrained handwritten numerals," *IEEE Transactions on Pattern Analysis and Machine Intelligence*, vol. 17, pp. 90-93, 1995
7. J. Kittler and F. M. Alkoot, "Relationship of Sum and Vote Fusion Strategies," *Multiple Classifier Systems (MCS)*, pp. 339-348, 2001
8. J. Kittler, M. Hatef, R. Duin and J. Matas, "On Combining Classifiers," *IEEE Transactions on Pattern Analysis and Machine Intelligence*, vol. 20, no. 3, pp. 226–239, 1998
9. L.I. Kuncheva, J.C. Bezdek and R.P.W. Duin, "Decision templates for multiple classifier fusion: an experimental comparison," *Pattern Recognition*, vol. 34, no. 2, pp. 299-314, 2001
10. L. I. Kuncheva and C. J. Whitaker, "Measures of Diversity in Classifier Ensembles and Their Relationship with the Ensemble Accuracy," *Machine Learning*, vol. 51, no. 2, pp. 181-207, 2003
11. S. Raudys, "Experts' boasting in trainable fusion rules," *IEEE Transactions on Pattern Analysis and Machine Intelligence*, vol. 25, no. 9, pp. 1178 - 1182, 2003
12. D. Ruta and B. Gabrys, "Analysis of the Correlation between Majority Voting Error and the Diversity Measures in Multiple Classifier Systems," *In Proceedings of the 4th International Symposium on Soft Computing*, 2001
13. D. Ruta and B. Gabrys, "Classifier Selection for Majority Voting," *International Journal of Information Fusion*, pp. 63-81, 2005
14. C. A. Shipp and L.I. Kuncheva, "Relationships between combination methods and measures of diversity in combining classifiers," *International Journal of Information Fusion*, vol.3, no. 2, pp. 135-148, 2002
15. D. M. J. Tax, M. Van Breukelen, R. P. W. Duin and J. Kittler, "Combining Multiple Classifiers by Averaging or by Multiplying," *Pattern Recognition*, vol.33, no. 9, pp.1475-1485, 2000
16. K. Turner and J. Ghosh, "Error Correlation and Error Reduction in Ensemble Classifiers," *Connection Science*, vol. 8, no. 3-4, pp. 385-404, 1996

17. K. D. Wernecke, "A coupling procedure for discrimination of mixed data," *Biometrics*, vol. 48, pp. 97-506, 1992

18. L. Xu, A. Krzyzak and C. Y. Suen, "Methods of combining multiple classifiers and their applications to handwriting recognition," *IEEE Transactions on Systems, Man and Cybernetics*, vol. 22, no. 3, pp. 418-435, 1992

19. H. Zouari, L. Heutte, Y. Lecourtier and A. Alimi, "Building Diverse Classifier Outputs to Evaluate the Behavior of Combination Methods: the Case of Two Classifiers," *Multiple Classifier Systems (MCS)*, pp. 273-282, 2004

Modelling Multiple-Classifier Relationships Using Bayesian Belief Networks

Samuel Chindaro, Konstantinos Sirlantzis, and Michael Fairhurst

Department of Electronics, University of Kent, Canterbury, Kent CT2 7NT, UK
{S.Chindaro,K.Sirlantzis,M.C.Fairhurst}@kent.ac.uk

Abstract. Because of the lack of a clear guideline or technique for selecting classifiers which maximise diversity and accuracy, the development of techniques for analysing classifier relationships and methods for generating good constituent classifiers remains an important research direction. In this paper we propose a framework based on the Bayesian Belief Networks (BBN) approach to classification. In the proposed approach the multiple-classifier system is conceived at a meta-level and the relationships between individual classifiers are abstracted using Bayesian structural learning methods. We show that relationships revealed by the BBN structures are supported by standard correlation and diversity measures. We use the dependency properties obtained by the learned Bayesian structure to illustrate that BBNs can be used to explore classifier relationships, and for classifier selection.

Keywords: Multiple Classifier Systems, Bayesian Belief Networks, Diversity.

1 Introduction

Theoretical and experimental results have established that to benefit from the use of ensemble systems constituent classifiers must be diverse. This has proven to be a difficult task as the relationship between combiners' accuracy and diversity has not been clearly established, and have been found to be weak [1]. However correlation and diversity properties in ensemble systems remains an area of importance, as there is no benefit in combining classifiers which make similar errors. Consequently, proper selection of constituent classifiers to use in an ensemble remains an important determinant of the overall performance of the ensemble. Classifier selection can be done by exhaustive search, using the performance of the ensemble as a target, but this is computationally intensive with an increasing number of constituent classifiers. Roli et al [2]have put forward the idea of 'overproduce and choose' for selecting classifiers. Genetic Algorithms have been used in [3, 4] for selecting classifiers and feature subsets. A number of measures have been put forward for quantifying the relationships between classifiers and using it as a measure of fitness for ensemble purposes. In [1] a number of diversity measures are presented, but their relationship with ensemble performance is not clearly established. There have also been proposal for explicitly using diversity for selecting classifier ensembles and for classifier selection in a meta-learning system [5]. A simulation experiment is presented in [6] for classifier selection using correlation measures.

M. Haindl, J. Kittler, and F. Roli (Eds.): MCS 2007, LNCS 4472, pp. 312–321, 2007.

Because of the lack of a clear guideline or technique for selecting classifiers which maximise diversity and accuracy, the development of techniques for analysing classifier relationships and methods for generating good constituent classifiers remains an important research direction. The problem of exploring and utilizing the relationship amongst classifier teams, therefore, remains fundamental. Thus we believe it is important to perform a structured, systematically designed investigation of these relationships. In this paper we propose a framework based on the Bayesian Belief Networks (BBN) approach to classification. It has been suggested [7] that a meta-framework seems to be needed to describe multi-classifier systems and characterize their properties. The Bayesian theory can be utilized to accommodate such ideas as well as offer graphical manipulation and illustration of the concepts. In the proposed approach the multiple-classifier system is conceived at a meta-level and the relationships between individual classifiers are abstracted. Because the conditional probability distribution can be calculated from the joint probability distribution, a Bayesian network consisting of a class variable and feature variables is readily applicable to the classification tasks, as demonstrated in [8, 9] .

The Bayesian network classifier [9] is distinguished from other classification methods by its ability to portray the probabilistic relationships between class and feature variables via a comprehensible graphical format [10]. In particular, key classifiers in the ensemble can easily be discriminated from redundant ones based on the network structure. Such a property is useful in the analysis of ensemble systems, where not only classification performance but also an understanding of the process by which the final decision is inferred is important. This will enable exploratory analysis for the development of more effective ensemble systems. Knowledge of these relationships allows us to make predictions in the presence of interventions; for example the effect of losing one data-source or classifier in an ensemble.

This paper explores the structural relationships of classifiers in a multiple-classifier architecture using Bayesian structural learning methods. We present experiments which produce graphical illustrations of the classifier relationships implied by various combination techniques. We show that relationships revealed by the BBN structures are supported by standard correlation and diversity measures. We use the dependency/independence properties obtained by the learned Bayesian structure to illustrate that BBNs can be used to explore classifier relationships. In the next section we give a summary of BBNs. This is followed by a description of the structural learning methods used, the composite classifiers and the database. This is followed by a description of the experimental work carried out on the use of BNs in modelling standard classifier combinations. The next section describes the experimental work we carried out on assessing the relationship between BBN structures and diversity. We then present a section on classifier selection using BBNs. Finally a discussion and a conclusion are presented.

2   Bayesian Belief Networks

Bayesian Belief Networks [9, 10] constitute a powerful probabilistic framework for reasoning under uncertainty. A Bayesian belief network structure consists a Directed Acyclic Graph (DAG) and nodes which represent domain variables and arcs between the nodes representing probabilistic dependency assumptions that must hold between the random variables. A variable in the Bayesian belief network structure may be continuous or discrete. In this paper, the experiments and results presented are focused on discrete variables. The key feature of belief networks is their explicit representation of the conditional independence among events. The concept makes a factorization of the probability distribution of the n-dimensional random variable $(X_1, ..., X_n)$ possible. The joint probability of any particular instantiation of all n variables in a belief network can be calculated as:

$$p(x_1..., x_n) = \prod_{i=1}^{n} p(x_i \mid pa(x_i)) \tag{1}$$

Where each x_i represents an instantiated variable and $pa(x_i)$ an instantiation of the parents of x_i. A BN is described by specifying its probability distribution. This is done by specifying the prior probability of all root nodes (nodes without predecessor or parents), and conditional probabilities for all the other nodes given all possible combinations of direct predecessors. It is however possible to learn all these from the data, this is discussed in the next section.

3 Structural Learning

Many heuristic methods have been proposed to determine the structure of a Bayesian network. A number of BN structural learning algorithms have been developed. One approach uses heuristic search method to construct a model and evaluates it using a scoring method. This process continues until the score of the new model is not significantly better than the old one. Different scoring criteria have been applied in these algorithms, such as, Bayesian scoring method [11], entropy based method [12], and minimum description length method [13]. The other category of algorithms constructs Bayesian networks by analyzing dependency relationships among nodes [14, 15]. The dependency relationships are measured by using some kind of conditional independence test. Successful examples of the later are the K2 [11] and MWST [16] algorithms.

The K2 algorithm [11] is a greedy search algorithm. Initially each node has no parents. It then adds incrementally that parent whose addition most increases the score of the resulting structure. When the addition of no single parent can increase the score, it stops adding parents to the node. The principle of the MWST algorithm [16] is rather different. This algorithm determines the best tree that links all the variables.). The aim is to find an optimal solution, but in a space limited to trees. The algorithm associates a weight (mutual information or BIC score) with each edge.

4 Composite Classifiers and Database Forms

In selecting multiple classifiers, the goal is to obtain diversity in their prediction given by each individual classifier, as well as good levels of accuracy [1]. In this study we used a set of five different classifiers from the PRTools Matlab toolbox [17]. We used a linear classifier built on the Karhunen-Loeve expansion of the common covariance matrix, a Parzen density based classifier, the nearest mean classifier, and two k-nearest neighbour classifiers (3 and 5 nearest neighbours). A description of each of the classifiers and how to apply them using Matlab and the PRTools can be found with the PRTools documentation. We deliberately chose k-nearest neighbour classifiers with varying parameters for our study in order to examine the effects of having potentially correlated classifiers. In this paper the classifiers are numbered as follows: nearest mean classifier (1), Parzen density classifier (2), k-nearest neighbour classifier with 3 neighbours (3), linear classifier built on the Karhunen-Loeve expansion of the covariance matrix (4) and k-nearest neighbour classifier (5 neighbours) (5).

The experiments here were carried out using 10 datasets from UCI repository [18].

Table 1. Characteristics of the datsets used in the study

Dataset	Samples	Classes	Dim
Vehicles (VH)	846	4	18
Wine (WN)	178	3	13
Iris (IR)	150	3	4
Heart (HRT)	270	2	13
Ionosphere (ION)	351	2	34
Liver (LV)	345	2	6
Winscon-breast-cancer (WDB)	569	2	30
Digits(Morphological) (DIGM)	1000	10	47
Digits(Zernike) (DIGM)	1000	10	6
Australian credit (AUS)	690	2	14

5 Modelling Classifier Relationships in Ensembles Using BBN

Our aim is to find out what are the implied relationships between the classifiers given the output obtained by the individual classifiers in the scheme and combination rule, what are the implied relationships between the classifiers? To do this, each of the nodes (variables) is assigned the outputs obtained from one classifier in the ensemble and the root node is assigned the output corresponding to the final decision in each case using one of the combination rules. The children nodes in the graphs (Fig. 1) correspond to the outputs of the individual constituent classifiers. The structure is first induced using the true output labels (groundtruth) of the training data. The same individual outputs are then used as the children nodes with the root node being the output obtained by using the different combination rules (product, mean, median and majority). The structural learning algorithms then induces a BBN structure based on the distribution of the constituent classifier outputs, and the corresponding class decision based on the groundtruth or a particular combination method.

The resulting DAGs (shown in Figs 1 and 2) admit different classifier dependencies for different combination rules. While this is not in itself surprising, the BBN structures give us an insight in the different ways the same classifier relationships are exploited by different combination methods. After a BBN structure is obtained using different classifier and combination outputs for a part of the data retained for training, the BBN can be tested (produce classifier decisions) using the outputs of the individual classifiers on a separate test set. That is the root node is assigned a class label (decision) based on the structure implied relationships of its children nodes values. In both datasets presented in Figure 2, the product and mean combination rules result in the same classifier dependency structure, similarly the pair of the median and majority rule. In both cases when these networks are tested using the same dataset, with the combination rules output as targets, the errors obtained are exactly the same.

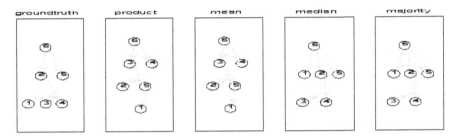

Fig. 1. Classifier relationships modeled by BBNs for different combination rules for the IRIS dataset

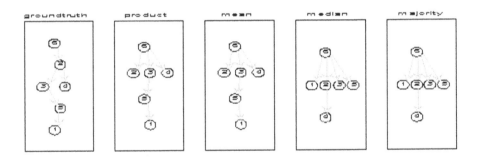

Fig. 2. Classifier relationships modeled by BBNs for different combination rules for the HRT dataset

6   Bayesian Networks Modelling and Diversity

Despite the existence of different ways of combining classifiers, both theoretical and empirical approaches have established that the vital ingredient for constructing a successful ensemble is the incorporation of team members which are both accurate and do not make similar errors (i.e. are diverse in their predictions). It is therefore not surprising that in order to construct more accurate ensembles, more research is now focusing on measures of diversity, similarities or dependencies within classifier teams[1, 5, 19] Consequently a number of diversity measures have been proposed and studied [1].The range of measures employed in ensemble analysis, even though targeting some form of diversity quantification, are based on different concepts. Basic differences arise from the nature of the measurement, where some are pair-wise measures (between classifier pairs), whilst others are non-pairwise (overall measures among all base classifiers).

The Bayesian network framework, described previously, when used in a multiple-classifier set-up allow us to explore the dependencies between different classifiers. They networks give an insight into these dependencies but do not quantify the extent of these. This part of our study is therefore aimed at exploring the relationship between some diversity measures and the dependencies as modelled by the Bayesian networks. Our study focused on calculating pair-wise measures between the different possible pairs of the multiple-classifier team. The aim was to examine if there were any correlation between the pair-wise diversity values obtained using these measures and the inter-classifier dependencies as modelled by the BBNs.

6.1 Pairwise Diversity Measures

In the experiments, we have included four measures: Yule's Q statistic [20], the correlation coefficient [21] the disagreement measure [22] and the double fault measure [23]. In our experiments we used all the 10 pairwise combinations possible with the 5 classifiers and calculated the corresponding diversities. We then compared the results with the relationships depicted by the BBNs. Our aim was to see if the relationships depicted by the BBNs were reflected on the measures of diversity; for example, if diversity measure 'A' shows classifier 1 to be correlated with classifier 2, is this reflected by the dependency structure of the BBN? We illustrate our results using BBN structures learnt using the MWST_BIC structural learning algorithm on eight of the datasets using the 'groundtruth' as the root node. For each dataset the dependent classifiers as identified by the BBNs were identified as:

VH(C15,C24,C35); **WN**(C14,C15,C23,C24); **IRIS**(C15,C24,C35); **HRT**(C15,C23,C24,C35); **ION**(C15,C35);**LV**(C13,C15); **WDBC**(C15,C35); **DIGM**(C15,C24,C35); **DIGZ**(C14,C24,C35); **AUST**(C15,C24,C35).

In the listing above, for example, C15 means classifier 1 and 5 were shown to have some dependency (had arcs linking the two) on the graph etc. for each corresponding dataset.

Figures 3 illustrate the Q statistic diversity measures for each pair of classifiers for each of the datasets. For example, for Dataset IRIS has pairs C15, C24 and C35 are dependent pairs on the DAG. Our hypothesis is that if the graphical interpretation of the multiple-classifier structure is consistent with the diversity measure, these pairs should be shown to be the least diverse, with those not dependant being the least diverse according to the measure. The Q statistic has the respective values as 0.898, 1.000 and 1.000 respectively which shows these pairs are not diverse at all, and has values of -1 for other pairs , meaning these pairs are highly diverse. In this case the dependences depicted by the DAG are consistent with the Q-statistic measure.

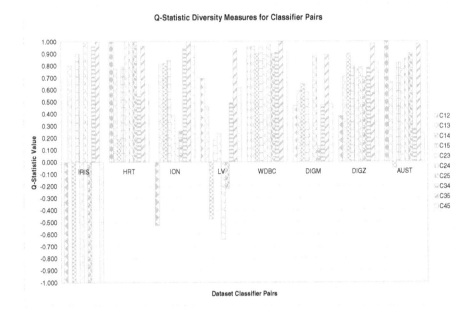

Fig. 3. Q –statistic diversity measures for different classifier pairs for each of the datasets

In few cases, the DAG dependent pairs have less diversity according to the measures, than the DAG non-dependent pairs. These are however exceptions rather than the norm in the cases we considered. A similar pattern was observed in the majority of cases for the other datasets and diversity measures, and illustrations of these have thus been omitted here for brevity. These results therefore illustrate that the learned DAGs do capture and can be used to explore the diversity in the participant classifiers.

7   Classifier Selection Using Bayesian Models

The majority of multiple classifier systems are based on the assumption that different classifiers make "independent" errors [2, 24]. However, in real pattern recognition applications, it is difficult to design a set of classifiers that should satisfy such an assumption. However the use of BNs enables us to explore the relationships between classifiers and as such it can be used to pursue the idea of selecting 'independent' classifiers. Having established that the dependencies depicted in DAGs are related to some diversity measures, the next step was to see if this could be exploited to select classifiers which are not dependent (diverse), and assess their performance.

In 5-fold experiments, the MWST_BIC structural learning algorithm was used to obtain DAGs for each run. Each DAG was then pruned of all children, leaving only nodes which were independent and were children of the root (class) node. Figure 7 below illustrates an example of how this was done. If all classifiers were descendants of one classifier, the result for that classifier was chosen as the final result (for example Figure4.b). The remaining nodes (classifiers) were then selected and used in standard combination algorithms, namely, the product, mean, median and majority rules. These results were then compared to the use of the same combination rules using the whole set of classifiers. The results are shown in Table 2.

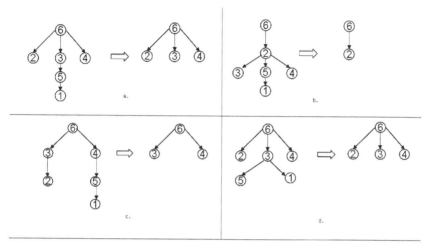

Fig. 4. Example of dependency-based multiple classifier structure pruning

Table 2. Classification error results obtained using all classifiers (AC) and selected classifiers (SC) with the root node being the output of each combination method

Dataset	Product		Mean		Median		Majority	
	AC	SC	AC	SC	AC	SC	AC	SC
VH	0.28±0.021	0.30±0.016	0.27±0.010	0.30±0.020	0.30±0.021	0.30±0.033	0.33±0.001	0.33±0.001
WN	0.01±0.003	0.01±0.021	0.02±0.003	0.02±0.006	0.17±0.004	0.02±0.004	0.18±0.001	0.05±0.001
IRIS	0.02±0.050	0.03±0.012	0.02±0.001	0.02±0.005	0.02±0.002	0.03±0.007	0.02±0.010	0.02±0.011
HRT	0.22±0.010	0.21±0.012	0.22±0.020	0.21±0.001	0.28±0.003	0.22±0.008	0.28±0.002	0.23±0.001
ION	0.05±0.026	0.05±0.004	0.09±0.006	0.09±0.005	0.13±0.115	0.10±0.102	0.13±0.002	0.10±0.002
LV	0.32±0.010	0.32±0.021	0.32±0.01	0.34±0.023	0.31±0.004	0.35±0.008	0.31±0.004	0.37±0.005
WDBC	0.04±0.002	0.05±0.006	0.04±0.009	0.04±0.007	0.05±0.006	0.05±0.061	0.05±0.041	0.05±0.032
DIGM	0.28±0.101	0.24±0.051	0.28±0.004	0.31±0.005	0.34±0.014	0.31±0.010	0.40±0.017	0.43±0.017
DIGZ	0.18±0.012	0.18±0.007	0.18±0.002	0.18±0.010	0.18±0.018	0.18±0.010	0.19±0.01	0.19±0.01
AUST	0.17±0.024	0.17±0.023	0.18±0.007	0.17±0.011	0.24±0.014	0.19±0.001	0.23±0.034	0.20±0.015

From the results it was observed that in a significant number of cases (at least 7/10 datasets, and at most 8/10 datsets), for each combination method considered, the performance of the combiners either improved, or did not change when a subset of classifiers chosen based on the proposed BN-based classifier selection method was used in the combination. This is shown by the highlighted results in Table 2. In such cases therefore, the BN-based selection method has successfully eliminated redundant classifiers, without deterioration in performance. In some cases, the performance of the combiners consisting the classifiers selected using the proposed selection method was not as good as that of the original combiner comprising all classifiers, and we believe there is scope for further investigations of the reason underpinning these observations

8 Conclusions

Combining different classifiers is an area of great interest in pattern recognition. In general, it is difficult to quantify the improvement in performance and robustness without a specific task and without specific classifiers at hand. In this paper we have carried out experiments using 10 benchmark datasets and applied BNs for exploring the relationships between these classifiers. We have also used standard diversity measures to analyse these relationships and established that the dependences depicted by the resulting BNs were related to some diversity measures. Having established this, the knowledge was then used in classifier selection for use with standard combiners. From the results it was observed that in at least 70% of the cases the performance of the combiners improved or remained the same when the classifiers chosen using the BN-based classifier selection method. This implies that a study in this direction can make a significant contribution in ensemble classifier selection.

The study of the relationships between classifier in ensemble systems is important for the design of more efficient classifiers. The search for techniques to explicitly use these relationships (for example using diversity) to improve the performance is on-going. In this paper we have shown that Bayesian Theory in the form of Bayesian Networks framework, can become a useful tool to implement such ideas, as well as offering, means for the graphical manipulation and illustration of these relationships.

Acknowledgements. We acknowledge the support of the UK Engineering and Physical Sciences Research Council (EPSRC) in carrying out this research.

References

1. Kuncheva, L.I. and C.J. Whitaker, Measures of Diversity in Classifier Ensembles and Their Relationship with the Ensemble Accuracy. Machine Learning, 2003. 51(2): p. 181-207.
2. Roli, F., G. Giacinto, and G. Vernazza. Methods for designing multiple classifier systems. in Proc. Second International Workshop on Multiple Classifier Systems. 2001. Cambridge, UK.: Springer-Verlag.
3. Yang, J. and V. Honavar. Feature subset selection using a genetic algorithm in Genetic Programming 1997: Proceedings of the Second Annual Conference. 1997. San Mateo, CA.
4. Stefano, C.D. and A. Marcelli. Exploiting Reliability for Dynamic Selection of Classifiers by Means of Genetic Algorithms. in Proceedings of the Seventh International Conference on Document Analysis and Recognition (ICDAR 2003. 2003.

5. Chindaro, S., K. Sirlantzis, and M.C. Fairhurst. Analysis and Modelling of Diversity Contribution to Ensemble-Based Texture Recognition Performance. in Proceedings of the 6th International Workshop on Multiple Classifier Systems, MCS 2005. 2005. Seaside, California, USA: LNCS 3541.

6. Kuncheva, L. and R. Kountch, Generating classifier outputs of fixed accuracy and diversity. Pattern Recognition Letters, 2002. 23: p. 593--600.

7. Ho, T.K., Multiple Classifier Combination: Lessons and Next Steps. Hybrid Methods in Pattern Recognition; World Scientific, 2002: p. 171-198.

8. Pavlovic, V., A. Garg, and S. Kasif, A Bayesian Framework for Combining Gene Predictions. Biinformatics, 2002. 1: p. 19-27.

9. Friedman, N., D. Geiger, and M. Goldszmidt, Bayesian network classifiers. Machine Learning 1997(29): p. 131--163.

10. Jordan, M.I., Learning Graphical Models. 1996, Dordrecht, The Netherlands: Kluwer Academic.

11. Cooper., G.F. and E. Herskovits, A Bayesian Method for the induction of probabilistic networks from data. Machine Learning, 1992. 9: p. 309-347.

12. Herskovits, E.H., Computer-based probabilistic network construction. Medical information sciences, , Doctoral dissertation., 1991. Stanford University, Stanford, CA.

13. Suzuki, J. Learning Bayesian belief networks based on the MDL principle: An efficient algorithm using the branch and bound technique. in Proceedings of the international conference on machine learning, , 1996. 1996. Bally, Italy.

14. R.M. Fung, R.M. and S.L. Crawford. Constructor: a system for the induction of probabilistic models. . in Proceedings of AAAI Boston, MA.: MIT Press.

15. Srinivas, S., S. Russell, and A. Agogino. Automated construction of sparse Bayesian networks from unstructured probabilistic models and domain information. in Uncertainty in artificial intelligence 5. 1990. Amsterdam: North-Holland.

16. Heckerman, D., D. Geiger, and D.Chickering, Learning Bayesian networks: The combination of knowledge and statistical data. . Machine Learning, 1995. 20: p. 197--243.

17. Duin, R.P.W., et al., PRTools 4, "A Matlab Toolbox for Pattern Recognition", Delft University of Technology. 2004.

18. UCI: Repository of machine learning databases, [http:// www. ics.uci. edu/~mlearn/ MLRepository.html],. University of California, Irvine, Dept. of Inform. and Comp. Sc., 1998.

19. Sirlantzis, K., S. Hoque, and M.C. Fairhurst. Classifier Diversity Estimation in a Multiclassifier Face Recognition System based on Binary Feature Quantisation. in Proceedings of the 4th International Conference on Recent Advances in Soft Computing (RASC 2002). 2002. Nottingham, UK.

20. Yule, G., On the association of attributes in statistics. Phil. Tansaction, 1900. A(194): p. 257-319.

21. Sneath, P. and R. Sokal, Numerical Taxonomy. 1973: W.H. Freeman and Company.

22. Ho, T.K., The Random Subspace Method for Constructing Decision Forests. IEEE Trans on Pattern Analysis and Machine Intelligence, 1998. 20(8): p. 832-844.

23. Giacinto, G. and F. Roli, Design of effective neural network ensembles for image classification processes. Image and Vision Computing Journal, 2001. 19(9/10): p. 699-707.

24. Dymitr Ruta, B.G. New Measure of Classifier Dependency in Multiple Classifier Systems in Multiple Classifier Systems: Third International Workshop, MCS 2002. Cagliari, Ital: Springer Berlin / Heidelberg.

Classifier Combining Rules Under Independence Assumptions*

Shoushan Li and Chengqing Zong

National Laboratory of Pattern Recognition, Institute of Automation, Chinese Academy of
Sciences, Beijing 100080, China
{sshanli,cqzong}@nlpr.ia.ac.cn

Abstract. Classifier combining rules are designed for the fusion of the results
from the component classifiers in a multiple classifier system. In this paper, we
firstly propose a theoretical explanation of one important classifier combining
rule, the sum rule, adopting the Bayes viewpoint under some independence
assumptions. Our explanation is more general than what did in the existed
previous by Kittler *et al.* [1]. Then, we present a new combining rule, named
SumPro rule, which combines the sum rule with the product rule in a weighted
average way. The weights for combining the two rules are tuned according to
the development data using a genetic algorithm. The experimental evaluation
and comparison among some combining rules are reported, which are done on a
biometric authentication set. The results show that the SumPro rule takes a
distinct advantage over both the sum rule and the product rule. Moreover, this
new rule gradually outperforms the other popular trained combining rules when
the classifier number increases.

Keywords: Pattern Classification, Multiple Classifier System, Combining
Rules.

1 Introduction

Combining multiple classifiers is a learning method where a collection of a finite
number of classifiers is trained for the same classification task. Over the past years,
this method has been considered as a more practical and effective solution for many
recognition problems than using one individual classifier [1] [2].

An important issue in combining classifiers is that of the combining rules which
are designed to fuse the results from the component classifiers. Generally, the
combining rules are usually categorized into two categories: fixed rules and trained
rules. The fixed rules combine the classification results in some fixed mode
independent of the application tasks, notably the sum rule and the product rule [1].
And the trained rules combine the results in a trained way, such as weighted sum rule
[3], Behavior-Knowledge Space algorithm [4], Decision Template method [5] and
Dempster-Shafer (DS) [2] [6] method. Some related experimental studies contribute

---

* This work has been partially funded by the Natural Science Foundation of China under Grant
Nos. 60575043 and 60121302.

M. Haindl, J. Kittler, and F. Roli (Eds.): MCS 2007, LNCS 4472, pp. 322–332, 2007.
© Springer-Verlag Berlin Heidelberg 2007

to the comparison between these two kinds of methods [7] [8]. Given their extensive experimental results, it is still difficult to draw a consistent conclusion about which kind or which particular rule performs better than the others. The difficulty mainly lies on the lack of explicit theoretical analysis of these rules. Therefore, some theoretical studies on these rules appear with the objective to explain why some combination methods work better and in what cases they perform better than the others. One important work of Kittler *et al.* [1] develops a common theoretical framework based on the different feature sets, where many fixed combining rules such as the product rule, sum rule, min rule, max rule and vote rule are derived. They report that the sum rule outperforms the other rules because of its resilience to estimation errors.

Although it is known that the fixed rules are obtained under strong assumptions, these assumptions still remain unclear. Furthermore, the sum rule takes favorable position in many experimental results, while the assumption for getting this rule is reported much stronger than the product rule [1]. In this paper, we focus on the combining rules based on the different feature sets. Our objective is to give a new explanation to the sum rule. Moreover, we present a new hybrid rule called SumPro which combine the sum rule with the product rule in a weighted average way.

The remainder of this paper is organized as follows. Section 2 presents our theoretical framework on the combining rules through the Bayes theorem under independence assumptions. In particular, we give the detailed analysis on the sum rule and demonstrate that our explanation for the sum rule is more general than that in Kittler *et al.* [1] (fully described in the **Appendix A**). Then, we propose a new combining rule, named as SumPro rule. In Section 3, the experimental study on one data set is given to compare some combining rules for evaluating the SumPro rule. The conclusions are drawn in Section 4.

2 Our Theoretical Framework

In statistical pattern recognition, a given pattern x is assigned to the i th class w_i among all the m classes $W = \{w_1,...,w_m\}$ with the maximum posterior probability. In a multiple classifier system, when the pattern x is represented by multiple feature sets, i.e., $x = (x_1, x_2,..., x_R)$, the pattern belonging to class w_i should satisfy the following equation:

$$i = \arg\max_k \ p(w_k \mid x_1, x_2,..., x_R) \tag{1}$$

2.1 Product Rule

According to the Bayes theorem, the posteriori probability can be rewritten as

$$p(w_k \mid x_1,..., x_R) = \frac{p(x_1,..., x_R \mid w_k)P(w_k)}{p(x_1,..., x_R)} \tag{2}$$

where, $p(x_1,..., x_R)$ is the joint probability density.

Assume that the feature sets are statistically independent given the class w_k, i.e.,

$$p(x_1,...,x_R \mid w_k) = \prod_{l=1}^{R} p(x_l \mid w_k) \tag{3}$$

Then the posteriori probability can be rewritten as

$$p(w_k \mid x_1,...,x_R) = \frac{p(w_k)\prod_{l=1}^{R} p(x_l \mid w_k)}{p(x_1,...,x_R)} \tag{4}$$

In terms of the posteriori probabilities yielded by the individual classifiers, we obtain the decision rule

$$p(w_k \mid x_1,...,x_R) = p^{-(R-1)}(w_k)\prod_{l=1}^{R} p(w_k \mid x_l) \cdot \frac{\prod_{l=1}^{R} p(x_l)}{p(x_1,...,x_R)} \tag{5}$$

Excluding the same factor of $\dfrac{\prod_{l=1}^{R} p(x_l)}{p(x_1,...,x_R)}$ for all the classes, we obtain the product rule

$$i = \arg\max_k p^{-(R-1)}(w_k)\prod_{l=1}^{R} p(w_k \mid x_l) \tag{6}$$

2.2 Sum Rule

In this section, we give the sum rule in two steps. First, we consider the case in which the system consists of two classifiers for combining ($R = 2$).

Note that the posteriori probability $p(w_k \mid x_1, x_2)$ can also be computed by the probability of $p(\overline{w_k} \mid x_1, x_2)$ as follows

$$p(w_k \mid x_1, x_2) = 1 - p(\overline{w_k} \mid x_1, x_2), \quad \overline{w_k} = W - \{w_k\} \tag{7}$$

Assume that the feature sets are statistically independent given the class set $\overline{w_k}$, i.e.,

$$p(x_1,...,x_R \mid \overline{w_k}) = \prod_{l=1}^{R} p(x_l \mid \overline{w_k}) \tag{8}$$

With the analogous operation for getting formula (5), we get

$$p(w_k \mid x_1, x_2) = 1 - p^{-1}(\overline{w_k})p(\overline{w_k} \mid x_1)p(\overline{w_k} \mid x_2) \cdot \lambda_2 \tag{9}$$

Where $\lambda_2 = \dfrac{p(x_1)p(x_2)}{p(x_1, x_2)}$.

Since the sum of $p(\overline{w_k} \mid x_j)$ and $p(w_k \mid x_j)$ equals one, formula (9) becomes

$$p(w_k \mid x_1, x_2) \cdot [1 - p(w_k)] = [1 - p(w_k)] - \lambda_2[1 - p(w_k \mid x_1)][1 - p(w_k \mid x_2)] \tag{10}$$

Applying formula (5), we expand the left of the above formula

$$\begin{aligned} &p(w_k \mid x_1, x_2) - \lambda_2 p(w_k \mid x_1)p(w_k \mid x_2) \\ &= 1 - p(w_k) - \lambda_2[1 - p(w_k \mid x_1)][1 - p(w_k \mid x_2)] \end{aligned} \tag{11}$$

With the further simplification, we get

$$p(w_k \mid x_1, x_2) = [1 - p(w_k) - \lambda_2] + \lambda_2 [p(w_k \mid x_1) + p(w_k \mid x_2)] \qquad (12)$$

The above formula shows that the combining posterior probability can be expressed as the sum of the individual probabilities in the two-classifier case. And the assumptions (3) and (8) are used in the deducing process.

Secondly, let us consider the case that the system consists of more than two classifiers ($R > 2$).

We can regard the ensemble of former $R-1$ component classifiers as one classifier. Then, according to formula (12), we get

$$p(w_k \mid x_1, ..., x_R) = [1 - p(w_k) - \lambda_R] + \lambda_R [p(w_k \mid x_1, ..., x_{R-1}) + p(w_k \mid x_R)] \qquad (13)$$

Where, $\lambda_R = \dfrac{p(x_1, ..., x_{R-1}) p(x_R)}{p(x_1, ..., x_R)}$.

By expanding the above formula, we get the following expression

$$p(w_k \mid x_1, ..., x_R) = \sum_{l=2}^{R} [(\prod_{q=l}^{q=R} \lambda_q) \cdot p(w_k \mid x_l)] + \prod_{q=2}^{q=R} \lambda_q \cdot p(w_k \mid x_1) + cont. \qquad (14)$$

Where, $\lambda_q = \dfrac{p(x_1, ..., x_{q-1}) p(x_q)}{p(x_1, ..., x_q)}$, and $cont.$ is the remaining terms which is only related to the class prior probability $p(w_k)$.

Formula (14) demonstrates that the classifiers using independent feature sets should be combined in a linear weighted way under the two assumptions (3) and (8). Since our objective is to get the sum rule, we would cut off the weights.

We assume that the feature measurements x_j ($j = 1, 2, ..., R$) are statistically independent, then the value of λ_j ($j = 1, 2, ..., R$) equals one, i.e.,

$$\lambda_j = 1 \ (j = 1, 2, ..., R) \qquad (15)$$

Under this assumption, the sum rule for multiple classifiers can be conclude from formula (14) that

$$i = \arg\max_k \{-(m-1) p(w_k) + \sum_{l=1}^{R} p(w_k \mid x_l)\} \qquad (16)$$

This formula implies that the prediction decision can be drawn according to the sum of the posterior probabilities yielded by the individual classifiers. This is the same sum rule that has been widely used in the multiple classifier system field. Compared to the product rule, two more independent assumptions, (8) and (15), are involved in the sum rule. To further understand these assumptions, some comments about these two rules are described as follows.

➤ The assumptions (3) and (8) are two conditional dependent assumptions and they are popularly used in pattern recognition literature (e.g., Naïve Bayes classifier) for simplifying the analysis. The difference between these two assumptions lies in their different conditions, i.e., one has the given class w_k while the other has the given class set $\overline{w_k}$. Note that, in two-class case, when the class set $\overline{w_k}$

merely consists of one class, these two assumptions are equivalent. It is also interesting to point out that this special case is a good explanation to one conclusion drawn in the previous work of Tax *et al.* [9], which states that, in a two-class problem, the sum rule and the product rule achieve comparable performance [9].

➤ Another assumption (15) involved in the sum rule is so strong that it would be violated in many applications. However, this independent assumption is actually a sufficient condition for the sum rule in our explanation. As shown in (12), in two-classifier case, this assumption is needless for the sum rule under equal prior assumption.

➤ Another important related work have been given by Kittler *et al.* [1], who also deduced the sum rule with a rather strong assumption. This assumption states that the posteriori probabilities computed by the respective classifiers will not deviate dramatically from the prior probabilities. It is not difficult to prove that our explanation is more general than theirs. A detailed proof can be found in the **Appendix A**.

➤ We must concede that to satisfy all the assumptions at the same time is really difficult in many applications. Nevertheless, the sum rule performs so well in error sensitivity that it outperforms other fixed rules in many experimental results [1] [10].

➤ Other common fixed rules, such as the max rule, the min rule and the vote rule can be easily obtained using the above two basic rules [1]. These rules are discussed in detail in Kittler *et al.* [1].

2.3 SumPro Rule

As mentioned above, the sum rule requires much stronger assumptions than the product rule but it takes lower error sensitivity than the product rule. In real problems (when approximated posteriors are used), it is interesting to look for a hybrid method of these two rules which could combine the strengths of the product and sum rules. In this section, we propose a new combining rule called the SumPro rule.

Firstly, let's consider the two-classifier case ($R = 2$).

Under the assumption (3) and (15), we get

$$p(w_k \mid x_1, x_2) = p^{-1}(w_k)p(w_k \mid x_1)p(w_k \mid x_2) \tag{17}$$

Under the assumption (15), formula (12) can be simplified as

$$p(w_k \mid x_1, x_2) = -p(w_k) + p(w_k \mid x_1) + p(w_k \mid x_2) \tag{18}$$

Thus, we have

$$p(w_k \mid x_1, x_2) = (1 - \omega) \cdot [-p(w_k) + p(w_k \mid x_1) + p(w_k \mid x_2)] \\ + \omega \cdot p^{-1}(w_k)p(w_k \mid x_1)p(w_k \mid x_2) \tag{19}$$

Where ω $(0 \le \omega \le 1)$, can be regard as a variable varying from zero to one.

Note that the sum rule and product rule expressions become the special cases when $\omega = 0$ and $\omega = 1$ respectively. In real applications, it is always possible to find a suitable value of ω under some criterion.

As to multiple-classifier case, the posterior probability can be computed by using following formula iteratively

$$p(w_k \mid x_1,...,x_R) = (1 - \omega_{R-1}) \cdot [-p(w_k) + p(w_k \mid x_1,...,x_{R-1}) + p(w_k \mid x_R)]$$
$$+ \omega_{R-1} \cdot p^{-1}(w_k) p(w_k \mid x_1,...,x_{R-1}) p(w_k \mid x_R) \tag{20}$$

Then, the SumPro rule can be defined as following

$$i = \arg \max_k \{(1 - \omega_{R-1}) \cdot [-p(w_k) + p(w_k \mid x_1,...,x_{R-1}) + p(w_k \mid x_R)]$$
$$+ \omega_{R-1} \cdot p^{-1}(w_k) p(w_k \mid x_1,...,x_{R-1}) p(w_k \mid x_R)\} \tag{21}$$

In real applications, one essential task is to find a way for training the values of ω_i $(i = 1,...,R-1)$. One simple way is an exhaustively search for the optimal values on the training set under some criterion. However, this is impracticable when the classifier's number is large. Considering that the genetic algorithm is a good tool for optimization problems [11], we apply genetic algorithm to tune the values of ω_i $(i = 1,...,R-1)$ according to some optimization criterion.

3 Empirical Study

In this section, we perform experimental study to compare the combining rules on a biometric authentication data set. A biometric authentication system is designed to verify the identity of a person based on biometric measures such as the person's face, voice, iris or fingerprints [10]. Use of multiple biometric indicators, known as multimodal biometrics, has been shown to increase the authentication accuracy [12]. A number of combining rules have been applied to combine the results of the multiple biometric indicators, where the sum rule, the DS rule, and the support vector machine (SVM) rule are usually reported as the champions [1] [13] [14].

Our experimental data set[1] is presented by Poh and Bengio [15] to encourage researchers to focus on the problem of biometric authentication score-level fusion. The scores are taken from the XM2VTS database, which contains video and speech data from 295 subjects. There exist two configurations called Lausanne Protocol I (LP1) and Protocol II (LP2) in the dataset with different partitioning approaches of the training and development sets. In both configurations, the test set is the same [15]. In our experiment, we pick the LP1 for our experimental study where eight different classifiers are available.

Two kinds of errors occur in a biometric authentication system, i.e., false acceptance of the impostors and false rejection of the clients. Correspondingly, there are two measures commonly used for evaluating the system, i.e., false acceptance rate (FAR) and false rejection rate (FRR). Generally, FAR and FRR are balanced by the threshold which is used for determining whether one person is an impostor or a client. Another evaluation criteria is defined as the mean value of FAR and FRR, called Half Total Error Rate ($HTER$), i.e., $HTER = (FAR + FRR)/2$ [15].

---

[1] It is available at http://www.idiap.ch/~norman/fusion/main.php?bodyfile=entry_page.html.

Table 1. Comparison of performances using different combining rules

Rules	N=2	N=3	N=4	N=5	N=6	N=7	N=8
Product	2.36	1.86	1.56	1.43	1.74	2.54	3.50
Sum	2.09	1.39	1.08	0.91	0.83	0.78	0.75
Max	2.51	2.02	1.76	1.52	1.36	1.23	1.13
Min	3.04	2.83	2.74	2.64	2.51	2.41	2.35
SumPro	2.03	1.28	0.82	0.74	**0.62**	**0.58**	**0.31**
wighted sum	1.82	1.15	0.88	0.76	0.70	0.66	0.63
DS	1.47	1.20	1.07	0.99	0.90	0.82	0.76
SVM	**1.44**	**0.90**	**0.74**	**0.68**	0.64	0.60	0.52

The development set is used to estimate both the threshold value for rejecting and the approximate optimal omega values ω_i $(i = 1,..., R-1)$ for the SumPro rule by the genetic algorithm. In our experiment, the genetic operators, including selection, crossover, and mutation are all set to the default values in the GA tool in Matlab 7.0. And the optimization criterion is to obtain the best *HTER* value in the development set.

The best and the worst *HTER* values over all the single classifiers are 1.53% and 7.60%. We perform the combining methods by combining all the possible combinations of N $(N = 2,3,...,8)$ classifiers taken from the eight ones. The mean *HTER* values of every aggregate of the N classifiers are shown in **Table 1**. Below we highlight some of our interesting findings from **Table 1**.

First, we find that combining classifier can contribute to the overall performance of the authentication system since, in the eight-classifier case, results with most combining rules are better than the best result of the single classifiers. In general, good trained rules usually outperform the fixed rules. In our experiment, the weighted sum rule, the DS rule and the SVM rule obtain superior results to the fixed rules, such as the product rule, the max rule and the min rule. However, the sum rule, as a fixed rule, achieves comparable performance with the trained rules.

Then, the SumPro rule is consistently preferable than both the sum rule and the product rule. This conclusion is encouraging because the sum rule has been reported as the best rule in many related studies. Moreover, this new rule gradually outperforms the other popular trained combining rules when the classifier number increases (when $N = 6, 7, 8$).

4 Conclusion

In summary, the contribution of this paper is twofold. At first, we give a theoretical analysis on the two fixed rules of the product and the sum rule which are often seen as two basic rules in the fixed rules. The proposed assumptions can help us to better understand the fixed rules. Second, we present a new combining rule called SumPro rule which combines the product rule with the sum rule. Experimental results reveal this new rule performs particularly well when the number of the classifiers is large.

References

1. J. Kittler, M. Hatef, R.P.W. Duin, and J. Matas, On Combining Classifiers. PAMI, vol.20, pp.226-239, 1998
2. L. Xu, A. Krzyzak, and C.Y. Suen, Methods of Combining Multiple Classifiers and Their Applications to Handwriting Recognition. IEEE Tran. Systems, Man and Cybernetics, vol.22(3), pp.418-435, May/June. 1992
3. G. Fumera, and F. Roli, A Theoretical and Experimental Analysis of Linear Combiners for Multiple Classifier Systems. IEEE Trans. PAMI, vol.27, pp.942 – 956, 2005
4. Y.S. Huang, and C.Y. Suen, A Method of Combining Multiple Experts for the Recognition of Unconstrained Handwritten Numerals. IEEE Trans. PAMI, vol.17(1), pp.90-94, 1995
5. L. I. Kuncheva, J. C. Bezdek, R. P.W. Duin, Decision templates for multiple classifier fusion: an experimental comparison. Pattern Recognition, vol.34, pp.299-314, 2001
6. Y. Sugie, and T. Kobayashi, Media-integrated Biometric Person Recognition Based on the Dempster-Shafer Theory. 16th International Conference on Pattern Recognition (ICPR), vol.4, pp.381-384, 2002
7. R.P.W. Duin, and D.M.J. Tax, Experiments with Classifier Combining rules. Proceedings of First International Workshop on Multiple Classifier System (MCS 2000), Lecture Notes in Computer Science, vol.1857 pp.16-29, 2000
8. F. Roli, S. Raudys, and G.L. Marcialis, An Experimental Comparison of Fixed and Trained Fusion Rules for Crisp Classifiers Outputs. Proceedings of First International Workshop on Multiple Classifier System (MCS 2002), Lecture Notes in Computer Science, vol.2364, 2002
9. D.M.J. Tax, M. van Breukelen, R.P.W. Duin, and J. Kittler, Combining Multiple Classifiers by Averaging or by Multiplying. Pattern Recognition, vol.33, pp.1475-1485, 2000
10. A. Ross and A.K. Jain, Information Fusion in Biometrics. Pattern Recognition Letters, vol.24, no.13, pp.2115-2125, 2003
11. D. E. Goldberg, Genetic Algorithm in Search, Optimization and Machine Learning, Addison Wesley, Reading, 1989
12. R. Snelick, U. Uludag, A. Mink, M. Indovina, and A. Jain, Large-Scale Evaluation of Multimodal Biometric Authentication Using State-of-the-Art Systems. IEEE Trans. PAMI, vol.27, no.3, pp.450-455, Mar., 2005
13. S. Ben-Yacoub, Y. Abdeljaoued, and E. Mayoran, Fusion of Face and Speech Data for Person Identity Verification. IEEE Trans. on Neural Networks, vol.10(5), pp.1065-1074, 1999
14. K. Chang, and K. W. Bowyer, Comparison and Combination of Ear and Face Images in Appearance-Based Biometrics. IEEE Trans. PAMI, vol.25, no.9, pp.1160-1165, 2003
15. N. Poh, and S. Bengio, A Score-level Fusion Benchmark Database for Biometric Authentication. AVBPA, Lecture Notes in Computer Science, vol.3546, pp.1059-1070, 2005

Appendix A

In this appendix, we demonstrate that our explanation for the sum rule is more general than the explanation in Kittler *et al.* [1]. In Kittler *et al.* [1], they presented an explanation of sum rule under the assumption that the posteriori probabilities computed by the respective classifiers will not deviate dramatically from the prior probabilities, i.e.,

$$p(w_k \mid x_j) = p(w_k)(1 + \delta_{kj}),\tag{22}$$

where δ_{kj} satisfies $\delta_{kj} \ll 1$. First, let us prove the following theorem.

Theorem 1. *Under the assumption (3), the assumption (22) is a sufficient condition for the assumption (8) and the assumption (15).*

Proof. *(a)* Firstly, we consider the assumption (15).

Substituting (22) into (3) and applying the Bayes theory, we get

$$p(x_1,...,x_r \mid w_j) = \prod_{l=1}^{r} p(x_l) + \sum_{l=1}^{r} \delta_{jl} \cdot \prod_{l=1}^{r} p(x_l)\tag{23}$$

Because of the basic character of the probability, we have

$$\sum_{j=1}^{m} p(w_j \mid x_l) = 1\tag{24}$$

Thus,

$$\sum_{j=1}^{m} p(w_j)(1 + \delta_{jl}) = 1\tag{25}$$

Because $\displaystyle\sum_{j=1}^{m} p(w_j) = 1$, we can find

$$\sum_{j=1}^{m} [p(w_j) \cdot \delta_{jl}] = 0\tag{26}$$

According to the law of the total probability,

$$p(x_1,...,x_r) = \sum_{j=1}^{m} p(w_j) p(x_1,...,x_r \mid w_j)\tag{27}$$

Substituting (23) into (27), we find

$$p(x_1,...,x_r) = \prod_{l=1}^{r} p(x_l) + \sum_{j=1}^{m} \{ p(w_j) \cdot [\sum_{l=1}^{r} \delta_{jl} \cdot \prod_{l=1}^{r} p(x_l)] \}\tag{28}$$

From formula (26), we have

$$\sum_{j=1}^{m} \{ p(w_j) \cdot [\sum_{l=1}^{r} \delta_{jl} \cdot \prod_{l=1}^{r} p(x_l)] \} = 0\tag{29}$$

Substituting (29) into (28), we obtain

$$p(x_1,...,x_r) = \prod_{l=1}^{r} p(x_l)\tag{30}$$

Formula (30) exactly implies that each feature set x_j ($j = 1, 2, ..., R$) is independent from each other, thus the assumption (15) can be satisfied.

(b) Then, we consider the assumption (8).

As discussed in Section 2.1, from formula (5) and the assumption (15), we get

$$p(w_k \mid x_1, x_2, ..., x_r) = p^{-1}(w_k) \prod_{j=1}^{r} p(w_k \mid x_j) \tag{31}$$

Substituting (22) into the above formula, we obtain

$$p(w_k \mid x_1, x_2, ..., x_n) = p(w_k)(1 + \sum_{j=1}^{R} \delta_{kj}) \tag{32}$$

Thus,

$$p(\overline{w_k} \mid x_1, x_2, ... x_n) = 1 - p(w_k \mid x_1, x_2, ..., x_n) = 1 - p(w_k)(1 + \sum_{j=1}^{R} \delta_{kj}) \tag{33}$$

On the other hand, when there are two classifiers for combination

$$\begin{aligned} p^{-1}(\overline{w_k}) p(\overline{w_k} \mid x_1) p(\overline{w_k} \mid x_2) &= p^{-1}(\overline{w_k})[(1 - p(w_k \mid x_1)][1 - p(w_k \mid x_2)] \\ &= p^{-1}(\overline{w_k})[(1 - p(w_k))(1 - p(w_k))(1 + \delta_{k1} + \delta_{k2})] \\ &= 1 - p(w_k)(1 + \delta_{k1} + \delta_{k2}) \end{aligned} \tag{34}$$

As to multiple classifiers, it is not difficult to get

$$p^{-(R-1)}(\overline{w_k}) \prod_{l=1}^{R} p(\overline{w_k} \mid x_l) = 1 - p(w_k)(1 + \sum_{j=1}^{R} \delta_{kj}) \tag{35}$$

From (32) and (35), we find

$$p(\overline{w_k} \mid x_1, x_2, ... x_n) = p^{-(R-1)}(\overline{w_k}) \prod_{l=1}^{R} p(\overline{w_k} \mid x_l) \tag{36}$$

According to the Bayes theorem, the left item and the right item of (36) can be expanded as

$$p(\overline{w_k} \mid x_1, x_2, ... x_n) = \frac{p(x_1, x_2, ..., x_n \mid \overline{w_k}) p(\overline{w_k})}{p(x_1, x_2, ..., x_n)} \tag{37}$$

and,

$$p^{-(R-1)}(\overline{w_k}) \prod_{l=1}^{R} p(\overline{w_k} \mid x_l) = \frac{p(\overline{w_k}) \prod_{l=1}^{R} p(x_l \mid \overline{w_k})}{\prod_{l=1}^{R} p(x_l)} \tag{38}$$

From (36), (37) and (38), we get

$$\frac{p(x_1, x_2, ..., x_n \mid \overline{w_k}) p(\overline{w_k})}{p(x_1, x_2, ..., x_n)} = \frac{p(\overline{w_k}) \prod_{l=1}^{R} p(x_l \mid \overline{w_k})}{\prod_{l=1}^{R} p(x_l)} \tag{39}$$

Applying (30) to the above formula, we get

$$p(x_1, x_2, ..., x_n \mid \overline{w_k}) = \prod_{l=1}^{R} p(x_l \mid \overline{w_k}) \tag{40}$$

The above expression is exactly the assumption (8).

Therefore, we can conclude that the assumption (22) is a sufficient condition for the assumption (8) and (15).

In our explanation, under the equal prior assumption, the sum rule can obtained by only using the assumption (3) when there exist two class labels and two classifiers (see formula (12) and the assumption (8) is the same as the assumption (3) in two-class problem). In other words, the assumption (22) is unnecessary for getting the sum rule in this special case.

Considering the **Theorem 1** and the special case above, we can conclude that our explanation with the independence assumptions is more general than the explanation by Kittler *et al.* [1].

Embedding Reject Option in ECOC Through LDPC Codes

Claudio Marrocco, Paolo Simeone, and Francesco Tortorella

DAEIMI, Università degli Studi di Cassino
Via G. Di Biasio 43, 03043 Cassino (FR), Italia
{c.marrocco,paolo.simeone,tortorella}@unicas.it

Abstract. Error Correcting Output Coding (ECOC) is an established technique to face a classification problem with many possible classes decomposing it into a set of two class subproblems. In this paper, we propose an ECOC system with a reject option that is performed by taking into account the confidence degree of the dichotomizers. Such a scheme makes use of a coding matrix based on Low Density Parity Check (LDPC) codes that can also be usefully employed to implement an iterative recovery strategy for the binary rejects. The experimental results have confirmed the effectiveness of the proposed approach.

Keywords: ECOC, reject option, LDPC, coding theory, multiple classifier systems.

1 Introduction

Error Correcting Output Coding (ECOC) is an established method to build effective multiway classifiers. A multiclass classification problem is decomposed into many binary classification tasks, and the results of the subtasks are combined to produce a possible solution to the original problem. In short, each multiclass label is associated to a binary string (*codeword*) and the defined codewords are collected in a *coding matrix*. Each column so defines a two class problem on which a dichotomizer is trained. The multiway decision is taken by choosing the codeword having the smallest Hamming distance from the bit string made up of the outputs of the dichotomizers on the sample to be classified. The effectiveness of the ECOC approach is related to the choice of the coding matrix, which is typically defined according to two main requirements [1]: **column separation** to reduce the correlation among the dichotomizers and **row separation** to achieve a high correction capability against the potential errors made by the dichotomizers. The ECOC approach is quite unaffected by the errors of the dichotomizers as long as the number of wrong bits does not exceed the correction capability of the code. Unfortunately, this is not the most frequent situation and much work has been done to improve the performance of ECOC in many respects. Several approaches have been proposed which focussed on coding and decoding strategies [2], on design of the coding matrix from the data [3], and on iterative decoding approach for the multiway decision [4].

M. Haindl, J. Kittler, and F. Roli (Eds.): MCS 2007, LNCS 4472, pp. 333–343, 2007.

In this paper we propose an alternative approach which aims at decreasing the wrong decisions forwarded by the dichotomizers toward the decoding stage. In order to reduce the errors produced by a classifier a well known technique is to withhold the decision when its reliability is estimated to be not sufficient (*reject option*) [5]. In this way the classifier, in addition to the possible outputs, can be in a state of abstention which is preferable to the wrong decision. For this reason, the reject option is actually employed in many applications [6] [7] since it can alleviate or remove the problem of a high misclassification rate. In principle, we could thus consider an ECOC classification system with dichotomizers provided with a reject option which decreases the number of errors reaching the decoding stage. The ECOC decoding algorithms currently used work with the Hamming distance or more sophisticated distances [2], but, in any case, they do not allow abstaining dichotomizers. Analyzing the techniques provided by Coding Theory, we found in the *Low Density Parity Check* (LDPC) codes a suitable theoretical framework which allowed us to exploit the redundancy of the code for recovering the rejects provided by the dichotomizers and, ultimately, to define an ECOC system with abstaining dichotomizers.

The following sections, after a brief look at linear coding basics, present the method based on LDPC to design ECOC systems which embed abstaining dichotomizers. Sect. 5 reports the experimental results obtained, while in sect. 6 some conclusions are drawn.

2   Snooping in Coding Theory

In the usual ECOC approach, each class label is represented by a bit string of length L, called *codeword*, with the only requirement that distinct classes are represented by distinct codewords. If M is the number of the original classes, a code is a $M \times L$ matrix $\mathbf{C} = \{c_{ij}\}$ where $c_{ij} \in \{0, 1\}$. Each row of $\mathbf{C}$ corresponds to a codeword for a class, while each column corresponds to a binary problem. In this way, the multiclass problem is reduced to L binary problems on which L dichotomizers have to be trained. In the training phase, each dichotomizer is trained with a finite set of samples. In the operating phase, a sample $\mathbf{x}$ to be classified is fed to all the dichotomizers and each of them produces a binary value: all such values are collected to make a vector of binary decisions (*output vector*) that is compared with the codewords of the coding matrix. The class chosen is the one with the codeword having the lowest Hamming distance from the output vector. The minimum Hamming distance $d = \min_{i,j} D_H(\mathbf{c}_i, \mathbf{c}_j)$ between any pair of codewords is a measure of the quality of the code. In fact, it is possible to have a correct decision even if some dichotomizer makes a wrong decision, provided that the single bit errors are no more than $\lfloor (d-1)/2 \rfloor$. However this usual setting in ECOC-based classifiers does not exploit all the typical features of an error correcting coding provided by Coding Theory. In order to highlight some useful properties of linear codes, we now introduce some basic concepts.

Let us consider the Galois field $GF(2)$, i.e. a set of two elements $\{0, 1\}$ where a sum and a product operations, both mod 2, are defined. Let us further denote with $GF^L(2)$ the vector space of all L-tuples over the field $GF(2)$. An (L, K, d) code $\mathcal{C}$ over $GF^L(2)$ is a K-dimensional vector subspace of $GF^L(2)$: the vectors of the subspace are the codewords of $\mathcal{C}$ and d is the minimum Hamming distance among them. If $\mathbf{u} = [u_0, u_1, ..., u_{K-1}]$ is a K-bit source message to be coded, it can be associated to a codeword $\mathbf{c} = [c_0, c_1, ..., c_{L-1}]$ of $\mathcal{C}$: therefore, the 2^K possible source messages with length K are associated with 2^K codewords with length L. The difference $L - K$ is called *redundancy*, while the ratio $r = K/L$ is the *transmission rate* of the code $\mathcal{C}$. The relation between the redundancy and d is regulated by an upper bound $d \leq L - K + 1$, which means that, for a smaller r, d can increase and thus the error correction capability. Since $\mathcal{C}$ is a K-dimensional vector subspace, there exist K linearly independent vectors belonging to $GF^L(2)$, let us call them $\mathbf{g}_0, \ldots, \mathbf{g}_{K-1}$, which form a basis for $\mathcal{C}$. In this way, the correspondence between the source message $\mathbf{u}$ and the codeword $\mathbf{c}$ can be put in terms of a linear combinations of the basis vectors through $\mathbf{u}$, i.e.

$$\mathbf{c} = \mathbf{uG} \tag{1}$$

where $\mathbf{G} = \left(\mathbf{g}_0 \cdots \mathbf{g}_{K-1} \right)^T$ is the $K \times L$ matrix having the basis vectors as rows. $\mathbf{G}$ is called the *generator matrix* of $\mathcal{C}$.

It is clear how this device is different from usual ECOC approach where the set of the codewords does not necessarily form a vector space and the correspondence between the class label and the associated codeword is not based on an algebraic relation. However the structure provided by a linear code $\mathcal{C}$ can be usefully exploited in the decoding phase to decide if a word transmitted by the channel is actually a codeword. To this aim, let us call $\mathcal{C}^\perp$ the orthogonal complement of $\mathcal{C}$, i.e. the set of vectors belonging to $GF^L(2)$ which are orthogonal to the codewords of $\mathcal{C}$. Moreover let $\mathbf{H} = \left(\mathbf{h}_0 \cdots \mathbf{h}_{L-K-1} \right)^T$ be the $(L-K) \times L$ matrix collecting the $L - K$ vectors $\mathbf{h}_i$ of the basis of $\mathcal{C}^\perp$. In this way, each codeword $\mathbf{c} = \mathbf{uG}$ of the code satisfies the condition $\mathbf{Hc}^T = \mathbf{0}$; for this reason, $\mathbf{H}$ is called the *parity check matrix* of $\mathcal{C}$. In other words, the parity check matrix defines $L - K$ equations which allow the received word to be checked to verify if it is actually a codeword of $\mathcal{C}$. In particular, if the received vector $\mathbf{o} = \mathbf{c} + \mathbf{e}$ is given by a codeword $\mathbf{c}$ corrupted by an error pattern $\mathbf{e}$, we get:

$$\mathbf{s} = \mathbf{Ho}^T = \mathbf{He}^T \neq \mathbf{0} \tag{2}$$

where $\mathbf{s}$ is a $L - K$-vector called the *syndrome* of $\mathbf{r}$. Since to distinct syndromes correspond distinct errors, it is possible to correct up to $\lfloor (d - 1)/2 \rfloor$ erroneous bits. This is a general feature of the linear codes and it is the basis for many different decoding techniques. In the next section we show how the particular structure of the parity check matrix of the LPDC codes allows an effective utilization of dichotomizers with reject option in an ECOC classification system.

3   Recovering the Rejects

Let us suppose that we can estimate the reliability of the output of each dichotomizer in the ECOC system. As an example, let us consider a model for the dichotomizer which provides a soft value ranging from 0 to 1. In this case, we should threshold the soft output to have a crisp response and the typical threshold value is 0.5. However, it is easy to see that a value for the soft output falling near the threshold will be much less reliable than a value near 0 or near 1. As a consequence, we can adopt a reject rule for each dichotomizer as:

$$o_j(\mathbf{x}, t) = \begin{cases} 1 & \text{if } f_j(\mathbf{x}) > 0.5 + t \\ 0 & \text{if } f_j(\mathbf{x}) < 0.5 - t \\ ? & \text{otherwise} \end{cases} \tag{3}$$

Since in this case the output vector can also contain rejected bits, i.e. $o_i \in \{0, 1, ?\}$, the condition (2) cannot be checked. Nevertheless we can assume that all the bits not rejected are correct and impose a null syndrome: in this way the parity check condition becomes a system of linear equations with the rejected bits as unknowns. In particular, if we denote with E the index set of the rejected bits and with $\bar{E}$ the index set of the bits not rejected, the parity check condition $\mathbf{Ho}^T = \mathbf{0}$ can be written as:

$$\mathbf{Ho}^T = \mathbf{H}_E \mathbf{o}_E^T + \mathbf{H}_{\bar{E}} \mathbf{o}_{\bar{E}}^T = \mathbf{0} \tag{4}$$

Since we are working with the arithmetic modulo 2, this is equivalent to:

$$\mathbf{H}_E \mathbf{o}_E^T = \mathbf{H}_{\bar{E}} \mathbf{o}_{\bar{E}}^T \tag{5}$$

where $\mathbf{H}_{\bar{E}} \mathbf{o}_{\bar{E}}^T$ is a known term. This system has a unique solution if and only if the matrix $\mathbf{H}$ has a subset of $|E|$ independent rows; in this case, the solution can be found by performing Gaussian elimination and back substitution.

An useful and intuitive graphical representation to show how each component of the output vector is involved in the parity check constraints is the Tanner graph [8]. This is a bipartite graph with L *variable nodes*, corresponding to every component of the output vector, and $L - K$ *check nodes*, corresponding to the parity check constraints, i.e. to the rows of $\mathbf{H}$. To build the graph, every check node i is connected to a variable node j if and only if $h_{ij} = 1$. The number of connections deriving from a node is usually referred as the *degree* of the node. An example of a parity check matrix through the corresponding Tanner graph is shown in fig. 1.

The parity check equations allow the rejects to be eliminated by means of an iterative procedure (*direct recovery algorithm*) which is shown in fig. 2 and that can be summarized this way [9]:

1. Initialize the values of all check nodes to zero;
2. FOR EACH variable node, IF the node has a value in $\{0, 1\}$ THEN add this value to the values of all adjacent check nodes and remove all the edges coming from it;
3. FOR EACH check node, IF the node has degree one THEN substitute its value into the unique adjacent variable node and remove the edge;
4. IF at least a check node with degree one has been found in the previous step THEN goto step 2 ELSE exit.

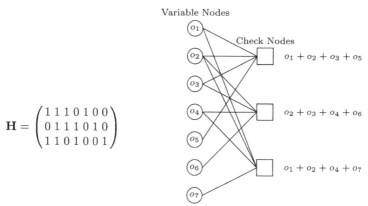

Fig. 1. An example of a Tanner graph for a generical code built starting from its Parity Check Matrix (left)

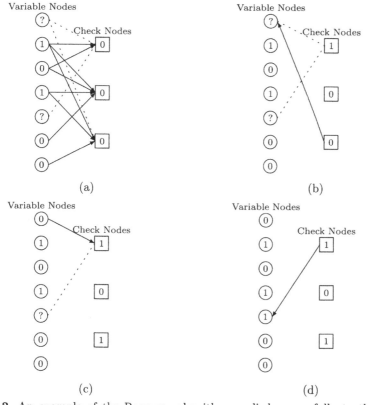

Fig. 2. An example of the Recovery algorithm applied successfully to the previous Tanner graph: (a) The variable nodes with no rejects transmit their values to the check nodes (b) The check nodes of degree one transmit back their values to the adjacent variable nodes with rejects (c) The recovered variable nodes transmit their values to the check nodes (d) Every new check node of degree one transmits back its value and the algorithm ends

It is worth noting that each check node with degree 1 singled out in step 3 can be only connected to a variable node with reject whose value is substituted in such a way to satisfy the constraint. The procedure ends when there are no more check nodes with degree 1. This means either all the check nodes have degree 0 (and thus all the rejects have been recovered) or there is some check node with degree greater than 1, i.e. a check node connected with two or more variable nodes with rejects which cannot be recovered. This case happens when $rank(\mathbf{H}_E) < |E|$. In order to have a high probability of recovering the rejected bits, the code to be chosen should have a sparse parity check matrix with the property that $\mathbf{H}_E$ has a triangular sub-matrix with high probability when $|E|$ is not too large [10]. In other words, this makes more practicable to recover the rejects directly through a back substitution instead of a Gaussian elimination.

Such features are provided by the *Low Density Parity Check* (LDPC) codes [11] which are characterized by a sparse pseudorandom matrix $\mathbf{H}$. An (a, b)-regular LDPC code is defined as a binary linear code such that in its Tanner graph every variable node has degree a and every check node has degree b. The term "low density" indicates that the number of edges in the Tanner graph is aL, where L is the length of the code. As L increases, the number of edges in the Tanner graph grows linearly in L, while for other codes it grows much faster.

4   From LDPC to LDPC-Based ECOC

Let us now describe how to integrate the LDPC codes into an ECOC framework provided with a reject option and discuss some issues rising during this process. The first point is the choice of L and K. If M is the number of the classes in the original multiclass problem, obviously we have $K \geqslant \lceil \log_2 M \rceil$; however, for a fixed L, it is convenient to keep K as low as possible so as to decrease the transmission rate and thus to increase the MHD d among the codewords. Once L and $K = \lceil \log_2 M \rceil$ are determined and the matrices $\mathbf{G}$ and $\mathbf{H}$ of the code $\mathcal{C}$ have been generated, we have to choose M codewords among the 2^K available. The safest choice is to select the M codewords with the highest MHD among them; in this way, if I_M is the index set of such codewords, the set of rows of the coding matrix $\mathbf{C}$ will be $\{\mathbf{c}_i \,|\, \mathbf{c}_i \in \mathcal{C}, i \in I_M\}$. To understand this choice, it is worth noting that the recovery algorithm does not necessarily output a codeword belonging to $\mathbf{C}$. In fact, in sec. 3 we made the assumption that all the bits not rejected were correct, but this is not always true. The recovered codeword $\tilde{\mathbf{c}}$ could thus contain some erroneous bits; moreover such errors could propagate during the recovery of the rejected bits, even though this problem is sensibly mitigated by the sparseness of the Tanner graph. As a result, the recovery could produce a codeword different from the correct one. However, a high MHD among the codewords of the coding matrix increases the probability that the erroneously recovered codeword does not represent another class, i.e. that $\tilde{\mathbf{c}} \in \mathcal{C}$ and $\tilde{\mathbf{c}} \notin \mathbf{C}$. In this case, an effective rule is to decide for the class corresponding to the codeword $\mathbf{c} \in \mathbf{C}$ with the lowest Hamming distance from the recovered codeword $\tilde{\mathbf{c}}$. Another point to be considered is that the recovery algorithm can fail because

$rank(\mathbf{H}_E) < |E|$ and the codeword cannot be recovered. In this case the final multiway decision cannot be taken and a *multiway reject* is produced. Therefore, our multiclass decision rule can be summarized this way:

$$r(\mathbf{C}, \mathbf{x}) = \begin{cases} \arg\min_{k \in I_M} (D_H(\mathbf{c}_k, \tilde{\mathbf{c}})) & \text{if } \tilde{\mathbf{c}} \text{ has no rejected bits,} \\ reject & \text{otherwise,} \end{cases} \tag{6}$$

where $\tilde{\mathbf{c}}$ is the codeword recovered starting from the outputs of the dichotomizers fed with the sample $\mathbf{x}$.

Let us now consider the coding matrix $\mathbf{C}$ produced by the chosen code $\mathcal{C}$ which, depending on the structure of the generator matrix, could contain similar (or even identical) columns as well as all-zeros or all-ones columns. Unlike the usual ECOC, in our approach we cannot eliminate such columns unless all the algebraic properties of the code do not hold and the recovery algorithm cannot be applied. Actually, the all-zeros/all-ones columns are not a big problem since they can be neglected during the training of the dichotomizers so that the number of needed dichotomizers becomes lower than L. The bits corresponding to all-zeros/all-ones columns can be then inserted within the output vector before the recovery algorithm starts. As for the similar columns, also this issue is less problematic than the usual ECOC. In fact, thanks to the sparseness of the parity check matrix, possible correlated outputs are likely to be forwarded to different check nodes and this makes the recovery robust to such circumstance. Nevertheless a further benefit for the robustness of the classification can be gained through the use of dichotomizers with learning algorithm incorporating some randomness into their execution.

5   Experimental Results

In order to evaluate the performance of the proposed ECOC classification system based on LDPC codes, some experiments have been performed on several data sets publicly available at the UCI Machine Learning Repository [12]; all of them have numerical input features and a variable number of classes. More details for each data set are given in table 1. To avoid any bias in the comparison, 12 runs of a multiple hold out procedure have been performed on all the data sets. In each run, the data set has been split in three subsets: a training set (containing the 70% of the samples of each class) to train the base classifiers, a tuning set and a test set (each containing the 15% of the samples of each class) respectively to normalize the dichotomizers output into the range $[0, 1]$ and to evaluate the performance for the multiclass classification. As base dichotomizers in the ECOC framework Modest AdaBoost [13] has been employed. A simple decision tree has been used as weak learner, with a random number of splits and a uniformly distributed random weight initialization in every run to provide a lower correlation among the different classifiers (see section 4).

First, the performance of different LDPC codes have been evaluated to verify how performance is affected by the code length. The coding matrices have been randomly generated so as to maximize the mean and minimize the standard deviation of the Hamming distance between columns. The first considered LDPC

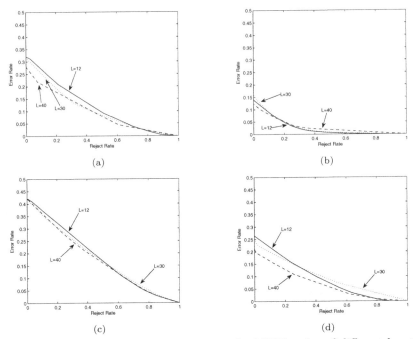

Fig. 3. Comparison of the error-reject curves for LDPC codes of different length on four data sets: (a) Glass, (b) SatImage, (c) Yeast, (d) Vowel

coding matrix has been determined so as to have the maximum code length without equal columns. For the value of $K = 4$ chosen for the considered data sets, a maximum of $L = 12$ different columns have been found. Successively, we have considered codes with greater length which could contain highly correlated columns into the coding matrix (and equal columns too). To this aim, coding matrices with $L = 30$ and $L = 40$ have been generated with $K = 3$ and $K = 4$ (we do not report the results obtained for higher values of L that do not give significant improvement and increase the computational complexity of the system). It is worth noting that these codes exhibit a low MHD between rows: a code with $K = 4$ and length $L = 40$ provides an achievable d larger($r = 0.1$) than the MHD obtained by a code with $K = 4$ and $L = 12$ ($r = 0.33$). However, it is not useful to consider values of r lower than 0.1 since, in this case, the increasing number of correlated columns leads to lower performance. The results in terms of error-reject curves relative to LDPC codes of different length are reported in fig. 3; the curves are produced with the threshold t in eq. (3) varying in the range $[0.5, 1]$ and evaluating the multiway reject rate according to eq. (6).

For low values of the reject rate a code with $L = 40$ has higher performance with respect to a code with all different columns ($L = 12$) for its higher error correcting capability; this behavior holds also for higher values of t except for the SatImage data set where the shorter code has slightly better performance. Therefore, the correlation between the columns of the coding matrix does not

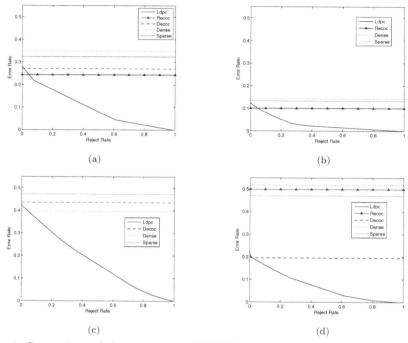

Fig. 4. Comparison of the error rate of DECOC, RECOC, dense and sparse ECOC and our method on four data sets: (a) Glass, (b) SatImage, (c) Yeast, (d) Vowel

affect the system performance thanks to the decorrelating effects provided by the sparseness of the parity check matrix (and partly to the employed dichotomizer with random initialization in the learning algorithm). It is worth noting that when the reject threshold becomes very high all the codes have quite similar performance since the sensibly increased number of rejects in the output vector lower the recovery capability for the longer codes.

For the sake of comparison, we have also contrasted the performance obtained by our approach with some relevant methods in literature in which the same data sets were employed for the experiments. In particular, since the reject option has never been employed, we report the results in terms of the error rate provided by the other considered methods. The value reported in these experiments are relative to the results obtained in [2] using a Dense and a Sparse random coding matrix, built respectively from the set of values $\{-1, 1\}$ and $\{-1, 0, 1\}$ and to the results of DECOC [3] and RECOC [4] approaches. The former introduces a coding technique derived from data distribution while the latter uses the LDPC codes with a sum-product algorithm as decoding technique. Fig. 4 shows the multiway error-reject curves obtained on the data sets. The characteristics of the LDPC matrix employed for each data set are reported in table 1. The last column refers to the number of dichotomizers actually employed, because the coding matrix can eventually include some all-zeros/all-ones columns that are not used in the training phase, but anyhow included in the final output vector. When the

Table 1. Data sets and codes used in the experiments

Data Set	#Classes	#Features	#Samples	Code	Dichotomizers needed
Glass	6	9	214	$\mathcal{C}(3,40)$	36
SatImage	6	36	6435	$\mathcal{C}(3,40)$	36
Yeast	10	8	1484	$\mathcal{C}(4,40)$	35
Vowel	11	10	435	$\mathcal{C}(4,40)$	35

reject rate is equal to zero the performance of our method are comparable to the other approaches. In particular, only in five cases the other methods are slightly better (RECOC on Glass and SatImage, DECOC on Glass and Vowel and Dense matrix on Yeast data set), but no any other method is definitely better than the proposed approach. Obviously, when the reject rate increases the error rate of our method becomes lower (if we accept a reject rate of 0.05 the error rate of the proposed method is lower than all the others). In other words, our approach gives the profitable opportunity to tune the error rate provided that a certain reject rate can be accepted and this is a relevant issue to be considered when using an ECOC system in real applications dealing with cost-sensitive classification problems.

6   Conclusions and Future Work

In this paper we have proposed an ECOC classification system based on Low Density Parity Check (LDPC) codes which allowed us to embed in the ECOC scheme dichotomizers with the reject option and to define an effective algorithm for recovering the rejects. Such approach gave us chance to verify that the framework of Coding Theory can be profitably used to design effective ECOC systems with strong theoretical foundations. There are some practical and theoretical issues that need to be addressed, however. As an example, a thorough analysis is required to verify to what extent the available classifier architectures fit the theoretical transmission channel models. This work hopes to be a first step toward further understanding how to use the results of Coding Theory in ECOC design.

References

1. Dietterich, T.G., Bakiri, G.: Solving multiclass learning problems via error-correcting output codes. Journ. Artif. Intell. Research, 2 (1995) 263–286
2. Allwein, E. L., Schapire, R. E., Singer, Y.: Reducing multiclass to binary: A unifying approach for margin classifiers. In: Proc. 17th Intl. Conf. on Mach. Learn. (2000) 9–16
3. Pujol, O., Radeva, P., Vitrià, J.: Discriminant ECOC: A heuristic method for application dependent design of error correcting output codes. IEEE Trans. Patt. Anal. and Mach. Intell., vol. 28 (6) (June 2006) 1001–1007
4. Tapia, E., Gonzàlez, J. C., Hütermann, A., Garcìa-Villalba, L. J.: Beyond boosting: Recursive ECOC learning machines. MCS 2004 62–71.

5. Chow, C.: On optimum recognition error and reject tradeoff. IEEE Trans. Inf. Theory, 16 (1970) 41–46
6. Karu, K., Jain, A.K.: Fingerprint Classification. Patt. Rec., 29 (1996) 389–404
7. Golfarelli, M., Maio, D., Malton, D.: On the error-reject trade-off in biometric verification systems. IEEE Trans. Patt. Anal. and Mach. Intell., 19 (1997) 786–796
8. Tanner, R. M.: A recursive approach to low complexity codes. IEEE Trans. Inf. Theory, vol. IT-27 (September 1981) 533–547
9. Shokrollahi, A.: LDPC Codes: An Introduction (April 2003)
10. Richardson, T., Urbanke, R.: Modern Coding Theory. (December 2006 draft)
11. Gallager, R.G.: Low-Density Parity-Check Codes. M.I.T. Press. (1963)
12. Blake, C., Keogh, E., Merz, C.J.: UCI Repository of Machine Learning Databases. (1998) [www.ics.uci.edu/~mlearn/MLRepository.html]
13. Vezhnevets, A., Vezhnevets,V.: Modest AdaBoost - Teaching AdaBoost to Generalize Better. Graphicon-2005, Novosibirsk Akademgorodok, Russia. (2005) [http://graphics.cs.msu.su/en/research/boosting/index.html]

On Combination of Face Authentication Experts by a Mixture of Quality Dependent Fusion Classifiers

Norman Poh[1], Guillaume Heusch[2], and Josef Kittler[1]

[1] CVSSP, University of Surrey, Guildford, GU2 7XH, Surrey, UK
[2] IDIAP-EPFL, Rue du Simplon 4, CH1920 Martigny, Switzerland
normanpoh@ieee.org, guillaume.heusch@epfl.ch,
j.kittler@surrey.ac.uk

Abstract. Face as a biometric is known to be sensitive to different factors, e.g., illumination condition and pose. The resultant degradation in face image quality affects the system performance. To counteract this problem, we investigate the merit of combining a set of face verification systems incorporating image-related quality measures. We propose a fusion paradigm where the quality measures are quantised into a finite set of discrete *quality states*, e.g., "good illumination vs. "bad illumination". For each quality state, we design a fusion classifier. The outputs of these fusion classifiers are then combined by a weighted averaging controlled by the *a posteriori* probability of a quality state given the observed quality measures. The use of quality states in fusion is compared to the direct use of quality measures where the density of scores and quality are jointly estimated. There are two advantages of using quality states. Firstly, much less training data is needed in the former since the relationship between base classifier output scores and quality measures is not learnt jointly but separately via the conditioning quality states. Secondly, the number of quality states provides an *explicit control* over the complexity of the resulting fusion classifier. In all our experiments involving XM2VTS well illuminated and dark face data sets, there is a *systematic* improvement in performance over the baseline method (without using quality information) and the direct use of quality in two types of applications: as a quality-dependent score normalisation procedure and as a quality-dependent fusion method (involving several systems).

1 Introduction

Face authentication is a process of verifying an identity claim using captured face images. While face as a biometric is well accepted by the general public and has already been in use in many applications using manual authentication, e.g., travel documents, it is still a very challenging task to replace this manual process by an automated one. This is because a captured face is inherently affected by the following factors: noise of the biometric device, e.g., a CCD camera operates slightly differently in different temperature; the interaction between the user and the device, e.g., a change of pose; the environmental (external) factors, e.g., the illumination conditions; and the natural physiological or behavioural change of face images principally originated by the user himself/herself, e.g., different face expressions. In general, these factors will lead to a

M. Haindl, J. Kittler, and F. Roli (Eds.): MCS 2007, LNCS 4472, pp. 344–356, 2007.

degradation in the face image quality and this will ultimately compromise the ability of the automatic face recognition system to verify the claim.

The goal of this paper is to devise a fusion algorithm that uses a set of quality measures derived from the face images to improve the fusion performance where several base face authentication systems may operate and exhibit different performance in different conditions. Combining several face verification systems in this context is especially useful when one baseline face verification system is robust to noise but does not perform well under good conditions and vice versa. Ideally, a fusion classifier should give more weight to the more reliable classifier in a given condition. The conventional fusion algorithm, unfortunately, does not have such a mechanism to do so. For instance, a linear fusion classifier weighs each base classifier output by the same weight for all the incoming samples regardless of their quality. It is clear that we should expect a better performance if the weight associated with each base system output changes *dynamically* as a function of image quality.

While several studies have shown that using quality measures as auxiliary information can improve the multimodal system performance at the score level, e.g., [1,2,3,4], as well as at the decision level [5], our experience is that this is *not necessarily* the case. This is because directly learning the relationship between base system output scores and quality measures may result in a more complex classifier, thus having a higher chance of overfitting the training data. Consequently, the resulting performance may be worse than the baseline system without using the quality information. Instead, we propose to first quantise the quality measures into a finite set of discrete *quality states* and then learn a fusion classifier for each state. The fused score output is given by a weighted sum of these fusion classifiers where the weight is the posterior probability of a quality state given a set of observed quality measures. Our experimental results carried out on the XM2VTS well illuminated and dark face images show that combining quality measures in fusion via the quality states generalises systematically better than by directly using the quality measures themselves. It is also superior to the baseline fusion approach without using the quality information. In comparison, our proposed fusion approach is much less likely to overfit on the training data, thus providing a good trade-off between complexity and generalisation performance.

2   Methodology

The proposed fusion approach via quality state is best explained in terms of a Bayesian network [6]. Graphical models representing three possible ways of using quality measures are shown in Figure 1. Model (a) is the conventional fusion without using quality measures. Model (b) is the state-of-the-art approach with quality measures. Finally, model (c) is the proposed fusion approach conditioned on quality states. A node in the graph represents a variable and its associated probability whereas an arrow from variable A to variable B specifies their causal relationship, i.e., the conditional probability of A given B. In the models just shown, the following variables are used:

- $k \in \{C, I\}$ is the true class label, i.e., being either a genuine user (also known as a client) or an impostor.

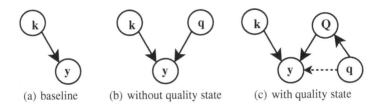

(a) baseline   (b) without quality state   (c) with quality state

Fig. 1. (a) A conventional fusion classifier without using quality information. (b) The state-of-the-art fusion classifier with raw quality measures. (c) The proposed method of incorporating quantised quality measures via quality states. The dashed arrow in (c) emphasises the *removed* casual relationship which is replaced by the newly introduced casual relationships (arrows) from q to Q and from Q to y. The dashed arrow will simply vanish in a conventional graphical model diagram.

- $q \in \mathbb{R}^{N_q}$ is the vector of quality measures output by N_q quality detectors. A quality detector is an algorithm designed to assess the quality of an image, e.g., the bit per pixel ratio, contrast and brightness as defined by the MPEG standards. In our case, these quality measures deal with face images describing, for instance, the orientation, illumination and spatial resolution of a face image. Both the general and face-related quality measures will be used in this paper.
- the quality state $Q \in \{1, \ldots, N_Q\}$ which signifies one of the N_Q discrete events[1] each describing a composite combination of quality degrading factors, e.g., {wearing glasses, back illumination, smile}, {no glasses, left illumination, neutral}, etc. In this study, we deal only with two quality states, i.e., well illuminated and side-illuminated face images. These states are obvious from a direct examination of a face image. However, from a computational point of view, Q is *not observable* when a biometric system operates without human intervention.
- $y \in \mathbb{R}^N$ is the vector of scores output by N base face authentication systems.

The three models shown in Figure 1 each describe the following joint probabilities, in increasing capability of modelling the quality information:

$$p(y, k) = p(y|k)p(k) \tag{1}$$
$$p(y, k, q) = p(y|k, q)p(k)p(q), \tag{2}$$
$$p(y, k, q, Q) = p(y|k, Q, q)p(k)p(Q|q)p(q),$$
$$= p(y|k, Q)p(k)p(Q|q)p(q). \tag{3}$$

Note that in our notation, we do not distinguish between discrete probability that is usually written with a capital "p" from the continuous one.

The first model does not consider the quality information; the second model uses the quality measures directly; and the third model uses the quality information via quality states. Using this Bayesian framework, the state-of-the-art algorithms exploiting quality

---

[1] Note that N_Q and N_q are different. We use the small letter "q" to denote a quality measure and the capital "Q" to denote a *cluster* of quality measures.

measures, e.g. [1,2,3,4], can be considered as belonging to the second model. In [1,3], the second model was implemented using discriminative classifiers whereas in [2,4], generative classifiers (hence approximating some probability density) were used. The last model thus assumes that the score y is *conditionally independent* of q given that Q is known, i.e., if one knows the state of Q, one does not need q. For this reason, we need to model only $p(y|k, Q)$ instead of $p(y|k, q, Q)$.

Using the first model where q is not considered, a conventional fusion classifier can be obtained by using the following log-likelihood ratio (LLR) test:

$$y_{bline}^{norm} = \log \frac{p(y|C)}{p(y|I)} \tag{4}$$

Similarly, for the second and third models, one can realise a *quality dependent* fusion classifier as follows:

$$y^{norm} = \log \frac{p(y|C, q)}{p(y|I, q)}. \tag{5}$$

Note that the state Q is not a conditioning variable in (5) because Q is not observed when inferring using the second and third models.

In (5), it can be assumed that the system outputs in y are dependent of each other. If one makes the independence assumption, the likelihood function can be written as:

$$y_{com} = \log \frac{\prod_i p(y_i|C, q)}{\prod_i p(y_i|I, q)} = \sum_i \log \frac{p(y_i|C, q)}{p(y_i|I, q)} = \sum_i y_i^{norm}. \tag{6}$$

where y_i is the i-th system that participates in fusion.

In the discussion that follows, we will consider y as a scalar, i.e., with $N = 1$. As a result, (5) can be considered a quality-dependent score normalisation procedure instead of a quality-dependent fusion classifier[2].

When one uses (5) as a quality-dependent score normalisation procedure, the resulting decision function should be:

$$\text{decision}(y^{norm}) = \begin{cases} accept & \text{if } y^{norm} > \Delta^{norm} \\ reject & \text{otherwise,} \end{cases} \tag{7}$$

where Δ^{norm} is a decision threshold after normalization. The decision function for the original score y can be written in exactly the same way by replacing y^{norm} with y. We argue that in theory, the performance due to y^{norm} is better than that due to y. In practice, however, this depends on how well one can estimate $p(y|k, q)$.

---

[2] We have considered both cases in our experiments but only to find that (6) generalises much better although in theory the vector case of (5) should perform similarly well, if not better. Since (5) has more parameters to estimate than (6), it is highly probable that (5) overfit the training data, thus resulting in inaccurate modeling of the dependency which in turn causes deteriorated generalisation performance. For better consistency with the experimental results to be presented at the end, we will refer to (5) as a quality-dependent score normalisation procedure.

Note that modeling $p(y|k,q)$ is difficult because the output variable y and the input variable q are continuous. This means that one should use a multivariate regression procedure since q has N_q dimensions. Fortunately, there are at least two ways to estimate $p(y|k,q)$ elegantly.

The first approach is to use $p(y,q|k)$ in place of $p(y|k,q)$, where all the continuous values are no longer in the conditioning set. This corresponds to model (b) shown in Figure 1. Therefore, $p(y,q|k)$ can be estimated using any multivariate density estimator. We used a mixture of Gaussian components or the Gaussian mixture model (GMM) [7] for this purpose. Other alternatives are Parzen windows [7], and the method of Gaussian Copulas that was first used in combining multimodal biometric systems in [8].

To show that using $p(y|k,q)$ is equivalent to using $p(y,q|k)$, we first note that:

$$p(y|k,q) = \frac{p(y,q|k)}{p(q|k)}.$$

Using the LLR framework, one obtains the following quality-dependent score normalisation procedure:

$$y^{norm}_{\text{with } q} = \log \frac{p(y,q|\mathtt{C})}{p(y,q|\mathtt{I})} \tag{8}$$

$$= \log \frac{p(y|\mathtt{C},q)}{p(y|\mathtt{I},q)} - \underbrace{\log \frac{p(q|\mathtt{C})}{p(q|\mathtt{I})}}$$

Since the quality measures are not expected to have any discriminative power to distinguish between the client and the impostor classes, the under-braced term will be zero. This is consistent with the models presented in Figure 1 where there is no link from k to q. We will therefore use (8) as the direct approach of quality-dependent score normalization procedure.

The second approach to estimating $p(y|k,q)$ is via the quality state, i.e., the third model shown in Figure 1. This can be done by computing the following probability:

$$p(y|k,q) = \sum_Q p(y|k,Q)p(Q|q) \tag{9}$$

where $p(Q|q)$ is the posterior probability of Q given q, i.e.,

$$p(Q|q) = \frac{p(q|Q)}{\sum_{Q_*} p(q|Q_*)}. \tag{10}$$

Using the LLR test in (5), the resulting score is obtained as follows:

$$y^{norm}_{\text{with } Q} = \log \frac{\sum_Q p(y|\mathtt{C},Q)p(Q|q)}{\sum_Q p(y|\mathtt{I},Q)p(Q|q)} \tag{11}$$

We will refer to the classifier due to (8) as a *joint quality-score* (JQS) normalisation procedure since for each example, the quality measures and scores must be present during training. The alternative classifier, i.e., due to (11) will be referred to as a *quality-state dependent* (QSD) score normalisation procedure since it is dependent on the quality state but not directly dependent on the quality measures. While these two quality-dependent score normalisation procedures are the same in principle, the latter has a much lower complexity. For instance, maximising the likelihood $p(y|k,Q)$ requires only the cluster index Q and *not* the actual observation q for each score y. In this case, $p(y|k,Q)$ has N dimensions, i.e., the number of dimensions in y. On the other hand, maximising the likelihood $p(y,q|k)$ requires both y and q to be present. Furthermore, $p(y,q|k)$ has $N + N_q$ dimensions. This implies that one may face the curse of dimensionality [7] when N_q is large. In brief, this curse means that modelling the increased number of dimensions may be less effective since this is not supported by the necessarily exponential increased number of training samples. In fact, there is only a fixed number of training samples to design a quality-dependent score normalisation procedure (or a fusion classifier). We argue that the higher complexity of $p(y,q|k)$ is not necessarily an advantage because this may result in overfitting. In contrast, by adjusting the number of discrete quality states N_Q, one can control the desired level of complexity adequately. As a result, (11) may be better in terms of generalisation performance than (8) given an appropriately adjusted N_Q.

We shall now discuss our particular implementation of the three models shown in Figure 1, i.e., the baseline system, realised using (4); the JQS approach, i.e., (8); and the QSD approach, i.e., (11). In all these three models, we have to estimate the probability distributions: $p(y|k)$, $p(y,q|k)$, $p(y|k,Q)$ and $p(q|Q)$ (from which the posterior $p(Q|q)$ is estimated via (10)). All these probability densities are multivariate and conditioned on some discrete variables. In our implementation, we use the Gaussian mixture model (GMM) [7] to estimate each of the multivariate probability distributions. Its parameters are estimated using the expectation maximisation algorithm. The number of Gaussian components is tuned by cross-validation.

3   Database and Experiments

3.1   Hypotheses to Verify

There are several claims in the Section 2 that need to be supported by experiments. The claims are:

1. The JQS normalisation procedure, i.e., due to (8) may overfit.
2. The QSD normalisation procedure, i.e., (11), achieves better generalisation than the baseline approach without using quality information.
3. A good estimate of $p(Q|q)$ is crucial to guarantee the success of the QSD score normalisation procedure.
4. The QSD fusion classifier generalises better than the JQS and the state-of-the-art fusion classifier which ignores quality information.

The first three hypotheses deal with quality-dependent score normalisation procedures. If they are true, the same conclusion can usually be applied to the fusion classifiers. For the ease of designing experiments, we will only show such coherence using hypothesis two and four where the former involves score normalisation procedures and the latter involves intramodal fusion of classifiers.

Since we have 11 quality detectors, to carry out the experiments with hypotheses 1–2, we will pick only the most discriminative quality detector so that the dimension of q is only one. This will simplify the comparison for the convenience of validating the experiments. This is not a limitation because we will test hypothesis 3 with all the quality measures available (to be discussed further).

3.2   The XM2VTS Standard and Darken Data Sets

We used the face images of the XM2VTS well-illuminated [9] and dark [10] data set. It contains 295 subjects, among which 200 are used as clients, 25 as impostors reserved for use for algorithm development, and 70 as impostors for the unique use of evaluation. For each subject, four sessions are acquired among which the first three sessions are used for algorithm development and the last one is reserved for algorithm evaluation. We consider the dark data sets with left illumination as the "fifth" session and the one with right illumination as the "sixth" session. Each session contains two mugshots of face images. In the results reported in [10], the protocol did not explicitly specify that the dark data set can be used for training although in one of the three submitted evaluations, the dark data set was possibly used for training. In this paper, however, in order to show the advantage of having observed some poor illumination data, we used the 25-impostor data set in which the well-illuminated and dark images are available for training. However, we could not obtain the scores for the dark client images. Given the fact that these scores can only be found in the 200-client data set, we further divided this data set into 20- and 180-client data set such that the 20-client data set is set aside uniquely for algorithm development and the 180-client for both algorithm development and evaluation. The consequence is that the data set for algorithm evaluation used in this paper will consist of sessions 4, 5 and 6 of the 180-client data set and sessions 1–6 of the 70-impostor data set[3].

3.3   Face Feature Representations and Classifiers

The classifiers used in this paper can be found in [11] and was implemented based on the open-source TorchVision[4]. There are two classifiers with three types of pre-processing, hence resulting in a matrix of six classifiers. The two classifiers used are Linear Discriminant Analysis (LDA) with correlation as a distance metric [12] and Gaussian Mixture Model (GMM) with maximum *a posteriori* adaptation, i.e., the same state-of-the-art system used in speaker verification [13]. The use of GMM in face authentication can be found in [14], for instance. The face pre-processing algorithms used are the photometric normalisation as proposed by Gross and Brajovic [15], histogram equalisation and local binary pattern (LBP), originally proposed by Ojala [16] but first used for pure pre-processing (and not recognition) in face authentication in [11]. Since the goal of this paper is to investigate intramodal fusion at the score-level, the absolute performance of the baseline systems is a secondary issue, whereas the relative performance with respect to the baseline systems as well as the baseline fusion methods as shown in models (b) and (c) is of particular importance. For this reason, neither the

---

[3] Due to lack of space, we could not show this protocol in a table.

[4] http://torch3vision.idiap.ch. See also http://www.idiap.ch/ marcel/labs/faceverif.php for a tutorial.

details of the three pre-processing procedures nor their verification performance in conjunction with the mentioned classifiers are reported here; the interested reader should refer to [11,14].

3.4   Quality Measures

In this paper, we use a set of proprietary quality detectors developed by Omniperception Ltd. The details of these quality detectors will thus not be discussed here. Note that some of them are defined by the MPEG standards. These quality detectors measure:

1. Overall quality
2. Frontal
3. Rotation
4. Reflection
5. Illumination
6. Spatial resolution
7. Bit per pixel
8. Focus
9. Contrast
10. Brightness
11. Reliability[5]

The overall quality is a combined measure using all the other quality measures. Only detectors 2–5 are face-related quality measures whereas the rest were developed as general purpose image quality detectors. It should be noted that none of these quality detectors were designed specifically to distinguish the three strong dominant quality states (by manual examination of face images in the XM2VTS database): good illumination, left illumination and right illumination. Although such a dedicated detector could have been designed easily, it would not reflect the real life situation where quality detectors are imperfect. Using the above quality detectors thus make the problem incorporating quality measures into a fusion classifier a more difficult one. For this reason, we did not further distinguish between left or right illumination but simply categorised them as "poor illumination" . The rest of the images were categorised as "good illumination". These are the two quality states and they are *observed* and used when training the QSD classifier but *inferred* via q during testing.

3.5   Experiments and Results

We first carried out independent experiments to find out the most discriminative quality measures to distinguish the quality states. Out of the 11 quality measures, the most discriminative one is the second one. It will be used for experiments designed to test hypotheses one and two. When we infer $P(Q|q)$, we consider the priors to be equal, i.e., $P(Q) = \frac{1}{N_Q}$ since for a general application, each state may be equally probable. This makes the task of distinguishing one Q state from another even harder, since there are more data acquired under good illumination conditions than those acquired under poor ones.

In order to show the first hypotheses, we conducted two sets of experiments: an unbiased training and a biased training. In the unbiased case, we trained the score normalisation procedure on the development set and applied the trained procedure to the evaluation score set. This approach corresponds to the default train/test procedure. For the *biased* training, we trained the procedure on the test set so that the score normalisation procedure fits the test data perfectly. We then compare the performance of the

---

[5] This reliability measure is probably different from what was proposed in [5].

Table 1. *A posteriori* EER of the baseline system (column 1) JQS (columns 2–3) and QSD (columns 4–6) score normalisation procedures obtained on the XM2VTS well-illuminated and darken data sets according to Lausanne Protocol I. The last column shows the relative change of EER between the baseline system (column 1) and the default QSD (column 5); larger negative values implies better improvement.

system	a posteriori EER (%)						rel. change of EER (%), Q
	baseline	unbiased q	biased q	Q, w/o quality	Q	Q, oracle	
lda-gross	11.41	13.94	9.05	11.41	10.12	9.91	-11.30
lda-heq	8.34	8.15	7.04	8.34	6.72	6.47	-19.38
lda-lbp	8.14	8.57	6.93	8.14	7.83	7.74	-3.74
gmm-gross	9.99	13.03	9.37	9.99	9.62	9.43	-3.67
gmm-heq	25.21	28.15	20.59	25.24	18.68	17.89	-25.93
gmm-lbp	17.01	18.01	13.05	17.06	14.55	13.72	-14.45

baseline (un-normalised scores) with the scores due to unbiased and biased training. These results are shown in the first three columns (containing *a posteriori* EER in percentage) of Table 1. Contrary to the results reported by [2,4], for almost all the cases of unbiased training of JQS procedure except lda-heq, their EERs increase with respect to the baseline unprocessed scores. In contrast, with the biased training of JQS, all resulting EERs decrease. Therefore, we conclude that that JQS over fits the training data. We repeated the same experiments to model $p(y, q|k)$ except that we constrained the number of Gaussian components to two. This corresponds to the observed two quality states, i.e., "good illumination" versus "poor illumination" instead of using cross validation (recalling that we used a GMM to model $p(y, q|k)$). Unfortunately, the resulting EERs are still not systematically better than that of the baseline systems. We therefore conclude that the JQS method has a too high complexity that cannot be adjusted easily even by imposing constraints on its density estimator.

We then used the usual unbiased train/test experimental approach for the QSD score normalisation procedure. We, however, introduced three variations, as follow:

– **without quality:** This variant ignores the quality information by integrating (11) with respect to q. We do so for two reasons. Firstly, this will support our claim that the baseline model can still be deduced from the advanced QSD model. Secondly, it also verifies the correctness of our implementation.
– **with quality:** This is the default QSD model where the state Q is inferred via $p(Q|q)$.
– **oracle:** This QSD model assumes that the state Q is known deterministically and so it is not inferred from the trained $p(Q|q)$. We expect that this oracle variant (so named due to the knowledge of the quality state) is expected to be better than the default QSD model (the second variant).

The results of these three variants of QSD models are shown in columns 4–6 of Table 1, respectively. The last column shows the relative change of *a posteriori EER* due to the default QSD model with respect to the baseline performance (column one). We observe that:

- There is no significant difference in terms of performance between the first variant of QSD compared to the baseline systems in which the scores are not processed.
- The oracle QSD variant is better than the default QSD model.
- The default QSD model is *systematically* better than the baseline systems (see the last column of Table 1). It is also better than the unbiasedly trained JQS model.

In order to show the third hypothesis, we chose the system whose relative performance gain (according to the last column of Table 1) is the highest. This system is gmm-heq. Instead of using the second quality measure, we replaced it with the other quality measures one by one. For each quality measure, we also measured the resulting performance in terms of EER due to distinguishing the good illumination from the poor one. Note that we used EER for this task for convenience only; the classification error could have been used. The EER performance of each quality measure and the relative change of EER performance of the resultant QSD model due to using $p(Q|q_*)$ for a given q_* is shown in Figure 2. As can be observed, the second quality measure gives the largest reduction of performance (its absolute and relative change of EER are shown in Table 1). There is indeed a dominant positive trend in this figure. We therefore conclude that the discriminative power of q to distinguish the quality state Q is important to guarantee good generalisation performance of the QSD model (hypothesis three).

In order to show the final hypothesis, we build a fusion classifier with the independence assumption as given by (6). Since we have six base systems, we can define $2^6 - 1 = 63$ fusion tasks by exhaustively making all possible combinations. This is

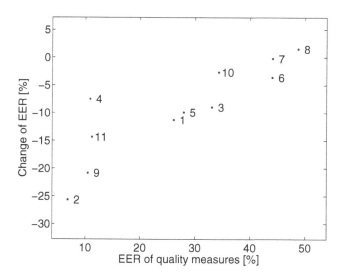

Fig. 2. Performance gain from quality state-dependent score normalisation (Y-axis) versus the discrimination power of quality measures (X-axis) to distinguish the quality state. The X-axis is the measure of EER (hence assuming equal priors) in the task of distinguishing between well illuminated and poor conditions due to the classifier $p(Q|q)$. The Y-axis is the measure of EER for the actual authentication task using the QSD score normalisation procedure. The higher the discriminative power of q to distinguish Q, the better the rate of improvement due to the use the QSD model.

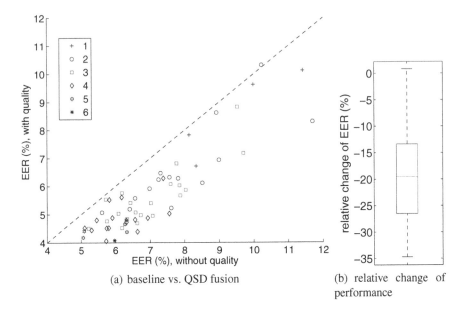

(a) baseline vs. QSD fusion

(b) relative change of performance

Fig. 3. Comparison of performance between the baseline and QSD fusion classifiers on the 63 exhaustive combinations of fusion tasks involving six base systems in terms of (a) absolute EER performance and of (b) relative change of EER from the baseline fusion classifier to the QSD one. The numbers 1–6 in the legend corresponds to the number of systems participating in a particular fusion task.

done by choosing one out of six, i.e., $^6C_1$; then choosing two out of six, i.e., $^6C_2$; then $^6C_3, \ldots$ and finally $^6C_6 = 1$ which is combining all six systems. The baseline fusion classifier is based on (4) where $p(y|k)$ is estimated by a GMM. We compared the performance of GMM with that of QSD models in terms of *a posteriori* EER. The pair of EERs are plotted in Figure 3(a). As can be observed, the QSD fusion classifiers *systematically* give better performance than the baseline fusion systems. We did not show the experiments using the JQS classifier because their performance are considerably worse than the baseline systems. In Figure 3(b), we measured the relative reduction of EER due to the two fusion classifiers examined. Negative values imply improvement due to the QSD fusion classifiers. Due to strong negative values (with median around -20%), we conclude that our proposed QSD fusion classifier is effective.

For the sake of convenience of the analysis, we showed only *a posteriori* EERs. We further visualised the DET curves of the baseline fusion (without quality), the QSD classifier and all the participating baseline systems and verified that indeed the QSD classifier is almost at least as good as, if not better than, the best participating base systems across all operating thresholds (examples of figures are not plotted due to lack of space).

3.6   Discussions

In the experiments, the posterior probability $p(Q|q)$ was estimated with (10) where $p(q|Q)$ is used. However, one could have used a direct estimation of $p(Q|q)$ using for instance a multi-layer perceptron [7] or a logistic regression function [17] since the quality state Q is directly observable in training. In our case, Q is either good or poor illumination. However, in general, the number of states N_Q is unlikely to be known. In this case, one should first find a number of clusters of quality measures and then verify that the performance for each cluster of data is indeed different. Using too many clusters N_Q is unlikely to be optimal because the resulting model as given by (11) may overfit the training data. Furthermore, the estimate of $p(y|k, Q)$ in each cluster may not be stable since using too many clusters will result in too few examples in each cluster.

4 Conclusions

Combining several face verification systems is a promising solution to increasing the reliability and robustness of face verification. However, to date, there is no satisfactory fusion solution that can *systematically* improve over the baseline performance over all the operating thresholds. The state-of-the-art approach, as exemplified by the JQS model, tends to overfit the training data. By introducing quality states, which are in fact clusters of the quality measures, we explicitly introduce a control parameter which regulates the complexity of the resulting algorithm that exploits quality measures. This is the main reason for the systematic improvement observed in almost all the 6 score normalisation and their resulting 63 exhaustive fusion experiments.

Acknowledgment

This work was supported partially by the prospective researcher fellowship PBEL2-114330 of the Swiss National Science Foundation, by the BioSecure project (www.biosecure.info) and by Engineering and Physical Sciences Research Council (EPSRC) Research Grant GR/S46543. This publication only reflects the authors' view.

References

1. J. Fierrez-Aguilar, J. Ortega-Garcia, J. Gonzalez-Rodriguez, and J. Bigun, "Kernel-Based Multimodal Biometric Verification Using Quality Signals," in *Defense and Security Symposium, Workshop on Biometric Technology for Human Identification, Proc. of SPIE*, 2004, vol. 5404, pp. 544–554.
2. J. Bigun, J. Fierrez-Aguilar, J. Ortega-Garcia, and J. Gonzalez-Rodriguez, "Multimodal Biometric Authentication using Quality Signals in Mobile Communnications," in *12th Int'l Conf. on Image Analysis and Processing*, Mantova, 2003, pp. 2–11.
3. K-A. Toh, W-Y. Yau, E. Lim, L. Chen, and C-H. Ng., "Fusion of Auxiliary Information for Multimodal Biometric Authentication," in *LNCS 3072, Int'l Conf. on Biometric Authentication (ICBA)*, Hong Kong, 2004, pp. 678–685.
4. K. Nandakumar, Y. Chen, S.C. Dass, and A.K. Jain, "Quality-based Score Level Fusion in Multibiometric Systems," in *Proc. 18th Int'l Conf. Pattern Recognition (ICPR)*, Hong Kong, 2006, pp. 473–476.
5. Krzysztof Kryszczuk, Jonas Richiardi, Plamen Prodanov, and Andrzej Drygajlo, "Error Handling in Multimodal Biometric Systems using Reliability Measures," in *Proc. 12th European Conference on Signal Processing*, Antalya, Turkey, September 2005.

6. F.V. Jensen, *An Introduction to Bayesian Networks*, Springer-Verlag, isbn = 0387915028, year = 1996, address = Secaucus, NJ, USA.

7. C. Bishop, *Neural Networks for Pattern Recognition*, Oxford University Press, 1999.

8. S. Dass, K. Nandakumar, and A. Jain, "A Principled Approach to Score Level Fusion in Multimodal Biometric Systems," in *5th Int'l. Conf. Audio- and Video-Based Biometric Person Authentication (AVBPA 2005)*, New York, 2005, pp. 1049–1058.

9. J. Matas, M. Hamouz, K. Jonsson, J. Kittler, Y. Li, C. Kotropoulos, A. Tefas, I. Pitas, T. Tan, H. Yan, F. Smeraldi, J. Begun, N. Capdevielle, W. Gerstner, S. Ben-Yacoub, Y. Abdeljaoued, and E. Mayoraz, "Comparison of Face Verification Results on the XM2VTS Database," in *Proc. 15th Int'l Conf. Pattern Recognition*, Barcelona, 2000, vol. 4, pp. 858–863.

10. K. Messer, J. Kittler, J. Short, G. Heusch, F. Cardinaux, S. Marcel, Y. Rodriguez, S. Shan Y. Su, and W. Gao, "Performance Characterisation of Face Recognition Algorithms and Their Sensitivity to Severe Illumination Changes," in *LNCS 3832, Proc. Int'l Conf. Biometrics (ICB'06)*, Hong Kong, 2006, pp. 1–11.

11. Guillaume Heusch, Yann Rodriguez, and Sebastien Marcel, "Local Binary Patterns as an Image Preprocessing for Face Authentication," in *Proc. 7th Int'l Conf. Automatic Face and Gesture Recognition (FGR06)*, Washington, DC, 2006, pp. 9–14, IEEE Computer Society.

12. J. Kittler, Y. Li, and J. Matas, "On Matching Scores for LDA-based Face Verification," in *British Machine Vision Conference (BMVC)*, 2000.

13. D. A. Reynolds, T. Quatieri, and R. Dunn, "Speaker Verification Using Adapted Gaussian Mixture Models," *Digital Signal Processing*, vol. 10, no. 1–3, pp. 19–41, 2000.

14. F. Cardinaux, C. Sanderson, and S. Bengio, "User Authentication via Adapted Statistical Models of Face Images," *IEEE Trans. on Signal Processing*, vol. 54, no. 1, pp. 361–373, January 2006.

15. R. Gross and V. Brajovic, "An Image Preprocessing Algorithm for Illumination Invariant Face Recognition," in *4th Intl. Conf. Audio- and Video-based Biometric Person Authentication, AVBPA'03*. June 2003, pp. 10–18, Springer.

16. T. Ojala, M. Pietikäinen, and T. Mäenpää, "Multiresolution Gray-scale and Rotation Invariant Texture Classification with Local Binary Patterns," *IEEE Trans. on Pattern Analysis and Machine Intelligence*, vol. 24, no. 7, pp. 971–987, 2002.

17. T. Hastie, R. Tibshirani, and J. Friedman, *The Elements of Statistical Learning*, Springer-Verlag, 2001.

Index Driven Combination of Multiple Biometric Experts for AUC Maximisation

Roberto Tronci, Giorgio Giacinto, and Fabio Roli

Department of Electric and Electronic Engineering, University of Cagliari,
Piazza D'Armi, I-09123 Cagliari, Italy
{roberto.tronci,giacinto,roli}@diee.unica.it

Abstract. A biometric system produces a matching score representing the degree of similarity of the input with the set of templates for that user. If the score is greater than a prefixed threshold, then the user is accepted, otherwise the user is rejected. Typically, the performance is evaluated in terms of the Receiver Operating Characteristic (ROC) curve, where the correct acceptance rate is plotted against the false authentication rate. A measure used to characterise a ROC curve is the Area Under the Curve (AUC), the larger the AUC, the better the ROC. In order to increase the reliability of authentication through biometrics, the combination of different biometric systems is currently investigated by researchers. In this paper two open problems are addressed: the selection of the experts to be combined and their related performance improvements. To this end we propose an index to be used for the experts selection to be combined, with the aim of the AUC maximisation. Reported results on FVC2004 dataset show the effectiveness of the proposed index.

1 Introduction

Biometric experts perform user authentication by the so-called matchers, i.e., algorithms that compare the acquired biometry to those stored during the enrolment phase. The output of a matcher is a *matching score*, i.e., a measure stating how much the acquired biometry is similar to the stored biometry. When a threshold is set, users with a matching score larger than the threshold are accepted (i.e., assigned to the so-called *genuine* class), otherwise they are rejected (i.e., assigned to the so-called *impostor* class).

In the pattern recognition field the combination of experts is widely used in many applications as it avoids the choice of the "best" expert, and typically provide better performance than those provided by individual experts [1]. The combination of experts also allows "fusing" experts based on different input sources, so that complementary information can be exploited, and the resulting combination is robust with respect to noise [1].

For the same reasons, in the biometric field there is an increasing interest in multi-biometrics, i.e., the combined use of different biometric traits and/or processing algorithms, as in many application the performance attained by individual sensors or processing algorithms does not provide the necessary reliability

M. Haindl, J. Kittler, and F. Roli (Eds.): MCS 2007, LNCS 4472, pp. 357–366, 2007.
© Springer-Verlag Berlin Heidelberg 2007

[2,3]. Combination of multiple biometric systems can be performed at different representation levels, i.e, the raw data level, the feature level, the score level, and the decision level [3].

An open problem for biometric experts combination is the choice of the experts to combine, and the decision whether to combine or not. For the combination at the decision level, the experts can be chosen using the same techniques developed for pattern classification [1]. At the score level, the performance of a biometric expert is evaluated in terms of the False Matching Rate (FMR, i.e., the percentage of impostors whose score is larger than the decision threshold) and the False Non-Matching Rate (FNMR, i.e., the percentage of genuines whose score is smaller than the decision threshold). As these errors vary according to the value of the chosen threshold, they are usually reported graphically in the Receiver Operating Characteristic (ROC) curve, where the value of $1 - FNMR$ (this value is equal to the True Matching Rate) is plotted against the value of FMR. Usually specific points of the ROC curve are used to evaluate the performance of experts as the 1% FMR (i.e., the rate of genuines rejected when the 1% of impostors are accepted), the 1% FNMR (i.e., the rate of impostors accepted when the 1% of genuines are rejected), and the Equal Error Rate (i.e., when FMR = FNMR).

Thus, at the score combination level, the ROC is the measure more apt to assess the performance of individual experts as it is not related to a particular value of the decision threshold. As a consequence, the choice of the experts to be combined is more difficult, as we have no information about the "errors" attained by the experts, and the techniques used for designing multiple pattern classifiers cannot be used [1].

In this paper we propose an index measure to be used for the selection of the experts to be combined, given that a set of different experts has been devised for the authentication problem attend. The index is derived from the formulation of the AUC through the Wilcoxon-Mann-Whitney statistic, and it has been designed to select the experts whose combination maximises the AUC. This index is independent from the combination method used. The rest of the paper is organised as follows: in Section 2 we describe the proposed index. Section 3 presents an ideal experts combination method that allows attaining the highest performance from the selected experts. The experimental results are presented in Section 4 and the conclusions are reported in Section 5.

2   Area Under the Curve

The Receiver Operating Characteristic (ROC) curve is the performance measure that allows having a global view of the trend of the errors of biometric experts for all possible acceptance threshold values. Unfortunately the ROC is a graphic measure, so when two biometric experts are compared it is usefull to use also a numeric performance measure, as it is more synthetic and allows automatic comparisons. Such a measure must be a summary index related to the ROC, or a brief index related to the degree of overlapping of the distributions of genuines and impostors. Moreover this measure must be a global measure, and not a specific measure as a ROC point. A measure with these characteristics is the Area Under the Curve (AUC) that is defined as follow:

$$AUC_{ROC} = \int (1 - FNMR(th)) \mathrm{d}FMR(th) \qquad (1)$$

The *Area Under the Curve* (AUC) is the most widely used measure for assessing the performance of a system because it is more discriminating than the accuracy when we analyse a ROC curve [4].

Let $U = \{u_i\}$ be the set of users, let also $f(\cdot)$ be the function associated to expert M that produces a score for each user u_i, $s_i = f(u_i)$. Let us denote with th a decision threshold so that users whose score is larger than th are assigned to the *genuine* class, while users whose score is smaller than th are assigned to the *impostor* class.

In the following the Wilcoxon-Mann-Whitney statistic [5] will be used to estimate the AUC as the integral value of the AUC is equivalent to the WMW statistic [6]. Given an expert M, let us divide all the scores $\{s_i\}$ obtained for all the $\{u_i\}$ users into two sets: $\{x_p\}$ the scores that belong to the genuine users and with $\{y_q\}$ the scores that belong to the impostor users. So the AUC is:

$$AUC = \frac{\sum_{p=1}^{n_+} \sum_{q=1}^{n_-} I(x_p, y_q)}{n_+ \cdot n_-} \qquad (2)$$

where n_+ is the number of genuine users and n_- is the number of impostors, and the function $I(x_p, y_q)$ is[1]:

$$I(x_p, y_q) = \begin{cases} 1 & x_p > y_q \\ 0 & x_p < y_q \end{cases}$$

It easy to see that if $x_p > y_q$ any threshold $th \in (y_q, x_p)$ allows accepting the genuine user and rejecting the impostor user.

Moreover the AUC can be statistically interpreted as follows: given two randomly chosen users, one belonging to the set of the genuine users and belonging to the set of the impostor users, the AUC is the probability $P(x_p > y_q)$, i.e., the probability of correct pair-wise ranking [6].

Now, let us consider two experts, M_1 and M_2, and all the possible pairs $\{\{x_{p1}, y_{q1}\}, \{x_{p2}, y_{q2}\}\}$ obtained from their matching algorithms. Let us divide these pairs into four subsets

$$S_{uv} = \{(p, q) | I(x_{p1}, y_{q1}) = u \quad and \quad I(x_{p2}, y_{q2}) = v\} \quad u, v \in \{0, 1\} \qquad (3)$$

i.e., S_{11} is made up of all the pairs where $x_{p1} > y_{q1}$ and $x_{p2} > y_{q2}$, S_{00} is made up of all the pairs where $x_{p1} < y_{q1}$ and $x_{p2} < y_{q2}$, S_{10} is made up of all the pairs where $x_{p1} > y_{q1}$ and $x_{p2} < y_{q2}$, and S_{01} is made up of all the pairs where $x_{p1} < y_{q1}$ and $x_{p2} > y_{q2}$. From Equations (2) and (3) using the S_{uv} subsets notation, the AUC of the single experts are computed as:

$$AUC_1 = \frac{card(S_{11}) + card(S_{10})}{n_+ \cdot n_-}, \quad AUC_2 = \frac{card(S_{11}) + card(S_{01})}{n_+ \cdot n_-} \qquad (4)$$

---

[1] For discrete values $I(x_p, y_q) = 0.5$ if $x_p = y_q$.

Let us explain the different contributions of the S_{uv} subsets to the value of the AUC when the combination of experts is performed. As an example, we use the linear combination because the value of the related AUC, say AUC_{lc}, can be computed by estimating the contributions of the pairs of outputs belonging to each of the four subsets $S_{uv}, u, v \in \{0, 1\}$ [7]. Let us consider the linear combination $f_{lc}(\cdot) = f_1(\cdot) + \alpha \cdot f_2(\cdot)$, where the fused outputs are computed as follows:

$$\xi_p = x_{p1} + \alpha \cdot x_{p2}$$
$$\eta_q = y_{q1} + \alpha \cdot y_{q2}$$

The contribution given by all the pairs belonging to S_{11} does not depend on the value of α as $\xi_p > \eta_q$ is always verified. Thus, the contribution to the AUC_{lc} from the pairs belonging to S_{11} is equal to $card(S_{11})$, i.e., the number of pairs belonging to S_{11}. Similarly, it is easy to see that the contribution given by all the pairs belonging to S_{00} does not depend on the value of α as $\xi_p < \eta_q$ is always verified. Thus, the pairs belonging to S_{00} give a nil contribution to the AUC_{lc}. The contribution given by all the pairs belonging to S_{10} depends on α and it is equal to $card(S_{10})$ only if there is a value of α such that for all the pairs $x_{i1} + \alpha \cdot x_{i2} > y_{i1} + \alpha \cdot y_{i2}$. The same reasoning can be used to estimate the contribution to the AUC_{lc} of pairs in S_{01}. It is worth noting that the value of α such that the contributions of S_{10} and S_{01} are equal respectively to $card(S_{10})$ and $card(S_{01})$ may not exists. Summing up, the maximum attainable value of AUC for the linear combination can be computed as follows:

$$AUC_{lc} = \frac{card(S_{11}) + card(S_{10}) + card(S_{01})}{n_+ \cdot n_-} \tag{5}$$

From the Equations (4) and (5) the following relation holds:

$$AUC_{lc} = AUC_1 + \frac{card(S_{01})}{n_+ \cdot n_-} = AUC_2 + \frac{card(S_{10})}{n_+ \cdot n_-}$$

so that the maximum increment attainable by AUC_{lc} with respect to AUC_1 depends on the cardinality of S_{01}, while the maximum increment attainable by AUC_{lc} with respect to AUC_2 depends on the cardinality of S_{10}. An analogous reasoning can be made for a score combination method that preserves the cardinality of S_{11} (it happens for the majority of the combination rules).

From the above discussion, it should be clear that the combination of expert is effective if it is able to "recover" those users belonging to S_{10} and S_{01}, i.e., the pairs of users correctly ranked by one expert and not by the other expert. So, if the cardinality of the two subsets S_{10} and S_{01} is small, than the two experts have similar behaviour, and few pairs of users could be "recovered" by the experts combination, as they exhibit a low degree of dissimilarity. The larger the cardinality of these two subsets, the larger the "recovery" factor achievable by a combination method, as the combined experts exhibit a high degree of dissimilarity.

We propose to use the sum of the cardinality of the subsets S_{10} and S_{01} as a *score dissimilarity* index,

$$SD = card(S_{10}) + card(S_{01}) \tag{6}$$

The larger the *score dissimilarity*, the larger the AUC that could be obtained by the combined scores with respect to the AUC of the single experts. Otherwise, if the *score dissimilarity* is small the AUC obtained by the combined scores is close to the AUC obtained by the single experts. It is worth nothing that actual increment value of AUC depends on the combination method used. To compute the value of SD for ensembles made up of 3 or more experts, the average SD computed over all pairs of experts can be used [1].

3   Ideal Score Selector

In this section we describe an ideal combination method called *ideal score selector* that allows attaining the highest performance from the combination of experts selected according to the index proposed in the previous section. This method had been already proposed by the authors in [8]. In this paper we will show the value of the AUC that is attained by the ideal score selector strategy in terms of the WMW statistics.

Given an ensemble of experts, the *ideal score selector* is defined as a selector that selects the maximum score for genuine users and the minimum score for impostor users. Using the notation of the previous section, the ideal selector for N experts can be written as follows:

$$\varphi_p = \max\{x_p^j\} \qquad j = \{1 \dots N\} \qquad (7)$$
$$\psi_q = \min\{y_q^j\}$$

The distributions of *genuine* and *impostor* scores produced by the ideal selector allows attaining smaller errors than those of individual experts. This result can be easily seen by the example shown in figure 1.

Let us now prove that the above defined ideal selector allows attaining an AUC that is larger than that of the individual experts. In particular, we will show that this selector allows exploiting the complementarity of experts selected according to the SD index. Following the line of reasoning of the previous section, let us consider two experts. The AUC of the ideal selector, say AUC_{sel}, can be computed as follows. Let us consider the contribution of all the pairs belonging to S_{11}. It is easy to see that for each pair the following relation holds: $\varphi_p > \psi_q$. Thus the contribution to the AUC_{sel} of S_{11} is equal to $card(S_{11})$, as for the linear combiner. By examining the pairs belonging to S_{00} we have to take into account two cases. One case is when φ_i and ψ_j come from the same expert. In this case, it follows that $\varphi_p < \psi_q$. The other case is when φ_p and ψ_q come from different experts. In this case, for some pair it may happen that $\varphi_p > \psi_q$. Let β be the ensemble of those pairs belonging to S_{00} that satisfy the above relation. It is easy to see that the contribution to the AUC of the pairs belonging to β is equal to $card(\beta)$. For the subsets S_{10} and S_{01}, it can be seen by using majority chains that for each pair $\varphi_p > \psi_q$ holds. As a consequence the contribution of S_{10} and S_{01} to the AUC is always $card(S_{10}) + card(S_{01})$. It is worth noting that in the case of the linear combiner this contribution of the pairs belonging to S_{10} and S_{01} is just an upper bound, as it may not exist a value of α allowing attaining

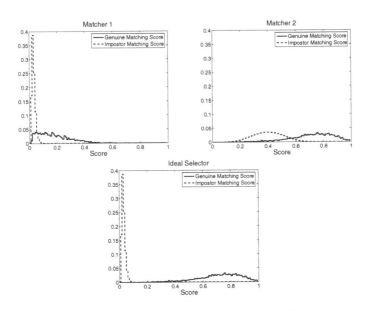

Fig. 1. An example of *ideal score selection* with two experts(matcher)

such performance. Summing up, the AUC of the ideal selector is computed as follows:

$$AUC_{sel} = \frac{card(S_{11}) + card(S_{10}) + card(S_{01}) + card(\beta)}{n_+ \cdot n_-} \tag{8}$$

and the following relations hold:

$$AUC_{sel} \geq AUC_1 , \quad AUC_{sel} \geq AUC_2$$

By comparing equations (5) and (8), it easy to see that

$$AUC_{sel} \geq AUC_{lc}$$

Thus we have proved that the proposed *ideal selector* always perform better than any expert of the ensemble. Moreover it allows attaining a larger AUC than the AUC that could be obtained by an optimal linear combiner. In addition, it can fully exploit the complementarity of experts selected according to the *SD* index proposed in the previous section as the selector can "recover" the pairs belonging to S_{10} and S_{01}.

4   Experimental Results

Experiments have been performed using the scores produced by a large number of experts during the third Fingerprint Verification Competition (FVC2004) [9] [10]. The competitors were divided into two categories *Open* and *Light*. The

Open category is composed by 41 experts, while the Light category is composed by 21 experts with restricted computing and memory usage. The fingerprint images consists of four different databases, three acquired with different sensors and one created with a synthetic fingerprint generator. For each sensor and for each matching algorithm, a set of 7750 matching scores is available related to 2800 authentication attempts of genuine users and 4950 authentication attempts of impostors. For the details on how the scores where obtained and normalised, the reader is referred to [9]. For our experiments we used only the Open category because the scores produced by the matchers belonging to the Light category are less reliable. As this database is not freely available, our algorithms were executed at the Biometric Systems Lab (University of Bologna, Italy) which organises the competition.

In the experiments we used five combination methods: the ideal score selector proposed in the previous section, the ideal linear combiner (see Section 2), the Mean rule, the Product rule and a weighted scores combination rule whose weights are computed through the Linear Discriminant Analysis (LDA) [11]. The *ideal score selector* and the *ideal linear combiner* are ideal in the sens that they use a posteriori information, as the values of actual errors, or the class each user belongs to. The performance of the ideal linear combiner are estimated by performing an exhaustive search on the value of the combination weight α, using values between 0 and 100 with a step of 0.01.

The LDA fusion rule needs a training set to estimate the weights of the combination. In order to create such training sets, we performed two different subdivisions of the users. One subdivision is performed by randomly dividing the set of users into four subsets of the same size. The other subdivision is performed by randomly dividing the set of users into two halves. The proportion of scores belonging to the "genuine" and "impostor" users has been kept equal to the one of the original dataset. In the first case, each of four subsets has been used for training, while the remaining three subsets have been used for testing. Analogously, in the second case, one halve has been used for training, and the other for testing, and then their roles have been reversed. This subdivision allowed to perform an extensive evaluation of the proposed techniques using training and test sets varying in size and composition. Reported results have been averaged over the six trials.

Using the above divisions of the dataset, we performed multi-modal (i.e., different sensors and/or different experts) combination experiments. For each experiment, we calculated the *SD* index, defined in Equation (6), for all the possible combinations of two experts avoiding duplications and repetitions: over 13300 pairs for trial were obtained. Then, we ordered all the pairs of experts according to the value of the *SD* index, and considered two subsets of pairs of experts. One subset is made up of the first 10 pairs with the largest values of *SD*, while the other subset is made up of the first 10 pairs with the smallest *SD*. The aim is to investigate the effectiveness of the *SD* index to selects which experts to combine.

The results are assessed in terms of the AUC, the Equal Error Rate (EER) and the d-prime. The EER is the error when FMR=FNMR, and it is currently used by researchers in the biometric field to assess the performance of biometric systems. The d-prime (d') is a measure of discriminability proposed, as the ROC, within the Signal Detection Theory [11]. Given the genuine and the impostor score distributions, the d' is defined as

$$d' = \frac{|\mu_{Gen} - \mu_{Imp}|}{\sqrt{\frac{\sigma_{Gen}^2}{2} + \frac{\sigma_{Imp}^2}{2}}}$$

where μ_{Gen} and μ_{Imp} are the means of the two score distributions, while σ_{Gen} and σ_{Imp} are the standard deviations of the score distributions of the genuine users and impostors, respectively. The larger the d', the better performance.

Tables (1) and (2) presents the results of the performed experiments. Results are reported in terms of the average and standard deviation of performance over the six subsets, and over the ten matching algorithms with largest/smallest SD value.

We expect that the combination of two experts with a small value of SD allows attaining only small improvements in AUC with respect to the performance of the single best expert. This idea is confirmed by the results in Table (1) where the value of AUC attained by the combination techniques are close to the AUC of the best single expert. This is due to the fact that the pairs of experts exhibiting a small value of SD exhibit a large value of AUC, thus allowing for small improvement in AUC. On the other hand, we can observe more significant improvements on the other performance measures taken into account. While improvements are small for the d', it is worth noting that the EER attained by the combination rules is always smaller than the EER obtained by the best single experts. In particular, the EER is at least halved by the combination rules compared to the EER of single experts. Summing up, this experiment showed that when the combined experts exhibit high performance and small SD, the Mean combination rule provides the best results with respect to the LDA and the Product rule, both in terms of AUC and EER. In addition, its performance are very close to those attained by the ideal linear combiner. On the other hand, the ideal score selector exhibits the highest performance as it allows exploiting the complementarity of the experts.

As we expected, the combination of two experts with a large value of the SD index allows increasing the AUC with respect to the AUC of the single best expert (Table 2). In this case the best combiner is the LDA, as its performance in terms of the AUC and the EER are higher than those attained by the Mean and the Product rules. However, the performance of combination rules in terms of the EER and the d' are close to those of the best single expert. An exception is the Product rule that exhibits lower performance than the best single expert either if we take into account pairs of experts with small values of the index, or pairs of experts with a large value of the index.

When the two ideal methods are taken into account, reported experiments point out another aspect: the *ideal score selector* exhibit higher performance than

Table 1. Combinations of pairs of experts with small values of the SD index. The results are in terms of the average and standard deviation computed over 10 pairs of experts, and 6 subsets of the original dataset.

	AUC	EER	d'
Single (best)	0.9973 ($\pm$0.0030)	0.0150 ($\pm$0.0077)	6.0339 ($\pm$1.6882)
Ideal Selector	0.9999 ($\pm$0.0004)	0.0015 ($\pm$0.0023)	9.2684 ($\pm$3.9873)
Linear Combiner	0.9992 ($\pm$0.0015)	0.0061 ($\pm$0.0059)	6.4045 ($\pm$2.1067)
Mean	0.9990 ($\pm$0.0017)	0.0067 ($\pm$0.0069)	6.5007 ($\pm$1.9761)
Product	0.9947 ($\pm$0.0066)	0.0122 ($\pm$0.0113)	4.3473 ($\pm$1.7307)
LDA	0.9978 ($\pm$0.0048)	0.0085 ($\pm$0.0072)	6.9904 ($\pm$1.7728)

Table 2. Combinations of pairs of experts with large values of the SD index. The results are in terms of the average and standard deviation computed over 10 pairs of experts, and 6 subsets of the original dataset.

	AUC	EER	d'
Single (best)	0.7924 ($\pm$0.1017)	0.2338 ($\pm$0.1181)	1.4678 ($\pm$0.6888)
Ideal Selector	0.9946 ($\pm$0.0127)	0.0123 ($\pm$0.0273)	7.3584 ($\pm$6.7999)
Linear Combiner	0.8339 ($\pm$0.0894)	0.2456 ($\pm$0.1258)	1.5098 ($\pm$0.7051)
Mean	0.8187 ($\pm$0.0976)	0.2429 ($\pm$0.0951)	1.5142 ($\pm$0.6653)
Product	0.7879 ($\pm$0.0936)	0.2418 ($\pm$0.1125)	1.3876 ($\pm$0.6468)
LDA	0.8246 ($\pm$0.0957)	0.2266 ($\pm$0.0970)	1.4950 ($\pm$0.7075)

the *ideal linear combiner* in all the performance measures, regardless of the value of the SD index. In particular, the performance attained for large values of the SD index clearly outperform other combination mechanisms. This means that a selection mechanism has the potentiality of exploiting the complementarity of experts better than mechanisms based on weighted combination. It is also worth noting that the selection mechanism allows increasing the value of d' more than other combination rules. At present, a selection mechanism based on the ideal mechanism has been proposed in the literature [8], but its performance are currently far away from those achievable by the ideal selector.

5   Conclusions

In this paper we proposed an index for selecting, among a set of biometric experts, the ones that are worth to be combined to attain performance improvements in terms of the AUC. This index has been derived from the formulation of the AUC through the Wilcoxon-Mann-Whitney statistic, and allows selecting those cases where large performance improvements can be attained. Reported results show that the combination of experts with small value of the index allows attaining small improvements of the AUC, while if the index has a large value, then the improvements in the AUC are more significant. However, in the reported experiments, the experts with small values of the index also exhibited high values of AUC, so that the combination could provide only small improvements. Nonetheless, the combination of experts with small value of the index and large individual performance allowed reducing the EER significantly using the Mean rule. This can be interpreted as the reduction of the "variance" in a "bias-variance" representation of errors, as the "bias" of the individual experts is very small. The experiments also showed that selection mechanisms can provide very high improvement in performance, when experts with large values of the proposed index are selected. Thus, in these cases the development of score selection mechanism should provide larger performance improvements than fusion mechanisms.

References

1. Kuncheva L.I.: Combining Pattern Classifiers: Methods and Algorithms. John Wiley & Sons, Inc. (2004)
2. Hong L. and Jain A.K. and Pankanti S.: Can Multibiometrics Improve Performance? In: AutoID'99. (1999) 59–64
3. Ross A., Nandakumar K., Jain A.: Handbook of Multibiometrics. Springer (2006)
4. Huang J. and Ling C.X.: Using AUC and Accuracy in Evaluating Learning Algorithms. IEEE Transactions on Knowledge and Data Engineering **17** (2005) 299–310
5. Mann H.B. and Whitney D.R.: On a test whether one or two random variable is stochastically larger than the other. Ann. Math. Statistic **18** (1947) 50 – 60
6. Hanley J.A. and McNeil B.J.: The meaning and the use of the area under a receiver operating charatheristic curve. Radiology **143** (1982) 29 – 36
7. Marrocco C., Molinara M., Tortorella F.: Exploiting AUC for optimal linear combinations of dichotomizers. Pattern Recognition Letters (**27**) 900 – 907
8. Giacinto G., Roli F., Tronci R.: Score Selection Techniques for Fingerprint Multimodal Biometric Authentication. In: Proc. of 13th ICIAP. (2005) 1018 – 1025
9. Maio D., Maltoni D., Cappelli R., Wayman J.L., Jain A.K.: FVC2004: Third Fingerprint Verification Competition. In: Proc. ICBA, Hong Kong (2004) 1 – 7
10. FVC2004 Website: (http://bias.csr.unibo.it/fvc2004/)
11. Duda R.O. and Hart P.E. and Stork D.G: Pattern Classification. John Wiley & Sons, Inc. (2001)

$Q-stack$: Uni- and Multimodal Classifier Stacking with Quality Measures

Krzysztof Kryszczuk and Andrzej Drygajlo

Swiss Federal Institute of Technology Lausanne (EPFL), Signal Processing Institute
http://scgwww.epfl.ch/

Abstract. The use of quality measures in pattern classification has recently received a lot of attention in the areas where the deterioration of signal quality is one of the primary causes of classification errors. An example of such domain is biometric authentication. In this paper we provide a novel theoretical paradigm of using quality measures to improve both uni- and multimodal classification. We introduce $Q-stack$, a classifier stacking method in which feature similarity scores obtained from the first classification step are used in ensemble with the quality measures as features for the second classifier. Using two-class, synthetically generated data, we demonstrate how $Q-stack$ helps significantly improve both uni- and multimodal classification in the presence of signal quality degradation.

Keywords: statistical pattern classification, quality measures, confidence measures, classifier ensembles, stacking.

1 Introduction

Noisy data is probably the most common problem that haunts pattern recognition systems [1]. One of the examples where researches are struggling with the negative effects of signal quality deterioration on classification performance is biometric identity verification [2].

It is often impossible to completely eliminate the effects of signal quality degradation by the means of preprocessing, normalization or marginalization of noisy signals, features or classifier scores [3,4,5]. One of the ways to reduce remaining classification errors is to combine multiple classifiers [1,6]. In biometric authentication, classifier fusion became particularly prominent as a natural consequence of the availability of multiple, presumably independent biometric traits that characterize an individual [7,2]. Multimodal systems in biometrics systematically outperform their unimodal counterparts [8,9].

Recently, researchers started to seek to incorporate auxiliary information into the fusion process, looking for improved robustness to degraded data quality. In particular, classifier confidence measures [10,11,9] and quality measures [5,12,10] have been recently put in the limelight.

An interesting attempt to incorporate the classifier confidence measures when combining multimodal classifiers was presented by Bengio et al. [9]. The authors

M. Haindl, J. Kittler, and F. Roli (Eds.): MCS 2007, LNCS 4472, pp. 367–376, 2007.

proposed to introduce different confidence measures next to the unimodal classifier scores as a feature when constructing the multimodal fusion classifier. Signal quality measures were not used.

In [13,5] the authors proposed to use quality measures in order to improve the performance of multimodal biometric fusion. Their approaches, albeit effective for their particular datasets, are heuristic in nature and therefore hard to generalize. The use of quality measures to improve unimodal classification was not considered.

A probabilistic approach to the use of quality measures in order to improve classifier fusion was presented by Kryszczuk et al [12,14] and by Richiardi et al. [10]. The notion of possible correction of decisions using quality-derived reliability measures has been first introduced in [12] and developed in [14] in the context of biometric identity verification. The reliability-based fusion was demonstrated to grant classification accuracy superior to any classifiers that did not use quality measures. Conceived as an error-predictor, the reliability estimation methods require explicit training of four error-conditional models and prior balancing. Its application to multimodal fusion of more than two classifiers is not straightforward.

In this paper we provide a theoretical analysis of the role that the quality measures play in the pattern classification process, in order to find a generic understanding of the problem. We present a novel theoretical approach to incorporating quality measures into the classification process, based on the concept of classifier stacking [6]. The essence of the presented approach, named $Q-stack$, is in the use of feature similarity scores together with the signal quality measures as classification features for a subsequent, stacked classifier. We notice that while class-nonspecific, the quality measures are causally linked to the classifier scores, which allows for increased class-separation in the score-quality measure space.

$Q-stack$ can be directly applied to uni- and multimodal dichotomization alike and therefore it can be seen as a general framework of incorporating quality information in classification. We show that in the unimodal case $Q-stack$ grants a higher classification accuracy than the baseline classifier, and in the multimodal case it delivers fusion performance superior to other known methods.

Nowadays, with the developments in multi-classifier systems, the published error rates on real-life data have been radically reduced and available databases do not anymore give the possibility to prove the minute improvements significant. We hence demonstrate the improvements granted by the proposed techniques on synthetic data in order to avoid ambiguities and deliver statistical soundness to our statements and conclusions.

Since most of the prior efforts and our own motivations derive from the field of multimodal biometric authentication the method presented in this paper is presented in the context of dichotomizer. This assumption comes without a loss of generality since a multi-class problem can be interpreted as a series of two-class problems [15].

The paper is structured as follows. Section 2 provides a theoretical and intuitive understanding of the role that quality measures and classifier confidence play in dichotomization. Section 3 describes the principles behind the proposed method of $Q - stack$. Sections 4 and 5 treat on its application to unimodal and multimodal classification problems, respectively. Section 6 concludes the paper with a discussion of presented results.

2   The Link Between Noise, Errors, Confidence, and Quality Measures

Consider a classifier C that computes the value x of a discriminant function $\Psi(f)$ for an observed feature vector f. The classification is done by comparing the score $x = \Psi(f)$ to a preset decision threshold τ [1]. The distance from the score x to the threshold τ for given feature set f is a measure of confidence of the classifier - the larger the distance, the more confident the classifier is about making the decision.

Now consider two random processes (classes), A and B, which generate observations x according to the probability density functions (pdf) $p(x|A)$ and $p(x|B)$, and noise-generating process N which generates noise instances n according to the pdf $p(n)$. In general, $p(x|A)$, $p(x|B)$ and $p(n)$ are not explicitly known. The process N and the class-generating processes A and B interact in an arbitrary way, producing noisy observations $x' = \Delta x = \Gamma(n, x)$. The nature of the function Γ does not need to be given explicitly.

The classifier C is deployed to classify potentially noisy *testing* data $S_{TS}(x')$ of unknown class alignment (groundtruth), and a set of *training* data $S_{TR}(x')$ of known class alignment is available. Here and further in the text let symbols with a subscript $_{TR}$ refer to the training data, and $_{TS}$ to the testing data. The training data by definition exemplifies the noisy data that may be encountered during testing. The class-conditional distributions of the noisy data $p(x'|A)$ and $p(x'|B)$ are estimated using the training set [1].

The upper graph in Figure 1 shows an example of $p(x|A)$, $p(x|B)$, $p(x'|A)$ and $p(x'|B)$. The lower graph in Figure 1 presents the posterior probabilities of classes A and B given observation x, with respect to the decision threshold τ.

A noiseless observation x_0 in Figure 1 is correctly assigned to class A since $p(x_0|B) < p(x_0|A)$. The classification error due to noise occurs if the same observation x_0 becomes biased by a noise influence $\Delta x = \Gamma(x_0, n)$, resulting in a noisy observation x'_0. If $\Delta x > (x_0 - \tau)$ the observation will be falsely assigned class label B, since $p(x_0|B) > p(x_0|A)$, as it is shown in Figure 1.

The confidence of the classifier C is given by $|x - \tau|$ [9,16]. The notion of the confidence alone does not allow to predict a possible misclassification: the observed score x'_0 could very well be a noiseless sample from class B. In order to distinguish between these two cases it is necessary to find a measure $QM(x_0) \sim \Delta x$ dependant on the actual amount of noise n that contaminated the original observation x. In our example, knowing Δx allows to compute the actual posterior probability $P(B|x' = x'_0)$. As shown in the lower graph in Figure 1 this probability falls below the chance level, $P(B|x' = x'_0) < 0.5$, and the inverse class label is more likely to be correct. Therefore it is possible to

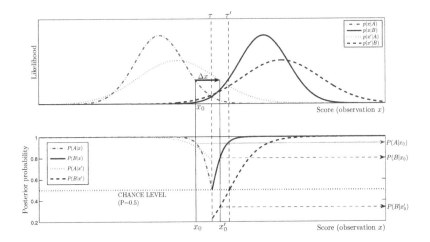

Fig. 1. Relationship between scores and quality measures. Upper graph: class-conditional probability density functions for training (solid lines) and development data (dashed lines). Lower graph: corresponding class-conditional posterior probabilities $P(A|x), P(B|x), P(A|x')$ and $P(B|x')$ for equal class priors.

invert the original classification decision and correctly assign x'_0 to A with the probability of $1 - P(B|x' = x'_0)$ (since $A \cap B = \emptyset$). Without the notion of Δx the only justified decision would be to keep the erroneous class label B with the probability of $P(B|x = x'_0) > 0.5$. Since the value of QM is encoding the effect of degradation in the signal quality, we refer to this measure as *quality measure*, following the established nomenclature in the field [5,12,10].

3 $Q - stack$ - Using Quality Measures to Improve Classification

Consider two class data-generating processes A and B, and a noise-generating random process N, as discussed in Section 2. Processes A and B generate features that are subjected to a classifier C of an arbitrary nature which returns similarity scores x'. The distributions of observed scores are affected by a noise-generating process that interacts with the class-generating processes A and B. This interaction manifests itself as the impact of noise n on the observed score x'.

In a classical paradigm, the classifier test scores x'_{TS} are compared to a decision threshold τ in order to obtain the classification decisions. The value of τ is optimized according to a criterion λ on the training scores x'_{TR}. The total Bayes' error of the classifier C, assuming optimal τ is given by Equation 1.

$$ER = \frac{1}{2} \int_{-\infty}^{\tau} p(x'|B)dx + \frac{1}{2} \int_{\tau}^{\infty} p(x'|A)dx \qquad (1)$$

The proposed $Q - stack$ method begins here. Assume we have a set of signal quality measure vectors qm. Each quality measure vector qm corresponds to a particular x' and may consist of one or more quality measures $qm = [qm_1, qm_2, ...]$.

Let us now concatenate the training scores x'_{TR} and the relevant quality measures qm_{TR} into evidence vectors $e_{TR} = [x'_{TR}, qm_{TR}]$. Resulting vectors have the dimensionality equal to the number of involved quality measures $+1$ (score x'). The evidence vectors e_{TR} have the same known class alignment (groundtruth) as the scores x'_{TR}. The essence of $Q - stack$ is to train a new, stacked classifier C' to separate $E_{TR}|A$ and $E_{TR}|B$. The nature of the classifier C' can be chosen arbitrarily according to the observed class-conditional distributions of $p(E_{TR}|A) = p(x'_{TR}, qm_{TR}|A)$ and $p(E_{TR}|B) = p(x'_{TR}, qm_{TR}|B)$.

The testing evidence vectors e_{TS} are formed in the same fashion, by concatenating $e_{TS} = [x'_{TS}, qm_{TS}]$. Now the previously trained classifier C' and corresponding new decision threshold χ is applied to provide class labels A or B to each of the vectors e_{TS}. Threshold χ is trained on E_{TS}, according to the criterion λ. The total Bayes' error of the stacked classifier C' is given by Equation 2.

$$ER' = \frac{1}{2} \int_{-\infty}^{\chi} p(x', qm|B)dx + \frac{1}{2} \int_{\chi}^{\infty} p(x', qm|A)dx \qquad (2)$$

Since x' and qm are dependant it can be analytically proven that $ER \geq ER'$ [17]. The intuition behind it is provided in the following Section 4. Since the proposed method uses a second classification step augmented by the quality information, the entire procedure can be thought of as classifier stacking and hence the coined name $Q - stack$.

In the following Sections we assume that the quality measures are linearly correlated with the magnitude of noise n present in x' at the correlation coefficient α. The value of $\alpha = 1$ corresponds to an undistorted measurement of the noise. The correlation assumption is for example clarity. In order for $Q - stack$ to improve classification, statistical dependance between qm and x', but not necessarily correlation is required.

4   Q-stack for Unimodal Classification

In this Section we demonstrate how $Q - stack$ operates on synthetic, one-dimensional noisy data generated by Gaussian processes. Two noise types are considered: additive (case a, $\Gamma = x + n$) and multiplicative (case b, $\Gamma = x \cdot n$). Our goal is to provide the reader with the intuitive understanding of $Q - stack$ and to show how it allows to reduce the error rates of a single classifier.

Two class data is generated by random Gaussian processes $p(x|A) = \mathcal{N}(\mu_A, \sigma_A^2)$ and $p(x|B) = \mathcal{N}(\mu_B, \sigma_B^2)$, where μ_{class} and σ_{class}^2 are the mean and variance parameters of the corresponding $class$. Let the noise-generating process N be also Gaussian, $\mathcal{N}(\mu_N, \sigma_N^2)$. The parameters of the processes A, B and N

in the given example are: $\mu_A = -1; \sigma_A^2 = \mu_B = \sigma_B^2 = \mu_N = \sigma_N^2 = 1$. We refer to them as *baseline* the experiments reported here. Two cases are considered: in the case a the noise is additive, $x' = n + x$. In the case b the noise is multiplicative, $x' = n \cdot x$. Since here the symbolic representation of the processes A and B are known their associated Bayes error bound can be computed analytically, and is $ER^{Bayes} \approx 0.1587$ for noiseless data x, $ER_a^{Bayes} \approx 0.2398$ for case a and $ER_b^{Bayes} \approx 0.2666$ for case b. The distributions of training and testing noisy observations $p(x'|A)$ and $p(x'|B)$ for cases a and b are shown in Figure 2.

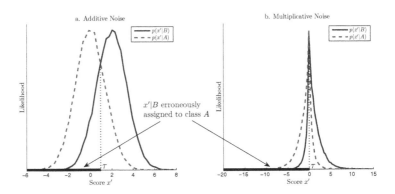

Fig. 2. Distributions of scores $x'|A$ and $x'|B$. Case a - additive noise, $\Gamma = x + n$. Case b - multiplicative noise, $\Gamma = x \cdot n$.

Let us now assume that we have available a quality measure qm that is correlated with the noise n (Section 2). Following the $Q - stack$ procedures described in Section 3 we concatenate the noisy scores x' and the quality measures qm into training and testing evidence vectors $e = [x', qm]$. Figure 3 shows the class-conditional distributions of testing evidence E_{TS} for the cases a and b.

To apply $Q - stack$, the stacked classifier C' is trained on evidence $E_{TR}|A$ and $E_{TR}|B$. The training and testing sets contained 20000 data samples each (40k total). In our example we used a Bayesian classifier using Gaussian Mixture Modeling (GMM) [1] as classifier C'. In order to minimize the impact of modeling the experiment was repeated 30 times (new dataset generated each time). The obtained accuracies for $\alpha = 1$ are listed in Table 5. As the results show, the proposed method allowed to classify the noisy data at an error rate reduced to the proximity of the Bayes error ER for clean data: a result that cannot possibly be obtained by classifying x' alone, without the use of quality measures in the $Q - stack$ scheme.

Based on the current example we wish to provide the reader with an intuitive understanding of $Q - stack$. Consider the marked areas in Figures 2 and 3. In Figure 2 the marked areas are the approximate loci of $x' < \tau$ generated by B, erroneously assigned to class A. The corresponding ellipsoids in Figure 3 mark the areas where thanks to the addition of the second dimension (qm) the same

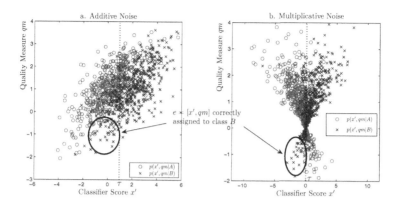

Fig. 3. Distributions of evidence $(x', qm)|A$ and $(x', qm)|B$. Case a - additive noise, $\Gamma = x + n$. Case b - multiplicative noise, $\Gamma = x \cdot n$. Figures show only 500 data points per class for clarity.

observations can be correctly assigned to class B, hence improving the overall classification accuracy. Consider a projection of the plotted data on the vertical qm axis: note that in both Figures 3a and b the dimension of qm provides no class-separation by itself.

In practical applications finding a quality measure at $\alpha = 1$ is rather difficult. Therefore we provide an experimental analysis of the influence of reduced α on the obtained classification gains. The change in obtained accuracy AC_a and AC_b are shown as a function of α in Figure 5.

5   Q-stack for Multimodal Classification

In this Section we demonstrate the application of $Q - stack$ for the task of multimodal fusion. For the clarity of the example, consider that processes A and B generate two independent, streams of identically distributed data x_1 and x_2. We will consider x_1 and x_2 as separate modalities. The noise-generating process N degrades x_1 and x_2 with two independent streams of noise instances n_1 and n_2. For this demonstration, let us take that one data stream is affected by additive, and the other one by multiplicative noise. Therefore the noisy observations are given by $x_1' = x_1 + n_1$ and $x_2' = x_2 \cdot n_2$. For the example presented, the parameters of the processes A, B and N are same as in Section 4. Quality measures qm_1 and qm_2 are collected for respective data streams. In total, 20000 data observations per class (total 40k samples) are collected for training, and another 20000 per class for testing.

The application of $Q - stack$ follows the steps described in Section 3. First, the evidence vectors are created for training and testing data. To do this, we concatenate all available pieces of evidence from both fused classifiers into one vector

$e = [x'_1, x'_2, qm_1, qm_2]$. The training evidence is used to train a Bayes/GMM stacked classifier C', which is then applied to classify the testing evidence. The obtained DET curves are shown in Figure 4, with a comparison with the results obtained using alternative fusion methods including the mean rule ($Mean Rule$), reliability-weighted mean ($Mean_{RW}$), quality-weighted mean ($Mean_{QW}$) [13] and Bayes/GMM without quality measures (GMM)[9,5,12,8]. The obtained mean error rates and their associated standard deviations after a 30-fold repetition of the experiment for the proposed method and the best approach to trained fusion without quality measures, GMM, [9], are summarized in Table 5.

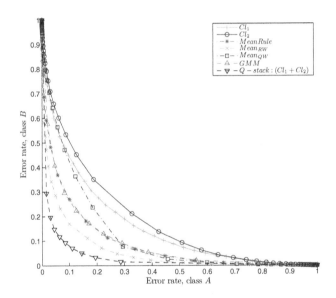

Fig. 4. DET curves showing the comparison of fusion algorithms, including proposed $Q - stack$-based fusion. The error bars correspond to standard deviation of the error rates after 30 experiment repetitions.

Table 1. Comparison of uni- and multimodal application of $Q - stack$ to a Bayesian classifier (GMM) trained without the use of quality measures.

	ER_{GMM}	σ_{GMM}	$ER_{Q-stack}$	$\sigma_{Q-stack}$
Additive Noise (a)	24.06%	0.30%	**15.88%**	0.26%
Multiplicative Noise (b)	28.41%	1.04%	**16.82%**	0.44%
Fusion($a+b$)	17.26%	0.27%	**8.75%**	0.22%

Like discussed in Section 4, here we provide an analysis of the sensitivity of the proposed fusion scheme to the correlation coefficient α. The achieved fusion accuracy as a function of α is shown in Figure 5.

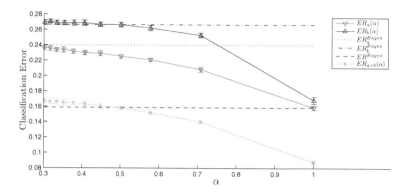

Fig. 5. Impact of the correlation coefficient α between the quality measure qm and the actual noise n, on the $Q - stack$ accuracy, for unimodal and multimodal classification. The error bars correspond to standard deviation of the error rates after 30 repetitions.

6 Discussion and Conclusions

The presented results obtained for uni- and multimodal classification show that incorporating the class-independent quality measures using the proposed method can greatly improve the classification accuracy. It is worth noticing that $Q - stack$ allowed for classification of noisy data at an accuracy much higher than that suggested by corresponding Bayes' error. In fact, for noisy data the proposed method is capable of recovering a close-to optimal accuracy computed for noiseless-data. This is achieved using exclusively noisy data and associated quality measures, regardless and without any assumptions of the noise type or noiseless data distributions.

The performance of the proposed method depends heavily on the available quality measures. Best performance can be achieved if the quality measures strongly depend on the noise that affects the class data - which can be reasonably demanded of a quality measure. However, as Figure 5 shows, as α changes towards zero the $Q - stack$ error rates asymptotically approach the error rates obtained without the use of quality measures. Hence, imperfect quality measures do improve accuracy, albeit to a smaller extent.

In this work we gave an example of one-dimensional data classification. However, the proposed methodology lends itself easily to more complex classification problems, as long as the baseline classifier C returns similarity scores. We have successfully applied $Q - stack$ to face, speech and fingerprint verification - a report on these experiments exceeds the theoretical frames of this paper.

Proposed method is easily scalable. If moving from one classifier to a fusion of two, as presented in this paper, required a mere concatenation of scores and quality measures, the same shall hold for multiple classifiers, and multiple quality measures. For a very large number of classifiers fused together dimensionality reduction techniques may be required. Last but not least, all existing normalization techniques can be applied before $Q - stack$ is used - the better the baseline classifier the higher performance can be expected after applying the proposed method.

References

1. Duda, R., Hart, P., Stork, D.: Pattern Classification. 2nd edn. Wiley Interscience, New York (2001)
2. Ross, A., Jain, A.: Multimodal biometrics: An overview. In: Proc. of 12th European Signal Processing Conference (EUSIPCO), Vienna, Austria (2004) 1221–1224
3. Kryszczuk, K., Drygajlo, A.: Gradient-based image segmentation for face recognition robust to directional illumination. In: Visual communications and image processing 2005 : 12-15 July 2005, Beijing, China. (2005)
4. Poh, N.: Multi-system Biometric Authentication: Optimal Fusion and User-Specific Information. PhD thesis, Swiss Federal Institute of Technology Lausanne $EPFL$ (2006)
5. Fierrez-Aguilar, J.: Adapted Fusion Schemes for Multimodal Biometric Authentication. PhD thesis, Universidad Politecnica de Madrid (2006)
6. Polikar, R.: Ensemble based systems in decision making. IEEE Circuits and Systems Magazine **6** (2006) 21–45
7. Jain, A.K., Ross, A.: Multibiometric systems. Commun. ACM **47** (2004) 34–40
8. Alkoot, F.M., Kittler, J.: Experimental evaluation of expert fusion strategies. Pattern Recogn. Lett. **20** (1999) 1361–1369
9. Bengio, S., Marcel, C., Marcel, S., Mariethoz, J.: Confidence measures for multimodal identity verification. Information Fusion **3** (2002) 267–276
10. Richiardi, J., Prodanov, P., Drygajlo, A.: Speaker verification with confidence and reliability measures. In: 2006 IEEE International Conference on Acoustics, Speech and Signal Processing, 2006. Volume 1. (2006) 641–644
11. Poh, N., Bengio, S.: Improving fusion with margin-derived confidence in biometric authentication tasks. In: Proceedings of the AVBPA, Rye Brook NY, USA (2005)
12. Kryszczuk, K., Richiardi, J., Prodanov, P., Drygajlo, A.: Error handling in multimodal biometric systems using reliability measures. In: 13th European Signal Processing Conference (EUSIPCO 2005), Antalya, Turkey (2005)
13. Toh, K.A., Yau, W.Y., Lim, E., Chen, L., Ng, C.H.: Fusion of auxiliary information for multi-modal biometrics authentication. In: Proceedings of International Conference on Biometrics. Lecture Notes in Computer Science, Hong Kong, Springer (2004) 678–685
14. Kryszczuk, K., Drygajlo, A.: Reliability measures and error prediction in biometric identity verification. submitted to: Journal of Signal Processing (2006)
15. Tax, D., Duin, R.: Using two-class classifiers for multiclass classification. In: Proceedings, 16th International Conference on Pattern Recognition. (2002)
16. Kryszczuk, K., Drygajlo, A.: On combining evidence for reliability estimation in face verification. In: Proc. of the EUSIPCO 2006, Florence (2006)
17. Koval, O., Voloshynovskiy, S., Pun, T.: Error exponent analysis of person identification based on fusion of dependent/independent modalities. In: In Proceedings of SPIE Photonics West, Electronic Imaging 2006, Multimedia Content Analysis, Management, and Retrieval 2006 (EI122). (2006)

Reliability-Based Voting Schemes Using Modality-Independent Features in Multi-classifier Biometric Authentication

Jonas Richiardi and Andrzej Drygajlo

Laboratory of IDIAP, Signal Processing Institute
Swiss Federal Institute of Technology Lausanne
jonas.richiardi@epfl.ch
http://scgwww.epfl.ch

Abstract. We present three new voting schemes for multi-classifier biometric authentication using a reliability model to influence the importance of each base classifier's vote. The reliability model is a meta-classifier computing the probability of a correct decision for the base classifiers. It uses two features which do not depend directly on the underlying physical signal properties, verification score and difference between user-specific and user-independent decision threshold. It is shown on two signature databases and two speaker databases that this reliability classification can systematically reduce the number of errors compared to the base classifier. Fusion experiments on the signature databases show that all three voting methods (rigged majority voting, weighted rigged majority voting, and selective rigged majority voting) perform significantly better than majority voting, and that given sufficient training data, they also perform significantly better than the best classifier in the ensemble.

1 Introduction

A voting combiner operating on the output of classifier ensembles with differing accuracies can be made more effective by supplying it with additional data to influence the importance of each base classifier's vote. A typical scheme is to weight the vote of each classifier proportionally to its accuracy, by training the weights on a development dataset. This paper is concerned with the use of other sources of information for improving voting schemes in biometric authentication.

It has previously been shown that using modality-specific, signal-level quality information can improve classifier combination [1,2]. These quality measures must be tailored to each signal to be used (for instance, image sharpness cannot be used with speech-based biometrics). In this paper, we show that other, modality-independent quality measures can be used in order to estimate the reliability of a classifier's decision, that is, the probability that the base classifier has taken a correct decision.

The estimate of reliability can be used for rejecting the sample (thus decreasing a base classifier's error rate via the reject-error tradeoff), providing a value

M. Haindl, J. Kittler, and F. Roli (Eds.): MCS 2007, LNCS 4472, pp. 377–386, 2007.

to a human layperson (useful in situations such as border control for biometric passports), or improving classifier combination (confidence information has been used to perform classifier selection [3,4,5,6] and classifier fusion [7,8]). In this paper, we propose different ways of using the reliability information in order to improve voting for classifier combination.

First, we introduce modality-independent quality measures in Section 2. We then discuss the process and limits of reliability modelling using the quality measures as features in Section 3. Section 4 proposes three voting schemes using the reliability information, and section 5 shows experimental results of reliability classification on signature and speech, and reliability-based voting for combining multiple signature classifiers. We close the paper by discussing theoretical points and further work in Section 6.

2   Modality-Independent Quality Measures

In order to predict the errors of the base classifiers in the ensemble, it is necessary to find quantities which are indicative of potential mistakes. We call these features *quality measures*. For example, in speaker recognition, a quality measure that is interesting to use is the signal-to-noise ratio (SNR), as a lower SNR tends to increase the probability of error[1] . The two quality measure we use, score and difference between user-specific and user-independent decision threshold, constitute features for the reliability classifier.

Most base classifiers can provide a continuous-valued output (measurement-level) indicating how close or far a particular sample is to a particular class, a quantity generally called score in biometrics. This can be a likelihood or posterior probability value for a probabilistic classifier, an Euclidean distance for a nearest-neighbour classifier, etc. Since the probability of classification error increases as the distance gets closer to the decision boundary between classes, this "soft" classifier output, and its distribution, constitute valuable data for error prediction, and are applicable to any biometric modality whose classifier is capable of producing measurement-level output. Estimation of classifier reliability based only on this soft classifier output is generally called *confidence estimation*.

In our experience on speech and signature, however, the boundary defined by the measurement-level output distribution between correct decisions and incorrect decisions of the base classifier is complex, and it is difficult (but not impossible) to train a meta-classifier that performs with fewer errors than the base classifier whose behaviour it models[2]. This is illustrated by the projections on the horizontal axis shown in Figure 1.

Thus, we introduce a second modality-independent quality measure, that is well correlated with errors and the score: the difference between the user-specific

---

[1] However, it is generally not the case that the relationship between quality measures and base classifier errors can be modelled effectively by linear or low-order polynomial regression.

[2] This is the likely reason for the lack of improvement in fusion mentioned in [8] when using a score-based confidence model.

threshold and the user-independent threshold. In a verification system using user-independent thresholds[3], some users will be more systematically subjected to false rejects, respectively false accepts, than others. As can be seen in Figure 1, this feature makes the reliability classification task easier for both the speech and signature modality.

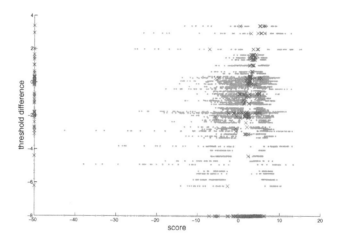

(a) Quality measures computed from the output of a signature base classifier using local features.

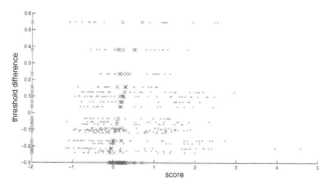

(b) Quality measures computed from the output of a speaker verification base classifier using Mel-frequency cepstral coefficients (MFCC) features.

Fig. 1. Score and threshold difference quality measures for signature verification (MCYT100) and speaker verification (BANCA, G2). Dots indicate reliable (correct) decisions, crosses indicate unreliable (erroneous) decisions of the base classifier. Each quality measure is also projected onto its axis.

---

[3] For instance because it has recently been deployed and there is not enough data for each user to reliably set a personalised threshold.

3 Reliability Estimation

Once the two features (score and threshold difference) are extracted, we can use nearly any classication algorithm to estimate the reliability of base decisions, with some limitations we discuss in section 3.1. In our case, we use an ensemble of decision trees, either a C4.5 pruned decision tree [9] with bagging or a random forest classifier [10]. In previous work, we have used Bayesian networks to perform reliability estimation [11]. The training data (development set) is separate from the base classifier's training data and the test data, and is generated by running the base classifiers on the development samples.

3.1 Limits of Reliability Modelling

Since we use measurement-level output of the base classifier as one of the features for modelling reliability of decisions, the reliability model is dependent on the accuracy of the base classifier. By definition a well-performing base classifiers has a lower density of soft outputs (which correspond to reliable or unreliable decisions) near the decision boundary than a base classifier with a higher error rate.

However, we can guarantee that the reliability classifier will perform better than the base classifier under certain conditions, which we will phrase in terms of confusion matrices (contingency tables). Let us define $\mathbf{B}$ as the confusion matrix of the base classifier, and $\mathbf{R}$ as the confusion matrix of the reliability classifier. The classes in $\mathbf{B}$, used by the base classifier, are *0—impostor* and *1—client*, while the classes in $\mathbf{R}$, used by the reliability model, are *0—unreliable* and *1—reliable*.

$$\mathbf{B} = \begin{pmatrix} a & b \\ c & d \end{pmatrix}, \mathbf{R} = \begin{pmatrix} e & f \\ g & h \end{pmatrix} \tag{1}$$

The two confusion matrices are linked by the fact that the reliability model has as class 0 (unreliable) the errors of the base classifier (off-diagonal elements in $\mathbf{B}$), and conversely as class 1 (reliable) the correct decisions of the base classifier (diagonal elements in $\mathbf{B}$):

$$b + c = e + f, \quad a + d = g + h \tag{2}$$

The condition for the reliability model to be able to improve on the output of the base classifier is that the reliability model must make less errors than the base classifier, meaning that the sum of the number of base errors considered reliable and the number of base correct decisions considered unreliable must be less than the sum of the base errors. Equivalently, the accuracy of the reliability model must be higher than that of the base classifier. This formulation can be written as in Equation (3) and simplified by using Equations (2) to obtain Equation (5).

$$\frac{e+h}{(e+f)+(g+h)} > \frac{a+d}{(a+d)+(b+c)} \tag{3}$$

$$\frac{e+h}{(e+f)+(g+h)} > \frac{g+h}{(g+h)+(e+f)} \tag{4}$$

$$e > g \tag{5}$$

Any reliability model whose confusion matrix satisfies the condition expressed in Equation (5) is guaranteed to have less errors than the base classifier it models, and to be useful in reducing base classifier error rates, even if the base classifier performs below chance. If, in addition to reducing base errors, we want the reliability model to perform above chance, we can add the condition

$$e + h > f + g \tag{6}$$

4 Using Reliability in Voting Combiners

While majority voting is an appealing combining scheme, its optimality depends on several assumptions[4], of which we will mention chiefly the fact that it assumes comparable expertise of the ensemble base classifiers. In biometric applications it is often not the case, especially when combining several modalities, with sometimes one or more orders of magnitude of difference between the error rates of the base classifiers. Therefore, we propose three schemes that use classifier-specific reliability models as an input to a controller driving the voting process to improve on majority voting.

4.1 Rigged Majority Voting

The first scheme we propose, rigged majority voting (RMV), uses the base classifier's reliability model to estimate, on an instance-by-instance basis, when its decision is likely to be unreliable. In such cases, the voting controller will rig the vote by inverting it (the role of prior probabilities in the inversion process is discussed in [12]). Denoting the base classifier decision by a binary variable CID (0 for impostors, 1 for clients), the reliability classification by a binary variable DR (0 for unreliable, 1 for reliable), and the rigged decision by RD, the voting controller implements the negative exclusive-or function: $RD = \overline{CID \oplus DR}$ This method works instance-by-instance, by estimating for each case the reliability of the decision.

If the reliability models satisfy Eq. (5), and assuming the correlation between the rigged votes is the same as the correlation between the votes of the base classifiers, this scheme guarantees a better lower and upper bounds on the achievable fused accuracy than simple majority voting on the base classifiers, because the rigged decisions will have higher individual accuracies. This result can be proved using the method in [13].

---

[4] Such as independence of ensemble members.

However, in the case of base classifiers with very different error rates (say, an order of magnitude), this scheme does not guarantee that we can outperform the best base classifier. We therefore introduce a variation on the voting controller by weighting the contributions of individual classifiers.

4.2 Weighted Rigged Majority Voting

The second scheme we introduce, weighted rigged majority voting (WRMV) is also based on rigged votes, which is an instance-specific method, but the rigged votes are subsequently weighted by a factor proportional to the accuracy of that classifier's reliability model. Thus, we also take into account the overall performance of the base classifier on a development set.

Even though the classifiers violate the independence assumption, and the weights may therefore be suboptimal [14, p.124], we set the classifier-specific weights w_n to

$$\sum_{n=1}^{N} w_n = 1, \quad w_n \propto \frac{acc_n}{1 - acc_n}, \tag{7}$$

where the accuracy of each reliability model acc_n is computed according to the confusion matrix $\mathbf{R}$ in Eq. (1).

The difference with standard practice for weighted majority voting is that the accuracy used in weighting is not that of the base classifier, but is replaced by the accuracy of the reliability model, which is higher. Thus, the weights are dependent on the effectiveness of the reliability model. However, since the accuracies of the reliability models may follow the same ordering as the accuracies of the base models, the results may not always differ significantly.

The majority threshold is changed from $\tau \geq \lfloor N/2 \rfloor + 1$ for unweighted majority voting to $\tau > \sum_{N_{worst}} w_n$. Thus, the vote of the worst N classifiers N_{worst} in the ensemble is insufficient to win the vote, and if reliabilities are unbalanced the opinion of the most reliable classifiers will count much more. N_{worst} can be chosen as $\lfloor N/2 \rfloor + 1$.

4.3 Selective Rigged Majority Voting

The selective rigged majority voting scheme (SRMV) operates on the same principle as the confidence gating method used in [3], the reliability-based decision table in [1], and the arbitration scheme of [4]: the classifier with the highest confidence gets to label the sample. The difference in our case is that we are operating on decisions that have been rigged by the voting controller before the selection.

Under some conditions (e.g. three classifiers, one of which clearly dominates for most patterns), selective voting can give results very close to weighted rigged majority voting. This is because the weights assigned to the members of the ensemble are proportional to the error rate of their associated reliability classifier.

5   Experiments

In these experiments, we first test the accuracy of the reliability model of each classifier for predicting errors (Section 5.2). Then, in Section 5.3 we apply reliability models to voting on a signature verification task.

5.1   Databases and Base Classifiers

For the signature modality, we use the 100-users MCYT-100 database [15] and the 40-users training set of the SVC2004 database [16]. For the speech modality we use the 52-users, English part of the BANCA database [17] and the 295-users XM2VTS database [18].

The base classifiers for signature are a Gaussian mixture model (GMM) using 15 local features [19] (abbreviated *LGMM*), a GMM using 12 global features (abbreviated *GGMM*), and a multi-layer perceptron (MLP) using the same 12 global features (abbreviated *GMLP*). Both the GMMs and the MLP are learned from 5 signatures, and the MLP is learned using discriminative training.

The base classifier for speaker verification is a GMM based on the Alize toolkit [20] (abbreviated *AGMM*), trained following each speech database's specific protocol (P for BANCA, configuration I for XM2VTS).

5.2   Reliability Prediction with Modality-Independent Quality Measures

The experiments are performed using 10-fold cross-validation and data from all users. Essentially, we want to verify whether we can learn a reliability model that will make less mistakes than the underlying base classifiers. If it is the case, then the reliability model can be used to enhance the performance of the base classifier.

Several types of classifiers were tested for reliability modelling, and the two most promising ones were: bagging of C4.5 trees (abbreviated *BC45*), and random forest classifiers (abbreviated *RF*). For space reasons we will report here only the best performing of the two. The results are reported in Table 1.

5.3   Voting Schemes with Reliability

We compare two baseline combiners, majority voting (abbreviated MV) and weighted majority voting (WMV), to three reliability-based voting combiners: rigged majority voting (RMV), weighted rigged majority voting (WRMV), and selective rigged majority voting (SRMV). The base classifiers are those presented above, with the decision thresholds computed a posteriori.

Table 2 presents the results of the tests on the SVC 2004 signature database. In addition, we performed the McNemar hypothesis test to assess whether the combiners presented are significantly different ($p = 0.05$). Despite the encouraging results, the small size of the dataset (40 users, 1400 cases available for fusion tests) means that the only significant difference (in the majority of the

Table 1. 10-fold cross-validation results of reliability prediction. *DB* indicates the database: S for SVC2004, M for MCYT100, B(G1/2) for BANCA G1 or G2, X(E/T) for XM2VTS Eval or Test set. *Classifier* refers to the type of base classifier used. *Rel Classifier* refers to the type of the reliability classifier used. *Err* is the error rate (in percent) of the base classifier. Err_r is the error rate (in percent) of the associated reliability model. *Decrease* shows the relative reduction in error rate that can be obtained by using the reliability model along with the base classifier. For BANCA G1, an AdaBoosted ensemble of C4.5 trees brings about a 21.4% relative improvement in the error rate.

DB	Classifier	Rel Classifier	Err [%]	Err_r [%]	Decrease [%]
S	LGMM	RF	8.5	4.0	53.0
S	GGMM	BC45	22.0	16.6	24.0
S	GMLP	BC45	23.8	19.8	17.0
M	LGMM	BC45	3.3	1.8	46.7
M	GGMM	BC45	19.0	12.4	34.7
M	GMLP	BC45	22.6	16.8	26.0
X(E)	AGMM	BC45	1.0	0.8	23.5
X(T)	AGMM	BC45	0.3	0.2	33.0
B(G1)	AGMM	RF=BC45	7.7	7.7	0
B(G2)	AGMM	RF	8.4	4.8	44.0

Table 2. 10-fold cross-validation results of reliability-based decision fusion on the SVC2004 signature database (denoted 'S') and the MCYT100 signature database (denoted 'M'). Baseline best is the best classifier in the ensemble. The standard deviation over the 10 folds is given along with the error rates. *FAR* is the false accept rate (impostor accepted as a client), *FRR* the false reject rate (client rejected as an impostor), and *HTER* is the half total error-rate, $HTER = \frac{FAR+FRR}{2}$.

DB	Scheme	FAR [%]	FRR [%]	$HTER$ [%]
S	Baseline best	8.6 ± 3.6	8.5 ± 3.0	8.6 ± 2.1
S	MV	10.3 ± 3.0	12.9 ± 3.9	11.6 ± 2.2
S	WMV	6.1 ± 3.9	15.9 ± 4.6	11.1 ± 2.0
S	RMV	4.9 ± 2.2	11.2 ± 4.9	8.0 ± 2.2
S	WRMV	2.2 ± 3.0	9.2 ± 5.2	5.7 ± 2.5
S	SRMV	3.3 ± 2.5	6.1 ± 3.4	4.7 ± 1.6
M	Baseline best	3.4 ± 1.1	3.3 ± 0.9	3.3 ± 0.8
M	MV	7.8 ± 1.2	9.0 ± 2.8	8.4 ± 1.2
M	WMV	3.4 ± 1.1	3.3 ± 0.9	3.3 ± 0.8
M	RMV	3.7 ± 1.0	5.0 ± 1.6	4.3 ± 0.8
M	WRMV	1.3 ± 0.8	2.3 ± 0.9	1.8 ± 0.5
M	SRMV	1.5 ± 0.8	2.4 ± 0.1	2.0 ± 0.4

cross-validation runs) is between the MV and SRMV combining schemes. Additionally, WMV and WRMV as well as WMV and SV are significantly different in 50% of the cross-validation folds. Note that using MV or WMV on this ensemble would actually degrade the performance.

Thus, we ran the same experiment on MCYT-100, a larger database comprising 4500 cases. The results are shown in Table 2. On this dataset, all three reliability-based schemes significantly outperform MV and WMV, and WRMV and SRMV both significantly outperform the best base classifier. This underlines the importance of properly assigning weights in imbalanced ensembles. As can be seen from the results for WMV, however, this is not always sufficient, and a finer modelling of the underlying classifier's behaviour can bring enhanced performance.

6   Conclusion

We have presented a new model for classifier reliability, based on features that can be applied independently of the underlying modality. We have used the new reliability model in three new decision-level fusion methods that take into account the overall reliability of individual classifiers on a development set, the instance-by-instance reliability of each classifier's decision, or both.

The rigged voting scheme improves over baseline methods by lowering the bias of the base classifiers. However, the current approach makes no guarantee about the remaining correlation between the rigged votes of the base classifiers, an important factor in voting-based schemes. It is likely that the results would be better with less correlation between base classifiers, as would be the case for majority voting in multimodal verification.

Also, to more clearly show the difference between the WRMV and the SRMV method, it would be interesting to perform experiments with more than 3 classifiers, and with more evenly matched classifiers.

Acknowledgements

We thank J. Ortega-Garcia and J. Fierrez-Aguilar for the provision of the MCYT-100 signature sub-corpus. The research on which this paper is based acknowledges the use of the Extended Multimodal Face Database and associated documentation. Further details of this software can be found in [18].

References

1. Kryszczuk, K., Richiardi, J., Prodanov, P., Drygajlo, A.: Error handling in multimodal biometric systems using reliability measures. In: Proc. 12th European Conference on Signal Processing (EUSIPCO), Antalya, Turkey (2005)
2. Fierrez-Aguilar, J., Ortega-Garcia, J., Gonzalez-Rodriguez, J., Bigun, J.: Discriminative multimodal biometric authentication based on quality measures. Pattern Recognition **38** (2005) 777–779
3. Sadeghi, M.T., Kittler, J.: Confidence based gating of multiple face authentication experts. In: Proc. Joint IAPR Int. Workshops, Structural, Syntactic, and Statistical Pattern Recognition 2006. Volume 4109/2006. (2006) 667–676

4. Ortega, J., Koppel, M., Argamon, S.: Arbitrating among competing classifiers using learned referees. Knowledge and Information Systems **V3** (2001) 470–490

5. Alpaydin, E., Kaynak, C.: Cascading classifiers. Kybernetika **34** (1998) 369–374

6. Koppel, M., Engelson, S.P.: Integrating multiple classifiers by finding their areas of expertise. In: Working Notes of the Workshop on Integrating Multiple Learned Models for Improving and Scaling Machine Learning Algorithms. (1996) held in conjunction with the 13th Nat. Conf. on Artificial Intelligence (AAAI-96).

7. Dutra, T., Canuto, A.M.P., de Souto, M.C.P.: Using weighted combination-based methods in ensembles with different levels of diversity. In: Proc. 13th Int. Conf. on Neural Information Processing (ICONIP 2006), Hong Kong, China (2006) 708–717

8. Bengio, S., Marcel, C., Marcel, S., Mariéthoz, J.: Confidence measures for multi-modal identity verification. Information Fusion **3** (2002) 267–276

9. Quinlan, J.: Induction of decision trees. Machine Learning **V1** (1986) 81–106

10. Breiman, L.: Random forests. Machine Learning **45** (2001) 5–32

11. Richiardi, J., Prodanov, P., Drygajlo, A.: Speaker verification with confidence and reliability measures. In: Proc. 2006 IEEE International Conference on Speech, Acoustics and Signal Processing, Toulouse, France (2006)

12. Kryszczuk, K., Drygajlo, A.: Reliability measures and error prediction in biometric identity verification. Journal of Signal Processing (2006) (submitted).

13. Matan, O.: On voting ensembles of classifiers (extended abstract). In: Working Notes of the Workshop on Integrating Multiple Learned Models for Improving and Scaling Machine Learning Algorithms, Portland, USA (1996) held in conjunction with the 13th Nat. Conf. on Artificial Intelligence (AAAI-96).

14. Kuncheva, L.I.: Combining Pattern Classifiers. Wiley and sons (2004)

15. J. Ortega-Garcia et al.: MCYT baseline corpus: a bimodal biometric database. IEE Proc. Vision, Image and Signal Processing **150** (2003) 395–401

16. Yeung, D.Y., Chang, H., Xiong, Y., George, S., Kashi, R., Matsumoto, T., Rigoll, G.: SVC2004: First international signature verification competition. In: Proceedings 2004 Biometric Authentication: First International Conference, (ICBA 2004), Hong Kong, China (2004) 16–22

17. Bailly-Bailliére, E., Bengio, S., Bimbot, F., Hamouz, M., Kittler, J., Mariéthoz, J., Matas, J., Messer, K., Popovici, V., Porée, F., Ruiz, B., Thiran, J.P.: The BANCA database and evaluation protocol. In Kittler, J., Nixon, M., eds.: Proceedings of 4th Int. Conf. on Audio- and Video-Based Biometric Person Authentication (AVBPA). Volume LNCS 2688. (2003) 625–638

18. Messer, K., Matas, J., Kittler, J., Luettin, J., Maitre, G.: XM2VTSDB: The extended M2VTS database. In: Proceedings of 2nd International Conference on Audio- and Video-Based Biometric Person Authentication (AVBPA). (1999) 72–77

19. Richiardi, J., Drygajlo, A.: Gaussian mixture models for on-line signature verification. In: Proc. ACM SIGMM Multimedia, Workshop on Biometrics methods and applications (WBMA), Berkeley, USA (2003) 115–122

20. Bonastre, J.F., Wils, F., Meignier, S.: ALIZE, a free toolkit for speaker recognition. In: Proceedings IEEE International Conference on Acoustics, Speech, and Signal Processing (ICASSP 2005), Philadelphia, USA (2005) 737–740

Optimal Classifier Combination Rules for Verification and Identification Systems

Sergey Tulyakov, Venu Govindaraju, and Chaohong Wu

Center for Unified Biometrics and Sensors (CUBS), SUNY at Buffalo, USA

Abstract. Matching systems can be used in different operation tasks such as verification task and identification task. Different optimization criteria exist for these tasks - reducing cost of acceptance decisions for verification systems and minimizing misclassification rate for identification systems. In this paper we show that the optimal combination rules satisfying these criteria are also different. The difference is caused by the dependence of matching scores produced by a single matcher and assigned to different classes. We illustrate the theory by experiments with biometric matchers and handwritten word recognizers.

1 Introduction

Traditionally, the goal of pattern classification algorithms is to minimize the misclassification rate or cost[7]. With the development of biometric field another type of optimization criteria became important - minimizing the cost of verifying the hypothesis of whether the input belongs to the prespecified class. In particular, for biometric verification system we need to determine whether the presented biometric input belongs to the claimed enrolled person. The verification problem is a two-class problem - the input does belong to the hypothesis class (genuine verification attempt) or does not (impostor). On the other hand, the traditional classification problem still takes place in biometrics as an identification problem: given biometric input determine the person among N enrolled persons. Note, that similar task division existed before in other pattern recognition tasks. As an example of verification system in a handwriting application, a bank check recognition system might hypothesize about the value of the check based on the legal field, and numeric string recognition module must confirm that courtesy value coincides with the legal amount[4]. Or, more frequently, a handwriting recognition module is used to identify each word between N words in the lexicon.

It turns out that different tasks might require different optimizations of recognition algorithms. Example 1 of this paper presents two hypothetical recognition algorithms with one more suited for verification task and another for identification task. Similarly, if we have two or more matching algorithms, and we want to combine their results, the best combination algorithms might be different for different tasks. The goal of this paper is to show that this is indeed the case. Whereas the optimal combination algorithm for verification systems corresponds to likelihood ratio combination rule, the optimal combination algorithm for identification systems might be different, and it is rather difficult to find.

M. Haindl, J. Kittler, and F. Roli (Eds.): MCS 2007, LNCS 4472, pp. 387–396, 2007.

1.1   Performance Measures

Different modes of operation demand different performance measures. For verification systems the performance is traditionally measured by means of Receiver Operating Characteristic (ROC) curves or by Detection Error Trade-off (DET) curve. These curves are well suited for describing the performance of two-class pattern classification problems. In such problems there are two types of errors: the samples of first class are classified to belong to second class, and samples of second class are classified to be in first class. The decision to classify a sample to be in one of two classes is usually based on some threshold. Both performance curves show the relationship between two error rates with regards to a threshold (see [2] for precise definition of above performance measures). In our case we will use ROC curves for comparing algorithm performance.

For measuring performance of identification systems we will use ranking approach. In particular, we are interested in maximizing the rate of correctly identifying the input, first-rank-correct rate. If we look at identification task as a pattern classification problem, this performance measure will directly correspond to the traditional minimization of the classification error. Note that there are also other approaches to measure performance in identification systems[2], e.g. Rank Probability Mass, Cumulative Match Curve, Recall-Precision Curve. Though they might be useful for some applications, in our case we will be more interested in correct identification rate.

2   Verification Systems

The problem of combining matchers in verification systems can be easily solved with pattern classification approach. As we already noted, there are two classes: genuine verification attempts and impostor verification attempts. The hypothesis identity of the input is provided before matching. Each matcher j outputs a score s^j corresponding to a match confidence between input sample and hypothesis identity. Assuming that we combine M matchers, our task is to perform two-class classification (genuine and impostor) in M-dimensional score space $\{s^1, \ldots, s^M\}$. If the number of combined matchers M is small, we will have no trouble in training pattern classification algorithm.

We employ the Bayesian risk minimization method as our classification approach[7]. This method states that the optimal decision boundaries between two classes can be found by comparing the likelihood ratio

$$f_{lr}(s^1, \ldots, s^M) = \frac{p_{gen}(s^1, \ldots, s^M)}{p_{imp}(s^1, \ldots, s^M)} \tag{1}$$

to some threshold θ where p_{gen} and p_{imp} are M-dimensional densities of score tuples $\{s^1, \ldots, s^M\}$ corresponding to two classes - genuine and impostor verification attempts. In order to use this method we have to estimate the densities p_{gen} and p_{imp} from the training data.

The likelihood ratio combination method is theoretically optimal for verification systems and its performance only limited by our ability to correctly estimate score densities. But, since our problem is the separation of genuine and impostor classes, we could apply many existing pattern classification techniques as well. For example, support vector machines have shown good performance in many tasks, and can be definitely used to improve the likelihood ratio method. In [8] we performed some comparisons of likelihood ratio method with SVMs on an artificial task and found that on average (over many random training sets) SVMs do have slightly better performance, but for a particular training set it might not be true. The difference in performance is quite small and decreases with the increasing number of training samples.

3   Identification Systems

In identification systems a hypothesis of the input sample is not available and we have to choose the input's class among all possible classes. Denote N as the number of classes. The total number of matching scores available for combination now is MN: N matching scores for N classes from each of M combined classifiers. If numbers M and N are not big, then we can use generic pattern classifiers in MN-dimensional score space to find the input's class among N classes. For some problems, e.g. digit or character recognition, this is an acceptable approach; the number of classes is small and usually there is a sufficient number of training samples to properly train pattern classification algorithms operating in MN score space.

But for our applications in handwritten word recognition and biometric person identification the number of classes is too big and the number of training samples is too small (there might be even no training samples at all for a particular lexicon word), so the pattern classification in the MN-dimensional score space seems to be out of the question. The traditional approach in this situation is to use some combination rules. The combination rule implies the use of some combination function f operating only on M scores corresponding to one class, $f(s^1, \ldots, s^M)$, and it states that the decision class C is the one which maximizes the value of a combination function:

$$C = \arg \max_{i=1,\ldots,N} f(s_i^1, \ldots, s_i^M) \tag{2}$$

Note that in our notation the upper index of the score corresponds to the classifier, which produced this score, and lower index corresponds to the class for which it was produced. The names of combination rules are usually directly derived from the names of used combination functions: the sum function $f(s^1, \ldots, s^M) = s^1 + \cdots + s^M$ corresponds to the sum rule, the product function $f(s^1, \ldots, s^M) = s^1 \ldots s^M$ corresponds to the product rule and so on.

Many combination rules have been proposed so far, but there is no agreement on the best one. It seems that different applications require different combination rules for best performance. Anyone wishing to combine matchers in real life has to test few of them and choose the one with best performance.

3.1 Likelihood Ratio Combination Rule

As we already know, likelihood ratio function is the optimal combination function for verification systems. We want to investigate whether it will be optimal for identification systems. Suppose we performed a match of the input sample by all M matchers against all N classes and obtained MN matching scores $\{s_i^j\}_{i=1,...,N;j=1,...,M}$. Assuming equal prior class probabilities, the Bayes decision theory states that in order to minimize the misclassification rate the sample should be classified as one with highest value of likelihood function $p(\{s_i^j\}_{i=1,...,N;j=1,...,M}|\omega_k)$. Thus, for any two classes ω_1 and ω_2 we have to classify input as ω_1 rather than ω_2 if

$$p(\{s_i^j\}_{i=1,...,N;j=1,...,M}|\omega_1) > p(\{s_i^j\}_{i=1,...,N;j=1,...,M}|\omega_2) \qquad (3)$$

Let us make an assumption that the scores assigned to each class are sampled independently from scores assigned to other classes; scores assigned to genuine class are sampled from M-dimensional genuine score density, and scores assigned to impostor classes are sampled from M-dimensional impostor score density:

$$
\begin{aligned}
p(\{s_i^j\}_{i=1,...,N;j=1,...,M}&|\omega_k) \\
&= p(\{s_1^1,...,s_1^M\},...,\{s_{\omega_k}^1,...,s_{\omega_i}^M\},...,\{s_N^1,...,s_N^M\}|\omega_k) \qquad (4) \\
&= p_{imp}(s_1^1,...,s_1^M)...p_{gen}(s_{\omega_k}^1,...,s_{\omega_k}^M)...p_{imp}(s_N^1,...,s_N^M)
\end{aligned}
$$

After substituting 4 into 3 and canceling out common factors we obtain the following inequality for accepting class ω_1 rather than ω_2:

$$p_{gen}(s_{\omega_1}^1,...,s_{\omega_1}^M)p_{imp}(s_{\omega_2}^1,...,s_{\omega_2}^M) > p_{imp}(s_{\omega_1}^1,...,s_{\omega_1}^M)p_{gen}(s_{\omega_2}^1,...,s_{\omega_2}^M)$$

or

$$\frac{p_{gen}(s_{\omega_1}^1,...,s_{\omega_1}^M)}{p_{imp}(s_{\omega_1}^1,...,s_{\omega_1}^M)} > \frac{p_{gen}(s_{\omega_2}^1,...,s_{\omega_2}^M)}{p_{imp}(s_{\omega_2}^1,...,s_{\omega_2}^M)} \qquad (5)$$

The terms in each part of the above inequality are exactly the values of the likelihood ratio function f_{lr} taken at the sets of scores assigned to classes ω_1 and ω_2. Thus, the class maximizing the MN-dimensional likelihood function of inequality 3 is the same as a class maximizing the M-dimensional likelihood ratio function of inequality 5. The likelihood ratio combination rule is the optimal combination rule under used assumptions of score independence.

The main assumption that we made while deriving likelihood ratio combination rule is that the score samples in each identification trial are independent. That is, genuine score is sampled from genuine score distribution and is independent from impostor scores which are independent and identically distributed according to impostor score distribution. We can verify if this assumption is true for our matchers.

Table 1 shows correlations between genuine score and some functions of the impostor score sets obtained in the same identification trial. $first_{imp}$ column

Table 1. Correlations between s_{gen} and different statistics of the impostor score sets produced during identification trials for considered matchers

Matchers	$first_{imp}$	$second_{imp}$	$third_{imp}$	$mean_{imp}$
CMR	0.4359	0.4755	0.4771	0.1145
WMR	0.7885	0.7825	0.7663	0.5685
li	0.3164	0.3400	0.3389	0.2961
C	0.1419	0.1513	0.1562	0.1440
G	0.1339	0.1800	0.1827	0.1593

has correlations between genuine and the best impostor score, and so on. Non-zero correlations indicate that the scores are dependent, and likelihood ratio combination rule will not necessarily be optimal for our applications.

The main reason for the dependence among matching scores produced during identification trial is that they are derived using same input signal. The next two examples will illustrate the effect of score dependences on the performance of identification systems. In particular, second example confirms that if identification system uses likelihood ratio combination, then its performance can be worse than the performance of a single matcher.

Example 1. Suppose we have an identification system with one matcher and, for simplicity, $N = 2$ classes. During each identification attempt a matcher produces two scores corresponding to two classes, and, since by our assumption the input is one of these two classes (closed set identification), one of these scores will be genuine match score, and another will be impostor match score. Suppose we collected a data on the distributions of genuine and impostor scores and reconstructed score densities (let them be gaussian) as shown in Figure 1.

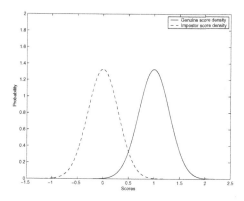

Fig. 1. Hypothetical densities of matching(genuine) and non-matching(impostors) scores

Consider two possible scenarios on how these densities might have originated from the sample of the identification attempts:

1. Both scores s_{gen} and s_{imp} are sampled independently from genuine and impostor distributions.
2. In every observed identification attempt : $s_{imp} = s_{gen} - 1$. Thus in this scenario the identification system always correctly places genuine sample on top. There is a strong dependency between scores given to two classes, and score distributions of Figure 1 do not reflect this fact.

If a system works in verification mode and we have only one match score to make a decision on accepting or rejecting input, we can only compare this score to some threshold. By doing so both scenarios would have same performance: the rate of false accepts (impostor samples having match score higher than threshold) and the rate of false rejects (genuine samples having match score lower than threshold) will be determined by integrating impostor and genuine densities of Figure 1 no matter what scenario we have. If system works in identification mode, the recognizer of the second scenario will be a clear winner: it is always correct while the recognizer of first scenario can make mistakes and place impostor samples on top.

This example shows that the performance of the matcher in the verification system might not predict its performance in the identification system. Given two matchers, one might be better for verification systems, and another for identification systems.

Example 2. Consider a combination of two matchers in two class identification system: one matcher is from the first scenario, and the other is from the second scenario. Assume that these matchers are independent. Let the upper score index refer to the matcher producing this score; s_i^j is the score for class i assigned by the classifier j. From our construction we know that the second matcher always outputs genuine score on the top. So the optimal combination rule for identification system will simply discard scores of first matcher and retain scores of the second matcher:

$$f(s^1, s^2) = s^2 \tag{6}$$

The input will always be correctly classified as $\arg\max_i s_i^2$.

Let us now use the likelihood ratio combination rule for this system. Since we assumed that matchers are independent, the densities of genuine $p_{gen}(s^1, s^2)$ and impostor $p_{imp}(s^1, s^2)$ scores are obtained by multiplying corresponding one-dimensional score densities of two matchers. In our example, impostor scores are distributed as a Gaussian centered at $(0, 0)$, and genuine scores are distributed as a Gaussian centered at $(1, 1)$. Figure 2(a) contains the contours of function $|p_{gen} - p_{imp}|$ which allows us to see the relative position of these gaussians. The gaussians have same covariance matrix, and thus the optimal decision contours are hyperplanes[7] - lines $s^1 + s^2 = c$. Correspondingly, the likelihood ratio combination function is equivalent to the combination function $f = s^1 + s^2$ (note, that true likelihood ratio function will be different, but if two functions have same contours, then their combination rules will be the same). Such combination improves the performance of the verification system relative to any single matcher; Figure 2(b) shows corresponding ROC curves for any single matchers and their combination.

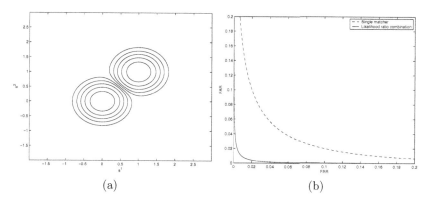

(a)   (b)

Fig. 2. (a) Two-dimensional distributions of genuine and impostor scores for examples 2 and 3 (b) ROC curves for single matchers and their likelihood ratio combination

Suppose that (s_1^1, s_1^2) and (s_2^1, s_2^2) are two score pairs obtained during one identification trial. The likelihood ratio combination rule classifies the input as a class maximizing likelihood ratio function:

$$\arg\max_{i=1,2} \frac{p_{gen}(s_i^1, s_i^2)}{p_{imp}(s_i^1, s_i^2)} = \arg\max_{i=1,2} s_i^1 + s_i^2 \qquad (7)$$

Let the test sample be $(s_1^1, s_1^2) = (-0.1, 1.0)$, $(s_2^1, s_2^2) = (1.1, 0)$. We know from our construction that class 1 is the genuine class, since the second matcher assigned score 1.0 to it and 0 to the second class. But its score pair $(1.1, 0)$ is located just above the diagonal $s^1 + s^2 = 1$, and the score pair $(-0.1, 1.0)$ corresponding to class 1 is located just below this diagonal. Hence class 2 has bigger ratio of genuine to impostor densities than class 1, and the likelihood ratio combination method would incorrectly classify class 2 as the genuine class.

Thus the optimal for verification system likelihood ratio combination rule (7) has worse performance than a single second matcher. On the other hand, the optimal for identification system rule (6) does not improve the performance of the verification system. Recall, that in section 3.1 we showed that if scores assigned by matchers to different classes are independent, then likelihood ratio combination rule is optimal for identification systems, as well as for verification systems. Current example shows that if there is a dependency between scores, this is no longer a case, and the optimal combination for identification systems can be different from the optimal combination for verification systems.

4   Experiments

We have performed three sets of experiments for this paper - one for combining two word recognizers and two for combining fingerprint and face biometric matchers. Two handwritten word recognizers are Character Model Recognizer (CMR)[3] and Word Model Recognizer (WMR)[5]. Both recognizers employ similar approaches to word recognition: they oversegment the word images, match the combinations of segments to characters and derive a final matching score for each lexicon word as a function of character matching scores. Still, the correct identification rates of these recognizers (see Table 2) reveal that these matchers produce somewhat complementary results and their combination might be beneficial.

Our data consists of three sets of 2654, 1723 and 1770 word images representing UK postal town and county names of approximately same quality (the data was provided as these three subsets and we did not regroup them). The word recognizers were run on these images and their match scores for the total of 1681 lexicon words were saved. Since our data was already separated into three subsets, we used this structure for producing training and testing sets. Each experiment was repeated three times, each time one subset is used as a training set, and two other sets are used as test sets. Final results are derived as averages of these three training/testing phases.

We used biometric matching score set BSSR1 distributed by NIST[1]. This set contains matching scores for a fingerprint matcher and two face matchers 'C' and 'G'. Fingerprint matching scores are given for left index 'li' finger matches and right index 'ri' finger matches. In this work we used both face matching scores and fingerprint 'li' scores and we do two types of combinations: 'li'&'C' and 'li'&'G'. We used bigger subsets of this data set with 6000 identification attempts to create a set of virtual persons and their matching scores. After discarding enrollees and identification trials with failed biometric enrollment we obtained two equal sets - 2991 identification trials with 2997 enrolled persons with each part used as training and testing sets in two phases.

For our applications the number of matchers M is 2 and the number of training samples is large (bigger than 1000), so we can successfully estimate the score densities for the likelihood ratio combination method. We approximate both densities as the sums of 2-dimensional gaussian Parzen kernels. The window parameter is estimated by the maximum likelihood method on the training set[6] using leave-one-out technique. Note that window parameter is different for genuine and impostor density approximations.

4.1   Identification System Experiments

Table 2 shows the performance of likelihood ratio rule on our data sets. Whereas the combinations of biometric matchers have significantly higher correct identification rates than single matchers, the combination of word recognizers has lower correct identification rate than a single WMR matcher. Example 2 provides an

Table 2. Correct identification rate for likelihood ratio and weighted sum combination rules

Matchers	Total	1st matcher is correct	2nd matcher is correct	Either one is correct	Likelihood Ratio Rule	Weighted Sum Rule
CMR&WMR	6147	3366	4744	5105	4293	5015
li&C	5982	4870	4856	5789	5817	5816
li&G	5982	4870	4635	5731	5737	5711

explanation to this result; there is a strong dependence in matching scores for WMR and it affects the performance of likelihood ratio combination.

We compare the performance of the likelihood ratio combination method with the weighted sum combination rule $f(s^1, \ldots, s^M) = w_1 s^1 + \cdots + w_M s^M$. We train the weights so that the number of successful identification trials on the training set is maximized. Since we have two matchers in all configurations we use brute-force method: we calculate the correct identification rate of combination function $f(s^1, s^2) = w s^1 + (1 - w) s^2$ for different values of $w \in [0, 1]$, and find w corresponding to highest rate.

The numbers of successful identification trials on the test sets is presented in Table 2. In all cases we see an improvement over the performances of single matchers. The combination of word recognizers is now successful and is in line with the performance of other combinations of matchers. Weighted sum method seems to perform slightly worse than likelihood ratio for biometric matchers, which can be explained by its simplicity. Another possible reason for this is that likelihood ratio combination rule is actually the optimal rule for classifiers with independent identification trial scores, and scores of biometric matchers show less dependence than scores of word recognizers.

4.2 Verification System Experiments

Figure 3 contains ROC curves likelihood ratio and weighted sum combination rules in verirification tasks. The weights in the weighted sum rule are the same as trained in identification experiments. In all cases we get slightly worse performance from the weighted sum rule than from the likelihood ratio rule. This

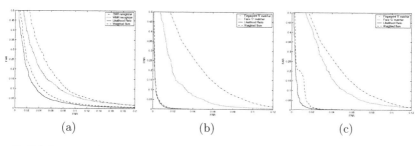

| (a) | (b) | (c) |

Fig. 3. ROC curves for combinations of (a) CMR and WMR, (b) 'li' and 'C', (c) 'li' and 'G'

confirms our assertion that the likelihood ratio is the optimal combination method for verification systems.

5 Conclusion

The combination of matchers for verification problems is relatively easy task with likelihood ratio combination rule being the optimal method, as well as many other two-class pattern classification methods. On the other hand, the combination in identification problems might require different methods, and it is rather difficult task. In practice, presented results argue that we can not effectively use same combination method for both verification and identification. Though the weighted sum rule shows good performance in identification systems, there is a need to develop more finely trainable combination methods.

References

1. Nist biometric scores set. http://www.nist.gov/biometricscores/.
2. Ruud M. Bolle, Jonathan H. Connell, Sharath Pankanti, Nalini K. Ratha, and Andrew W. Senior. *Guide To Biometrics*. Springer, New York, 2004.
3. J.T. Favata. Character model word recognition. In *Fifth International Workshop on Frontiers in Handwriting Recognition*, pages 437–440, Essex, England, 1996.
4. G.Kim and V.Govindaraju. Bank check recognition using cross validation between legal and courtesy amounts. *Int'l J. Pattern Recognition and Artificial Intelligence*, 11(4):657–674, 1997.
5. G. Kim and V. Govindaraju. A lexicon driven approach to handwritten word recognition for real-time applications. *Pattern Analysis and Machine Intelligence, IEEE Transactions on*, 19(4):366–379, 1997.
6. B W Silverman. *Density estimation for statistics and data analysis*. Chapman and Hall, London, 1986.
7. S. Theodoridis and Koutroumbas K. *Pattern Recognition*. Academic Press, 1999.
8. S. Tulyakov and Govindaraju V. Using independence assumption to improve multimodal biometric fusion. In *6th International Workshop on Multiple Classifiers Systems (MCS2005)*, Monterey, USA, 2005. Springer.

Exploiting Diversity in Ensembles: Improving the Performance on Unbalanced Datasets

Nitesh V. Chawla[1] and Jared Sylvester[2]

[1] Department of Computer Science and Engineering
University of Notre Dame, IN 46556, USA
nchawla@cse.nd.edu
[2] Department of Computer Science
University of Maryland, College Park, MD 20742, USA
jsylvest@umd.edu

Abstract. Ensembles are often capable of greater predictive performance than any of their individual classifiers. Despite the need for classifiers to make different kinds of errors, the majority voting scheme, typically used, treats each classifier as though it contributed equally to the group's performance. This can be particularly limiting on unbalanced datasets, as one is more interested in complementing classifiers that can assist in improving the true positive rate without signicantly increasing the false positive rate. Therefore, we implement a genetic algorithm based framework to weight the contribution of each classifier by an appropriate fitness function, such that the classifiers that complement each other on the unbalanced dataset are preferred, resulting in significantly improved performances. The proposed framework can be built on top of any collection of classifiers with different fitness functions.

1 Introduction

Ensemble techniques are becoming increasingly important as they have repeatedly demonstrated the capacity to improve upon the accuracy of a single classifier in practice and theory [1,2,3]. Ensembles can either be homogeneous, in which every base classifier is constructed with the same algorithm, or heterogeneous, in which different algorithms are used to learn the ensemble members. Once multiple classifiers have been constructed, their predictions are typically combined through some method of voting. Many of the popular ensemble techniques use a simple majority vote of every classifier. It stands to reason that not every member contributes equally to the group performance, and as such, not every member should be given equal weight in the decision making. However, the question remains how best to determine the relative worth of every classifier.

A simple solution would be to weight each individual according to its accuracy on some validation set. However, for an ensemble to be more accurate than its members, they need only be more accurate than a random guess [3]. It is not necessarily true that the most accurate classifiers contribute the most to an ensemble — diversity also plays an important role [4]. Diversity is the degree to

M. Haindl, J. Kittler, and F. Roli (Eds.): MCS 2007, LNCS 4472, pp. 397–406, 2007.

which classifiers disagree in the errors they make. This allows the voted accuracy to be greater than the accuracy of any single classifier.

Learning from unbalanced datasets can impose more exacting requirements on the diversity in types of errors among classifiers, because we are interested in the collection of classifiers that help in reducing the false negatives without significantly increasing the false positives. There is a non-uniformity in the types of errors that can be made, given the interest in increasing the true positives even if at the expense of increasing the false positives. Moreover, the classifiers themselves are learned with the objective criterion of reducing the overall error, and not necessarily the error on the positive class, which is typically the minority class. The goal then is to be able to discover a weighting scheme for individual classifiers such that the collective classification helps in improving the true positive rate. One could potentially weight each classifier by a metric that is more amenable to evaluating classifiers on unbalanced datasets, but that does not help in realization of diversity. In this case, each classifier is independently evaluated on a validation set and that independent evaluation becomes the weight, but it does not help in realization of their performance as a collective.

Thus, the problem we face is: *how to best set the weights of each classifier to maximize the performance of the entire ensemble on unbalanced datasets?* To that effect, we utilize an evolutionary framework using a genetic algorithm to assign weights for each classifier in an ensemble [5]. The goal is to assign weights that reflect the relative contribution of each classifier in improving the overall performance of the ensemble. The genetic algorithm starts with random weight assignment to the classifiers, and after multiple generations, these weights come to reflect the relative contribution of the corresponding classifiers. Such an evolutionary combination of members can be more effective than considering all members equally. The evolutionary scheme uses positive (or minority) class f-measure [6] for its fitness function. It is more attuned with the evaluation on unbalanced datasets. Furthermore, by separating the stages of learning classifiers and forming ensemble, our meta-learner does not need any knowledge of the structure or type of the base classifiers, just their predictions.

Contributions: We posited the following questions in our evaluation of ensembles learned on unbalanced datasets.

1. What is the improvement offered by the proposed evolutionary framework over uniform voting, weighted voting, and the best member-classifier of the ensemble?
2. What is the impact of using a technique designed for countering imbalance in data as a pre-processing stage before learning ensembles? We used an over-sampling method, SMOTE [7], that generates synthetic minority (positive) class instances.
3. Is there a relationship among the classifiers selected by our proposed framework and the classifiers on the ROC convex hull [8]? Utilizing the probabilistic version of C4.5 [9] and different levels of SMOTE, we study the nature of the classifiers selected in terms of the ROC space.

1.1   Related Work

Genetic algorithms have a history of use in data mining, especially as wrapper technique of feature selections [10,11,12] that use genetic algorithms as an iterative search technique to identify the best performing feature subset on a validation set. Kim et al. [13] proposed creating meta-evolutionary ensembles, in which both classifiers and ensembles are evolved simultaneously. However, only neural networks were considered as potential classifiers. In a similar vein, Menczer et al. [14] proposed a local selection methodology for evolving neural networks in which they seek to minimize the interaction among members. Liu et al. [15] also explored evolutionary techniques for neural networks. They evolved both ensembles and neural networks simultaneously, and focused on speciation to minimize the interactions between ensembles members. Kuncheva and Jain [16] designed a multiple classifier fusion system using genetic algorithms, albeit genetic algorithms were used to first select the features and then on those selected feature subsets they learned three different types of classifiers (linear and quadratic discriminant classifiers and the logistic classifier). Langdon and Buxton [17] used genetic programming to fuse linear classifiers to achieve a "maximum realizable ROC". Our work differs from the above in not only the number of classifiers, but also on the special focus on unbalanced datasets.

2   Building Evolutionary Ensembles

We implemented a framework that we call EVEN (EVolutionary ENsembles) [5], which uses a genetic algorithm to carry out the meta-learning. EVEN utilizes the individual classifier predictions on the validation set as input. EVEN's output comprises weights for each individual classifier and the final composite testing set predictions based on those weights. EVEN uses the minority class *f-measure* [6] as the fitness function, which can be defined as follows.

$$precision = \frac{TP}{TP + FP} \tag{1}$$

$$recall = \frac{TP}{TP + FN} \tag{2}$$

$$f - measure = \frac{(1 + \beta^2) \times precision \times recall}{\beta^2 \times (recall + precision)} \tag{3}$$

EVEN is implemented as follows. A dataset is partitioned into three disjoint subsets, one for training, one for validation and one for testing. The base classifiers are learned on the training sets, and then evaluated on the validation data and the testing data. Their predictions for both validation and testing sets were recorded. The predictions on the validation sets are used to train EVEN, and the predictions on the testing set are used to evaluate EVEN's final performance. It is important to note that all EVEN knows of the base classifiers is the predictions they made; EVEN does not have any information regarding either the decision making process of the classifiers or the features of the original data sets. Once the appropriate weights have been learned on the validation set those weights are used to combine the predictions of the base classifiers made on the testing set. The weight vector of classifiers as generated by EVEN is $W = w_1, w_2, ..., w_C$, where C is the number of classifiers in the ensemble. Then the prediction for a test instance j:

$$\hat{y}_j = \sum_{i=1}^{C} w_i \times \hat{y_{i,j}} \tag{4}$$

where $\hat{y_{i,j}}$ is the prediction by classifier i on the test instance j. The pseudo-code for EVEN is contained in *Evolution*.

Algorithm. *Evolution*(G,p,C)
Input: Number of generations G; Population size p; Number of classifiers C
Output: Weight vector W; Predictions X
1. (∗ Let P_g denote the population in generation g, and let $P_g.i$ be *member$_i$* of that population. ∗)
2. $P_0 = Random\_population(p)$
3. **for** $g \leftarrow 1$ **to** G
4.   **for** $i \leftarrow 0$ **to** p
5.   Compute: $fitness_i = fmeasure(P_g.i)$
6.   **endfor**
7.   Sort P_g by $fitness$
8. $P_{g+1} = interbreed(P_g) + mutations(P_g) + survivors(P_g)$
9.   **endfor**
10. Select $P_{G-1}.i$ from P_{G-1} such that
       $fitness(P_{G-1}.i) = max(fitness(P_{G-1}.1), ..., fitness(P_{G-1}.p))$
11. **return** $W = weights(P_{G-1}.i)$
12. **return** $Y = predictions(P_{G-1}.i)$

3   Experiments

We ran a variety of experiments to demonstrate the efficacy of EVEN. We used heterogeneous ensembles comprised of different learning techniques as individual members, and homogeneous ensembles comprising the same underlying learning technique but with each classifier trained on a modified version of the dataset. We included a variety of datasets with different sizes and characteristics. We preprocessed the datasets by randomly dividing each into the training/validation/testing sets *ten* different times, and ran as many experiments.

3.1   Datasets

Our experiments featured five publicly available datasets stemming from different domains with differing levels of class imbalance. Table 1 shows the varying characteristics of the datasets, which are comprised of a mixture of continuous and nominal values.

Table 1. Datasets. Ordered by the increasing amount of skew.

Dataset	Number of examples	Number of Features	Class Distribution (Negative:Positive)
Pima	768	8	0.6510:0.3490
Phoneme	5404	5	0.7065:0.2935
Satimage	6435	36	0.9027:0.0973
Covtype	35,754	54	0.9287:0.0713
Mammography	11,183	6	0.9768:0.0232

3.2   Experiment-1: Heterogeneous Ensemble on Unbalanced Datasets

We used 12 different learning algorithms, as implemented in Weka, for constructing the base ensemble: ID3 decision trees, J48 decision trees (C4.5), JRIP rule learner (Ripper), Naïve Bayes, NBTree (Naïve Bayes trees), 1R, logistic model trees, logistic regression, decision stumps, multi-layer perceptron, SMO (support vector machine), and 1BK (k-nearest neighbor). We chose to work with many different classification algorithms because each displays a different inductive bias, and therefore provides a potentially more independent and diverse set of predictions to build upon. In order to enlarge the ensembles to more interesting sizes, ten full size bootstraps were made on the training data. Each classifier was learned on each bootstrap, creating a total of 120 classifiers for EVEN to work with. The purpose of constructing bootstraps was just to generate more members of the ensembles. For each of the runs, EVEN maintained a population of size 250 for 1000 generations.

Our experimental set-up included results from EVEN voted classifiers to an un-weighted uniform vote of classifier; a weighted vote where the weight was equal to the validation set accuracy of the classifier; a weighted vote where the weight was set equal to the validation set measure of each classifier; and the *f-measure* of the best performing single classifier. We chose to compare to a simple majority vote because that is the most common voting form in ensembles. The weighted vote was included to verify that the classifiers' individual performance was not a sufficient indicator of its relative contribution. Finally, the single best classifier, as defined by performance on the validation set, was also used for comparison to ensure that the added overhead of using multiple classifiers was justified.

However, for space considerations, we elided the results on the accuracy weighted vote, as the *f-measure* and uniformly voted classifiers sufficed for the comparisons with EVEN. *f-measure* weighted voting outperformed accuracy weighted voting, as one would expect, and there was no statistical difference, if any, between uniform voting and accuracy weighted voting. However, we do report all the statistical significance comparisons, subsequently. Table 2 shows the average *f-measure* and the standard deviations. It is evident from Table 2 that EVEN obtains the best average *f-measure* as compared to the other considered schemes.

Table 2. *f-measure* of ensemble of 120 classifiers. The following convention is used in the Table: FMW-V is *f-measure* weighted voting; U-V is uniform voting; and Best is the best classifier in the ensemble.

Dataset	EVEN	FMW-V	U-V	Best
Pima	**0.6528 ± 0.0705**	0.6411 ± 0.0561	0.6315 ± 0.0546	0.6345 ±0.0600
Phoneme	**0.8221 ± 0.0373**	0.7553 ± 0.0182	0.7351 ± 0.0174	0.7849 ± 0.0435
Satimage	**0.6682 ± 0.0369**	0.6636 ± 0.0402	0.4625 ± 0.0525	0.6599 ± 0.0328
Covtype	**0.9022 ± 0.0157**	0.8828 ± 0.0086	0.8508 ± 0.0120	0.8748 ± 0.0080
Mammography	**0.6186 ± 0.0590**	0.5950 ± 0.0501	0.5669 ± 0.0529	0.5731 ± 0.0750

EVEN always significantly outperforms uniform voting and accuracy weighted voting. It statistically significantly better than *f-measure* weighted voting in 4 out of 5 datasets. This presents empirical evidence that it is not the individual worth of a classifier that provides the classification improvement, but it is their relative worth as a collective. As an example, we show the weights versus *f-measure* distribution for the phoneme dataset in Figure 1. Firstly, there is no obvious correlation observed between the weights and the corresponding *f-measure*. Classifiers with similar *f-measures* have a range of weights, and the classifiers with higher weights can also have lower *f-measures*. Similar trends were observed for the other datasets.

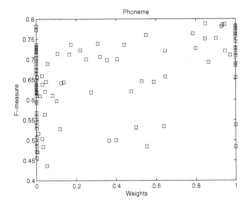

Fig. 1. Weights versus *f-measure* distribution across all the classifiers for the Phoneme dataset

We are more interested in classifiers that make different types of errors, canceling out each others mistakes, leading to an overall improvement in the ensemble's performance. Based on these weights one can also establish a cut-off for the classifiers that will vote together, thus reducing the size of the ensemble, which can be very relevant when the ensemble sizes are in thousands. To evaluate this, we established a cut-off value of 0.8 on the weights. Table 3 shows the number of the selected classifiers and the corresponding average *f-measure*. Applying the cut-off results in a significantly reduced number of classifiers, approximately 20 – 25% of the original ensemble size, for all the datasets, without any significant drop in the *f-measure*. This shows the effectiveness of EVEN in assigning relevant weights to the classifiers and identifying the maximally contributing subset.

Table 3. Average *f-measure* and Size (including standard deviations) of ensemble after applying a cutoff value of 0.8 to classifier weights in the original ensemble of 120 classifiers

Dataset	$EVEN_{0.8}$	# Classifiers
Pima	0.6483 ± 0.0650	27.9 ± 5.7436
Phoneme	0.8142 ± 0.0194	24.5 ± 3.8370
Satimage	0.6696 ± 0.0430	28.4 ± 2.8752
Covtype	0.9079 ± 0.0122	27.3 ± 4.2177
Mammography	0.5817 ± 0.0921	27.8 ± 4.4096

In accordance with the Free Lunch Theorem [18], no single classifier was consistently best on all the datasets or even within the set of runs within a single dataset. Thus, it becomes very important to have a collection of classifiers to apply to any given dataset. But if one utilizes an ensemble voting framework like ours, then the selection of a single classifier becomes unimportant, as each classifier is assigned a weight based on its relative contribution in the collective.

Table 4. *f-measure* of ensemble of classifiers learned after applying SMOTE. Same convention as Table 2 applies.

Dataset	EVEN	FMW-V	U-V	Best
Pima	$\mathbf{0.7027 \pm 0.0515}$	0.6966 ± 0.0550	0.7002 ± 0.052	0.6874 ± 0.0569
Phoneme	$\mathbf{0.8160 \pm 0.0161}$	0.7742 ± 0.0147	0.7653 ± 0.0137	0.8193 ± 0.0223
Satimage	$\mathbf{0.6459 \pm 0.0403}$	0.6663 ± 0.0443	0.5816 ± 0.0421	0.6560 ± 0.0490
Covtype	$\mathbf{0.9063 \pm 0.0202}$	0.8954 ± 0.0135	0.8611 ± 0.0189	0.8865 ± 0.0261
Mammography	$\mathbf{0.6937 \pm 0.1122}$	0.6655 ± 0.1194	0.6649 ± 0.1223	0.6172 ± 0.1217

3.3   Experiment-2: Effect of SMOTE on Ensemble Generation

For this set of experiments we did not bootstrap the data. Instead we applied SMOTE at 5 different levels, 100%, 200%, 300%, 400%, and 500%, to synthetically generate new positive class instances. This resulted in different dataset sizes and class distributions for members of the ensemble. We also included classifiers learned on the original distribution, thus giving us a total of 6 classifiers on a dataset. This resulted in an ensemble of 72 classifiers. The main purpose of this experiment was to study the behavior of the ensemble when the dataset has been pre-treated with a technique to counter the class imbalance and its impact on different voting schemes. We used exactly the same training, validation, and testing sets as in Experiment-1. This allowed easy juxtaposing of the two results from both the experiments. Table 4 shows the results on this set of experiments. Again, we included the same set of comparisons as in the previous subsection. It is evident that the initial preprocessing of data by applying an oversampling technique such as SMOTE, clearly benefits all the voting schemes.

The most significant improvements are for uniform voting and accuracy weighted voting. This is not surprising as now the classifier's inductive bias is manipulated towards the minority class because of oversampling, which leads to improved true positives, but at the expense of false positives. We also note that there is not much difference in the *f-measure* values obtained by EVEN in Experiment-1 and Experiment-2. This is very interesting in the light of improvements offered by SMOTE in all other schemes. The best classifier performance also improves. EVEN is, nevertheless, able to capture the diversity among the classifiers in their predictions and exploit it, despite classifiers' inductive bias towards the majority class. If we compare the results on Experiment-2 and Experiment-1 (as the testing sets remain the same), SMOTE with EVEN helps in performance improvement only for two datasets — pima and mammography. EVEN is thus able to exploit the differences in the errors to generate weights for optimizing the *f-measure* performance, irrespective of the prior oversampling.

3.4   EVEN and ROC Space

We are also interested in understanding the classifiers selected via EVEN for unbalanced datasets and their relationship in the ROC space. Ideally, the ROC convex hull represents the family of classifiers that are optimal in the different operating conditions [8]. The compelling question then is: *How many of the higher weighted EVEN classifiers lie on the ROC convex hull?* To that end, we use C4.5 decision trees from our family of classifiers to understand the phenomenon. We smoothed the C4.5 leaf frequencies using the LaPlace estimate [9], and then constructed ROC curves from the leaf estimates. Moreover, having just a single type of classifier in the ensemble made the ROC space more tractable for the purpose of this experiment. Now to construct an ensemble, we first applied different levels of SMOTE to each of the datasets.

As an example, Figure 2 shows the family of ROC curves and the ROC convex hull for mammography dataset. Due to space considerations, we only show the ROC curves for the most unbalanced dataset. Clearly, not all classifiers are falling on the ROC convex hull. $SMOTE = 500$ classifier is the most dominating one with the most number of points on the ROC space (approximately 72% of the ROC convex hull is occupied by points belonging to $SMOTE = 500$). That particular classifier also carried the maximum voting weight assigned by EVEN: 0.99521. But, one might ask what if we just vote the classifiers on the convex hull. The *f-measure* then obtained is 0.56, whereas the *f-measure* obtained

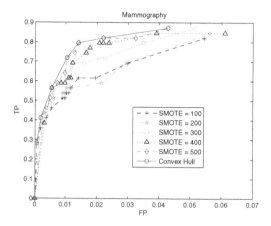

Fig. 2. ROC curves for Mammography dataset

by EVEN is 0.592 (a 5.7% improvement offered by EVEN). It is indicative of the value added by the EVEN weighted participation of all the classifiers. As part of future work, we are including comparisons to the work of Langdon and Buxton [17].to compare the maximum realizable AUROCs.

4   Conclusions

Ensemble generation using EVEN offers a significant advantage over the different voting schemes and the best classifier member of the ensemble. EVEN is effectively able to weight each individual classifier of the ensemble on the basis of its relative contribution to the overall performance, and these weights carry no obvious correlation to the independent performance of the classifier. This underlines the fact that the key is not the individual merit of the classifier, but their diversity in making different types of errors. We also generated ensembles after applying SMOTE, which significantly helped all the voting methods. Essentially, we are introducing inherent diversity in the SMOTE-based ensembles by learning classifiers on different amounts and instances of SMOTE. This increases the capability of the ensemble to optimize on *f-measure*, since the individual classifies are learned on different class distributions and demonstrate different biases in their predictions.

As part of future work, we are also incorporating other metrics such as AU-ROC within the classifier selection framework. A framework like EVEN allows for incorporation of any evaluation metric, given the data/class distribution. This offers flexibility to incorporate any evaluation metric as a fitness function, since the classifiers don't have to be re-learned; all we are interested in is the relative contribution of the classifier given a different objective function.

References

1. Y. Freund and R. Schapire, "Experiments with a new boosting algorithm," in *Thirteenth International Conference on Machine Learning*, 1996.
2. L. Breiman, "Bagging predictors," *Machine Learning*, vol. 24, no. 2, pp. 123–140, 1996.
3. T. Dietterich, "Ensemble methods in machine learning," *Lecture Notes in Computer Science*, vol. 1857, pp. 1–15, 2000.
4. L. Kuncheva and C. Whitaker, "Measures of diversity in classifier ensembles and their relationship with the ensemble accuracy," *Machine Learning*, vol. 51, pp. 181–207, 2003.
5. J. Sylvester and N. V. Chawla, "Evolutionary ensemble creation and thinning," in *International Joint Conference on Neural Networks*, pp. 5148 – 5155, 2006.
6. C. J. van Rijsbergen, *Information Retrieval*. London: Butterworths, 1979.
7. N. Chawla, L. Hall, B. K.W., and W. Kegelmeyer, "SMOTE: Synthetic Minority Oversampling TEchnique," *Journal of Artificial Intelligence Research*, vol. 16, pp. 321–357, 2002.
8. F. Provost and T. Fawcett, "Robust Classification for Imprecise Environments," *Machine Learning*, vol. 42/3, pp. 203–231, 2001.
9. F. Provost and P. Domingos, "Tree induction for probability-based rankings," *Machine Learning*, vol. 52(3), 2003.
10. D. Opitz, "Feature selection for ensembles," in *AAAI/IAAI*, pp. 379–384, 1999.
11. C. Guerra-Salcedo and L. Whitley, "Genetic approach to feature selection for ensemble creation," in *International Conference on Genetic and Evolutionary Computation*, pp. 236–243, 1999.
12. J. Yang and V. Honavar, "Feature subset selection using A genetic algorithm," in *Genetic Programming 1997: Proceedings of the Second Annual Conference*, p. 380, 13–16 1997.
13. Y. Kim, N. Street, and F. Menczer, "Meta-evolutionary ensembles," in *IEEE Intl. Joint Conf. on Neural Networks*, pp. 2791–2796, 2002.
14. F. Menczer, W. N. Street, and M. Degeratu, "Evolving heterogeneous neural agents by local selection," in *Advances in the Evolutionary Synthesis of Neural Systems* (V. Honavar, M. Patel, and K. Balakrishnan, eds.), Cambridge, MA: MIT Press, 2000.
15. Y. Liu, X. Yao, and T. Higuchi, "Evolutionary ensembles with negative correlation learning," *IEE Transactions on Evolutionary Computation*, vol. 4.4, pp. 380–387, 2000.
16. L. I. Kuncheva and L. C. Jain, "Designing classifier fusion systems by genetic algorithms," *IEEE-EC*, vol. 4, pp. 327 – 336, November 2000.
17. W. B. Langdon and B. F. Buxton, "Genetic programming for combining classifiers," in *Proceedings of the Genetic and Evolutionary Computation Conference (GECCO-2001)*, pp. 66–73, 2001.
18. D. H. Wolpert and W. G. Macready, "No free lunch theorems for optimization," *IEEE Transactions on Evolutionary Computation*, vol. 1, pp. 67–82, April 1997.

On the Diversity-Performance Relationship for Majority Voting in Classifier Ensembles

Yun-Sheng Chung[1], D. Frank Hsu[2,*], and Chuan Yi Tang[1]

[1] Department of Computer Science, National Tsing Hua University, Hsinchu, Taiwan
300, ROC
yschung@algorithm.cs.nthu.edu.tw, cytang@cs.nthu.edu.tw
[2] Department of Computer and Information Sciences, Fordham University, LL813,
113 West 60th Street, New York, NY 10023, USA
hsu@cis.fordham.edu

Abstract. Combining multiple classifier systems (MCS') has been shown to outperform single classifier system. It has been demonstrated that improvement for ensemble performance depends on either the diversity among or the performance of individual systems. A variety of diversity measures and ensemble methods have been proposed and studied. It remains a challenging problem to estimate the ensemble performance in terms of the performance of and the diversity among individual systems. In this paper, we establish upper and lower bounds for P^m (performance of the ensemble using majority voting) in terms of $\bar{P}$ (average performance of individual systems) and $\bar{D}$ (average entropy diversity measure among individual systems). These bounds are shown to be tight using the concept of a performance distribution pattern (PDP) for the input set. Moreover, we showed that when $\bar{P}$ is big enough, the ensemble performance P^m resulting from a maximum (information-theoretic) entropy PDP is an increasing function with respect to the diversity measure $\bar{D}$. Five experiments using data sets from various applications domains are conducted to demonstrate the complexity, richness, and diverseness of the problem in estimating the ensemble performance.

1 Introduction

Multiple classifier systems (MCS), or classifier ensembles, have been recognized as an effective classification method. It is often observed that MCS can outperform single classification systems (e.g., [1, 2, 3, 4, 5]). One of the key factors for the success of combination is often attributed to *diversity* [5, 6, 7, 8, 9, 10, 11, 12, 13, 14, 15, 16, 17, 18]. In addition, the performance of the component systems also has significant impact on the combined performance [9, 10, 11, 19, 20]. One of the most extensively applied and studied combination methods for MCS is majority voting (e.g., [6, 8, 19, 20, 21, 22, 23, 24, 25]). It is hence an important issue to understand how diversity and individual performance affect the ensemble performance. We also refer to the two special issues edited by Roli and Kittler [26]

---

[*] Corresponding author.

M. Haindl, J. Kittler, and F. Roli (Eds.): MCS 2007, LNCS 4472, pp. 407–420, 2007.

and Kuncheva [27] and the book by Kuncheva [3] which give excellent treatises of combining pattern classifiers and diversity in classifier ensembles (see Ch.10 in [3]).

In this paper, we study the following problem:

- Suppose we have p classifier systems $C_1, \ldots, C_p$ where each classifier produces a class label, and classifier performance is measured by the zero-one loss function. Let $\bar{P}$ and $\bar{\Delta}$ be the average performance and average diversity of the classifiers over all input, respectively. Let P^m be the performance of ensemble classifier C^m using majority voting. What is the strongest possible relationship for P^m in terms of $\bar{P}$ and $\bar{\Delta}$?

A relationship is established for P^m in terms of $\bar{P}$ and $\bar{\Delta} = \bar{D}$, where $\bar{D}$ is a non-pairwise diversity measure defined in [3,6] (see Theorems 1 and 2 in Sec. 4). In particular, tight upper and lower bounds of P^m in terms of $\bar{P}$ and $\bar{D}$ are established. The tight upper and lower bounds will be denoted as $U^m(\bar{P}, \bar{D})$ and $L^m(\bar{P}, \bar{D})$, respectively. When the classifiers are independent, majority voting has been studied quite thoroughly [8,20,23]. We also showed that when $\bar{P}$ is large enough, the ensemble performance P^m resulting from a performance distribution pattern (PDP) with maximum entropy is an increasing function in terms of $\bar{D}$.

The remainder of this paper is organized as follows. In Sec. 2, we review other related works on ensemble performance in terms of systems diversity and performance. Section 3 covers various fundamental terms related to performance, diversity, and ensemble performance, and inlcudes the partition of the input set and the notion of a performance distribution pattern (PDP). In Sec. 4, we give bounds of P^m and show their tightness. Section 5 includes experiments on five data sets to illustrate our results in Sec. 4. Section 6 concludes our paper with further work discussed.

2   Related Works

In regression, Krogh and Vedelsby [9] had established an elegant equation relating the combination performance to the average performance and diversity of the individual systems:

$$E = \bar{E} - \bar{A}$$

where E is the quadratic error of the combined estimation, $\bar{E}$ is the average quadratic error of the individual estimations, and $\bar{A}$ measures the variance among the individual estimations.

However, in classification, the relationship is not as clear. Tumer and Ghosh [10] studied the case that the classifiers estimate the posterior probabilities of the classes. They derived an equation for the added error of a linear combination of correlated unbiased classifiers:

$$E_{add}^{ave} = E_{add} \left(\frac{1 + \delta(p-1)}{p} \right)$$

where δ is the average correlation coefficient among the individual classifiers, E_{add}^{ave} is the added error of the linear combination, and E_{add} is the added error of the individual systems. Fumera and Roli [11] released some of the assumptions in [10] and obtained more general results.

When the classifiers produce class labels, the results in [10,11] do not apply. One of the most frequently used combination methods and error measures for this case are majority voting and the zero-one loss function, respectively. In this setting, extensive experiments using various diversity measures have been conducted by Kuncheva and Whitaker [6] to study the desired relationship. Scatter-plots of the majority voting accuracy versus the diversity for some fixed member accuracy are produced in [6] (see also Fig. 10.6 in [3]). Some other experimental or simulation results are also given in [6,19].

Breiman [28] proved an upper bound of the error made by random forests, which also applies to majority voting ensembles in general:

$$1 - P^{\mathrm{m}} \leq \bar{\rho}(1 - s^2)/s^2$$

where $\bar{\rho}$ is the correlation coefficient averaged over all pairs of classifiers and over all inputs, and s is the "strength" (average margin) of the classifiers. In the two-class case, $s = 2\bar{P} - 1$. Hence in the two-class case the above bound can be expressed as $P^{\mathrm{m}} \geq 1 - \bar{\rho}/(2\bar{P} - 1)^2 + \bar{\rho}$. This bound has the desirable property of decreasing with $\bar{\rho}$ (higher $\bar{\rho}$ means lower diversity). However, it is not tight [3]. In fact, from a tight bound it is easy to derive a bound (at the expense of tightness) that is increasing with diversity.

When diversity is not involved, the relationship between P^{m} and the individual accuracy is relatively simpler and had been studied by several researchers. One of the first analytical results is due to Matan [29], where tight bounds of P^{m} are obtained in terms of the individual system accuracy. Let P_i be the performance of the ith classifier over all input, and let $P_1 \leq P_2 \leq \cdots \leq P_p$, where p is the number of classifiers. Also let $\ell = \lfloor p/2 \rfloor$. Matan proved that

$$\max\{0, \xi(\ell + 1), \xi(\ell), \ldots, \xi(1)\} \leq P^{\mathrm{m}} \leq \min\{1, \Sigma(\ell + 1), \Sigma(\ell), \ldots, \Sigma(1)\}$$

where $\Sigma(j) = \frac{1}{j} \sum_{i=1}^{\ell+j} P_i$ and $\xi(j) = \frac{1}{j} \sum_{i=\ell+2-j}^{p} P_i - \frac{\ell}{j}$. Independently, in [19], Kuncheva et al. defined "pattern of success" and "pattern of failure". The majority voting accuracy for the pattern of success (resp. failure) is the tight upper (resp. lower) bound of majority voting accuracy for all possible ensembles with the given member accuracy. The upper and lower bounds are:

$$\max\left\{0, p/(\ell + 1) \times \bar{P} - \ell/(\ell + 1)\right\} \leq P^{\mathrm{m}} \leq \min\left\{1, p/(\ell + 1) \times \bar{P}\right\} \quad (1)$$

Roughly speaking, the upper bound in (1) is about $2\bar{P}$, and the lower bound in (1) is about $2\bar{P} - 1$. Ruta and Gabrys [20] further refined the patterns of success and failure to define "stable" versions which are claimed to be more likely to occur (and attain the same bounds in (1)).

Bounds of P^{m} involving only diversity (measured by Q statistic) but not $\bar{P}$ are also given in [19]. Instead of obtaining explicit bounds of P^{m} analytically as in [19, 20, 28, 29], Narasimhamurthy [16, 25] used linear programming to study (numerically) the relationship between P^{m} and individual system performance or diversity. The size of the linear program can be exponential in the number of classifiers, which may restrict the scale of permissible analyses.

3   Performance, Diversity, and the Performance Distribution Pattern

3.1   Performance and Diversity

We assume that the number p of classifiers is odd. Let $\Omega = \{\omega_1, \omega_2, \ldots, \omega_q\}$ be the set of class labels. Let C^* be the classifier that always gives the true class label. On input $x \in \mathcal{I}$, $\mathcal{I}$ being the set of inputs, let $C_j(x)$ (resp. $C^*(x)$ and $C^{\mathrm{m}}(x)$) be the output of C_j (resp. C^* and C^{m}). Denote as $\#(\omega_i, x)$ the quantity $|\{j : C_j(x) = \omega_i\}|$. Let $\omega_{\max}(x) = \arg\max_{\omega_i}\{\#(\omega_i, x)\}$. Then define $C^{\mathrm{m}}(x)$ as

$$C^{\mathrm{m}}(x) = \begin{cases} \omega_{\max}(x) & \text{if } \#(\omega_{\max}(x), x) > \frac{p}{2} \\ \omega_{q+1} & \text{otherwise.} \end{cases}$$

where $C^{\mathrm{m}}(x) = \omega_{q+1}$ indicates its rejection on the input. For $x \in \mathcal{I}$, the performance $P_j(x)$ of classifier C_j, and the average performance $\bar{P}(x)$ of the p classifiers, are defined as

$$P_j(x) = \begin{cases} 1 & \text{if } C_j(x) = C^*(x); \\ 0 & \text{otherwise;} \end{cases} \quad \text{and} \quad \bar{P}(x) = \frac{1}{p}\sum_{j=1}^{p} P_j(x).$$

The average of $\bar{P}(x)$ over $\mathcal{I}$ is denoted as $\bar{P}$. For C^{m}, the definition of $P^{\mathrm{m}}(x)$ is similar to $P_j(x)$. When the ensemble classifier rejects on input x, we have $P^{\mathrm{m}}(x) = 0$. The performance of C^{m}, averaged over all input, is denoted as P^{m}. Throughout this paper let $\ell - \lfloor \frac{p}{2} \rfloor$. On $x \in \mathcal{I}$, define $\bar{D}(x)$ as

$$\bar{D}(x) = \min\{\bar{P}(x), 1 - \bar{P}(x)\}.$$

Then let $\bar{D}$ be the average of $\bar{D}(x)$ taken over $\mathcal{I}$. This diversity measure follows Kuncheva and Whitaker [6] where diversity measures are defined on oracle outputs, and $\bar{D}$ is called entropy diversity. By definition, it can be seen that $\bar{P} + \bar{D} \le 1$, $\bar{D} \le \frac{\ell}{p}$, $\bar{D} \le \bar{P}$ and $\bar{D} \le 1 - \bar{P}$.

3.2   Performance Distribution Pattern

Given p classifiers $C_1, C_2, \ldots, C_p$ and the input set $\mathcal{I}$, let C^* be the classifier as defined in Sec. 3.1. Let $P^*(x)$ be the performance of C^* on input x. Clearly, $P^*(x) = 1$ for all $x \in \mathcal{I}$. We call C^* an **ideal classifier** for $\mathcal{I}$. Let $\bar{P}(x)$ be defined in terms of C^* as in Sec. 3.1. We can partition the input set $\mathcal{I}$ into $p+1$

disjoint subsets $\mathcal{I}_k$, $k = 0, 1, \ldots, p$ such that $\mathcal{I}_k = \{x \in \mathcal{I} : \bar{P}(x) = \frac{k}{p}\}$. This partition of the input set $\mathcal{I}$ gives rise to a partition vector $\boldsymbol{\pi} = (\pi_0, \pi_1, \ldots, \pi_p)^{\mathrm{T}}$ such that $\pi_k = \Pr\{x \in \mathcal{I}_k\}$, $k = 0, 1, \ldots, p$. We now define the Partition of Input set using Performance (PIP) and the Performance Distribution Pattern (PDP) (see also [8, 20]):

Definition 1. *Given an input set $\mathcal{I}$, suppose that there exists an ideal classifier C^* such that $P^*(x) = 1$ for every $x \in \mathcal{I}$. For a set $\mathcal{C} = \{C_1, \ldots, C_p\}$ of p classifiers and $\mathcal{I}_k = \{x \in \mathcal{I} : \bar{P}(x) = \frac{k}{p}\}$ where $\bar{P}(x)$ is defined in Sec. 3.1, we define the PIP partition and the PDP pattern as:*
(a) the input set $\mathcal{I}$ has a PIP partition, $\mathcal{I} = \bigcup_{k=0}^{p} \mathcal{I}_k$ where $\mathcal{I}_i \cap \mathcal{I}_j = \emptyset$ for $i \neq j$, and
(b) the performance distribution pattern (PDP) of $\mathcal{C}$ is the vector $\boldsymbol{\pi} = (\pi_0, \ldots, \pi_p)^{\mathrm{T}}$, where $\pi_k = \Pr\{x \in \mathcal{I}_k\}$.

It follows from Definition 1(a) and 1(b) that there is an one-one correspondence between the PIP partition and the PDP pattern. Definition 1(a) deals with partitions of the input set $\mathcal{I} = \bigcup_{k=0}^{p} \mathcal{I}_k$, while Definition 1(b) gives a corresponding partition of $\Pr\{x \in \mathcal{I}\}$ such that $1 = \Pr\{x \in \mathcal{I}\} = \sum_{k=0}^{p} \Pr\{x \in \mathcal{I}_k\} = \sum_{k=0}^{p} \pi_k$. Since $\mathcal{I}_k$ is defined to be the set of those inputs in $\mathcal{I}$ so that $\bar{P}(x) = \frac{k}{p}$, both Definitions 1(a) and 1(b) require an ideal classifier C^* to define $\bar{P}(x)$ for the input set $\mathcal{I}$ and the set $\mathcal{C}$ of p classifiers. We can show, under an input set $\mathcal{I}$ and an ideal classifier C^*, the following equivalence between the existence of a set $\mathcal{C}$ of p classifiers $\{C_1, \ldots, C_p\}$ and the existence of a probability vector $\boldsymbol{\pi}$ associating with a partition of $\mathcal{I}$. The proof is omitted due to page constraint.

Lemma 1. *Let $\mathcal{I}$ be an input set and C^* be an ideal classifier for $\mathcal{I}$. For each $x \in \mathcal{I}$ let $\bar{P}(x)$ be defined as in Sec. 3.1 for an ensemble of classifiers. The following two statements are equivalent:*

(a) There exists a set $\mathcal{C}$ of p classifiers $\mathcal{C} = \{C_1, \ldots, C_p\}$ so that $\Pr\{\bar{P}(x) = \frac{k}{p}\} = \pi_k$.
(b) There exists a probability vector $\boldsymbol{\pi} = (\pi_0, \ldots, \pi_p)^{\mathrm{T}}$ such that for some partition $\{\mathcal{J}_k : k = 0, \ldots, p\}$ of $\mathcal{I}$, $\Pr\{x \in \mathcal{J}_k\} = \pi_k$ for all k.

What underlines the statements (a) and (b) in Lemma 1 is a PIP partition of the input set $\mathcal{I}$ into $p + 1$ disjoint subsets $\mathcal{I} = \bigcup_{k=0}^{p} \mathcal{I}_k$, where $\mathcal{I}_i \cap \mathcal{I}_j = \emptyset$ if $i \neq j$. Moreover, in this partition, we have $\Pr\{x \in \mathcal{I}_k\} = \pi_k$ and $\mathcal{I}_k = \{x \in \mathcal{I} : \bar{P}(x) = \frac{k}{p}\}$. This partition will be very useful in Sec. 4.2 to construct multiple classifier systems which achieve the tight upper or lower bound. We define vectors $\mathbf{v}_P$ and $\mathbf{v}_m$ in $\mathbb{R}^{p+1}$ as follows (where the components are numbered from 0 to p): $\mathbf{v}_P[k] = \frac{k}{p}$, $0 \leq k \leq p$, and $\mathbf{v}_m[k] = 1$ if $\ell < k \leq p$, and $\mathbf{v}_m[k] = 0$ otherwise. Then, since $\boldsymbol{\pi} = (\pi_0, \ldots, \pi_p)^{\mathrm{T}}$, we have $\bar{P} = \sum_{k=0}^{p} \frac{k}{p} \cdot \pi_k = \langle \mathbf{v}_P, \boldsymbol{\pi} \rangle$, and $P^m = \sum_{k=\ell+1}^{p} \pi_k = \langle \mathbf{v}_m, \boldsymbol{\pi} \rangle$, where $\langle \cdot, \cdot \rangle$ is the inner product operation.

4 The Upper and Lower Bounds

4.1 The Bounds

In this section, four linear equations of P^m in terms of $\bar{P}$, $\bar{D}$ and some third terms are given. Based on these equations, bounds of P^m involving only $\bar{P}$ and $\bar{D}$ can be derived. The proof of Lemma 2 is omitted due to space limitation.

Lemma 2. *Given p classifiers $C_1, \ldots, C_p$ with input set $\mathcal{I}$, let C^m be the ensemble classifier of $C_1, \ldots, C_p$ using majority voting. Let $\bar{P}(x)$, $P^m(x)$ be defined as above for $x \in \mathcal{I}$. Let $\bar{D}$ and $\bar{P}$ be the average of $\bar{D}(x)$ and $\bar{P}(x)$ over $\mathcal{I}$, respectively. The following statements hold:*

(a) *Let $R_1(x) = 0$ if $\bar{P}(x) > \frac{\ell}{p}$, and $R_1(x) = 2\bar{P}(x)$ if $\bar{P}(x) \leq \frac{\ell}{p}$. Let R_1 be the average of $R_1(x)$ over $\mathcal{I}$. Then $P^m = \bar{P} + \bar{D} - R_1$.*

(b) *Let $R_2(x) = 0$ if $\bar{P}(x) \leq \frac{\ell}{p}$, and $R_2(x) = 2(1 - \bar{P}(x))$ if $\bar{P}(x) > \frac{\ell}{p}$. Let R_2 be the average of $R_2(x)$ over $\mathcal{I}$. Then $P^m = \bar{P} - \bar{D} + R_2$.*

(c) *Let $R_3(x) = 0$ if $\bar{P}(x) \leq \frac{\ell}{p}$ and $R_3(x) = 2p\bar{P}(x) - p - 1$ if $\bar{P}(x) > \frac{\ell}{p}$. Let R_3 be the average of $R_3(x)$ over $\mathcal{I}$. Then $P^m = p(\bar{P} - \bar{D}) - R_3$.*

(d) *Let $R_4(x) = p - 1 - 2p\bar{P}(x)$ if $\bar{P}(x) \leq \frac{\ell}{p}$ and $R_4(x) = 0$ if $\bar{P}(x) > \frac{\ell}{p}$. Let R_4 be the average of $R_4(x)$ over $\mathcal{I}$. Then $P^m = p(\bar{P} + \bar{D}) + R_4 + 1 - p$.*

Using Lemma 2 and the characteristics of the terms R_i, $i = 1, 2, 3$ and 4, we are able to establish upper bound and lower bound for P^m in terms of $\bar{P}$ and $\bar{D}$.

Theorem 1. $\max\{\bar{P} - \bar{D}, p(\bar{P} + \bar{D}) + 1 - p\} \leq P^m \leq \min\{\bar{P} + \bar{D}, p(\bar{P} - \bar{D})\}$.

Proof. First observe that $R_i \geq 0$ for all $i = 1, 2, 3, 4$. Hence Lemma 2(a) implies that $P^m \leq \bar{P} + \bar{D}$, and Lemma 2(c) implies $P^m \leq p(\bar{P} - \bar{D})$. Therefore the upper bound follows. Similarly, the lower bound follows from Lemma 2(b) and (d).   □

4.2 Tightness of the Bounds

Given a set of p classifiers and input set $\mathcal{I}$, we have, by Definition 1, the PDP $\boldsymbol{\pi} = (\pi_0, \pi_1, \ldots, \pi_p)^T$, where $\pi_k = \Pr\{x \in \mathcal{I}_k\}$ and $\mathcal{I}_k = \{x \in \mathcal{I} : \bar{P} = \frac{k}{p}\}$. On the other hand, given a probability vector $\boldsymbol{\pi}$, we can construct $\mathcal{I}$ which has a partition $\{\mathcal{I}_k : 0 \leq k \leq p\}$ with $\Pr\{x \in \mathcal{I}_k\} = \pi_k$, and then by Lemma 1, $\boldsymbol{\pi}$ corresponds to a set $\mathcal{C}$ of multiple classifier systems whose PDP is $\boldsymbol{\pi}$. Define $\mathbf{v}_D \in \mathbb{R}^{p+1}$ to be such that $\mathbf{v}_D[k] = \min\{\frac{k}{p}, 1 - \frac{k}{p}\}$, and we have $\bar{D} = \langle \mathbf{v}_D, \boldsymbol{\pi} \rangle$.

Lower Bound. Now consider the lower bound in Theorem 1. First we state the following lemma without proof due to space limitation.

Lemma 3. *(a) If $\bar{D} \leq \frac{\ell}{\ell+1}(1 - \bar{P})$, then there exists PDP $\boldsymbol{\pi}'$ such that $\langle \mathbf{v}_P, \boldsymbol{\pi}' \rangle = \bar{P}$, $\langle \mathbf{v}_D, \boldsymbol{\pi}' \rangle = \bar{D}$, and $\pi'_k = 0$ for all $k \notin \{0, \ell, p\}$.*

(b) If $\bar{D} \geq \frac{\ell}{\ell+1}(1 - \bar{P})$, then there exists a PDP $\boldsymbol{\pi}'$ such that $\langle \mathbf{v}_P, \boldsymbol{\pi}' \rangle = \bar{P}$, $\langle \mathbf{v}_D, \boldsymbol{\pi}' \rangle = \bar{D}$, and $\pi'_k = 0$ for all $k \notin \{\ell, \ell+1, p\}$.

We are ready to prove the tightness of the lower bound stated in Theorem 1.

Lemma 4. *The tight lower bound of P^{m} is*

$$P^{\mathrm{m}} \geq \begin{cases} \bar{P} - \bar{D} & \text{if } \bar{D} \leq \frac{\ell}{\ell+1}(1 - \bar{P}); \\ p\left(\bar{P} + \bar{D}\right) + 1 - p & \text{if } \bar{D} \geq \frac{\ell}{\ell+1}(1 - \bar{P}). \end{cases} \tag{2}$$

Proof. When $\bar{D} \leq \frac{\ell}{\ell+1}(1 - \bar{P})$, the lower bound $\max\{\bar{P} - \bar{D}, p(\bar{P} + \bar{D}) + 1 - p\}$ is $\bar{P} - \bar{D}$. Let $\mathbf{v}_{R_2} \in \mathbb{R}^{p+1}$ be such that $\mathbf{v}_{R_2}[k] = 0$ if $k \leq \ell$, and $\mathbf{v}_{R_2}[k] = \frac{2(p-k)}{p}$ if $k > \ell$. Then $R_2 = \langle \mathbf{v}_{R_2}, \boldsymbol{\pi} \rangle$. Note that $\mathbf{v}_{R_2}[k] = 0$ for $k \in \{0, \ell, p\}$. Since the PDP $\boldsymbol{\pi}'$ specified in Lemma 3(a) is orthogonal to $\mathbf{v}_{R_2}$, and $\langle \mathbf{v}_P, \boldsymbol{\pi}' \rangle = \bar{P}$ and $\langle \mathbf{v}_D, \boldsymbol{\pi}' \rangle = \bar{D}$, it follows from Lemma 2(b) that $\langle \mathbf{v}_{\mathrm{m}}, \boldsymbol{\pi}' \rangle = \langle \mathbf{v}_P, \boldsymbol{\pi}' \rangle - \langle \mathbf{v}_D, \boldsymbol{\pi}' \rangle + \langle \mathbf{v}_{R_2}, \boldsymbol{\pi}' \rangle = \bar{P} - \bar{D}$. Hence the lower bound in this case is achieved by $\boldsymbol{\pi}'$.

When $\bar{D} \geq \frac{\ell}{\ell+1}(1 - \bar{P})$, $\max\{\bar{P} - \bar{D}, p(\bar{P} + \bar{D}) + 1 - p\} = p(\bar{P} + \bar{D}) + 1 - p$. Let $\mathbf{v}_{R_4} \in \mathbb{R}^{p+1}$ be such that $\mathbf{v}_{R_4}[k] = p - 1 - 2k$ if $k \leq \ell$, and $\mathbf{v}_{R_4}[k] = 0$ if $k > \ell$. Then $R_4 = \langle \mathbf{v}_{R_4}, \boldsymbol{\pi} \rangle$. In this case, the lower bound can be achieved by the PDP specified in Lemma 3(b), since it is orthogonal to $\mathbf{v}_{R_4}$. $\qquad\square$

Upper Bound. Now consider the upper bound in Theorem 1. The following lemma is stated without proof.

Lemma 5. *(a) If $\bar{D} \leq \frac{\ell}{\ell+1} \times \bar{P}$, then there exists a PDP $\boldsymbol{\pi}'$ such that $\langle \mathbf{v}_P, \boldsymbol{\pi}' \rangle = \bar{P}$, $\langle \mathbf{v}_D, \boldsymbol{\pi}' \rangle = \bar{D}$, and $\pi'_k = 0$ for all $k \notin \{0, \ell+1, p\}$.*
(b) If $\bar{D} \geq \frac{\ell}{\ell+1} \times \bar{P}$, then there exists a PDP $\boldsymbol{\pi}'$ such that $\langle \mathbf{v}_P, \boldsymbol{\pi}' \rangle = \bar{P}$, $\langle \mathbf{v}_D, \boldsymbol{\pi}' \rangle = \bar{D}$, and $\pi'_k = 0$ for all $k \notin \{0, \ell, \ell+1\}$.

Now we can establish the tightness of the upper bound stated in Theorem 1. The proof is similar to that of Lemma 4 and is omitted.

Lemma 6. *The tight upper bound of P^{m} is*

$$P^{\mathrm{m}} \leq \begin{cases} p(\bar{P} - \bar{D}) & \text{if } \bar{D} \geq \frac{\ell}{\ell+1} \times \bar{P}; \\ \bar{P} + \bar{D} & \text{if } \bar{D} \leq \frac{\ell}{\ell+1} \times \bar{P}. \end{cases} \tag{3}$$

The desired relationship among P^{m}, $\bar{P}$ and $\bar{D}$ have thus been established, which we restate as follows. The bounds are plotted in Fig. 1 for $p = 3$.

Theorem 2. *The tight bounds for majority voting performance P^{m} are:*
(a) If $\bar{P} \geq 0.5$, then the tight bounds are

$$\begin{cases} \bar{P} - \bar{D} \leq P^{\mathrm{m}} \leq \bar{P} + \bar{D} & \text{if } \bar{D} \leq \frac{\ell}{\ell+1}(1 - \bar{P}), \\ p(\bar{P} + \bar{D}) + 1 - p \leq P^{\mathrm{m}} \leq \bar{P} + \bar{D} & \text{if } \frac{\ell}{\ell+1}(1 - \bar{P}) < \bar{D} \leq \frac{\ell}{\ell+1} \times \bar{P}, and \\ p(\bar{P} + \bar{D}) + 1 - p \leq P^{\mathrm{m}} \leq p(\bar{P} - \bar{D}) & \text{if } \bar{D} > \frac{\ell}{\ell+1} \times \bar{P}. \end{cases}$$

(b) If $\bar{P} < 0.5$, then the tight bounds are

$$\begin{cases} \bar{P} - \bar{D} \leq P^{\mathrm{m}} \leq \bar{P} + \bar{D} & \text{if } \bar{D} \leq \frac{\ell}{\ell+1} \times \bar{P}, \\ \bar{P} - \bar{D} \leq P^{\mathrm{m}} \leq p(\bar{P} - \bar{D}) & \text{if } \frac{\ell}{\ell+1} \times \bar{P} < \bar{D} \leq \frac{\ell}{\ell+1}(1 - \bar{P}), and \\ p(\bar{P} + \bar{D}) + 1 - p \leq P^{\mathrm{m}} \leq p(\bar{P} - \bar{D}) & \text{if } \bar{D} > \frac{\ell}{\ell+1}(1 - \bar{P}). \end{cases}$$

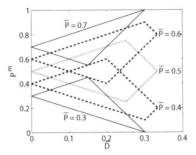

Fig. 1. Bounds for majority voting accuracy. Here $p = 3$. The dashed and dotted lines are for $\bar{P} \in (\frac{\ell}{p}, \frac{\ell+1}{p})$, while the solid lines are for $\bar{P} \notin (\frac{\ell}{p}, \frac{\ell+1}{p})$. The bounds have different spans in $\bar{D}$ since $\bar{D} \leq \min\{\bar{P}, 1 - \bar{P}, \frac{\ell}{p}\}$.

The lower and upper bounds in (1) established in [19, 20] can be derived from (2) and (3), respectively. This is shown in the following corollary.

Corollary 1. *The tight bounds of P^{m} involving $\bar{P}$ but not $\bar{D}$ are*

$$\max\left\{0, p/(\ell+1) \times \bar{P} - \ell/(\ell+1)\right\} \leq P^{\mathrm{m}} \leq \min\left\{1, p/(\ell+1) \times \bar{P}\right\}$$

Proof. For the lower bound, we need simply to find $\min_{\bar{D}} L^{\mathrm{m}}(\bar{P}, \bar{D})$. If $\bar{P} \geq \frac{\ell}{p}$, then $\bar{D}$ can achieve $\frac{\ell}{\ell+1}(1 - \bar{P})$, and at this value of $\bar{D}$, $L^{\mathrm{m}}(\bar{P}, \bar{D})$ is minimized. Then by Lemma 4, in this case, $\min_{\bar{D}} L^{\mathrm{m}}(\bar{P}, \bar{D}) = L^{\mathrm{m}}(\bar{P}, \frac{\ell}{\ell+1}(1 - \bar{P})) = \bar{P} - \frac{\ell}{\ell+1}(1 - \bar{P}) = \frac{p}{\ell+1} \times \bar{P} - \frac{\ell}{\ell+1}$. Similarly, in the case $\bar{P} < \frac{\ell}{p}$, it can be shown that the minimum is 0. In both cases, the bound is tight since $L^{\mathrm{m}}(\bar{P}, \bar{D})$ is tight by Lemma 4. The upper bound can be similarly obtained by evaluating $\max_{\bar{D}} U^{\mathrm{m}}(\bar{P}, \bar{D})$, where $U^{\mathrm{m}}(\bar{P}, \bar{D})$ is as given in Lemma 6.   □

4.3   Maximum Entropy PDP's and Discussion

In the following we consider maximum entropy PDPs (**maxent PDPs** for short) satisfying the given $\bar{P}$ and $\bar{D}$. That is, PDP $\boldsymbol{\pi}^*$ maximizing the information-theoretic entropy $\mathcal{H}(\boldsymbol{\pi}^*) = -\sum_{k=0}^{p} \pi_k^* \log \pi_k^*$, with $\langle \mathbf{v}_P, \boldsymbol{\pi}^* \rangle = \bar{P}$ and $\langle \mathbf{v}_D, \boldsymbol{\pi}^* \rangle = \bar{D}$. To motivate maxent PDPs, suppose that $|\mathcal{I}| = n$. The number of ways that any PDP $\boldsymbol{\pi}$ can be realized follows the multinomial coefficient $\binom{n}{n_0, \ldots, n_p}$, where $n_k = \pi_k \cdot n$. The maxent PDP $\boldsymbol{\pi}^*$ corresponds to the PDP with the maximum number of ways of being realized (see, e.g., Sec. V.B of [8] and Sec. 11.2 of [30]). By Theorem 11.1.1 of [30], the kth component of $\boldsymbol{\pi}^*$ is $\pi_k^* = \exp(\lambda_0 + \lambda_1 k + \lambda_2 \min\{k, p - k\})$, where λ_0, λ_1 and λ_2 are constants.

For simplicity, we only consider the case where $p = 3$. Then $\boldsymbol{\pi}^*$ satisfies the following system of equations:

$$\begin{cases} e^{\lambda_0} + e^{\lambda_0+\lambda_1+\lambda_2} + e^{\lambda_0+2\lambda_1+\lambda_2} + e^{\lambda_0+3\lambda_1} = 1, \\ e^{\lambda_0+\lambda_1+\lambda_2} + 2e^{\lambda_0+2\lambda_1+\lambda_2} + 3e^{\lambda_0+3\lambda_1} = 3\bar{P}, \text{ and} \\ e^{\lambda_0+\lambda_1+\lambda_2} + e^{\lambda_0+2\lambda_1+\lambda_2} = 3\bar{D}, \end{cases} \quad (4)$$

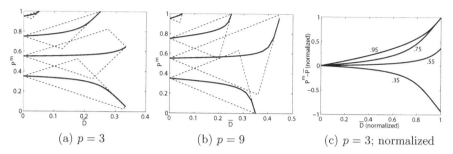

(a) $p = 3$ \qquad (b) $p = 9$ \qquad (c) $p = 3$; normalized

Fig. 2. P^{m} vs $\bar{D}$ and normalized $P^{\mathrm{m}} - \bar{P}$ vs normalized $\bar{D}$ for maxent PDPs. Here $\bar{P} \in \{0.95, 0.75, 0.55, 0.35\}$. In (a) and (b), solid curves are P^{m} of the maxent PDPs, while the dashed curves are tight bounds of P^{m}. (c) $P^{\mathrm{m}} - \bar{P}$ vs $\bar{D}$, both normalized.

in which we have $e^{\lambda_1} = [e^{-\lambda_0}(1 - 3\bar{D}) - 1]^{1/3}$ and $e^{\lambda_2} = e^{-\lambda_0}(3\bar{P} - 3\bar{D})e^{-2\lambda_1} - 3e^{\lambda_1}$. Since π_k^*, $k = 0, 1, 2, 3$ can be obtained in terms of λ_0, λ_1 and λ_2 which can be solved by (4), one of the issues in which we are most interested is whether $P^{\mathrm{m}} = \langle \mathbf{v}_{\mathrm{m}}, \boldsymbol{\pi}^* \rangle$ is increasing in $\bar{D}$. It follows from (4) that $\langle \mathbf{v}_{\mathrm{m}}, \boldsymbol{\pi}^* \rangle = e^{\lambda_0 + 2\lambda_1 + \lambda_2} + e^{\lambda_0 + 3\lambda_1} = 3\bar{P} - 3\bar{D} - 2(1 - 3\bar{D} - e^{\lambda_0})$. Hence $\frac{d \langle \mathbf{v}_{\mathrm{m}}, \boldsymbol{\pi}^* \rangle}{d\bar{D}} = 3 + 2 \cdot \frac{de^{\lambda_0}}{d\bar{D}}$. We can show that $\frac{de^{\lambda_0}}{d\bar{D}} > -\frac{3}{2}$ if $\bar{P} > \frac{3}{5}$ and $\bar{D} \in (0, \min\{\frac{1}{3}, 1 - \bar{P}\})$, from which it follows that $\langle \mathbf{v}_{\mathrm{m}}, \boldsymbol{\pi}^* \rangle$ is increasing in $\bar{D}$. We state the following remark without proof due to page constraint.

Remark 1. Let $p = 3$, $\bar{P} > 0.6$ and $\bar{D} \in (0, \min\{\frac{1}{3}, 1 - \bar{P}\})$. Then the ensemble performance P^{m} of the maximum entropy PDP $\boldsymbol{\pi}^*$ satisfying $\langle \mathbf{v}_P, \boldsymbol{\pi}^* \rangle = \bar{P}$ and $\langle \mathbf{v}_D, \boldsymbol{\pi}^* \rangle = \bar{D}$ is increasing in terms of $\bar{D}$.

In Fig. 2, we observe that when $\bar{P} \in (0.5, 0.6]$ or $p > 3$, the increasing pattern also holds. These results indicate that for $\bar{P} > 0.5$, it would be quite likely to see P^{m} and $P^{\mathrm{m}} - \bar{P}$ increase in $\bar{D}$. This is one of the main reasons for taking advantage of the diversity measure in trying to improve ensemble performance. However, when $\bar{P} < 0.5$, we have $P^{\mathrm{m}} < \bar{P}$ and $P^{\mathrm{m}} - \bar{P}$ decreases with $\bar{D}$.

The upper and lower bounds of $P^{\mathrm{m}} - \bar{P}$, as well as the possible range of $\bar{D}$, vary with $\bar{P}$. For example, for higher $\bar{P} > 0.5$, the range of $\bar{D}$ is smaller, and the upper bound of $P^{\mathrm{m}} - \bar{P}$ is also lower. This would become a systematic factor affecting the relationship between diversity and improvement. To reduce this effect, in the existence of various $\bar{P}$ values, we may consider $P^{\mathrm{m}} - \bar{P}$ and $\bar{D}$ in normalized terms. In this work, $P^{\mathrm{m}} - \bar{P}$ and $\bar{D}$ are normalized to lie in $[-1, 1]$ and in $[0, 1]$, respectively (see Fig. 2(c)).

In general we do not expect to see the PDPs on hand exactly match the maxent PDPs. Nevertheless the maxent PDPs enable us to qualitatively observe some interesting relationship between $\bar{D}$ and $P^{\mathrm{m}} - \bar{P}$ (Fig. 2). Remark 2 discusses the situation with (a) a fixed $\bar{P}$, (b) a fixed $\bar{D}$, and (c) both $\bar{P}$ and $\bar{D}$ in Fig. 2.

Remark 2. Let $\bar{P}$, $\bar{D}$ and P^{m} be as in Fig. 2 where $\boldsymbol{\pi}^*$ is the maxent PDP.
(a) For a fixed $\bar{P} > 0.5$, $P^{\mathrm{m}} - \bar{P}$ increases faster when $\bar{D}$ is higher. When $\bar{P} < 0.5$, the opposite is true (Fig. 2(c)).

Table 1. A summary of the datasets

Experiment	I	II	III	IV	V
Dataset	WDBC[1]	Cone-Torus	Multi-Feature	Digit Liver Disorders	Glass
No. Instances	569	800	2000	345	214
No. Classes	2	3	10	2	7
No. Attributes	30	2	6	6	9

[1] Wisconsin Diagnostic Breast Cancer data set.

(b) For a fixed normalized $\bar{D}$ and $\bar{P} > 0.5$, $P^m - \bar{P}$ has a higher increasing rate for larger $\bar{P}$ if the normalized $\bar{D}$ is in the lower part (say < 0.65). However, if normalized $\bar{D}$ belongs to the higher end, the situation is the opposite.
(c) When $\bar{P}$ and $\bar{D}$ both vary, the increase or decrease rate for P^m (Fig. 2(a), (b)) and for normalized $P^m - \bar{P}$ (Fig. 2(c)) can go higher or lower with respect to normalized $\bar{D}$.

Theorem 1 gives a general upper and lower bound for P^m in terms of $\bar{P}$ and $\bar{D}$. Theorem 2 showed that these specific bounds can be achieved. What makes the bounds complicated is that both upper bounds and lower bounds all involve $\bar{P} + \bar{D}$ and $\bar{P} - \bar{D}$. As can be seen in Fig. 1, the values of P^m falls in the region boounded by a triangle or trapezoid. In addition, that the largest angle in the region is facing down or up depends on the values of $\bar{P}$ which is less or greater than 0.5 respectively. In either case, $P^m - \bar{P}$ can be either positive, negative or zero. However, some necessary or sufficient condition for $P^m > \bar{P}$ can be derived. For example if $\bar{D} > (1 - \frac{1}{p})(1 - \bar{P})$ then $P^m > \bar{P}$ by (2). In this case, it is necessary that $\bar{P} > 0.5$ and $\bar{D} < (1 - \frac{1}{p})\bar{P}$. On the other hand, if $\bar{D} \geq (1 - \frac{1}{p})\bar{P}$, then by (3) we have $P^m \leq \bar{P}$. These results are stated in the following remark.

Remark 3. Let $\bar{P}$, $\bar{D}$ and P^m be defined as in Sec. 3. We have
(a) If $\bar{D} > (1 - 1/p)(1 - \bar{P})$, then $P^m > \bar{P}$ (sufficient condition). $\qquad(5)$
(b) If $P^m > \bar{P}$, then $\bar{D} < (1 - 1/p)\bar{P}$ (necessary condition). $\qquad(6)$

5   Experiments

In this section we include experiments using five datasets to investigate the diversity-performance relationship for majority voting. The datasets used are summarized in Table 1, which include a variety of application domains: Exp. I: breast cancer diagnostics, Exp. II: cone-torus discrimination, Exp. III: handwritten digit recognition, Exp. IV: liver disorders, and Exp. V: glass classification. Dataset for Exp. II is described in [31]. The others are taken from the UCI ML repository (http://www.ics.uci.edu/~mlearn/MLRepository.html).

Half of each dataset is used for training, and the remaining for testing. For experiments other than II and III, the partition is done randomly. In experiment II the designated usage of the original dataset is followed, and in III the training set is obtained by randomly choosing 100 instances from each class. In all five experiments, Breiman's ARC-X4 algorithm [32], a variation of ADABOOST, is

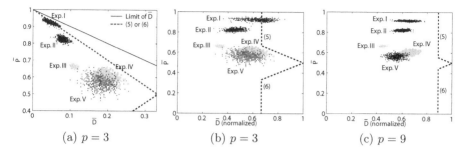

Fig. 3. Scatterplots of $\bar{P}$ versus $\bar{D}$ (a) and $\bar{P}$ versus normalized $\bar{D}$ ((b) and (c)) for the experiments. Dotted lines represent the sufficient condition and the necessary condition in (5) and (6), respectively.

Table 2. Spearman's rho coefficient of rank correlation between normalized $P^m - \bar{P}$ and normalized $\bar{D}$

Exp.	I	II	III	IV	V	Exp.	I	II	III	IV	V
$p = 3$	.681**	.398**	.017	.159**	.078	$p = 9$	.433**	.410**	.144*	.407**	.200**

* Significant at the level of 0.005; ** significant at the level of 0.001.

adopted to train CART trees. For $p = 3$ and $p = 9$, 300 and 900 CART trees are trained, respectively. Then 500 random subsets (of sizes 3 and 9, respectively) of these base classifiers are chosen to form 500 ensembles. For each ensemble, $\bar{P}$, P^m and $\bar{D}$ are examined on the test set.

Figure 3 shows the scatterplots of $\bar{P}$ versus $\bar{D}$ (Fig. 3(a)) and normalized $\bar{D}$ (Fig. 3(b), (c)). From Fig. 3(a), (b), we observe that a significant portion of the ensembles in Exp. I satisfy the sufficient condition (5). Table 2 summarizes the correlation between normalized $P^m - \bar{P}$ and normalized $\bar{D}$, as measured using Spearman's rho coefficient of rank correlation [33]. The correlation is significantly positive in most cases, in line with what were observed from the maximum entropy PDPs (Remark 1 and Fig. 2). The two possible exceptions are experiments III and V, where each is not significantly different from 0 when $p = 3$ and has weaker significance than other experiments for $p = 9$. In Fig. 3(c), we observe that normalized diversity values for Exp. III and V are lower. Exp. III also has a much smaller spread of diversity. These could be reasons leading to a lower correlation, as observed in Remark 2. However those significant positive correlations still suggest that diversity is beneficial to various extents in most cases.

We also compare the normalized $P^m - \bar{P}$ of these experiments. The Mann-Whitney statistic is applied to determine whether the normalized $P^m - \bar{P}$ for the ensembles in one experiment are larger than those in another. At the significance level of 0.001, the result for $p = 3$ is I $\rightarrow$ II $\sim$ IV $\rightarrow$ III $\sim$ V, and that for $p = 9$ is I $\rightarrow$ IV $\rightarrow$ II $\rightarrow$ III $\rightarrow$ V, where "$\rightarrow$" indicates "larger than", and "$\sim$" indicates "not significantly different from".

From Fig. 3, Table 2, and the discussion above, it can be seen that if an experiment has both higher $\bar{P}$ and higher normalized $\bar{D}$, then both its normalized

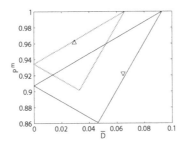

Fig. 4. Ensembles from the experiments that are closest to the upper and lower bounds: (a) The upper-left triangle is the ensemble closest to the upper bound (in normalized terms) where $\bar{P} = 0.9343$, and (b) the lower-right triangle is the ensemble closest to the lower bound where $\bar{P} = 0.9073$.

$P^m - \bar{P}$ and the diversity-ensemble improvement correlation are also higher. This phenomenon is also reflected by the fact that the ensembles for Exp. I, II and IV have higher $\bar{P} + \nu(\bar{D})$ values (Fig. 3(b), (c)), where $\nu(\bar{D})$ is the normalized $\bar{D}$. We also observed that all experiments except Exp. I have higher diversity, higher ensemble performance, and higher Spearman's rho for $p = 9$ than those for $p = 3$. This perhaps is a clear indication that majority voting is favored for a large set of MCS'.

We also examine how close can P^m in these experiments be to the tight upper and lower bounds in Theorem 2. The ensembles from these experiments that are closest to the tight bounds in normalized terms are found. That is, for the lower bound, we find the ensemble with the smallest $(P^m - L^m(\bar{P}, \bar{D}))/(U^m(\bar{P}, \bar{D}) - L^m(\bar{P}, \bar{D}))$. Similar result is obtained for the upper bound. In Fig. 4, the resulting ensembles are plotted. These ensembles are quite close to the upper bound with $\bar{P} = 0.9343$ (Fig. 4(a)) and to the lower bound with $\bar{P} = 0.9073$ (Fig. 4(b)).

6   Conclusion and Further Work

This paper addresses the fundamental problem of estimating ensemble performance in terms of the performance of and diversity among the multiple individual classifier systems. In particular, we give upper and lower bounds for the ensemble performance when the method of combination is majority voting and diversity measure the entropy diversity. These bounds are shown to be tight in the sense that they are achievable by certain input data set.

The notions of a partition of the input set by performance (PIP) and a performance distribution pattern (PDP) are defined in this paper. Using the concepts of a PIP $\mathcal{I} = \bigcup_{k=0}^{p} \mathcal{I}_k$, where $\mathcal{I}_k = \{x \in \mathcal{I} : \bar{P}(x) = \frac{k}{p}\}$, and of a PDP $\boldsymbol{\pi} = (\pi_0, \ldots, \pi_p)^{\mathrm{T}}$, where $\pi_k = \Pr\{x \in \mathcal{I}_k\}$, we are able to obtain tight bounds for P^m, which is the average ensemble performance over the data set $\mathcal{I}$, in terms of the average performance $\bar{P}$ and average diversity $\bar{D}$. It is also shown that the majority voting accuracy P^m of maximum entropy PDPs is increasing with the diversity $\bar{D}$. From maximum entropy PDPs some observations regarding the non-uniformity of the relationship between diversity and improvement are also made. Experiments on five datasets as summarized in Table 1 are included to illustrate our results.

As reviewed in Sec. 2, several important results have been obtained to estimate the ensemble performance [6, 10, 11, 16, 19, 20, 25, 28, 29]. As far as we know, our results are the first to give explicit tight bounds for ensemble performance in terms of both parameter $\bar{P}$ and $\bar{D}$ which are average performance of and average diversity among MCS' (where labels are classes) using majority voting and entropy diversity (Theorems 1 and 2). It represents the first of several ongoing studies on the general problems of estimating ensemble performance. As pointed out in Ho [2], Kuncheva [3], and Sec. 3–5 of this paper, there are several factors involved in improving the ensemble performance. These include (among others): diversity measures, combination methods, and the number of individual classifier systems (see also [13, 14, 15]). Recently, tight bounds of P^m in terms of $\bar{P}$ and Dis (the pairwise disagreement diversity measure) have been established [34]. These results will be extended to other pairwise and non-pairwise diversity measures. On the other hand, we have also obtained similar results for the ensemble performance in terms of $\bar{P}$ and $\bar{D}$ when combination method of plurality voting is used [34]. Moreover, we are working on the generalization of the current techniques and results to the problem of combining multiple scoring systems (see e.g.; [17, 18]). These results will be reported in the future.

References

1. Ho, T., Hull, J., Srihari, S.: Decision combination in multiple classifier systems. IEEE Transactions on Pattern Analysis and Machine Intelligence **16** (1994) 66–75
2. Ho, T.K.: Multiple classifier combination: Lessons and next steps. In Bunke, H., Kandel, A., eds.: Hybrid Methods in Pattern Recognition. World Scientific (2002) 171–198
3. Kuncheva, L.I.: Combining Pattern Classifiers: Methods and Algorithms. John Wiley & Sons, Inc. (2004)
4. Sharkey, A., ed.: Combining Artificial Neural Nets. Springer-Verlag (1999)
5. Dietterich, T.G.: Ensemble methods in machine learning. In Kittler, J., Roli, F., eds.: Multiple Classifier Systems. Volume 1857 of LNCS. (2000) 1–15
6. Kuncheva, L.I., Whitaker, C.J.: Measures of diversity in classifier ensembles and their relationship with the ensemble accuracy. Machine Learning **51** (2003) 181–207
7. Kuncheva, L.: That elusive diversity in classifier ensembles. In López, F.J.P., Campilho, A.C., de la Blanca, N.P., Sanfeliu, A., eds.: IbPRIA. Volume 2652 of LNCS., Springer (2003) 1126–1138
8. Hansen, L., Salamon, P.: Neural network ensembles. IEEE Transactions on Pattern Analysis and Machine Intelligence **12**(10) (1990) 993–1001
9. Krogh, A., Vedelsby, J.: Neural network ensembles, cross validation, and active learning. In Tesauro, G., Touretzky, D.S., Leen, T.K., eds.: Advances in Neural Information Processing Systems. Volume 7., MIT Press (1995) 231–238
10. Tumer, K., Ghosh, J.: Linear and order statistics combiners for pattern classification. In Sharkey, A., ed.: Combining Artificial Neural Nets. Springer-Verlag (1999) 127–162

11. Fumera, G., Roli, F.: A theoretical and experimental analysis of linear combiners and multiple classifier systems. IEEE Transactions on Pattern Analysis and Machine Intelligence **27**(6) (2005) 942–956
12. Aksela, M., Laaksonen, J.: Using diversity of errors for selecting members of a committee classifier. Pattern Recognition **39** (2006) 608–623
13. Partridge, D., Krzanowski, W.: Refining multiple classifier system diversity. Technical report, Computer Science Department, University of Exeter, UK (2003)
14. Ruta, D.: Classifier Diversity in Combined Pattern Recognition Systems. PhD thesis, University of Paisley, Scotland, UK (2003)
15. Shipp, C., Kuncheva, L.: Relationships between combination methods and measures of diversity in combining classifiers. Information Fusion **3**(2) (2002) 135–148
16. Narasimhamurthy, A.: Evaluation of diversity measures for binary classifier ensembles. In: Multiple Classifier Systems. Volume 3541 of LNCS. (2005) 267–277
17. Hsu, D.F., Chung, Y.S., Kristal, B.S.: Combinatorial fusion analysis: Methods and practices of combining multiple scoring systems. In Hsu, H.H., ed.: Advanced Data Mining Technologies in Bioinformatics. Idea Group Inc. (2006) 32–62
18. Hsu, D.F., Taksa, I.: Comparing rank and score combination methods for data fusion in information retrieval. Information Retrieval **8**(3) (2005) 449–480
19. Kuncheva, L.I., Whitaker, C.J., Shipp, C.A., Duin, R.P.W.: Limits on the majority vote accuracy in classifier fusion. Pattern Analysis and Applications **6** (2003) 22–31
20. Ruta, D., Gabrys, B.: A theoretical analysis of the majority voting errors for multiple classifier systems. Pattern Analysis and Applications **5** (2002) 333–350
21. Kittler, J., Hatef, M., Duin, R.P., Matas, J.: On combining classifiers. IEEE Transactions on Pattern Analysis and Machine Intelligence **20**(3) (1998) 226–239
22. Kittler, J., Alkoot, F.: Sum versus vote fusion in multiple classifier systems. IEEE Transactions on Pattern Analysis and Machine Intelligence **25**(1) (2003) 110–115
23. Lam, L., Suen, C.Y.: Application of majority voting to pattern recognition: An analysis of its behaviour and performance. IEEE Transactions on Systems, Man, and Cybernetics **27**(5) (1997) 533–568
24. Zenobi, G., Cunningham, P.: Using diversity in preparing ensembles of classifiers based on different feature subsets to minimize generalization error. In: European Conference on Machine Learning. Volume 2167 of LNCS., Springer (2001) 576–587
25. Narasimhamurthy, A.: Theoretical bounds of majority voting performance for a binary classification problem. IEEE Transactions on Pattern Analysis and Machine Intelligence **27**(12) (2005) 1988–1995
26. Roli, F., Kittler, J.: Fusion of multiple classifiers. Information Fusion **3**(4) (2002) 243 Editorial.
27. Kuncheva, L.I.: Diversity in multiple classifier systems. Information Fusion **6**(1) (2005) 3–4 Editorial.
28. Breiman, L.: Random forests. Machine Learning **45** (2001) 5–32
29. Matan, O.: On voting ensembles of classifiers. In: Proc. AAAI-96, Integrating Multiple Learned Models Workshop. (1996) 84–88
30. Cover, T.M., Thomas, J.A.: Elements of Information Theory. John Wiley & Sons, Inc. (1991)
31. Kuncheva, L.I.: Fuzzy Classifier Design. Springer-Verlag (2000)
32. Breiman, L.: Arcing classifiers. The Annals of Statistics **26**(3) (1998) 801–849
33. Kendall, M., Gibbons, J.D.: Rank Correlation Methods. Edward Arnold (1990)
34. Chung, Y.S., Hsu, D.F., Tang, C.Y.: On the diversity-performance relationship for plurality voting and disagreement diversity in classifier ensembles. (2006) manuscript.

Hierarchical Behavior Knowledge Space

Hubert Cecotti and Abdel Belaïd

READ Group , LORIA/CNRS
Campus Scientifique BP 239,
54506 Vandoeuvre-les-Nancy cedex France
{cecotti,abelaid}@loria.fr

Abstract. In this paper we present a new method for fusing classifiers output for problems with a number of classes $M > 2$. We extend the well-known Behavior Knowledge Space method with a hierarchical approach of the different cells. We propose to add the ranking information of the classifiers output for the combination. Each cell can be divided into new sub-spaces in order to solve ambiguities. We show that this method allows a better control of the rejection, without using new classifiers for the empty cells. This method has been applied on a set of classifiers created by bagging. It has been successfully tested on handwritten character recognition allowing better-detailed results. The technique has been compared with other classical combination methods.

1 Introduction

In any recognition system, an optimal reliability is one of the main requirements. In order to obtain such high reliability, the system must be able to consider the rejection. We distinguish three main ways to build a system able to reject:

- A single classifier, which also considered a rejection class (trained with junk patterns for example).
- A single classifier, which does not consider a rejection class, but uses some rejection rules for rejecting or not the results.
- A multi-classifiers system (MCS), where the rejection is processed by the module that fuses each classifier output.

Among these solutions, we consider in this paper the third solution for several reasons. We consider that for a high reliability several classifiers must take part into the recognition, to have several points of view of the problem. In this work, we will consider a specific MCS type: MCS with a parallel topology. In this case, the outputs of each classifier are combined thanks to a fusing module [5,11]. Usually, classifiers are combined by voting methods, belief functions, statistical techniques or Dempster-Shafer evidence theory. We distinguish several types of fusing rules:

- Fixed rules: majority voting, Borda count method... These rules are usually simple, fast and they are well-suited for classifiers ensembles that have similar performances and low correlated errors.

M. Haindl, J. Kittler, and F. Roli (Eds.): MCS 2007, LNCS 4472, pp. 421–430, 2007.
© Springer-Verlag Berlin Heidelberg 2007

– Trained rules: Bayesian, behavior knowledge space, neural network... These rules are potentially better than the fixed rules as they use knowledge about how to combine. These rules allow taking more into account the complementarities between classifiers.

This paper will focus on the behavior knowledge space method and its potential issues [6,12]. We will show that it is possible to improve this method by adding information about the ranking output of each classifier. Accordingly, in the second section, the initial fusing rule using the behavior knowledge space will be defined. Its possible improvements are described in the third section. Then the hierarchical behavior knowledge space is described in the fourth section. The fifth section will present the different classifiers. Finally, we exhibit the improvement given by the method with experiments.

2   Behavior Knowledge Space

We consider a problem with M classes: C_i, $1 \leq i \leq M$ and D classifiers: e_i, $1 \leq i \leq D$.

For applying the Bayes rule, classifiers must be independent. Each classifier must act separately in a total independent way. This condition cannot be always verified. The method using the history of the classifiers behavior allows getting free from this condition. The BKS (Behavior-Knowledge Space) method allows determining a belief degree of a proposition $x \in C_i$ based on the combination of the first best answer of each classifier $e_k = j_k$, $k \in \{1, \ldots, D\}$:

$$bel(C_i) = \frac{P(e_1(x) = j_1, \ldots, e_D(x) = j_D, x \in C_i)}{P(e_1(x) = j_1, \ldots, e_D(x) = j_D)}$$

This equation corresponds to the degree of belief definition by a Bayesian approach. It can be represented in a behavior knowledge space (BKS) [6]. This space represents the behavior for all the possible combinations in the training database. The BKS is a D dimensional space where each dimension represents the decision of a classifier. Each classifier has $M + 1$ possible outputs (M classes and 1 rejection class). The intersection of the decision of each classifier corresponds to a cell of the BKS. This method will estimate M^D posterior probabilities.

Each cell of the space is noted by $BKS(j_1, j_2, \ldots, j_D)$ with $j_i \in \{1, \ldots, M+1\}$ $\forall i \in \{1, \ldots, D\}$. Each cell of the BKS is defined by 3 features:

– $n(j_1, \ldots, j_D)(i)$: the total number of samples x such that $e_1(x) = j_1, \ldots, e_D$ $(x) = j_D$ and $x \in C_i$ $i \in \{1, \ldots, M\}$.
– $S(j_1, \ldots, j_D)$: the total number of samples x such that $e_1(x) = j_1, \ldots, e_D(x) = j_D$ and

$$S(j_1, \ldots, j_D) = \sum_{i=1}^{M} (n(j1, \ldots, jD)(i))$$

$S(j_1, \ldots, j_D)$ corresponds to the total sum of the samples that have as combination result the configuration $j1, \ldots, jD$.

- $B_{j1,...,jD}$ is the best representative class of the cell $j_1, \ldots, j_D$ of the BKS
  then:

$$n(j_1, \ldots, j_D)(B(j_1, \ldots, j_D)) = max_i(n(j_1, \ldots, j_D)(i))$$

$$B(j_1, \ldots, j_D) = Argmax_i(n(j_1, \ldots, j_D)(i))$$

with $i \in \{1, \ldots, M\}$.

In an implementation view, the BKS space can be represented by a space BKS' of dimension $D + 1$, where D dimensions correspond to the classifiers outputs and the last dimension represents the final optimal result of the combination. The BKS' is a space where all the extracted results are represented. In this case, each cell of $BKS'(j_1, \ldots, j_{D+1})$ is a natural positive number such that:

$$BKS'(j_1, \ldots, j_{D+1}) = n(j_1, \ldots, j_D)(j_{D+1})$$

The degree of belief that a sample x belongs to the class C_i denoted by $bel(C_i)$ $i \in \{1, \ldots, M\}$ is defined by:

$$bel(C_i) = \frac{P(e_1(x) = j_1, \ldots, e_D(x) = j_D, x \in C_i)}{P(e_1(x) = j_1, \ldots, e_D(x) = j_D)}$$

$$= \frac{BKS'(j_1, \ldots, j_D, i)}{\sum_{k=1}^{M} BKS'(j_1, \ldots, j_D, k)}$$

$$= \frac{n(j_1, \ldots, j_D)(i)}{S(j_1, \ldots, j_D)}$$

Finally, the combination E of the classifiers will give to the input x the following class:

$$E(x) = \begin{cases} R(j_1, \ldots, j_D) \; if \; (S(j_1, \ldots, j_D) > 0) \\ \qquad\qquad and \; (bel(C_{R_{j1,...,jD}}) \geq \alpha) \\ M + 1 \qquad\quad else \end{cases}$$

where α is a rejection threshold; $0 \leq \alpha \leq 1$.

During the test phase, it is possible to access to an empty cell. In this case, it means that the classifiers output combination has been never seen during the creation of the space. The input x is rejected.

In a statistical point of view, the BKS method tries to estimate the probability distribution of the classifiers outputs thanks to the frequencies of its occurrences. Although the BKS does not require a special dependency between each classifier, several observations can be made for this method.

3   Possible Improvements

The BKS method suffers of several defaults [12]:

- The size of the database is the first issue. In order to estimate the distribution of each classifier output, a large database is needed for representing all the possible combinations. However, this observation is mostly valid for weak classifiers that cannot offer a good recognition. For strong classifiers, all the non-empty cells are expected to stay close to the diagonal of the behavior space. Weak classifiers may lead to a better generalization thanks to their cover of the input space, but they will require much more samples to fill the space. Because of the statistical nature of the BKS, the quality of the database is very important for obtaining a good generalization.

- The confusion of BKS cells where the representative class R has a very low probability, is the second issue. If such cell exists, the result remains ambiguous. Although this cell will propose the best solution, many patterns will obtain a bad class. For the training database, in each cell, $S(j_1, \ldots, j_D) - max_i(n(j_1, \ldots, j_D)(i))$ samples, with $i \in \{1, \ldots, M\}$, will not be recognized correctly. In order to solve this problem, it is possible to add a new classifier specialized for dealing with the confusion problem involved by the ambiguous cell. Instead of using such process, we propose to extract more knowledge contained in the classifiers output: the ranking.

In the BKS method, only the first result of each classifier is considered during the combination. The confidence value and the ranking of the different classes are unfortunately not considered. We propose to use more information in order to improve the description of the ideal combination.

4   Hierarchical Behavior Knowledge Space

The Hierarchical Behavior Knowledge Space is based on the hypothesis that the ranking of the different classes, for each classifier, may bring relevant information for improving the quality of the combination. During the creation of the behavior space, the only information is the first best answer. The addition of new information to the space will lead to the creation of new cells. The $HBKS$ is totally equivalent to the BKS space for 2 classes. Indeed, for a two classes problem, with C_0 and C_1, we have $P(C_0) = 1 - P(C_1)$. Thus there is no information in the second best answer as it is dependent of the first. For taking advantage of the cell splitting, we must have $M > 2$. The new space becomes a tree of sub-spaces. The root of the space is defined by the initial BKS. For each cell $j_1, \ldots, j_D$ if $bel(C_{R_{j_1, \ldots, j_D}}) \geq \alpha$ then the cell is split into $(M - i + 1)^D$ cells where i is the actual rank of the cell.

Each cell of the space is noted by $HBKS((j_{1,1}, \ldots, j_{1,k}), \ldots, (j_{D,1}, \ldots, j_{D,k}))$ with $j_{i,k} \in \{1, \ldots, M+1\} \ \forall (i,k) \in (\{1, \ldots, D\} \times \{1, \ldots, M-1\})$. k is the rank of the output.

For the following definition, we note by J the cell
$(j_{1,1}, \ldots, j_{1,k}), \ldots, (j_{D,1}, \ldots, j_{D,k})$
Each cell of the $HBKS$ is defined by 3 features:

- $n'(J)(i)$: the total number of samples x such that the best answer of $e_d(x)$ is $j_{d,1}$, the kth best answer of $e_d(x)$ is $j_{d,1}$ with $d \in \{1, \ldots, D\}$ and $x \in C_i$ $i \in \{1, \ldots, M\}$. We note $e_{d,k}(x)$ the kth best answer of $e_d(x)$.

- $S'(J)$: the total number of samples x such that $e_{d,1}(x)$ is $j_{d,1}$ and $e_{d,k}(x)$ is $j_{d,k}$.

$$S'(J) = \sum_{i=1}^{M} (n'(J)(i))$$

$S'(J)$ corresponds to the total sum of the samples that have as outputs the configuration J.

- $B'(J)$ is the best representative class of the cell J of the $HBKS$ then:

$$n'(J)(B'(J)) = max_{(i \in \{1,...,M\})}(n'(J)(i))$$

$$B'(J) = Argmax_{(i \in \{1,...,M\})}(n'(J)(i))$$

The creation of such sub-spaces can denoise the initial cells and discover evidence of confusion between classes. For example, the rejection of a cell can be due to the noise of the different outputs. It is the case where always the same 2 classes are confused and the combination can solve the ambiguity. If a couple of classes is confused, which has never happened, the creation of sub-spaces in the BKS may solve this problem.

$$E(x) = \begin{cases} R'(j_1,\ldots,j_D) \; if \; (S'(j_1,\ldots,j_D) > 0) \\ \qquad and \; (bel(C_{R'_{j_1,\ldots,j_D}}) \geq \alpha) \\ Split \; the \; cell \quad else \end{cases}$$

$$\begin{aligned} bel(C_i) &= \frac{P(e_1(x) = j_{1,1},\ldots,e_D(x) = j_D, x \in C_i)}{P(e_1(x) = j_1, e_2(x) = j_2,\ldots,e_D(x) = j_D)} \\ &= \frac{BKS'(j_1,\ldots,j_D,i)}{\sum_{k=1}^{M} BKS'(j_1,\ldots,j_D,k)} \\ &= \frac{n(j_1,\ldots,j_D)(i)}{S(j_1,\ldots,j_D)} \end{aligned}$$

The number of cells of the $HBKS$ is defined by:

$$M^D + \sum_{k=1}^{M-1} l_k((M-k)^D)$$

where l_k is the number of new sub-spaces at the step k or the number of ambiguous cells at the step $k-1$.

The maximum number of cells of the $HBKS$ is defined by:

$$M^D + \sum_{k=1}^{M-1} (M-k+1)^D * (M-k)^D - (M-k+1)^D$$

When a sub-space is created for a cell, the sub-space replaces its corresponding cell.

The creation of the $HBKS$ can be built this way:

```
k ← 1
Fill the HBKS with the training database
While (∃J|((S'(J) > 0) and (bel(C_R'(J)) ≤ α))
{
    For all J|((S'(J) > 0) and (bel(C_R'(J)) ≤ α))
        Create a sub-space for the cell J
    Fill the new HBKS sub-spaces with the training database
    k ← k + 1
}
```

The table 1 presents an example for a problem with 2 classifiers and 3 classes (A,B and C). Each cell of the table represents $n(j_1, \ldots, j_D)(i)$. In the BKS cell AB, there is an ambiguity between the answers A and B. In the classical BKS, this cell could have been considered as being too ambiguous. The table 2 shows the subspace involved by the split of the cell AB. In these new cells, some cells remain ambiguous (c1,c4) but for some others the problem may be solved (c2,c3).

Table 1. Example of some cells in a BKS

top 1	AA	AB	AC	BA	BB	BC	CA	CB	CC
A	90	50	80	40	9	30	20	0	0
B	5	51	12	60	80	30	20	30	0
C	5	0	8	0	11	40	60	70	100

Table 2. Example for a subspace in a HBKS

cell	c1	c2	c3	c4
top 1	AB	AB	AB	AB
top 2	BA	BC	CA	CA
A	21	20	5	1
B	20	2	20	2
C	0	4	3	2

5   Classifiers

In this section, the different classifiers used for the combination are described. They are based on the same architecture: a convolutional neural network. This type of classifier has been already successfully used on handwritten digits recognition and word recognition [13].

5.1   Convolutional Neural Network

The used neural network is composed of 5 layers, it is based on the topology given in [13]:

- The first one corresponds to the input image. The image is normalized by its center and reduced to a size of 29*29 [10].
- The next two layers correspond to the information extraction, performed by convolutions. The second layer is composed of 10 maps, each one corresponds to a specific image transformation by convolution and sub-sampling reducing its size. The third layer is composed of 50 maps. For these 2 layers, the activation function is $f(\sigma) = 1.7159 * tanh((2.0/3.0) * \sigma)$ [9]
- The last two layers are fully connected. For these 2 layers, the activation function is $f(\sigma) = 1/(1 + exp(-\sigma))$.
- The last one corresponds to the output: 10 neurons, for the number of classes.

For a neuron n, weights are initialized with values w such that $|w| \leq 1/\sqrt{N_{input}}$ where N_{input} represents the number of inputs. During the back propagation, shared weights are corrected by the factor $2/\sqrt{N_{share}}$ where N_{share} represents the number of neurons that share the same set of weights.

5.2   Creation of the Classifiers

Each classifier is built on the same architecture that was described previously. D classifiers are created, each classifier being trained on a different versions of the initial database. For creating the ensemble of classifiers, we did use the bagging technique [3]. This method is based on obtaining different training sets of equal size as the original one, by using the statistical bootstrap method.

6   Experiments

6.1   Database Description

The system has been tested on the MNIST handwritten digits database [8]. This database contains separated handwritten digit images of $28 * 28$ in gray level. The learning set contains 60000 images and the test set contains 10000 images. In the learning set, 50000 images are used for real learning; 10000 images are used to find the best parameters. For the experiments, 3 classifiers have been created. Each one is trained with 33151 images.

6.2   Results

The results obtained on each classifier are presented in the table 3. We present the best result on the test database and the obtained results with the same network on the training database. For a single classifier or MCS, the results are defined by a triplet $\tau_r/\tau_s/\tau_q$ where τ_r, τ_s and τ_q are the recognition rate, the error rate and the rejection rate respectively.

The results obtained on the whole training database and test database are presented in the table 3. For each classifier, the results correspond to the network that gives the best result on the validation database. Although these classifiers do not offer the best results on this database function to the state-of-the-art [8,13], they still provide all a high accuracy. The table 4 illustrates the results on the test database for the different tops. The good result is almost always in the first three best answers, which justifies the choice of our approach for the problem.

Table 3. Results

	Training	Test
C1	99.28 / 0.72 / 0	98.51 / 1.49 / 0
C2	99.32 / 0.68 / 0	98.56 / 1.44 / 0
C3	99.27 / 0.73 / 0	98.61 / 1.39 / 0

Table 4. Recognition rate

	Top 1	Top 2	Top 3	Top 4	Top 5	Top 6
C1	98.51	99.63	99.83	99.92	99.99	100
C2	98.56	99.63	99.90	99.94	99.97	99.98
C3	98.61	99.58	99.89	99.96	99.97	99.99

The 3 classifiers have been combined with classical fixed rules:

– The Majority Voting; 2 classifiers must agree to accept the answer.
– The Oracle illustrates the result of an optimal output selection.
– The Maximum rule.
– The combination by outputs sums.
– The combination by outputs products.
– The Borda Count method, which takes into account the outputs ranking [2,4].

The results of these combinations on the test database are shown in the table 5. The Borda Count method, which uses rank-level information, gives one of the best results. It is again a proof for considering the ranking during the combination for our problem.

For the learning database, we did observe that the $HBKS$ is an optimal combination: each sub-spaces lead to the good answer. It may lead to the creation of a sub-space with only one pattern in the space. Such sub-spaces have however

Table 5. Combination results

	MNIST Test
Majority voting	98.64 / 1.29 / 0.07
Oracle	99.13 / 0.87 / 0
Max	98.69 / 1.31 / 0
Sum	98.68 / 1.32 / 0
Product	98.64 / 1.36 / 0
Borda Count	98.66 / 1.34 / 0
BKS	98.45 / 1.41 / 0.14

Table 6. BKS and HBKS results

Rejection threshold	Number of sub-spaces	Number of cells	BKS	HBKS	Sub-spaces results
0.4	2	223	98.45 / 1.41 / 0.14	98.45 / 1.41 / 0.14	(0,0,0)
0.5	5	230	98.43 / 1.40 / 0.17	98.44 / 1.41 / 0.15	(1,1,1)
0.6	58	362	98.31 / 1.29 / 0.40	98.35 / 1.31 / 0.34	(4,2,20)
0.7	107	485	98.23 / 1.20 / 0.57	98.31 / 1.25 / 0.44	(8,5,30)
0.8	137	590	98.11 / 1.14 / 0.75	98.21 / 1.21 / 0.44	(10,7,44)
0.9	166	702	98.10 / 1.02 / 0.88	98.20 / 1.08 / 0.72	(10,6,58)

no generalization power. The table 6 presents for different thresholds the results with the BKS and $HBKS$ methods. For the $HBKS$, we give the number of sub-spaces and non-empty cells. The sub-spaces results describe the special effect of the $HBKS$. These results are defined by a triplet (ξ_r, ξ_s, ξ_q) where ξ_r, ξ_s and ξ_q are the number of well recognized patterns, errors and rejected patterns respectively. For a low threshold (0.4), the $HBKS$ has no effect compared to the BKS. In the general case, $HBKS$ is expected to give better result than $HBKS$ if the ranking has a real meaning, like in handwritten word recognition. In classification tasks where the ranking cannot add knowledge, $HBKS$ may have too much knowledge for an optimal generalization. When the threshold is higher, the number of processed patterns by the $HBKS$ is higher. Although the addition of information may be risky, we show that information can be added by the sub-spaces while keeping a good reliability.

7   Conclusion

In this paper, a new fusing method has been presented for multi-classifiers systems with a parallel topology for problems with M classes ($M > 2$). It corresponds to an improvement of the existing BKS method by adding knowledge about the rank of the results. Function to a fixed confidence threshold value, each cell is divided into sub-spaces in order to solve ambiguities. We have shown that the proposed method can allow an optimal rejection control for the training database. It also provides new information for some ambiguous cells, without using new classifiers for the non-empty cells. For an optimal use of this method classifiers must provide ranking results, which have a real sense. Further works would deal with the optimal use of the $HBKS$ method and the threshold selection for getting the best generalization.

References

1. Alpaydin, E.: Improved classification accuracy by training multiple models and taking a vote. In: 6th Italian Workshop. Neural Nets Wirn Vietri-93. (1994) 180–185
2. Borda, J-C.: Mmoire sur les lections au scrutin, Histoire de l'acadmie royale des sciences, Paris, (1781)

3. Breiman, L.: Bagging Predictors, Machine Learning 24 (2), (1996) 123–140
4. Van Erp M., and Schomaker L.: Variants of the Borda count method for combining ranked classifier hypotheses. In Proc. of the Seventh International Workshop on Frontiers in Handwriting Recognition (2000) 443–452
5. Gunes, V., Ménard, M., Loonis, P., Petit-Renaud, S.: Systems of classifiers: state of the art and trends. International Journal of Pattern Recognition and Artificial Intelligence 17 (8) World-Scientific, (2004)
6. Huang, Y.S., Suen, C.Y.: A method of combining multiple experts for the recognition of unconstrained handwritten numerals. IEEE Trans Pattern Anal Mach Intell 17 (1), (1995) 90–94
7. Lam, L., Suen, C.Y.: Application of majority voting to pattern recognition: an analysis of its behavior and performance. IEEE Trans Pattern Anal Mach Intell 27 (5), (1997) 553–568
8. LeCun Y., Bottou L., Bengio Y., Haffner P.: Gradient-Based Learning Applied to Document Recognition. Proceedings of the IEEE 86 (11), (1998) 2278–2324
9. LeCun, Y., Bottou, L., Orr, G., and Muller, K.: Efficient BackProp, in Neural Networks: Tricks of the trade (G. Orr and Muller K., eds.) (1998)
10. Liu, C.-L., Nakashima K., Sako H., Fujisawa H.: Handwritten digit recognition: investigation of normalization and feature extraction techniques, Pattern Recognition 37 (2004) 265–279
11. Rahman, A.F.R., Fairhurst, M.C: Multiple classifier decision combination strategies for character recognition: A review. International Journal on Document Analysis and Recognition 5, (2003) 166–194
12. Raudys, S., Roli, F.: The Behavior Knowledge Space Fusion Method: Analysis of Generalization Error and Strategies for Performance Improvement. Multiple Classifier Systems 4 (2003) 55–64
13. Simard, P.Y., Steinkraus, D., Platt, J.C.: Best Practices for Convolutional Neural Networks Applied to Visual Document Analysis. 7th International Conference on Document Analysis and Recognition. (2003) 958–962

A New Dynamic Ensemble Selection Method for Numeral Recognition

Albert Hung-Ren Ko, Robert Sabourin, and Alceu de Souza Britto Jr.

LIVIA, ETS, University of Quebec
1100 Notre-Dame West Street, Montreal, Quebec, H3C 1K3 Canada
PPGIA, Pontifical Catholic University of Parana
Rua Imaculada Conceicao, 1155, PR 80215-901, Curitiba, Brazil
`albert@livia.etsmtl.ca`, `robert.sabourin@etsmtl.ca`,
`alceu@ppgia.pucpr.br`

Abstract. An ensemble of classifiers (EoC) has been shown to be effective in improving classifier performance. To optimize EoC, the ensemble selection is one of the most imporatant issues. Dynamic scheme urges the use of different ensembles for different samples, but it has been shown that dynamic selection does not give better performance than static selection. We propose a dynamic selection scheme which explores the property of the oracle concept. The result suggests that the proposed scheme is apparently better than the selection based on popular majority voting error.

Keywords: Fusion Function, Combining Classifiers, Diversity, Confusion Matrix, Pattern Recognition, Majority Voting, Ensemble of Learning Machines.

1 Introduction

The purpose of pattern recognition systems is to achieve the best possible classification performance. A number of classifiers are tested in these systems, and the most appropriate one is chosen for the problem at hand. Different classifiers usually make different errors on different samples, which means that, by combining classifiers, we can arrive at an ensemble that makes more accurate decisions [11,1,8]. In order to have classifiers with different errors, it is advisable to create diverse classifiers. For this purpose, diverse classifiers are grouped together into what is known as an Ensemble of Classifiers (EoC). There are several methods for creating diverse classifiers, among them Random Subspaces [6], Bagging and Boosting [10]. The Random Subspaces method creates various classifiers by using different subsets of features to train them. Because problems are represented in different subspaces, different classifiers develop different borders for the classification. Bagging generates diverse classifiers by randomly selecting subsets of samples to train classifiers. Intuitively, based on different sample subsets, classifiers would exhibit different behaviors. Boosting uses parts of samples to train classifiers as well, but not randomly; difficult samples have a greater probability of being selected, and easier samples have less chance of being used for training. With this mechanism, most created classifiers will focus on hard samples and can be more effective.

M. Haindl, J. Kittler, and F. Roli (Eds.): MCS 2007, LNCS 4472, pp. 431–439, 2007.

There are two levels of problems in optimizing the performance of an EoC. First, how are classifiers selected, given a pool of different classifiers, to construct the best ensemble? Second, given all the selected classifiers, what is the best rule for combining their outputs? These two problems are fundamentally different, and should be solved separately to reduce the complexity of optimization of EoCs; the former focuses on ensemble selection [11, 1, 12] and the latter on ensemble combination, i.e. the choice of fusion functions [8, 12, 13]. For ensemble selection, the problem can be considered in two steps: (a) find a pertinent objective function for selecting the classifiers; and (b) use a pertinent searching algorithm to apply this criterion. Obviously, a correct criterion is one of the most crucial elements in selecting pertinent classifiers [11, 1, 12]. It is considered that, in a good ensemble, each classifier is required to have different errors, so that they will be corrected by the opinions of the whole group [11, 10, 8, 12, 15]. This property is regarded as the diversity of an ensemble. Diversity is thus widely used as objective function to select ensembles, but since diversity is not itself a fusion function, other authors proposed to directly use fusion functions such as a simple majority voting error rule (MVE) for ensemble selection.

However, the use of all these objective functions for ensemble selection is meant to construct one ensemble for all the samples. Intuitively, this is not the best way to combine classifiers, because different samples might be fit to different EoCs. Dynamic scheme explores the use of different classifiers for different samples [5, 4, 2, 3, 16, 7]. Based on different features or different decision regions of each sample, a classifier is selected and assigned to the sample, some popular methods are a priori selection, a posteriori selection, overall local accuracy and local class accuracy [4, 2, 3, 16]. In general, their performances are compared with oracle, which is defined as the proportion of test samples that are at least correctly classified by one classifier in EoC. Nevertheless, against all expectations, it has been shown that dynamic selection has a large performance gap from the oracle [2], and moreover, it does not necessarily give better performance than static selection [4].

We note that most of dynamic selection schemes use the concept of the classifier accuracy on a defined neighborhood or region, such as local accuracy a priori or local accuracy a posteriori schemes [2]. These classifier accuracies are usually calculated with the help of KNN, and the use of these accuracies aims to realize an optimal Bayesian decision, but it is still outperformed by some static ensemble selection rule, such as MVE. This indicates a dilemma in estimation of these local accuracies, because their distribution might be too complicated to be well estimated. Interestingly, dynamic selection is regarded as an alternative of EoC [2, 3, 16], and is supposed to select the best classifier instead of the best EoC for a given sample. But, in fact, dynamic selection and EoC are not mutually exclusive. We believe that dynamic selection can also explore the strength of EoC.

We also note that, the oracle is usually regarded as a possible upper bound for EoC performances, and as far as we know, there is no effort made to explore the property of the oracle for dynamic selection. We argue that the complicated local classifier accuracy estimation can be actually carried out by oracle on a validation data set, and a simple KNN method can allow the test data set to obtain the approximated local classifier accuracy from the validation data set. Here are the key questions that need to be addressed:

1. Can the concept of oracle be useful for dynamic selection?
2. Should we use the best classifier or the best EoC for dynamic selection?
3. Can dynamic selection outperform static selection?

To answer these questions, we propose a dynamic selection scheme which explores the property of the oracle concept, and compare the scheme with the static ensemble selection guided by different objective functions.

2   Dynamic Classifier Selection Methods

2.1   Overall Local Accuracy (OLA)

The basic idea of this scheme is to estimate each individual classifier's accuracy in local regions of feature space surrounding a test sample, and then use the decision of the most locally accurate classifier [16]. The local accuracy is estimated as the percentage of training samples in the region that are correctly classified.

2.2   Local Class Accuracy (LCA)

This method is similar to the OLA, the only difference is that the local accuracy is estimated as the percentage of training samples with the respect to output classes [16]. In other words, we consider the percentage of the local training samples assigned to a class cl_i by this classifier that have been correctly labeled.

2.3   A Priori Selection Method (a Priori)

Instead of simply counting the percentage of training samples in the region that are correctly classified, we can calculate the average of probability outputs from correct classifiers. The probability can be further weighted by the distances between the training samples in the local region and the test sample. Consider the sample $x_j \in \omega_k$ as one of the k-nearest neighbors of the test pattern X, the $\hat{p}(\omega_k|x_j, c_i)$ provided by the classifier c_i can be regarded as a measure of the classifier accuracy for the test pattern X based on its neighbor x_j. Suppose we have N training samples in the neighborhood, then the best classifier C_* to classify the sample X can be selected by [2,4]:

$$C_* = \arg_i \max \frac{\sum_{j=1}^{N} \hat{p}(\omega_k|x_j \in \omega_k, c_i)W_j}{\sum_{j=1}^{N} W_j} \tag{1}$$

where $W_j = \frac{1}{d_j}$ is the distance between the test pattern X and the its neighbor sample x_j.

2.4   A Posteriori Selection Method (a Posteriori)

If the class assigned by the classifier c_i is known, $c_i(X) = \omega_k$, then this information can be exploited as well. Suppose we have N training samples in the neighborhood, and let us consider the sample $x_j \in \omega_k$ as one of the k-nearest neighbors of the test pattern X, then the best classifier $C_*(\omega_k)$ with the output class ω_k to classify the sample X can be selected by [2,4]:

$$C_*(\omega_k) = \arg_i \max \frac{\sum_{x_j \in \omega_k} \hat{p}(\omega_k | x_j, c_i) W_j}{\sum_{j=1}^{N} \hat{p}(\omega_k | x_j, c_i) W_j} \tag{2}$$

where $W_j = \frac{1}{d_j}$ is the distance between the test sample and the training sample.

3   K-Nearest-Oracles (KNORA) Dynamic Classifier Selection

All the above dynamic selection methods intend to find the most possibly correct classifier for a sample in a pre-defined neighborhood. But we propose another approach: Instead of finding the most suitable classifier, we select the most suitable ensemble for each sample.

The concept of the K-Nearest-Oracles (KNORA) is similar to those of OLA, LCA, a priori and a posteriori in terms of the consideration of the neighborhood of test patterns, but it distinguishes itself from the others by using directly the property of the oracle of the training samples in the region in order to find the best ensemble for a given sample. For any test data point, KNORA simply finds its nearest K neighbors in the validation set, figure out which classifiers correctly classify these neighbors in the validation set, and use them as the ensemble to classify the given pattern in the test set.

We propose four different schemes using KNORA:

1. KNORA-ELIMINATE (KN-E)
   Given K neighbors $x_j, 1 \leq j \leq K$ of a test pattern X, and suppose that a set of classifiers $C(j), 1 \leq j \leq K$ correctly classifies all its K nearest neighbors, then every classifier $c_i \in C(j)$ belonged to this correct classifier set $C(j)$ should gives a vote on the sample X. In case that none classifier can correctly classifies all K nearest neighbors of the test pattern, then we simply decrease the value of K until at least one classifier correctly classifies its neighbors.

2. KNORA-UNION (KN-U)
   Given K neighbors $x_j, 1 \leq j \leq K$ of a test pattern X, and suppose that the j nearest neighbor has been correctly classified by a set of classifiers $C(j), 1 \leq j \leq K$, then every classifier $c_i \in C(j)$ belonged to this correct classifier set $C(j)$ should gives a vote on the sample X. Note that since K nearest neighbors are considered, a classifier can have more than one vote if it correctly classifies more than one neighbor. The more neighbors that one classifier correctly classifies, the more votes this classifier will have for a test pattern.

3. KNORA-ELIMINATE-W (KN-E-W)
   The same as KNORA-ELIMINATE, but each vote is weighted by the distance between neighbor pattern x_j and test pattern X.

4. KNORA-UNION-W (KN-U-W)

The same as KNORA-UNION, but each vote is weighted by the distance between neighbor pattern x_j and test pattern X.

4   Experiments for Dynamic Selection on Handwritten Numerals

4.1   Experimental Protocol for KNN

We carried out experiments on a 10-class handwritten numeral problem. The data were extracted from $NIST\ SD19$, essentially as in [14], based on the ensembles of KNNs generated by the Random Subspaces method. We used nearest neighbor classifiers ($K = 1$) for KNN, each KNN classifier having a different feature subset of 32 features extracted from the total of 132 features.

To evaluate the static ensemble selection and the dynamic ensemble selection, four databases were used: the training set with 5000 samples ($hsf\_\{0 - 3\}$) to create 100 KNN in Random Subspaces. The optimization set containing 10000 samples ($hsf\_\{0 - 3\}$) was used for genetic algorithm (GA) searching for static ensemble selection. To avoid overfitting during GA searching, the selection set containing 10000 samples ($hsf\_\{0 - 3\}$) was used to select the best solution from the current population according to the objective function defined, and then to store it in a separate archive after each generation. Using the best solution from this archive, the test set containing 60089 samples ($hsf\_\{7\}$) was used to evaluate the EoC accuracies.

We need to address the fact that the classifiers used were generated with feature subsets having only 32 features out of a total of 132. The weak classifiers can help us better observe the effects of EoCs. If a classifier uses all available features and all training samples, a much better performance can be observed [2, 3]. But, since this is not the objective of this paper, we focus on the improvement of EoCs by optimizing fusion functions on combining classifiers. The benchmark KNN classifier uses all 132 features, and so, with $K = 1$ we can have 93.34% recognition rates. The combination of all 100 KNN by simple MAJ gives 96.28% classification accuracy. The possible upper limit of classification accuracy (the oracle) is defined as the ratio of samples which are classified correctly by at least one classifier in a pool to all samples. The oracle is 99.95% for KNN.

4.2   Static Ensemble Selection with Classifier Performance

The majority voting error (MVE) was tested because of its reputation as one of the best objective functions in selecting classifiers for ensembles [12], it evaluates directly the global EoC performance by the majority voting (MAJ) rule. Based on this reason we tested the MAJ as the objective function for the ensemble selection. Furthermore, we tested the mean classifier error (ME) as well. The MAJ is also used as the fusion function.

In table 1 we observe that the MVE performs better than ME as an objective function for the static ensemble selection. The ensemble selected by MVE also outperforms that of all 100 KNNs.

Table 1. The recognition rates on test data of ensembles searched by GA with the Mean Classifier Error, Majority Voting Error

Objective Functions	Min	Q_L	Median	Q_U	Max
Mean Classifier Error (ME)	94.18 %	94.18 %	94.18 %	94.18 %	94.18 %
Majority Voting Error (MVE)	96.32 %	96.41 %	96.45 %	96.49 %	96.57 %

It is clear that the MVE achieved the best performance as the objective function compared with traditional diversity measures. Given that the MAJ is used as the fusion function, this is not surprising.

4.3 Dynamic Ensemble Selection

Even though the MVE can so far find the best ensemble for the all samples, this does not mean that a single ensemble is the best solution for combining classifiers. In other words, each sample may have a different most suitable ensemble. It is our purpose to know whether the use of different ensembles on different samples can further increase the accuracy of the system.

Table 2. The best recognition rates of proposed dynamic ensemble selection methods within the neighborhood sizes $1 \leq k \leq 30$. RR= Recognition Rates

	KN-E	KN-E-W	KN-U	KN-U-W
RR	97.52 %	97.52 %	97.25 %	97.25 %
K-value	7,8	7,8	1	1

Note that the dynamic ensemble selection does not use any search algorithm for the ensemble selection, because each sample has its own ensemble for the classifier combination. As a result, the repetition of the search was also not necessary.

For the dynamic selection, only three databases were used: the training set with 5000 samples ($hsf\_\{0-3\}$) to create 100 KNN in Random Subspaces, The optimization set containing 10000 samples ($hsf\_\{0-3\}$) was used for the dynamic ensemble selection, and the test set containing 60089 samples ($hsf\_\{7\}$) was used to evaluate the EoC accuracies. We tested our KNORA algorithm and compared it with other proposed schemes: the overall local accuracy (OLA), the local class accuracy (LCA), the local class accuracy a priori (a priori), and the local class accuracy a posteriori (a posteriori).

We note that most of the dynamic schemes are so far better than all tested objective functions for the static ensemble selection, except OLA and a priori methods. Both LCA and a posteriori schemes achieved very good performances, with 97.40% of the recognition rates. But the KNORA-ELIMINATE and KNORA-ELIMINATE-W have good performance as well, and with 97.52% it is the best dynamic selection scheme in our handwritten numeral problems (Table 2, 3).

If we compare their performances in different neighborhood sizes, we can notice that while LCA and a posteriori dynamic selection schemes outperform the static GA selection with MVE as the objective function in a small neighborhood, their performances

Table 3. The best recognition rates of each dynamic ensemble selection methods within the neighborhood sizes $1 \leq k \leq 30$ on Dynamic Ensemble Selection

Methods	KNORA	OLA	LCA	a priori	a posteriori
Recognition Rates	97.52 %	94.11 %	97.40 %	94.12 %	97.40 %
K-value	7,8	30	1	30	1

declined when the value k augments (Fig. 1). In this case, the static GA selection with MVE may still be better than LCA and a posteriori dynamic selection schemes. By contrast, KNORA-ELIMINATE has a more stable performance even when the value of k increases. It gives a better recognition rates than all other schemes on our experimental study, except when $k = 1$. But still, the stable performance of KNORA-ELIMINATE suggests that the dynamic selection schemes are worth for more attention.

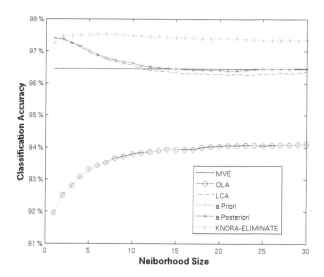

Fig. 1. The performances of various ensemble selection schemes based on different neighborhood sizes $1 \leq k \leq 30$ on NIST SD19 database. In the figure OLA overlaps with a priori selection.

5   Discussion

In this paper, we propose a new dynamic ensemble selection scheme applying directly the concept of the oracle. Different from other dynamic selections, which use the estimated best classifier for a certain data point, the K-nearest oracle uses the estimated best EoCs for dynamic ensemble selection.

In our study of handwritten numeral digits, the proposed method apparently outperforms the static ensemble selection schemes such as the use of MVE or ME as the objective function in a GA search. Using the GA search, MVE can achieve 96.45% of the recognition rates, and ME attain can 94.18%. Nevertheless, with 97.52% of the recognition rates, KNORA-ELIMINATE is better then the evaluated static ensemble selection methods.

We note that OLA and a priori dynamic selection schemes were not as good as the static GA selection scheme with MVE. The OLA takes into account neither the class dependence, nor the weighting with the each classifier, and the a priori method ignores the class dependence. Since our experiment has high class dimension (10) and the ensemble pool size is quite large (100), it is not surprising that they do not perform well.

We also observe that KNIORA-UNION and KNORA-UNION-W are less performing than KNORA-ELIMINATE and KNORA-ELIMINATE-W. This might be due to the extreme elitism in the behavior of oracle.

Moreover, the KNORA-ELIMINATE also performs slightly better than other dynamic selection schemes. LCA and a posteriori schemes can achieve 97.40%, which is better than other static methods but inferior to the KNORA-ELIMINATE. However, the performance of the KNORA is still far from the oracle, which can achieve 99.95% of the recognition rates.

This might indicate that the behavior of the oracle is much more complex than a simple neighborhood approach can achieve, and it is not an easy task to figure out its behavior merely based on the pattern feature space.

6   Conclusion

We describe a methodology to dynamically select an ensemble for each data points. We find that by using directly the concept of the oracle, the proposed scheme has apparently better performances than the static ensemble selection schemes such as GA with MVE as the objective function. Moreover, the proposed schemes also perform slightly better than other dynamic selection methods in our study.

Besides this, the dynamic ensemble selection scheme has some additional advantages over the static ensemble selection schemes. For one, dynamic selection is pretty faster than some static selection - such as GA and exhaustive search. Also, the parameters embedded in the dynamic selection are much less than those of static selection. For example, considering the single GA search we need to adjust the mutation rate, the number of generation, the size of population size, and so on. All these make the optimization of the dynamic selection much easier.

Our study shows that a dynamic ensemble selection scheme can, in some cases, perform better than some static ensemble selection methods. Furthermore, our study suggests that an ensemble of classifier might be more stable than a single classifier in the case of a dynamic selection. Yet our method is limited by the uncertainty of the behavior of the oracle, since the attained recognition rates are still not close to that of the oracle. We believe that this methodology can be much enhanced with theoretical studies on the connection between the feature subspaces and the classifier accuracies, the influence of geometrical and topological constraints on the oracle, better statistical studies to quantify the uncertainty of the oracle's behavior, and empirical studies in more real-world problems with various ensemble generation methods.

Acknowledgment

This work was supported in part by grant OGP0106456 to Robert Sabourin from the NSERC of Canada.

References

1. G. Brown, J. Wyatt, R. Harris and X. Yao, "Diversity Creation Methods: A Survey and Categorisation," *International Journal of Information Fusion*, vol. 6, no. 1, pp. 5-20, 2005
2. L. Didaci, G. Giacinto, F. Roli, G. L. Marcialis, "A study on the performances of dynamic classifier selection based on local accuracy estimation," *Pattern Recognition*, vol. 38, no. 11, pp. 2188-2191, 2005
3. L. Didaci, G. Giacinto, "Dynamic Classifier Selection by Adaptive k-Nearest-Neighbourhood Rule," *International Workshop on Multiple Classifier Systems (MCS 2004)*, pp. 174-183, 2004
4. G. Giacinto, F. Roli, "Methods for Dynamic Classifier Selection," *International Conference on Image Analysis and Processing (ICIAP 1999)* , pp. 659-664, 1999
5. T. Hastie, R. Tibshirani, "Discriminant Adaptive Nearest Neighbor Classification," *IEEE Transactions on Pattern Analysis and Machine Intelligence*,vol. 18, no. 6, pp. 607-616, 1996
6. T.K. Ho, "The random space method for constructing decision forests," *IEEE Transactions on Pattern Analysis and Machine Intelligence*, vol. 20, no. 8, pp. 832-844, 1998
7. T. K. Ho, J. J. Hull, and S. N. Srihari, "Decision combination in multiple classifier systems",*IEEE Transactions on Pattern Analysis and Machine Intelligence*, vol. 16, no. 1, pp. 66- 75, 1994
8. J. Kittler, M. Hatef, R. Duin, and J. Matas, "On Combining Classifiers," *IEEE Transactions on Pattern Analysis and Machine Intelligence,* vol. 20, no. 3, pp. 226–239, 1998
9. A. H. R. Ko, R. Sabourin, A. Britto Jr, "Combining Diversity and Classification Accuracy for Ensemble Selection in Random Subspaces" , *IEEE World Congress on Computational Intelligence (WCCI 2006) - International Joint Conference on Neural Networks (IJCNN 2006)*, 2006.
10. L. I. Kuncheva, M. Skurichina, and R. P. W. Duin, "An Experimental Study on Diversity for Bagging and Boosting with Linear Classifiers," *International Journal of Information Fusion*, vol. 3, no. 2, pp. 245-258, 2002
11. L. I. Kuncheva and C. J. Whitaker, "Measures of Diversity in Classifier Ensembles and Their Relationship with the Ensemble Accuracy," *Machine Learning*, vol. 51, no. 2, pp. 181-207, 2003
12. D. Ruta and B. Gabrys, "Classifier Selection for Majority Voting," *International Journal of Information Fusion*, pp. 63-81, 2005
13. D. M. J. Tax, M. Van Breukelen, R. P. W. Duin, and J. Kittler, "Combining Multiple Classifiers by Averaging or by Multiplying," *Pattern Recognition*, vol. 33, no. 9, pp.1475-1485, 2000
14. G. Tremblay, R. Sabourin, and P. Maupin, "Optimizing Nearest Neighbour in Random Subspaces using a Multi-Objective Genetic Algorithm," *In Proceedings of the 17th International Conference on Pattern Recognition (ICPR 2004)*, pp 208-211, 2004
15. D. Ruta and B. Gabrys, "Analysis of the Correlation between Majority Voting Error and the Diversity Measures in Multiple Classifier Systems," *In Proceedings of the 4th International Symposium on Soft Computing*, 2001
16. K. Woods, W. P. Kegelmeyer Jr, and K. Bowyer, "Combination of multiple classifiers using local accuracy estimates," *IEEE Transactions on Pattern Analysis and Machine Intelligence*, vol. 19, no. 4, pp. 405–410, 1997

Ensemble Learning in Linearly Combined Classifiers Via Negative Correlation

Manuela Zanda[1], Gavin Brown[1], Giorgio Fumera[2], and Fabio Roli[2]

[1] School of Computer Science, University of Manchester, UK
{zandam,gbrown}@cs.man.ac.uk
[2] Dept of Electrical and Electronic Engineering, University of Cagliari, Italy
{fumera,roli}@diee.unica.it

Abstract. We investigate the theoretical links between a regression ensemble and a linearly combined classification ensemble. First, we reformulate the Tumer & Ghosh model for linear combiners in a regression context; we then exploit this new formulation to generalise the concept of the "Ambiguity decomposition", previously defined only for regression tasks, to classification problems. Finally, we propose a new algorithm, based on the Negative Correlation Learning framework, which applies to ensembles of linearly combined classifiers.

1   Introduction

The field of Multiple Classifier Systems (MCSs) has now firmly established itself as able to produce state-of-the-art learning techniques. It enjoys an abundance of heuristic methods for improving performance, though on the whole is lacking in theoretical contributions. As such, one of the most highly cited references in the MCS literature is Tumer & Ghosh [1]; this was the first work to show that *correlations* between classifier outputs[1] had a quantifiable effect on the ensemble error. A parallel field to MCS is that of *regression ensembles*; that is, ensembles of estimators that solve a regression problem. In this field, the theoretical framework is far more established and can claim a heritage as far back as Laplace [2], or further. A central result here is the *bias-variance-covariance* decomposition of the mean squared error (MSE). This illustrated that the performance of the ensemble is critically dependent on the three-way balance between bias, variance, and covariance; the latter accounting for correlations between estimators. This trade-off is the analog of the often cited "diversity" in the MCS literature.

In previous work we proposed a learning algorithm, Negative Correlation (NC) learning [3] which *explicitly manages* the bias-variance-covariance (diversity) trade-off using a penalty term in the error function. In this work we extend this to the classification domain, by clearly relating the Tumer & Ghosh model to the bias-variance-covariance decomposition, and deriving a novel learning method based on NC learning.

---

[1] It should be noted that the model applies only to ensembles that average class probability estimates—the equivalent work for ensembles using majority voting is an outstanding question in the MCS community.

M. Haindl, J. Kittler, and F. Roli (Eds.): MCS 2007, LNCS 4472, pp. 440–449, 2007.

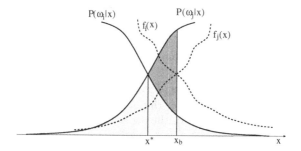

Fig. 1. Estimating posterior probabilities shifts the ideal decision boundary x^* by a quantity $b = x_b - x^* > 0$. Misclassification error is due to irreducible error (light-grey area) and added error (dark-grey area).

2 Background

In this section we describe the background of our research. Firstly we introduce a framework developed by Tumer & Ghosh [1,4] for linearly combined classifiers, and then discuss the equivalent problem in a regression framework.

2.1 Tumer & Ghosh Framework for Linearly Combined Classifiers

It is well known that for a given class k a classifier can only provide an estimate $f_k(\boldsymbol{x})$ of the posterior probability $P(\omega_k|\boldsymbol{x})$. Therefore if we choose the maximum probability class, non-optimal decisions are taken for patterns where $arg\ max_k\ f_k(\boldsymbol{x}) \neq arg\ max_k\ P(\omega_k|\boldsymbol{x})$. In a series of studies [1,4] Tumer & Ghosh analysed the case in which there is a shift of the ideal class boundary. This is shown in Fig. 1 for a two class problem.

According to their framework, the estimated posterior probability for a class ω_i is the sum of the true posterior probability $P(\omega_i|x)$ and an estimation error ϵ_i. Under the simplifying assumptions of

- a shift of the decision boundary x_b around the ideal decision boundary x^* caused by estimation errors
- a first order approximation of the posterior probabilities
- a zero order approximation of the input space distribution x around the ideal decision boundary x^*

they showed that the added error for a single classifier is proportional to the square of the boundary shift b

$$E = \frac{p(x^*)t}{2}b^2 \qquad (1)$$

and that the shift itself can be expressed as a function of the estimation errors $\epsilon_i(x_b)$ and $\epsilon_j(x_b)$:

$$b = \frac{\epsilon_i(x_b) - \epsilon_j(x_b)}{t}, \qquad (2)$$

where t is the difference between derivatives of posteriors at the optimal boundary: $t = P'(\omega_j|x^*) - P'(\omega_i|x^*)$.[2]

They proved that the expected added error $\mathrm{E}_{add} = \mathcal{E}\{E\}$ for a single classifier can be decomposed in terms of the bias and variance of this shift b. The authors then extended this to an expression of the expected added error for a simple average combination of M classifiers, deriving an expression that accounted for the effect of classifier correlations on the added error. As shown in Fig. 1, the added error in (1) is just a portion of the overall misclassification error evaluated around the decision boundary x^*.

2.2   The Regression Context

In a regression context quantifying diversity among component individuals of an ensemble is a well defined problem. Here, the combiner function is a linear combination (as in the Tumer & Ghosh model) and the loss function of interest is not the classification error, but instead the MSE.

In this context, Geman et al. [6] showed that the MSE can be broken into separate components, termed *bias and variance*:

$$\mathcal{E}\left\{(f-d)^2\right\} = (\mathcal{E}\{f\} - d)^2 + \mathcal{E}\left\{(f - \mathcal{E}\{f\})^2\right\} \qquad (3)$$

where f denotes the estimator, d the target, and the expectation is with respect to all possible training sets. Ueda and Nakano [7] extended this concept for a linearly combined regression ensemble (i.e. where the estimator is $\bar{f} = \frac{1}{M}\sum_{m=1}^{M} f^m$), providing the *bias-variance-covariance* decomposition. Krogh and Vedelsby [8] developed another important decomposition for the MSE, termed the *Ambiguity decomposition*. They proved that at a single data point the MSE can be broken into an accuracy and Ambiguity term:

$$\left(\bar{f}-d\right)^2 = \frac{1}{M}\sum_{m=1}^{M}\left(f^m - d\right)^2 - \frac{1}{M}\sum_{m=1}^{M}\left(f^m - \bar{f}\right)^2 . \qquad (4)$$

The first term is an index of the accuracy of the individuals, while the second one characterizes diversity among individuals, being a measure of how individual answers differ from the ensemble answer on this single data point.

What is interesting to point out is that Brown et al. [3] showed that the expectation of the Ambiguity decomposition leads strictly to the bias-variance-covariance decomposition, and there exists a common term which quantifies the accuracy-diversity trade-off in this case. The diversity cannot be maximized without affecting the accuracy of the individual components, and the often cited 'diversity dilemma' is in fact a three-way balance between bias, variance, and covariance.

---

[2] In this paper we follow the notation used by Fumera and Roli in [5].

3   Linking the Regression and Classification Frameworks

The equivalence between the Ambiguity and the bias-variance-covariance decomposition [9] and its exploitation through the NC framework [3] represent a well-grounded theoretical basis for the understanding of MCSs in terms of the accuracy-diversity trade-off between its individual components. The classification context lacks such a neat theory. The main result reached so far is the Tumer & Ghosh model, that shows how correlation among individual classifiers can affect the performance of a MCS. It would be then useful to understand how they relate to each other. In this section we will show that *a regression problem is implicit* in the Tumer & Ghosh model, but it is not obvious what is the estimator and what is the target that are to be considered. Our contribution will be to make it clear.

3.1   Which Random Variable to Consider?

As we already mentioned in Sect. 2.2, in regression contexts we want to minimise the MSE, that is the squared difference between the estimator function f and the true target d. Thanks to well known bias-variance decomposition [6], the expected mean squared error can be decomposed into bias and variance, as illustrated in (3).

In the Tumer & Ghosh model, the random variable (RV) in question is the boundary shift b in Fig. 1. Intuitively, b can be regarded as the 'key' variable to reformulate this in a regression framework. As b decreases towards 0, the added error drops accordingly; though bias and variance of b are discussed, it should be noted that this model differs from other bias-variance decompositions for classification problems, e.g. [10], because it treats the error as a regression random variable.

The connection between the bias-variance-covariance and the Tumer & Ghosh model is not immediately apparent; the main question is: *what are the corresponding 'estimator' and 'target' variables in this framework?*

In order to answer this question, we can first observe that the shaded area in Fig. 1 has approximately the shape of a *triangle*. The area S of a triangle is $S = \frac{1}{2}$ (base × height).

After some manipulations we can rewrite (1) as

$$E = p\left(x^*\right) \frac{1}{2}\left(\epsilon_i - \epsilon_j\right) \frac{\epsilon_i - \epsilon_j}{t} \ . \tag{5}$$

If we do not take into consideration the constant $p(x^*)$, it is easy to see that the added error is the area of a triangle having base $(\epsilon_i - \epsilon_j)$ and height $b = \frac{\epsilon_i - \epsilon_j}{t}$.

Let us denote $P_i = P(\omega_i|x)$ and $P_j = P(\omega_j|x)$ the posterior probabilities of classes ω_i and ω_j conditioned on point x. The posterior probability for the k-th class can be written as:

$$f_k = P_k + \epsilon_k \ . \tag{6}$$

The base $(\epsilon_i - \epsilon_j)$ of the triangle can be expressed as:

$$\epsilon_i - \epsilon_j = (f_i - f_j) - (P_i - P_j) \ . \tag{7}$$

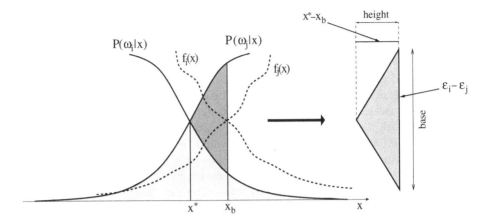

Fig. 2. The added error has approximately the shape of a triangle

If we look at the picture in Fig. 2 the base of the triangle is not only proportional to b (it is t times b) but is also a more meaningful random variable. Indeed the error, that is proportional to b^2 is equal to 0 whenever b is equal to 0. At the optimum boundary, the base of the triangle is equal to 0:

$$(f_i - f_j) - (P_i - P_j) = 0 \ . \tag{8}$$

The error drops to 0 when the difference between the two function estimation equals the difference between the posterior probabilities.

Tumer & Ghosh model can be interpreted as a regression problem by simply considering the base instead of the height of the triangle. In this case we have an estimator $f_{ij} = (f_i - f_j)$, that is the difference between two posterior probability estimators. Furthermore we can think of the difference $d_{ij} = (P_i - P_j)$ as the target of our new regression problems. The aim of the regression problem is to make the function estimator $(f_i - f_j)$ as close as possible to the new target $(P_i - P_j)$. This is true for every point $x \in \mathbb{R}$, as shown in Fig. 2.

This change of random variables increases the understanding of the model, because it makes possible to point out a valid estimator function and target for the Tumer & Ghosh model. Indeed this looking at the Tumer & Ghosh model from another perspective determines to re-define not only the RV of interest, but also its bias-variance decomposition as summarised in Table 1.

Table 1. Some key aspects of the original T & G model are compared with our new interpretation in a regression context

	T & G Model	New Interpretation
RV	$b = \frac{1}{t}[(f_i - f_j) - (P_i - P_j)]$	$f_i - f_j$
Target	0	$P_i - P_j$
Bias	$\beta_b = \frac{\beta_i - \beta_j}{t}$	$\beta_{ij} = t\beta_b + (P_i - P_j)$
Variance	$\sigma_b^2 = \frac{\sigma_i^2 + \sigma_j^2}{t^2}$	$\sigma_{ij}^2 = t^2\sigma_b^2$

Now that we have found a formulation of the Tumer & Ghosh model in a regression context, it would be interesting to investigate the idea of diversity and to develop an algorithm able to show significative improvements whenever we try to minimise the added error.

4   Optimizing Diversity by NC Learning

A way of exploiting this inter-dependency is through the Negative Correlation algorithm [11]. Removing an assumption made by Liu [11], Brown [9] proved that NC learning can be seen to be exploiting the Ambiguity decomposition. In his formulation [3] NC algorithm uses the Ambiguity decompositon as it tries to minimize a "diversity-encouraging" error function:

$$e^{\text{div}} = \frac{1}{M} \sum_{m=1}^{M} \frac{1}{2} \left(f^m - d \right)^2 - \gamma \frac{1}{M} \sum_{m=1}^{M} \frac{1}{2} \left(f^m - \bar{f} \right)^2 . \tag{9}$$

The algorithm works iteratively by performing a single weight update for each neural network in the ensemble, according to (9), proceeding in a pattern-by-pattern updating scheme. The error function in (9) allows to train a simple averaged ensemble of estimators in parallel, in contrast to the alternative of training each network independently, by putting $\gamma = 0$ [3]. In a number of benchmark studies [9,3] it was found that a γ value less than 1 showed significant improvements in both convergence speed and generalization ability. It is easy to notice that, except for linear scaling factors, the last term is equal to the Ambiguity term from (4). Given this, we now show how this algorithm can be extended to work on linearly combined ensembles exploiting the theoretical framework described earlier.

Given an ensemble of M classifiers combined by simple averaging and two classes i and j, let us denote with $\bar{f}_i$ is the ensemble estimator function for class i

$$\bar{f}_i = \frac{1}{M} \sum_{m=1}^{M} f_i^m , \tag{10}$$

and with $\bar{f}_{ij} = \bar{f}_i - \bar{f}_j$

$$\bar{f}_{ij} = \frac{1}{M} \sum_{m=1}^{M} \left(f_i^m - f_j^m \right) . \tag{11}$$

Following Krogh and Vedelsby [8], we define the Ambiguity decomposition for the Tumer & Ghosh model as:

$$\left(\bar{f}_{ij} - d_{ij} \right)^2 = \frac{1}{M} \sum_{m=1}^{M} \left(f_{ij}^m - d_{ij} \right)^2 - \frac{1}{M} \sum_{m=1}^{M} \left(f_{ij}^m - \bar{f}_{ij} \right)^2 . \tag{12}$$

---

[3] Equation 9 is equal to an independent MSE function for each network when $\gamma = 0$.

The NC framework applied to this gives us:

$$\mathrm{E_{ij}} = \left(\bar{f}_{ij} - d_{ij} \right)^2 = \frac{1}{M} \sum_{m=1}^{M} \left(f_{ij}^m - d_{ij} \right)^2 - \gamma \left\{ \frac{1}{M} \sum_{m=1}^{M} \left(f_{ij}^m - \bar{f}_{ij} \right)^2 \right\} , \quad (13)$$

where γ is a scaling factor that allows us to vary the covariance component on E_{ij}. If we adopt a gradient descent procedure on (13), it follows that given two classes i and j the partial derivative for the m-th classifier and the i-th class is

$$\frac{\partial \mathrm{E_{ij}}}{\partial f_i^m} = \frac{2}{M} \left(f_{ij}^m - d_{ij} \right) - \frac{2}{M} \gamma \left(f_{ij}^m - \bar{f}_{ij} \right) . \quad (14)$$

In a real multi-class problem it is unknown which pair of classes will contribute to the added error around any point of the feature space. In this case, we have to take into account every possible pair of classes $i, j \mid j \neq i$ and $i, j = 1 \ldots C$:

$$\mathrm{E_{TOT}} = \sum_{i=1}^{C} \sum_{j>i} \left[\frac{1}{M} \sum_{m=1}^{M} \left(f_{ij}^m - d_{ij} \right)^2 \right] - \gamma \sum_{i=1}^{C} \sum_{j>i} \left[\frac{1}{M} \sum_{m=1}^{M} \left(f_{ij}^m - \bar{f}_{ij} \right)^2 \right] . \quad (15)$$

The partial derivative of the overall error with respect to the class i and the estimator function m is

$$\frac{\partial \mathrm{E_{TOT}}}{\partial f_i^m} = \frac{2}{M} \sum_{\substack{j=1 \\ j \neq i}}^{C} \left(f_{ij}^m - d_{ij} \right) - \gamma \left[\frac{2}{M} \sum_{\substack{j=1 \\ j \neq i}}^{C} \left(f_{ij}^m - \bar{f}_{ij} \right) \right] . \quad (16)$$

Nevertheless, (14) still holds for each pair of classes, and is the true added error for the two class involved around a decision boundary. Equations (14) and (16) can be used for training in parallel a simple averaged system of neural networks, like (9) does in regression problems as an alternative to the standard independent training with the error function $\frac{1}{2} \sum_{m=1}^{M} \left(f^m - d \right)^2$.

5   Experiments

The aim of these experiments was to assess the performance of the NC ensemble learning algorithm we derived from the new interpretation of Tumer & Ghosh model in a regression context. We have applied this new NC algorithm on three real-world classification problems. The first dataset we used is a random sample of 3602 items from Phoneme dataset, from the ELENA project. The aim of the dataset is phoneme recognition—to distinguish between nasal (class 0) and oral sounds (class 1). There are 3602 data items, 5 continuous features, and the class distribution is approximately 70% class 0 and 30% class 1. The other two datasets were taken from the UCI repository. The Wine dataset has 178 instances, 13 continuous features, and 3 classes; the Heart Disease dataset has 270 instances, 13 features (mixture of continuous/discrete), and 2 classes. In both cases the input features were rescaled to zero mean and unit variance.

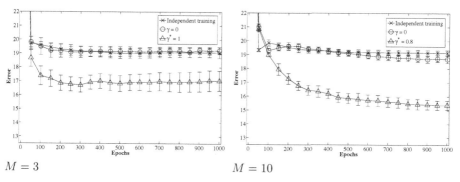

$M = 3$ $M = 10$

Fig. 3. Phoneme test error for an ensemble with relatively simple MLPs (each has 3 hidden nodes). On the left is an ensemble of size $M = 3$ (optimum $\gamma^* = 1$). On the right is a larger ensemble of size $M = 10$ (optimum $\gamma^* = 0.8$). The larger ensemble clearly faster convergence.

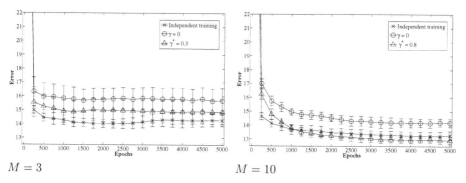

$M = 3$ $M = 10$

Fig. 4. Phoneme test error for an ensemble with relatively complex MLPs (each has 10 hidden nodes). On the left is an ensemble of size $M = 3$ (optimum $\gamma^* = 0.3$). On the right is a larger ensemble of size $M = 10$ (optimum $\gamma^* = 0.8$). The NC technique shows no significant improvements over independent training with such complex networks.

Experiments have been conducted with multilayer perceptrons, with a single hidden layer, two outputs and logistic activation functions on all nodes. In order to understand the inter-dependency between the number of networks M and the complexity H of networks[4] we have tested four different possible combinations of small/large systems made of low/high complexity neural networks, where we consider 3 and 10 to respectively be a suitable value for small/low and for large/high. Ten runs of the algorithm have been done for each of these combinations. Then, results have been compared with the performance of a single classifier (neural network with two outputs) and with an identical system[5] of individuals trained independently.

---

[4] i.e. The number of hidden nodes H, considered that every single component of MCS has the same configuration, that is the same number of hidden nodes.
[5] That is same size and same complexity.

Table 2. Mean (and 95% confidence intervals) improvement of systems trained with the NC algorithm over independent training after 1000 epochs for low complexity systems ($H = 3$) and after 5000 epoch for high complexity systems ($H = 10$). Note that the best gains are made with large ensembles of relatively simple networks.

Dataset	M = 3, H = 3	M = 10, H = 3	M = 3, H = 10	M = 10, H = 10
Phoneme	2.0 (0.7)	3.8 (0.4)	−0.6 (1.1)	0.4 (0.3)
Wine	20.5 (2.1)	16.2 (1.4)	1.4 (0.5)	0.9 (0.1)
Heart	1.7 (0.1)	3.4 (0.5)	2.7 (0.4)	3.0 (0.2)

Figure 3 shows results on Phoneme dataset for ensembles of simple networks, while Fig. 4 illustrates results obtained with ensembles of complex networks. In these figures the performance of the independent training MCS, and both performances for the special case $\gamma = 0$ and the optimum γ value γ^{*6} on the test dataset have been reported. Table 2 summarises results—the largest improvement is from a large ensemble of relatively simple networks (3.76%); whereas a small ensemble of complex networks is 0.73% worse than the independent case.

It can also be observed that system improvements can be always obtained for optimum γ values $\gamma^* > 0$. Furthermore, every system has always shown better performances than a single network. Results obtained on Phoneme dataset illustrates that the NC learning algorithm applied in the Tumer & Ghosh framework behaves very similarly to the NC algorithm on regression problems [9]. The observations are consistent with the commonly held idea in the field that MCS benefits are best levied from a large system of relatively simple classifiers. This principle of using a large ensemble of weak classifiers is echoed by other works, such as Boosting or Stochastic Discrimination [12].

6   Discussion and Conclusions

We have run several experiments by testing our NC algorithm on real classification problems. The work done so far, shows that our interpretation is consistent with results obtained, that is the NC learning applied to the new interpretation of the Tumer & Ghosh model shows improvements in terms of performance with reference to a system of networks trained independently. Its success supports the original Tumer & Ghosh idea of decreasing correlations among classifiers as a tool for increasing MCS accuracy, also illustrating that this "diversity" can be *engineered* by an appropriate technique, in this case, the Negative Correlation Learning framework.

An important point to note in this discussion is the assumptions of noise on the target data. If we wish to maximise the log-likelihood of the data, under the assumption of Gaussian noise, the appropriate error function is the mean squared error. For classification problems it is usual to assume binomial/multinomial noise, leading to the cross-entropy error function. It should be noted here that in adopting the regression framework we have implicitly made the assumption

---

[6] the γ that gives the best performance of the ensemble.

of *Gaussian* distributed noise on the posterior probability estimates. We leave the analysis under different noise assumptions for future work.

A full empirical investigation is out of the scope of this paper and will be conducted in later work. The main contribution of this paper has been to investigate the theoretical links between two different frameworks, that is: the well known regression ensemble and a linearly combined classifier ensemble.

References

1. Tumer, K., Ghosh, J.: Analysis of decision boundaries in linearly combined neural classifiers. Pattern Recognition **29** (1996) 341–348
2. de Laplace, P.S.: Deuxieme supplement a la theorie analytique des probabilites. Paris, Gauthier-Villars (1818) Reprinted (1847) in Oeuvres Completes de Laplace, vol. 7.
3. Brown, G., Wyatt, J., Tino, P.: Managing diversity in regression ensembles. Journal of Machine Learning Research **6** (2005) 1621–1650
4. Tumer, K., Ghosh, J.: Linear and order statistics combiners for pattern classification. In Sharkey, A.J.C., ed.: Combining Artificial Neural Nets: Ensemble and Modular Multi-Net Systems. Springer-Verlag, London (1999) 127–162
5. Fumera, G., Roli, F.: A theoretical and experimental analysis of linear combiners for multiple classifier systems. IEEE Trans. Pattern Anal. Mach. Intell. **27** (2005) 942–956
6. Geman, S., Bienenstock, E., Doursat, R.: Neural networks and the bias/variance dilemma. Neural Computation **4** (1992) 1–58
7. Ueda, N., Nakano, R.: Generalization error of ensemble estimators. In: Proceedings of International Conference on Neural Networks. (1996) 90–95
8. Krogh, A., Vedelsby, J.: Neural network ensembles, cross validation, and active learning. NIPS **7** (1995) 231–238
9. Brown, G.: Diversity in Neural Network Ensembles. PhD thesis, School of Computer Science, University of Birmingham (2004)
10. Kohavi, R., Wolpert, D.H.: Bias plus variance decomposition for zero-one loss functions. In Saitta, L., ed.: Machine Learning: Proceedings of the Thirteenth International Conference, Morgan Kaufmann (1996) 275–283
11. Liu, Y., Yao, X.: Ensemble learning via negative correlation. Neural Networks **12** (1999) 1399–1404
12. Kleinberg, E.M.: Stochastic discrimination. Annals of Mathematics and Artificial Intelligence **1** (1990)

Naïve Bayes Ensembles with a Random Oracle

Juan J. Rodríguez and Ludmila I. Kuncheva

[1] Departamento de Ingeniería Civil, Universidad de Burgos, Burgos, Spain
jjrodriguez@ubu.es
[2] School of Electronics and Computer Science, University of Wales, Bangor, UK
l.i.kuncheva@bangor.ac.uk

Abstract. Ensemble methods with Random Oracles have been proposed recently (Kuncheva and Rodríguez, 2007). A random-oracle classifier consists of a pair of classifiers and a fixed, randomly created oracle that selects between them. Ensembles of random-oracle decision trees were shown to fare better than standard ensembles. In that study, the oracle for a given tree was a random hyperplane at the root of the tree. The present work considers two random oracles types (linear and spherical) in ensembles of Naive Bayes Classifiers (NB). Our experiments show that ensembles based solely upon the spherical oracle (and no other ensemble heuristic) outrank Bagging, Wagging, Random Subspaces, AdaBoost.M1, MultiBoost and Decorate. Moreover, *all* these ensemble methods are better with any of the two random oracles than their standard versions without the oracles.

1 Introduction

Given its name and simplicity, the performance of the Naïve Bayes Classifier is often described as surprising [8,10,13]. A simple and accurate method is ideally suited as a base classifier for classifier ensembles. Nevertheless, NB is very stable and does not work well with some ensemble methods, such as Bagging [1]. The random oracle makes it possible to destabilize NB, introducing diversity in the classifiers of an ensemble.

Methods for constructing ensembles are often designed so as to inject randomness in the learning algorithm [6]. For instance, a Random Forest [4] is Bagging using random trees as base classifiers instead of standard decision trees. A random oracle makes it possible to introduce randomness for any base classifier model. Thus it can be considered that the presented approach consists of using an ensemble method with a different base classifier.

The paper is organised as follows. Section 2 details the random oracle approach to ensemble construction and the two random oracles considered. The experimental validation and results are given in Section 3. Finally, Section 4 concludes the study.

M. Haindl, J. Kittler, and F. Roli (Eds.): MCS 2007, LNCS 4472, pp. 450–458, 2007.
© Springer-Verlag Berlin Heidelberg 2007

2   Ensembles with a Random Oracle

A random oracle classifier is a mini-ensemble formed by a pair of classifiers and a random oracle that chooses between them. It can be thought of as a random discriminant function which splits the data into two subsets with no regard of any class labels or cluster structure. A random oracle classifier can be used as the base classifier of any ensemble method. Given a classification method, the training of a random oracle classifier consists of:

- Select the random oracle (sample its parameters from a uniform distribution).
- Split the training data in two subsets using the random oracle.
- For each subset of the training data, train a classifier.

The random oracle classifier is formed by the pair of classifiers and the oracle itself. The classification of a test instance is done in the following way:

- Use the random oracle to select one of the two classifiers.
- Return the classification given by the selected classifier.

If the computational complexity of the oracle is low, both in training and classification, the computational complexity of a random oracle classifier is very similar to the complexity of the base classifier. In the classification phase, only one of the two classifiers is used. In the training phase, two classifiers are built. Nevertheless, they are trained with a disjoint partition of the training examples and the training time of any classification method depends, at least linearly, on the number of training examples.

In this work, two random oracles are considered: the linear and the spherical oracles.

2.1   The Linear Oracle

This oracle divides the space into two subspaces using a hyperplane. To build the oracle, two different training objects are selected at random (these can be from the same class). The oracle is the hyperplane delineating the Voronoi regions of the two objects, i.e., the hyperplane passing through the middle of the segment joining the objects and orthogonal to that segment. Using objects from the data set for constructing the oracle, we ensured that there will be training instances in both subspaces.

Since the data sets used in the experiment contain both numeric and nominal attributes, we used distances to the two selected objects rather than the computationally cheaper calculation of the hyperplane. We consider Euclidean space; all numerical attributes are scaled within [0,1]. The distance between two values of a nominal attribute is 0 if the values are equal and 1 otherwise.

2.2   The Spherical Oracle

The space is divided into two regions: inside and outside a hypersphere in a random subspace. The procedure for selecting the sphere is:

– Draw a random feature subset containing at least 50% of the features.
– Select a random training instance as the center of the sphere.
– Find the radius of the sphere as the median of the distances from the center to K randomly selected training instances. (For no specific reason, here we use $K = 7$.)

The objective of this procedure is to have training instances inside and outside of the sphere. The selection of a feature subset seeks to increase the diversity of the oracles (and therefore, of the random oracle classifiers). The effect of using such subset is that the distance between two objects can be different for different oracles. If the distances are always the same for a pair of objects, two close objects would be in the same subspace for the majority of random oracles.

2.3   Why Does Random Oracle Work?

Figure 1 shows an artificial data set and the classification regions for NB, NB with linear and spherical random oracles and two NB ensembles with random oracle. Clearly, NB on its own is not adequate for this kind of data. Classical ensemble methods of NB classifiers do not help on this data. The training error of the NB classifier on this data is 57.2%. AdaBoost needs weak classifiers with errors smaller than 50%. The base classifiers from Bagging are trained from samples of the data, they will be similar to the classifier obtained from all the data.

A random oracle classifier with two NB classifiers is better for this data, but the accuracy depends substantially on the randomly selected oracle. An ensemble or 25 Random Oracle classifiers approximates rather well the optimal classification boundary.

This example illustrates two possible reasons for the success of random oracles. First, the oracle splits the training data into two subsets and the classification task can be easier in the subsets than in the original data. This may lead to a better classifier (mini-ensemble) than the original NB.

The second reason for the success of random oracle is that the base classifiers can be much more diverse than the classifiers obtained with other ensemble methods. Classical ensemble methods are not able to introduce diversity in NB classifiers. The example shows that it is possible to obtain accurate ensembles from random oracle classifiers.

3   Experiments

3.1   Settings

The data sets used in the experiments, from the UCI Repository [7], are shown in table 1. The experiments were carried out using Weka [16] and our own code.

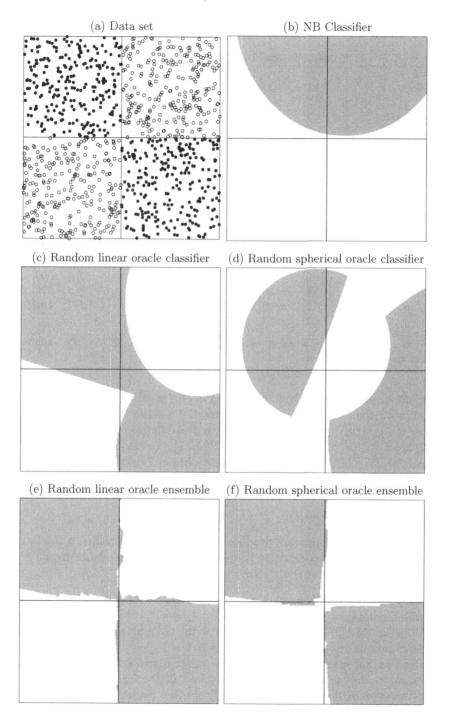

(a) Data set

(b) NB Classifier

(c) Random linear oracle classifier

(d) Random spherical oracle classifier

(e) Random linear oracle ensemble

(f) Random spherical oracle ensemble

Fig. 1. Data set and classification regions for NB, NB with random oracle and NB ensembles with random oracle. Each ensemble consists of 25 classifiers.

Table 1. Summary of the 35 UCI Datasets used in the experiment

Data set	Classes	Objects	D	C	Data set	Classes	Objects	D	C
anneal	6	898	32	6	letter	26	20000	0	16
audiology	24	226	69	0	lymphography	4	148	15	3
autos	7	205	10	16	mushroom	2	8124	22	0
balance-scale	3	625	0	4	pima-diabetes	2	768	0	8
breast-cancer	2	286	10	0	primary-tumor	22	339	17	0
cleveland-14-heart	2	303	7	6	segment	7	2310	0	19
credit-rating	2	690	9	6	sick	2	3772	22	7
german-credit	2	1000	13	7	sonar	2	208	0	60
glass	7	214	0	9	soybean	19	683	35	0
heart-statlog	2	270	0	13	splice	3	3190	60	0
hepatitis	2	155	13	6	vehicle	4	846	0	18
horse-colic	2	368	16	7	vote	2	435	16	0
hungarian-14-heart	2	294	7	6	vowel-context	11	990	2	10
hypothyroid	4	3772	22	7	vowel-nocontext	11	990	0	10
ionosphere	2	351	0	34	waveform	3	5000	0	40
iris	3	150	0	4	wisconsin-bc	2	699	0	9
kr-vs-kp	2	3196	36	0	zoo	7	101	16	2
labor	2	57	8	8					

Note: 'D' stands for the number of discrete features and 'C' for the number of continuous-valued features.

There are several methods for handling continuous attributes in NB classifiers [2]; in this work the "Normal" method was used. The class-conditional pdf for attribute x_i, $p(x_i|\omega_j)$ is approximated as a normal distribution, and the discriminant function for class ω_j is $g_j(\mathbf{x}) = P(\omega_j)\prod_i p(x_i|\omega_j)$. Each ensemble was formed by 25 classifiers. The results were obtained using a 10-fold stratified cross validation, repeated 10 times.

3.2   Ensemble Methods

As the random oracle approach produces, in effect, a base classifier, it can be used with any ensemble heuristic or on its own. The ensemble methods considered in this work are:

- Bagging [3]. Each base classifier is trained on a bootstrap sample of the training data.
- Wagging [15,1]. For each base classifier, the training examples are weighted randomly using the Poisson distribution.
- Random Subspaces [11]. Each base classifier is trained with all the training examples, but using only a random subset of the features. Two values are considered for the number of randomly selected features here: 50% and 75%.
- AdaBoost.M1 [9]. This is the most well-known variant of Boosting. The training samples are also weighted. It is an incremental method; the weight on an object depends on the correctness of the classifications given by the

previous base classifiers. Both the re-sampling and the re-weighting version are considered here, denoted (S) and (W), respectively.

- MultiBoost [15]. This is a combination of Boosting and Wagging. It follows the AdaBoost method, but after a number of iterations the training examples are reweighted using the Wagging approach. The size of the sub-committees for this method was set to 5. It has the same two variants as AdaBoost.M1, both of them used in the experiment.
- Decorate [14]. This is an incremental method based on the boosting method. Each base classifier is trained using all training examples plus artificially generated examples. The method seeks diversity among the base classifiers by constructing the artificial examples in a specific way.

The total number of different methods together with their variants is 9 (6 methods, 3 of them with 2 options). Each method will be used with three base classifiers: NB, random linear oracle with NB and random spherical oracle with NB. Hence, the number of different configurations is 27.

Included in the experiments were also the following three methods: a single NB (denoted further as 'Single') and ensembles obtained using *only* the random oracle heuristic, linear (denoted L-Ensemble) or spherical (denoted S-Ensemble).

3.3 Results

Table 2 shows a summary of the experimental results. The methods are sorted according to their average rank, following the method described in [5]. For each data set, all the methods are sorted. The best method has rank 1, the second best has rank 2, and so on. If there are ties, the methods are assigned average ranks. The overall value of a method is measured by its average rank across all data sets.

The best 7 methods use a Random Oracle. The top ranks are for MultiBoost with a Random Oracle and re-weighting or re-sampling. The best method without an oracle is the re-sampling version of MultiBoost.

The last column of the table, the benefit, represents the difference between the average ranks of a method with an oracle and the corresponding method without the oracle. The length of the bars is proportional to that difference. For *all the methods*, the benefit is positive.

The table also shows that the random oracle can be used as the only heuristic for ensemble construction. The spherical oracle ensemble has a better rank than all the methods that do not use a random oracle. The linear oracle ensemble is not as good, but the only method, without a random oracle, with better rank than L-Ensemble is MultiBoost.

Table 2 also includes, for the methods with a random oracle, the number of data sets where that method is better, equal and worse than the corresponding version without the oracle. For all the methods, the versions with an oracle are better than the version without the oracle for at least 21 of 35 data sets.

When comparing two methods over 35 data sets, the differences are statistically significant, according to a sign test [5], for a level $\alpha = 0.05$, if the number

Table 2. Ensemble methods with and without Random Oracle sorted by their average ranks. The ensemble size, L, is 25.

Method	Total Rank	Win-tie -loss	Benefit	Method	Total Rank	Win-tie -loss	Benefit
S-MultiBoost (W)	8.41	•26-0-9	▬	S-AdaBoostM1 (W)	15.00	•24-2-9	▬
S-MultiBoost (S)	8.43	•27-0-8	▬	L-Rand. Subs. (75%)	15.03	•25-0-10	▬
L-MultiBoost (S)	8.64	•26-0-9	▬	L-AdaBoostM1 (W)	15.56	•25-1-9	▬
L-MultiBoost (W)	9.33	•25-0-10	▬	L-Rand. Subs. (50%)	15.73	•29-0-6	▬▬
S-Bagging	11.23	•31-0-4	▬▬	S-Rand. Subs. (50%)	15.93	•27-1-7	▬
S-Wagging	12.44	•27-0-8	▬▬	L-Decorate	18.03	23-0-12	▬
S-Ensemble	12.77			AdaBoostM1 (S)	18.63		
MultiBoost (S)	13.11			AdaBoostM1 (W)	19.03		
S-Rand. Subs. (75%)	13.63	•26-0-9	▬	Bagging	20.19		
L-Bagging	13.93	•26-0-9	▬	Rand. Subs. (75%)	20.44		
S-AdaBoostM1 (S)	14.09	23-0-12	▬	S-Decorate	20.74	21-0-14	▪
MultiBoost (W)	14.33			Wagging	20.83		
L-Wagging	14.46	•24-0-11	▬▬	Single	21.13		
L-Ensemble	14.63			Decorate	21.81		
L-AdaBoostM1 (S)	14.71	•24-1-10	▬	Rand. Subs. (50%)	22.79		

Note 1: 'L-' indicates that the linear oracle is present, 'S-' that the spherical oracle is present.
Note 2: '•' indicates that the difference between the method with oracle and without oracle is statistically significant at $\alpha = 0.05$ (using sign test).

Table 3. Ensemble methods with and without Random Oracle sorted by their average ranks. The ensemble size, L, is 25 for the methods with oracle and 50 for the methods without oracle.

Method	Total Rank	Win-tie -loss	Benefit	Method	Total Rank	Win-tie -loss	Benefit
S-MultiBoost (W)	8.36	•28-1-6	▬▬	MultiBoost (S)	15.37		
S-MultiBoost (S)	8.43	•27-0-8	▬▬	L-AdaBoostM1 (W)	15.37	•26-1-8	▬
L-MultiBoost (S)	8.57	•26-0-9	▬▬	L-Rand. Subs. (50%)	15.60	•25-0-10	▬▬
L-MultiBoost (W)	9.16	•28-0-7	▬▬	S-Rand. Subs. (50%)	15.81	•28-0-7	▬▬
S-Bagging	11.11	•30-0-5	▬▬	MultiBoost (W)	16.87		
S-Wagging	12.26	•27-1-7	▬▬	L-Decorate	18.04	23-0-12	▬
S-Ensemble	12.54			AdaBoostM1 (S)	18.56		
S-Rand. Subs. (75%)	13.51	•28-0-7	▬▬	AdaBoostM1 (W)	19.19		
L-Bagging	13.79	•25-0-10	▬	Bagging	19.46		
S-AdaBoostM1 (S)	14.09	23-0-12	▬	Wagging	19.97		
L-Wagging	14.23	•24-0-11	▬▬	S-Decorate	20.66	21-0-14	▪
L-AdaBoostM1 (S)	14.61	23-1-11	▬	Single	21.00		
L-Ensemble	14.67			Rand. Subs. (75%)	21.00		
L-Rand. Subs. (75%)	14.73	•28-0-7	▬▬	Rand. Subs. (50%)	21.27		
S-AdaBoostM1 (W)	14.87	•24-2-9	▬	Decorate	21.90		

Note: 'L-' indicates that the linear oracle is present, 'S-' that the spherical oracle is present.
Note 2: '•' indicates that the difference between the method with oracle and without oracle is statistically significant at $\alpha = 0.05$ (using sign test).

of wins (plus half the number of ties) is greater or equal than 24. Those cases are marked with a bullet in the table. From 18 tests, only in 3 cases the difference is not significant.

In the previous comparison, the number of base classifiers for all the ensembles was 25. It could be argued that the setting is favourable to the random oracle variants because these ensembles are formed by 50 NB classifiers (25 Random Oracles with 2 NB classifiers) while the variants without the oracle are formed by 25 NB classifiers. That setting was selected because in the variants with and without the Random Oracle, each training instance was used to construct, at most, 25 NB classifiers and each testing instance was classified by, at most, 25 NB classifiers.

The experiments were repeated with all the ensembles without the random oracle using 50 NB classifiers. Table 3 shows the results. Interestingly, the results are even more favourable to the versions with the Random Oracle. This unexpected finding indicates that some classical methods performed worse with $L = 50$ classifiers than with $L = 25$ classifiers. One possible explanation is over-training of the ensemble. As the results are based on ranking, the behaviour of one or two ensembles would affect the overall score for all methods. The suspect here is MultiBoost. In both tables, this is the best method without random oracle. In Table 2 this method was the 7th best method, with an average rank of 13.11. In Table 3 the method is at 16th place with an average rank of 15.37, showing that MultiBoost with $L = 50$ has been outperformed by more ensemble methods than MultiBoost with $L = 25$.

4   Conclusion

Here we study ensembles of NB classifiers with random oracle. Previously a random linear oracle was used to improve ensembles of decision trees [12]. Our results indicate that random oracles are even more suitable for NB classifiers than for decision trees.

Most ensemble methods rely on unstable base classifiers. It is known that NB are more stable than decision trees. The random oracle introduces the desired instability of NB, which makes random-oracle NB a good base classifier for constructing ensembles.

Nine ensemble models were considered (6 methods, 3 of them with 2 variants). For each of them, there were 3 variants: without random oracle, with the linear oracle and with the spherical oracle. 35 UCI data sets were used in this study. The spherical oracle ensemble method (based only on the random oracle heuristic) showed better results than any of the 9 ensemble models without oracle. Moreover the random oracle improved the performance of *all* nine ensemble models. Best method appeared to be MultiBoost with a spherical oracle. For NB base classifiers, the spherical oracle is generally better than the linear oracle.

There is further room for improvement; the 'best' random oracle to use can depend on the base classifier, the ensemble method and the data set. Also, the diversity of the classifiers in an ensemble could be improved using different random oracles in the same ensemble.

Acknowledgements. This work has been partially supported by the Spanish MCyT project DPI2005–08498, and the "Junta de Castilla y León" project VA088A05.

References

1. E. Bauer and R. Kohavi. An empirical comparison of voting classification algorithms: Bagging, boosting, and variants. *Machine Learning*, 36(1–2):105–139, 1999.
2. R.R. Bouckaert. Naive Bayes classifiers that perform well with continuous variables. In *17th Australina Conference on AI (AI 04)*, Lecture Notes in AI. Springer, 2004.
3. L. Breiman. Bagging predictors. Technical Report 421, Department of Statistics, University of California, Berkeley, 1994.
4. L. Breiman. Random forests. *Machine Learning*, 45(1):5–32, 2001.
5. J. Demšar. Statistical comparison of classifiers over multiple data sets. *Journal of Machine Learning Research*, 7:1–30, 2006.
6. T.G. Dietterich. Ensemble methods in machine learning. In *Multiple Classifier Systems 2000*, pages 1–15, 2000.
7. C.L. Blake D.J. Newman, S. Hettich and C.J. Merz. UCI repository of machine learning databases, 1998.
8. P. Domingos and M. Pazzani. On the optimality of the simple bayesian classifier under zero-one loss. *Machine Learning*, 29:103–130, 1997.
9. Y. Freund and R. E. Schapire. A decision-theoretic generalization of on-line learning and an application to boosting. *Journal of Computer and System Sciences*, 55(1):119–139, 1997.
10. D.J. Hand and K. Yu. Idiot's bayes — not so stupid after all? *International Statistical Review*, 69:385–399, 2001.
11. T. K. Ho. The random space method for constructing decision forests. *IEEE Transactions on Pattern Analysis and Machine Intelligence*, 20(8):832–844, 1998.
12. L. I. Kuncheva and J. J. Rodríguez. Classifier ensembles with a random linear oracle. *IEEE Transactions on Knowledge and Data Engineering*, 19(4):500–508, 2007.
13. L.I. Kuncheva. On the optimality of naïve bayes with dependent binary features. *Pattern Recognition Letters*, 27:830–837, 2006.
14. P. Melville and R. J. Mooney. Creating diversity in ensembles using artificial data. *Information Fusion*, 6(1):99–111, 2005.
15. G. I. Webb. Multiboosting: A technique for combining boosting and wagging. *Machine Learning*, 40(2):159–196, 2000.
16. I. H. Witten and E. Frank. *Data Mining: Practical Machine Learning Tools and Techniques.* Morgan Kaufmann, 2nd edition, 2005. http://www.cs.waikato.ac.nz/ml/weka.

An Experimental Study on Rotation Forest Ensembles

Ludmila I. Kuncheva[1] and Juan J. Rodríguez[2]

[1] School of Electronics and Computer Science, University of Wales, Bangor, UK
l.i.kuncheva@bangor.ac.uk
[2] Departamento de Ingeniería Civil, Universidad de Burgos, 09006 Burgos, Spain
jjrodriguez@ubu.es

Abstract. Rotation Forest is a recently proposed method for building classifier ensembles using independently trained decision trees. It was found to be more accurate than bagging, AdaBoost and Random Forest ensembles across a collection of benchmark data sets. This paper carries out a lesion study on Rotation Forest in order to find out which of the parameters and the randomization heuristics are responsible for the good performance. Contrary to common intuition, the features extracted through PCA gave the best results compared to those extracted through non-parametric discriminant analysis (NDA) or random projections. The only ensemble method whose accuracy was statistically indistinguishable from that of Rotation Forest was LogitBoost although it gave slightly inferior results on 20 out of the 32 benchmark data sets. It appeared that the main factor for the success of Rotation Forest is that the transformation matrix employed to calculate the (linear) extracted features is sparse.

Keywords: Pattern recognition, Classifier ensembles, Rotation Forest, Feature extraction.

1 Introduction

Classifier ensembles usually demonstrate superior accuracy compared to that of single classifiers. Within the classifier ensemble models, *AdaBoost* has been declared to be the best off-the-shelf classifier [4]. A close rival to AdaBoost is *bagging* where the classifiers in the ensemble are built independently of one another, using some randomisation heuristic [3,5]. Bagging has been found to outperform AdaBoost on noisy data [1] but is generally perceived as the less accurate of the two methods. To encourage diversity in bagging, further randomisation was introduced in the Random Forest model [5]. A Random Forest ensemble consists of decision trees trained on bootstrap samples from the data set. Additional diversity is introduced by randomising the feature choice at each node. During tree construction, the best feature at each node is selected among M randomly chosen features, where M is a parameter of the algorithm.

Rotation Forest [15] draws upon the Random Forest idea. The base classifiers are also independently built decision trees, but in Rotation Forest each tree

M. Haindl, J. Kittler, and F. Roli (Eds.): MCS 2007, LNCS 4472, pp. 459–468, 2007.

is trained on the whole data set in a rotated feature space. As the tree learning algorithm builds the classification regions using hyperplanes parallel to the feature axes, a small rotation of the axes may lead to a very different tree. A comparative experiment by Rodriguez et al. [15] favoured Rotation Forest to bagging, AdaBoost and Random Forest. Studying kappa-error diagrams it was discovered that Rotation Forest would often produce more accurate classifiers than AdaBoost which are also more diverse than those in bagging.

This paper explores the effect of the design choices and parameter values on the performance of Rotation Forest ensembles. The rest of the paper is organized as follows. Section 2 explains the Rotation Forest ensemble method and the design choices within. Sections 3 to 6 comprise our lesion study. Experimental results are reported also in Section 6. Section 7 offers our conclusions.

2   Rotation Forest

Rotation Forest is an ensemble method which trains L decision trees independently, using a different set of extracted features for each tree [15]. Let $\mathbf{x} = [x_1, \ldots, x_n]^T$ be an example described by n features (attributes) and let X be an $N \times n$ matrix containing the training examples. We assume that the true class labels of all training examples are also provided. Let $\mathcal{D} = \{D_1, \ldots, D_L\}$ be the ensemble of L classifiers and F be the feature set.

Rotation Forest aims at building accurate *and* diverse classifiers. Bootstrap samples are taken as the training set for the individual classifiers, as in bagging. The main heuristic is to apply feature extraction and to subsequently reconstruct a full feature set for each classifier in the ensemble. To do this, the feature set is split randomly into K subsets, principal component analysis (PCA) is run separately on each subset, and a new set of n linear extracted features is constructed by pooling all principal components. The data is transformed linearly into the new feature space. Classifier D_i is trained with this data set. Different splits of the feature set will lead to different extracted features, thereby contributing to the diversity introduced by the bootstrap sampling.

We chose decision trees as the base classifiers because they are sensitive to rotation of the feature axes and still can be very accurate. The effect of rotating the axes is that classification regions of high accuracy can be constructed with fewer trees than in bagging and AdaBoost. Our previous study [15] reported an experiment whose results were favourable to Rotation Forest compared to bagging, AdaBoost and Random Forest with the same number of base classifiers. The design choices and the parameter values of the Rotation Forest were picked in advance and not changed during the experiment. These were as follows

– Number of features in a subset: $M = 3$;
– Number of classifiers in the ensemble: $L = 10$;
– Extraction method: principal component analysis (PCA);
– Base classifier model: decision tree (hence the name "forest").

Thirty two data sets from UCI Machine Learning Repository [2], summarized in Table 1, were used in the experiment. The calculations and statistical

Table 1. Characteristics of the 32 data sets used in this study

data set	c	N	n_d	n_c	data set	c	N	n_d	n_c
anneal	6	898	32	6	labor	2	57	8	8
audiology	24	226	69	0	lymphography	4	148	15	3
autos	7	205	10	16	pendigits	10	10992	0	16
balance-scale	3	625	0	4	pima-diabetes	2	768	0	8
breast-cancer	2	286	10	0	primary-tumor	22	239	17	0
cleveland-14-heart	5	307	7	6	segment	7	2310	0	19
credit-rating	2	690	9	6	sonar	2	208	0	60
german-credit	2	1000	13	7	soybean	19	683	35	0
glass	7	214	0	9	splice	3	3190	60	0
heart-statlog	2	270	0	13	vehicle	4	846	0	18
hepatitis	2	155	13	6	vote	2	435	16	0
horse-colic	2	368	16	7	vowel-context	11	990	2	10
hungarian-14-heart	5	294	7	6	vowel-nocontext	11	990	0	10
hypothyroid	4	3772	22	7	waveform	3	5000	0	40
ionosphere	2	351	0	34	wisc-breast-cancer	2	699	0	9
iris	3	150	0	4	zoo	7	101	16	2

Notes: c is the number of classes, N is the number of objects, n_d is the number of discrete (categorical) features and n_c is the number of contiunous-valued features

comparisons were done using Weka [20]. Fifteen 10-fold cross-validations were used with each data set.

Statistical comparisons in Weka are done using a corrected estimate of the variance of the classification error [14].

The remaining sections of this paper address the following questions.

1. Is splitting the features set F essential for the success of Rotation Forest?
2. How does K (respectively M) affect the performance of Rotation Forest? Is there a preferable value of K or M?
3. How does Rotation Forest compare to bagging and AdaBoost for various ensemble sizes L?
4. Is PCA the best method to rotate the axes for the feature subsets? Since we are solving a classification problem, methods for linear feature extraction which use discriminatory information may be more appropriate.

3   Is Splitting Essential?

Splitting the feature set, F, into K subsets is directed towards creating diversity. Its effect is that each new extracted feature is a linear combination of $M = \lfloor n/K \rfloor$ original features. Then the "rotation matrix", R, used to transform a bootstrap sample T of the original training set into a new training set $(T' = TR)$ is sparse. [1]

---

[1] Here we refer to random projections broadly as "rotations", which is not technically correct. For the random projections to be rotations, the rotation matrix must be orthonormal. In our case we only require this matrix to be non-degenerate. The choice of terminology was guided by the fact that random projections are a version of the rotation forest idea, the only difference being that PCA is replaced by a non-degenerate random linear transformation.

To find out how a sparse rotation matrix compares to a full rotation matrix we used two approaches.

We call the first approach Random Projections. L random (nondegenerate) transformation matrices of size $n \times n$ were generated, denoted $R_1, \ldots, R_L$, with entries sampled from a standard normal distribution $\sim N(0, 1)$. There is no loss of information in this transformation as R_i can be inverted and the original space restored. However, any such transformation may distort or enhance discriminatory information. In other words, a rotation may simplify or complicate the problem, leading to very different sizes of the decision trees in the two cases.

In the second approach, which we call Sparse Random Projections, sparse transformation matrices were created so as to simulate the one in the Rotation Forest method. The non-zero elements of these matrices were again sampled randomly from a standard normal distribution. L such matrices were generated to form the ensemble.

For ensembles with both pruned and unpruned trees, Sparse Random Projections were better than Random Projections on 24 of the 32 data sets, where 7 of these differences were statistically significant. Of the remaining 8 cases where Random Projections were better than Sparse Random Projections, none of the differences were statistically significant.

Next we look at the reasons why Sparse Random Projections are better than Random Projections.

3.1 Accuracy of the Base Classifiers

One of the factors contributing to the accuracy of an ensemble is the accuracy of its base classifiers. Hence, one of the possible causes for the difference between the performances of Random Projections and Sparse Random Projections may be due to a difference in the accuracies of the base classifiers. We compared the results obtained using a single decision tree with the two projection methods. As in the main experiment, we ran 15 10-fold cross-validations on the 32 data sets. The results displayed in Table 2 show that

- Decision trees obtained with the projected data are worse than decision trees obtained with the original data.
- Decision trees obtained after a non-sparse projection are worse than decision trees obtained after a sparse projection.

One possible explanation of the observed relations is that projecting the data randomly is similar to introducing noise. The degree of non-sparseness of the projection matrix gauges the amount of noise. For instance, a diagonal projection matrix will only rescale the axes and the resultant decision tree will be equivalent to a decision tree built on the original data.

3.2 Diversity of the Ensemble

Better accuracy of the base classifiers alone is not sufficient to guarantee better ensemble accuracy. For the ensemble to be successful, accuracy has to be coupled

Table 2. Comparison of the results obtained with a single decision tree, using the original and the projected data. The entry $a_{i,j}$ shows the number of datasets for which the method of column j gave better results than the method of row i. The number in the parentheses shows in how many of these cases the difference has been statistically significant.

| | With pruning | | | Without pruning | | |
	original	non-sparse	sparse	original	non-sparse	sparse
original	-	3 (0)	8 (0)	-	4 (0)	9 (0)
non-sparse	29 (17)	-	30 (13)	28 (15)	-	28 (11)
sparse	24 (8)	2 (0)	-	23 (7)	4 (0)	-

with diversity. To study further the effect due to splitting the feature set, we consider kappa-error diagrams with sparse and with non-sparse projections.

Kappa-error diagrams is the name for a scatterplot with $L(L-1)/2$ points, where L is the ensemble size. Each point corresponds to a pair of classifiers. On the x-axis is a measure of diversity between the pair, κ. On the y-axis is the averaged individual error of the classifiers in the pair, $E_{i,j} = \frac{E_i+E_j}{2}$. As small values of κ indicate better diversity and small values of $E_{i,j}$ indicate better accuracy; the most desirable pairs of classifiers will lie in the bottom left corner.

Figure 1 plots the kappa-error diagrams for two data sets, audiology and vowel-context, using Random Projections and Sparse Random Projections with pruned trees. The points come from a 10-fold cross-validation for ensembles of size 10. We chose these two data sets because they are typical examples of the two outcomes of the statistical comparisons of sparse and non-sparse random projections. For the audiology data set, sparse projections are substantially better while for vowel-context data the two methods are indistinguishable.

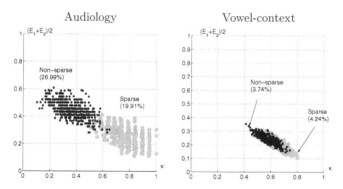

Fig. 1. Kappa-error diagrams for two data sets for sparse and non-sparse random projections. The ensemble errors are marked on the plots.

The figure shows that the success of the sparse projections compared to non-sparse projections is mainly due to maintaining high accuracy of the base classifiers. The additional diversity obtained through the "full" random projection is not useful for the ensemble.

The results presented in this section show that splitting the feature set is indeed essential for the success of Rotation Forest.

4   Number of Feature Subsets, K

No consistent relationship between the ensemble error and K was found. The patterns for different data sets vary from clear steady decrease of the error with K (audiology, autos, horse-colic, hypothyroid, segment, sonar, soybean, splice, vehicle and waveform datasets), through non-monotonic (almost horizontal) lines, to marked increase of the error with K (balance-scale, glass, vowel-nocontext and wisconsin-breast-cancer datasets). The only regularity was that for $K = 1$ and $K = n$ the errors were larger than these with values in-between. This is not unexpected. First, for $K = 1$, we have non-sparse projections, which were found in the previous section to give inferior accuracy to that when sparse projections were used. Splitting the feature set into $K = 2$ subsets immediately makes the rotation matrix 50% sparse, which is a prerequisite for accurate individual classifiers and ensembles thereof. On the other hand, if $K = n$, where n is the number of features, then any random projection reduces to rescaling of the features axes, and the decision trees are identical. Thus for $K = n$ we have a single tree rather than an ensemble.

As with K, there was no consistent pattern or regularity for M ranged between 1 and 10. In fact, the choice $M = 3$ in [15] has not been the best choice in terms of smallest cross-validation error. It has been the best choice for only 4 data sets out of the 32, and the worst choice in 8 data sets! Thus $M = 3$ has not been a serendipitous guess in our previous study. As Rotation Forest outperformed bagging, AdaBoost and Random Forest for this rather unfavourable value of M, we conclude that Rotation Forest is robust with respect to the choice of M (or K).

5   Ensemble Size, L

All our previous experiments were carried out with $L = 10$ ensemble members. Here AdaBoost.M1, Random Forest and Rotation Forest were run with L varying from 1 (single tree) to 100. Only unpruned trees were used because Random Forest only operates with those. Since the classification accuracies vary significantly from dataset to dataset, ranking methods are deemed to provide a more fair comparison [7]. In order to determine whether the ensemble methods were significantly different we ran Friedman's two-way ANOVA. The ensemble accuracies for a fixed ensemble size, L, were ranked for each dataset. Figure 2 plots the average ranks of the four methods versus ensemble size, L. All results shown are from a single 10-fold cross-validation. If the ensemble methods are equivalent, then their ranks would be close to random for the different data sets. According to Friedman's test, the ensemble methods are different at significance level 0.005 for all values of L. However, the differences are largely due to the rank of bagging being consistently the worst of the four methods. A further pairwise comparison was carried out. With significance level of 0.1, Rotation Forest was found to be significantly better than bagging for $L \in \{3, 6, 10 - 100\}$, better than AdaBoost

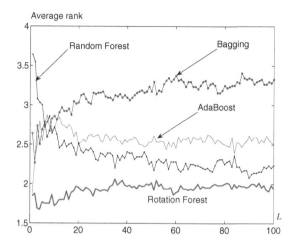

Fig. 2. The average ranks ($\bar{R}$) of the four ensemble methods as a function of the ensemble size (L)

for $L \in \{4, 7, 11, 12\}$, and better than Random Forest for $L \in \{1 - 5, 7, 8\}$. The differences are more prominent for small ensemble sizes. However, we note the consistency of Rotation Forest being the best ranking method across all values of L, as shown in Figure 2.

6   Suitability of PCA

6.1   Alternatives to PCA

Principal Component Analysis (PCA) has been extensively used in statistical pattern recognition for dimensionality reduction, sometimes called Karhunen-Loéve transformation. PCA has also been used to extract features for classifier ensembles [16, 17]. Unlike the approaches in the cited works, we do not employ PCA for dimensionality reduction but for rotation of the axes while keeping all the dimensions.

It is well documented in the literature since the 1970s that PCA is not particularly suitable for feature extraction in classification because it does not include discriminatory information in calculating the optimal rotation of the axes. Many alternative linear transformations have been suggested based on discrimination criteria [11,9,13,19,18]. Sometimes a simple random choice of the transformation matrix has led to classification accuracy superior to that with PCA [8].

To examine the impact of PCA on Rotation Forest, we substitute PCA by Sparse Random Projections and Nonparametric Discriminant Analysis (NDA) [12,10,6]. The Sparse Random Projections were all non-degenerate but were not orthogonal in contrast to PCA.

We compared Rotation Forest (with PCA, NDA, Random Projections and Sparse Random Projections), denoted respectively RF(PCA), RF(NDA), RF(R) and RF(SR), with bagging, AdaBoost, and Random Forest. We also decided to include in the comparison two more ensemble methods, LogitBoost and Decorate, which have proved to be robust and accurate, and are available from Weka [20].

6.2 Win-Draw-Loss Analysis

Tables 3 and 4 give summaries of the results.

Table 3. Comparison of ensemble methods

	(2)	(3)	(4)	5)	(6)	(7)	(8)	(9)	(10)*
(1) Decision Tree	11/21/0	12/19/1	18/14/0	11/19/2	8/22/2	9/20/3	19/13/0	17/15/0	20/12/0
(2) Bagging		4/27/1	10/21/1	2/27/3	3/27/2	4/24/4	6/26/0	7/25/0	9/23/0
(3) AdaBoost			7/24/1	1/26/5	1/28/3	3/23/6	5/26/1	5/26/1	8/23/1
(4) LogitBoost				0/24/8	0/24/8	1/21/9	0/29/2	2/26/3	2/28/1
(5) Decorate					5/27/0	2/25/5	6/26/0	6/26/0	7/25/0
(6) Random Forest						2/26/4	6/26/0	8/24/0	9/23/0
(7) RF(R)							7/25/0	8/24/0	9/23/0
(8) RF(SR)								1/31/0	1/31/0
(9) RF(NDA)									0/32/0

*(10) RF(PCA)

Table 4. Ranking of the methods using the significant differences from all pairwise comparisons

Number	Method	Dominance	Win	Loss	Average rank
(10)	RF(PCA)	63	65	2	2.750
(4)	LogitBoost	59	66	7	3.656
(9)	RF(NDA)	50	54	4	3.938
(8)	RF(SR)	44	49	5	4.219
(3)	AdaBoost.M1	2	34	32	6.219
(6)	Random Forest	-19	21	40	6.281
(1)	Bagging	-23	22	45	6.500
(4)	Decorate	-25	19	44	6.844
(7)	RF(R)	-34	21	55	5.719
(1)	Decision Tree	-117	8	125	8.875

The three values in each entry of Table 3 refer to how many times the method of the column has been significantly-better/same/significantly-worse than the method of the row. The corrected estimate of the variance has been used in the test, with level of significance $\alpha = 0.05$.

Table 4 displays the overall results in terms of ranking. Each of the methods being compared receives a ranking in comparison with the other methods. The Dominance Rank of method 'X' is calculated as Wins–Losses, where Wins if the total number of times method 'X' has been significantly better than another method and Losses is the total number of times method 'X' has been significantly worse than another method.

To our surprise, PCA-based Rotation Forest scored better than both NDA and Random Projections (both sparse and non-sparse). It is interesting to note that there is a large gap between the group containing Rotation Forest models and LogitBoost on the one hand and the group of all other ensemble methods on the other hand. The only representative of Rotation Forest in the bottom group is Random Projections, which is in fact a feature extraction ensemble. It does not share one of the most important characteristic of the rotation ensembles: sparseness of the projection. We note though that if the problem has $c > 2$ classes, LogitBoost builds c trees at each iteration, hence Lc trees altogether, while in Rotation Forest the number of trees is L.

The last column of the table shows the average ranks. The only anomaly in the table is the rank of RF(P) which places the method further up in the table, before Adaboost.M1. The reason for the discrepancy between Dominance and Average rank is that RF(P) has been consistently better than Adaboost.M1 and the methods below it but the differences in favour of RF(P) have not been statistically significant. On the other hand, there have been a larger number of statistically significant differences for the problems where Adaboost.M1, Random Forest, bagging and Decorate have been better than RF(R). PCA seems to be slightly but consistently better than the other feature extraction alternatives. Sparse random projections are the next best alternative being almost as good as NDA projections but substantially cheaper to run.

7 Conclusions

Here we summarize the answers to the four questions of this study

1. Is splitting the features set F into subsets essential for the success of Rotation Forest? Yes. We demonstrated this by comparing sparse with non-sparse random projections; the results were favourable to sparse random projections.
2. How does K (respectively M) affect the performance of Random Forest? No pattern of dependency was found between K (M) and the ensemble accuracy which prevent us from recommending a specific value. As $M = 3$ worked well in our experiments, we propose to use the same value in the future.
3. How does Rotation Forest compare to bagging, AdaBoost and Random Forest for various ensemble sizes? Rotation Forest was found to be better than the other ensembles, more so for smaller ensembles sizes (Figure 2).
4. Is PCA the best method to rotate the axes for the feature subsets? PCA was found to be the best method so far.

In conclusion, the results reported here support the heuristic choices made during the design of the Rotation Forest method. It appears that the key to its robust performance lies in the core idea of the method – to make the individual classifiers as diverse as possible (by rotating the feature space) and at the same time not compromising on the individual accuracy (by choosing sparse rotation, keeping all the principal components in the rotated space and using the whole training set for building each base classifier).

References

1. E. Bauer and R. Kohavi. An empirical comparison of voting classification algorithms: Bagging, boosting, and variants. *Machine Learning*, 36:105–142, 1999.
2. C. L. Blake and C. J. Merz. UCI repository of machine learning databases, 1998. `http://www.ics.uci.edu/~mlearn/MLRepository.html`.
3. L. Breiman. Bagging predictors. *Machine Learning*, 26(2):123–140, 1996.
4. L. Breiman. Arcing classifiers. *The Annals of Statistics*, 26(3):801–849, 1998.
5. L. Breiman. Random forests. *Machine Learning*, 45:5–32, 2001.
6. M. Bressan and J. Vitrià. Nonparametric discriminant analysis and nearest neighbor classification. *Pattern Recognition Letters*, 24:2743–2749, 2003.
7. J Demšar. Statistical comparison of classifiers over multiple data sets. *Journal of Machine Learning Research*, 7:1–30, 2006.
8. X. Z. Fern and C. E. Brodley. Random projection for high dimensional data clustering: A cluster ensemble approach. In *Proc. 20th International Conference on Machine Learning, ICML*, pages 186–193, Washington,DC, 2003.
9. F.H. Foley and J.W. Sammon. An optimal set of discriminant vectors. *IEEE Transactions on Computers*, 24(3):281–289, 1975.
10. K. Fukunaga. *Introduction to Statistical Pattern Recognition*. Academic Press, Boston, MA, 2nd edition, 1990.
11. K. Fukunaga and W.L.G. Koontz. Application of the karhunen-loeve expansion to feature selection and ordering. *IEEE Transactions on Computers*, 19(4):311–318, April 1970.
12. K. Fukunaga and J. Mantock. Nonparametric discriminant analysis. *IEEE Transactions on Pattern Analysis and Machine Intelligence*, 5(6):671–678, 1983.
13. J.V. Kittler and P.C. Young. A new approach to feature selection based on the karhunen-loeve expansion. *Pattern Recognition*, 5(4):335–352, December 1973.
14. C. Nadeau and Y. Bengio. Inference for the generalization error. *Machine Learning*, 62:239–281, 2003.
15. J. J. Rodríguez, L. I. Kuncheva, and C. J. Alonso. Rotation forest: A new classifier ensemble method. *IEEE Transactions on Pattern Analysis and Machine Intelligence*, 28(10):1619–1630, Oct 2006.
16. M. Skurichina and R. P. W. Duin. Combining feature subsets in feature selection. In *Proc. 6th International Workshop on Multiple Classifier Systems, MCS'05*, volume LNCS 3541, pages 165–175, USA, 2005.
17. K. Tumer and N. C. Oza. Input decimated ensembles. *Pattern Analysis and Applications*, 6:65–77, 2003.
18. F. van der Heijden, R. P. W. Duin, D. de Ridder, and D. M. J. Tax. *Classification, Parameter Estimation and State Estimation*. Wiley, England, 2004.
19. A. Webb. *Statistical Pattern Recognition*. Arnold, London, England, 1999.
20. I. H. Witten and E. Frank. *Data Mining: Practical Machine Learning Tools and Techniques*. Morgan Kaufmann, 2nd edition, 2005.

Cooperative Coevolutionary Ensemble Learning

Daniel Kanevskiy and Konstantin Vorontsov

Computing Center of the Russian Academy of Sciences.
Vavilov st. 40, 119991, Moscow GSP-1, Russia
`kanevskiy@forecsys.ru, voron@ccas.ru`

Abstract. A new optimization technique is proposed for classifier fusion — Cooperative Coevolutionary Ensemble Learning (CCEL). It is based on a specific multipopulational evolutionary algorithm — cooperative coevolution. It can be used as a wrapper over any kind of weak algorithms, learning procedures and fusion functions, for both classification and regression tasks. Experiments on the real-world problems from the UCI repository show that CCEL has a fairly high generalization performance and generates ensembles of much smaller size than boosting, bagging and random subspace method.

1 Introduction

Combining classifiers is one of the most prominent techniques currently used to augment the accuracy of learning machines. A large number of combination schemes have been proposed in the literature [1].

Boosting is probably the most popular combination technique [2]. Base classifiers are trained in a sequence so that each focuses its attention on the "hardest" examples poorly classified by the previous ones. Outputs of the base classifiers are aggregated by the weighted voting. Boosting is simple and powerful, yet it suffers from certain disadvantages. First, the greedy sequential strategy takes into account only the previous classifiers but not the next ones, thus making the classifier trained be suboptimal in the composition. Second, outliers become the "hardest" examples with high probability, so concentrating on them may weaken the base classifiers. To compensate for these drawbacks boosting generates exhaustively large number of base classifiers. Generalization error of boosting may reach its minimum at thousands of base classifiers [3].

Bagging trains classifiers independently on different parts of the training set, thus making them sufficiently diverse [4]. Training subsets are created by drawing objects randomly with replacement from the initial training set. Base classifiers trained on these subsets are aggregated using simple or weighted voting. Bagging is rather effective on small data sets and when base learning algorithm is instable, that means small changes in the training set may lead to significantly different classifiers [5]. If it is not the case, bagging does not improve the performance of a single classifier much [6]. Also, though the bootstrapping procedure helps maintain the diversity, no optimization is made to select training subsets. Then the resulting composition may be rather far from optimal. Like boosting, these drawbacks are compensated for by taking an exhaustive number of classifiers.

M. Haindl, J. Kittler, and F. Roli (Eds.): MCS 2007, LNCS 4472, pp. 469–478, 2007.

Random Subspace Method (RSM) trains base classifiers independently on the same training set using different random subsets of features [7]. Outputs of the obtained classifiers are aggregated by simple majority voting. RSM helps struggle with the curse of dimensionality and is useful when the number of training objects is small compared to the number of features [8]. Again, the disadvantage is that little optimization is made to select feature subsets carefully, that again leads to a very large number of base classifiers.

Evolutionary Algorithms are frequently used in pattern recognition for feature selection and classifier fusion. For example, [9] exploits a genetic optimization technique to choose different subsets of features for the constituents of the ensemble, and also the type of each base classifier. The fitness function used in this approach is claimed to be advantageous, because it evaluates the performance of the combination, not the single classifiers. But the encoding of the chromosome strongly depends on the number of classifiers in the ensemble, so it must be prespecified. This often leads to another branch of resource-intensive research aimed at choosing the best ensemble size. A canonical genetic algorithm is used in [10] to independently choose a separate feature subset for each base classifier. After the subsets are chosen, one of the known fusion techniques (boosting, bagging) is applied without further ensemble optimization. This approach implicitly feeds different base classifiers with different subsets of objects and features, but no global optimization is used to choose the subsets, that would optimize the performance of the ensemble as a whole.

Some contributions use genetic optimization to choose a subset of classifiers from a wider set of pretrained ones. They may strongly depend on the type of the learning machine such as neural networks [11], or exploit some additional information such as reliability measures [12]. Both approaches do not optimize the ensemble globally, leaving this task to the local optimization.

The latter two approaches are combined in [13], where a two-level multi-objective genetic algorithm is suggested. The first level finds the Pareto-optimal front of feature subsets, while the second chooses the best ensemble of classifiers among those trained on the Pareto-optimal feature subsets. The chosen classifiers are then averaged to produce the final output. This also reduces the fusion problem to a number of independent optimization tasks, and no global optimization is held to make classifiers work together. And still the number of classifiers can not be chosen automatically.

There is also a technique specific to neural networks that incorporates the power of evolutionary optimization with thoroughly selected heuristics [14]. This technique automatically determines the number of hidden neurons in NN and the number of NNs in the ensemble. But a greedy optimization technique (though with feedback) does not make it possible to take advantage of classifier cooperation.

In this paper we use a special kind of evolutionary algorithm, inspired by the symbiosis in nature, and called *cooperative coevolution* [15]. It makes it possible to optimize all base operators and fusion function simultaneously, learns base operators to cooperate rather than to solve the problem individually, and chooses the number of operators dynamically, thus obtaining an accurate small size ensemble.

This technique is appropriate to any type of base classifiers and fusion functions for both binary and multiclass classification. It can be easily propagated to regression tasks also. We embody this approach into a new ensemble learning algorithm called *Cooperative Coevolutionary Ensemble Learning* (CCEL). Section 2 introduces the necessary notation. Section 3 describes the universal CCEL framework. Section 4 specifies it for the linear fusion. Section 5 presents the experimental results and compares CCEL with other popular linear fusion techniques.

2 Definitions and Notation

We consider an input space X, an output space Y and a given finite dataset $D = \{x_i, y_i\}_{i=1}^{\ell}$ of pairs from $X \times Y$. Elements of X are described by n features $g_j \colon X \to V_j$, $j = 1, \ldots, n$, where V_j is a set of all permissible values of the feature g_j. The goal is to learn a function $a \colon X \to Y$ that approximates the unknown dependence of outputs on inputs. Approximation quality of a function a on a finite set $U \subset D$ is measured by the *empirical error*:

$$Q(a, U) = \frac{1}{|U|} \sum_{x_i \in U} L(a(x_i), y_i),$$

where $L(y, y')$ is a real-valued *loss function* that penalties the deviation of the output $a(x_i)$ from the truth y_i.

For the sake of generality and following algebraic approach to pattern recognition [16] we introduce an intermediate space R and suppose that function a has a form of a superposition: $a(x) = C(b(x))$ for any $x \in X$, where $b \colon X \to R$ is called *base learner*, and $C \colon R \to Y$ is a fixed function. For example, in the binary classification task $Y = \{-1, +1\}$, if $R = \mathbb{R}$, $C(b) = \text{sgn}(b)$, then $b(x)$ is a real-valued classifier. In the multiclass task with $Y = \{1, \ldots, M\}$, the reasonable choice is $R = \mathbb{R}^M$, $C(b_1, \ldots, b_M) = \text{argmax}_{y \in Y} b_y$. Regression and binary classification are trivial examples with the most natural choice $R = Y$, $C(b) = b$.

An ensemble of base learners $b_1(x), \ldots, b_p(x)$, aggregated by a *fusion function* $F \colon R^p \to R$ is defined as a superposition:

$$a(x) = C\big(F\big(b_1(x), \ldots, b_p(x)\big)\big). \tag{1}$$

The most well-known example is the linear fusion, also called *weighted voting*:

$$F(b_1, \ldots, b_p) = \alpha_1 b_1 + \cdots + \alpha_p b_p. \tag{2}$$

Here the usual requirement $\alpha_i \geq 0$ means that F must be a monotone function of its arguments. Less known are non-linear monotone fusion functions for both classification and regression tasks [17].

Learning algorithm is a mapping $\mu \colon (U, G) \mapsto b$ that generates base learner $b \colon X \to R$ using a finite subset of objects $U \subseteq D$ described by a finite subset of features $G \subseteq \{g_1, \ldots, g_n\}$. For example, μ may be an empirical error minimizer:

$$\mu(U, G) = \underset{a \in A(G)}{\text{argmin}}\, Q(a, U),$$

where $A(G)$ is a set of functions that uses only features from G.

3   Cooperative Coevolutionary Ensemble Learner

In this section we propose a generalized evolutionary algorithm for the global optimization of composition (1). It uses a fixed learning algorithm μ to train base learners $b_1, \ldots, b_p$. We do not restrict neither the family of algorithms $A(G)$ nor the optimization technique that the learning algorithm μ may apply.

The algorithm forms a set of $p(t)$ isolated populations $\Pi_1(t), \ldots, \Pi_{p(t)}(t)$ at each iteration $t = 1, \ldots, t_{\max}$. Each population $\Pi_j(t)$ is a set of N_0 individuals. Each individual is a binary vector of the length $\ell + n$, which encodes a subset of objects $U \subseteq D$ and a subset of features $G \subseteq \{g_1, \ldots, g_n\}$. So, each individual v_j from $\Pi_j(t)$ can be considered as a pair $v_j = (U, G)$ and thus can be fed to the learning algorithm μ to obtain a base learner $b_j = \mu(v_j)$.

The evolutionary process starts from a single population initialized at random, see step 1 of Algorithm 1. Populations evolve independently except one but very important thing: the fitness $\varphi(v_j)$ of the individual v_j is evaluated as the quality of the ensemble (1), in which j-th position is occupied by b_j, and others are the most fitted base learners b_s^*, taken from other populations $\Pi_s(t)$, $s \neq j$:

$$\varphi(v_j) = Q\big(F(b_1^*, \ldots, b_{j-1}^*, \mu(v_j), b_{j+1}^*, \ldots, b_{p(t)}^*), D\big).$$

This is the main distinguishing property of the cooperative coevolution. Another ways exist to choose representatives from other populations, but the fittest ones are argued to be better if the evaluation involves only one collaboration [18].

All populations go through a common generational loop. Genetic operations (crossover and mutation) are applied to the individuals, creating offsprings, that form an intermediate population Π_j''. The main population for the next generation consists of a number of most fitted individuals, selected from the intermediate population, and a few elite individuals, transferred from the previous main population unchanged. For each generation t the best composition $F(b_1, \ldots, b_{p(t)})$ is selected and saved.

Populations may be added or erased during the evolution, changing the size p of the ensemble. A population is erased when its contribution into the ensemble remains too small for a number of generations. New population is created when the evolution comes into stagnation. The evolutionary process stops, when changing the size p does not cease the stagnation.

Now we give details of the heuristics governing the evolutionary process. There is quite a number of ways to define them, and our choice is based on either our or other available empirical observations.

Init(N_0) generates N_0 random individuals. Its parameters are the probabilities of adding an object p_x and a feature p_g. We've chosen these to be 0.5 both, but prohibited the chromosomes with less than 25% of objects or features.

Select(Π, N) is chosen to be the deterministic truncation selection. It returns a subset of N fittest individuals from the population Π. In CCEL it is used twice: first, when N_2 elite individuals are transferred to the next generation (step 4); second, when N_0 best individuals from intermediate population are taken to form the population of the next generation (step 6).

Algorithm 1. Cooperative Coevolutionary Ensemble Learner (CCEL).

Require:
  Sample $D = \{x_i, y_i\}_{i=1}^{\ell}$;
  Base learning algorithm μ;
  Parameters: $t_{\max}$, p_x, p_g, p_m, N_0, N_1, N_2, d_1, ε_1, d_2, ε_2, d_3, ε_3;
Ensure:
  ensemble $F(b_1, \ldots, b_p)$;

1: initialize a single population:
      $p(1) := 1$; $\Pi_1(1) := \mathrm{Init}(N_0)$;
2: **for all** generations $t := 1, \ldots, t_{\max}$ **do**
3:     **for all** populations $\Pi_j(t)$, $j := 1, \ldots, p(t)$ **do**
4:         create an intermediate population:
              $\Pi'_j := \mathrm{Crossover}(\Pi_j(t), N_1)$;
              $\Pi''_j := \mathrm{Mutation}(\Pi'_j) \cup \mathrm{Select}(\Pi_j(t), N_2)$;
5:         fix the best individual v_j^* and corresponding b_j^*:
              $v_j^* := \arg \min_{v \in \Pi''_j} \varphi(v)$; $b_j^* := \mu(v_j^*)$; $Q_t := \varphi(v_j^*)$;
6:         keep top N_0 individuals:
              $\Pi_j(t+1) := \mathrm{Select}(\Pi''_j, N_0)$;
7:         **if** $\mathrm{Contribution}(\Pi_j)$ is small **then**
8:             delete population Π_j; $p(t+1) := p(t) - 1$;
9:     **if** $\mathrm{Stagnation}(Q, t)$ **then**
10:        add population $\Pi_{p(t)+1}(t+1) := \mathrm{Init}(N_0)$; $p(t+1) := p(t) + 1$;
11:    **if** $\mathrm{Termination}(Q, t)$ **then**
12:        exit;
13: **return** ensemble $F(b_1^*, \ldots, b_{p(t)}^*)$.

$\mathrm{Crossover}(\Pi, N_1)$ is the uniform crossover operator, generating N_1 new individuals (offsprings) in the following way. Two individuals (parents) are taken at random from the population Π and the offspring inherits every chromosome bit equiprobably from one of the parents.

$\mathrm{Mutation}(\Pi)$ is the usual bit-flip operator that makes random changes in the bits of the individuals in Π. The canonical choice for the bit-flip probability is $p_m = \frac{1}{k}$, where k is the length of the chromosome. In our experiments we used a greater value, which seems to provide better exploration of the search space in combination with the elitist strategy [19].

$\mathrm{Contribution}(\Pi_j)$ evaluates the contribution of the population Π_j to the ensemble using the *take-one-out* procedure. Two ensembles are constructed: with and without the j-th base learner, and their respective qualities Q_{jt} and $\bar{Q}_{jt}$ are estimated. The contribution is defined as their average difference for the last d_1 generations: $\frac{1}{d_1} \sum_{\tau = t - d_1 + 1}^{t} (\bar{Q}_{j\tau} - Q_{j\tau})$. If the contribution is smaller than ε_1, the population is erased and the size of the ensemble decreases by one.

$\mathrm{Stagnation}(Q, t)$ checks the stagnation criterion for the sequence $Q = \{Q_t\}$ at the time t. New population is created when no significant quality growth happens last d_2 generations: $Q_{t-d_2}^* - Q_t^* < \varepsilon_2$, where $Q_t^* = \min\{Q_1, \ldots, Q_t\}$.

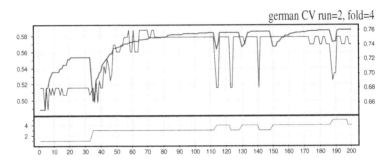

Fig. 1. The main characteristics of the evolutionary process as the functions of the generation number t. On the top chart: the thick curve is the margin functional $\tilde{Q}$ on the training set with values along the left vertical axis; the thin curve is the correct answers rate on the test set with the values along the right vertical axis. The bottom chart shows the number of populations $p(t)$ that is equal to the ensemble size.

$\mathtt{Termination}(Q,t)$ is a criterion of a lingering stagnation: $Q^*_{t-d_3} - Q^*_t < \varepsilon_3$, where $d_3 \gg d_2$ is assumed. At least several unsuccessful changes of the ensemble size p should be made before stopping the whole process.

The contribution, stagnation and termination criteria enable one to control the number of populations dynamically [15]. Fig. 1 shows s typical example of how CCEL works. Here several attempts to create and erase population were made before termination criterion has stopped the process. Note, that the structural change of a composition always leads to a significant drop of the quality on both training and test samples, but after a few generations it rehabilitates.

Now the universal CCEL framework is fully defined, except one thing: nothing was said about the optimization of the fusion function F. Although this framework makes it possible to add another population of fusion parameters and proceed in the same manner, this approach is computationally ineffective. Instead we suggest one should use fast optimization procedures specific to the chosen fusion function. In the next section we demonstrate this for the weighted voting (2).

4   CCEL for Linear Fusion

In this section we consider the linear fusion functions (2) for binary classification task assuming $Y = \{-1, +1\}$, $C(b) = \mathrm{sgn}(b)$.

A wide variety of weight optimization techniques is known [1]. The trivial one is the simple voting, when $\alpha_j = 1$ and no tuning is necessary. The other end of the stick is the Support Vector Machine (SVM), that allows one to obtain near-optimal weights, but seems to be too slow for evolutionary algorithms. In this work we used the naïve Bayes assumption that the base classifiers are independent, making it possible to calculate the weights explicitly:

$$\alpha_j = \ln \frac{|S| - E_j + 1}{E_j + 1},$$

where E_j is the number of errors that the classifier b_j makes on a sample $S \subseteq D$. In CCEL each base algorithm is trained on its own subsample $U \subset D$, therefore three variants of weight estimation are possible: from training $S = U$, from testing $S = D \setminus U$, or from the full sample $S = D$. Our preliminary experiments have shown that the second variant is the best. Additionally, if $E_j \geq \frac{1}{2}|S|$, then α_j is taken to be zero, so the algorithm b_j is excluded from the ensemble.

The quality functional $Q(a, U)$ is commonly defined as the error rate of an ensemble a on a sample U. Yet linear classifiers are known to generalize better when the direct maximization of margins is used [20]. For the composition (2) the *margin* of an object x_i is defined as

$$M(x_i) = \frac{y_i \sum_{j=1}^p \alpha_j b_j(x_i)}{\sum_{j=1}^p \alpha_j}.$$

The margin $M(x_i)$ can be thought of as a distance from the object x_i to the classes boundary. If the margin is negative, $M(x_i) < 0$, then the composition makes an error, $a(x_i) \neq y_i$. Hence we suggest the quality functional $\widetilde{Q}$, defined as the average margin of the training objects:

$$\widetilde{Q}(a, U) = \frac{1}{|U|} \sum_{x_i \in U} M(x_i) \rightarrow \max_a.$$

A number of our preliminary experiments has shown, that $\widetilde{Q}$ really outperforms both the standard error rate functional and its combinations with the explicit diversity measures [21].

The following heuristic simplifies the `Contribution` procedure in the case of linear fusion: the contribution of Π_j can be evaluated as the average weight of the j-th base classifier for the last d_1 generations: $\frac{1}{d_1} \sum_{\tau=t-d_1+1}^t \alpha_j(\tau)$. When this value becomes too small, the population is erased.

Yet another linear-specific heuristic is the "1-3 rule". As the weighted voting of two classifiers makes no sense (the one with larger weight always wins), a 1-element ensemble is always increased to a 3 elements one.

Finally, note that the multiclass version of the margins functional is also available due to [22], thus making it possible to use the algorithm described for the multiclass problems.

5   Experimental Results

In this section the linear fusion CCEL is compared experimentally with other linear methods: boosting, bagging, and RSM.

The base algorithm was taken to be the naïve Bayes classifier [1]. Its learning algorithm is very fast, what is very important for the resource-intensive evolutionary techniques. On the other hand, the quality of this algorithm is rather moderate, because the underlying assumption of feature independence does not hold for most real-world problems. Also note that the naïve Bayes classifier is rarely used as an

Table 1. Bias and variance estimations through 10 runs of 10-fold cross-validation for 12 problems from the UCI repository

Problem	Naïve Bayes		CCEL		boosting		bagging		RSM	
	bias	var	bias	var	bias	var	bias	var	bias	var
Cancer	5.24	**0.37**	**3.14**	**0.32**	**3.01**	1.74	5.32	**0.36**	4.17	0.77
Credit-a-1	14.07	1.15	**11.50**	**1.46**	14.80	1.59	14.13	1.07	13.76	2.53
Credit-a-2	15.05	**0.85**	**12.74**	1.42	13.81	4.85	14.81	1.05	14.77	1.56
Credit-g	28.23	**3.84**	**21.04**	4.74	24.46	5.02	27.57	**3.73**	27.61	4.54
DBC	11.04	**0.47**	**4.64**	0.74	9.29	15.71	10.82	0.57	10.64	0.64
Heart	16.78	**2.64**	15.44	**2.71**	**13.73**	10.38	16.45	**2.87**	16.60	**2.83**
Hepatitis	15.11	**1.82**	**14.12**	4.27	15.25	4.65	**14.40**	2.40	15.19	2.26
Liver	28.51	**7.90**	**23.77**	11.06	24.50	10.34	28.25	8.31	28.40	8.18
Diabetes	29.27	2.49	21.60	**2.06**	**18.40**	12.99	28.76	2.69	28.44	3.13
Survival	23.69	7.60	23.01	**4.67**	**21.03**	6.09	23.87	6.34	23.51	8.99
Tic-tac-toe	24.61	4.30	**18.82**	5.80	32.56	**0.73**	25.01	4.02	24.51	4.73
Voting	5.82	0.79	**4.03**	**0.57**	4.94	1.31	5.81	0.73	6.09	0.92

Table 2. The test error rates with standard deviations (in percents) averaged through 10 runs of 10-fold cross-validation for 12 problems from the UCI repository. For CCEL the average size of the ensemble is written in parentheses.

Problem	Naïve Bayes	CCEL	boosting	bagging	RSM
Cancer	5.55 ± 0.26	**3.46 ± 0.37** (3.16)	4.14 ± 1.48	5.63 ± 0.24	4.97 ± 0.40
Credit-a-1	15.22 ± 0.39	**12.96 ± 0.57** (2.48)	25.23 ± 6.65	15.20 ± 0.42	15.31 ± 0.62
Credit-a-2	15.94 ± 0.40	**14.16 ± 0.53** (2.99)	17.72 ± 2.86	15.87 ± 0.45	16.12 ± 0.48
Credit-g	32.07 ± 0.67	**25.78 ± 0.65** (1.74)	29.48 ± 0.93	31.30 ± 0.67	32.11 ± 0.71
DBC	11.50 ± 0.30	**5.38 ± 0.44** (2.66)	25.00 ± 7.22	11.40 ± 0.27	11.24 ± 0.35
Heart	19.42 ± 0.92	**18.15 ± 0.85** (3.32)	24.11 ± 6.47	19.31 ± 1.16	19.35 ± 1.19
Hepatitis	**16.93 ± 1.06**	18.38 ± 1.43 (2.87)	19.90 ± 1.80	**16.80 ± 1.14**	17.32 ± 1.46
Liver	36.42 ± 1.86	**34.38 ± 0.95** (1.95)	**34.84 ± 2.45**	36.56 ± 1.88	36.48 ± 1.77
Diabetes	31.76 ± 0.63	**23.66 ± 0.43** (2.30)	31.39 ± 2.05	31.45 ± 0.68	31.53 ± 0.58
Survival	31.29 ± 2.58	**26.21 ± 1.02** (2.02)	27.12 ± 1.56	30.22 ± 2.77	32.41 ± 3.24
Tic-tac-toe	28.92 ± 1.02	**24.61 ± 1.11** (2.59)	33.29 ± 0.40	29.03 ± 0.96	29.20 ± 1.07
Voting	6.61 ± 0.60	**4.60 ± 0.46** (3.53)	6.25 ± 0.65	6.54 ± 0.40	7.0 ± 0.75

ensemble building block because of its very low variance, which prevents standard fusion techniques from improving its quality. The low variance leaves the only way of significant performance improvement: reducing a bias. Both bagging and RSM are known to fail in reducing bias, while boosting sometimes effectively trades off bias for variance and vice versa [6,5]. To estimate how CCEL works in these terms we made an empirical evaluation of bias and variance using a standard technique from [23]. The results are summarized in Table 1.

We compared CCEL with the base classifier, AdaBoost, bagging, and RSM. For the latter three methods the ensemble size was fixed to be $p = 250$ [4]. The experiments were made on 12 two-class problems from the UCI repository [24]. Table 2 summarizes the average test error.

The results verify the assumption that bagging and RSM fail to improve the quality of the low-variance base classifier. CCEL competes with boosting in bias reduction, while preserving substantially lower level of variance. As a result, CCEL outperforms others in 11 problems out of 12.

6 Conclusion

Cooperative coevolution is a very natural approach to ensemble learning. It trains base learners to cooperate with each other rather than to solve the problem independently. Each base learner tends to specialize on its own subset of objects and subspace of features. This results in significant reduction of the ensemble size compared to standard techniques. CCEL takes 3–6 base learners whereas boosting, bagging and RSM require hundreds. CCEL is applicable to base learning algorithms and fusion functions of any type, though it is also open to any type-specific heuristics. CCEL yields good results even for such stable and inaccurate algorithm as naïve Bayes. Finally, analysis of the CCEL results can tell much about the structure of the problem. For example, one can determine most important features and filter out some useless objects (outliers). The only disadvantage of CCEL is the training speed: the solution of a middle-size problem takes a few minutes on a usual PC. On the other hand, CCEL is very suitable as an "anytime" learning algorithm that may be interrupted at any moment to return a solution, and then continued to learn more.

References

1. Kuncheva, L.I.: Combining Pattern Classifiers: Methods and Algorithms. John Wiley and Sons, Inc. (2004)
2. Schapire, R.: The boosting approach to machine learning: An overview. In: MSRI Workshop on Nonlinear Estimation and Classification, Berkeley, CA. (2001)
3. Freund, Y., Schapire, R.E.: Experiments with a new boosting algorithm. In: International Conference on Machine Learning. (1996) 148–156
4. Breiman, L.: Arcing classifiers. The Annals of Statistics **26** (1998) 801–849
5. Dietterich, T.G.: An experimental comparison of three methods for constructing ensembles of decision trees: Bagging, boosting, and randomization. Machine Learning **40** (2000) 139–157
6. Bauer, E., Kohavi, R.: An empirical comparison of voting classification algorithms: Bagging, boosting, and variants. Machine Learning **36** (1999) 105–139
7. Ho, T.K.: The random subspace method for constructing decision forests. IEEE Transactions on Pattern Analysis and Machine Intelligence **20** (1998) 832–844
8. Skurichina, M., Duin, R.P.W.: Limited bagging, boosting and the random subspace method for linear classifiers. Pattern Analysis & Applications (2002) 121–135
9. Kuncheva, L.I., Jain, L.C.: Designing classifier fusion systems by genetic algorithms. IEEE-EC **4** (2000) 327

10. Guerra-Salcedo, C., Whitley, D.: Genetic approach to feature selection for ensemble creation. In Banzhaf, W., Daida, J., Eiben, A.E., Garzon, M.H., Honavar, V., Jakiela, M., Smith, R.E., eds.: Proceedings of the Genetic and Evolutionary Computation Conference. Volume 1., Orlando, Florida, USA, Morgan Kaufmann (1999) 236–243

11. Z.-H. Zhou, J.-X. Wu, Y.J., Chen, S.F.: Genetic algorithm based selective neural network ensemble. Proceedings of the 17th International Joint Conference on Artificial Intelligence 2 (2001) 797–802

12. De Stefano, C., et al.: Exploiting reliability for dynamic selection of classifiers by means of genetic algorithms. Proceedings of the Seventh International Conference on Document Analysis and Recognition (ICDAR) (2003)

13. Oliveira, L., Sabourin, R., Bortolozzi, F., Suen, C.: Feature selection for ensembles : A hierarchical multi-objective genetic algorithm approach (2003)

14. Islam, M., Yao, X., Murase, K.: A constructive algorithm for training cooperative neural network ensembles. (2003)

15. Potter, M.A., De Jong, K.A.: Cooperative coevolution: An architecture for evolving coadapted subcomponents. Evolutionary Computation 8 (2000) 1–29

16. Zhuravlev, J.I.: An algebraic approach to recognition or classifications problems. Pattern Recognition and Image Analysis 8 (1998) 59–100

17. Rudakov, K.V., Vorontsov, K.V.: Methods of optimization and monotone correction in the algebraic approach to the recognition problem. Doklady Mathematics 60 (1999) 139

18. Wiegand, R.P., Liles, W.C., De Jong, K.A.: An empirical analysis of collaboration methods in cooperative coevolutionary algorithms. In Proceedings of the Genetic and Evolutionary Computation Conference (GECCO) (2001)

19. Andre's Pen a-Reyes, C.: (Coevolutionary fuzzy modeling)

20. Mason, L., Bartlett, P., Baxter, J.: Direct optimization of margins improves generalization in combined classifiers. Technical report, Deparment of Systems Engineering, Australian National University (1998)

21. Kuncheva, L., Whitaker, C.: Measures of diversity in classifier ensembles and their relationship with the ensemble accuracy. Machine Learning 51 (2003) 181–207

22. Allwein, E.L., Schapire, R.E., Singer, Y.: Reducing multiclass to binary: A unifying approach for margin classifiers. In: Proc. 17th International Conf. on Machine Learning, Morgan Kaufmann, San Francisco, CA (2000) 9–16

23. Webb, G.I.: MultiBoosting: A technique for combining Boosting and Wagging. Machine Learning 40 (2000) 159–196

24. Blake, C., Merz, C.: UCI repository of machine learning databases. Technical report, Department of Information and Computer Science, University of California, Irvine, CA (1998)

Robust Inference in Bayesian Networks with Application to Gene Expression Temporal Data

Omer Berkman and Nathan Intrator

School of Computer Science, Tel-Aviv University,
Ramat Aviv 69978, Israel
nin@tau.ac.il

Abstract. We are concerned with the problem of inferring genetic regulatory networks from a collection of temporal observations. This is often done via estimating a Dynamic Bayesian Network (DBN) from time series of gene expression data. However, when applying this algorithm to the limited quantities of experimental data that nowadays technologies can provide, its estimation is not robust. We introduce a weak learners' methodology for this inference problem, study few methods to produce Weak Dynamic Bayesian Networks (WDBNs), and demonstrate its advantages on simulated gene expression data.

Keywords: Genetic Networks, Time Series Data, Dynamic Bayesian Networks, Weak Learners.

1 Introduction

1.1 Biological Background

The genome plays a central role in the control of cellular processes. Genes are involved in the control of intracellular and intercellular processes. Gene expression is a complex process regulated at several stages in the synthesis of proteins. A protein synthesized from DNA may function as a transcription factor which fulfills these regulatory functions. This gives rise to genetic regulatory systems that can be modeled by networks of regulatory interactions. These systems determine which genes are expressed and when. A central goal of molecular biology is to understand these regulatory mechanisms of gene transcription. Gaining an understanding of the interactions between genes in a regulatory network raises a scientific challenge with potentially industrial rewards. So far, researchers have gained only partial success in trying to discover temporal structure of an underlying causal network.

1.2 Bayesian Networks

Graphical models use graphs to model regulatory network where the nodes of the graph represent random variables (genes), and the edges represent regulation interaction between them. Bayesian (belief) Networks (BNs) [1] generalize the Boolean network model, Hidden Markov Models, and other models widely used in

M. Haindl, J. Kittler, and F. Roli (Eds.): MCS 2007, LNCS 4472, pp. 479–489, 2007.

the computational biology community [2]. The BN approach is attractive because of its solid basis in statistics, which enables it do deal with the stochastic aspects of gene expression and noisy data (typically inherent in both the biological processes and the measurements) in a natural way. They were first applied to this kind of problem by Friedman et al. [3] and has been widely used since (e.g. [4-9]). BN provides interpretable and flexible models for representing probabilistic relationships between multiple interacting genes. Two major limitations of this approach have been discussed: first is the problem of assigning direction of causation to edges [1] and second is the acyclic constraint of BN, which rules out recurrent structures. Both of these limitations can be overcome by using Dynamic Bayesian Networks (DBN) which extends BN for the case of temporal data.

1.3   Ensemble of Weak Learners

It turns out that a robust inference and model interpretation using DBN, requires large amounts of temporal observations, which currently, are difficult to achieve. Several statistical methods were developed to extend the original datasets by effectively increasing the number of observations. We can mention "re-sampling" methods such as Leave-K-Out, Bootstrapping and Noisy Bootstrapping, and Boosting technologies. These methods often use several different learners, regard them as "weak" learners, and combine them into one solution. Learners can utilize different learning algorithms (e.g. Neural Network and CART); they can be of different architectures (e.g. Neural Networks with different number of hidden units) or can be learned from data that is manipulated in various ways. The goal is to make them more likely to converge to different local minima, and so produce a more independent set of results. Better performance is then often achieved by assembling their products into one result [10]. These methods showed that such ensemble results in lower variance when the learners forming them are not sharing the same errors (e.g. [11-14]).

Weak Learner methods are popular in solving classification and regression problems but have not been extended to Dynamic Bayesian Networks. Few early studies have tried averaging methods [15-17], but only for the static case. Our approach is a more comprehensive one. We introduce novel algorithms to generate Weak Dynamic Bayesian Networks (WDBN) Learners. These Learners use the same DBN inference procedure, but manipulate the raw data differently. We demonstrate how to generate inference from multiple networks and show that the ensemble of these algorithms' results increases the robustness of the inference.

1.4   Simulations

Bayesian networks, as well as other models, are often evaluated by comparing the predicted regulatory interactions with those known from the biological literature. This approach is problematic due to the absence of known gold standards. In addition, the available not-synthetic data sets are not rich enough for this kind of inference models. The inference methods require a costly gene expression data that is not feasible nowadays. This has led to an increasing interest with the simulative approach, where the inference results are easy to evaluate. We demonstrate our results on *in silico* data.

This approach has been successfully used to evaluate algorithm performances on different network topologies and data sampling schemes [6, 7].

2 Methods

2.1 Simulating a Regulatory Network

Our approach is to apply network inference procedures to multiple copies of data sampled from the same simulated network, and to evaluate the performances by comparing the recovered networks to the original network used by the simulator. A simple way to model a system of interacting components is to assume that the change of each one of them over time is given by a weighted sum of all other components. In our simulator the expression at one time point determines the expression observed at the next time point. The simulator was written in MATLAB and provides gene expression levels at discrete time points, using a given gene network. Its design is based on the simulator presented by Yu et al [9, 18], where updates to values at each time point are governed by the stochastic process:

$$Y_{t+1} - Y_t = f(Y_t) = A(Y_t - Thr) + \varepsilon \qquad (1)$$

Where Y_t is the vector representing the expression levels of all genes at time t, with expression levels ranging from 0 to 100, restricted by a floor and ceiling functions. Expression levels are initialized to random values uniformly sampled from this range. A is a matrix of gene regulatory interactions which underlies the regulatory network. This matrix provides information about relationships between genes and can be used to reconstruct the underlying gene expression network. The absolute value of A_{ij} represents the strength of the regulation of regulator gene i upon a target gene j. The sign of A_{ij} indicates the type of regulation: positive values indicating up-regulation and negative values indicating down-regulation. We used only three values of interaction: 0 for no interaction and 0.15, -0.15 for positive and negative interactions respectively.

Thr is a vector of threshold regulating values for each gene: a regulator gene exerts an influence on its target gene when it is above or below its threshold value. Therefore the influence of each gene on its target is proportional to its deviation from this threshold value. Following previous studies [9, 18], all gene thresholds have been set to half of the maximum value, namely 50 is their "steady state". If the regulator gene is present at a level above its steady state value, then its regulatory effect on its target genes occurs as specified in A. When the regulator gene value is below its threshold value, then its effect is in the opposite direction of that specified in A to return the gene to its basal level. The noise term ε is drawn uniformly at random from the interval -15 to 15. This term is meant to capture all sources of noise (inherent biological noise and measurement errors) and its amplitude is a reasonable approximation for this kind of experiments. If a gene has no regulator (all corresponding entries in A are zero), then it will move in a random walk, governed only by values of ε.

2.2   Architecture Inference of the Regulatory Network

In this study we provide the simulator with an architecture that was used in previous studies ([9, 19, 20]). It is illustrated in Figure 1, Left. There are few dozens of genes, but only twelve assemble a network, while the others have no regulatory connections and therefore are used as destructors. There are 13 gene regulatory interactions within this architecture: six of them are negative and seven are positive. The model has one negative feedback loop.

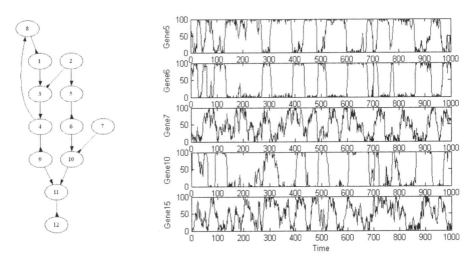

Fig. 1. Left: illustration of the architecture. Arrows represent an influence of the upstream variable's value at one time step on the downstream variable's value at the next time step. A regular arrowhead indicates a positive influence, while upside down arrowhead indicates a negative influence. Right: Simulated data for 1000 time points. Depicted are gene expression time sequence plot for 5 arbitrary genes. The results are consistent with the original structure.

2.3   Data Acquisition

The simulator produces data, corresponding to the following parameters: Architecture, Number of observations (time points), noise amplitude and influence score (the values within the transition matrix, A). As the simulation runs, the data is sampled in pre-specified intervals as one would do in an actual experiment. We define the sampling interval to be 5 time units (as discussed in [18]), and so the sampled output is the series of expression level vectors (Y_0, Y_5, Y_{10} ,......), analogous to data gathered in a micro-array time course experiment. An example for the simulator output is illustrated in Figure 1, Right.

2.4   Inference Packages

For the core inference problem, we used BANJO ([21]) - a software package for the inference of Bayesian networks. We set BANJO's parameters as following: discretization is quantile and uses three states (as discussed in [18]). The scoring method was the Bayesian Dirichlet scoring metric for discrete variables (BDe) that computes the relative posterior probability of a network structure given data. This scoring method has been shown as superior to the BIC scoring method with respect to micro-array data in limited quantities [18]. The graph space was explored using simulated annealing algorithm with evaluation of a single random local move (one addition, deletion, or reversal of a single edge is "proposed" in each iteration) - the search examines a single, randomly selected change to the network and keeps the new network if it scores better than the current network, or discards the change if it scores lower. This search heuristic has been shown to be as good as other search heuristics [18]. BANJO is capable to provide any number of highest scoring networks found by the search, instead of a single one.

2.5 Inference Evaluation

Based on their existence and nonexistence in the recovered network and the true network, we classified the edges into four categories: true positive (TP, an edge that exists in both networks), true negative (TN, an edge that does not exist in either network), false positive (FP, an edge that exists only in the recovered network) and false negative (FN, an edge that exists only in the true network). We study the inference algorithms' performances by a metric of sensitivity, precision and error:

Sensitivity (known also as *Recall*) = TP / (TP + FN). This measure shows how much of the true network was discovered.

Precision = TP / (TP + FP). This measure shows how much of the inferred network is true. We chose precision over the common specificity metric (measuring how many of the false edges were wrongly inferred) because of the large number of potential interactions in a network that makes it a less relevant metric [18, 19].

Error = FP + FN. This error function sums up the number of false edges that were detected and the number of true edges that were not detected. It gives equal weight to the sensitivity and precision, as we are concerned about the general case.

One should keep in mind that some false positives are more informative than others, in that they link genes that are still nearby in the pathway. With the strict metric described above, we regard them as false, just like the other false detections.

2.6 Generating Weak Bayesian Networks (WDBN)

To demonstrate our approach of ensemble of weak learners, we compare it to the regular DBN inference, as implemented by BANJO. We regard its output edges as binary ones: an edge can be included within the network or be kept out from it.

Averaging Inference Iterations. The search space of this inference problem exceeds the ability of the inference algorithm to produce robust solutions and there is no guarantee that two different inference iterations will provide two identical outputs. Instead of regarding the DBN output as a single inference network, we can regard it as a weak learner. We investigate two methods to produce such weak learners:

DBN iterations - we execute separate and independent inference iterations.

DBN N-best networks - we observe the N best networks that the algorithm provides.

In both cases we can average the weak learners' networks and get scoring function for the edges. The averaging gives a more continuous score, varying from 0 for edges that were not detected to 1 for edges that were detected by all of the learners.

Leave Observations Out (LOO) WDBN. In this procedure observations are taken out of the original data before executing the inference algorithm. For every inference iteration, we take out different subset of the dataset. The LOO algorithm has a partition parameter, α, which determines how much of the data will be dropped in each iteration. For example, if this parameter is set to be 10, then 10 inference iterations are executed where ten percent of the data is dropped in each. Several approaches can be implemented to decide how to choose the data that is dropped: a continuous section of observations, every i-th observation, random observations etc'. We chose the first option due to the small advantage it showed (lower error). If the raw dataset consists of t observations, $(X_1, ..., X_t)$, we can formalize the creation of the datasets as follows:

$$\text{Dataset}_i = (X_1, ..., X_{(i-1)t/\alpha}, X_{it/\alpha}, ..., X_t) \quad _{i=1,...,\alpha} \tag{2}$$

LOO execute the inference procedure for each of the α datasets and gives the edges a score representing the proportion of its number of detections from the total number of iterations. To fetch a single network one should set a threshold to define the minimal score an edge should achieve in order to be included within this inferred graph. Naturally, a low threshold is more permissive criteria and will result in high sensitivity and low precision, and high threshold will cause the opposite. The sense behind this method is to create datasets that "behave" different, and to ensemble them to improve the inference.

Leave Genes Out (LGO) WDBN. LGO is a similar WDBN algorithm. It is implemented by executing inference iterations, where in each we take out data rows (genes) instead of columns (observations). The act of taking out genes from the data seems to be more influential than taking out observations. The sense is that strong regulators might screen out weaker ones and by taking a gene out of the dataset we may "encourage" the learner to find genes that would have been ignored otherwise. Note that the influence of the dropped genes still exists within the data, as it still has its part within the simulated dynamics, only its values are obscured to the learner. We executed a single iteration for each gene we had chosen to drop; meaning in each iteration only one gene is missing from the data. Instead of executing iteration for each gene in the original dataset, we start from some estimated set. In this study, we repeat the inference procedure for every gene that was detected by the LOO (regarding zero threshold value), and drop it out of the data in the corresponding iteration.

Leave Edges Out (LEO) WDBN. Another way to generate weak Bayesian networks is the LEO algorithm which performs iteration for edges and obscures them from the inference procedure, each edge in its corresponding iteration. Like the LGO, the LEO procedure does not repeat the regular inference procedure for every possible edge, but considers only the edges that were detected by the LOO procedure (got positive scores). The edges, modeling regulatory connections, are the most fundamental features of the DBN model and by focusing on them we expect to achieve more exact results.

3 Results

3.1 Searching Time and N Best Networks

One of the most interesting aspects of the DBN inference procedure is the time we let the searcher look for optimal network. As the search is heuristic, we should guarantee that it is able to find good networks. We used here 50 simulated datasets and executed the inference on subsets of 100, 150 and 200 time points. We observed the inference after 60, 120 and 180 seconds. BANJO can provide as many high-scored networks as defined, and we used this feature to compare the quality of the 50 best networks, to averaged networks based on the 2, 5, and the 10 best networks for every inference iteration. As can be seen in figure 2, the inference is steady already after one minute and longer searching time does not make it better. This is due to the difficulty in inference from this short temporal structure. While a single inference network can not be improved, we observe that fusing more inferred networks results in better inference performances; Averaging 5 or 10 best networks (green curves) provides better networks than the best scored one (blue curve). Naturally, when averaging networks, one should set a threshold value to determine for an edge if it is to be included in the inference result or not. We examined the threshold values and found the optimal ones regarding the error, for each subset size, searching time and number of averaged networks (shown within the legends). We could see that low threshold values result in lower error levels. For averaging up to 5 networks, threshold of 0.1 was the optimal and for 10 networks, threshold value of 0.2.

3.2 DBN – Iterations

As a representative method for DBN-iterations, we executed five inference iterations for every dataset, for the same datasets sizes. The iterations were independent from each other and the output network was obtained by averaging their output networks. The total time for each procedure (run time of the BANJO's algorithm) was kept to be 3 minutes, therefore 3/5 minutes for each iteration. We could verify that the larger the dataset is, the lower the error gets. The trade off between the sensitivity and the precision is determined by the threshold value. Low threshold value of 0.1 (every edge that was detected at least once is included within the output network) results in lower error rates for all the checked dataset sizes.

3.3 LOO, LGO and LEO

We used the 50 simulated datasets to study the LOO, LGO and LEO inference performances. We limited the search to three minutes for every WDBN inference procedure (overall time for all the procedure's iterations). We checked their performances according to the number of averaged networks. This has showed stronger effect for smaller datasets. Naturally when we were using more networks for the averaging, the sensitivity becomes higher and the precision becomes lower. This tradeoff was consistent for all of these three methods.

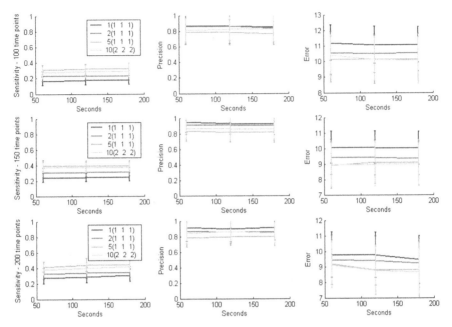

Fig. 2. Performances of the DBN versus searching time. Different colors represent different numbers of averaged networks: 1 (only best scored network), 2, 5 and 10 best networks. The columns represent the sensitivity, precision and error. Within the legends one can observe also the optimal threshold values, for each time limit, multiplied by 10 (regarding low error levels).

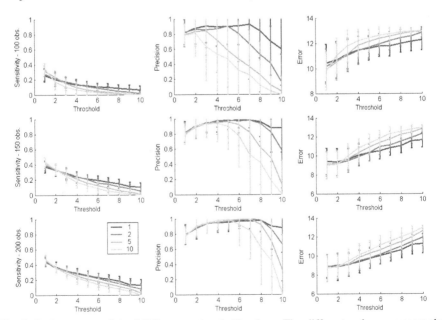

Fig. 3. Performances of the LGO versus threshold values. The different colors represent the different averaged networks, done by averaging 1, 2, 5 and 10 best networks.

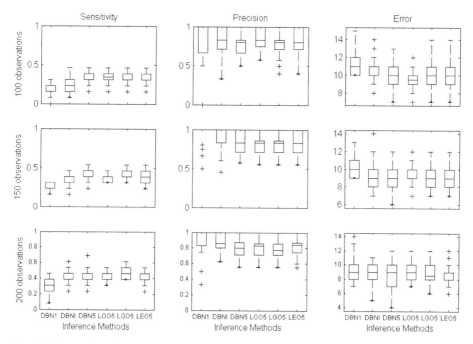

Fig. 4. Comparison between regular DBN, DBN-iterations, DBN-5-best-networks, LOO-5-best-networks, LGO-5-best-networks and LEO-5-best-networks as described in text

As can be seen in figure 3 (shown only for LGO), small threshold values (left side of the x-axis) results in lower error rates (right column), and when considering the smallest threshold value (0.1), the difference between the number of averaged networks (the four different colors) is negligible.

3.5 DBN Versus WDBNs

Figure 4 illustrates a comparison between six representative inference methods: DBN1, which considers only the highest scored networks (regular DBN), DBNI, where the number of iterations was 5 for every dataset, DBN5, LOO5, LGO5 and LEO5 that averages the best five networks found by the corresponding inference algorithms (hence averaged methods). For the LOO we consider iteration parameter of 8. For all of the averaged methods, we used threshold value of 0.1 and limited the search to three minutes (overall searching time for all the iterations). It can be clearly seen that the averaged methods outperformed DBN1.

In table 1 one can explore the significance of the improvement, by considering the P-values of the coupled t-tests. The improvement is more significant for smaller datasets, however still significant for all of the checked datasets sizes. The only exception for the zero-rates-P-values is the DBN-iterations for datasets of 100 observations. This is explained by the fact that the DBN-iterations' learners are much less independent, namely the regular DBN inference in this case is quite consistent.

Table 1. P-values of the coupled t-tests with the distributions of the methods' errors. Every method averaged five best networks and compared to the regular DBN1. The threshold values of the averaged methods were 0.1.

	100	150	200
DBNI	0.0275	0.0001	0.0002
DBN5	0	0	0.0026
LOO5	0	0.0006	0.0103
LGO5	0	0.0002	0.0024
LEO5	0	0.0001	0.0001

4 Discussion

The known approach of ensemble of weak learners was used for the problem of inferring genetic network from gene expression temporal data. Using a simulated data, we have introduced five methods for constructing WDBNs and illustrated their superiority regarding regular DBN, mainly achieved for small number of time observations, namely more realistic data sets. We evaluate the quality of inference and conclude that it is still infeasible to fully uncover underlying regulatory networks based only on expression data. However, as the DBN model is one of the most popular models for this case, especially when combining the data with prior biological knowledge, the discussed methods can improve the inference results.

References

1. Pearl, J., *Probabilistic Reasoning in Intelligent Systems*, in *Morgan Kaufmann*. 1988: San Francisco, CA.
2. Murphy, K., Mian, S., *Modelling Gene Expression Data using Dynamic Bayesian Networks*. Technical Report, MIT Artificial Intelligence Laboratory, 1999.
3. Friedman, N., Linial, M., Nachman, I., Pe'er, D., *Using Bayesian Networks to Analyze Expression Data*. Journal of Computational Biology., 2000.
4. Hartemink, A.J., Gifford, D.K, Jaakkola T.S., Young, R.A., *Using graphical models and genomic expression data to statistically validate models of genetic regulatory networks*. Pacific Symp. Biocomput., 2001: p. 422-433.
5. Hartemink, A., et al., *Combining location and expression data for principled discovery of genetic regulatory network models*. Pac. Symp. Biocomput, 2002. **7**: p. 437–449.
6. Husmeier, D., *Sensitivity and specificity of inferring genetic regulatory interactions from microarray experiments with dynamic Bayesian networks*. Bioinformatics, 2003. **19**,: p. 2271-2282.
7. Smith, V.A., Jarvis, E. D., Hartemink, A. J., *Influence of Network Topology and Data Collection on Network Infernece*. Pacific Symp Biocomput., 2003. **8**: p. 164-175.
8. Smith, V.A., Jarvis, E. D., Hartemink, A. J., *Evaluating functional network inference using simulations*. Bioinformatics, 2002. **18**: p. S216-S224.
9. Yu, J., Smith, V. A., Wang, P. P., Hartemink, A. J., Jarvis, E. D., *Using Bayesian Network Inference Algorithms to Recover Molecular Genetic Regulatory Networks*. 3rd International Conference on System Biology (Karolinska Institute, Stockholm, Sweden). 2002.
10. Jacobs, R.A., Jordan, M.I., Nowlan, S.J., Hinton, G.R., *Adaptive Mixtures of Local Experts*. Neural Computation, 1991. **3**: p. 79-87.

11. Hansen, L.K., Salamon, P., *Neural network ensembles.* IEEE Transactions on Pattern Analysis and Machine Intelligence, 1990. **12**: p. 993-1001.

12. Tumer, K., Ghosh, J., *Error Correlation and Error Reduction in Ensemble Classifiers.* Connection Science, 1996. **8**: p. 385-404.

13. Sharkey , A.J.C., *On Combining Artificial Neural Nets.* Connection Science, 1996. **8**.

14. Raviv, Y., Intrator, N., *Bootstrapping with Noise: An Effective Regularization Technique.* Connection Science, 1996. **8**: p. 355-372.

15. Pe'er, D., et al., *Inferring subnetworks from perturbed expression profiles.* Bioinformatics, 2001. **17**(Suppl 1): p. S215-24.

16. Hartemink, A.J., Gifford, D.K, Jaakkola T.S. & Young, R.A., *Combining location and expression data for principled discovery of genetic regulatory network models.* Pacific Symp. Biocomput., 2002. **7**: p. 437-449.

17. Friedman, N. and D. Koller, *Being Bayesian about Network Structure. A Bayesian Approach to Structure Discovery in Bayesian Networks.* Machine Learning, 2003. **50**(1): p. 95-125.

18. Yu, J., Smith, V. A., Wang, P. P., Hartemink, A. J., Jarvis, E. D., *Advances to Bayesian network inference for generating causal networks from observational biological data.* Bioinformatic., 2004. **20**(18): p. 3594-3603.

19. Basso, K., Margolin, A. A., Stolovitzky, G., Klein, U., Dalla-Favera, R., Califano, A., *Reverse engineering of regulatory networks in human B cells.* Nat Genet, 2005.

20. Hartemink, A.J., *Reverse engineering gene regulatory networks.* Nat Biotechnol, 2005. **23**(5),: p. 554-5.

21. Hartemink, A.J., *BANJO.* 2005.

An Ensemble Approach for Incremental Learning in Nonstationary Environments

Michael D. Muhlbaier and Robi Polikar[*]

Signal Processing and Pattern Recognition Laboratory
Electrical and Computer Engineering, Rowan University, Glassboro, NJ 08028 USA
muhlbaier@ieee.org, polikar@rowan.edu

Abstract. We describe an ensemble of classifiers based algorithm for incremental learning in nonstationary environments. In this formulation, we assume that the learner is presented with a series of training datasets, each of which is drawn from a different snapshot of a distribution that is drifting at an unknown rate. Furthermore, we assume that the algorithm must learn the new environment in an incremental manner, that is, without having access to previously available data. Instead of a time window over incoming instances, or an aged based forgetting – as used by most ensemble based nonstationary learning algorithms – a strategic weighting mechanism is employed that tracks the classifiers' performances over drifting environments to determine appropriate voting weights. Specifically, the proposed approach generates a single classifier for each dataset that becomes available, and then combines them through a dynamically modified weighted majority voting, where the voting weights themselves are computed as weighted averages of classifiers' individual performances over all environments. We describe the implementation details of this approach, as well as its initial results on simulated non-stationary environments.

Keywords: Nonstationary environment, concept drift, Learn[++].NSE.

1 Introduction

The problem of learning in nonstationary environments (NSE) has traditionally received much less attention than its stationary counterpart. It is perhaps due to inherent difficulty of the problem: after all, machine learning algorithms require a formal and precise definition of the problem, and in this case, it is even difficult to define the problem: what exactly is a nonstationary environment? Informally, it refers to the variation of the underlying data distribution that defines the concept to be learned: the environment subsequently provides new data, for which the input/output mapping (decision boundary) is different than those of the previous datasets. Early work in NSE learning, also known as *concept drift*, have concentrated on formalizing exactly what kind of drift and/or how fast of a drift can be learned [1-4].

Therein lies the difficulty with this problem; change can be slow or fast, abrupt or gradual, random or systematic, cyclical or expanding or contracting in the feature space.

---

[*] Corresponding author.

M. Haindl, J. Kittler, and F. Roli (Eds.): MCS 2007, LNCS 4472, pp. 490–500, 2007.
© Springer-Verlag Berlin Heidelberg 2007

Several approaches have been proposed for various combinations of such changes, which typically include a mechanism to (i) detect the drift and/or its magnitude; (ii) learn the change in the environment; and/or (iii) forget what is no longer relevant.

Many algorithms specifically designed for concept drift are generally based in part on the ideas used in FLORA [3]: use a timing window (fixed or variable) to choose a block of (new) instances as they come in, and then train a new classifier. The window size can be increased or decreased depending on how fast the environment is changing. Of course, such algorithms have a built-in forgetting mechanism with the implicit assumption that those instances that fall outside of the window are no longer relevant, and the information carried by them can be forgotten. Other approaches try to detect when a substantial change has occurred (*novelty detection*), and then update the classifier [5-8], or find the extreme examples that carry most relevant and novel information to train a classifier (partial instance memory) [9]; still others detect and purge those instances that no longer carry relevant information, and train a new classifier with the remaining block of data [10]. A different group of approaches treat the nonstationary learning as a prediction problem, and use appropriate classification (e.g., PNN) [11] or tracking algorithms (such as Kalman filters) [12].

More recently, ensemble based approaches have also been proposed. As reviewed by Kuncheva in [13], such algorithms typically fall into one of the following categories: (i) *dynamic combiners* where, for a previously trained fixed ensemble, the combination rule is changed to track the concept drift, e.g., weighted majority voting or Winnow based algorithms [14]; (ii) algorithms that use the new training to *update* an online learner or all members of an ensemble, e.g. online boosting [15]; and (iii) algorithms that add new ensemble members [16] and/or replace the least contributing member of an ensemble with a classifier trained on new data [17,18].

In this paper we propose an alternative formulation, Learn[++].NSE, built upon our previously introduced incremental learning algorithm Learn[++] [19], by suitably modifying it for nonstationary environments. Learn[++].NSE does not completely fit into any of the above categories, but rather combines ideas from each. It does use new data to create new ensemble members, and it also adjusts the combination rule by dynamically modifying voting weights. It does not use a timing window, or any of the previously seen data (hence an incremental learning approach), and it does not discard old classifiers, in case old classifiers become relevant again in the future. It simply reweighs them based on their predicted expertise on the current environment.

It is reasonable to question whether there is need for yet another ensemble based algorithm for nonstationary learning, in particular considering that we make no claim on the superiority of Learn[++].NSE over any of the other algorithms – ensemble based or otherwise. In the spirit of the no-free-lunch theorem, we believe that no single algorithm can outperform all others on all applications, that the success depends much on the match of the characteristics of the algorithm with those of the problem, and therefore it is best to have access to a toolbox of algorithms each with its own particular strengths and weaknesses. Considering the differences of Learn[++].NSE mentioned above, along with the promising initial results and outcomes discussed later in this paper, we believe that Learn[++].NSE can be a beneficial alternative on a variety of nonstationary learning scenarios. The algorithm is described in detail in Section 2, followed by a description of our simulation tests and results in Section 3. Specific nonstationary environment scenarios in which the algorithm is expected to be particularly useful are discussed in Section 4.

2 Learn^{++}.NSE

Learn^{++}.NSE uses a similar structural framework as Learn^{++}: incrementally build an ensemble of classifiers from new data that are combined by weighted majority voting, and the existing ensemble decides on the contribution of each successive classifier. There are a number of differences, however, instituted for suitably modifying the algorithm for nonstationary environments.

In summary, we assume that each new dataset represents a new snapshot of the environment. The amount of change in the environment since the previous dataset may be minor or substantial, and is tracked by the performance of the existing ensemble on the current dataset. Learn^{++}.NSE creates a single classifier for each dataset that becomes available from the new environment, and a weighted performance measure (based on its error) is computed for each classifier on each environment it has experienced. Each performance measure represents the expertise of that classifier on a particular snapshot of the environment. These performance measures are then averaged using a nonlinear (sigmoidal) function, giving higher weights to the performances of the classifier on the more recent environments. At any time, the classifiers can be combined through weighted majority voting, using the most recent averaged weights, to obtain the final hypothesis.

In Learn^{++}.NSE, the change in the environment is tracked both by addition of new classifiers, as well as the voting weights of existing classifiers, and no classifier is ever discarded. If cyclical drift makes earlier classifiers once again relevant, the algorithm recognizes this change, and assigns higher weights to earlier classifiers. The algorithm is described in detail below, with its pseudocode given in Fig. 1.

We assume that an oracle provides us with a training dataset at certain intervals, (not necessarily uniform). At each interval, the distribution from which the oracle draws the training data changes in some manner and rate, also unknown to us. The training dataset D^t of cardinality m^t at time t provides us with a snapshot of the then current environment. Learn^{++}.NSE generates one classifier for each such new dataset that becomes available. To do so, the algorithm first evaluates the classification accuracy of the currently available composite hypothesis H^{t-1} on the newly available data D^t. H^{t-1}, obtained by the weighted majority voting of all classifiers generated during the previous $t-1$ iterations, represents the existing ensemble's knowledge of the environment. The error of the composite hypothesis E^t is computed as a simple ratio of the correctly identified instances of the new dataset. We demand that this error be less that a threshold, say ½, to ensure that it has a meaningful classification capacity. For this selection of the threshold, we normalize the error so that the normalized error B^t remains between 0 and 1 (Step 1 inside the Do loop). We then update a set of weights for each instance, that is normally initialized to be uniform ($1/m^t$): the weights of the instances misclassified by the ensemble are reduced by a factor of B^t. The weights are then normalized to obtain a distribution D^t (step 2).

Input: For each dataset D^t $t=1,2,...$ representing a new environment
- Sequence of $i=1,...,m^t$ instances x_i with labels $y_i \in Y = \{1,...,c\}$
- Supervised learning algorithm **BaseClassifier**.

Do for $t=1,2,...$

If $t=1$ **Initialize** $D^1(i) = w^1(i) = 1/m^1$, $\forall i$, skip to step 3. $\qquad$ (1)

1. Compute error of existing ensemble on new data

$$E^t = \sum_{i=1}^{m^t}(1/m^t)\cdot \left[\!\left[H^{t-1}(x_i) \neq y_i \right]\!\right] \qquad (2)$$

Normalize error $B^t = E^t/(1-E^t)$ $\qquad$ (3)

2. Update instance weights

$$w_i^t = \frac{1}{m^t} \times \begin{cases} B^t, & H^{t-1}(x_i) = y_i \\ 1, & otherwise \end{cases} \qquad (4)$$

Set $D^t = w^t / \sum_{i=1}^{m^t} w_i^t$ so that D^k is a distribution. $\qquad$ (5)

3. Call **BaseClassifier** with D^t, obtain $h_t : X \to Y$
4. Evaluate all existing classifiers on new dataset D^t

$$\varepsilon_k^t = \sum_{i=1}^{m^t} D^t(i) \cdot \left[\!\left[h_k(x_i) \neq y_i \right]\!\right], \quad for\ k=1,...,t \qquad (6)$$

If $\varepsilon_{k=t}^t > 1/2$, generate a new h_t. If $\varepsilon_{k<t}^t > 1/2$, set $\varepsilon_k^t = 1/2$

$$\beta_k^t = \varepsilon_k^t/(1-\varepsilon_k^t), \quad for\ k=1,...,t \qquad (7)$$

5. Compute a weighted sum of all normalized errors for k^{th} classifier h_k

$$\omega_k^t = 1/\left(1+e^{-a(t-k-b)}\right), \qquad \omega_k^t = \omega_k^t/\sum_{j=0}^{t-k}\omega_k^{t-j} \qquad (8)$$

$$\overline{\beta}_k^t = \sum_{j=0}^{t-k} \omega_k^{t-j}\beta_k^{t-j}, \quad for\ k=1,...,t \qquad (9)$$

6. Calculate classifier voting weights

$$W_k^t = \log\left(1/\overline{\beta}_k^t\right), \quad for\ k=1,...,t \qquad (10)$$

7. Obtain the composite hypothesis as the current final hypothesis

$$H^t(x_i) = \arg\max_c \sum_k W_k^t \cdot \left[\!\left[h_k(x_i) = c \right]\!\right] \qquad (11)$$

Fig. 1. The pseudocode of the algorithm Learn^{++}.NSE

The algorithm then calls the BaseClassifier and asks it to create the tth classifier h_t using data drawn from the current training dataset D^t provided by the oracle (step 3). All classifiers generated thus far h_k, $k=1,...,t$ are then evaluated on the current dataset, by computing their weighted error (Equation 6, step 4). Note that at current time step t, we now have t error measures, one for each classifier generated thus far. Hence the error term ε_k^t represents the error of the kth classifier h_k at the tth time step.

The errors are again assumed to be less than ½. Here, we make a distinction: if the error of the most recent classifier (on its native training set) is greater than ½, then we discard that classifier and generate a new one. For any of the other (older) classifiers, if its error is greater than ½, it is set to ½. This effectively sets the normalized error of that classifier at that time step to 1, which in turn removes all of its voting power later during the weighted majority voting. Note that unlike AdaBoost and similar algorithms that use such an error threshold, Learn^{++}.NSE does not abort, nor does it throw away (the previously generated) classifiers when their error exceeds ½. This is because, it is not unreasonable for a classifier to perform poorly if the environment has changed drastically since it was created, and furthermore, it does not mean that this classifier will never be useful again in the future. Should the environment goes through a cyclical change and becomes similar to the time when the classifier in question was generated, its error will then be less than ½ , and it will contribute to the current decision of the ensemble.

In order to combine the classifiers, however, we need one weight for each, even though the algorithm maintains a set of t such error measures ε_k^t for each classifier $k=1,...,t$. The error measures are therefore combined through a weighted averaging (step 5). The weighting is done through a sigmoid function (Equation 8), which gives a large weight to errors on most recent environments, and less to errors on older environments. We emphasize, however, that this process does *not* give less weight to old classifiers. It is their *error on old environments* that is weighted less. Therefore, a classifier generated long time ago can in fact receive a large voting weight, if its error on the *recent* environments is low.

The errors so weighted as described above are then combined to obtain a weighted average error (Eq. 9). The logarithm of the inverse of this weighted error average then constitutes the final voting weight W_k^t for classifier k at time instant t (Step 6, Eq. 10). Finally all classifiers are combined through weighted majority voting (Step 7, Eq. 11).

3 Experiments and Results

Two experiments were designed to test the ability of the algorithm to track a nonstationary environment. In both experiments, data was drawn from Gaussian distributions so that the optimal Bayes error could be computed and compared – at each time step – against the Learn^{++}.NSE ensemble as well as single classifier performances. Naive Bayes was used as the base classifier in all experiments.

In the first experiment, conceptually illustrated in Fig. 2, the distributions for two of the three classes were moved in a concept drift scenario, where both the means and the variances of the distributions were changed. In fact, the distribution of one class has completely replaced the other. The entire change was completed in 50 time steps, however, in each case, we allowed the algorithm to see very little of the environment: a mere 20 samples per class. The distribution for the third class left unchanged.

We then tracked the performance of the Learn^{++}.NSE ensemble, a single classifier, and the Bayes classifier, at each time step. Figure 3 shows four independent trials of the percent classification performances on the entire feature space, calculated with

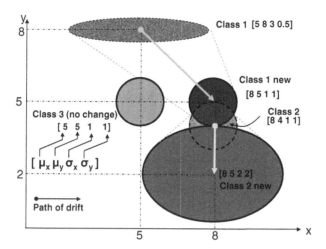

Fig. 2. Concept drift simulation – 3-class experiment. Classes 1 and 2 move and change variance.

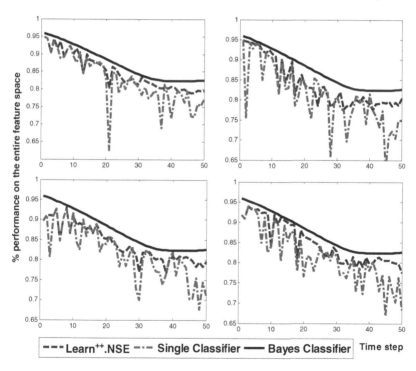

Fig. 3. Comparative performances on four independent single trials

respect to individual instances' probability of occurrence (to prevent instances away from decision boundaries artificially increasing the performance).

Several interesting observations can be made. First, all four performance trends indicate that the Learn[++].NSE tracks the Bayes classifier very closely, and as expected, it has smaller performance variance than the single classifier.

Second, the ensemble performance is, in general, better than the single classifier, and more closely follows the Bayes classifier. This is important since a single Naïve Bayes classifier tested on the most recent data on which it was trained would normally be expected to do very well. The ensemble is using its combined knowledge from all training sessions to correctly identify those areas that have changed due to concept drift as well as those that have not changed. Third, the performance gap between the ensemble and the single classifier appear to be widening in time, in favour of the ensemble. That is, the performances of single classifier and Learn[++].NSE start similar, but in time the ensemble increasingly outperforms the single classifier despite occasional good single classifier performances. Since the large variance in the single classifier performance makes it difficult to determine the validity of such a claim, we looked at the average performance of 100 independent trials of the same experiment. Performance results in Figure 4 indicate that the Learn[++].NSE ensemble increasingly and significantly outperforms the single classifier.

Finally, note that what appears to look like an overall performance decline (from 90% to 70%-80% range) in Fig.2 and Fig. 4 is irrelevant for our purposes. Such a decline merely indicates that the underlying classification problem is getting increasingly difficult in time (see Fig. 2), as evidenced by the declining optimal Bayes classifier performance. We are primarily concerned with how well Learn[++].NSE tracks Bayes classifier, as we cannot expect any algorithm to do any better.

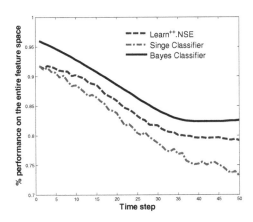

Fig. 4. Comparative performances - average of 100 independent trials

We have also designed a second, four-class experiment, the non-stationary environment of which was substantially more challenging, including classes switching places, changing variances, drifting in and out of their original distributions in a cyclical manner. Figure 5 provides snapshots of the distributions of four classes $c_1 \sim c_4$ at $t=0$, $t=T/3$, $t=2T/3$ and $t=T$, where T indicates the time of the last environment update. During $t=0$ to $t=T/3$, the variances of the class distributions were modified; then the means of the class distributions drifted until $t=2T/3$, and finally both the variances and means were changed during the last third section of the simulation. There were a total of 120 time steps from $t=0$ to $t=T$, during which the distributions briefly returned to the vicinity of their original neighbourhoods twice, before drifting again in other directions. Hence, the design simulated a semi-cyclical non-stationary behaviour.

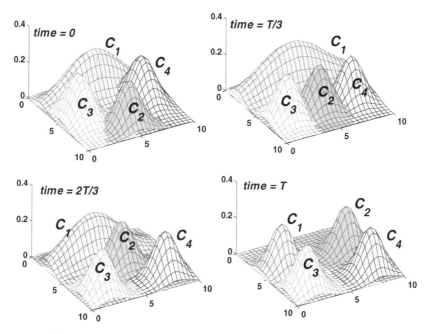

Fig. 5. The snapshots of the drifting distributions at four time steps

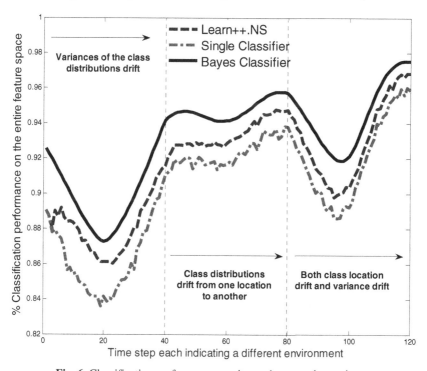

Fig. 6. Classification performance results on the second experiment

The classification performance results of Learn^{++}.NSE, single classifier and the Bayes classifier are shown in Figure 6, where all performances are averages of 100 independent trials. Once again, the ensemble was able to track the Bayes classifier much closer than the single classifier, despite the convoluted changes in the environment. The ensemble performance was also significantly better than the single Naïve Bayes classifier at the 95% level for all $t>5$ steps.

4   Conclusions and Discussions

We described an ensemble based algorithm for nonstationary environments. The algorithm creates a single classifier for each dataset that becomes available, and keeps a record of the performance of each classifier on all environments throughout the training. The classifiers are then combined through a modified dynamically weighted majority voting, where the voting weights are determined as a measure of each classifier's performance on the current environment, weighted along with the performances on previous environments. All classifiers are retained, which allows the previously generated classifiers to make significant contributions to the ensemble decision, if such classifiers provide relevant information for the current environment.

The algorithm has many characteristics that are deemed desirable for online learners [13]: (i) the algorithm learns from only single pass of each dataset, without revisiting them. This property of the algorithm is inherited from its predecessor Learn^{++}, as it was designed to learn incrementally without requiring access to previously seen data; (ii) the algorithm has a relatively small computational complexity that is linear in the number of datasets, or even possibly in the data size, depending on the base classifier (since it can be used with any supervised classifier); (iii) the algorithm possesses *any-time-learning* capability, i.e., if the algorithm is stopped at time t, the algorithm provides the current best representation of the environment at that time.

As mentioned earlier in our justification for another ensemble based nonstationary learning algorithm, the success of any algorithm depends much on how well its characteristics match those of the problem. It is therefore appropriate, and in fact necessary, to establish what such characteristics are for Learn^{++}.NSE. Specifically, when would we expect this algorithm to do well? The structure of Learn^{++}.NSE makes it particularly useful if the nonstationary environment provides a sequence of relatively small data, that by itself is not sufficient to adequately represent the current state of the environment. Then, a single classifier generated with such data would not be able to appropriately characterize the decision boundary. Only a subset of classes being represented in each dataset is another scenario of nonstationary learning, and the performance of Learn^{++}.NSE on such scenarios is part of our planned future work.

The algorithm described here is certainly not fully developed yet, and much work needs to be done. The algorithm, while intuitive, is based on heuristic ideas, and there are no theoretical performance guarantees. This is in part because we have not placed any restrictions on the environment. However, a careful analysis of the algorithm is necessary to determine how it reacts to different scenarios of nonstationary environments, and specifically to different rates of change. Of particular interest is how well the algorithm would be able to track the nonstationary environment, if the environment changed faster, say for example, it made the same total change in $T/2$ or $T/4$ time steps rather than in T steps?

While the algorithm is at its early stages of development, its initial performance has been promising, motivating us for further optimization and development. Future efforts will include the above mentioned analysis for tracking / estimating the environment's rate of change, and the algorithm's response to such change.

Acknowledgments. This material is based upon work supported by the National Science Foundation under Grant No. ECS-0239090.

References

[1] Schlimmer, J. C. and Granger, R. H.; Incremental Learning from Noisy Data. Machine Learning 1 (1986) 317-354.

[2] Helmbold, D. P. and Long, P. M.; Tracking drifting concepts by minimizing disagreements. Machine Learning 14 (1994) 27-45.

[3] Widmer, G. and Kubat, M.; Learning in the presence of concept drift and hidden contexts. Machine Learning 23 (1996) 69-101.

[4] Case, J., Jain, S., Kaufmann, S., Sharma, A., and Stephan, F.; Predictive learning models for concept drift. Theoretical Computer Science 268 (2001) 323-349.

[5] Liao, Y., Vemuri, V. R., and Pasos, A.; Adaptive anomaly detection with evolving connectionist systems. Journal of Network and Computer Applications 30 (2007) 60-80.

[6] Castillo, G., Gama, J., and Medas, P.; Adaptation to Drifting Concepts. Progress in Artificial Intelligence, Lecture Notes in Computer Science 2902 (2003) 279-293.

[7] Gama, J., Medas, P., Castillo, G., and Rodrigues, P.; Learning with Drift Detection. Advances in Artificial Intelligence - SBIA 2004, Lecture Notes in Computer Science 3171 (2004) 286-295.

[8] Cohen, L., Avrahami-Bakish, G., Last, M., Kandel, A., and Kipersztok, O.; Real-time data mining of non-stationary data streams from sensor networks. Information Fusion In Press, (2007).

[9] Maloof, M. A. and Michalski, R. S.; Incremental learning with partial instance memory. Artificial Intelligence 154 (2004) 95-126.

[10] Black, M. and Hickey, R.; Learning classification rules for telecom customer call data under concept drift. Soft Computing - A Fusion of Foundations, Methodologies and Applications 8 (2003) 102-108.

[11] Rutkowski, L.; Adaptive probabilistic neural networks for pattern classification in time-varying environment. IEEE Transactions on Neural Networks 15 (2004) 811-827.

[12] Cheng-Kui, G., Zheng-Ou, W., and Ya-Ming, S.; Encoding a priori information in neural networks to improve its modeling performance under non-stationary environment. International Conference on Machine Learning and Cybernetics (ICMLC 2004) 5 (2004) 3068-3072.

[13] Kuncheva, L. I.; Classifier Ensembles for Changing Environments. Multiple Classifier Systems (MCS 2004), Lecture Notes in Computer Science 3077 (2004) 1-15.

[14] Blum, A.; Empirical Support for Winnow and Weighted-Majority Algorithms: Results on a Calendar Scheduling Domain. Machine Learning 26 (1997) 5-23.

[15] Oza, N.; Online Ensemble Learning, Ph.D. Dissertation, (2001) University of California, Berkeley.

[16] Kyosuke, N., Koichiro, Y., and Takashi, O.; ACE: Adaptive Classifiers-Ensemble System for Concept-Drifting Environments. Multiple Classifier Systems (MCS 2005), Lecture Notes in Computer Science 3541 (2005) 176-185.

[17] Street, W. N. and Kim, Y.; A streaming ensemble algorithm (SEA) for large-scale classi-fication. Seventh ACM SIGKDD International Conference on Knowledge Discovery & Data Mining (KDD-01), (2001) 377-382.

[18] Chu, F. and Zaniolo, C.; Fast and Light Boosting for Adaptive Mining of Data Streams. Advances in Knowledge Discovery and Data Mining, Lecture Notes in Computer Science 3056 (2004) 282-292.

[19] Polikar, R., Upda, L., Upda, S. S., and Honavar, V.; Learn++: an incremental learning al-gorithm for supervised neural networks. Systems, Man and Cybernetics, Part C, IEEE Transactions on 31 (2001) 497-508.

Multiple Classifier Systems in Remote Sensing: From Basics to Recent Developments

Jon Atli Benediktsson[1], Jocelyn Chanussot[2], and Mathieu Fauvel[1,2]

[1] University of Iceland, Hjardarhagi 2-6, 107 Reykjavik, Iceland
benedikt@hi.is
[2] GIPSA-Lab, INP Grenoble, BP 46 - 38402 St Martin d'Heres, France
jocelyn.chanussot@lis.inpg.fr, mathieu.fauvel@lis.inpg.fr

Abstract. In this paper, we present some recent developments of Multiple Classifiers Systems (MCS) for remote sensing applications. Some standard MCS methods (boosting, bagging, consensus theory and random forests) are briefly described and applied to multisource data (satellite multispectral images, elevation, slope and aspect data) for landcover classification. In the second part, special attention is given to Support Vector Machines (SVM) based algorithms. In particular, the fusion of two classifiers using both spectral and the spatial information is discussed in the frame of hyperspectral remote sensing for the classification of urban areas. In all the cases, MCS provide a significant improvement of the classification accuracies. In order to address new challenges for the analysis of remote sensing data, MCS provide invaluable tools to handle situations with an ever growing complexity. Examples include extraction of multiple features from one data set, use of multi-sensor data, and complementary use of several algorithms in a decision fusion scheme.

1 Introduction

Over the past decades, remote sensing has become a central source of information for the observation of the Earth. Numerous satellites have been launched, providing images in different modalities. On one hand, active imagery systems use radar sensors (e.g., synthetic aperture radar, polarimetric or interferometric imagery): an electromagnetic wave is generated and the sensor records the information reflected by the ground surface when illuminated. On the other hand, passive imagery systems use optical sensors (panchromatic, multispectral or hyperspectral images) where the sensor records the information naturally emitted by the ground when illuminated by the sun. Multisource data can also include geographic data such as elevation and slope [7]. All these data have different characteristics, e.g., different spatial and spectral resolutions, different angle of view, and different dates of acquisition. They thus provide complementary information.

Remote sensing data are used in a wide range of applications, including monitoring of the environment, management of major disasters, urban planning, precision agriculture, and strategic defense issues. In most of these applications,

M. Haindl, J. Kittler, and F. Roli (Eds.): MCS 2007, LNCS 4472, pp. 501–512, 2007.
© Springer-Verlag Berlin Heidelberg 2007

an automatic analysis of the data is required. The first step of the analysis usually consists in a classification at pixel-level, be it (semi-)supervised or not. Numerous algorithms have been proposed in the geoscience and remote sensing community to address these emerging issues. Considering the complexity of the data and the variety of available algorithms, multiple classifier systems (MCS) proved to be of the utmost interest in numerous remote sensing applications, significantly improving the classification performances. The aim of this paper is to present some of the recent issues addressed by multiple classifier systems in remote sensing. Special attention will be paid to classification algorithms based on Support Vector Machines.

Several multiclassifier systems have been used in remote sensing research. Bagging, boosting and consensus theory are among the most commonly used such approaches. Their application to multisource remote sensing data is discussed in Section 2. Based on these approaches, ensemble of classification and regression tree classifiers can be formed, leading to random forest classifier. This strategy used for land cover classification is presented in Section 3.

Support Vector Machines (SVM) have been widely used of late in classification of remote sensing data. Section 4 briefly presents the principle of this machine learning algorithm. The fusion of SVM for classification of hyperspectral data is then addressed, making a joint use of spatial and spectral information. In the conclusion, we also discuss the new trends in the use of MCS for remote sensing applications, such as decision fusion schemes.

2   Boosting, Bagging and Consensus Theory for Multisource Data

The combination of multisource remote sensing and geographic data offers improved accuracies in land cover classification. For such classification, the conventional parametric statistical classifiers, which have been applied successfully in remote sensing for the last two decades, are not appropriate, since a convenient multivariate statistical model does not exist for the data. In [1], several single and multiple classifiers, that are appropriate for the classification of multisource remote sensing and geographic data are considered. The focus is on multiple classifiers; bagging, boosting, and consensus-theoretic classifiers. These multiple classifiers have different characteristics.

2.1   Boosting

Boosting is a general and well known method which is used to increase the accuracy of any classifier. In this study, we use the AdaBoost.M1 method which can be used on classification problems with more than two classes [17]. In the beginning of AdaBoost, all patterns have the same weight and the classifier C_1 is the same as the base classifier. If the classification error is greater than 0.5, then the method does not work and the procedure is stopped. A minimum accuracy is thus required for the base classifier, which can be of considerable disadvantage in multiclass problems. Iteration by iteration, the weight of the samples which are correctly classified goes down. The algorithm consequently concentrates on the difficult samples. At the end of the procedure, T weighted training sets and T base classifiers have been generated. In most cases, the overall accuracy is increased. Many practical classification problems include samples which are not equally difficult to classify. AdaBoost is suitable for such problems. It tends to exhibit virtually no overfitting when the data is noiseless. Other advantages of boosting include that the algorithm has a tendency to reduce both the variance and the bias of the classification. On the other hand, AdaBoost is computationally more demanding than other simpler methods. The lack of robustness to noise is another shortcoming.

2.2 Bagging

Bagging is an abbreviation of ***bootstrap aggregating*** [18]. Bootstrap methods are based on randomly and uniformly collecting m samples with replacement from a sample set of size m. Many different bags are constructed by performing bootstrapping iteratively, classifying each bag, and computing some type of an average of the classifications of each sample via a vote. Bagging is in some ways similar to boosting since both methods design a collection of classifiers and combine their conclusions with a vote. However, the methods are different, e.g., because bagging always uses resampling instead of re-weighting, it does not change the distribution of the samples and all classes in the bagging algorithm have equal weights during the voting. Furthermore, bagging can be done in parallel, i.e., all the bags can be designed at once. On the other hand, boosting is always done in series, and each sample set is based on the latest weights.

For a particular bag S_i, the probability that a sample from the training set S is selected at least once in m tries is $1-(1-1/m)^m$. For a large m, the probability is approximately $1 - 1/e \approx 0.632$, indicating that each bag only includes about 63.2% of the samples in S. If the base classifier is unstable, that is, when a small change in training samples can result in a large change in classification accuracy, then bagging can improve the classification accuracy significantly. If the base classifier is stable, like e.g., a k-NN classifier, then bagging can actually reduce the classification accuracy because each classifier receives less of the training data. The bagging algorithm is also not very sensitive to noise in the data. The algorithm uses the instability of its base classifier in order to improve the classification accuracy. Therefore, it is of great importance to select the base classifier carefully. This is also the case for boosting since it is sensitive to small changes in the input signal. Bagging reduces the variance of the classification (just as boosting does) but in contrast to boosting, bagging has little effect on the bias of the classification.

2.3 Consensus Theory

Consensus theory aims at combining single probability distributions to summarize estimates from multiple experts with the assumption that the experts make decisions based on Bayesian decision theory [8]. The combination formula is called a consensus rule. These rules are used in classification by applying a *maximum* rule, i.e., the summarized estimate is obtained for all the information classes and the pattern X is assigned to the class with the highest summarized estimate. The most common consensus rule is the linear opinion pool (LOP) which is based on a weighted linear combination of the posterior probabilities from each data source. Another consensus rule, the logarithmic opinion pool (LOGP), is based on the weighted product of the posterior probabilities. The LOGP is unimodal and less dispersed than the LOP and it processes the data sources independently.

The simplest approach of the weighting scheme consists in giving all the data sources equal weights. Measures of reliability of the different sources can also be used for heuristic weighting. Furthermore, the weights can be chosen to not only weight the individual sources but also the individual classes. For such a scheme both linear and nonlinear optimization can be used. In [9], the statistical consensus models are optimized with neural networks, and achieve improved classification.

2.4   Experimental Results

Experiments [1] were conducted on multisource remote sensing and geographic data from Colorado. These data were originally acquired, preprocessed by Dr. Roger Hoffer from the Colorado State University. Access to the data set is gratefully acknowledged.

The classification was performed on a data set consisting of the following four data sources:

1. Landsat MSS data (4 spectral data channels).
2. Elevation data (in 10 m contour intervals, 1 data channel).
3. Slope data (0-90 degrees in 1 degree increments, 1 data channel).
4. Aspect data (1-180 degrees in 1 degree increments, 1 data channel).

Each channel comprised an image of 135 rows and 131 columns, and all channels were spatially co-registered. The area used for classification is a mountainous area in Colorado. It has 10 ground-cover classes: one class is water; the others are forest types (namely Colorado Blue Spruce, Mountane/Subalpine Meadow, Aspen, Ponderosa Pine, Ponderosa Pine/Douglas Fir, Engelmann Spruce, Douglas Fir/White Fir, Douglas Fir/Ponderosa Pine/Aspen and Douglas Fir/White Fir/Aspen). It is very difficult to distinguish among the forest types using the Landsat MSS data alone since the forest classes show very similar spectral response. Reference data were compiled for the area by comparing a cartographic map to a color composite of the Landsat data and also to a line printer output of each Landsat channel. By this method, 2019 reference points (11.4% of the area) were selected comprising two or more homogeneous fields in the imagery for each class. Approximately 50% of the reference samples were used for training, and the rest was used as a test set.

Several single classifiers were applied to the data, namely the minimum Euclidean Distance (MED) classifier and conjugate gradient backpropagation (CGBP) with two and three layers. The base classifiers which were used for bagging and boosting were also trained as single classifiers on the data. These base classifiers were: a decision table, the j4.8 decision tree [19] and the simple classifier 1R [20]. The results are summarized in Table 1.

Table 1. Training and Testing Accuracies in Percentage for the Different Classification Methods

Method	Average Accuracy Training set	Overall Accuracy Training set	Average Accuracy Test set	Overall Accuracy Test set
MED	37.8	40.3	35.5	38.0
Decision Table	73.0	82.8	63.4	77.0
j4.8	81.3	88.0	63.4	77.4
1R	35.9	60.3	34.0	58.8
CGBP (40 hidden neurons)	95.6	96.3	67.0	78.4
LOP (equal weights)	49.3	68.1	46.5	66.4
LOP (heuristic weights)	55.8	74.2	54.9	73.4
LOP (optimal linear weights)	66.2	80.3	66.1	80.2
LOP (optimized with CGBP)	74.6	83.5	72.9	82.2
LOGP (equal weights)	69.2	79.0	69.0	78.7
LOGP (heuristic weights)	69.2	80.5	66.8	79.6
LOGP (optimal linear weights)	65.1	79.7	64.3	80.0
LOGP (optimized with CGBP)	89.1	91.4	75.1	82.3
Bagging with DecisionTable	79.5	88.3	69.3	82.5
Bagging with j4.8	84.3	90.4	69.5	81.7
Bagging with 1R	61.5	74.9	58.9	73.6
Boosting with Decision Table	89.6	91.4	76.1	83.8
Boosting with j4.8	97.6	97.5	72.6	81.5
Boosting with 1R	88.7	90.9	79.4	85.3
Number of Samples		1008		1011

For the LOP and LOGP, ten data classes were defined in each data source. The multispectral remote sensing data sources were modeled to be Gaussian but the topographic data sources were modeled by Parzen density estimation with Gaussian kernels. Several different weighting schemes were used for the LOP and LOGP.

In the case of bagging, 100 iterations were selected for the decision table, 10 iterations for j4.8 and 200 iterations for 1R. Adaboost.M1 was employed, with 50 iterations for the decision table, 200 iterations for j4.8 and 60 iterations for 1R. In each case, the 10 class problem was converted into multiple two class problems.

The obtained overall and average accuracies are shown in Table 1 for both the training and the test sets. The multiple classifiers show improvement over all the single classifiers. The highest training accuracies were obtained by boosting the j4.8 decision tree. However, the highest overall and average test accuracies were obtained by boosting the 1R base classifier, which gave far worse training and test accuracies on its own than the other base classifiers. In contrast, bagging the 1R gave poor accuracies. The best overall and average accuracies for consensus theoretic classifiers were achieved with the LOGP optimised by conjugate gradient backpropagation. Those results were comparable in terms of overall accuracies to the best results achieved using bagging.

3   Random Forests

To further improve the classification performances and overcome the shortcomings of the previous approaches (e.g., sensitivity to noise, computational load and the need for parametric statistical modeling of each data source), random forests have been proposed. Random forests are ensembles of tree-type classifiers, that use a similar but improved method of bootstrapping as bagging, and can be considered an improved version of bagging. Random forests have been shown to be comparable to boosting in terms of accuracies, but without the drawbacks of boosting [11]. In addition, the random forests are computationally much less intensive than boosting. Recently, random forests have been applied to classification of hyperspectral remote sensing data [10]. Their approach is implemented within a multiclassifier system arranged as a binary hierarchy and provides good results for a hyperspectral data set with limited training data. Here, we consider random forests for classification of multisource remote sensing and geographic data [2]. It is of great interest since it is not only nonparametric [12], but it also provides a way of estimating the importance of the individual variables (data channels) in the classification.

Random forest is a general term for ensemble methods using tree-type classifiers $h(x, \theta_k), k = 1, \ldots$ where the θ_k are independent identically distributed random vectors and x is an input pattern [11]. In training, the random forest algorithm creates multiple CART-like trees, each trained on a bootstrapped sample of the original training data, and searches only across a randomly selected subset of the input variables to determine a split (for each node). For classification, each tree in the random forest casts a unit vote for the most popular class at input x. The output of the classifier is determined by a majority vote of the trees.

The number of variables is a user-defined parameter that is often blindly selected to the square root of the number of inputs. By limiting the number of variables used for a split, the computational complexity of the algorithm is reduced, and the correlation between trees is also decreased. Finally, the trees in random forests are not pruned, further reducing the computational load. As a result, the random forest algorithm can handle high dimensional data and use a large number of trees in the ensemble. As each tree is only using a portion of the input variables in a random forest, the algorithm is considerably lighter than conventional bagging with a comparable tree-type classifier.

A random forest classifier was applied to the same data set as boosting, bagging and consensus theory, considering the same 10 classes (see Section 2.4). It performed well (overall test set accuracy: 83%), outperforming the single CART classifier (78%), and being comparable to the accuracies obtained by other ensemble methods (Bagging: 83%-decision table, 82%-j4.8, 74%-1R ; Boosting: 84%-decision table, 82%-j4.8, 85%-1R) [2]. However, the random forest classifier was much faster in training when compared to the ensemble methods, especially boosting. The random forest algorithm does not overfit, and it does not require guidance (although its accuracy can be tweaked slightly by altering the number of variables used for a split). Furthermore, the algorithm can estimate the importance of variables for the classification. Such estimation is of value for feature extraction and/or feature weighting in multisource data classification. The random forest algorithm can also detect outliers, which can be very useful when some of the cases may be mislabeled. With this combination of efficiency and accuracy, along with very useful analytical tools, the random forest classifier is very desirable for multisource classification of remote sensing and geographic data, where no convenient statistical models are usually available.

4   Support Vector Machines (SVM) and Multiple Classifier Systems

4.1   SVM Formulation and the Use of Different Kernel Functions

We first briefly recall the general formulation of SVM classifiers [13]. Let us first consider a two-class problem in a n-dimensional space $\mathbb{R}^n$. We assume that l training samples, $\mathbf{x}_i \in \mathbb{R}^n$ (vector of attributes, or pixel vectors in the case of hyperspectral analysis) are available with their corresponding class labels given by $y_i = \pm 1$, $S = \{(\mathbf{x}_i, y_i) \mid i \in [1, l]\}$. The SVM method consists in finding the hyperplane that maximizes the margin (see Fig. 1), $i.e.$, the distance to the closest training data points in both classes. Noting $\mathbf{w} \in \mathbb{R}^n$ as the vector normal to the hyperplane and $b \in \mathbb{R}$ as the bias, the hyperplane H_p is defined as

$$\langle \mathbf{w}, \mathbf{x} \rangle + b = 0, \ \forall \mathbf{x} \in H_p \tag{1}$$

where $\langle \mathbf{w}, \mathbf{x} \rangle$ is the inner product between $\mathbf{w}$ and $\mathbf{x}$. If $\mathbf{x} \notin H_p$ then $f(\mathbf{x}) = \langle \mathbf{w}, \mathbf{x} \rangle + b$ is the distance of $\mathbf{x}$ to H_p. The sign of f corresponds to decision function $y = sgn\,(f(\mathbf{x}))$. Such a hyperplane has to satisfy:

$$y_i(\langle \mathbf{w}, \mathbf{x}_i \rangle + b) \geq 1, \ \forall i \in [1, l]. \tag{2}$$

For the non-linearly separable case, $slack$ variables ξ are introduced to deal with misclassified samples, and (2) becomes:

$$y_i(\langle \mathbf{w}, \mathbf{x}_i \rangle + b) \geq 1 - \xi_i, \ \xi_i \geq 0, \ \forall i \in [1, l]. \tag{3}$$

Finally, the optimal hyperplane has to jointly maximize the margin $2/\|\mathbf{w}\|$ and minimize the sum of errors $\sum_{i=1}^{l} \xi_i$. This is a convex optimization problem:

$$\min_{\mathbf{w}, \xi_i, b} \left[\frac{\|\mathbf{w}\|^2}{2} + C \sum_{i=1}^{l} \xi_i \right], \ \text{subject to (3)} \tag{4}$$

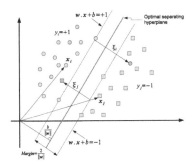

Fig. 1. Classification of non-linearly data by SVMs

where the parameter C balances the minimization of errors and the smoothness (regularization) of the solution, thus directly affecting the generalization capability of the classifier. This primal problem can be solved by considering the dual optimization problem through the use of Lagrange multipliers α_i:

$$\max_\alpha \sum_{i=1}^{l} \alpha_i - \frac{1}{2} \sum_{i,j=1}^{l} \alpha_i \alpha_j y_i y_j \langle \mathbf{x}_i, \mathbf{x}_j \rangle$$
$$\text{subject to } 0 \leq \alpha_i \leq C \quad \forall i \in [1,l] \tag{5}$$
$$\sum_{i=1}^{l} \alpha_i y_i = 0.$$

The relation between the primal ($\mathbf{w}$) and the dual parameters (α_i) is given by $\mathbf{w} = \sum_{i=1}^{l} \alpha_i y_i \mathbf{x}_i$ [14]. The solution vector is a linear combination of the samples of the training set associated with non-null α_i, which are called *support vectors*. The hyperplane decision function can thus be written as $y_u = sgn\left(\sum_{i=1}^{l} y_i \alpha_i \langle \mathbf{x}_u, \mathbf{x}_i \rangle + b\right)$ where $\mathbf{x}_u$ is an unseen sample. To address non-linear problems while preserving the simplicity of linear models, the input space is projected in higher dimensional feature Hilbert space $\mathcal{H}$ according to a non-linear mapping Φ [15]. The SVM algorithm can be simply considered with the following training samples: $\Phi(S) = \{(\Phi(\mathbf{x}_i), y_i) \mid i \in [1,l]\}$, which leads to a new solution, in which the inner product is: $\langle \Phi(\mathbf{x}_i), \Phi(\mathbf{x}_j) \rangle$. Inner products in feature spaces are computed using the *kernel trick* [13], which allows one to work in the mapped kernel space without knowing explicitly the mapping Φ, but only the kernel function k: $\langle \Phi(\mathbf{x}_i), \Phi(\mathbf{x}_j) \rangle = k(\mathbf{x}_i, \mathbf{x}_j)$. This way, the decision function is given by $y_u = sgn\left(\sum_{i=1}^{l} y_i \alpha_i k(\mathbf{x}_u, \mathbf{x}_i) + b\right)$.

The most popular kernels are presented below:

- *Polynomial*. The inner product is computed in the space of all monomials up to degree d: $k_{poly}(\mathbf{x}, \mathbf{z}) = (\langle \mathbf{x}, \mathbf{z} \rangle + \theta)^d$. The parameter θ tunes the weight of the higher order polynomial.

– *Gaussian Radial Basis Functions.* This kernel is given by $k_{gauss}(\mathbf{x}, \mathbf{z}) = \exp\left(-\gamma\|\mathbf{x} - \mathbf{z}\|^2\right)$. For this kernel, $k_{gauss}(\mathbf{x}, \mathbf{x}) = 1$. The parameter γ tunes the flexibility of the kernel.

SVMs are designed to solve binary classification problems. Two main approaches have been proposed to address multiclass (N classes) problems [14]:

– *One versus the rest:* N binary classifiers are applied to each class against the others. Each sample is assigned to the class with the *maximum* output.
– *Pairwise classification:* $\frac{N(N-1)}{2}$ binary classifiers are applied on each pair of classes. Each sample is assigned to the class getting the highest number of votes.

The aforementioned multiclass architectures as well as other multicategory strategies that can be applied to classification of hyperspectral images are presented and discussed in [16].

4.2   Joint Spatial and Spectral SVMs

A recent trend in multi- and hyperspectral remote sensing tends to use simultaneously spatial and spectral information, for improved classification performances. One way to address this issue consists in designing a decision fusion scheme. In [6], a landcover multiclass problem is considered on ROSIS data provided by the German Aerospace Agency (DLR) from urban area (N=9 classes, 115 spectral bands ranging from 0.43 to 0.86 μm, 1.3 m per pixel for the spatial resolution). The hyperspectral images are first preprocessed to extract some spatial information and the data are classified using Support Vector Machines (SVM). Another SVM classifier is applied on the initial spectral values, with no spatial information. As a matter of fact, it has been demonstrated that both the spatial and the spectral information are required to actually achieve good classification performances.

Using the *one versus one* classification strategy, 36 binary classifiers are used for each classifier. The standard method consists in combining the results with a majority voting scheme. However, a better multiclassifier system can be designed by storing for each result the actual distance to the hyperplane, following the general idea that it is more useful to have access to the belief of the classifiers rather than the final decision [5]. For a given sample, the larger is the distance to the hyperplane, the more reliable is the label. The most reliable source is thus the one that gives the largest *absolute* distance.

Let us consider that m SVM classifiers are used (in our case 2 classifers: one based on spatial features, one based on spectral information). We have the following results: $\{S_1, S_2, \ldots, S_m\}$, where $S_1 = d_{ij}^1$ is the distance provided by the first SVM classifier which separates class i from class j. The *absolute maximum* decision rule is defined as follows:

$$S_f = AbsMax(S_1, \ldots, S_m) \tag{6}$$

where *AbsMax* is the logical rules:

$$\begin{aligned} &\textbf{if}(|S_1| > |S_2|, \ldots, |S_m|) \textbf{ then } S_1 \\ &\textbf{else if}(|S_2| > |S_1|, \ldots, |S_m|) \textbf{ then } S_2 \\ &\qquad\qquad\qquad\vdots \\ &\textbf{else if}(|S_m| > |S_1|, \ldots, |S_{m-1}|) \textbf{ then } S_m. \end{aligned} \qquad (7)$$

The agreement of the classifiers can also be taken into account. Each distance is multiplied by the *maximum* probability associated to the two considered classes [21]: $p_i = \frac{2}{N(N-1)} \sum_{j=0, j\neq i}^{N} I(d_{ij})$,where I is the indicator function. The absolute *maximum* rule is applied on these weighted results:

$$S_f = AbsMax \left(\max(p_i^1, p_j^1) S_1, \ldots, \max(p_i^m, p_j^m) S_m \right). \qquad (8)$$

A last approach consists in simply applying a majority voting on the $m *$ $N(N-1)/2$ binary classifers used when each of the m classifiers uses the *one versus one* strategy.

The results are summarized on Table 2: the overall and average accuracies are clearly improved by the decision fusion, as well as the Kappa coefficient, with some variations among the different classes.

Table 2. Classification accuracies (%) for the SVMs based on the spectral or the spatial info, or with the 3 fusion operators

	Spectral info. only	Spatial info. only	Abs. Max.	Weighted Abs. max.	Maj. Vot.
Overall Accuracy	81.0	85.2	89.6	**89.7**	86.1
Avergae Accuracy	88.3	90.8	93.6	**93.7**	88.5
Kappa Coefficient	76.2	80.9	86.6	**86.7**	81.8
Asphalt	83.7	**95.4**	93.2	93.0	94.0
Meadows	70.3	80.3	83.9	84.0	**85.3**
Gravel	70.3	**87.6**	82.1	82.2	64.9
Trees	97.8	98.4	**99.7**	**99.7**	99.67
Metalsheets	99.4	**99.5**	**99.5**	99.4	**99.5**
Bare soil	**92.3**	63.7	91.2	91.8	61.6
Bitumen	81.6	**98.9**	97.0	97.2	93.0
Bricks	92.6	95.4	96.4	96.4	**98.8**
Shadows	96.6	97.7	**99.6**	**99.6**	**99.6**

5 Conclusion and Future Trends

Over the past years, multiple classifiers systems have been designed to address numerous applications in remote sensing. Dealing with land cover classification, this paper briefly presented the use of standard algorithms (boosting, bagging and consensus theory) in the case of multi-source data. Random forests is a valuable extension of these algorithms. The focus was then on classifiers based on Support Vector Machines. They provide very promising results in various remote sensing applications and one application was presented in the frame of hyperpsectral data from urban areas.

Future trends in the use of MCS in remote sensing arise from the three following items:

– **Multi-sensor data:** As stated in the introduction, numerous imaging satellites have been launched in the last decades and a lot of new ones are scheduled for the next few years. As a consequence, in many applications, images provided by different sensors are available and MCS can help taking advantage of their complementary characteristics. For instance, in [3], SVM classifiers working on multitemporal radar and optical data, respectively, are aggregated with excellent results.

– **Multiple feature extraction:** To address the difficulty and complexity of the emerging remote sensing applications, such as the accurate classification of very high resolution images from urban areas, multiple features are required. For instance, the spectral information (characterizing the physical nature of the different materials) is complementary to the spatial information (characterizing the shape and geometry of the different objects in the picture). Again, MCS can help taking advantage of their complementary characteristics. An example was described in section 4.2. Another strategy is described in [4], i.e., the spatial features are aggregated with the spectral information prior to classification using feature extraction and dimension reduction techniques. More generally speaking, the joint use of spatial and spectral features for a better understanding of the content of an image, be it multi- or hyperspectral, is one of the key problems in the close future of remote sensing.

– **Fusion of multiple algorithms (*decision fusion*):** Many different algorithms have been proposed in remote sensing research to address various applications. In most of the cases, none of these algorithms strictly outperforms all others. Every algorithm has its own merits, and, again, MCS can help taking advantage of their complementary characteristics. A key issue when designing a decision fusion scheme lies in the reliability of each source (a source being the result of one algorithm). How can one assess this reliability? In the case of SVM classifiers, as previously described, the distance to the separating hyperplane can be used. In [5], a general framework based on fuzzy logic is presented. A fusion rule incorporating in a flexible way prior knowledge on the different sources and local reliability estimated from the classifiers outputs for each pixel is proposed and tested in the frame of urban areas classification.

The future for novel remote sensing classifiers is closely tied to the design of appropriate MCS, enabling an optimal use of all the available information, with some key issues: 1) How can one handle very high dimensional data?, 2) How can one assess the reliability of one given classifier?, and 3) How can one handle temporal variability in the data?

Acknowledgement. This work was supported in part by the Research Fund of the University of Iceland and in part by the Jules Verne Program of the French and Icelandic governments.

References

[1] Briem G.J., Benediktsson J.A., Sveinsson J.R., Multiple classifiers applied to multisource remote sensing data. IEEE Trans. on Geoscience and Remote Sensing. **vol.40 n.10** (2002) 2291–2299

[2] Gislason P.O., Benediktsson J.A., Sveinsson J.R., Random forests for land cover classification. Pattern Recognition Letters **vol.27** (2006) 294–300

[3] Waske B., Benediktsson J.A., Fusion of support vector machines for classification of multisensor data. to appear in IEEE Trans. on Geoscience and Remote Sensing

[4] Palmason J.A., Benediktsson J.A., Sveinsson J.R., Chanussot J., Fusion of morphological and spectral information for classification of hyperspectral urban remote sensing data. IEEE Geoscience and Remote Sensing Symposium (IEEE IGARSS'06) (2006), Denver, Colorado

[5] Fauvel M., Chanussot J., Benediktsson J.A., Decision fusion for the classification of urban remote sensing images. IEEE Trans. on Geoscience and Remote Sensing. **vol.44 n.10** (2006) 2828–2838

[6] Fauvel M., Chanussot J., Benediktsson J.A., A combined support vector machines classification based on decision fusion. IEEE Geoscience and Remote Sensing Symposium (2006), Denver, Colorado

[7] Benediktsson J.A., Swain P.H., Ersoy, O.K., Neural network approaches versus statistical methods in classification of multisource remote sensing data. IEEE Trans. on Geoscience and Remote Sensing. **vol.28** (1990) 540–542

[8] Benediktsson J.A., Swain P.H., Consensus theoretic classification methods. IEEE Trans. Systems, Man Cybernet.**vol. 22** (1992) 688–704.

[9] Benediktsson J.A., Sveinsson J.R., Swain P.H., Hybrid consensus theoretic classification. IEEE Trans. on Geoscience and Remote Sensing. **vol.35** (1997) 833–843.

[10] Ham J., Chen Y., Crawford M.M., Gosh J., Investigation of the random forest framework for classification of hyperspectral data. IEEE Trans. on Geoscience and Remote Sensing. **vol.43** (2005) 492–501.

[11] Breiman L., Random Forests. Mach. Learn. **vol.40** (2001) 5-32.

[12] Duda R.O., Hart P.E., Stork D., Pattern Classification, second ed. (2001) Wiley, New York.

[13] Boser B. E., Guyon I. M., Vapnik V. N., A training algorithm for optimal margin classifier. *Fifth ACM Annual Workshop on Computational Learning* (1992) 144–152.

[14] Scholkopf B., Smola J., Learning with kernels (2002) MIT Press.

[15] Muller K. R., Mika S., Ratsch G., Tsuda K., Scholkopf B., An introduction to kernel-based learning algorithms. IEEE Trans. on Neural Networks. **vol.12** (2001) 181–202.

[16] Melgani F., Bruzzone L., Classification of hyperspectral remote-sensing images with support vector machines. IEEE Trans. on Geoscience and Remote Sensing. **vol.42** (2004) 1778–1790.

[17] Freund Y., Schapire R. E., Experiments with a new boosting algorithm. Proc. 13th Int. Conf. Machine Learning (1996).

[18] Breiman L., Bagging predictors. Univ. California, Dept. Stat., Berkeley, Tech. Rep. 421 (1994).

[19] Witten I. H., Frank E., Data MiningPractical Machine Learning Tools With Java Implementations. San Francisco, CA: Morgan Kaufmann (2000).

[20] Holte R. C., Very simple classification rules perform well on most commonly used datasets. Mach. Learn. **vol.11** (1993) 63-91.

[21] Wu T., Lin C., Weng R., Probability estimates for multiclass classification by pairwise coupling. Journal of Machine Learning. **vol.5** (2004) 975-1005.

Biometric Person Authentication Is a Multiple Classifier Problem[*]

Samy Bengio[1] and Johnny Mariéthoz[2]

[1] Google Inc, Mountain View, CA, USA
bengio@google.com
[2] IDIAP Research Institute, Martigny, Switzerland
marietho@idiap.ch

Abstract. Several papers have already shown the interest of using multiple classifiers in order to enhance the performance of biometric person authentication systems. In this paper, we would like to argue that the core task of Biometric Person Authentication is actually a multiple classifier problem as such: indeed, in order to reach state-of-the-art performance, we argue that all current systems , in one way or another, try to solve several tasks simultaneously and that without such joint training (or sharing), they would not succeed as well. We explain hereafter this perspective, and according to it, we propose some ways to take advantage of it, ranging from more parameter sharing to similarity learning.

1 Introduction

Biometric authentication is the task of verifying the identity of someone according to his or her claim, by using some of his or her biometric information (voice record, face photo, fingerprint, etc). A Biometric authentication system is thus trained to accept or reject an access request of one of the registered clients. This can be done efficiently by solving a two-class classification problem for each client separately.

When using more than one biometric information [1,2,3], the underlying verification system is said to be a *multiple classifier system*, as it merges several data sources coming from various biometric scanning devices, and hence, fits very well the topic of this workshop.

In this paper, we would like to argue that even when trying to solve a biometric authentication system based on a single modality and using a single classifier per client, one still needs to solve several classifier tasks jointly in order to reach state-of-the-art performance. We will argue in the following that there are several ways to solve these tasks jointly, ranging from the so-called world model approach, which is used to share common knowledge among several client models, to the learning of specialized distances or representation spaces, that can then be used for each client to take an accept/reject decision.

---

[*] This research was partially funded by the European PASCAL Network of Excellence and the Swiss OFES. Part of this work was done while Samy Bengio was at IDIAP Research Institute, Martigny, Switzerland.

M. Haindl, J. Kittler, and F. Roli (Eds.): MCS 2007, LNCS 4472, pp. 513–522, 2007.

The paper goes as follows: in Section 2 we explain the main argument of the paper, giving several examples of how it is already used in the various state-of-the-art approaches of the literature. In Section 3, we propose yet another way to use this new perspective of the biometric authentication task, and finally, in Section 4, we briefly conclude.

2   A Multiple Classifier Problem

The purpose of this paper is to show that the essence of a biometric authentication task is by nature a **multiple classifier problem**. This is not to be mixed up with the fact that multiple classifier systems often yield better performance for the task of biometric authentication [1,2,3].

Instead, we would like to advocate that, while biometric authentication can be seen as a two-class classification problem (each access should either be accepted or rejected), it is in fact *several two-class classification problems (one for each client model) that are inter-connected to each other* and one should take this into account in order to better design such systems.

Indeed, the general setup of a biometric authentication task is to be able to recognize whether a legitimate client is or is not who he or she claims to be by showing some biometric information. The expected resulting system should be able to accommodate for a growing number of clients[1], and should be able to enroll a new client with as little as possible of this new client's biometric material (be they voice, face, finger, or other modality prints).

2.1   Global Cost Function

The best way to illustrate that person authentication is a multiple classifier problem is to look at how such systems are evaluated in the research community. The most used measures of performance evaluate not only the performance of a single client model, but that of a large set of client models. Furthermore, this performance is not additive with respect to these apparently separate problems: indeed performance measures in person authentication always involve information such as False Acceptance Rate (FAR), False Rejection Rate (FRR), aggregates of them such as Half Total Error rate (HTER) or Detection Cost function (DCF) [4], and curves summarizing them, such as Detection Error Trade-off (DET) [5] and Expected Performance Curves (EPC) [6]. In all these cases, the global performance of a (set of) system(s) is not simply the sum of the performance of each client model (as the number of accesses per client model, be they legitimate or impostor, varies greatly from one client to another).

Hence, in order to train a good set of client models, one should select the corresponding parameters in order to maximize the joint performance of all models, and not separately the performance of each model. In this sense, it is clear that one needs to solve a **multiple classifier problem** jointly.

---

[1] It is expected that it should scale at most linearly with the number of clients, in terms of training time, and should be constant in terms of access time.

2.2   Parameter Sharing

Furthermore, given the inherent constraints of biometric authentication systems already discussed (scarce available data for each client, need for efficient access time, etc) most (if not all) of the state-of-the-art approaches in biometric authentication try to make use of a large quantity of previous client information in order to build a generic model, out of which each new client model starts from.

In order to illustrate this phenomenon, we will concentrate on the task of text-independent speaker verification, but bear in mind that the explanation is valid for any biometric authentication system. We can divide most of the current approaches into (apparently) generative approaches and discriminant approaches[2]. Let us review these two broad families of approaches.

The most well-known generative approach and still state-of-the-art method for text-independent speaker verification is based on adapted Gaussian Mixture Models (GMMs)[8]. It starts by training by Expectation-Maximization a generic GMM over a large quantity of voice data, and then adapts this generic model, using for instance Maximum A Posteriori (MAP) techniques, for each new client. Moreover, not only some parameters from the client model are adapted from a generic model (this usually applies to Gaussian means), but several other parameters of client models are simply *copied* from the generic model (this usually applies to Gaussian variances and weights). This approach turns out to be the most efficient way to make the best use of the small amount of each client's information. Furthermore, it is also state-of-the-art for many other biometric authentication problems, including face verification [9].

Several experiments have shown in the past that if one tries to solve the speaker verification problem by training a new GMM for each client instead of starting from a generic model and adapting it, then the performance results are poorer, even when tuning the number of Gaussians for each client separately.

Other evidences of the same phenomenon can be seen in various enhancements of the basic GMM based approach that have been proposed in the biometric authentication literature over the years, including the use of normalization techniques (Z-norm, T-norm, etc) which aim at trying to normalize the obtained score to make it more robust to several kinds of variations (intra-speaker, inter-speaker, inter-session, channel, etc) [10]. Once again, in order to compute efficient normalization parameters, one needs to use a large number of previous client information. This has already been demonstrated empirically.

For instance, one can see in Table 1 and in Figures 1 and 2 the comparative performance of three systems on the NIST database described in appendix A. One system is trained using the classical EM training approach (also called *maximum likelihood approach*, or ML), the second one is trained using the MAP adaptation technique, and the third one is trained using MAP and applying the T-norm normalization technique. Table 1 shows the *a priori* performance of all three systems on the test set in terms of FAR, FRR, and HTER, after selecting the threshold that minimized the Equal Error Rate (EER) on the development

---

[2] Note that actually, generative approaches that effectively work usually implement several tricks that make the overall system quite discriminant in various aspects [7].

set. Figure 1 shows the DET curves on the development set (the lower to the left the better). Finally, Figure 2 shows the EPC curves on the test set. The latter curves provide unbiased estimates of the HTER performance of all three systems for various expected ratios of FAR and FRR (represented on the X-axis of the graph by γ). The lower part of the graph also shows whether one of the three models was statistically significantly better than another one, according to the statistical test described in [11].

In all cases (table results, DET and EPC curves), it is clear that the more one shares information among client models, the better the expected performance on new client models becomes.

Table 1. Point-wise performance results, in terms of FAR, FRR and HTER (%), on the test set of the NIST database using classical ML training, MAP training and MAP plus T-normalization procedure. These results where obtained by selecting the threshold that minimized the EER on the development set.

	FAR	FRR	HTER
ML	3.23	30.80	17.02
MAP	4.79	16.38	10.59
MAP + T-norm	7.06	10.29	8.68

In all these cases, one could never obtain a good authentication system for a given client if no information was shared among various clients. Hence, while it is never explicitly said, **all successful generative approaches to person authentication systems are built by sharing some information among several classifier systems**.

While generative approaches have been used successfully for many years, there are good reasons to think that direct discriminant approaches should perform better; one of them, advocated by Vapnik [12], is that *one should never try to solve a more difficult task than the target task*. Hence if the task is to decide whether to accept or reject an access, there should be no reason to first train a generic model that describes everything about what is a correct access and what is an incorrect access, as the only thing that matters is the decision boundary between these two kinds of accesses.

More recently thus, several discriminant approaches have started to provide state-of-the-art performance in various person authentication tasks.

For instance, the *Nuisance Attribute Projection* (NAP) approach [13] tries to find a linear transformation of the access data into a space where accesses of the same client are near each others, in terms of the L2-norm. In order to refrain from finding an obvious bad solution, the size of the target space (or more specifically its Co-rank) is controlled by cross-validation. This transformation is learned on a large set of clients (hence, similarly to learning a generic GMM in the generative approach). After this step is performed, a standard linear support vector machine (SVM) [14] is trained for each new client over the transformed access data. This approach provided very good performance in the recent NIST evaluations.

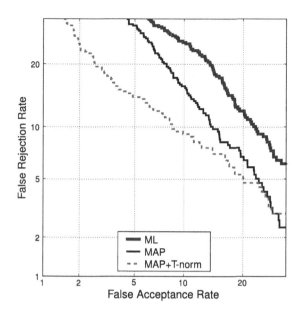

Fig. 1. DET curves on the development set of the NIST database using classical ML training, MAP training and MAP plus T-normalization procedure

This shows even more the fact that one has to share some information among many clients in order to obtain good performance. In this case, the shared information is used to learn how to transform the original data into a space which will be invariant to various aspects, such as the channel, and concentrate on the important topic, the client specific information.

Unfortunately, one thing in the NAP approach is somehow disappointing: the transformation function is not learned using the criterion that is directly related to the task; rather, it tries to minimize the mean squared distance between accesses of the same client to get rid of the *channel effect*, but do nothing about accesses from different clients for instance. In other words, we might still try to do more than the expected task, which is not optimal, according to Vapnik.

Another recent approach that also goes in the right direction and that obtains similar and state-of-the-art performance as the NAP approach is the Bayesian Factor Analysis approach [15]. In this case, one assumes that the mean vector of a client model is a linear combination of a generic mean vector, the mean vector of the available training data for that client, and the mean vector of the particular channel used in this training data. Once again, the linear combination parameters are trained on a large amount of access data, involving a large amount of clients. While this approach is nicely presented theoretically (and obtains very good empirical performance), it still does not try to find the optimal parameters of client models and linear combination by taking into account the global cost function.

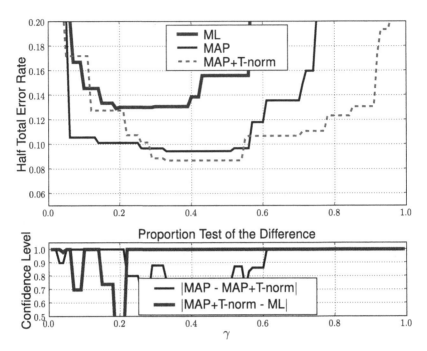

Fig. 2. Expected Performance Curves (EPC, the lower the better) on the test set of the NIST database using classical ML training, MAP training and MAP plus T-normalization procedure. The lower graph shows the confidence level of one model being statistically significantly better than another one in each part of the EPC curve.

3 Similarity Learning

In this section, we would like to propose at least one idea that would directly take into account the *multiple classifier problem* dimension of biometric authentication tasks.

We advocated in the previous section that one should try to learn jointly some information about several clients that would directly help in the final task of accepting or rejecting accesses. We also advocated that a promising approach should be discriminant, as the NAP approach is or similarly to Campbell's polynomial expansion for sequence kernel approach based on support vector machines (SVMs)[16].

We also acknowledge that the SVM approach to speaker verification is discriminant but given that each client SVM is trained separately, the currently only parameters that can be shared among clients in this approach are through the transformation of the input space (as it is done in the NAP approach)[3].

---

[3] Actually, another way the SVMs share information among them is through the same list of negative examples, or impostor accesses.

We would like to propose here another discriminant method based on SVMs, but that would use a particular kernel (or similarity measure between two accesses) that would be learned on several clients' accesses. Indeed, if we knew in advance a distance or similarity measure that would quantify reasonably well whether two accesses are coming from the same client or not, and even assuming this measure to be noisy, putting it into an SVM and training the SVM to solve the final authentication task would yield a better performance than using the standard Gaussian or polynomial kernel for the same task, as it is done in Campbell's approach for instance.

Hence, our proposed approach is the following. Using a large base of accesses for which one knows the correct identity, train a parametric similarity measure that will assess whether two accesses are coming from the same person or not. That can be done efficiently by stochastic gradient descent using a scheme similar to the so-called *Siamese neural network* [17] and a margin criterion with proximity constraints, as follows.

Let $\phi(\cdot)$ be a mapping of a given access into a space where two accesses of the same client are near while two accesses from different clients are far. More formally, given a triplet (x, x^+, x^-) such that x is a vector representation of a given access, x^+ is a vector representation of an access of the same client as x and x^- a vector representation of an access of a client different from that of x, we would like the scalar product of the similar ones in the $\phi(\cdot)$ space to be higher than that of the dissimilar ones:

$$\phi(x) \cdot \phi(x^+) > \phi(x) \cdot \phi(x^-). \tag{1}$$

Let $\phi(\cdot)$ be a multi-layer perceptron (MLP), the following ranking loss function L [18,19,20] can be used to search for a good candidate for (1):

$$L = |1 - [\phi(x) \cdot \phi(x^+) - \phi(x) \cdot \phi(x^-)]|_+ \tag{2}$$

where $|a|_+ = \max(0, a)$.

Finally, let us consider for the moment that a given access can be transformed into a vector representation using a trick such as the one used in Campbell's polynomial expansion approach [16]. That constraint could be relaxed to any other sequence kernel technique that have been proposed in the literature, such as in [7].

We now have all the ingredients to learn efficiently $\phi(\cdot)$ by stochastic gradient descent. One simply needs to prepare, out of a database of several client accesses, a training set of triplets (x, x^+, x^-); one then needs to select a particular form for the parametric function $\phi(\cdot)$ noting that the only constrains here is that it should be positive and differentiable with respect to its parameters (in particular, $\phi(\cdot)$ can be non-linear, which is not the case for the NAP and Bayesian Factor Analysis approaches). One can then train $\phi(\cdot)$ using stochastic gradient descent to optimize (2) on that data. The chosen loss function (2) involves a *security* margin, as not only do we want similar accesses to be nearer each other than dissimilar ones in that space, we also want the difference between the two similarity measures to be at least 1 (or any positive constant, for that matter).

Once $\phi(\cdot)$ is trained on a reasonably large database, one can then use it to create the following kernel k for each client SVM, similarly to the NAP and Campbell's approaches:

$$k(x, y) = \phi(x) \cdot \phi(y) \tag{3}$$

which guaranties Mercer's conditions for proper SVM training [14], as long as we put some mild constraint on $\phi(\cdot)$ such as being continuous and positive, which is straightforward to enforce.

4   Conclusion

In this paper, we have presented a somehow novel view of the task of biometric person authentication, advocating that it should be solved by taking into account that one needs to create simultaneously several two-class classifiers, one for each client, and that parameter sharing of one sort or another during this process is of paramount importance. We have shown that all currently state-of-the-art approaches to several biometric authentication tasks are indeed following this approach while never referring to it specifically. We have then proposed a novel approach, based on learning a similarity measure between two accesses, trained by a margin criterion on a large set of previous client accesses, that can then be plugged in an SVM for each client to replace standard kernels such as the polynomial or the Gaussian kernel. A nice extension of the following framework could be to incorporate the transformation of an access (which is normally a variable size sequence of feature vectors such as MFCCs) into a vector representation. A standard Time Delay Neural Network (TDNN) [21] could be used inside the $\phi(\cdot)$ function to accomplish this.

A   The NIST Database Used in This Paper

The NIST database used here is similar to the one described in [7] and its description goes as follows: it is a subset of the database that was used for the *NIST 2002 and 2003 Speaker Recognition Evaluation*, which comes from the second release of the cellular switchboard corpus, Switchboard Cellular - Part 2, of the Linguistic Data Consortium. This data was used as test set while the world model data and the development data comes from previous NIST campaigns. For both development and test clients, there were about 2 minutes of telephone speech used to train the models and each test access was less than 1 minute long. Only female data are used and thus only a female world model is used. The development population consisted of 100 females, while the test set is composed of 191 females. 655 different records are used to compute the world model or as negative examples for the discriminant models. The total number of accesses in the development population is 3931 and 17578 for the test set population with a proportion of 10% of true target accesses.

Table 2 gives a summary of the hyper-parameters used for GMM based experiments after selection based on minimizing EER on the development set.

Table 2. Summary of the hyper-parameters for GMMs based systems on the NIST database

ML Hyper-Parameters		
# of Iterations	# of Gaussians	Variance Flooring (%)
25	75	60

MAP Hyper-Parameters		
# of ML Iterations	# of Gaussians	Variance Flooring (%)
25	100	60
# of MAP Iterations	MAP Factor	Variance Flooring (%)
5	0.5	60

References

1. Hong, L., Jain, A.: Multi-Model Biometrics. In: Biometrics: Person Identification in Networked Society. (1999)
2. Kittler, J., Matas, G., Jonsson, K., Sanchez, M.: Combining Evidence in Personal Identity Verification Systems. Pattern Recognition Letters **18**(9) (1997) 845–852
3. Kittler, J., Messer, K., Czyz, J.: Fusion of Intramodal and Multimodal Experts in Personal Identity Authentication Systems. In: Proc. Cost 275 Workshop, Rome (2002) 17–24
4. Martin, A., Przybocki, M.: The NIST 1999 speaker recognition evaluation - an overview. Digital Signal Processing **10** (2000) 1–18
5. Martin, A., Doddington, G., Kamm, T., Ordowski, M., M.Przybocki: The DET curve in assessment of detection task performance. In: Proceedings of Eurospeech'1997. (1997) 1805–1809
6. Bengio, S., Mariéthoz, J.: The expected performance curve: A new assessment measure for person authentication. In: Proceedings of Odyssey 2004: The Speaker and Language Recognition Workshop. (2004)
7. Mariéthoz, J.: Discriminant models for text-independent speaker verification. Technical Report IDIAP-RR 06-70, IDIAP (2006)
8. Reynolds, D.A., Quatieri, T.F., Dunn, R.B.: Speaker verification using adapted gaussian mixture models. Digital Signal Processing **10**(1–3) (2000)
9. Cardinaux, F., Sanderson, C., Bengio, S.: User authentication via adapted statistical models of face images. IEEE Transactions on Signal Processing **54**(1) (2006) 361–373
10. Auckenthaler, R., Carey, M., Lloyd-Thomas, H.: Score normalization for text-independent speaker verification systems. Digital Signal Processing **10** (2000) 42–54
11. Bengio, S., Marithoz, J.: A statistical significance test for person authentication. In: Proceedings of Odyssey 2004: The Speaker and Language Recognition Workshop. (2004)
12. Vapnik, V.N.: The nature of statistical learning theory. second edn. Springer (2000)
13. Solomonoff, A., Campbell, W.M., Quillen, C.: Channel compensation for SVM speaker recognition. In: Proceedings of Odyssey 2004: The Speaker and Language Recognition Workshop. (2004)

14. Burges, C.: A tutorial on support vector machines for pattern recognition. Data Mining and Knowledge Discovery **2**(2) (1998) 1–47
15. Kenny, P., Boulianne, G., Dumouchel, P.: Eigenvoice modeling with sparse training data. IEEE Transactions on Speech and Audio Processing **13**(3) (2005)
16. Campbell, W.M.: Generalized linear discriminant sequence kernels for speaker recognition. In: Proceedings of the IEEE International Conference on Audio Speech and Signal Processing, ICASSP. (2002) 161–164
17. Chopra, S., Hadsell, R., LeCun, Y.: Learning a similarity metric discriminatively, with application to face verification. In: Proc. of Computer Vision and Pattern Recognition Conference. (2005)
18. Schultz, M., Joachims, T.: Learning a distance metric from relative comparison. In: Advances in Neural Information Processing Systems 16. (2003)
19. Burges, C., Shaked, T., Renshaw, E., Lazier, A., Deeds, M., Hamilton, N., Hullender, G.: Learning to rank using gradient descent. In: ICML. (2005) 89–96
20. Grangier, D., Bengio, S.: Exploiting hyperlinks to learn a retrieval model. In: NIPS Workshop on Learning to Rank. (2005)
21. Weibel, A., Hanazawa, T., Hinton, G., Shikano, K., Lang, K.: Phoneme recognition using time-delay neural networks. IEEE Transactions on Accoustics, Speech and Signal Processing **37**(3) (1989) 328–339

Author Index

Atiya, Amir F.   93

Babalik, Ahmet   62
Bai, Li   141
Banfield, Robert E.   161
Baykan, Ömer Kaan   62
Belaïd, Abdel   421
Benediktsson, Jon Atli   501
Bengio, Samy   513
Berkman, Omer   479
Bertolami, Roman   72
Bicego, Manuele   190
Bielskis, Antanas Andrius   62
Biggio, Battista   292
Bowyer, Kevin W.   161
Britto Jr., Alceu de Souza   52, 302, 431
Brown, Gavin   440
Bunke, Horst   72, 220

Cabello, Enrique   141
Cecotti, Hubert   421
Chanussot, Jocelyn   501
Chawla, Nitesh V.   397
Chindaro, Samuel   312
Christensen, Hans Ulrich   82
Chung, Yun-Sheng   407
Conde, Cristina   141

Denisov, Vitalij   62
DePasquale, Joseph   251
Drygajlo, Andrzej   367, 377
Duin, Robert P.W.   22, 190

Ebrahimpour, Reza   131
El Gayar, Neamat   93
Eliseyev, Andrey   13

Fairhurst, Michael   312
Fauvel, Mathieu   501
Fink, Gernot A.   42
Foggia, Pasquale   282
Fred, Ana   261
Fumera, Giorgio   292, 440
Furlanello, Cesare   32

García-Osorio, César   231
Giacinto, Giorgio   357
Govindaraju, Venu   387

Hadjitodorov, Stefan T.   200
Haindl, Michal   210
Hall, Lawrence O.   161
Heusch, Guillaume   344
Hsu, D. Frank   407
Huang, Thomas S.   180

Intrator, Nathan   479

Jurman, Giuseppe   32

Kabir, Ehsanollah   131
Kanevskiy, Daniel   469
Kegelmeyer, W. Philip   161
Khoshrou, Samaneh   121
Kittler, Josef   121, 344
Ko, Albert Hung-Ren   52, 302, 431
Krasotkina, Olga   1
Kryszczuk, Krzysztof   367
Kudo, Mineichi   241
Kuncheva, Ludmila I.   200, 450, 459

Lee, Wan-Jui   22
Li, Shoushan   322
Lienemann, Kai   42
Lu, Yijuan   180

Marcialis, Gian Luca   151
Mariéthoz, Johnny   513
Marrocco, Claudio   333
Martín de Diego, Isaac   141
Maudes, Jesús   231
Merler, Stefano   32
Meynet, Julien   171
Mikeš, Stanislav   210
Mohamed, Tawfik A.   93
Mottl, Vadim   1, 13
Muhlbaier, Michael D.   490

Ortiz-Arroyo, Daniel   82

Pękalska, Elżbieta   190
Percannella, Gennaro   282

Plötz, Thomas   42
Poh, Norman   344
Polikar, Robi   251, 490
Prior, Matthew   271

Raudys, Sarunas   62
Richiardi, Jonas   377
Riesen, Kaspar   220
Rodríguez, Juan J.   231, 450, 459
Roli, Fabio   151, 292, 357, 440

Sabourin, Robert   52, 302, 431
Sadeghi, Mohammad T.   121
Sansone, Carlo   282
Seredin, Oleg   1
Serrano, Ángel   141
Shen, Linlin   141
Shirai, Satoshi   241
Silva, Hugo   261
Simeone, Paolo   333
Sirlantzis, Konstantinos   312
Sulimova, Valentina   1

Sun, Shiliang   103, 113
Sylvester, Jared   397

Tang, Chuan Yi   407
Tatarchuk, Alexander   1, 13
Tenmoto, Hiroshi   241
Thiran, Jean-Philippe   171
Tian, Qi   180
Tortorella, Francesco   333
Tronci, Roberto   357
Tulyakov, Sergey   387

Vento, Mario   282
Verzakov, Sergey   22
Vorontsov, Konstantin   469

Windeatt, Terry   271
Windridge, David   13
Wu, Chaohong   387

Yousefi, Mohammad Reza   131

Zanda, Manuela   440
Zong, Chengqing   322

Lecture Notes in Computer Science

For information about Vols. 1–4371

please contact your bookseller or Springer

Vol. 4510: P. Van Hentenryck, L. Wolsey (Eds.), Integration of AI and OR Techniques in Constraint Programming for Combinatorial Optimization Problems. X, 391 pages. 2007.

Vol. 4486: M. Bernardo, J. Hillston (Eds.), Formal Methods for Performance Evaluation. VII, 469 pages. 2007.

Vol. 4483: C. Baral, G. Brewka, J. Schlipf (Eds.), Logic Programming and Nonmonotonic Reasoning. IX, 327 pages. 2007. (Sublibrary LNAI).

Vol. 4482: A. An, J. Stefanowski, S. Ramanna, C.J. Butz, W. Pedrycz, G. Wang (Eds.), Rough Sets, Fuzzy Sets, Data Mining and Granular Computing. XIV, 585 pages. 2007. (Sublibrary LNAI).

Vol. 4481: J.T. Yao, P. Lingras, W.-Z. Wu, M. Szczuka, N.J. Cercone, D. Ślęzak (Eds.), Rough Sets and Knowledge Technology. XIV, 576 pages. 2007. (Sublibrary LNAI).

Vol. 4480: A. LaMarca, M. Langheinrich, K.N. Truong (Eds.), Pervasive Computing. XIII, 369 pages. 2007.

Vol. 4472: M. Haindl, J. Kittler, F. Roli (Eds.), Multiple Classifier Systems. XI, 524 pages. 2007.

Vol. 4470: Q. Wang, D. Pfahl, D.M. Raffo (Eds.), Software Process Change – Meeting the Challenge. XI, 346 pages. 2007.

Vol. 4464: E. Dawson, D.S. Wong (Eds.), Information Security Practice and Experience. XIII, 361 pages. 2007.

Vol. 4463: I. Măndoiu, A. Zelikovsky (Eds.), Bioinformatics Research and Applications. XV, 653 pages. 2007. (Sublibrary LNBI).

Vol. 4462: D. Sauveron, K. Markantonakis, A. Bilas, J.-J. Quisquater (Eds.), Information Security Theory and Practices. XII, 255 pages. 2007.

Vol. 4459: C. Cérin, K.-C. Li (Eds.), Advances in Grid and Pervasive Computing. XVI, 759 pages. 2007.

Vol. 4453: T. Speed, H. Huang (Eds.), Research in Computational Molecular Biology. XVI, 550 pages. 2007. (Sublibrary LNBI).

Vol. 4452: M. Fasli, O. Shehory (Eds.), Agent-Mediated Electronic Commerce. VIII, 249 pages. 2007. (Sublibrary LNAI).

Vol. 4450: T. Okamoto, X. Wang (Eds.), Public Key Cryptography – PKC 2007. XIII, 491 pages. 2007.

Vol. 4448: M. Giacobini et al. (Ed.), Applications of Evolutionary Computing. XXIII, 755 pages. 2007.

Vol. 4447: E. Marchiori, J.H. Moore, J.C. Rajapakse (Eds.), Evolutionary Computation,Machine Learning and Data Mining in Bioinformatics. XI, 302 pages. 2007.

Vol. 4446: C. Cotta, J. van Hemert (Eds.), Evolutionary Computation in Combinatorial Optimization. XII, 241 pages. 2007.

Vol. 4445: M. Ebner, M. O'Neill, A. Ekárt, L. Vanneschi, A.I. Esparcia-Alcázar (Eds.), Genetic Programming. XI, 382 pages. 2007.

Vol. 4444: T. Reps, M. Sagiv, J. Bauer (Eds.), Program Analysis and Compilation, Theory and Practice. X, 361 pages. 2007.

Vol. 4443: R. Kotagiri, P.R. Krishna, M. Mohania, E. Nantajeewarawat (Eds.), Advances in Databases: Concepts, Systems and Applications. XXI, 1126 pages. 2007.

Vol. 4440: B. Liblit, Cooperative Bug Isolation. XV, 101 pages. 2007.

Vol. 4439: W. Abramowicz (Ed.), Business Information Systems. XV, 654 pages. 2007.

Vol. 4438: L. Maicher, A. Sigel, L.M. Garshol (Eds.), Leveraging the Semantics of Topic Maps. X, 257 pages. 2007. (Sublibrary LNAI).

Vol. 4433: E. Şahin, W.M. Spears, A.F.T. Winfield (Eds.), Swarm Robotics. XII, 221 pages. 2007.

Vol. 4432: B. Beliczynski, A. Dzielinski, M. Iwanowski, B. Ribeiro (Eds.), Adaptive and Natural Computing Algorithms, Part II. XXVI, 761 pages. 2007.

Vol. 4431: B. Beliczynski, A. Dzielinski, M. Iwanowski, B. Ribeiro (Eds.), Adaptive and Natural Computing Algorithms, Part I. XXV, 851 pages. 2007.

Vol. 4430: C.C. Yang, D. Zeng, M. Chau, K. Chang, Q. Yang, X. Cheng, J. Wang, F.-Y. Wang, H. Chen (Eds.), Intelligence and Security Informatics. XII, 330 pages. 2007.

Vol. 4429: R. Lu, J.H. Siekmann, C. Ullrich (Eds.), Cognitive Systems. X, 161 pages. 2007. (Sublibrary LNAI).

Vol. 4427: S. Uhlig, K. Papagiannaki, O. Bonaventure (Eds.), Passive and Active Network Measurement. XI, 274 pages. 2007.

Vol. 4426: Z.-H. Zhou, H. Li, Q. Yang (Eds.), Advances in Knowledge Discovery and Data Mining. XXV, 1161 pages. 2007. (Sublibrary LNAI).

Vol. 4425: G. Amati, C. Carpineto, G. Romano (Eds.), Advances in Information Retrieval. XIX, 759 pages. 2007.

Vol. 4424: O. Grumberg, M. Huth (Eds.), Tools and Algorithms for the Construction and Analysis of Systems. XX, 738 pages. 2007.

Vol. 4423: H. Seidl (Ed.), Foundations of Software Science and Computational Structures. XVI, 379 pages. 2007.

Vol. 4422: M.B. Dwyer, A. Lopes (Eds.), Fundamental Approaches to Software Engineering. XV, 440 pages. 2007.

Vol. 4421: R. De Nicola (Ed.), Programming Languages and Systems. XVII, 538 pages. 2007.

Vol. 4420: S. Krishnamurthi, M. Odersky (Eds.), Compiler Construction. XIV, 233 pages. 2007.

Vol. 4419: P.C. Diniz, E. Marques, K. Bertels, M.M. Fernandes, J.M.P. Cardoso (Eds.), Reconfigurable Computing: Architectures, Tools and Applications. XIV, 391 pages. 2007.

Vol. 4418: A. Gagalowicz, W. Philips (Eds.), Computer Vision/Computer Graphics Collaboration Techniques. XV, 620 pages. 2007.

Vol. 4416: A. Bemporad, A. Bicchi, G. Buttazzo (Eds.), Hybrid Systems: Computation and Control. XVII, 797 pages. 2007.

Vol. 4415: P. Lukowicz, L. Thiele, G. Tröster (Eds.), Architecture of Computing Systems - ARCS 2007. X, 297 pages. 2007.

Vol. 4414: S. Hochreiter, R. Wagner (Eds.), Bioinformatics Research and Development. XVI, 482 pages. 2007. (Sublibrary LNBI).

Vol. 4412: F. Stajano, H.J. Kim, J.-S. Chae, S.-D. Kim (Eds.), Ubiquitous Convergence Technology. XI, 302 pages. 2007.

Vol. 4411: R.H. Bordini, M. Dastani, J. Dix, A.E.F. Seghrouchni (Eds.), Programming Multi-Agent Systems. XIV, 249 pages. 2007. (Sublibrary LNAI).

Vol. 4410: A. Branco (Ed.), Anaphora: Analysis, Algorithms and Applications. X, 191 pages. 2007. (Sublibrary LNAI).

Vol. 4409: J.L. Fiadeiro, P.-Y. Schobbens (Eds.), Recent Trends in Algebraic Development Techniques. VII, 171 pages. 2007.

Vol. 4407: G. Puebla (Ed.), Logic-Based Program Synthesis and Transformation. VIII, 237 pages. 2007.

Vol. 4406: W. De Meuter (Ed.), Advances in Smalltalk. VII, 157 pages. 2007.

Vol. 4405: L. Padgham, F. Zambonelli (Eds.), Agent-Oriented Software Engineering VII. XII, 225 pages. 2007.

Vol. 4403: S. Obayashi, K. Deb, C. Poloni, T. Hiroyasu, T. Murata (Eds.), Evolutionary Multi-Criterion Optimization. XIX, 954 pages. 2007.

Vol. 4401: N. Guelfi, D. Buchs (Eds.), Rapid Integration of Software Engineering Techniques. IX, 177 pages. 2007.

Vol. 4400: J.F. Peters, A. Skowron, V.W. Marek, E. Orłowska, R. Słowiński, W. Ziarko (Eds.), Transactions on Rough Sets VII, Part II. X, 381 pages. 2007.

Vol. 4399: T. Kovacs, X. Llorà, K. Takadama, P.L. Lanzi, W. Stolzmann, S.W. Wilson (Eds.), Learning Classifier Systems. XII, 345 pages. 2007. (Sublibrary LNAI).

Vol. 4398: S. Marchand-Maillet, E. Bruno, A. Nürnberger, M. Detyniecki (Eds.), Adaptive Multimedia Retrieval: User, Context, and Feedback. XI, 269 pages. 2007.

Vol. 4397: C. Stephanidis, M. Pieper (Eds.), Universal Access in Ambient Intelligence Environments. XV, 467 pages. 2007.

Vol. 4396: J. García-Vidal, L. Cerdà-Alabern (Eds.), Wireless Systems and Mobility in Next Generation Internet. IX, 271 pages. 2007.

Vol. 4395: M. Daydé, J.M.L.M. Palma, Á.L.G.A. Coutinho, E. Pacitti, J.C. Lopes (Eds.), High Performance Computing for Computational Science - VECPAR 2006. XXIV, 721 pages. 2007.

Vol. 4394: A. Gelbukh (Ed.), Computational Linguistics and Intelligent Text Processing. XVI, 648 pages. 2007.

Vol. 4393: W. Thomas, P. Weil (Eds.), STACS 2007. XVIII, 708 pages. 2007.

Vol. 4392: S.P. Vadhan (Ed.), Theory of Cryptography. XI, 595 pages. 2007.

Vol. 4391: Y. Stylianou, M. Faundez-Zanuy, A. Esposito (Eds.), Progress in Nonlinear Speech Processing. XII, 269 pages. 2007.

Vol. 4390: S.O. Kuznetsov, S. Schmidt (Eds.), Formal Concept Analysis. X, 329 pages. 2007. (Sublibrary LNAI).

Vol. 4389: D. Weyns, H.V.D. Parunak, F. Michel (Eds.), Environments for Multi-Agent Systems III. X, 273 pages. 2007. (Sublibrary LNAI).

Vol. 4385: K. Coninx, K. Luyten, K.A. Schneider (Eds.), Task Models and Diagrams for Users Interface Design. XI, 355 pages. 2007.

Vol. 4384: T. Washio, K. Satoh, H. Takeda, A. Inokuchi (Eds.), New Frontiers in Artificial Intelligence. IX, 401 pages. 2007. (Sublibrary LNAI).

Vol. 4383: E. Bin, A. Ziv, S. Ur (Eds.), Hardware and Software, Verification and Testing. XII, 235 pages. 2007.

Vol. 4381: J. Akiyama, W.Y.C. Chen, M. Kano, X. Li, Q. Yu (Eds.), Discrete Geometry, Combinatorics and Graph Theory. XI, 289 pages. 2007.

Vol. 4380: S. Spaccapietra, P. Atzeni, F. Fages, M.-S. Hacid, M. Kifer, J. Mylopoulos, B. Pernici, P. Shvaiko, J. Trujillo, I. Zaihrayeu (Eds.), Journal on Data Semantics VIII. XV, 219 pages. 2007.

Vol. 4379: M. Südholt, C. Consel (Eds.), Object-Oriented Technology. VIII, 157 pages. 2007.

Vol. 4378: I. Virbitskaite, A. Voronkov (Eds.), Perspectives of Systems Informatics. XIV, 496 pages. 2007.

Vol. 4377: M. Abe (Ed.), Topics in Cryptology – CT-RSA 2007. XI, 403 pages. 2006.

Vol. 4376: E. Frachtenberg, U. Schwiegelshohn (Eds.), Job Scheduling Strategies for Parallel Processing. VII, 257 pages. 2007.

Vol. 4374: J.F. Peters, A. Skowron, I. Düntsch, J. Grzymała-Busse, E. Orłowska, L. Polkowski (Eds.), Transactions on Rough Sets VI, Part I. XII, 499 pages. 2007.

Vol. 4373: K. Langendoen, T. Voigt (Eds.), Wireless Sensor Networks. XIII, 358 pages. 2007.

Vol. 4372: M. Kaufmann, D. Wagner (Eds.), Graph Drawing. XIV, 454 pages. 2007.